W9-BCO-103

# Java Programmer's Reference

© 2000 Wrox Press

All rights reserved. No part of this book may be reproduced, stored in a retrieval
system or transmitted in any form or by any means, without the prior written
permission of the publisher, except in the case of brief quotations embodied in critical
articles or reviews.

The authors and publisher have made every effort in the preparation of this book to
ensure the accuracy of the information. However, the information contained in this
book is sold without warranty, either express or implied. Neither the authors, Wrox
Press nor its dealers or distributors will be held liable for any damages caused or
alleged to be caused either directly or indirectly by this book.

First Reprint    April 2000

Published by Wrox Press Ltd,
Arden House, 1102 Warwick Road, Acocks Green, Birmingham B27 6BH, UK.
Printed in Canada
2 3 4 5 TRI 04 03 02 01 00
ISBN 1-861004-22-2

# Java
# Programmer's Reference

**Grant Palmer**

**Wrox Press Ltd. ®**

# About the Author

Grant has worked as a scientific programmer in the Space Technology Division at the NASA Ames Research Center for the past 15 years. He has worked with Java since 1996 developing programs for scientific applications as well as converting older FORTRAN and C codes to the Java platform.

Grant lives in Chandler, Arizona with his wife, Lisa, and his two sons, Jackson and Zachary. In his spare time, Grant enjoys skiing and gardening, and is a competitive swimmer. He also likes to watch movies and read historical fiction.

# Acknowledgements

I would like to acknowledge Eric Nagler for helping me to learn Java and for encouraging me to pursue this project.

I would like to dedicate this book to Lisa, Jackson, and Zachary, the three shining lights in my life.

## Trademark Acknowledgements

Wrox has endeavored to provide trademark information about all the companies and products mentioned in this book by the appropriate use of capitals. However, Wrox cannot guarantee the accuracy of this information.

## Credits

**Author**
Grant Palmer

**Technical Editors**
Jon Duckett
Richard Huss

**Development Editor**
Timothy Briggs

**Managing Editor**
Paul Cooper

**Project Manager**
Chandima Nethisinghe

**Index**
Andrew Criddle

**Technical Reviewers**
Raj Betapudi
Michael Boerner
Ivor Horton
David Hudson
Rick Jacoby
Songmuh Jong
Jeff Luszcz
Jim MacIntosh
Eric Nagler
Sanjeev Navalkar
Stephen Potts

**Design / Layout**
Tom Bartlett
William Fallon
Jonathan Jones
Laurent Lafon

**Cover Design**
Chris Morris

# Table of Contents

# Table of Contents

# Table of Contents

# Table of Contents

# Table of Contents

# Table of Contents

# Introduction

Java is a platform-netural, Object-Oriented programming language which provides a large number of predefined library classes that greatly simplify common programming tasks.

This book is a quick reference to the parts of the language and libraries you'll need 90% of time time - the language has grown so large that it is not possible to cover the entire class library in one book. Instead, this book covers the commonly-used packages: the Java language, utility, I/O, and network programming classes, together which those for GUI development using the Abstract Windowing Toolkit and Swing, applets, event handling, and Java Beans.

In each chapter the important classes and methods within the package are presented, along with clear, concise examples that demonstrate how to use them.

## History of Java

Development of the Java language, initially named **Oak**, was begun at Sun Microsystems, Inc. in 1991. The first public announcement of the language, and the change of name to Java, occurred in 1995. The initial intent for the language was somewhat mundane. It was intended to be a platform independent language for use in consumer electronic devices. The language was designed to produce code that would run on a variety of CPU's and under different operating environments.

The thing that propelled Java into prominence was the advent of the World Wide Web. With people running many different operating systems and browsers wishing to access programs made available on the Internet, platform independent programming became very important. The developers at Sun realized that they had been working on a programming language that had the capability to embed intelligent, interactive content into a Web page. The focus of the language development changed from consumer electronics to Internet programming.

The key to the portability of the Java language is that the output of the Java compiler is not standard executable code. Instead, the Java compiler generates an optimized set of instructions called bytecodes. The bytecodes are interpreted by the Java run-time system which is referred to as the **Java Virtual Machine (JVM)**. The only requirement to run a compiled Java program on the system is that the system must have the JVM installed. Furthermore, while the specifics of the JVM will differ from platform to platform they all interpret the same Java bytecodes. This allows a program compiled on, say, a Mac to be run on a PC.

From its beginnings as a tool to generate Web-based applications, Java has expanded into many different areas areas from network programming, to creating graphical user interfaces, to programs for scientific applications. The creation of standalone and enterprise applications has become the driving force behind the evolution of the Java language. Today Java is used for large scale enterprise applications, as well as for programming smaller devices such as phones.

# General Characteristics of the Java Language

Java is an interpreted language. When you write a Java program, either in a development environment or in a text editor, it needs to be **compiled** into an optimized set of instructions called a **bytecode program**. This bytecode is platform independent and cannot be executed directly by the processor. Instead, a **Java Virtual Machine (JVM)** runs (interprets) the bytecodes. There are JVMs available for a variety of platforms, which enable Java programs to be platform independent. For instance, a Java program compiled on a UNIX workstation can be run on a Macintosh.

*In reality, you need to be aware that not all JVMs support all features of the language.*

Another strength of Java comes from its built-in libraries. The packages that come with the **Java Development Kit (JDK)** contain many hundreds of built-in classes, with many thousands of methods. These classes and methods contain commonly used functionality, meaning that a good deal of the programming work has already been done. It remains for the developer to integrate the built-in classes for his or her specific application.

Java is a **strongly-typed** language; this means that the compiler performs a lot of checking to make sure that the data types you are using match up correctly. This helps to catch a lot of common programming errors.

Java is an Object Oriented programming language. All executable code must be contained within a class. Java incorporates such object-oriented concepts as inheritance, enscapsulation, and polymorphism. Inheritance allows classes to be written that are extensions of other classes. Encapsulation is implemented by packaging the data, and methods to manipulate the data, together at class scope. Polymorphism is achieved through the use of interfaces to define a general class of action.

The Java language is intended to be secure. Java enables the construction of virus-free, tamper-free programs. A Java program cannot corrupt memory outside of its process space. Java applets cannot access the disks of other computers.

Java also supports multi-threaded programming which is important when designing interactive, networked programs, when running multiple applets in a web page, or in spinning off any activity that would other wise bog down the application.

Java borrowed a good deal of syntax from C and C++. The developers of Java wanted to produce a simple language, so many of the less useful, more esoteric features of C and C++ were removed. Section 1.1.13 details some of the differences between Java and C++.

# What Does This Book Cover?

With the evolution of the Java language from Java 1.0, to 1.1, to Java 2, the size of the language has expanded drastically. The Java 2 SDK Standard Edition version 1.3 contains 76 packages and over 2000 classes.

It is not feasible for a single book to cover the entire class library in detail. The first chapter presents some fundamental features of the Java language, and the subsequent chapters discuss the details of 12 of the most commonly used packages, covering basic Java language and utility classes, I/O, network programming, GUI development using the Abstract Windowing Toolkit and Swing, applets, event handling, and Java Beans.

Each chapter presents the important classes and methods within the package, along with clear, concise examples that demonstrate how to use them.

# Who Is This Book For?

This book is for experienced, professional Java developers, and anyone else who uses Java on a regular basis, who want a quick solutions reference. Assuming a good knowledge of the language, it covers the Java you'll need 90% of the time – essential rather than exhaustive.

Unlike complete reference guides that are huge and as a consequence almost always out of date, this is the book a developer has by his side that helps him solve his problems quickly – focusing on Java 2 Standard Edition (J2SE) and the soon to be released JDK 1.3 (Java Developers Kit). It provides examples, syntax, and concept clarification in an accessible format to speed you to the solution you need.

# What You Need to Use this Book

The code in this book was tested with the Java 2 Platform Standard Edition SDK (JDK 1.3 Release Candidate 1). This can be obtained from Sun's Java web site at

http://java.sun.com

At the time of writing, JDK 1.3 Release Candidate 1 is available from this site for Windows 95/98/NT 4.0, and will shortly be available for Solaris, while the previous version (JDK 1.2.2) is available for the same platforms and Linux.

The complete source code from the book is available for download from

http://www.wrox.com

# Running the Examples

This book contains many examples that detail the classes, methods, and concepts described in this book. There are two types of examples: standalone applications and web-based applications (applets). In either case, the source code must either be downloaded from the FTP site or typed in by hand. Section 1.1.11 on page 14 gives instructions for compiling and running Java programs.

# Conventions

To help you get the most from the text and keep track of what's happening, we've used a number of conventions throughout the book.

For instance:

> These boxes hold important, not-to-be forgotten information which is directly relevant to the surrounding text.

*While the background style is used for asides to the current discussion.*

As for styles in the text:

- ❏ When we introduce them, we highlight **important words**.
- ❏ We show keyboard strokes like this: *Ctrl-A*.
- ❏ We show filenames, and code within the text like so: doGet()
- ❏ Text on user interfaces, and URLs, are shown as: **Menu**.

We present code in various different ways. Definitions of methods, properties, and so on are shown in tables, like this with the method names shown in bold and parameter names in *italic*:

| Method | Syntax |
|---|---|
| getName() | public final String **getName**() |
| setName() | public final void **setName**(String *name*) |

Code is shown with a shaded background, sometimes important lines of code and modifications to earlier examples are shown with bolded fonts:

```
public class TestMain {
  public static void main(String args[]) {
    System.out.println("This is main");
  }
}
```

# Tell Us What You Think

We've worked hard to make this book as useful to you as possible, so we'd like to know what you think. We're always keen to know what it is you want and need to know.

We appreciate feedback on our efforts and take both criticism and praise on board in our future editorial efforts. If you've anything to say, let us know on:

feedback@wrox.com

Or via the feedback links on:

http://www.wrox.com

1

# Java Fundamentals

The rest of this book is a reference for the class libraries which are an integral part of the Java platform. To be able to make use of them, however, you need to be able to use the language itself. This chapter provides a quick introduction and reference to the language.

This chapter covers:

# 1.1 A (Brief) Introduction to Java

Before we get into the details of the language, a brief overview would be of benefit. This section gives a *very* quick look at the main features of the language, without going too far into the details or showing you any actual Java syntax, to give you a feel for the main concepts behind Object-Oriented programming in Java.

## 1.1.1 What is a Java Program?

A Java program is a collection of **classes**. Some of these you write; some are provided as part of the Java language. (Indeed, the rest of this book is a reference to some of the classes provided as part of the Java language.)

## 1.1.2 Classes

Almost everything in Java is an **object**: an object typically stores ("**encapsulates**") related data and provides operations which can be performed on it. A class defines the capabilities of a group of objects which share certain characteristics: they store the same sorts of data and can perform the same operations. Each **instance** of an object of the same class stores the same types of data and can perform the same operations, but each object can store different actual values, and represents a particular occurrence of that class of objects.

A **class** is like a template from which you create **objects**. When writing a Java program, you write classes, and then create objects of those classes (or of those provided as part of the language), known as **instances** of those classes, which can then be manipulated as required.

A class may contain a variety of sorts of **members**. The most important are:

❑   **Constructors**. These create an object of a particular class and are used to initialize the object's state.

❑   **Instance variables**. These store information about the object's state.

❑   **Methods**. These perform some operation on an object.

❑   **Static variables**. These store information that is related to the whole class, rather than to a particular object.

❑   **Static methods**. These perform some operation that is related to the whole class, rather than to a particular object.

A particular class doesn't need to have members of all of these sorts. Each member may have an **access modifier** to control which other classes and methods can access it.

Classes are described in more detail in Section 1.10 on page 57.

# 1.1.3 Inheritance

Classes do not exist in isolation; Java, being an Object-Oriented language, allows one class to **extend** another. Any class that does not explicitly state which class it extends automatically extends the class Object.

You can see this in the predefined Java classes. For example, the Button class (used to create an on-screen button as part of a graphical user interface) extends the Component class, which extends Object. Object provides the basic operations that every class needs, such as comparing itself with another object, making a copy of itself, converting itself to a String, and so on.

In other words inheritance allows you, with the minimum of extra work, to take what one class does, and then write a new class that:

❑ adds extra features to that class, and/or

❑ modifies how existing features work.

Unless you find that you need to change how the class works, you just say nothing and you get access to the previously defined versions thrown in for free in your new class.

Another way of describing this is to say that your new class (called a **sub-class**) **inherits** the features (methods, variables, etc.) of another (called its **super-class**). Your new class can then be extended by another class, and so on.

Inheritance is important, and understanding which classes are extended by the class you are using is essential if you want to find out all about how to use it. In this book, we use diagrams like this:

```
Object
  DatagramSocket
    MulticastSocket
```

to show this "chain of inheritance". The DatagramSocket class extends the Object class, and is itself extended by the MulticastSocket class.

For more detail on inheritance, see Section 1.11 on page 62.

# 1.1.4 Interfaces

**Interfaces** provide specifications of methods (that is, what inputs they require and what sorts of values they return) without actually implementing (providing the code for) the methods themselves. It is up to the individual classes to **implement** an interface, which means that they undertake to provide actual implementations of the methods listed in the interface. In this way, a common functionality can be imposed on a number of different classes. You can't create an object of an interface, only of a class that implements that interface. Interfaces can also extend other interfaces.

In this book, we illustrate interfaces being implemented like this:

```
Object
    InetAddress
```

### *Interfaces*
```
Serializable
```

This shows that the class `InetAddress` extends `Object` and implements the interface `Serializable`.

Interfaces are covered in more detail in Section 1.12 on page 67.

# 1.1.5 Special Sorts of Classes

As well as ordinary classes of the sort we have been talking about up to now, there are some special sorts of classes: abstract classes, final classes, and inner classes.

**Abstract classes** are classes where some (or maybe all) of the methods don't have any code written for them, because another class will extend the abstract class and provide the implementations of those methods. Such methods are called **abstract methods**, and act as a placeholder for the methods implemented in the subclasses.

Abstract classes are a bit like interfaces, in that they are used to impose a common functionality on a number of different classes, but they are definitely classes: they can extend **concrete classes** (a class which isn't abstract is called a concrete class) and their subclasses can be concrete classes. But you can't create an object of an abstract class, only of a concrete class that extends that abstract class.

**Final classes** are classes which can't be extended; sometimes this is useful if you never want your class to be changed by a subclass.

**Inner classes** are classes which are defined, for convenience, within the definition of another class.

All these sorts of classes are described in more detail in Section 1.13 on page 69.

# 1.1.6 Packages

With lots of classes, keeping everything organised can get confusing. So Java provides **packages**, which let you organise classes in a hierarchy. Java has plenty of predefined packages (and the other chapters of this book each cover one such package), but you can also create your own packages. If you do not explicitly put a class in a particular package, it will be in the default, un-named, package.

When you want to use a class or interface that is defined in a different package, you **import** either the class or interface itself, or the whole package.

The full name of a class is the name of the package it's in, followed by a period, followed by the class's name. For example, the Object class is part of the java.lang package, and its full name is java.lang.Object. The java.lang package provides various classes which are a core part of the Java language; it is imported automatically.

To ensure that package names are kept unique, Sun proposes that you use your internet domain name, with its elements reversed, as the first part of new package names. For example, Wrox Press Limited would start all its Java package names with com.wrox.

Packages are covered in Section 1.14 on page 74.

# 1.1.7 Data types and Variables

Every item of data in a Java program has a type; the types can be divided into two basic kinds:

❑ **Primitive types** that store basic data of a variety of simple types (such as characters and numbers).

❑ **Reference types** that store references to objects. Note that reference types do *not* store objects: they store *references to objects*. It is possible for several variables to refer to the same object. When an object has no references to it, the Java runtime system's garbage collector will destroy it.

There are a whole variety of different sorts of variables. The main differences between the different sorts are:

❑ Where they are declared in a program:

    ❑ **instance variables** belong to a particular object

    ❑ **static variables** belong to a whole class

    ❑ **local variables** belong only to a particular block of code.

❑ What type of information they store; as we have already said, the types of data are divided into primitive types and reference types.

An important point is that a reference variable can hold a reference to the particular class it was declared as holding, or any of its subclasses. Alternatively, a reference variable can be declared as holding a reference to an object of any class that implements a particular interface.

However, when a reference of a particular type points to an object of a subclass of that type, only the features of the superclass can be accessed. For example, if a variable which holds a reference to an Object in fact refers to a String object, only the methods and instance variables of the Object class can be used, even though the object is in fact a String. This can be got around by **casting** the object to the required type.

Section 1.3 on page 18 covers data types and variables.

# 1.1.8 Methods

A method is a collection of **statements**, which are instructions to be performed when the method is **called**. A method may need to be passed a number of **parameters**, and may **return** a value.

A method can also **throw an exception** if an error arises while the method is being performed. If an exception is possible, the method must declare that it can do so, and the code calling the method must either deal with it by **catching** the exception or it must itself throw the same exception, passing responsibility for catching the exception to a higher level within the program. Certain types of run-time errors, however, do not need to be declared or caught, as they are so serious that the program must terminate if they occur.

Parameters are passed by value: that is, when a parameter is passed to a method, a copy of the parameter value is given to the method, and can't be changed by the method. *However*, if you pass a reference to an object to a method, although you can't change the reference (that is, you can't change which object is referred to), you *can* change the object itself.

For details of how to define and call methods, refer to Section 1.8 on page 41.

# 1.1.9 Programs and Applets

A Java program consists of a number of classes, including one which contains a static method called `main()`. You start the program by specifying the name of this class to the Java runtime system, which calls the `main()` method.

Alternatively, you can write an **applet**. Applets run inside a web browser program. Within the code for a web page, a class is specified which extends `Applet`. The web browser creates an object of this class and calls its `init()` method.

# 1.1.10 Java Development Kit (JDK)

The **Java Software Development Kit**, or **SDK**, can be downloaded from Sun's website, http://java.sun.com. It is also known as the **Java Development Kit (JDK)**. The current version of the JDK is version 1.3.

The JDK includes, amongst others, the following tools:

| Tool | Use |
| --- | --- |
| javac | Java compiler |
| java | Java interpreter, used to run compiled program |
| appletviewer | Used for displaying the applet as it would be seen by the browser |
| jdb | Debugger |
| javadoc | Documentation generator |

# 1.1.11 Compiling and Running Java Programs

To create, compile and run a Java program, the necessary steps are:

**1.** Create the necessary Java source files. Each public class must go in a separate source file, which must have the same name as the class followed by ".java". For example, the class MyProg should be contained the file MyProg.java.

**2.** Compile the Java source (.java) file to create a .class file. For example:

```
javac MyProg.java
```

**3.** Run the program using the java interpreter; the name of the class providing the main() method must be given. For example:

```
java MyProg <command line arguments>
```

Note that it would be wrong to type java MyProg.class; you specify the class name, rather than the name of the file containing the compiled bytecodes.

# 1.1.12 The Sun Java Website and Online Documentation

The Sun Java website is located at: http://java.sun.com. It contains tutorials, new development announcements, and other useful information. You can also download the Java Development Kit from there, and view (or download) the JDK documentation.

Using the JDK documentation, and in particular the Java API Documentation, is one of the most important skills of the Java programmer. The JDK documentation can be found on the web, or downloaded from the Sun Java web site.

To view the JDK documentation on-line, see
http://java.sun.com/products/jdk/1.3/docs/index.html

and for the Java API documentation see
http://java.sun.com/products/jdk/1.3/docs/api/index.html

The following screenshot shows the front page of the API documentation. The browser window is divided into three frames, containing:

❑ On the right, documentation for the chosen class or package.

❑ Top left, an alphabetical list of packages, plus the option to list all classes.

❑ Bottom left, alphabetical lists of classes and interfaces. If a particular package is chosen, this will show only those classes and interfaces within that package, plus an option to see an overview of the whole package.

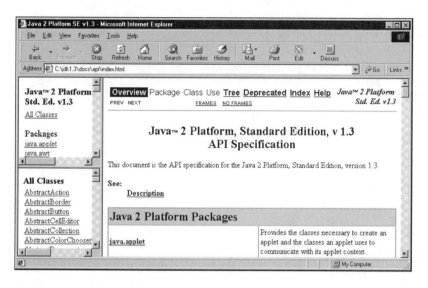

In the next screenshot, the `java.lang` package has been selected in the top left frame, then the `String` class from the bottom left frame. The documentation for the `String` class is displayed in the right hand frame.

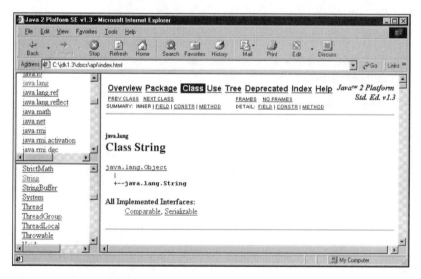

A couple of other interesting Java websites are the on-line Java magazine, JavaWorld, which can be found at http://www.javaworld.com, and the TeamJava Discussion Forum, containing answers to frequently asked questions about Java, which is located at http://www.www-net.com/java/faq/.

# 1.1.13 Differences from C++

Java is similar in many ways to C++, but there are also many important differences. If you are learning Java as your first language, don't despair: you do not have to have any C++ knowledge to learn Java. This section is primarily for people moving over from a C++ environment to Java, or for people who are trying to convert C++ code to Java. Java does not have:

- ❑ pointers
- ❑ structs
- ❑ typedefs
- ❑ sizeof function
- ❑ templates
- ❑ default function arguments
- ❑ enumerated types
- ❑ operator overloading
- ❑ global data and functions
- ❑ macros
- ❑ need to free memory
- ❑ multiple inheritance
- ❑ destructors
- ❑ object types - only object reference types

Java does, however, have:

- ❑ basic types independent of the underlying machine
- ❑ interfaces
- ❑ Unicode characters

# 1.2 Syntax Basics

We start off with a few of the basic constructs of the Java language.

## 1.2.1 Comments

Comments in Java are of three sorts:

❑ Single-line comments start // and continue to the end of the line.

❑ Multi-line comments start with /* and continue until the characters */

❑ Documentation comments are a special sort of multi-line comments, starting with /**. They are used to embed in the source code documentation about a class, and can be read, along with the source code itself, by the javadoc tool to generate HTML documentation for your classes. The online Java API Documentation is generated using javadoc.

## 1.2.2 Keywords

Certain words are reserved by java for internal use, these are called **keywords** and cannot be used for variable names:

abstract, boolean, break, byte, case, catch, char, class, const, continue, default, do, double, else, extends, final, finally, float, for, goto, if, implements, import, instanceof, int, interface, long, native, new, package, private, protected, public, return, short, static, super, switch, sychronized, this, throw, throws, transient, try, void, volatile, while.

In addition to these keywords, Java reserves false, null, and true as values defined in the language.

## 1.2.3 Expressions and Statements

**Expressions** combine values and operators (see Section 1.5 on page 26) and are evaluated by the Java interpreter to compute a value.

**Statements** are the individual commands that the Java interpreter executes. The types of statements available in Java include:

❑ Certain kinds of expression may be used as statements by following them with a semicolon:

❑ Assignment of a value to a variable

❑ Use of increment and decrement operators

❑ Method invocation

❑ Creation of a new object

❑ The various sorts of control statements described in Section 1.6, on page 30.

❑ The `return` statement described in Section 1.8.3, on page 44.

❑ The `try` statement, described in Section 1.7.1, on page 37.

❑ The `throw` statement described in Section 1.7.3, on page 38.

❑ The `synchronized` statement, described in Section 2.3.5, on page 105 .

❑ A **block**, which is a series of statements enclosed within curly brackets:

```
{
  Statement 1
  Statement 2
  etc.
}
```

❑ A local variable declaration.

❑ An empty statement, which consists simply of a semicolon, and does nothing.

❑ A labeled statement, which consists of a label used to identify the statement, a colon, and a statement.

# 1.3 Data Types and Variables

Variables are used to store data. There are two general categories of variables in Java:

❑ **Primitive variables** are used to store primitive datatypes. The primitive datatypes in Java are described in Section 1.3.1 on page 19.

❑ **Reference variables** that store a reference to an object. When a reference type has the value `null`, it means that it does not refer to an actual object.

Primitive variables and class objects may also be static, and/or final. (See Section 1.3.4 on page 21 and Section 1.3.5 on page 22.)

Variables must be declared and used within a class, and may be initialized when they are declared. Variables have scope within the block in which they reside, designated by curly braces; variables locally defined within a method can have the same name as a variable declared at class level. Java does not have global variables.

This class HW shown below demonstrates the visibility of variables declared at class level and within methods.

```
class HW {
  int j;              // j is visible to both method1 and method 2

  void method1() {
    double x;         // x is visible only to method1
  }
```

```
void method2() {
    double y;        // y is visible only to method2
    }
}
```

Variables of the same name cannot be re-declared within a nested scope: the code below would not compile.

```
public static void main(String args[]) {
    int a = 0;
    {
        int a = 0;        // error in java, permitted in C and C++
    }
}
```

# 1.3.1 Primitive Data Types and Their Storage Requirements

Primitive variables represent the simplest data types in Java: integer values, floating point values, bytes of data, and characters. The primitive datatypes and their storage requirements are:

| Data type | Used to store | Storage Requirement |
|-----------|---------------|---------------------|
| boolean | a logical variable that has a value either true or false | 1 bit |
| byte | one byte of data | 1 byte |
| char | a UNICODE character | 2 bytes |
| double | a double-precision floating point number between 1.7e-308 and 1.7e+308 | 8 bytes |
| float | a single-precision floating point number between 3.4e-38 and 3.4e+38 | 4 bytes |
| int | an integer number between -2,147,483,648 and 2,147,483,647 | 4 bytes |
| long | an integer number between -9,223,372,036,854,775,808 and 9,223,372,036,854,775,807 | 8 bytes |
| short | an integer number between -32,768 and 32,767 | 2 bytes |

For each of these primitive data types, there is also a **wrapper class** provided which allows a value of the primitive type to be encapsulated within an object; these classes are part of the java.lang package and are described in Section 2.4 on page 110.

Two other datatypes are worthy of note:

❑ void is used to describe the value returned by a method which returns no value.

❑ String is a class used to store strings of characters. A String literal may be created by enclosing characters within quotation marks:

```
"This is a String literal"
```

# 1.3.2 Declaring Variables

Different types of variables require different amounts of storage. Also, certain methods are reserved for certain variable types. For instance, the concat() method defined in the String class requires a String argument. To identify the variable type and to inform the compiler how much memory to reserve for the variable, a variable must be declared before it is used. The declaration consists of the variable name preceded by the variable type. Unlike in C, Java variables can be declared anywhere in the code as long as the declaration is performed before the variable is used.

## Example: Declaring Variables

In this example, a String object is declared and initialized with a reference to the String "blah" at the top of the main() method. An int named k is declared after the String object but is not given a value until later in the program. Another int named j is declared and intialized in the for loop. This variable will not be accessible outside of the for loop.

```java
public class TestDeclare {
  public static void main(String args[]) {
    String str = "blah";
    int k;

    System.out.println(str);
    k = 2;

    for (int j = 0; j < 2; ++j) {
      System.out.println("j is " + j);
    }
  }
}
```

# 1.3.3 Variable Access Modifiers

Variables can be provided with an access modifier keyword that determines the availibility of the variable to other classes. The modifier can be `public`, `private`, `protected`, or it can be absent.

❑ A variable declared as `public` is accessible anywhere inside or outside of the class and package in which the variable is defined.

❑ A variable declared as `private` can only be accessed by methods contained in the class in which the variable is defined.

❑ A variable declared as `protected` is accessible to all classes contained in the same package as the variable but outside of the package it is accessible only to sub-classes.

❑ If no access modifier is provided, the default access privilege is used, which means that it is accessible to all classes contained in the same package but is not accessible outside that package.

# 1.3.4 Static Variables

Java does not support global variables. However, a variable can be given some of the characteristics of a global variable by declaring it to be static using the `static` keyword. `Static` variables can be accessed without reference to a class object; they belong to their class and not to the various objects created of the class type, and can be used to maintain information about the class as a whole. Static variables must be declared at class scope; they are not allowed to be defined at method scope. To access a static variable from another class, use the class name before the variable name.

Both class (static) and instance variables are initialized by default. Data members of a basic type are initialized to 0 (`false` in the case of `boolean` variables), and members of a class type are initialized to `null`. Local variables are not initialized by default.

**Example: Using Static Variables**

In this example, the `Box` class contains a static variable, `numBoxes`, which is incremented each time a `Box` object is created. The `main()` method of the `TestStaticVar` class creates two `Box` objects, then prints out the value of the static variable.

```
class Box {
   double width;
   static int numBoxes = 0;  // static variable is declared and initialized

   public Box() {
      width = 5.0;
      numBoxes++;   // numBoxes is incremented to count number of objects.
   }
```

```
    }

public class TestStaticVar {
  public static void main (String args[]) {
    Box box1 = new Box();
    Box box2 = new Box();

    System.out.println("Number of objects = " + Box.numBoxes);
  }
}
```

**Output**
```
Number of objects = 2
```

## 1.3.5 Final Variables

Variables that are declared `final` must be initialized when they are declared and cannot then be changed. For example:

```
static final int MAX_COUNT = 10;
```

At method scope, all final data members must be non-static.

## 1.3.6 Casting

Values can be converted, or cast, into other datatypes. A widening conversion (for example, `float` to `double`) is performed implicitly and no cast is needed. A narrowing conversion (for example, `double` to `float`) requires a cast.

### Example: Casting Variables

The `double` variable a is cast to a `float`, and assigned to the variable b.

```
double a = 5.0;
float b;
b = (float)a;
```

Primitive variables can never be cast to a class object:

```
String str_obj = (String)0;  // error
```

To convert an integer to a string, add an empty string literal:

```
String str_obj = 0 + "";  // The + operator here means concatenation
```

`boolean` variables can never by cast. Objects can be cast to another class if they are instances of that class or any of its subclasses.

# 1.4 Arrays

An array is an associated group of primitive datatypes or references to class objects. The different elements contained in an array are given an index and are accessed using their index; array indices start at 0. Arrays can be multi-dimensional, and, like class objects, are created using the new keyword

## 1.4.1 Creating One-Dimensional Array Objects

**Syntax**

```
variableType arrayName[] = new variableType[arraySize];
variableType[] arrayName = new variableType[arraySize];
```

This creates an array object. Array objects are class objects which mean they are created using the new keyword. There are two equivalent syntax structures for creating an array.

The first places the empty brackets after the array name:

```
int[] data = new int[12];
```

The second places the brackets after the variable type. As with other class objects, the two parts of the instantiation syntax can be placed on separate lines:

```
int data[];
data = new int[12];
```

## 1.4.2 Initializing Array Values

**Syntax**

```
variableType[] arrayName = {val1, val2, ..., valN};
```

This creates an N-element array and initializes it with the values contained in the curly braces. The full syntax is:

**Syntax**

```
variableType[] arrayName = new variableType[]{val1, val2, ..., valN};
```

but the new variableType[] syntax is implied and can be omitted.

---

### Example: Initializing Array Values

This example creates a four element array with 1, 2, 3, 4 as the values. The length of the array, and the element at index 2, are printed out.

```
public class TestArray {
   public static void main(String args[]) {
      int[] data = {
         1, 2, 3, 4
      };

      System.out.println("The length of the array is " + data.length);
      System.out.println("The element at index 2 is " + data[2]);
   }
}
```

**Output**

```
The length of the array is 4
The element at index 2 is 3
```

## 1.4.3 Accessing and Assigning Values to Array Elements

### Syntax

```
arrayName[index]
```

This syntax retrieves the member of *arrayName* at the specified *index*, and can be used within expressions.

### Syntax

```
arrayName[index] = value;
```

This syntax assigns value to the member of *arrayName* at the specified *index*. For example:

```
data[0] = 31;
```

## 1.4.4 Two-Dimensional Arrays

Two-dimensional arrays, and more generally multi-dimensional arrays, are treated as arrays of one-dimensional arrays. Each one-dimensional array can have a different number of array elements. In the two-dimensional case, this means that every row can have a different number of columns.

# Creating a Two-Dimensional Array Object

**Syntax**

```
variableType[][] arrayName = new variableType [numRows][numCols];
```

This creates a two-dimensional array object. Two-dimensional arrays are really arrays of one-dimensional arrays. If the number of columns is left blank, the array can have a different number of columns for each row. In a two-dimensional array, the left index indicates the row and the right index indicates the column.

## Example: Creating a Two-Dimensional Array

This example creates a two-dimensional array with 9 rows and a variable number of columns for each row. The first row is given 21 columns. The second row is given 5000 columns.

```
class Test2Darray2 {
  public static void main(String args[]) {
    int[][] multD = new int[9][];
    multD[0] = new int[21];
    multD[1] = new int[5000];
  }
}
```

# Initializing Two-Dimensional Arrays

**Syntax**

```
variableType[][] arrayName = { {val1, val2, ...}, {val1, val2, ...} };
```

This creates a two-dimensional array and initializes the columns with the values contained in the curly brackets. Each set of curly brackets represents a row of the two-dimensional array.

## Example: Initializing a Two-Dimensional Array

A two-dimensional array of int values is initialized, and the element at [0][2] is displayed.

```
public class Test2Darray {
  public static void main(String args[]) {
    int[][] multiD = {
      { 1, 2, 3, 4 },
      { 5, 6, 7 }
    };
```

```
        System.out.println("The element at [0][2] is " + multiD[0][2]);
    }
}
```

**Output**

```
The element at [0][2] is 3
```

## 1.4.5 The length Variable

All one-dimensional arrays have an instance variable named `length` associated with them. This variable contains the length of the array. Because a multi-dimensional array is just an array of arrays, the `length` of a multi-dimensional array is the length of its first dimension.

### Example: Using the length Variable

The length variable is used to access the length of the first row of a two-dimensional array.

```
public class TestLength {
    public static void main(String args[]) {
        int[][] multiD = {
            { 1, 2, 3, 4 },
            { 5, 6, 7 }
        };

        System.out.println("The length of the first row is "+multiD[0].length);
    }
}
```

**Output**

```
The length of the first row is 4
```

See also example *Initializing Array Values* on page 24.

## 1.5 Operators

Java provides a large collection of operators that can be used to manipulate data, including arithmetic, assignment, boolean, casting, and logical operators.

# 1.5.1 Arithmetic Operators

These operators provide basic mathematical operations.

| Operator | Meaning |
| --- | --- |
| + | addition |
| - | subtraction |
| * | multiplication |
| / | division |
| % | modulus |
| ++ | increment by 1 |
| - - | decrement by 1 |

The increment and decrement operators can appear in prefix (++*variable*) or postfix (*variable*- -) form. In prefix form, the variable is incremented or decremented before any other operations are performed. In postfix form, the variable is incremented or decremented after any other operations have been performed.

## Example: Using Arithmetic Operators

An int variable is declared, and initialized with the value 2. The ++ operator is used to increment its value.

```
public class TestArith {
  public static void main(String args[]) {
    int j = 2;
    System.out.println("j is " + j);

    ++j;
    System.out.println("j is now " + j);
  }
}
```

**Output**

```
j is 2
j is now 3
```

## 1.5.2 Assignment Operators

The simple assignment operator = is used to assign a value to a variable. The other operators combine assignment with an arithmetic operation. For example, x += y is equivalent to x = x + y.

| Operator | Meaning |
|---|---|
| = | simple assignment |
| += | assignment and addition |
| -= | assignment and subtraction |
| *= | assignment and multiplication |
| /= | assignment and division |
| %= | assignment and modulus, returns the remainder of the value of the left hand expression divided by the value of the right hand expression |

### Example: Assignment Operators

An int variable is declared, and initialized with the value 2. The *= operator is used to multiply it by 4.

```
public class TestAssign {
    public static void main(String args[]) {
        int j = 2;
        System.out.println("j is " + j);

        j *= 4;
        System.out.println("j is now " + j);
    }
}
```

**Output**
```
j is 2
j is now 8
```

## 1.5.3 Boolean Operators

The boolean operators are used to manipulate boolean values.

| Operator | Meaning |
|---|---|
| && | logical and |
| & | evaluation and |
| \|\| | logical or |
| \| | evaluation or |

& always evaluates both expressions. && will evaluate the first expression and will only evaluate the second if the first expression is true.

## Example: Using the && Operator

The && operator is used to evaluate two boolean expressions. If they are both true, a message is printed to standard output. Note the use of the == operator and the special character sequence \" to denote double quotation marks. See Section 1.5.5 on page on page 30 and Section 1.9.4 on page 56 for more details.

```
public class TestBool {
  public static void main(String args[]) {
    int j = 2;
    String str = "Jackson";

    if (j == 2 && str.equals("Jackson")) {
      System.out.println("j is 2 and str is \"Jackson\" ");
    }
  }
}
```

*Output*
```
j is 2 and str is "Jackson"
```

# 1.5.4 Casting Operator

The casting operator is a set of curved brackets enclosing a variable type. It is used to convert one data type to another.

## Example: Casting Variables

A float variable is divided by an int variable, and the result assigned to another int variable. Without the integer cast, (int), Java will return an error because Java does not allow an implicit conversion of float to int. (The result of dividing two int values is a float.)

```
public class TestCast {
  public static void main(String args[]) {
    float x = 10;
    int y = 3;
    int i = (int) (x / y);
    System.out.println("i is " + i);
  }
}
```

*Output*
```
i is 3
```

## 1.5.5 Relational Operators

The relational operators are used to compare values; they return a `boolean` value and are typically used in conditional statements.

| Operator | Meaning |
|----------|---------|
| == | equal to |
| != | not equal to |
| < | less than |
| <= | less than or equal to |
| > | greater than |
| >= | greater than or equal to |

Note that to test if an `int` value was equal to 2, the code would not be written as:

```
if (j = 2)
```

This would not compile, because the expression `j = 2` is of type `int` whereas the `if` statement requires a `boolean` expression. The proper syntax is:

```
if (j == 2)
```

This compares the current value of `j` with the value 2.

**Example: Using Relational Operators**

See example *Using the && Operator* on page 29.

# 1.6 Control Structures

Control structures provide a means to control the flow of code execution within a method.

## 1.6.1 if-else if-else

The `if - else if - else` syntax tests one or more conditions. If a condition is met, the code contained in the subsequent block is executed. The condition is a `boolean` expression.

**Syntax**

```
if (condition1) {
  some code;
} else if (condition2) {
  some code;
} else {
  some code;
}
```

## Example: Using an if Statement

This example demonstrates the use of the if statement to execute one of two blocks of code depending on whether y is equal to 2.

```
public class TestIf {
  public static void main(String args[]) {
    int y = 2;

    if (y == 2) {
      System.out.println("y is 2");
    } else {
      System.out.println("y is not 2");
    }
  }
}
```

**Output**

```
y is 2
```

# 1.6.2 while

A while loop is used to execute a block of code for as long as a specified boolean condition is true.

**Syntax**

```
while (boolean expression) {
  body of loop;
}
```

### Example: Using a while Loop

This example demonstrates the use of a while loop to execute a block of code while y is less than 5. Within the block of code, y is incremented, so that the block of code is executed five times.

```java
public class TestWhile {
  public static void main(String args[]) {
    int y = 0;

    while (y < 5) {
      System.out.println("y is " + y);
      ++y;
    }
  }
}
```

#### Output

```
y is 0
y is 1
y is 2
y is 3
y is 4
```

## 1.6.3 do-while

A do-while loop is similar to a while loop, except the body of the loop is always executed at least once.

### Syntax

```
do {
  body of loop;
} while (boolean expression);
```

### Example: Using a do Loop

This example demonstrates the use of a do-while loop to execute a block of code while y is less than 1. Although y initially has the value 1, the block of code is still executed once.

```java
public class TestDoWhile {
  public static void main(String args[]) {
    int y = 1;
```

```
      do {
        System.out.println("y is " + y);
        ++y;
      } while (y < 1);
    }
  }
```

**Output**

```
  y is 1
```

# 1.6.4 for

A for loop is used to execute a block of code a number of times.

**Syntax**

```
for (initialization; condition; increment) {
  body of loop;
}
```

A variable is given an initial value. As long as the variable meets a certain condition, the code in the subsequent block will execute. Normally the variable is incremented or decremented each time the block executes. The three parts of the for loop conditional statement are separated by semi-colons.

**Example: Using a for Loop**

This example demonstrates the use of a for loop to execute a block of code three times.

```
public class TestFor {
  public static void main(String args[]) {
    for (int i = 0; i < 3; ++i) {
      System.out.println("i is " + i);
    }
  }
}
```

**Output**

```
  i is 0
  i is 1
  i is 2
```

More than one variable can be initialized and incremented. The multiple values are separated by commas, for example:

```
for (i=0, j=100; i < 10; i++, j--) {
```

# 1.6.5 break

break exits the current loop; it can also be used to exit a labeled block.

**Syntax**

```
break;
```

**Example: Using break**

This example uses break to prematurely break out of a for loop.

```
public class TestBreak {
    public static void main(String args[]) {
        int n;

        for (n = 0; n < 5; ++n) {
            if (n == 3) {
                break;
            }
        }

        System.out.println("n is " + n);
    }
}
```

*Output*

```
n is 3
```

# 1.6.6 continue

continue returns to the top of the current loop.

**Syntax**

```
continue;
```

# 1.6.7 switch

The switch statement is used to compare an expression to a series of possible cases.

**Syntax**

```
switch (expression) {
case value1:
  some code;
  break;
case value2:
  some code;
  break;
default:
  final code;
}
```

If the expression matches the case, the code below the case statement is executed. A break statement is used to exit the switch block once a case has been matched. If the expression matches none of the case statements, the code below the default statement is run. The break and default statements are not mandatory.

The expression must be an int, byte, or char. A colon (not semi-colon) is placed at the end of the case statements.

**Example: Using a switch Statement**

This example demonstrates the use of a switch statement to compare a char with a number of possible values.

```
public class TestCase {
   public static void main(String args[]) {
      char letter = 'B';
      int points;

      switch (letter) {
      case 'A':
        points = 90;
        break;
      case 'B':
        points = 80;
        break;
      default:
        points = 0;
      }
      System.out.println("points = " + points);
   }
}
```

**Output**

```
points = 80
```

## 1.6.8 Ternary Operator (? :)

The ternary operator can be used within an expression to return one of two values depending on the value of a `boolean` expression.

**Syntax**

```
(conditional expression) ? var1 : var2;
```

The conditional statement is evaluated. If it is `true`, then the operator gives value `var1`; if it is `false`, then its value is `var2`.

**Example: Using the Ternary Operator**

This example demonstrates the use of the ternary operator within an expression.

```
public class TestTernary {
  public static void main(String args[]) {
    double a = 3.0;
    double b = 2.0;

    double max = (a > b) ? a : b;
    System.out.println("max value is " + max);
  }
}
```

*Output*

```
max value is 3.0
```

# 1.7 Exception Handling

Exception handling allows a program to keep running when otherwise catastrophic errors occur. A user-defined exception handler can process the exception and allow the code to keep running; otherwise, it will be handled by the default system handler, which will result in program termination.

Exception handling is performed one of two ways: by including the code that might throw an exception within a `try-catch` block, or by adding the exception type to the method's `throws` list.

There are two types of exceptions in Java:

- ❏ **Checked** exceptions, which must be caught or added to the method's `throws` list.

- ❏ **Unchecked** exceptions, which do not have to be handled. The compiler does not check to see if the method handles this type of error. Unchecked exceptions are not included in the syntax information in Chapters 2 - 13 of this book.

# 1.7.1 try-catch Block

One way to handle a thrown exception is through the use of a try-catch block. A try block is a block of code preceded by the keyword try. Any code that can throw an exception is enclosed in the try block. Once an exception is thrown, any statements in the try block below where the exception was thrown will not be executed.

### Syntax

```
try {
    some code;
} catch (exception e) {
    some more code;
}
```

A try block acts like an inner block of code. Any variables declared or objects instantiated within a try block will not be available to the program once the code leaves the try block.

The catch block catches the exception. It consists of a block of code preceded by the keyword catch and an exception type. The code inside the catch block may provide a detailed error message or it may try to correct the error. There can be multiple catch blocks associated with a given try block. There can also be no catch block at all if the try block is followed by a finally block. If an exception is thrown in the try block, the Java Virtual Machine will try to match the type of thrown object with the type specified in each catch block.

There should never be any code between a try block and a catch block. If the code in a try block throws an exception, the code between the try and catch blocks will not be executed.

### Example: Catching an Exception

In this example, an exception is deliberately caused, and the exception is handled in a try-catch block which prints the exception to the command line.

```
public class TestException {
    public static void main(String args[]) {
        int[] a = {
            0, 1, 2, 3, 4
        };

        try {
            for (int i = 0; i <= 5; ++i) {
                System.out.println("a[" + i + "] is " + a[i]);
            }
        } catch (Exception e) {
            System.out.println("Exception: " + e);
        }
        System.out.println("more code can be run");
    }
}
```

> **Output**
> ```
> a[0] is 0
> a[1] is 1
> a[2] is 2
> a[3] is 3
> a[4] is 4
> Exception: java.lang.ArrayOutOfBoundsException
> more code can be run
> ```

In this code, an inappropriate array index is deliberately passed to the `println()` method. This throws an `ArrayIndexOutOfBoundsException`. The `catch` block has an `Exception` object as an argument, meaning the block can catch any `Exception` sub-class object. Sending the `Exception` object to the `println()` method in the catch block calls the `toString()` method which identifies the type of exception thrown. If the exception were not caught, the program would stop running and `"more code can be run"` would never be printed.

# 1.7.2 finally Keyword

> **Syntax**
> ```
> finally {
>     some code;
> }
> ```

The `finally` keyword is used at the end of a `try` block to designate a block of code that will be executed whether an exception is thrown or not, and whether the exception is caught or not. (If the exception is caught, the `catch` block will be executed first.) A `try` block can have zero or more `catch` blocks, and an optional `finally` block, but must have one or the other.

# 1.7.3 throw Keyword

> **Syntax**
> ```
> throw throwableObject;
> ```

The `throw` keyword, followed by a reference to an `Exception` object, is used to throw an exception; this is useful if a method in a class you are writing can produce some error which must be handled elsewhere in the program. The exception must be of type `Throwable` or one of its sub-classes. The `throw` keyword is often used to rethrow a caught exception.

## Example: Throwing an Exception

In this example, an inappropriate array index is sent to the println() method in
the printArray() method. This causes an ArrayIndexOutOfBoundsException to
be thrown. The exception is caught in the catch block of the printArray() method.
The throw statement then re-throws the exception back to the main() method
where it is re-caught in the catch block of the main() method

```
public class TestThrow {
   public static void printArray(int[] a) {
     try {
        for (int i = 0; i <= 5; ++i) {
           System.out.println("a[" + i + "] is " + a[i]);
        }
     } catch (ArrayIndexOutOfBoundsException e) {
        System.out.println(e + " caught in printArray");
        throw e;
     }
   }

   public static void main(String args[]) {
     int[] array = {
        0, 1, 2, 3, 4
     };

     try {
        printArray(array);
     } catch (ArrayIndexOutOfBoundsException e) {
        System.out.println(e + " re-caught in main");
     }
   }
}
```

### *Output*

```
a[0] is 0
a[1] is 1
a[2] is 2
a[3] is 3
a[4] is 4
java.lang.ArrayIndexOutOfBoundsException caught in printArray
java.lang.ArrayIndexOutOfBoundsException re-caught in main
```

# 1.7.4 throws Keyword

**Syntax**

```
... methodName throws Exception1, Exception2, ...
```

If a possible exception is not caught within a try-catch block, it must instead be allowed to propogate up from the current method to the method calling it. The throws keyword is used to declare that a method can throw an exception; it is followed by a list of exceptions the method is capable of throwing. Error or RuntimeException subclass exceptions do not need to be included in the throws list, because they are typically so serious as to require program termination.

**Example: Using throws**

```java
public class TestThrows {
  public static void throwError() throws InterruptedException {
    throw new InterruptedException();
  }

  public static void main(String args[]) {
    try {
      throwError();
    } catch (InterruptedException e) {
      System.out.println("" + e + " caught in main");
    }
    System.out.println("code continues on");
  }
}
```

*Output*

```
java.lang.InterruptedException caught in main
code continues on
```

The method throwError() creates an InterruptedException object and throws it. Because InterruptedException is part of the throws list, the exception propagates through the throwError() method back to the main() method where it is caught. This program will not compile without the throws syntax.

# 1.8 Methods

**Syntax**

```
accessType returnType methodName(parameterList) {
  // Body of method

  return value; // Not necessary if return value is void
}
```

A method is a block of code that has a name, access type, return type, and a list of arguments. It may also have keywords associated with it such as `static`, `abstract`, and `final`. Methods in Java are the equivalent of C++ class functions. With the exception of variable and object declaration statements and static initialization blocks, all executable code in Java is placed within a method.

The name can be any legal string of characters. A method name cannot be the same as one of the keywords reserved by Java. The convention is to use lower case for the first letter of method names. Care must be taken when selecting a name not to choose one unintentionally that is already being used to describe a method or the previously described method will be overridden.

With the exception of constructors (see Section 1.10.2 on page 59), every method must be given a return type. Only one primitive variable, class object, or array of primitive variables or class objects can be returned. In other words, a method can return an `int` or a `float` but cannot return both an `int` and a `float`. If no data is returned by the method, the return type is `void`.

Methods can be overloaded - two methods with different parameter lists can be given the same name.

# 1.8.1 Method Access

Every method has an access type associated with it that is used to control the access to the method. The access type can be absent (as in none specified), `public`, `private`, or `protected`.

❑ A `public` method can be called by any code that has access to the class. The `main()` method, for instance, is declared `public` because it is called by the Java run-time system.

❑ A `private` method can only be called by an object of the class in which the `private` method is defined.

❑ A `protected` method can be called by an object of the class in which the `protected` method is defined and by any class objects of classes that inherit from the class in which the method is defined. They are also available to any class objects from classes inside the same package as the class in which the method is defined.

❑ If no access type is specified, a default access level is used, which means that the method is accessible to all classes contained in the same package but is not accessible outside that package.

## Example: Method Access

A class named Message is defined, and contains a constructor and one other method, getMessage(), which has public access, returns a String object, and takes no arguments. getMessage() can be accessed from the TestMeth class because it has been declared public.

```
public class TestMeth {
  public static void main(String args[]) {
    Message m = new Message("Hello there");

    System.out.println("Message is: " + m.getMessage());
  }
}

class Message {
  private String message;

  public Message(String msg) {
    message = msg;
  }

  public String getMessage() {
    return message;
  }
}
```

A Message object is created in the main() method the TestMeth class, and its getMessage() method is invoked. If getMessage() had been declared private, the Message object would not have been able to call the getMessage() method because the Message object was created outside of class Message.

### Output

```
Message is: Hello there
```

# 1.8.2 main() Method

| Method | Syntax |
| --- | --- |
| main() | public static void main(String args[]) |

All Java applications begin by calling the main() method which is placed in the class whose name is provided to the Java Virtual Machine to begin execution of the program. Not every class needs a main() method, only the class that is the starting point of the program. The main() method is declared static because it is called by the Java run-time machine before any objects are created. The arguments passed to the main() method are any command line arguments that are typed when the program is executed.

## Example: Using main()

This is the simplest of all Java applications. The TestMain class contains only the main() method. The main() method contains only one line of code.

```
public class TestMain {
  public static void main(String args[]) {
    System.out.println("This is main");
  }
}
```

### Output

```
This is main
```

Command line arguments are read in as the arguments to the main() method. Unlike C, the program name is not the first argument passed. The command line arguments are stored in the args[] String array that is passed to the main() method.

## Example: Using command-line arguments

This example demonstrates the use of command-line arguments within the main() method. The arguments that are entered after typing in java TestCLA are printed. Because args is a String array, the number of arguments can be obtained using the length variable.

```
public class TestCLA {
  public static void main(String args[]) {
    for(int i=0; i<args.length; ++i) {
      System.out.println("argument "+i+" is " + args[i]);
    }
  }
}
```

### Output

When the program is invoked using the command java TestCLA Hello There, the output is:

```
argument 0 is Hello
argument 1 is there
```

If a space is needed inside an argument, enclose the argument in double quotes, for example java Main "Hi there".

# 1.8.3 return Statement

### Syntax

```
return;
return object;
```

return is used to exit from the current method, and returns the value specified by the return type of the method. If the method return type is void, the return keyword is used by itself.

### Example: Using Return

In this example, the getArea() method of class Box is used to return the area of a box.

```
public class TestReturn {
  public static void main(String args[]) {
    Box b = new Box(2.0, 5.0);
    System.out.println("area is " + b.getArea());
  }
}

class Box {
  double width, height;

  public Box(double w, double h) {
    width = w;
    height = h;
  }

  public double getArea() {
    return width*height;
  }
}
```

### Output

```
area is 10.0
```

# 1.8.4 Abstract Methods

Abstract methods are used in abstract classes (see Section 1.13.1 on page 69) to impose a certain functionality on sub-classes of the abstract class. Abstract methods are designated by the abstract keyword and have no body.

The implementation of the abstract methods is left to sub-classes. For instance, in the example below, a class called Figure defines an abstract method getArea(), which returns the area of the Figure object. Rectangle and Triangle classes can be defined as sub-classes of Figure. Because the area of a rectangle and a triangle are computed using different mathematical formulae, the Rectangle and Triangle classes would provide their own implementation of the getArea() method.

A class object cannot be instantiated if the class contains or inherits any abstract methods.

## Example: Using Abstract Methods

The abstract class Figure defines the abstract method getArea(). Two sub-classes of Figure, Rectangle and Triangle, provide different implementations of getArea(). The TestAbs class provides the main() method. Inside main(), a Rectangle and a Triangle object are instantiated. The areas are returned using the individual getArea() methods implemented by the Triangle and Rectangle classes.

```
public class TestAbs {
  public static void main(String args[]) {
    Rectangle r = new Rectangle(5, 4);
    Triangle t = new Triangle(4, 3);

    System.out.println("Rectangle area is " + r.getArea());
    System.out.println("Triangle area is " + t.getArea());
  }
}


abstract class Figure {
  double idim, jdim;

  Figure(double a, double b) {
    idim = a;
    jdim = b;
  }

  abstract double getArea();   // getArea() is an abstract method
}


class Rectangle extends Figure {
  Rectangle(double a, double b) {
    super(a, b);               // The class Figure constructor is called
  }
```

**45**

```
      double getArea() {              // The getArea() method is overridden
        return idim * jdim;
      }
    }


class Triangle extends Figure {
  Triangle(double a, double b) {
    super(a, b);
  }

      double getArea() {              // The getArea() method is overridden
        return 0.5 * idim * jdim;
      }
    }
```

**Output**
```
Rectangle area is 20.0
Triangle area is 6.0
```

# 1.8.5 Final Methods

A method that is declared as final cannot be overridden in a sub-class. The final keyword is written after the access type and before the return type.

## Example: Using Final Methods

See example *Using the final Keyword* on page 74.

# 1.8.6 Static Methods

A static method is similar to a static variable in that it is assigned to a class and not to an object of that class. Static methods may not access non-static variables declared at class scope and may not invoke non-static methods. Static methods may only use static variables at class scope and can only call other static methods. Static methods do not have access to the "this" reference.

A static method within a class can be called even if there has not been an instantiation of the class. An example of this is the main() method. The syntax for calling a static method is the method name plus whatever arguments the method requires. To invoke a static method from another class use the class name followed by the method.

## Example: Using Static Methods

In this example, the main() method calls a static method, getBlah(), that is defined in the class AnotherClass. Because getBlah() has been defined as static it can be called directly without first creating an instance of class AnotherClass.

```
public class TestStatic {
  public static void main(String args[]) {
    String str = AnotherClass.getBlah();
    System.out.println(str);
  }
}

class AnotherClass {
  public static String getBlah() {
    return "Blah";
  }
}
```

### Output

```
Blah
```

See also example *Calling a Static Method Defined in Another Class* on page 48.

# 1.8.7 Calling Methods

Methods are called in different ways depending on whether the methods are static or non-static, and whether the methods are called from within or outside the class in which they are defined.

## Calling Class Methods From Within the Same Class

To call a class method from within the class, just use the method name.

## Example: Calling a Class Method from Within the Same Class

A static method can only invoke other static methods, so printBlah must be declared static. If printBlah() was not static, it could still be called from the main() method using the techniques described in *Calling Non-Static Methods from Main* on page 49.

```
public class TestCall1 {
  public static void main(String args[]) {
    printBlah();   // method call
  }
```

```
    public static void printBlah() {
      System.out.println("Blah, Blah, Blah");
    }
  }
```

*Output*

```
Blah, Blah, Blah
```

# Calling Class Methods Defined in Another Class

To call a class method defined in another class, use a class object to invoke the method.

## Example: Calling a Class Method Defined in Another Class

In this example, the method printBlah() in the PrintBlah class is called from the main() method of the TestCall2 class by first creating a PrintBlah object.

```
public class TestCall2 {
  public static void main(String args[]) {
    PrintBlah pb = new PrintBlah();
    pb.printBlah(); // method call
  }
}

class PrintBlah {
  public void printBlah() {
    System.out.println("Blah, Blah, Blah");
  }
}
```

*Output*

```
Blah, Blah, Blah
```

# Calling Static Methods Defined in Another Class

To call a static method defined in another class, use the class name in front of the method call.

## Example: Calling a Static Method Defined in Another Class

The sleep() method is a static method defined in the Thread class. It causes the program to go to sleep for the specified number of milliseconds. For a description of the try-catch syntax, see Section 1.7.1 on page 37.

```
public class TestCall3 {
  public static void main(String args[]) {
    System.out.println("I'll think for three seconds");
```

```
    try {
        Thread.sleep(3000);   // call to static method sleep()
    } catch (InterruptedException ie) {}
    System.out.println("I'm done");
    }
  }
```

**Output**

```
I'll think for three seconds
I'm done
```

# Calling Non-Static Methods From main()

The main() method is a static method which means only static methods can be called from within main() unless a class object is created. To allow non-static methods to be called from main(), create a class object in main() and either directly call the non-static methods of that object or put the non-static method calls in the class constructor.

## Example: Calling Non-Static Methods from Main

The printMessage() method is non-static. It is called from main() in two ways: by placing the method call in class constructor, and by calling the method directly from main() once a TestCall4 object has been instantiated.

```
public class TestCall4 {
  public TestCall4() {
    printMessage();
  }

  public void printMessage() {
    System.out.println("I'm non-static");
  }

  public static void main(String args[]) {
    TestCall4 tc = new TestCall4();
    tc.printMessage();
  }
}
```

**Output**

```
I'm non-static
I'm non-static
```

# 1.8.8 Passing Arguments to Methods

Arguments are passed to methods in Java by value. A copy of the primitive datatype, or the reference to the class object or array, is made and the copy is passed to the method.

## Passing Variable Arguments to Methods

Primitive datatypes are passed to methods by value: a copy is made and passed to the method. The method is never able to modify the actual argument.

A variable of a class type is stored as a reference, and the reference is passed to the method by value: a copy of the *reference* is made and passed to the method. The copy refers to the same object as the original, and so the object can be modified through the copy of the reference.

### Example: Passing Variable Arguments to Methods

This example demonstrates how to pass arguments to methods, and how class objects may be changed within a method using the copy of the reference.

```
import java.util.*;

public class TestPass {
  public TestPass(Vector v, int i) {
    change(v, i);
  }

  public void change(Vector v, int i) {
    v.add("Lisa");
    i = i + i;
  }

  public static void main(String args[]) {
    int value = 3;
    Vector names = new Vector();
    names.add("Jackson");
    names.add("Zachary");

    TestPass tp = new TestPass(names, value);

    System.out.println("value is " + value);
    System.out.println("names are " + names);
  }
}
```

A Vector object and an int are given initial values in the main() method and passed to a method called change(). In the change() method an element is added to the Vector and the int is added to itself. Even though the change() method has return type void, the Vector object in the main() method is permanently changed because reference passed to the method by value refers to the same object as the original. The value of the int in the main() method is not changed.

**Output**

```
value is 3
names are [Jackson, Zachary, Lisa]
```

## Passing Array Arguments to Methods

Arrays are passed to methods by passing a copy of the reference to it. The array elements can then be modified by using the copy of the reference.

### Example: Passing Array Arguments to Methods

A three element int array is created and intialized with the values 1, 2, and 3. The array is passed by reference to a method called change() where the values stored in the array are changed. Because the change() method is non-static, it cannot be called directly from the main() method, but instead is called from the constructor.

```java
public class TestPass2 {
  private int[] intArray;

  public TestPass2() {
    intArray = new int[] {
      1, 2, 3
    };
    change(intArray);
  }

  public void change(int[] ia) {
    for (int i = 0; i < intArray.length; ++i) {
      intArray[i] = 9 - intArray[i];
    }
  }

  public int getZero() {
    return intArray[0];
  }

  public static void main(String args[]) {
    TestPass2 tp = new TestPass2();

    System.out.println("zeroth element is " + tp.getZero());
  }
}
```

**Output**

```
zeroth element is 8
```

# 1.8.9 Method Chaining

Method chaining, or cascading, is when multiple method calls are placed on a single line. The return value of the left-most method is used to call the method to its right and so on.

## Example: Using Method Chaining

In this example, a String object is converted into a double value by first converting the String into a Double object. Method chaining is used to put this entire operation on one line of code.

```
public class TestChain {
  public static void main(String args[]) {
    double d = Double.valueOf("45.3").doubleValue();
    double d2 = 2.0*d;
    System.out.println("value is " + d2);
  }
}
```

The valueOf() method is a static method defined in the Double class that returns a Double object containinge double value corresponding to the String "45.3". The resulting Double object then calls the doubleValue() method, which returns the double primitive.

**Output**
```
value is 90.6
```

# 1.8.10 Overloading Class Methods and Constructors

Java class methods can be overloaded meaning multiple methods can be given the same name. The compiler determines which method to call based on the arguments passed. A call to an overloaded method must be unambiguous, meaning the compiler must be able to decide which to call. Constructors are often overloaded.

There is no implicit type conversion from a primitive to a reference type.

## Example: Using Overloaded Class Methods

A class named Rect is defined that represents a rectangle. Three constructors are provided. The no-argument constructor assigns the width and height to 1. The one argument constructor assigns the width and height to the same value. The two argument constructor allows the width and height to be set to different values. The compiler calls the appropriate version of the constructor based on the number of arguments provided.

```
public class TestOver {
  public static void main(String args[]) {
    Rect r1 = new Rect();
    Rect r2 = new Rect(5);
    Rect r3 = new Rect(2, 3);

    System.out.println("area of r1 is " + r1.getArea());
    System.out.println("area of r2 is " + r2.getArea());
    System.out.println("area of r3 is " + r3.getArea());
  }
}

class Rect {
  int width, height;

  public Rect() {
    width = 1;
    height = 1;
  }

  public Rect(int w) {
    width = w;
    height = w;
  }

  public Rect(int w, int h) {
    width = w;
    height = h;
  }

  public int getArea() {
    return width * height;
  }
}
```

**Output**
```
area of r1 is 1
area of r2 is 25
area of r3 is 6
```

# 1.8.11 Static Initialization Blocks

**Syntax**
```
static {
  initialization code;
}
```

A static initialization block is a block of code that is only executed once when the class is first loaded, and is preceded by the keyword static. Static initialization blocks are used to initialize static data members.

# 1.9 Basic Printing

While Java's input and output facilities are described more fully in Chapter 4, the basic facilities for printing a message to the command prompt are sufficiently widely used to warrant a short description here.

## 1.9.1 Standard Output Stream

**Syntax**

```
public static final PrintStream out
```

The standard output stream allows access to the basic printing methods `print()` and `println()` from the `PrintStream` class. It provides a reference to a `PrintStream` object that can access those methods.

The `out` variable is a member of the `System` class (see Section 2.6.3 on page ). Because it is a static variable, to retrieve a reference to the `out` variable use the syntax:

```
System.out
```

## 1.9.2 print() Method

| Method | Syntax |
|--------|--------|
| print() | `public void print(String s)` |
| | `public void print(boolean b)` |
| | `public void print(char c)` |
| | `public void print(char[] charArray)` |
| | `public void print(double d)` |
| | `public void print(float f)` |
| | `public void print(int i)` |
| | `public void print(long l)` |
| | `public void print(Object obj)` |

`print()` prints the passed argument to standard output (generally the console) without an end-of-line character or sequence. If anything other than a `String` object is passed as an argument, the argument is converted to a `String` representation of itself.

## Example: Using print()

This example uses print() to output String data without an end-of-line sequence, so the successive items of output run together.

```
public class TestPrint {
  public static void main(String args[]) {
    for(int i=1; i<3; ++i) {
      System.out.print("This is line " + i);
    }
  }
}
```

*Output*

```
This is line 1This is line 2
```

# 1.9.3 println() Method

| Method | Syntax |
|--------|--------|
| println() | public void **println**(String *s*) |
| | public void **println**(boolean *b*) |
| | public void **println**(char *c*) |
| | public void **println**(char[] *charArray*) |
| | public void **println**(double *d*) |
| | public void **println**(float *f*) |
| | public void **println**(int *i*) |
| | public void **println**(long *l*) |
| | public void **println**(Object *obj*) |

println() is similar to the print() method except an end-of-line character or sequence is added to the end. The println() method also flushes the output buffer when finished.

## Example: Using println()

This example uses print() to output String data, together with an end-of-line sequence, so the successive items of output appear on separate lines.

```
public class TestPrintln {
  public static void main(String args[]) {
    for(int i=1; i<3; ++i) {
      System.out.println("This is line " + i);
    }
  }
}
```

*Output*
```
This is line 1
This is line 2
```

# 1.9.4 Special Characters

| Syntax | Meaning |
|--------|---------|
| \' | single quote |
| \" | double quote |
| \\ | backslash |
| \b | backspace |
| \f | formfeed |
| \n | newline |
| \r | carriage return |
| \t | tab |
| \d*ee* | octal representation |
| \x*dd* | hexadecimal representation |
| \u*dddd* | Unicode character |

Special characters are used to denote characters that would otherwise be difficult to represent. The special characters can also be assigned to a variable for clarity.

## Example: Using Special Characters

The quotes in the syntax "Hello you" below do not represent double quotes but instead indicate a String object. In order to print double quotes, the appropriate special character must be used.

```
public class TestSpecChar {
    public static void main(String args[]) {
        char doubleQuote = '\"';
        System.out.println(doubleQuote + "Hello you" + doubleQuote);
        System.out.println("here is a " + '\t' + " tab");
    }
}
```

*Output*
```
"Hello you"
here is a       tab
```

# 1.9.5 The + Operator

| Operator | Meaning |
|----------|---------|
| + | Arithmetic addition or string concatenation |

The + operator is a String concatenation operator when either of the two operands is a String, otherwise it represents arithmetic addition.

## Example: Using the + Operator

This example shows the difference between String concatenation and arithmetic addition. The argument passed to the println() method is evaluated from left to right. In the first instance, the sequence 1 + 2 + 3 is evaluated as arithmetic addition. The result, 6, is then concatenated with the String "go". In the second instance, a String is the first operand so the entire argument is evaluated as a String concatenation.

```
public class TestSpecOp {
   public static void main(String args[]) {
      System.out.println(1 + 2 + 3 + " go");
      System.out.println("Testing " + 1 + 2 + 3);
   }
}
```

### Output

```
6 go
testing 123
```

# 1.10 Classes

### Syntax

```
accessType class className {
   variable1;
   variable2;
   //etc.

   method1(parameterList) {
      method body;
   }

   // additional methods
}
```

A class is a collection of data members and methods that define a particular object. It is the fundamental construct of the Java language. Other than import and package statements, every piece of code in a Java program must be contained within a class. A class can be either user-defined or provided by one of the built-in Java packages. The naming convention for classes is to use upper case letter for first letter of class names.

A file may contain any number of classes but only one class in each file can be declared public. The name of the file must be the same as the public class name with the .java extension. (For example, a class declared as public class Main must be stored in a file called Main.java.)

In any Java program, one class will contain the main() method. The main() method is the starting point of the code. The class that contains the main() method is known as the driver or starting class. See Section 1.8.2 on page 42 for more information on the main() method.

Access to data members within a class, other than final and static data members, should be done only through class member functions. The convention is for a get() or is() method to return the current value of the variable and a set() method is used to change the value of the variable. See example *Defining a Constructor* on page 59 for a demonstration of how get() methods are used.

Java class objects, whether user-defined or library objects, are always stored on the heap and must be created using the new command.

## Example: Using Classes

In this example, two classes are defined. The BoxText class contains the main() method. Inside the main() method, a Box class object is created using the new keyword. The Box object then calls the getVolume() method which is defined in the Box class. The Box class contains three data members named width, height, and depth. It also has two methods, a constructor and the aforementioned getVolume() method.

```java
public class BoxText {
    public static void main(String args[]) {
        Box b = new Box(3.0, 4.0, 2.0);
        System.out.println("volume is " + b.getVolume());
    }
}

class Box {
    double width, height, depth;

    public Box(double w, double h, double d) {
        width = w;
        height = h;
        depth = d;
    }

    public double getVolume() {
        return width * height * depth;
    }
}
```

### Output

```
volume is 24.0
```

# 1.10.1 Access Privileges

The access can be absent (unspecified) or public. There may only be one public class present in a file and the name of this public class must be the same as the name of the source file in which it is located.

If the access is absent, then the class and its members are only accessible by other classes within the same package. A public class is accessible to all other classes.

Inner classes (see Section 1.13.2 on page 69) may be declared private or protected.

# 1.10.2 Constructors

The constructor is a non-static method with the same name as the class. Constructors have no return type and are automatically called when a class object is created. The function of the constructor is to initialize the non-static data members of the class.

The constructor can be overloaded to give multiple constructors with different types of passed arguments. The compiler figures out which to call based on the arguments passed. Constructors are generally defined as public.

Values are passed to the constructor by placing them within the parentheses of the class object creation (instantiation) statement.

The system will provide a no-argument constructor if no constructor is provided. If any constructor is present, the system-provided default constructor is not available.

### Example: Defining a Constructor

In this example, a class is written that defines two data members, a String and an int. A public constructor is used to initialize the data members. getName() and getAge() methods are provided to retrieve the values of the name and age members.

```
public class TestConstr {
    private String name;
    private int age;

    public TestConstr(String str, int a) {
        name = str;
        age = a;
    }

    public String getName() {
        return name;
    }

    public int getAge() {
        return age;
    }
```

```
public static void main(String args[]) {
    TestConstr tc = new TestConstr("Jackson", 4);

    System.out.println("name is " + tc.getName());
    System.out.println("age is " + tc.getAge());
  }
}
```

**Output**

```
name is Jackson
age is 4
```

# 1.10.3 Creating (Instantiating) a Class Object

All class objects are dynamically allocated on the heap. A class object is created using the new keyword. Class objects are created in two steps. The first step declares a variable of the class type and creates a null pointer to the object. The second step creates an object of the class type:

```
Box b;
b = new Box(2.0, 3.0, 4.0);
```

The two steps can be combined into a single line of code.

```
Box b = new Box(2.0, 3.0, 4.0);
```

The values in parentheses are passed to the constructor. The parentheses are mandatory even if there are no arguments to be passed.

A class object can also be created without declaring a variable of the class type by placing the new syntax in an expression.

**Example: Creating an Object without Declaring a Variable**

In this example, two Integer objects are added to a Vector. The Vector class, defined in the java.util package, represents a dynamic array that is used to store objects. The Integer objects are created using the new syntax without declaring variables of type Integer.

```
import java.util.*;

public class TestClassCreate {
  public static void main(String args[]) {
    Vector v = new Vector();

    v.addElement(new Integer(4));
    v.addElement(new Integer(7));
```

```
        System.out.println("contents of v: " + v);
    }
}
```

*Output*

```
contents of v: [4, 7]
```

# 1.10.4 Instantiating Arrays of Class Objects

With arrays of primitive datatypes, the values themselves are stored in the array. With arrays of classes, first an array of references of the class type are created, then the class objects themselves are instantiated. Thus, an array of objects does not contain the objects themselves but *references* to the objects.

## Example: Instantiating Arrays of Objects

In this example, an array of Integer objects is created and its contents are then printed out.

```
public class TestObjArray {
    public static void main(String args[]) {

        Integer[] intObjArray = new Integer[5]; // references are created

        for (int i=0; i<5; ++i) {
            intObjArray[i] = new Integer(i);      // Integer objects are created
        }

        for( int i=0; i<5; ++i) {
            System.out.println("value at index " + i + " is " + intObjArray[i]);
        }
    }
}
```

*Output*

```
value at index 0 is 0
value at index 1 is 1
value at index 2 is 2
value at index 3 is 3
value at index 4 is 4
```

## 1.10.5 this Keyword

The this keyword represents a reference that is implicitly passed to every non-static method. The reference is to the invoking object itself.

### Example: Using the this Keyword

The this keyword is used to differentiate between the class variables x and y that are associated with the Point object and the variables x and y that are passed as arguments to the constructor.

```
public class TestThis {
  public static void main(String args[]) {
    Point pt = new Point(4, 5);
    System.out.println("x is " + pt.getX());
    System.out.println("y is " + pt.getY());
  }
}

class Point {
  int x, y;

  Point(int x, int y) {
    this.x = x;
    this.y = y;
  }

  int getX() {
    return x;
  }
  int getY() {
    return y;
  }
}
```

**Output**

```
x is 4
y is 5
```

## 1.11 Inheritance

The Java language supports the concept of inheritance. Inheritance allows a class, known as the sub-class or child class, to be written as an extension of another class, known as the super-class or parent class. A sub-class object has access to the public and protected methods and data members defined in the super-class. The super-class can be used to implement common methods that are used by any number of sub-classes. Thus, inheritance is a useful quality in that it minimizes redundant code.

Java Fundamentals

**Syntax**

```
accessType class className extends superClassName {
  // Methods and data members
}
```

A sub-class is given access to the public and protected methods of a super-class by using the extends keyword. Multiple inheritance is not allowed in Java: only one super class can be referenced after the extends keyword.

## Example: Using Inheritance

Three classes are defined in this example. The Coin class defines one data member, an int named value, and one method. The Quarter class extends the Coin class and provides a constructor that assigns a number to the int value. In the main() method of the TestInher class, a Quarter object is instantiated. Because the Quarter class inherits from the Coin class, the Quarter object has access to the getValue() method which is defined in the Coin class.

```
public class TestInher {
  public static void main(String args[]) {
    Quarter q = new Quarter();
    System.out.println("Value is " + q.getValue());
  }
}

class Coin {
  int value;

  public int getValue() {
    return value;
  }
}

class Quarter extends Coin {
  public Quarter() {
    value = 25;
  }
}
```

**Output**

```
Value is 25
```

## 1.11.1 Access Privileges and Inheritance

The table below summarizes which types of classes can access methods with the different access types.

| | Accessible to class defining the member | Accessible to another class in the same package | Accessible to subclass in a different package | Accessible to non-subclass in a different package |
|---|---|---|---|---|
| public access | Yes | Yes | Yes | Yes |
| protected access | Yes | Yes | Yes | No |
| default access | Yes | Yes | No | No |
| private access | Yes | No | No | No |

## 1.11.2 Using a Super-Class Reference Refer to a Sub-Class Object

A reference of a super-class type can refer to a sub-class object, but only the super-class part of the sub-class object is accessible through the super-class reference unless a narrowing reference cast is used.

### Example: Using a Super-Class Reference with a Sub-Class Object

This example demonstrates the use of a super-class variable to hold a reference to a sub-class object. A variable of type SuperClass is used to hold a reference to a SubClass object, but the field b cannot be accessed unless the reference is cast to type SubClass.

This example will not compile.

```
class SuperClass {
  protected int a;
}

class SubClass extends SuperClass {
  protected int b;
}

public class TestBind {
  public static void main(String args[]) {
    SuperClass ref = new SubClass();

    ref.a = 0;              // OK, super-class data member
    ref.b = 0;              // Error, sub-class data member
    (SubClass)ref.b = 0;    // OK, narrowing reference cast used.
  }
}
```

# 1.11.3 The super Keyword

Sub-class and super-class objects are responsible for initializing their own non-static data members. To initialize super-class data members inside a sub-class, the super-class constructor must be called as the first statement in the sub-class constructor using the super keyword. If this is not done explicitly, the no-argument constructor of the super-class will be called; if a constructor is not explicitly specified, a no-argument constructor will be generated automatically by the compiler which calls the no-argument constructor of the super-class.

Note that the super-class constructor is executed first so a sub-class object cannot be one of the arguments passed to the super-class constructor.

## Example: Using super to call the Super-Class Constructor

A class named SubClass is defined as a sub-class of a class named SuperClass. A SubClass object has access to the data member named superValue that is defined in SuperClass. When a SubClass object is created, the superValue data member is initialized by calling the SuperClass constructor and passing it the appropriate value.

```
public class TestSuper {
  public static void main(String args[]) {
    SubClass sc = new SubClass(4,3);
    System.out.println("superValue is " + sc.getSuperValue());
    System.out.println("subValue is " + sc.getSubValue());
  }
}

class SuperClass {
  protected int superValue;

  public SuperClass(int supv) {
    superValue = supv;
  }

  public int getSuperValue() {
    return superValue;
  }
}

class SubClass extends SuperClass {
  private int subValue;

  public SubClass(int subv, int supv) {
    super(supv); // calls Super_class constructor
    subValue = subv;
  }
```

```
      public int getSubValue() {
        return subValue;
      }
    }
```

**Output**

```
superValue is 3
subValue is 4
```

The super keyword can also be used to refer to super-class data members or to super class methods.

## Example: Using super to Refer to Super-Class Data Members

In this example, class TestChild and its super-class define a data member named data. The super-class data member can be accessed using the super keyword.

```
public class TestChild extends Parent {
    int data;

    public TestChild() {
      data = 3;        // Refers to data defined in TestChild class
      super.data = 4;  // Refers to data defined in Parent class
    }

    public static void main(String args[]) {
      TestChild tc = new TestChild();

      // This will print out 3 since it refers to data defined in TestChild
      System.out.println("data value is " + tc.data);
    }
}

class Parent {
    int data;
}
```

**Output**

```
data value is 3
```

# 1.11.4 Method Overloading

A sub-class method that has the same name but different arguments from a super-class method is treated as an overloaded function. The compiler will decide which is the most appropriate method based on the argument list and the object type making the call.

When an overloaded method is called from within a subclass, the version written in the sub-class is called. An example of this is the toString() method, which has a default version in the Object class that is almost always overwritten in the user-defined subclass.

## Example: Using Method Overloading

The getMessage() method is contained by both a sub-class and super class. When a sub-class object invokes the getMessage() method, the compiler decides the most appropriate version to call is the one defined in the sub-class.

```
public class TestOL {
   public static void main(String args[]) {
     SubClass s = new SubClass();
     System.out.println("message is " + s.getMessage());
   }
}

class SuperClass {
   public String getMessage() {
     return "Super message";
   }
}

class SubClass extends SuperClass {
   public String getMessage() {
     return "Sub message";
   }
}
```

### Output

```
message is Sub message
```

# 1.12 Interfaces

## Syntax

```
accessType interface interfaceName {
   method1(parameterList);
   method2(parameterList);
   // other methods

   variable1 = value;
   variable2 = value;
}
```

Interfaces are used to impose a certain functionality on the classes that implement them: they specify what such classes must do. They are also used to provide constants that can be used by the classes that implement the interface. Interfaces contain constant variables and method declarations, but the implementation of the methods is left to the classes that implement the interface. A class can implement any number of interfaces.

The access type can be either `public` or unspecified. If the access is unspecified, the interface is only available to other members of the package in which it is declared, whereas a public interface is available to any other code. If the interface is `public`, all methods and variables defined by it are implicitly `public`. Variables declared inside interfaces are implicitly `static` and `final`. Only one class or interface may be declared `public` in a given file.

## Example: Using Interfaces

A class named `Circle` implements two interfaces. The `Area` interface defines a method `getArea()` that must be implemented in class `Circle`. The `MathConstants` interface contains the value of pi. Because the class is declared `public` and the class and interfaces are contained in the same file, the interfaces cannot also be declared `public`. To declare the interfaces `public`, they would have to be placed in separate files.

```
public class Circle implements Area, MathConstants {
    double radius;

    public Circle(double r) {
        radius = r;
    }

    public double getArea() {
        return pi * radius * radius;
    }

    public static void main(String args[]) {
        Circle c = new Circle(2.0);
        System.out.println("area is " + c.getArea());
    }
}


interface Area {
    double getArea();
}

interface MathConstants {
    double pi = 3.14159265;
    // A more accurate value is available as Math.PI and would normally be
    // used. This is here only as a demonstration.
}
```

### Output

```
area is 12.5663706
```

# 1.13 More Types of Classes

As described in Section 1.1.5 on page 11, there are several special types of classes that can be defined in Java: abstract classes, inner classes, and final classes.

## 1.13.1 Abstract Classes

Abstract classes are used to define the general structure of a family of derived classes. They are designated by using the keyword abstract before the keyword class in the class declaration statement. Abstract classes cannot be instantiated, but references of an abstract type can be used to point to an instance of a concrete sub-class object.

Abstract classes can define both abstract and concrete methods. Any concrete sub-class of an abstract class must implement the abstract methods from the abstract class.

> **Example: Using Abstract Classes**
>
> See example *Using Abstract Methods* on page 45.

## 1.13.2 Inner Classes

Since Java 1.1, the language has allowed for **Inner Classes**. Inner classes allow one class to be contained inside another, for convenience. There are four types of inner class:

❑ **Static member classes** are defined within a top-level class. Apart from where they are declared, they are very much like ordinary top-level classes except that they can access static members of the class they are contained in. Static member interfaces may also be defined in the same way.

❑ **Member classes** are defined within a top-level class and an instance is always associated with a particular instance of the top-level class. A member class has access to all the members of the class it is contained in.

❑ **Local classes** are defined within a block of code, and are only visible within that block. In addition to the members of the class they are contained in, they can access any final local variables and parameters of the enclosing block of code.

❑ **Anonymous classes** are a special type of local class which is provided for convenience. An anonymous class has no name and the class definition is combined with instantiation of an object of the class; this allows a class to be defined and an instance created once, exactly where it is needed within an expression. Since definition of the anonymous class is combined with instantiation, they are not appropriate if more than one instance of the class will be required.

### Static Member Classes

**Syntax**

```
accessType class OuterClass extends SuperClass implements Interfaces {
   accessType static class StaticMemberClass extends SuperClass
      implements Interfaces {
      // Members of the static member class
   }
   // Other members of the top-level class
}
```

The static member class may be referred to outside the outer class as
*OuterClass.StaticMemberClass*.

Static member classes and interfaces may only be contained within top-level classes, or
other static member classes or interfaces.

## Example: Using a Static Member Class

The class TestStaticMember contains a static member class, StaticMember, which
contains one method, printHello(). The main() method creates a StaticMember
object and calls its printHello() method.

```
public class TestStaticMember {
   public static void main(String args[]) {
      StaticMember sm = new StaticMember();
      sm.printHello();
   }

   static class StaticMember {
      void printHello() {
         System.out.println("Hello");
      }
   }

}
```

**Output**

```
Hello
```

*Member Classes*

```
accessType class OuterClass extends SuperClass implements Interfaces {
  accessType class MemberClassName extends SuperClassName
    implements Interfaces {
    // Members of the member class
  }
  // Other members of the top-level class
}
```

The member class may be referred to outside the outer class as
*OuterClass.MemberClass*.

Member classes may not contain any static members, except for static final data
members. Since this will refer to the member class instance, the containing class
instance may be referred to using the special syntax *OuterClassName*.this.

**Example: Using a Member Class**

A Square class is written that contains a member class Box. When a Square class
object invokes the go3D() method, a Box object is instantiated. The Box object calls
the getVolume() method defined in the Box class. The getVolume() method has
access to the width and height variables that are defined in the Square class.

```
public class TestMember {
  public static void main(String args[]) {
    Square sq = new Square(3.0);
    sq.go3D();
  }
}

class Square {
  double width, height;

  public Square(double w) {
    width = w;
    height = w;
  }

  public void go3D() {
    Box b = new Box(2.0);
    System.out.println("volume is " + b.getVolume());
  }
```

```
class Box {
  double depth:

  public Box(double d) {
    depth = d:
  }

  public double getVolume() {
    return width * height * depth:
  }
 }
}
```

**Output**

```
volume is 18.0
```

### Local Classes

**Syntax**

```
{ // Beginning of block of code
  // Statements
  class LocalClass extends SuperClass implements Interfaces {
    // Members of the local class
  }
  // Statements
}
```

Local classes may not have an access type specified (since they are only visible within the containing block of code) and cannot contain static members except for static final data members. They can use any final local variables and parameters of the enclosing block of code.

## Example: Using a Local Class

The main() method of class TestLocalClass contains a local class, LocalClass, which contains one method, printHello(). The main() method creates a LocalClass object and calls its printHello() method.

```
public class TestLocalClass {

  public static void main(String args[]) {

    class LocalClass {
      void printHello() {
        System.out.println("Hello"):
      }
    }
```

```
        LocalClass lc = new LocalClass();
        lc.printHello();
    }

}
```

**Output**

```
Hello
```

### Anonymous Classes

#### Syntax

```
new SuperClass(parameters) {
  // Members of the anonymous class
}
```

The syntax above both defines an anonymous class and instantiates an object of that class. Anonymous classes cannot have constructors as they have no name; any parameters specified after the name of the super-class are passed to the super-class constructor.

Anonymous classes may not have an access type specified, and cannot contain static members except for static final data members. They can use any final local variables and parameters of the enclosing block of code.

## Example: Using an Anonymous Class

The main() method of class TestLocalClass defines and instantiates a local class which extends Object and overrides its toString() method to return the String "Hello". The object's toString() method is invoked.

```
public class TestAnonymousClass {

  public static void main(String args[]) {

    Object obj = new Object() {
      public String toString() {
        return "Hello";
      }
    };

    System.out.println(obj);
  }

}
```

**Output**

```
Hello
```

# 1.13.3 Final Classes

The final keyword can be used to prevent a sub-class method from overriding (same name, same argument list) a super-class method. The final keyword is written before the return type in the super-class declaration.

The final keyword can also prevent a class from being inherited by sub-classes. The final keyword is written before the class keyword in the class definition.

### Example: Using the final Keyword

The getMessage() method defined in SuperClass is declared to be final. It cannot be overwritten in SubClass. This program will not compile.

```java
public class TestFinal {
  public static void main(String args[]) {
    SubClass s = new SubClass();
    System.out.println("message is " + s.getMessage());
  }
}


class SuperClass {
  public final String getMessage() {
    return "Super message";
  }
}


class SubClass extends SuperClass {
  public String getMessage()  // Error: getMessage() can't be overridden
  {
    return "Sub message";
  }
}
```

# 1.14 Packages

Packages are used to partition the class name space: a less fancy way of thinking about packages is to consider them as folders that contain a group of related Java classes.

They are used as both a naming and visibility control mechanism. Two classes with the same name can happily co-exist as long as they are placed in different packages, and classes can be defined so they are only accessible to other classes contained in the same package.

If no package is specified in a Java source file, the resulting .class file(s) will be placed in a default package, which is unnamed.

The contents of a package are made accessible to a Java source file using an import statement.

# 1.14.1 Accessing Library Packages

### Syntax

```
import packageName.className;
import packageName;
```

Library packages and classes are accessed using the import keyword.

### Example: Accessing Library Packages

The Date class, contained in the java.util package, can be used to provide a snapshot of the current time. It is accessed by importing it into the program. To import the entire java.util package, the syntax would be import java.util.*;

```java
import java.util.Date;

public class TestLibPack {
  public static void main(String args[]) {
    Date d = new Date();
    System.out.println("The time is " + d.toString());
  }
}
```

**Output** *(will vary between runs)*
```
The time is Thu Feb 17 12:58:43 PST 2000
```

# 1.14.2 Creating a Package

### Syntax

```
package packageName;
package pkg1.pkg2.pkg3;
```

The package statement is put as the first statement in a Java source file. Any classes contained in the file will be associated with the package packageName. The second version creates a package hierarchy; the java.util package described in the previous example is an example of a package hierarchy.

The .class files that are created as part of a package must be stored in a directory that has the same name as the package. For a package hierarchy, a series of nested directories corresponding to the components of the package name must be used. For example, the .class files for classes in the com.wrox package must be stored in a directory called wrox within a directory called com.

## Example: Creating a Package

This code places a class named Blah1 in a package named Blah.

```
package Blah;

public class Blah1 {
  String message;

  public Blah1() {
    message = "This is Blah1";
  }

  public String getMessage() {
    return message;
  }
}
```

To add the file to the package, place the source code in the Blah directory and compile it from the parent directory:

```
javac Blah/Blah1.java
```

## Example: Using the Contents of a User-Defined Package

This example creates an instance of class Blah1 (described in example *Creating a Package* above) from the package Blah; the Blah1 class is accessed by importing it from the Blah package.

Unless the CLASSPATH environment variable has been set to include the Blah directory, the TestPack class should be compiled and run in the directory above the Blah directory.

```
import Blah.Blah1;

public class TestPack {
  public static void main(String args[]) {
    Blah1 b1 = new Blah1();
    System.out.println(b1.getMessage());
  }
}
```

*Output*

```
This is Blah1
```

# 1.14.3 Package Directory Structure

The Java .class files for a given package must be stored in a directory of the same name. If a package myPackage is created in a directory Java, the .class files contained in myPackage must reside in the directory Java/myPackage.

To locate the .class files contained in the myPackage package from anywhere in the system, the CLASSPATH environment variable must be changed to include the path to the myPackage directory. The CLASSPATH variable lists the directories that Java will use to search for the .class files.

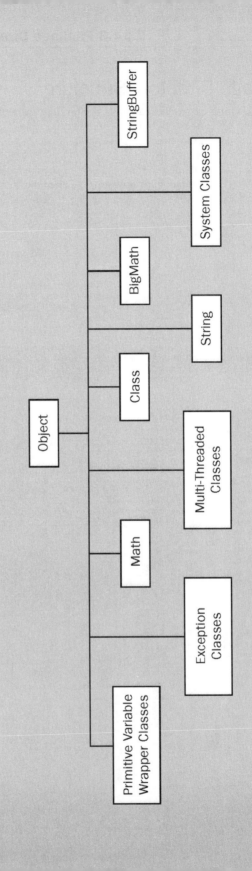

# 2

# java.lang

The java.lang package contains the main language support classes for Java. Included in the package are primitive variable wrapper classes, the classes for multi-threaded programming, the system classes, the String class, and the error and exception classes. The java.lang package is implicitly imported into every Java program; no import statement is needed.

In this Chapter we will cover:

# 2.1 Top-Level Classes and Interfaces

The `Object` and `Class` classes and the `Cloneable` interface provide basic functionality required in Java programs.

## 2.1.1 Object Class

```
public class Object
```

The `Object` class is the superclass of every other class in Java. Every other class implicitly "extends `Object`". Every method defined in `Object` is available to all of its subclasses.

The methods provided by the `Object` provide some basic functionality to copy, compare, or return information about the invoking object. They are often overridden to suit the needs of the individual sub-class.

The `Object` class provides a no-argument constructor but an `Object` object is rarely created.

### clone() Method

| Method | Syntax |
|---|---|
| clone() | protected Object clone()<br>                     throws CloneNotSupportedException |

`clone()` creates a shallow copy of the invoking object. A shallow copy means that if the invoking object contains a reference variable, the clone will point to the same object. Because the `clone()` method provides a shallow copy of the invoking object, it should be used with caution.

To override this method within a class (to provide a deep copy, for instance) the class must implement the `Cloneable` interface.

The `protected` keyword means that the `clone()` method can only be called from a method defined by a class that implements the `Cloneable` interface or it must be overridden within the class.

The `clone()` method can throw a `CloneNotSupportedException` if the invoking object is from a class that does not implement the `Cloneable` interface, or an `OutOfMemoryError` if there is not sufficient memory to create the cloned object.

## Example: Using clone()

This example uses the `clone()` method to create a copy of a `Rectangle1` object.

```
public class Rectangle1 implements Cloneable {
  double width, height;

  Rectangle1(double w, double h) {
    width = w;
    height = h;
  }

  public Object clone() {
    try {
      return super.clone();
    } catch (CloneNotSupportedException e) {
      System.out.println("Clone failed");
      return this;
    }
  }

  public static void main(String args[]) {
    Rectangle1 s1 = new Rectangle1(4.0, 2.0);
    Rectangle1 s2;

    s2 = (Rectangle1) s1.clone();

    System.out.println("Rectangle 1: width = " + s1.width
                     + " height = " + s1.height);
    System.out.println("Rectangle 2: width = " + s2.width
                     + " height = " + s2.height);
  }
}
```

### Output

```
Rectangle 1: width = 4.0  height = 2.0
Rectangle 2: width = 4.0  height = 2.0
```

In this example the `clone()` method is overridden within the `Rectangle1` class. The `clone()` method in the `Rectangle` class calls the `clone()` method from the `Object` class using the `super` keyword. Because the `clone()` method must return an `Object`, if the clone fails and an exception is caught, the invoking object is returned to the `main()` method. The return value from the `clone()` method is of type `Object` and is cast to a `Rectangle1` object.

## equals() Method

| Method | Syntax |
|--------|--------|
| equals() | public boolean equals(Object *obj*) |

`equals()` returns `true` if the invoking object and the object passed to the method argument have the same reference. This is known as a shallow comparison. This method is often overridden to provide a more meaningful comparison. For instance, the `String` class overrides this method to provide a comparison based on the contents of the two `String`s.

### Example: Overriding equals()

In this example, the `Rectangle2` class overrides the `equals()` method so that two `Rectangle2` references can be compared according to whether the `Rectangle2` objects have the same `width` and `height` rather than whether the references are to the same object.

```
public class Rectangle2 {
   double width, height;

   Rectangle2(double w, double h) {
     width = w;
     height = h;
   }

   public boolean equals(Object obj) {
     Rectangle2 r = (Rectangle2) obj;

     if ((this.width == r.width) && (this.height == r.height)) {
       return true;
     } else {
       return false;
     }
   }

   public static void main(String args[]) {
     Rectangle2 s1 = new Rectangle2(4.0, 2.0);
     Rectangle2 s2 = new Rectangle2(4.0, 2.0);

     if (s1.equals(s2)) {
       System.out.println("Rectangles are the same");
     } else {
```

```
      System.out.println("Rectangles are different");
    }
  }
}
```

***Output***

```
Rectangles are the same
```

In this example, two Rectangle2 objects are created and given the same width and height. The equals() method has been overridden to compare the widths and heights, returning true if they are the same. The argument to the equals() method is of type Object and must be cast to type Rectangle before the comparison can be made. If the equals() method were not overridden, the output from this program would be "Rectangles are different" because the equals() method from the Object class compares references and the two Rectangle objects would have different references.

# getClass() Method

| Method | Syntax |
|---|---|
| getClass() | public final Class getClass() |

getClass() returns the Class object associated with the invoking object. Each object has a Class object associated with it containing information about the object's class.

## Example: Using getClass()

This example demonstrates use of the getClass() method to find out the class of an object.

```
public class GetClass {
  public static void main(String args[]) {
    String str = "Jackson Palmer";
    System.out.println("The class of str is "
                       + str.getClass().getName());
  }
}
```

***Output***

```
The class of str is java.lang.String
```

The getName() method is from the Class class (see section 2.1.2 on page 85) and returns a String containing the name of the invoking Class object, in this case the Class object that is returned when str calls the getClass() method.

## hashCode() Method

| Method | Syntax |
|--------|--------|
| hashCode() | public int hashCode() |

hashCode() returns the hash code associated with the invoking Object object. Whenever possible, this method will return distinct integers for distinct objects.

## Multi-threaded Programming Methods

| Method | Syntax |
|--------|--------|
| notify() | public final void notify() |
| notifyAll() | public final void notifyAll() |
| wait() | public final void wait() throws InterruptedException |
| | public final void wait(long *millis*) throws InterruptedException |
| | public final void wait(long *milliseconds*, int *nanoseconds*) throws InterruptedException |

These methods are used with multi-threaded programming. See Section 2.3 on page 93 for complete details.

## toString() Method

| Method | Syntax |
|--------|--------|
| toString() | public String toString() |

toString() returns a String representation of the invoking object. If a String is required, say in a print statement, the compiler will automatically invoke the toString() method. This method is often overridden within a sub-class.

### Example: Using toString()

In this example, the Rectangle3 class overrides the toString() method so that it returns useful information about the state of a Rectangle3 object.

```
public class Rectangle3 {
  double width, height;

  Rectangle3(double w, double h) {
    width = w;
    height = h;
  }

  public String toString() {
    String str = "width = " + width + " height = " + height;
    return str;
  }
```

```
    public static void main(String args[]) {
        Rectangle3 s1 = new Rectangle3(4.0, 2.0);

        System.out.println(s1.toString());
    }
}
```

**Output**

```
width = 4.0  height = 2.0
```

The toString() method has been overridden to print out information about the invoking Rectangle object. If it is not overridden, the toString() method provided by the Object class returns the object reference. The statement "System.out.println(s1);" would also have called the toString() method

# 2.1.2 Class Class

```
public final class Class extends Object implements Serializable
```

```
Object
    Class
```

**Interfaces**

```
Serializable
```

For every class, Java maintains a Class object that contains information about the class and its interfaces. A Class object is never instantiated directly but is usually obtained using the getClass() method from the Object class or by invoking the forName() method defined in the Class class.

## Class Class Methods

| Method | Syntax |
|---|---|
| forName() | public static Class forName(String *className*) throws ClassNotFoundException |
| | public static Class forName(String *className*, boolean *initialize*, ClassLoader *loader*) throws ClassNotFoundException |
| getClasses() | public Class[] getClasses() |
| getConstructors() | public Constructor[] getConstructors() throws SecurityException |
| getDeclaredClasses() | public Class[] getDeclaredClasses() throws SecurityException |
| getDeclaredConstructors() | public Constructor[] getDeclaredConstructors() throws SecurityException, NoSuchMethodException |

| Method | Syntax |
|---|---|
| getDeclaredFields() | public Field[] getDeclaredFields() throws SecurityException |
| getDeclaredMethods() | public Method[] getDeclaredMethods() throws SecurityException |
| getField() | public Field getField(String *name*) throws NoSuchFieldException, SecurityException |
| getFields() | public Field[] getFields() throws SecurityException |
| getInterfaces() | public Class[] getInterfaces() |
| getMethods() | public Method[] getMethods() throws SecurityException |
| getName() | public String getName() |
| getSuperClass() | public Class getSuperClass() |
| isArray() | public boolean isArray() |
| isInterface() | public boolean isInterface() |
| isPrimitive() | public boolean isPrimitive() |
| toString() | public String toString() |

These methods return information about the invoking Class object. The Constructor, Field, and Method classes are defined in java.lang.reflect package, which must be imported to access these classes.

forName() returns the Class object associated with the given String name. The boolean determines if the class will beinitialized. The ClassLoader object is used to load the class or interface

get() methods return the public fields, interfaces, methods, name, and super-class including the methods and fields inherited from the superclass.

getDeclared() methods return the public, protected, and private entities but not those inherited from the superclass.

isArray(), isInterface(), and isPrimitive() return true if the invoking Class object represents an array, interface, or primitive type.

toString() overrides the one defined in the Object class.

## Example: Using the Class class to examine Class attributes

This example uses the Class class to examine the java.lang.Boolean class and prints out details of its constructors, fields and methods.

```
import java.lang.reflect.*;
public class TestClass {
  public static void main(String args[]) {
    try {
      Class c = Class.forName("java.lang.Boolean");
      String name = c.getName();
      Constructor[] constructors = c.getConstructors();
      Field[] fields = c.getFields();
```

```
      Method[] methods = c.getMethods();
      System.out.println(name + " has " + constructors.length
                  + " constructors");
      for (int i = 0; i < constructors.length; ++i) {
        System.out.println("" + constructors[i]);
      }
      System.out.println(name + " has " + fields.length + " fields");
      for (int i = 0; i < fields.length; ++i) {
        System.out.println("" + fields[i]);
      }
      System.out.println(name + " has " + methods.length
                  + " methods");
      for (int i = 0; i < methods.length; ++i) {
        System.out.println("" + methods[i]);
      }
    } catch (ClassNotFoundException e) {
      System.out.println("Class not found");
    }
  }
}
```

### Output

```
java.lang.Boolean has 2 constructors
public java.lang.Boolean(java.lang.String)
public java.lang.Boolean(boolean)
java.lang.Boolean has 4 fields
public static final long java.io.Serializable.serialVersionUID
  (more output follows)
```

The forName() method requires the entire name of the class, including the package name. It can throw a ClassNotFoundException and is therefore contained in a try-catch block. The java.lang.reflect package must be imported in order to use the getConstructors(), getFields(), and getMethods() methods. Passing a Constructor, Field, or Method argument to the println() method calls the toString() method of the Class class.

# 2.1.3 Cloneable Interface

```
public interface Cloneable
```

The Cloneable interface has no methods or variables. It is used like a keyword and indicates that an object from a class that implements the interface can be cloned using the clone() method defined in the Object class.

## 2.2 The Exception Classes

The exception classes define objects that represent particular exceptions, or errors, that can occur during the execution of a Java program. When the error occurs, an exception object is created and thrown. The exception object is then caught and processed either by a user-defined block of code or by the system default handler. In addition to the error and exception classes provided by Java, it is also possible to create user-defined exceptions. The following diagram shows the hierarchy of the exception classes:

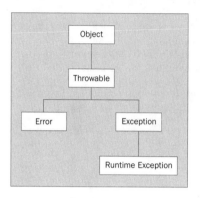

## 2.2.1 Error Class

```
public class Error extends Throwable
```

```
Object
    Throwable
        Error
```

### Interfaces

```
Serializable
```

The Error class is the super-class of exceptions that are thrown by the class loader, Java Virtual Machine, or other support code. An out of memory error would be one example of this type of exception. Since these exceptions are generally non-recoverable, they cannot usually be handled by the program, and we will not discuss the Error class in detail here.

## 2.2.2 Exception Class

```
public class Exception extends Throwable implements Serializable
```

```
Object
    Throwable
        Exception
```

### Interfaces

```
Serializable
```

The Exception class is the super-class of the exception objects that should be caught by the Java program. There are two general types of Exception sub-class objects:

❏ **Unchecked** exceptions – which do not have to be included in a method's throws list or caught. The compiler does not check to see if the method handles this type of error.

❏ **Checked** exceptions – which must be caught or included in a method's throws list.

# Exception() Constructor

| Constructor | Syntax |
|---|---|
| Exception() | public Exception() |
| | public Exception(String *message*) |

If a message is passed as an argument it will be associated with the Exception object.

# Exception Class Sub-Classes

| Sub Classes |
|---|
| public class ClassNotFoundException extends Exception |
| public class CloneNotSupportedException extends Exception |
| public class IllegalAccessException extends Exception |
| public class InstantiationException extends Exception |
| public class InterruptedException extends Exception |
| public class IOException extends Exception |
| public class NoSuchFieldException extends Exception |
| public class NoSuchMethodException extends Exception |

These are exception classes that are sub-classes of class Exception. Their names are pretty much self-explanatory. They are all checked exceptions, meaning that if a method can throw them, the method call must either be included in a try-catch block or the exception must be included in the throws list of the method calling them.

Each of these classes has two constructors:

❏ A no-argument constructor

❏ A constructor that is passed a String as an argument. The String represents a message that is associated with the class object

just like the Exception class.

# 2.2.3 RuntimeException Class

```
public class RuntimeException extends Exception implements Serializable
```

```
Object
  Throwable
    Exception
      RuntimeException
```

### Interfaces

```
Serializable
```

The RuntimeException class is the super-class of the runtime exception objects. Because a runtime exception can occur in any method, runtime exceptions are unchecked, meaning they do not need to be included in the throws list of a method.

Because RuntimeException is a sub-class of Exception which is a sub-class of Throwable, a RuntimeException object and all of the sub-class objects of RuntimeException have access to the Throwable class methods.

## RuntimeException() Constructor

| Constructor | Syntax |
| --- | --- |
| RuntimeException() | public RuntimeException() |
| | public RuntimeException(String message) |

RuntimeException object constructor. If a message is passed as an argument it will be associated with the Exception object.

## RuntimeException Class Sub-Classes

| Sub Classes |
| --- |
| public class ArithmeticException extends RuntimeException |
| public class ArrayIndexOutOfBoundsException extends RuntimeException |
| public class ArrayStoreException extends RuntimeException |
| public class ClassCastException extends RuntimeException |
| public class IllegalArgumentException extends RuntimeException |
| public class IllegalMonitorStateException extends RuntimeException |
| public class IllegalStateException extends RuntimeException |
| public class IllegalThreadStateException extends RuntimeException |
| public class IndexOutOfBoundsException extends RuntimeException |
| public class NegativeArraySizeException extends RuntimeException |
| public class NullPointerException extends RuntimeException |
| public class NumberFormatException extends RuntimeException |
| public class SecurityException extends RuntimeException |
| public class StringIndexOutOfBoundsException extends RuntimeException |
| public class UnsupportedOperationException extends RuntimeException |

2

java.lang

These are exception classes that are sub-classes of the `RuntimeException` class. Their names are self-explanatory. They are all unchecked exceptions, meaning they do not need to be included in the `throws` list of a method.

Each of these classes have two constructors, a no-argument constructor and a constructor that is passed a `String` as an argument. The `String` represents a message that is associated with the class object.

# 2.2.4 Throwable Class

```
public class Throwable extends Object implements Serializable
```

```
Object
    Throwable
```

### Interfaces
```
Serializable
```

This is the parent class of the `Error` and `Exception` classes and provides all of the methods used by those classes. For an object to be thrown using the `throw` keyword, it must be a sub-class of `Throwable`.

## Throwable( ) Constructor

| Constructor | Syntax |
|---|---|
| Throwable( ) | public Throwable( ) |
| | public Throwable(String *message*) |

`Throwable` object constructor. If a message is passed as an argument it will be associated with the `Throwable` object.

## fillInStackTrace( ) Method

| Method | Syntax |
|---|---|
| fillInStackTrace( ) | public Throwable fillInStackTrace( ) |

`fillInStackTrace( )` fills in the execution stack trace and can be used to obtain additional information about the invoking error or exception. It returns a `Throwable` object with the additional information that can be re-thrown.

## getLocalizedMessage( ) Method

| Method | Syntax |
|---|---|
| getLocalizedMessage( ) | public String getLocalizedMessage( ) |

`getLocalizedMessage( )` is overridden in sub-classes of `Throwable` to provide a localized message different from that passed to the object's constructor.

## getMessage() Method

| Method | Syntax |
|---|---|
| getMessage() | public String getMessage() |

getMessage() returns the String object associated with the invoking Throwable object by its constructor.

## printStackTrace() Method

| Method | Syntax |
|---|---|
| printStackTrace() | public void printStackTrace() |
| | public void printStackTrace(PrintStream ps) |
| | public void printStackTrace(PrintWriter pw) |

printStackTrace() writes a String representation of the invoking Throwable object and a stack trace. The no-argument version sends the information to System.err.

## toString() Method

| Method | Syntax |
|---|---|
| toString() | public String toString() |

toString() returns a String containing the name of the invoking Throwable object and its associated message.

# 2.2.5 User-Defined Exception Classes

```
public class MyExceptionName extends Exception
```

It is possible to create exception classes to suit a specific need. User-defined exception classes are sub-classes of class Exception. A user-defined Exception object is thrown using the throw keyword.

### Example: User-Defined Exceptions

In this example, a user-defined exception is created that is thrown if the int value passed to the testValue() method is negative.

```
class MyException extends Exception {
   public String toString() {
      return "negative value";
   }
}
```

```
class ExceptionTest {
  public static void testValue(int value) throws MyException {
    if (value < 0) {
      throw new MyException();
    }
  }

  public static void main(String args[]) {
    try {
      testValue(-5);
    } catch (MyException e) {
      System.out.println("" + e + " caught in main");
    }
    System.out.println("code continues on");
  }
}
```

**Output**

```
negative value caught in main
code continues on
```

The user-defined exception consists simply of an overridden toString() method. The throw, throws, try, and catch keywords are described in Section 1.7 on page 36.

# 2.3 Multi-Threaded Programming

A **thread** is another name for a Java 'process' that is running under the control of the Java Virtual Machine. Every Java thread is under the control of a Thread object.

Normally, there is only one thread. It is associated with the main() method or with the applet. The thread executes the commands sequentially with the entire CPU devoted to each operation until that operation is completed.

Sometimes it is desirable to run several threads in parallel, each process being controlled by a different Thread object. For instance, in a web application it might be desirable to have a continuously updated clock, an animation, and other features all running at the same time. This is facilitated by multi-threaded programming.

There are two ways to create a thread:

❑   Instantiate an object that implements the Runnable interface. This class must also override the run() method. Any code that the thread is to execute is placed in the run() method. The Thread or Runnable object then calls the start() method, which calls the run() method.

❑   Instantiate an object that extends the Thread class. The new class must override the run() method from the Runnable interface.

# 2.3.1 Runnable Interface

```
public interface Runnable
```

The Runnable interface declares the run() method that is used by Thread objects. Any class that implements the Runnable interface must implement the run() method.

## run() Method

| Method | Syntax |
|--------|--------|
| run() | public void run() |

run() is called whenever a Thread object is started by invoking the start() method. The run() method is overridden by the Runnable or Thread class object. Whatever code is to be executed by the Thread object is placed inside the run() method.

## Creating a Thread Using the Runnable Interface

Java does not permit multiple inheritance. If a class extends a super-class, it cannot also extend the Thread class. If its super-class does not extend the Thread class, the only way to turn the class into a thread is to have the class implement the Runnable interface. The run() method from the Runnable interface must be overridden in the local class.

### Example: Creating threads using Runnable

This example demonstrates how to create a thread using a class (MyThread) which implements the Runnable interface.

```
public class TestT2 {
  public static void main(String args[]) {
    Thread t1 = new Thread(new MyThread(5, 500));
    Thread t2 = new Thread(new MyThread(10, 500));
    Thread t3 = new Thread(new MyThread(10, 500));

    t1.setName("Thread one");
    t2.setName("Thread two");
    t3.setName("Thread three");

    t2.setPriority(7);

    t1.start();
    t2.start();

    try {
      t1.join();
      t3.start();
    } catch (InterruptedException ie) {}
  }
}
```

```
class MyThread implements Runnable {
  int maxCount, sleepTime;

  public MyThread(int c, int t) {
    maxCount = c;
    sleepTime = t;
  }

  public void run() {
    for (int i = 0; i < maxCount; ++i) {
      System.out.println(Thread.currentThread().getName() + " " + i);
      try {
        Thread.sleep(sleepTime);
      } catch (InterruptedException ie) {}
    }
  }
}
```

**Output** *(will vary between runs)*

```
Thread two 0
Thread one 0
Thread two 1
Thread one 1
. . .
Thread one 4
Thread two 5
Thread three 0
Thread two 6
Thread three 1
. . .
```

Three threads are created by passing a reference to a Runnable object to the Thread class constructor. The first two threads are started. The second thread has a higher priority. Because the first thread invokes the join()method before the third thread invokes the start() method, the third thread doesn't start until the first thread is finished. The join() method, defined in the Thread class, causes the invoking Thread object to finish before subsequent commands are executed.

One of the disadvantages of using an object that implements the Runnable interface is that object will not directly have access to the methods of the Thread class.

# 2.3.2 Thread Class

```
public class Thread extends Object implements Runnable
```

```
Object
  Thread
```

### Interfaces

    Runnable

A Thread object controls a thread or process running under the Java Virtual Machine. Threads have a priority associated with them that determines whether they have preferred access to the CPU.

# Thread() Constructor

| Constructor | Syntax |
|---|---|
| Thread() | public Thread() |
| | public Thread(String threadName) |
| | public Thread(Runnable r) |
| | public Thread(Runnable r, String threadName) |
| | public Thread(ThreadGroup group, Runnable r) |
| | public Thread(ThreadGroup group, Runnable r, String threadName) |
| | public Thread(ThreadGroup group, String threadName) |

A ThreadGroup is an object that groups Thread or ThreadGroup objects together. The variable r is a reference to an object that implements the Runnable interface. This object will override the run() method. The default constructor creates a Thread object with the same ThreadGroup as the current thread with the same priority and a default name.

# currentThread() Method

| Method | Syntax |
|---|---|
| currentThread() | public static Thread currentThread() |

currentThread() returns a reference to the currently executing thread.

# join() Method

| Method | Syntax |
|---|---|
| join() | public final void join() throws InterruptedException |
| | public final void join(long milliseconds) throws InterruptedException |
| | public final void join(long milliseconds, int nanoseconds) throws InterruptedException |

join() causes the invoking Thread object to finish before subsequent commands are executed. If a time argument is provided, the subsequent commands are executed when the invoking Thread object finishes or the time limit expires, whichever comes first. Note that some systems have a large system clock granularity.

## Name Methods

| Method | Syntax |
|--------|--------|
| getName() | public final String getName() |
| setName() | public final void setName(String *name*) |

A Thread may be given a name.

getName() returns the name of the invoking Thread object.

setName() changes the name of the invoking Thread object.

## Priority Methods

| Method | Syntax |
|--------|--------|
| getPriority() | public final int getPriority() |
| setPriority() | public final void setPriority(int *newPriority*) |

getPriority() returns the priority of the invoking Thread object.

setPriority() sets the priority of the invoking Thread object.

The priority is set to an integer value between 1 and 10. The higher the priority value, the higher the CPU allocation to that thread. There are three priority constants defined by the Thread class:

❑  Thread.MAX_PRIORITY

❑  Thread.NORM_PRIORITY

❑  Thread.MIN_PRIORITY

They have values of 10, 5, and 1 respectively.

## resume() Method

| Method | Syntax |
|--------|--------|
| resume() | public final void resume() |

resume() resumes execution of the invoking Thread object if it was suspended; it has no effect if the invoking Thread object wasn't suspended. This method has been deprecated because the suspend() method has been deprecated.

## run() Method

| Method | Syntax |
|--------|--------|
| run() | public void run() |

run() implements the run() method from the Runnable interface. Whatever code is to be executed by the thread is placed in this method.

## sleep() Method

| Method | Syntax |
|--------|--------|
| sleep() | public static native void **sleep**(long *milliSeconds*) throws InterruptedException |
| | public static void **sleep**(long *milliSeconds*, int *nanoSeconds*) throws InterruptedException |

sleep() causes the currently running Thread object to sleep for the specified amount of time. The sleeping Thread object retains whatever locks it may possess.

## start() Method

| Method | Syntax |
|--------|--------|
| start() | public void **start**() |

start() starts the Thread object by calling the run() method from the Runnable object passed to the constructor or the run() method provided by the Thread object.

## Methods to Determine the State of a Thread

| Method | Syntax |
|--------|--------|
| isAlive() | public final boolean **isAlive**() |
| isDaemon() | public final boolean **isDaemon**() |
| isInterrupted() | public boolean **isInterrupted**() |

These methods return information about the state of the invoking Thread object. A thread is alive if it has started and not yet died. The Java virtual machine exits when all non-daemon threads have stopped running, regardless of how many daemon threads are still running.

## Methods Used to Stop a Thread

| Method | Syntax |
|--------|--------|
| destroy() | public void **destroy**() |
| interrupt() | public void **interrupt**() |
| stop() | public final void **stop**() |
| stop() | public final void **stop**(Throwable *t*) |
| suspend() | public final void **suspend**() |

destroy() is a clumsy termination of the invoking Thread object. It is currently not implemented and therefore does nothing.

interrupt() interrupts the invoking Thread object.

stop() causes the invoking Thread object to stop executing and throws a ThreadDeath object. This method has been deprecated because it can result in inconsistent or 'damaged' objects and should not be used in new code.

suspend() suspends the execution of the invoking Thread object. It can be restarted by calling the resume() method. This method has been deprecated because it is dead-lock prone and should not be used for new code.

## ThreadGroup Methods

| Method | Syntax |
|---|---|
| activeCount() | public static int activeCount() |
| getThreadGroup() | public final ThreadGroup getThreadGroup() |

activeCount() returns the current number of active threads in the invoking Thread object's threadgroup.

getThreadGroup() returns the ThreadGroup object to which the invoking Thread object belongs.

## toString()Method

| Method | Syntax |
|---|---|
| toString() | public String toString() |

toString() overrides the toString() method from the Object class to provide a String representation of the thread including the thread name, priority, and threadgroup.

## yield() Method

| Method | Syntax |
|---|---|
| yield() | public static void yield() |

yield() causes the currently running Thread object to give up control of the CPU.

## Creating Threads by Extending the Thread Class

```
public class ClassName extends Thread
```

A thread may be created using a class that extends the Thread class and overrides the run() method. Whatever code is to be executed is placed inside this method. The thread is started by having the sub-class object invoke the start() method.

### Example: Creating a thread by extending Thread

This example demonstrates how to creating new threads using a class MyThread which extends Thread.

```
public class TestT {
  public static void main(String args[]) {
    MyThread t1 = new MyThread(5, 500, "Thread one");
```

```
    MyThread t2 = new MyThread(10, 500, "Thread two");
    MyThread t3 = new MyThread(10, 500, "Thread three");

    t2.setPriority(7);

    t1.start();
    t2.start();

    try {
      t1.join();
      t3.start();
    } catch (InterruptedException ie) {}
  }
}

class MyThread extends Thread {
  int maxCount, sleepTime;

  public MyThread(int c, int t, String name) {
    maxCount = c;
    sleepTime = t;
    setName(name);
  }

  public void run() {
    for (int i = 0; i < maxCount; ++i) {
      System.out.println(getName() + " " + i);
      try {
        Thread.sleep(sleepTime);
      } catch (InterruptedException ie) {}
    }
  }
}
```

**Output** (will vary between runs)

```
Thread two 0
Thread one 0
Thread two 1
Thread one 1
...
Thread one 4
Thread two 5
Thread three 0
Thread two 6
Thread three 1
...
```

Three threads are created. The first two threads are started. The second thread has a higher priority, and it started execution first. Because the first thread invokes the join() method before the third thread invokes the start() method, the third thread doesn't start until the first thread is finished.

# Creating a Thread Using an Inner Thread Class

A section of code can be spun off as a separate thread by enclosing it in the run() method of an inner Thread class.

## Example: Creating threads using Inner Classes

```java
public class TestT3 {
    public static void main(String args[]) {
        Thread t1 = new Thread() {
            public void run() {
                for (int i = 0; i < 10; ++i) {
                    System.out.println(Thread.currentThread().getName() + " "
                                       + i);
                    try {
                        Thread.sleep(500);
                    } catch (InterruptedException ie) {}
                }
            }
        };
        t1.setName("Thread one");
        t1.start();

        for (int i = 0; i < 10; ++i) {
            System.out.println("Main method " + i);
            try {
                Thread.sleep(500);
            } catch (InterruptedException ie) {}
        }
    }
}
```

**Output** (will vary between runs)

```
Main method 0
Thread one 0
Main method 1
Thread one 1
...
```

Using an inner Thread class is a good quick-and-dirty way of spinning off part of a program as a separate thread.

# 2.3.4 Thread Communication

Often one thread has to wait for another thread to do something before it can perform its task. The threads need to communicate between each other when they have completed their task, and this **inter-thread communication** is achieved using three methods from the Object class: wait(), notify(), and notifyAll(). These methods must be called from within a synchronized method. A synchronized method is one that can only be called by one thread at a time.

## Deadlock

A deadlock or race condition occurs when two or more threads have a circular dependency on each other, where each thread is in a wait state and needs the other to issue a notify() or notifyAll() call. A program in a deadlock condition is paralyzed.

## Thread Communciation Methods from the Object Class

### notify() Method

| Method | Syntax |
|--------|--------|
| notify() | public final void notify() |

notify() notifies a thread in a wait state that the condition it is waiting for has been achieved. If more than one thread is waiting, the notify() method will arbitrarily awaken just one of the threads. If the awakened thread cannot proceed, the system can deadlock.

### notifyAll() Method

| Method | Syntax |
|--------|--------|
| notifyAll() | public final void notifyAll() |

notifyAll() performs similarly to the notify() method except that all the waiting threads are awakened. The thread with the highest priority will run first.

### wait() Method

| Method | Syntax |
|--------|--------|
| wait() | public final void wait() throws InterruptedException |
|  | public final void wait(long *milliseconds*) throws InterruptedException |
|  | public final void wait(long *milliseconds*, int *noseconds*) throws InterruptedException |

wait() causes the invoking thread to wait for a condition to occur. This occurence is indicated by another thread invoking the notify() or notifyAll() method. If a time is provided, that is the maximum time that the thread will wait.

## Example: Thread Communication: A Producer/Consumer Program

```java
public class TestPC {
  private static final int MAX_COUNT = 5;

  public static void main(String args[]) {
    Counter counter = new Counter(MAX_COUNT);

    Consumer consumer = new Consumer(counter);
    Producer producer = new Producer(counter);

    consumer.start();
    producer.setPriority(7);
    producer.start();
  }
}

class Consumer extends Thread {
  private Counter counter;

  public Consumer(Counter c) {
    counter = c;
  }

  public void run() {
    for (int i = 0; i < 20; ++i) {
      counter.subtractFromCount();
    }
  }
}

class Producer extends Thread {
  private Counter counter;

  public Producer(Counter c) {
    counter = c;
  }

  public void run() {
    for (int i = 0; i < 20; ++i) {
      counter.addToCount();
    }
  }
}

class Counter {
  private int maxCount;
  private int count = 0;
```

```
    public Counter(int mct) {
      maxCount = mct;
    }

    public synchronized void subtractFromCount() {
      while (count < 1) {
        try {
          wait();
        } catch (InterruptedException ie) {}
      }
      --count;
      System.out.println("count is " + count);
      notifyAll();
    }

    public synchronized void addToCount() {
      while (count > maxCount) {
        try {
          wait();
        } catch (InterruptedException ie) {}
      }
++count;
      System.out.println("count is " + count);
      notifyAll();
    }
}
```

## Output

```
count is 1
count is 2
count is 3
count is 4
count is 5
count is 6
count is 5
count is 6
...
```

The Producer and Consumer objects share a Counter object. If the count is less than 1, the subtractFromCount() method waits until the addToCount() method adds one to the count and issues the notifyAll() command. The reverse situation occurs when the count is equal to maxCount. Because the producer thread is given a higher priority, initially production outpaces consumption.

# 2.3.5 Thread Synchronization

Normally, threads run asynchronously. While their access to CPU time is influenced by their priority, they will run somewhat independently. This can cause problems. For instance, sometimes a method should only by called by one thread at a time. Access to a method or block of code can be synchronized through the use of the `synchronized` keyword.

## Synchronized Blocks

A block of code can be **synchronized**; meaning that only one thread at a time is given access to the block. A sychronized block is created using the `synchronized` keyword, and is provided with a reference to the object being synchronized.

### Example: Using Synchronized Blocks

This example demonstrates the use of synchronized blocks to prevent more than one thread accessing a `StringWriter` object at the same time.

```
public class TestT4 {
  public static void main(String args[]) {
    StringWriter sw = new StringWriter();
    MyThread t1 = new MyThread(sw, "Thread one");
    MyThread t2 = new MyThread(sw, "Thread two");

    t1.start();
    t2.start();
  }
}

class MyThread extends Thread {
  StringWriter swr;
  String msg;

  public MyThread(StringWriter sw, String name) {
    swr = sw;
    msg = name;
  }

  public void run() {
    synchronized (swr) {
      swr.writeString(msg);
    }
  }
}

class StringWriter {
  public void writeString(String name) {
    System.out.println(name + " starting");
```

```
        try {
          Thread.sleep(500);
        } catch (InterruptedException ie) {}
        System.out.println(name + " ending");
      }
    }
```

**Output**

```
Thread one starting
Thread one ending
Thread two starting
Thread two ending
```

In this example, the call to the writeString() method is contained in a synchronized block. The first thread calls writeString() method. The second thread cannot call the writeString() method until the first thread exits the method. The writeString() method itself is not synchronized. For the synchronization to work, both threads must be passed a reference to the same StringWriter object. Because of encapsulation, if each thread is given a different StringWriter object, then each thread will have its own version of the writeString() method to access and synchronization will not come into play.

Without the synchronized block, both can be inside the writeString() method at the same time. The output from this code would be:

```
Thread one starting
Thread two starting
Thread one ending
Thread two ending
```

## Synchronized Methods

Declaring a method to be synchronized prevents more than one thread calling the method at any one time. The synchronized keyword is written before the method return type. The Java Virtual Machine will queue up any and all threads waiting to call the synchronized methods.

Synchronized methods don't have exclusive access to the CPU. A non-synchronized method of a class can be executing at the same time as a synchronized method.

### Example: Using Synchronized Methods

This example demonstrates the use of synchronized blocks to prevent more than one thread calling the writeString method of a StringWriter object at the same time.

```java
public class TestT5 {
  public static void main(String args[]) {
    StringWriter sw = new StringWriter();
    MyThread t1 = new MyThread(sw, "Thread one");
    MyThread t2 = new MyThread(sw, "Thread two");

    t1.start();
    t2.start();
  }
}

class MyThread extends Thread {
  StringWriter swr;
  String msg;

  public MyThread(StringWriter sw, String name) {
    swr = sw;
    msg = name;
  }

  public void run() {
    swr.writeString(msg);
  }

}

class StringWriter {
  public synchronized void writeString(String name) {
    System.out.println(name + " starting");
    try {
      Thread.sleep(500);
    } catch (InterruptedException ie) {}
    System.out.println(name + " ending");
  }
}
```

**Output**

```
Thread one starting
Thread one ending
Thread two starting
Thread two ending
```

In this example, two threads try to access the writeString() method. Because writeString() has been declared to be synchronized, only one thread at a time can access it. For the synchronization to work, both threads must be passed a reference to the same StringWriter object. Because of encapsulation, if each thread is given a different StringWriter object, then each thread will have its own version of the writeString() method to access and synchronization will not come into play.

Without the synchronized keyword, both can be inside the writeString() method at the same time. The output from this code would be:

```
Thread one starting
Thread two starting
Thread one ending
Thread two ending
```

# 2.3.8 ThreadGroup Class

```
public class ThreadGroup extends Object
```

```
Object
    ThreadGroup
```

A ThreadGroup object represents a collection of Thread and ThreadGroup objects. The methods contained in the ThreadGroup class work on all of the ThreadGroup elements. For example, when a ThreadGroup object invokes the interrupt() method, all of the Thread and ThreadGroup objects contained in the invoking ThreadGroup object are interrupted.

Thread objects are associated with a ThreadGroup object when the Thread object is instantiated. See section 2.3.2 on page 95.

## ThreadGroup() Constructor

| Constructor | Syntax |
|---|---|
| ThreadGroup() | public ThreadGroup(String *name*) |
| | public ThreadGroup(ThreadGroup *parent*, String *name*) |

A parent ThreadGroup and a name can be provided.

## ThreadGroup Property Methods

| Method | Syntax |
|---|---|
| activeCount() | public int activeCount() |
| activeGroupCount() | public int activeGroupCount() |
| getMaxPriority() | public final int getMaxPriority() |
| getName() | public final String getName() |
| getParent() | public final ThreadGroup getParent() |
| setDaemon() | public final void setDaemon(boolean *daemon*) |
| setMaxPriority() | public final void setMaxPriority(int *priority*) |

activeCount() returns an estimate of the number of active threads controlled by the invoking ThreadGroup object.

activeGroupCount() returns an estimate of the number of active groups in the invoking ThreadGroup object.

getMaxPriority() returns the maximum priority that threads in the ThreadGroup can have.

getName() returns the name associated with the invoking ThreadGroup object.

getParent() returns the parent ThreadGroup of the invoking ThreadGroup object.

setDaemon() specifies whether the invoking ThreadGroup object is a daemon ThreadGroup.

setMaxPriority() specifies the maximum priority that threads in the ThreadGroup can have.

# resume() Method

| Method | Syntax |
|---|---|
| resume() | public final void resume() |

resume() resumes execution of the threads in the invoking ThreadGroup object. This method is used in conjunction with the suspend() method and has been deprecated. It should not be used for new code.

# Methods to Determine the State of a ThreadGroup Object

| Method | Syntax |
|---|---|
| allowThreadSuspension() | public boolean allowThreadSuspension(boolean b) |
| isDaemon() | public final boolean isDaemon() |
| isDestroyed() | public boolean isDestroyed() |
| parentOf() | public final boolean parentOf( ThreadGroup group) |

allowThreadSuspension() determines whether the invoking ThreadGroup object can be suspended. Because the suspend() method has been deprecated, this method is also deprecated and should not be used for new code.

isDaemon() returns true if the invoking ThreadGroup object is a daemon ThreadGroup.

isDestroyed() returns true if the invoking ThreadGroup object has been destroyed. parentOf() returns true if the invoking ThreadGroup object is the parent of ThreadGroup group.

# Methods Used to Stop a ThreadGroup

| Method | Syntax |
|---|---|
| destroy() | public final void destroy() |
| stop() | public final void stop() |
| interrupt() | public final void interrupt() |
| suspend() | public final void suspend() |

`destroy()` destroys the invoking `ThreadGroup` object and all of its sub-groups. All threads contained in the invoking `ThreadGroup` object must be stopped before this method is called.

`interrupt()` interrupts all of the threads in the invoking `ThreadGroup` object.

`stop()` causes the threads in the invoking `ThreadGroup` object to stop executing. This method is unsafe because it can produce inconsistent or 'damaged' objects and has been deprecated. It should not be used for new code.

`suspend()` suspends the execution of the threads in the invoking `ThreadGroup` object. They can be restarted by calling the `resume()` method. This method has been deprecated because it is deadlock-prone. It should not be used for new code.

### toString() Method

| Method | Syntax |
| --- | --- |
| toString() | public String toString() |

`toString()` overrides the `toString()` method from the `Object` class to provide a String representation of the invoking `ThreadGroup` object.

# 2.4 Primitive Variable Wrapper Classes

Primitive datatypes are not objects. They are passed by value and cannot be passed by reference. Sometimes class methods require an `Object` reference as an argument. The `java.lang` package provides wrapper classes to convert primitive data types into objects. The following diagram shows the primitive variable wrapper class hierarchy.

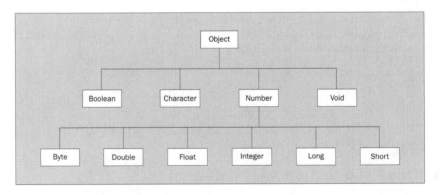

# 2.4.1 Boolean Class

`public final class Boolean extends Object implements Serializable`

```
Object
    Boolean
```

*Interfaces*

    Serializable

2

java.lang

The Boolean class is the wrapper class for the primitive type boolean. It contains a single field of type boolean.

## Boolean() Constructor

| Constructor | Syntax |
|---|---|
| Boolean() | public Boolean(boolean *b*)<br>public Boolean(String *trueOrFalse*) |

Creates a Boolean object based on either a boolean or String argument. If the String is not "true" or "True", the Boolean object will be created with the value false.

## booleanValue() Method

| Method | Syntax |
|---|---|
| booleanValue() | public boolean booleanValue() |

booleanValue() returns true if the invoking Boolean object has the value true or false if it contains the value false.

## equals() Method

| Method | Syntax |
|---|---|
| equals() | public boolean equals(Object *obj*) |

equals() compares the boolean values in the invoking and specified Boolean objects and returns true if they are the same.

## hashCode() method

| Method | Syntax |
|---|---|
| hashCode() | public int hashCode() |

hashCode() returns the hash code associated with the invoking Boolean object.

## toString() Method

| Method | Syntax |
|---|---|
| toString() | public String toString() |

toString() returns "true" if the value of the invoking Boolean object is true, or "false" if the value is false.

## valueOf() Method

| Method | Syntax |
|--------|--------|
| valueOf() | public static Boolean valueOf(String *str*) |

valueOf() returns a Boolean object based on parsing the passed String. If the String contains the string "true" or "True", the resulting Boolean object has the boolean value true.

### Example: Using Boolean

This example demonstrates the use of the Boolean wrapper class to encapsulate boolean values.

```
public class TestB {
  public static void main(String args[]) {
    Boolean b1 = new Boolean(true);
    Boolean b2 = Boolean.valueOf("true");
    if (b1.equals(b2) && b1.booleanValue()) {
      System.out.println("b1 and b2 are " + b1.toString());
    }
  }
}
```

*Output*

```
b1 and b2 are true
```

# 2.4.2 Byte Class

```
public final class Byte extends Number implements Comparable, Serializable
```

```
Object
  Number
    Byte
```

### Interfaces

```
Comparable, Serializable
```

The Byte class is the wrapper class for the primitive type byte.

## Byte() Constructor

| Constructor | Syntax |
|-------------|--------|
| Byte() | public Byte(byte *b*) |
|  | public Byte(String *s*) throws NumberFormatException |

Creates a Byte object based on a byte or String argument. The String must represent an appropriate byte value.

## Static Methods that Create Byte Objects

| Method | Syntax |
|---|---|
| decode() | public static Byte decode(String s)<br>                              throws NumberFormatException |
| valueOf() | public static Byte valueOf(String s)<br>                              throws NumberFormatException |
| | public static Byte valueOf(String s, int radix)<br>                              throws NumberFormatException |

decode() returns a Byte object based on parsing the String argument. The String can represent a decimal, hexadecimal, or octal number.

valueOf() return a Byte object using the String argument to set the value. The radix is the base of the number system being used. For the standard decimal system, radix would be 10.

## Methods to Compare Byte Objects

| Method | Syntax |
|---|---|
| equals() | public boolean equals(Object obj) |
| compareTo() | public int compareTo(Byte b) |
| | public int compareTo(Object obj) |

equals() overrides the equals() method from the Object class and returns true if the invoking Byte object is the same as Object obj.

compareTo() compares the invoking Byte object to the specified Byte or Object object. It returns 0 if the invoking Byte object is equal to, a negative value if the invoking Byte object is numerically less than, or a positive value if the invoking Byte object is numerically greater than the argument object.

## Methods to Convert Byte Objects to Primitive Types

| Method | Syntax |
|---|---|
| byteValue() | public byte byteValue() |
| doubleValue() | public double doubleValue() |
| floatValue() | public float floatValue() |
| intValue() | public int intValue() |
| longValue() | public long longValue() |
| shortValue() | public short shortValue() |

These methods return a primitive data type from the value of the invoking Byte object.

## hashCode() Method

| Method | Syntax |
|--------|--------|
| hashCode() | public int hashCode() |

hashCode() overrides the hashCode() method from the Object class to return the hash code associated with the invoking Byte object.

## parseByte() Method

| Method | Syntax |
|--------|--------|
| parseByte() | public static byte parseByte(String s)<br>                  throws NumberFormatException |
| | public static byte parseByte(String s, int radix)<br>                  throws NumberFormatException |

parseByte() returns a primitive byte using the String argument to set the value. The method is static, so it can be invoked without creating a Byte object.

## toString() Method

| Method | Syntax |
|--------|--------|
| toString() | public static String toString(byte b) |
| | public String toString() |

toString() overrides the toString() method from the Object class to return the String representation of the value of the invoking Byte object. The static version returns a String representation of the specified byte.

# 2.4.3 Character Class

public final class **Character** extends Object implements Comparable, Serializable

    Object
      Character

### Interfaces

    Comparable, Serializable

The Character class is the wrapper class for the primitive type char. It contains a single field of type char.

## Character() Constructor

| Constructor | Syntax |
|-------------|--------|
| Character() | public Character(char c) |

Creates a Character object with the specified char as its value.

## charValue() Method

| Method | Syntax |
|---|---|
| charValue() | public char charValue() |

charValue() returns the char value of the invoking Character object.

## Methods to Compare Character Objects

| Method | Syntax |
|---|---|
| equals() | public boolean equals(Object *obj*) |
| compareTo() | public int compareTo(Character c) |
| | public int compareTo(Object *obj*) |

equals() overrides the equals() method from the Object class and returns true if Object obj is a Character object with the same value as the invoking Character object.

compareTo() compares the invoking Character object to the specified Character or Object object. It returns 0 if the invoking Character object is equal to, a negative value if the invoking Character object is numerically less than, or a positive value if the invoking Character object is numerically greater than the argument object.

## Methods to Change the Case of a Character

| Method | Syntax |
|---|---|
| toLowerCase() | public static char toLowerCase(char c) |
| toTitleCase() | public static char toTitleCase(char c) |
| toUpperCase() | public static char toUpperCase(char c) |

toLowerCase() changes the case of the character passed as an argument to lower case. If there is no lower case for the character, the original character is returned.

toTitleCase() changes the case of the character passed as an argument to title case. If there is no title case for the character, the original character is returned.

toUpperCase() changes the case of the character passed as an argument to upper case. If there is no upper case for the character, the original character is returned.

## Methods to Convert Chars to Ints and Ints to Chars

| Method | Syntax |
|---|---|
| digit() | public static int digit(char *ch*, int *radix*) |
| forDigit() | public static char forDigit(int *digit*, int *radix*) |

digit() converts a character to an int.

forDigit() converts an int to a char.

The radix is the base of the number. In the standard decimal system, radix would be 10.

## Methods to Determine Character Type

| Method | Syntax |
|---|---|
| isDigit() | public static boolean isDigit(char c) |
| isLowerCase() | public static boolean isLowerCase(char c) |
| isUpperCase | public static boolean isUpperCase(char c) |
| isTitleCase | public static boolean isTitleCase(char c) |
| isDefined | public static boolean isDefined(char c) |
| isLetter | public static boolean isLetter(char c) |
| isLetterOrDigit | public static boolean isLetterOrDigit(char c) |
| isSpaceChar | public static boolean isSpaceChar(char c) |
| isWhitespace | public static boolean isWhitespace(char c) |

These methods are used to determine the nature of the character passed to the method.

## hashCode() Method

| Method | Syntax |
|---|---|
| hashCode() | public int hashCode() |

hashCode() overrides the hashCode() method from the Object class to return the hash code associated with the invoking Character object.

## toString() Method

| Method | Syntax |
|---|---|
| toString() | public String toString() |

toString() returns a one-character String containing the character value of the invoking Character object.

# 2.4.4 Double Class

```
public final class Double extends Number implements Comparable, Serializable
```

```
Object
  Number
    Double
```

### Interfaces

```
Comparable, Serializable
```

The Double class is the wrapper class for the primitive type double.

## Double() Constructor

| Constructor | Syntax |
|---|---|
| Double() | public Double(double d) |
| | public Double(String s) throws NumberFormatException |

Creates a `Double` object based on a `double` or `String` argument. The `String` must be a representation of a `double`, for example `"45.33"`.

## Methods to Compare Double Objects

| Method | Syntax |
|--------|--------|
| equals() | public boolean equals(Object *obj*) |
| compareTo() | public int compareTo(Double *d*) |
| | public int compareTo(Object *obj*) |

`equals()` overrides the `equals()` method from the `Object` class and returns `true` if `Object obj` is a `Double` object with the same value as the invoking `Double` object.

`compareTo()` compares the invoking `Double` object to the specified `Double` or `Object` object. It returns 0 if the invoking `Double` object is equal to, a negative value if the invoking `Double` object is numerically less than, or a positive value if the invoking `Double` object is numerically greater than the argument object.

## Methods to Convert Double Objects to Primitive Types

| Method | Syntax |
|--------|--------|
| byteValue() | public byte byteValue() |
| doubleValue() | public double doubleValue() |
| floatValue() | public float floatValue() |
| intValue() | public int intValue() |
| longValue() | public long longValue() |
| shortValue() | public short shortValue() |

These methods return a primitive data type from the value of the invoking `Double` object.

## hashCode() Method

| Method | Syntax |
|--------|--------|
| hashCode() | public int hashCode() |

`hashCode()` overrides the `hashCode()` method from the `Object` class and returns the hash code associated with the invoking `Double` object.

## parseDouble() Method

| Method | Syntax |
|--------|--------|
| parseDouble() | public static double parseDouble(String *s*) throws NumberFormatException |

`parseDouble()` returns a `double` value based on parsing the `String` argument.

## toString() Method

| Method | Syntax |
|--------|--------|
| toString() | public static String toString(double *d*)<br>public String toString() |

toString() overrides the toString() method from the Object class to return the String representation of the value of the invoking Double object. The static version returns a String representation of the specified double.

## valueOf() Method

| Method | Syntax |
|--------|--------|
| valueOf() | public static Double valueOf(String *s*)<br>    throws NumberFormatException |

valueOf() returns a Double object using the String argument to set the value.

### Example: Converting a String to a Double

This example demonstrates the use of the valueOf() and doubleValue() methods of the Double class to convert a String to a double value.

```
public class TestD {
  public static void main(String args[]) {
    Double D = Double.valueOf("45.3");
    double d = D.doubleValue();
    d = 2.0 * d;
    System.out.println("Value of d is " + Double.toString(d));
  }
}
```

**Output**

```
Value of d is 90.6
```

The String is first converted to a Double object and the Double object is then converted to a primitive double. The two methods could have been cascaded and written as:

```
double d = Double.valueOf("45.3").doubleValue();
```

The valueOf() and toString() methods are invoked using the "Double." syntax to tell the compiler which valueOf() and toString() methods to use.

# 2.4.5 Float Class

2

java.lang

```
public final class Float extends Number implements Comparable
```

```
Object
    Number
        Float
```

### Interfaces
```
Comparable, Serializable
```

This is the wrapper class for the primitive type float.

## Float() Constructor

| Constructor | Syntax |
|---|---|
| Float() | public Float(double *d*) |
| | public Float(float *f*) |
| | public Float(String *s*) throws NumberFormatException |

Creates a Float object based on a double, float, or String argument. The String must be a representation of a float, for example "45.3".

## Methods to Compare Float Objects

| Method | Syntax |
|---|---|
| equals() | public boolean equals(Object *obj*) |
| compareTo() | public int compareTo(Float *f*) |
| | public int compareTo(Object *obj*) |

equals() overrides the equals() method from the Object class and returns true if Object obj is a Float object with the same value as the invoking Float object.

compareTo() compares the invoking Float object to the specified Float or Object object. It returns 0 if the invoking Float object is equal to, a negative value if the invoking Float object is numerically less than, or a positive value if the invoking Float object is numerically greater than the argument object.

## Methods to Convert Float Objects to Primitive Types

| Method | Syntax |
|---|---|
| byteValue() | public byte byteValue() |
| doubleValue() | public double doubleValue() |
| floatValue() | public float floatValue() |
| intValue() | public int intValue() |
| longValue() | public long longValue() |
| shortValue() | public short shortValue() |

These methods return a primitive data type from the value of the invoking Float object.

## hashCode() Method

| Method | Syntax |
|---|---|
| hashCode() | public int hashCode() |

hashCode() overrides the hashCode() method from the Object class and returns the hash code associated with the invoking Float object.

## parseFloat() Method

| Method | Syntax |
|---|---|
| parseFloat() | public static float parseFloat(String s) throws NumberFormatException |

parseFloat() returns a float value based on parsing the argument String argument.

## toString() Method

| Method | Syntax |
|---|---|
| toString() | public static String toString(float f) public String toString() |

toString() overrides the toString() method from the Object class to return the String representation of the value of the invoking Float object. The static version returns a String representation of the specified float.

## valueOf() Method

| Method | Syntax |
|---|---|
| valueOf() | public static Float valueOf(String s) throws NumberFormatException |

valueOf() returns a Float object using the argument String to set the value.

# 2.4.6 Integer Class

```
public final class Integer extends Number
    implements Comparable, Serializable
```

```
Object
   Number
      Integer
```

### Interfaces

```
Comparable, Serializable
```

The Integer class is the wrapper class for the primitive type int.

# Integer() Constructor

| Method | Syntax |
|--------|--------|
| Integer() | public Integer(int *i*) |
|           | public Integer(String *s*) throws NumberFormatException |

Creates an Integer object based on an int or String argument. The String must be a representation of an int, for example "45".

# Static Methods to Create Integer Objects

| Method | Syntax |
|--------|--------|
| decode() | public static Integer decode(String *s*) throws NumberFormatException |
| valueOf() | public static Integer valueOf(String *s*) throws NumberFormatException |
| valueOf() | public static Integer valueOf(String *s*, int *radix*) throws NumberFormatException |

decode() returns an Integer object based on parsing the argument String. The String can represent a decimal, hexadecimal, or octal number.

valueOf() returns an Integer object based on parsing the argument String. The String must represent an integer value, for example "45". The radix is the base of the number system used. In the decimal system, the radix would be 10.

# Methods to Compare Integer Objects

| Method | Syntax |
|--------|--------|
| equals() | public boolean equals(Object *obj*) |
| compareTo() | public int compareTo(Integer *i*) |
|             | public int compareTo(Object *obj*) |

equals() overrides the equals() method from the Object class and returns true if Object obj is an Integer object with the same value as the invoking Integer object.

compareTo() compares the invoking Integer object to the specified Integer or Object object. It returns 0 if the invoking Integer object is equal to, a negative value if the invoking Integer object is numerically less than, or a positive value if the invoking Integer object is numerically greater than the argument object.

# Methods to Convert Integer Objects to Primitive Types

| Method | Syntax |
|--------|--------|
| byteValue() | public byte byteValue() |
| doubleValue() | public double doubleValue() |
| floatValue() | public float floatValue() |
| intValue() | public int intValue() |
| longValue() | public long longValue() |
| shortValue() | public short shortValue() |

These methods return a primitive data type from the value of the invoking `Integer` object.

## hashCode() Method

| Method | Syntax |
|--------|--------|
| hashCode() | public int hashCode() |

`hashCode()` overrides the `hashCode()` method from the `Object` class and returns the hash code associated with the invoking `Integer` object.

## parseInt() Method

| Method | Syntax |
|--------|--------|
| parseInt() | public static int parseInt(String s)<br>                          throws NumberFormatException |
|  | public static int parseInt(String s, int radix)<br>                          throws NumberFormatException |

`parseInt()` returns a primitive `int` using the `String` argument to set the value. The `radix` is the base of the number system used. In the decimal system, the radix would be 10.

## toString() Method

| Method | Syntax |
|--------|--------|
| toString() | public static String toString(int i) |
|  | public static String toString(int i, int radix) |
|  | public String toString() |

`toString()` overrides the `toString()` method from the `Object` class to return the `String` representation of the value of the invoking `Integer` object. The static version returns a `String` representation of the specified `int`. The `radix` is the base of the number system used. In the decimal system, the radix would be 10. The default radix is 10.

## Other toString() Methods

| Method | Syntax |
|--------|--------|
| toBinaryString() | public static String toBinaryString(int i) |
| toHexString() | public static String toHexString(int i) |
| toOctalString | public static String toOctalString(int i) |

`toBinaryString()` returns a `String` representation of the argument `int` as an unsigned integer in base 2.

`toHexstring()` returns a `String` representation of the argument `int` as an unsigned integer in base 16.

toOctalstring() returns a String representation of the argument int as an unsigned integer in base 8.

---

### Example: Converting a String to an int

This example demonstrates the use of the parseInt() method to convert a String to an int.

```
public class TestI {
    public static void main(String args[]) {
        int i = Integer.parseInt("9");
        i = i + 2;
        System.out.println("Value of i is " + Integer.toString(i));
    }
}
```

#### Output

```
Value of i is 11
```

The parseInt() and toString() methods are invoked using the "Integer." syntax to tell the compiler which parseInt() and toString() methods to use.

---

# 2.4.7 Long Class

```
public final class Long extends Number implements Comparable
```

```
Object
    Number
        Long
```

### Interfaces

```
Comparable, Serializable
```

The Long class is the wrapper class for the primitive type long.

## Long() Constructor

| Constructor | Syntax |
|---|---|
| Long() | public Long(long l) |
| | public Long(String s) throws NumberFormatException |

Creates a Long object based on a long or String argument. The String argument must be a String representation of a long.

## Static Methods to Create Long Objects

| Method | Syntax |
|--------|--------|
| decode() | public static Long decode(String s)<br>                              throws NumberFormatException |
| valueOf() | public static Long valueOf(String s)<br>                              throws NumberFormatException |
| valueOf() | public static Long valueOf(String s, int radix)<br>                              throws NumberFormatException |

decode() returns a Long object based on parsing the argument String. The String can represent a decimal, hexadecimal, or octal number.

valueOf() returns a Long object based on parsing the argument String. The String must represent a long value. The radix is the base of the number system used. In the decimal system, the radix would be 10.

## Methods to Compare Long Objects

| Method | Syntax |
|--------|--------|
| equals() | public boolean equals(Object obj) |
| compareTo() | public int compareTo(Long l) |
|  | public int compareTo(Object obj) |

equals() overrides the equals() method from the Object class and returns true if Object obj is a Long object with the same value as the invoking Long object.

compareTo() compares the invoking Long object to the specified Long or Object object. It returns 0 if the invoking Long object is equal to, a negative value if the invoking Long object is numerically less than, or a positive value if the invoking Long object is numerically greater than the argument object.

## Methods to Convert Long Objects to Primitive Types

| Method | Syntax |
|--------|--------|
| byteValue() | public byte byteValue() |
| doubleValue() | public double doubleValue() |
| floatValue() | public float floatValue() |
| intValue() | public int intValue() |
| longValue() | public long longValue() |
| shortValue() | public short shortValue() |

These methods return a primitive data type from the value of the invoking Long object.

## hashCode() Method

| Method | Syntax |
|--------|--------|
| hashCode() | public int hashCode() |

hashCode() overrides the hashCode() method from the Object class and returns the hash code associated with the invoking Long object.

## parseLong() Method

| Method | Syntax |
|---|---|
| parseLong() | public static long parseLong(String s)<br>               throws NumberFormatException |
| | public static long parseLong(String s, int radix)<br>               throws NumberFormatException |

parseLong() returns a primitive long using the String argument to set the value. The radix is the base of the number system used. In the decimal system, the radix would be 10.

## toString() Method

| Method | Syntax |
|---|---|
| toString() | public static String toString(long l) |
| | public static String toString(long l, int radix) |
| | public String toString() |

toString() overrides the toString() method from the Object class to return the String representation of the value of the invoking Long object. The static version returns a String representation of the specified long. The radix is the base of the number system used. In the decimal system, the radix would be 10. The default radix is 10.

## Other toString() Methods

| Method | Syntax |
|---|---|
| toBinaryString() | public static String toBinaryString(long l) |
| toHexString() | public static String toHexString(long l) |
| toOctalString | public static String toOctalString(long l) |

toBinaryString() returns a String representation of the argument long as an unsigned integer in base 2.

toHexstring() returns a String representation of the argument long as an unsigned integer in base 16.

toOctalstring() returns a String representation of the argument long as an unsigned integer in base 8.

# 2.4.8 Number Class

```
public abstract class Number extends Object implements Serializable
```

```
Object
    Number
```

### Interfaces

```
Serializable
```

This is an abstract super-class for the primitive number wrapper classes Byte, Short, Integer, Long, Float, and Double. It has no constructors and no data members.

The Number class defines six methods which are implemented by the Number class sub-classes. The six methods are:

| Method | Syntax |
|--------|--------|
| byteValue() | public byte byteValue() |
| doubleValue() | public abstract double doubleValue() |
| floatValue() | public abstract float floatValue() |
| intValue() | public abstract int intValue() |
| longValue() | public abstract long longValue() |
| shortValue() | public short shortValue() |

# 2.4.9 Short Class

```
public final class Short extends Number implements Comparable
```

```
Object
    Number
        Short
```

### Interfaces

```
Comparable, Serializable
```

The Short class is the wrapper class for the primitive type short.

## Short() Constructor

| Constructor | Syntax |
|-------------|--------|
| toString() | public Short(short s) |
| | public Short(String s) throws NumberFormatException |

Creates a Short object based on a short or String argument. The String must be a String representation of a short.

## Static Methods to Create Short Objects

| Method | Syntax |
|---|---|
| decode() | public static Short decode(String s)<br>throws NumberFormatException |
| valueOf() | public static Short valueOf(String s)<br>throws NumberFormatException |
| valueOf() | public static Short valueOf(String s, int radix)<br>throws NumberFormatException |

decode() returns a Short object based on parsing the argument String. The String can represent a decimal, hexadecimal, or octal number.

valueOf() returns a Short object based on parsing the argument String. The String must represent a short value. The radix is the base of the number system used. In the decimal system, the radix would be 10.

## Methods to Compare Short Objects

| Method | Syntax |
|---|---|
| equals() | public boolean equals(Object obj) |
| compareTo() | public int compareTo(Short s) |
| | public int compareTo(Object obj) |

equals() overrides the equals() method from the Object class and returns true if Object obj is a Short object with the same value as the invoking Short object.

compareTo() compares the invoking Short object to the specified Short or Object object. It returns 0 if the invoking Short object is equal to, a negative value if the invoking Short object is numerically less than, or a positive value if the invoking Short object is numerically greater, than the argument object.

## Methods to Convert Short Objects to Primitive Types

| Method | Syntax |
|---|---|
| byteValue() | public byte byteValue() |
| doubleValue() | public double doubleValue() |
| floatValue() | public float floatValue() |
| intValue() | public int intValue() |
| longValue() | public long longValue() |
| shortValue() | public short shortValue() |

These methods return a primitive data type from the value of the invoking Short object.

## hashCode() Method

| Method | Syntax |
|---|---|
| hashCode() | `public int hashCode()` |

`hashCode()` overrides the `hashCode()` method from the `Object` class and returns the hash code associated with the invoking `Short` object.

## parseShort() Method

| Method | Syntax |
|---|---|
| parseShort() | `public static short parseShort(String s)`<br>`                            throws NumberFormatException` |
| | `public static short parseShort(String s, int radix)`<br>`                            throws NumberFormatException` |

`parseShort()` returns a primitive `short` using the `String` argument to set the value. The `radix` is the base of the number system used. In the decimal system, the radix would be 10.

## toString() Method

| Method | Syntax |
|---|---|
| toString() | `public static String toString(short s)` |
| | `public String toString()` |

`toString()` overrides the `toString()` method from the `Object` class to return the `String` representation of the value of the invoking `Short` object. The static version returns a `String` representation of the specified `short`.

# 2.5 String and StringBuffer Classes

`String` and `StringBuffer` represent sequences of characters. A `String` is immutable, meaning that once a `String` object has been created it cannot be changed, whereas a `StringBuffer` represents a changeable, growable sequence of characters.

# 2.5.1 String Class

```
public final class String extends Object
  implements Serializable, Comparable
```

```
Object
  String
```

**Interfaces**

```
Comparable, Serializable
```

A String object represents a sequence of characters. A String object is immutable meaning that once it is created the sequence of characters cannot be changed. Any text enclosed in double quotes is considered to be of type String and is automatically converted to a String object.

String objects are static strings whose individual characters cannot be changed. Look at the following code:

```
String str = "abc";
str = "def";
```

In the second line, a new String object is created and assigned to the variable str. Java makes String objects immutable because it is easier to implement them that way.

## String() Constructor

| Constructor | Syntax |
|---|---|
| String() | String() |
| | String(char[] charArray) |
| | String(char[] charArray, int startIndex, int numChars) |
| | String(byte[] byteArray) |
| | String(byte[] byteArray, String encodingScheme) |
| | String(byte[] byteArray, int startIndex, int numBytes) |
| | String(String stringObject) |
| | String(StringBuffer sbObject) |

Creates a String object.

## Creating String Objects Using a Literal String

String objects can also be created by equating a String reference to some text surrounded in double quotes. The expression:

```
String s = "hello";
```

produces the same result as writing:

```
String s = new String("hello");
```

## Static Methods to Create String Objects

| Method | Syntax |
|---|---|
| valueOf() | public static String valueOf(boolean b) |
| | public static String valueOf(char c) |
| | public static String valueOf(char[] charArray) |
| | public static String valueOf(char[] charArray, int startIndex, int count) |

| Method | Syntax |
|---|---|
| valueOf() | `public static String valueOf(double d)` |
| | `public static String valueOf(float f)` |
| | `public static String valueOf(int i)` |
| | `public static String valueOf(long l)` |
| | `public static String valueOf(Object obj)` |
| copyValueOf() | `public static String copyValueOf(char[] charArray)` |
| | `public static String copyValueOf(char[] charArray, int startIndex, int numChars)` |

These methods return a String object based on the passed argument. If a boolean is passed, the String object will be either "true" or "false". The methods that take an index argument can throw a StringIndexOutOfBoundsException if the index is less than 0 or greater than or equal to the length of the String.

## String Concatenation

The + operator and the concat() method can be used to concatenate String objects.

### The + Operator

| Operator | Meaning |
|---|---|
| + | Concatenates two or more String objects. Can also be used to join strings with other data types. |

### Example: Using the + Operator

This example demonstrates the use of the + operator to concatenate strings and other data types.

```
public class TestPlusOper {
  public static void main(String args[]) {
    int i = 9;
    String str = "his age is " + i + " years old";
    System.out.println(str);
  }
}
```

**Output**

```
his age is 9 years old
```

### concat() Method

| Method | Syntax |
|---|---|
| concat() | `public String concat(String str)` |

concat() returns the argument String concatenated to the invoking String.

## Example: Using concat()

```
public class TestConcat {
  public static void main(String args[]) {
    String a = "Jackson";
    String b = " and Zachary";

    System.out.println(a.concat(b));
  }
}
```

**Output**

```
Jackson and Zachary
```

# Converting String Objects to Primitive Datatypes

### String to boolean

```
boolean b = Boolean.valueOf(String booleanString).booleanValue()
```

The static method valueOf() from the Boolean class returns a Boolean object based on the String booleanString. The booleanValue() method from the Boolean class returns true if the invoking Boolean object has the value true, and false if the invoking Boolean object has the value false. This syntax uses method cascading. Another way to write this would be:

```
Boolean B = Boolean.valueOf(String booleanString);
boolean b = B.booleanValue();
```

## Example: Converting a String to a boolean

This example demonstrates the use of the valueOf() and booleanValue() methods from the Boolean class to convert a String to a boolean.

```
public class TestStrToBoo {
  public static void main(String args[]) {
    boolean b = Boolean.valueOf("true").booleanValue();

    if (b) {
      System.out.println("b is true");
    }
  }
}
```

**Output**

```
b is true
```

### String to Double or Float

```
double d = Double.valueOf(String doubleString).doubleValue()
float f = Float.valueOf(String floatString).floatValue()
```

The static method valueOf() from the Double class returns a Double object based on the String doubleString. It can throw a NumberFormatException if doubleString does not represent an appropriate double value. The doubleValue() method from the Double class returns a primitive double that is set to the value contained by the invoking Double object. This syntax makes use of method cascading. Another way to write this would be:

```
Double Dobj = Double.valueOf(String doubleString);
double d = Dobj.doubleValue();
```

The valueOf() and floatValue() methods from the Float class work in a similar fashion.

## Example: Converting a String to a double

This example demonstrates the use of the valueOf() and doubleValue() methods from the Double class to convert a String to a double.

```
public class TestStrToDouble {
    public static void main(String args[]) {
        double d = Double.valueOf("45.3").doubleValue();
        double twoD = 2.0*d;
        System.out.println("twice d is "+twoD);
    }
}
```

### Output

```
twice d is 90.6
```

### String to int, long, or short

```
int i = Integer.parseInt(String intString)
long l = Long.parseLong(String longString)
short s = Short.parseShort(String shortString)
```

The static method parseInt() from the Integer class takes a String argument and returns an int based on that String argument. The static methods parseLong() and parseShort() from the Long and Short classes work in a similar fashion. These methods can throw a NumberFormatException if an inappropriate String argument is provided.

### Example: Converting a String to an int

This example demonstrates the use of the parseInt() method from the Integer class to convert a String to an int.

```
public class TestStrToInt {
  public static void main(String args[]) {
    int i = Integer.parseInt("45");
    int twoI = 2*i;
    System.out.println("twice i is "+twoI);
  }
}
```

*Output*

```
twice i is 90
```

## getBytes() Method

| Method | Syntax |
| --- | --- |
| getBytes() | public byte[] getBytes()<br>public byte[] getBytes(String *encodingScheme*)<br>　　　　　　throws UnsupportedEncodingException |
| | public byte[] getBytes(int *srcStart*, int *srcEnd*,<br>　　　　　　byte[] *dest*, int *destStart*)<br>　　　　throws StringIndexOutOfBoundsException |

getBytes() returns a byte array generated from the sequence of characters in the invoking String object. The third version has been deprecated because it does not properly convert characters into bytes and should not be used for new code.

## getChars() Method

| Method | Syntax |
| --- | --- |
| getChars() | public void getChars(int *sourceStart*, int *sourceEnd*,<br>　　　　　　char[] *ch*, int *chStart*) |

getChars() extracts a subset of the invoking String object and places the characters into a char array.

### Example: Using getChars()

This example demonstrates the use of getChars() to obtain a char array from a String.

```
public class TestGetChars {
  public static void main(String args[]) {
```

```
    String a = "Jackson";
    char[] charArray = new char[10];

    a.getChars(0, 2, charArray, 0);

    System.out.println("First two letters are " + charArray[0]
                        + " and " + charArray[1]);
  }
}
```

*Output*

```
    First two letters are J and a
```

## hashCode() Method

| Method | Syntax |
|--------|--------|
| hashCode() | public int hashCode() |

hashCode() overrides the hashCode() method from the Object class and returns the hash code associated with the invoking String object.

## length() Method

| Method | Syntax |
|--------|--------|
| length() | public int length() |

length() returns the length of the invoking String object. The length is equal to the number of 16-bit Unicode characters in the String.

### Example: Using length()

This example demonstates using the length() method to find out the length of a String.

```
public class TestLength {
  public static void main(String args[]) {
    String str = "Jackson";
    System.out.println("Length of string is " + str.length());
  }
}
```

*Output*

```
    Length of string is 7
```

## Methods to Change the Case of a String Object

| Method | Syntax |
|---|---|
| toLowerCase() | public String toLowerCase() |
| | public String toLowerCase(Locale *locale*) |
| toUpperCase() | public String toUpperCase() |
| | public String toUpperCase(Locale *locale*) |

toLowerCase() returns a String object in lower case. A Locale object can be provided to use the lower case rules of that locale.

toUpperCase() returns a String object in upper case. A Locale object can be provided to use the lower case rules of that locale.

### Example: Using toLowerCase()

This example demonstrates the use of toLowerCase() to convert a String to lower case.

```
public class TestCase {
  public static void main(String args[]) {
    String str = "Jackson";

    System.out.println("Lowercase string is " + str.toLowerCase());
  }
}
```

*Output*

```
Lowercase string is jackson
```

## Methods to Compare Two String Objects

| Method | Syntax |
|---|---|
| compareTo() | public int compareTo(String *s*) |
| compareTo() | public int compareTo(Object *obj*) |
| compareToIgnoreCase() | public int compareToIgnoreCase(String *s*) |
| equals() | public boolean equals(Object *obj*) |
| equalsIgnoreCase() | public boolean equalsIgnoreCase(String *s*) |

These methods are used to compare the argument String or Object to the invoking String object.

compareTo() returns a positive value if the invoking String object comes before the argument object alphabetically, 0 if the two String objects are the same, and a negative value if the passed String object comes before the invoking String object alphabetically.

compareToIgnoreCase() performs similarly to compareTo() except case is ignored.

equals() overrides the equals() method in class Object and returns true if the Object obj is a String and has the same sequence of characters as the invoking String object.

equalsIgnoreCase() behaves the same as equals() except case is ignored.

## Example: Comparing String objects

This example uses the equalsIgnoreCase() method to compare two String objects.

```
public class TestCompare {
  public static void main(String args[]) {
    String str1 = "Zachary";
    String str2 = "zaCHarY";

    if (str1.equalsIgnoreCase(str2)) {
      System.out.println("strings are equal ignoring case");
    }
  }
}
```

*Output*

```
strings are equal ignoring case
```

## Methods to Examine the Elements of a String Object

| Method | Syntax |
| --- | --- |
| charAt() | public char charAt(int *index*) |
| endsWith() | public boolean endsWith(String *str*) |
| indexOf() | public int indexOf(int *ch*) |
| | public int indexOf(int *ch*, int *fromIndex*) |
| | public int indexOf(String *s*) |
| | public int indexOf(String *s*, int *fromIndex*) |
| lastIndexOf() | public int lastIndexOf(int *ch*) |
| | public int lastIndexOf(int *ch*, int *fromIndex*) |
| | public int lastIndexOf(String *s*) |
| | public int lastIndexOf(String *s*, int *fromIndex*) |
| startsWith() | public boolean startsWith(String *str*) |
| | public boolean startsWith(String *str*, int *offset*) |

charAt() returns the character at the specified index in the invoking String object.

endsWith() returns true if the invoking String object ends with the specified String.

indexOf() searches the invoking String object for the first occurrence of the char or String passed as an argument and returns the index, or -1 if the char or String is not found. A starting index for the search can be specified.

lastIndexOf() searches the invoking String object for the last occurrence of the char or String passed as an argument and returns the index, or -1 if the char or String is not found. A starting index for the search can be specified.

startsWith() returns true if the invoking String object starts with the specified String.

# replace() Method

| Method | Syntax |
|---|---|
| replace() | public String replace(char *oldChar*, char *newChar*) |

replace() replaces all occurrences of oldChar with newChar in the invoking String object.

## Example: Using replace()

This example uses replace() to replace all occurrences of the letter 'a' with 'o' in the String.

```
public class TestReplace {
  public static void main(String args[]) {
    String str1 = "Zachary";
    String str2 = str1.replace('a', 'o');
    System.out.println("new string is " + str2);
  }
}
```

*Output*

```
new string is Zochory
```

# substring() Method

| Method | Syntax |
|---|---|
| substring() | public String substring(int *startIndex*) |
| | public String substring(int *startIndex*, int *endIndex*) |

substring() returns a String object containing a substring of the invoking String object. The first version returns a String from startIndex to the end of the String.

## Example: Using substring()

This example uses substring() to extract a portion of a String.

```
public class TestSubstring {
  public static void main(String args[]) {
    String str1 = "Jackson";
    String str2 = str1.substring(0, 4);

    System.out.println("new string is " + str2);
  }
}
```

### Output

```
new string is Jack
```

The second int passed to the substring() method is the first char that is not included in the substring. Calling substring(0,4) results in a four character substring.

## toCharArray() Method

| Method | Syntax |
|---|---|
| toCharArray() | public char[] toCharArray() |

toCharArray() returns a char array containing the sequence of characters from the invoking String object.

## Example: Using toCharArray()

This example uses toCharArray() to convert a String into an array of characters.

```
public class TestToCharArray {
  public static void main(String args[]) {
    String str = "Jackson";
    char[] charArray = str.toCharArray();

    System.out.println("First two letters are " + charArray[0]
                        + " and " + charArray[1]);
  }
}
```

### Output

```
First two letters are J and a
```

# trim() Method

| Method | Syntax |
|--------|--------|
| trim() | public String trim() |

trim() returns a String object the same as the invoking String object except all leading and trailing whitespace is removed.

## Example: Using trim()

This example demonstrates the use of trim() to remove whitespace characters from the beginning and end of a String.

```
public class TestTrim {
  public static void main(String args[]) {
    String str = "    Jackson    ";

    System.out.println("The trimmed string is =" + str.trim() + "=");
  }
}
```

### Output

```
The trimmed string is =Jackson=
```

# toString() Method

| Method | Syntax |
|--------|--------|
| toString() | public String toString() |

toString() overrides the toString() method from the Object class. In this case, it simply returns the invoking String object.

# 2.5.2 StringBuffer Class

```
public final class StringBuffer extends Object implements Serializable
```

```
Object
  StringBuffer
```

### Interfaces

```
serializable
```

A String object is an immutable, fixed-length series of characters. A StringBuffer object is a changeable, growable sequence of characters. Java uses StringBuffer objects internally, for instance, when two String objects are concatenated. If you are working with a string that keeps changing, then it is more efficient to use a StringBuffer initially, then convert it to a String at the end of the process.

## StringBuffer() Constructor

| Constructor | Syntax |
|---|---|
| StringBuffer() | public StringBuffer()<br>public StringBuffer(int capacity)<br>public StringBuffer(String str) |

Creates a StringBuffer object. The no-argument version creates an empty
StringBuffer object with a capacity of 16 characters. The capacity is automatically
increased if the size of the StringBuffer object exceeds its capacity.

## Methods to Access or Change Elements of a StringBuffer Object

| Method | Syntax |
|---|---|
| charAt() | public char charAt(int *index*) |
| getChars() | public void getChars(int *sourceStart*, int *sourceEnd*,<br>char[] *ch*, int *chStart*) |
| setCharAt() | public void setCharAt(int *index*, char *c*) |

charAt() returns the character at the specified index. It is synchronized, meaning that
only one Thread can access the method at any one time.

getChars() extracts a subset of the invoking String object and places the characters
into a character array.

setCharAt() changes the character at the specified index to the char passed as an
argument.

### Example: Accessing StringBuffer Elements

This example uses getChars() and setCharAt() to access StringBuffer elements.

```
public class TestSBcharAt {
  public static void main(String args[]) {
    StringBuffer str = new StringBuffer("Jackson");
    char[] charArray = new char[10];

    char c = str.charAt(3);
    str.getChars(0, 4, charArray, 0);
    str.setCharAt(0, 'j');

    System.out.println("character at index 3 is " + c);
    System.out.println("the first character in charArray is "
                       + charArray[0]);
    System.out.println("The new StringBuffer string is " + str);
  }
}
```

*Output*

```
character at index 3 is k
the first character in charArray is J
The new StringBuffer string is jackson
```

# append() Method

| Method | Syntax |
|--------|--------|
| append() | public StringBuffer append(boolean *b*) |
| | public StringBuffer append(char *c*) |
| | public StringBuffer append(char[] *charArray*) |
| | public StringBuffer append(char[] *charArray*, int *startIndex*, int *length*) |
| | public StringBuffer append(double *d*) |
| | public StringBuffer append(float *f*) |
| | public StringBuffer append(int *i*) |
| | public StringBuffer append(long *l*) |
| | public StringBuffer append(Object *obj*) |
| | public StringBuffer append(String *str*) |

append() appends a character or String representation of the passed argument to the end of the sequence of characters contained in the invoking StringBuffer object. The method has been overloaded to accept primitive variables, Object, or String arguments.

The version of append() that takes an index argument appends the specified subarray of the char array.

These methods return a StringBuffer object and therefore can be cascaded.

## Example: Using append()

This example uses append() to append a String and an int to a StringBuffer.

```java
public class TestSBappend {
  public static void main(String args[]) {
    StringBuffer sb = new StringBuffer("Jackson");
    String str = " Palmer ";
    int i = 4;

    sb = sb.append(str).append(i);

    System.out.println("The new StringBuffer string is " + sb);
  }
}
```

**Output**
```
The new StringBuffer string is Jackson Palmer 4
```

Because the append() method returns a StringBuffer object, it can be cascaded. Passing a StringBuffer object (sb) to the println() method calls the toString() method which returns a String representation of the StringBuffer object.

## Capacity Methods

| Method | Syntax |
| --- | --- |
| capacity() | public int capacity() |
| ensureCapacity() | public void ensureCapacity(int *minimumCapacity*) |

capacity() returns the current capacity of the invoking StringBuffer object.

ensureCapacity() sets the minimum capacity of the invoking StringBuffer object.

### Example: Determining StringBuffer Capacity

This example uses the capacity() method to determine the capacity of a StringBuffer.

```
public class TestSBcapacity {
  public static void main(String args[]) {
    StringBuffer sb = new StringBuffer(" Jackson ");
    int i = sb.capacity();

    System.out.println("capacity is " + i);
  }
}
```

**Output**
```
capacity is 27
```

The capacity of the StringBuffer object sb set by the constructor is 16 plus the length of the String argument. The leading and trailing whitespace counts as part of this length.

# Methods to Delete Characters

| Method | Syntax |
|--------|--------|
| delete() | public StringBuffer delete(int *startIndex*, int *endIndex*) |
| deleteCharAt() | public StringBuffer deleteCharAt(int *index*) |

delete() removes the characters from startIndex to endIndex in the invoking StringBuffer object. The StringBuffer containing the modified sequence of characters is returned.

deleteCharAt() removes the characters at the specified index from the invoking StringBuffer object. A StringBuffer containing the modified sequence of characters is returned.

## Example: Using deleteCharAt()

This example uses deleteCharAt() to delete a character from a StringBuffer.

```
public class TestSBdelete {
  public static void main(String args[]) {
    StringBuffer sb = new StringBuffer("Lisa");
    sb.deleteCharAt(2);

    System.out.println("string is *" + sb.toString() + "*");
  }
}
```

### Output:

```
string is *Lia*
```

# insert() Method

| Method | Syntax |
|--------|--------|
| insert() | public StringBuffer insert(int *startIndex*, boolean *b*) |
| | public StringBuffer insert(int *startIndex*, char *c*) |
| | public StringBuffer insert(int *startIndex*, char[] *charArray*) |
| | public StringBuffer insert(int *startIndex*, char[] *charArray*, int *offset*, int *length*) |
| | public StringBuffer insert(int *startIndex*, double *d*) |
| | public StringBuffer insert(int *startIndex*, float *f*) |
| | public StringBuffer insert(int *startIndex*, int *i*) |
| | public StringBuffer insert(int *startIndex*, long *l*) |
| | public StringBuffer insert(int *startIndex*, Object *bj*) |
| | public StringBuffer insert(int *startIndex*, String *tr*) |

insert() methods insert a character or String representation of the passed argument to the sequence of characters contained in the invoking StringBuffer object starting at startIndex. The version that takes an offset and length inserts the specified subarray of the char array.

---

### Example: Using insert()

This example uses insert() to insert the elements of a char array into a StringBuffer.

```
public class TestSBinsert {
    public static void main(String args[]) {
        StringBuffer sb = new StringBuffer("Lisa");
        char[] charArray = {
            'M', 's', ' '
        };

        sb = sb.insert(0, charArray);

        System.out.println("string is *" + sb.toString() + "*");
    }
}
```

*Output*
```
string is *Ms Lisa*
```

Because the offset passed to the insert() method was 0, the characters 'M', 's', and ' ' were inserted at the beginning of the StringBuffer object character sequence.

---

## Length Methods

| Method | Syntax |
|---|---|
| length() | public int length() |
| setLength() | public synchronized void setLength(int length) throws IndexOutOfBoundsException |

length() returns the number of characters contained in the invoking StringBuffer object.

setLength() changes the length of the invoking StringBuffer object, deleting characters if the length is made smaller than the current length or adding null characters if the length is made longer than the current length.

### Example: Using setLength()

```
public class TestSBLength {
  public static void main(String args[]) {
    StringBuffer sb = new StringBuffer("Lisa");
    sb.setLength(3);

    System.out.println("string is *" + sb.toString() + "*");
  }
}
```

**Output**

```
string is *Lis*
```

When the length is decreased to 3, the 'a' is deleted from the StringBuffer object.

## replace() Method

| Method | Syntax |
| --- | --- |
| replace() | public StringBuffer replace(int *startIndex*, int *endIndex*, String *str*) |

replace() replaces the characters in the invoking StringBuffer object from startIndex to endIndex with the specified String.

### Example: Using replace()

This example uses replace() to replace some of the characters in a StringBuffer.

```
public class TestSBreplace {
  public static void main(String args[]) {
    StringBuffer sb = new StringBuffer("Lisa");
    sb.replace(1,2,"owee");
    System.out.println("string is *" + sb.toString() + "*");
  }
}
```

**Output**

```
string is *Loweesa*
```

## reverse() Method

| Method | Syntax |
|--------|--------|
| reverse() | public StringBuffer reverse() |

reverse() returns a StringBuffer object with the reverse order of characters contained in the invoking StringBuffer object.

### Example: Using reverse()

This example uses reverse() to reverse the order of the characters in a StringBuffer.

```java
public class TestSBreverse {
  public static void main(String args[]) {
    StringBuffer sb = new StringBuffer("Lisa");

    sb = sb.reverse();

    System.out.println("reverse string is " + sb.toString());
  }
}
```

*Output*

```
reverse string is asiL
```

## substring() Method

| Method | Syntax |
|--------|--------|
| substring() | public String substring(int *startIndex*) |
|  | public String substring(int *startIndex*, int *endIndex*) |

substring() returns a String object containing the specified substring. If no endIndex is provided, the substring will continue to the last character contained in the invoking StringBuffer object.

## toString() Method

| Method | Syntax |
|--------|--------|
| toString() | public String toString() |

toString() returns a String object with the same sequence of characters as the invoking StringBuffer object.

# 2.6 System Classes

The system classes provide objects to access information about the system, the runtime environment and processes. The following diagram shows the system classes hierarchy:

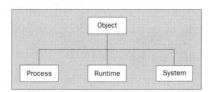

# 2.6.1 Process Class

```
public abstract class Process extends Object
```

```
Object
    Process
```

The Process class describes processes started by the exec() command of the Runtime class. Process is an abstract class so a Process object is never created directly. Process objects are returned by the exec() method.

## destroy() Method

| Method | Syntax |
|---|---|
| destroy() | public abstract void **destroy**() |

destroy() kills the process controlled by the invoking object.

## Exit Status Methods

| Method | Syntax |
|---|---|
| exitValue() | public abstract int **exitValue**() |
| waitFor() | public abstract int **waitFor**()<br>                              throws InterruptedException |

exitValue() returns the exit value of the process that the invoking object is controlling. (Some systems return dummy exit values.)
waitFor() waits until the process is finished before returning the exit value.

---

### Example: Using waitFor()

See example *Using exec()* on page 149.

---

## I/O Stream Methods

| Method | Syntax |
|---|---|
| getErrorStream() | public abstract InputStream getErrorStream() |
| getInputStream() | public abstract InputStream getInputStream() |
| getOutputStream() | public abstract OutputStream getOutputStream() |

getErrorStream() returns the error stream associated with the process.

getInputStream() returns the input stream associated with the process.

getOutputStream() returns the output stream associated with the process.

# 2.6.2 Runtime Class

```
public class Runtime extends Object
```

```
Object
  Runtime
```

The Runtime class provides access to various information about the environment in which a program is running.

Runtime class methods and variables provide access to platform specific features. Supported operations include spawning a child process, memory usage and management, loading dynamic libraries, and exiting the runtimeenvironment. The Runtime class also defines the exec() method which can be used to execute external programs or commands.

The Runtime class has no public constructors. A program must call the getRuntime() method to return a reference to the current Runtime object.

## getRuntime() Method

| Method | Syntax |
|---|---|
| getRuntime() | public static Runtime getRuntime() |

getRuntime() returns a reference to the current Runtime object.

### Example: Using getRuntime()

This example uses getRuntime() to obtain a reference to the current Runtime object.

```
public class TestRuntime {
  public static void main(String args[]) {
    Runtime r = Runtime.getRuntime();
  }
}
```

The getRuntime() method is static which means it can be called without having to first instantiate a Runtime object.

# exec() Method

| Method | Syntax |
|--------|--------|
| exec() | public Process **exec**(String command)<br>      throws IOException |
| | public Process **exec**(String command,<br>      String[] envVariables)<br>      throws IOException |
| | public Process **exec**(String command,<br>      String[] envVariables, File dir)<br>      throws IOException |
| | public Process **exec**(String[] commandArray,<br>      String[] envVariables)<br>      throws IOException |
| | public Process **exec**(String[] commandArray,<br>      String[] envVariables, File dir)<br>      throws IOException |
| | public Process **exec**(String[] commandArray)<br>      throws IOException |

exec() starts a new process to execute the command or commands passed as an argument. The commands passed to the exec() method will depend on the operating system being used.

## Example: Using exec()

This example demonstrates the use of exec() to start an external process. The command "ping bad" is run. The standard error and output streams are read and their contents printed out, along with the command's exit value.

```java
import java.io.*;

public class TestExec {

  public static void main(String args[]) {
    Runtime r = Runtime.getRuntime();
    Process p = null;
    String cmd = "ping bad";
    InputStream inp = null;
    InputStream inpE = null;

    // Run the command
    try {
      p = r.exec(cmd);
      p.waitFor();
      inp = p.getInputStream();
      inpE = p.getErrorStream();
    } catch (Exception e) {
      System.out.println("error executing command");
    }

    // Try to read Standard Error and Standard Output
    try {
      int count = inp.available();
      int countE = inpE.available();
```

**149**

```
            if (countE > 0) {
              // There was output to Standard Error
              byte[] bufferE = new byte[countE];
              inpE.read(bufferE);

              String stderr = new String(bufferE);
              System.out.println("Standard Error:");
              System.out.println(stderr);
            } else {
              System.out.println("No output to Standard Error");
            }

            if (count > 0) {
              // There was output to Standard Output
              byte[] buffer = new byte[count];
              inp.read(buffer);
              System.out.println("Standard Output:");
              String stdout = new String(buffer);
              System.out.println(stdout);
            } else {
              System.out.println("No output to Standard Output");
            }
          } catch (Exception e) {
            System.out.println("Error capturing output");
          }

          System.out.println("command finished, exit value = "
                         + p.exitValue());
      }
    }
```

**Output**

```
No output to Standard Error
Standard Output:
Unknown host bad.

command finished, exit value = 1
```

## Other Runtime Class Methods

| Method | Syntax |
|---|---|
| runFinalization() | public void runFinalization() |
| exit() | public void exit(int *status*) |
| freeMemory() | public long freeMemory() |
| gc() | public void gc() |
| halt() | public void halt(int *status*) |
| load() | public void load(String *filename*) |

| Method | Syntax |
|---|---|
| loadLibrary() | public void loadLibrary(String *libraryName*) |
| totalMemory() | public long totalMemory() |
| traceInstructions() | public void traceInstructions(boolean *on*) |
| traceMethodCalls() | public void traceMethodCalls(boolean *on*) |

runFinalization() runs the finalization methods of any objects waiting finalization.

exit() terminates the Java program.

freeMemory() returns the amount of free memory left in the system.

gc() suggests that the garbage collector be run. This eliminates unused objects in order to make the memory they currently occupy available for quick reuse.

halt() forcibly terminates the Java application.

load() loads the specified file as a dynamic library.

loadLibrary() loads the dynamic library with the specified library name.

totalMemory() returns the total amount of memory in the Java Virtual Machine.

traceInstructions() determines whether instruction tracing will be enabled.

traceMethodCalls() determines whether method calls will be traced.

# 2.6.3 System Class

```
public final class System extends Object
```

```
Object
    System
```

System provides access to information about the operating system environment in which a program is running. It also provides platform independent resources such as the standard input, output, and error streams.

Since all methods and variables in the System class are public and static, the class need not be instantiated. A system object is never created; the public static methods are simply invoked.

## arraycopy() Method

| Method | Syntax |
|---|---|
| arraycopy() | public static void arraycopy(Object *src*, int *srcOffset*, Object *dst*, int *dstOffset*, int *count*) |

arraycopy() copies part of the src array starting at element srcOffset into the dst array beginning at element dstOffset. count is the number of elements to be copied. This method is useful for copying primitive datatype arrays.

## Example: Using arraycopy()

This example uses arraycopy() to copy 3 elements from one int array to another.

```java
public class TestArrayCopy {
  public static void main(String args[]) {
    int[] array1 = {
      1, 2, 3, 4, 5
    };
    int[] array2 = new int[3];

    System.arraycopy(array1, 1, array2, 0, 3);

    System.out.println("array2 elements " + array2[0] + ", "
                        + array2[1] + ", " + array2[2]);
  }
}
```

### Output

```
array2 elements 2, 3, 4
```

## currentTimeMillis() Method

| Method | Syntax |
|---|---|
| currentTimeMillis() | public static long currentTimeMillis() |

currentTimeMillis() returns the current time in milliseconds from Jan 1, 1970. This method is used to initialize a Date object with the current date. When the Date object calls the toString() method it returns the current date in a readable form. The Date class is in the java.util package, which must be imported.

## Example: Using currentTimeMillis()

This example uses currentTimeMillis() and the Date class to print out the current time.

```java
import java.util.*;

public class TestTimeMillis {
  public static void main(String[] args) {
```

```
Date now = new Date(System.currentTimeMillis());
    System.out.println("The time is " + now.toString());
  }
}
```

**Output** *(will vary between runs)*

```
The time is Sat Nov 20 12:32:36 PST 1999
```

# exit() Method

| Method | Syntax |
|--------|--------|
| exit() | public static void exit(int *status*) |

exit() causes the Java virtual machine to exit the program. A non-zero status
generally indicates an abnormal termination.

## Example: Using exit()

This example demonstrates the use of the exit() method to exit the program.

```
public class TestExit {
  public static void main(String args[]) {
    System.out
      .println("I'm waiting five seconds and then I'm exiting");
    try {
      Thread.sleep(5000);
    } catch (InterruptedException e) {}

    System.exit(0);
    System.out.println("this never executes");
  }
}
```

**Output**

```
I'm waiting five seconds and then I'm exiting
```

The message "this never executes" is not printed, because exit() has been
called.

## Standard I/O Streams

### Syntax

```
public static final PrintStream err
public static final InputStream in
public static final PrintStream out
```

These are the standard I/O streams. The standard error is generally an unbuffered output stream that is sent to the console. The standard input stream used to read a stream of characters from the keyboard and, similar to the getchar() method in C, waits for a carriage return before making the data available to the program. The standard output stream writes character output to the console.

### Example: Using the Standard I/O Streams

This example demonstrates the use of the System.in, System.out, and System.err streams.

```java
import java.io.*;

public class TestStdIO {
  public static void main(String[] args) {
    try {
      char ch = (char) System.in.read();
      if (Character.isDigit(ch)) {
        System.out.println("Character " + ch + " is a digit");
      }
    } catch (IOException e) {
      System.err.println("Error reading from standard input");
    }
  }
}
```

**Output** (will vary between runs)

```
Character 4 is a digit
```

(*4* was typed on the keyboard.)

## Methods to Re-Assign the Standard I/O Streams

| Method | Syntax |
|--------|--------|
| setErr() | public static void setErr(PrintStream err) |
| setIn() | public static void setIn(InputStream in) |
| setOut() | public static void setOut(PrintStream out) |

setErr() reassigns the standard error stream to the specified stream.

setIn() reassigns the standard input stream to the specified stream.

setOut() reassigns the standard output stream to the specified stream.

# System Property Methods

| Method | Syntax |
|---|---|
| getProperties() | public static Properties getProperties() |
| getProperty() | public static String getProperty<br>(String *propertyName*) |
| getProperty() | public static String getProperty(String *property*,<br>String *default*) |
| setProperties() | public static void setProperties(Properties *p*) |
| setProperty() | public static String setProperty(String *property*,<br>String *value*) |

getProperties() returns a Properties object containing the system properties. Examples of properties that can be accessed by this methods are file.separator, java.home, java.version, line.separator, os.name, os.version, path.separator, usr.dir, usr.home, and usr.name.

getProperty() returns the value associated with the specified property name. A default value can be provided.

setProperties() and setProperty() are used to change system properties.

## Example: Getting System Properties

```
public class TestSysProp {
  public static void main(String args[]) {
    System.out.println("Java version is " +
                  System.getProperty("java.version"));
  }
}
```

**Output** *(may vary)*
```
Java version is 1.3.0rc1
```

# Other System Class Methods

| Method | Syntax |
|---|---|
| gc() | public static void gc() |
| load() | public static void load(String *pathname*) |
| loadLibrary() | public static void loadLibrary(String *libname*) |
| getSecurityManager() | public static SecurityManager<br>getSecurityManager() |
| setSecurityManager() | public static void<br>setSecurityManager(SecurityManager *sm*) |

gc() suggests that the garbage collector be run.

load() and loadLibrary() load a dynamically linked library.

getSecurityManager() and setSecurityManager() return or set the
SecurityManager.

# 2.7 Miscellaneous Classes

The Math and StrictMath classes provide common mathematical functions.

## 2.7.1 Math Class

```
public final class Math extends Object
```

```
Object
  Math
```

Provides constants and static methods for basic math operations including
trigonometric, exponential, rounding, and transcendental math functions. All of the
constants and methods defined in the Math class are static, meaning they can be called
directly without instantiating a Math object.

### pi and e Constants

| Constant |
| --- |
| public static final double PI |
| public static final double E |

These constants contain the values of pi and e.

---

**Example: Using PI**

This example demonstrates the use of the Math.PI constant.

```java
public class TestPi {
  public static void main(String args[]) {
    double radius = 2.0;
    double area = Math.PI * radius * radius;
    System.out.println("The area is " + area);
  }
}
```

**Output**
```
The area is 12.566370614359172
```

---

# abs() Method

| Method | Syntax |
|--------|--------|
| abs() | `public static double abs(double d)` |
| | `public static float abs(float f)` |
| | `public static int abs(int i)` |
| | `public static long abs(long l)` |

abs() returns the absolute value of the argument. This method has been overloaded to handle double, float, int, and long data types. The compiler determines which version to call based on the argument type.

## Example: Using abs()

This example demonstrates the use of the abs() method.

```
public class TestAbs {
  public static void main(String args[]) {
    int a = -4;
    double b = -32.3;

    System.out.println("The absolute value of a is " + Math.abs(a));
    System.out.println("The absolute value of b is " + Math.abs(b));
  }
}
```

### Output

```
The absolute value of a is 4
The absolute value of b is 32.3
```

# exp() Method

| Method | Syntax |
|--------|--------|
| exp() | `public static double exp(double d)` |

exp() returns the value of e raised to the power d.

## Example: Using exp()

This example demonstrates the use of the exp() method.

```
public class TestE {
  public static void main(String args[]) {
    System.out.println("e squared is " + Math.exp(2.0));
  }
}
```

**157**

**Output**

```
e squared is 7.38905609893065
```

## IEEEremainder() Method

| Method | Syntax |
|--------|--------|
| IEEEremainder() | public static double IEEEremainder(double a, double b) |

IEEEremainder() returns the remainder of a divided by b as defined by the IEEE 754 standard. It first divides a by b and rounds the result to the nearest whole number. It takes this value, multiplies it by b and subtracts the result from a.

### Example: Using IEEEremainder()

This example demonstrates the use of the IEEEremainder() method.

```java
public class TestIEEE {
    public static void main(String args[]) {
    double a = 7.0;
        double b = 3.0;

        System.out.println("The remainder is "
                        + Math.IEEEremainder(a, b));
    }
}
```

**Output**

```
The remainder is 1.0
```

## log() Method

| Method | Syntax |
|--------|--------|
| log() | public static double log(double d) |

log() returns the natural logrithm of d.

## Example: Using log()

This example demonstrates the use of the log() method.

```
public class TestLog {
  public static void main(String args[]) {
    System.out.println("The natural log of 0.5 is " + Math.log(0.5));
  }
}
```

**Output**

```
The natural log of 0.5 is -0.6931471805599453
```

# max() Method

| Method | Syntax |
|--------|--------|
| max() | public static double max(double a, double b) |
| | public static float max(float a, float b) |
| | public static int max(int a, int b) |
| | public static long max(int a, int b) |

max() returns the greater of a and b. This method has been overloaded to handle double, float, int, and long data types. The compiler determines which version to call based on the argument type.

## Example: Using max()

This example demonstrates the use of the max() method.

```
public class TestMax {
  public static void main(String args[]) {
    double a = 3.5;
    double b = 4.0;

    System.out.println("The maximum of a and b is " + Math.max(a, b));
  }
}
```

**Output**

```
The maximum of a and b is 4.0
```

## min() Method

| Method | Syntax |
|--------|--------|
| min() | public static double min(double *a*, double *b*) |
|        | public static float min(float *a*, float *b*) |
|        | public static int min(int *a*, int *b*) |
|        | public static long min(int *a*, int *b*) |

min() returns the lesser of a and b. This method has been overloaded to handle double, float, int, and long datatypes. The compiler determines which version to call based on the argument type.

### Example: Using min()

This example demonstrates the use of the min() method.

```
public class TestMin {
  public static void main(String args[]) {
    double a = 3.5;
    double b = 4.0;
    System.out.println("The minimum of a and b is " + Math.min(a, b));
  }
}
```

### Output

```
The minimum of a and b is 3.5
```

## pow() Method

| Method | Syntax |
|--------|--------|
| pow() | public static double pow (double a, double b) |

pow() returns the value of the first argument raised to the power of the second argument.

### Example: Using pow()

This example demonstrates the use of the pow() method.

```
public class TestPow {
  public static void main(String args[]) {
    double circleRadius = 1.0;
    double circleArea = Math.PI * Math.pow(circleRadius, 2.0);
```

```
System.out.println("The area of the circle is " + circleArea);
    }
  }
```

**Output**

```
The area of the circle is 3.141592653589793
```

# random() Method

| Method | Syntax |
|--------|--------|
| random() | public static double random() |

random() returns a random number between 0.0 and 1.0. Generally speaking the Random class should be used to generate random numbers because it allows more control of the distribution of random numbers.

# Rounding Methods

| Method | Syntax |
|--------|--------|
| ceil() | public static double ceil(double *d*) |
| floor() | public static double floor(double *d*) |
| rint() | public static double rint(double *d*) |
| round() | public static long round(double *d*) |
|  | public static int round(float *f*) |

ceil() returns the nearest whole number greater than or equal to d.

floor() returns the nearest whole number less than or equal to d.

rint() returns the nearest whole number to d. If d is halfway between two numbers the method returns the even number.

round() returns a long or int representing the nearest whole number to the argument double or float. If the argument is halfway between the two numbers the method returns the larger of the two.

## Example: Rounding Numbers

This example demonstrates the use of the ceil() and floor() methods.

```
public class TestRound {
  public static void main(String args[]) {
    double a = 7.3;

    System.out.println("a rounded up is " + Math.ceil(a));
    System.out.println("a rounded down is " + Math.floor(a));
  }
}
```

**Output**
```
a rounded up is 8.0
a rounded down is 7
```

## sqrt() Method

| Method | Syntax |
|--------|--------|
| sqrt() | public static double sqrt(double *d*) |

sqrt() returns the square root of the argument d.

### Example: Using sqrt()

This example demonstrates the use of the sqrt() method.

```
public class TestSqrt {
  public static void main(String args[]) {
    double circleArea = 16.0;
    double circleRadius = Math.sqrt(circleArea / Math.PI);

    System.out.println("The radius of the circle is " + circleRadius);
  }
}
```

**Output**
```
The radius of the circle is 2.256758334191025
```

## Trigonometric Functions

| Method | Syntax |
|--------|--------|
| acos() | public static double acos(double *value*) |
| asin() | public static double asin(double *value*) |
| atan() | public static double atan(double *value*) |
| atan2() | public static double atan2(double *x*, double *y*) |
| cos() | public static double cos(double *angle*) |
| sin() | public static double sin(double *angle*) |
| tan() | public static double tan(double *angle*) |

acos() provides the trigonometric function arccosine. The return value is an angle in radians.

asin() provides the trigonometric function arcsine. The return value is an angle in radians.

atan() provides the trigonometric function arctangent. The return value is an angle in radians.

`atan2()` returns the angle whose tangent is x/y. The return value is an angle in radians.

`cos()` provides the trigonometric function cosine. It requires as an argument an angle expressed in radians.

`sin()` provides the trigonometric function sine. It requires as an argument an angle expressed in radians.

`tan()` provides the trigonometric function tangent. It requires as an argument an angle expressed in radians.

## Example: Using Trigonometric Functions

This example demonstrates the use of the `sin()` and `acos()` methods.

```
public class TestTrig {
  public static void main(String args[]) {
    double angle, value;

    value = Math.sin(30.0 * Math.PI / 180.0);
    angle = Math.acos(0.1) * 180.0 / Math.PI;

    System.out.println("The sine of 30 is " + value);
    System.out.println("The angle whose cosine is 0.1 is " + angle);
  }
}
```

**Output**

```
The sine of 30 is 0.49999999999999994
The angle whose cosine is 0.1 is 84.26082952273322
```

# Methods to Convert Between Degrees and Radians

| Method | Syntax |
| --- | --- |
| toDegrees() | public static double **toDegrees**(double *radians*) |
| toRadians() | public static double **toRadians**(double *degrees*) |

`toDegrees()` converts the specified number of radians to degrees.

`toRadians()` converts the specified number of degrees to radians.

**Example: Converting from Radians to Degrees**

This example demonstrates the use of the toDegrees() method.

```
public class TestRadToDeg {
  public static void main(String args[]) {
    double deg = Math.toDegrees(Math.PI);
    System.out.println("pi radians is "+deg+" degrees");
  }
}
```

**Output**

```
pi radians is 180.0 degrees
```

# 2.7.2 StrictMath Class

```
public final class StrictMath extends Object
```

```
Object
  StrictMath
```

The StrictMath class provides the same mathematical methods as the Math class except the definitions of many of the numeric functions in this package require that they produce the same bit-for-bit results as certain published algorithms. This is to ensure the portability of Java programs. This strict reproducibility comes at a slight performance cost.

The methods in the StrictMath class have the same names and provide the same functions as the methods in the Math class. See the Math class section on page 156 for a description of these methods.

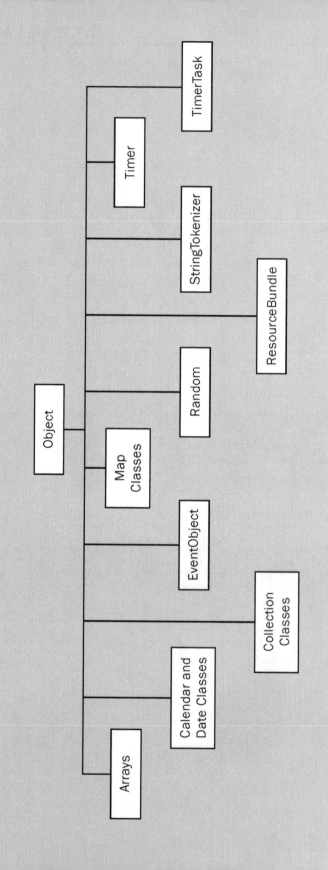

# 3

# java.util

The java.util package provides a collection of classes and interfaces that provide a lot of useful functionality. Included in the package are classes and interfaces to manipulate collections of objects, parse Strings, generate random numbers, and work with dates and times. Recent additions (in Java 1.3) to the java.util package are the Timer and TimerTask classes that can be used to schedule tasks for future execution in a background thread. The java.util package class hierarchy is shown in the figure opposite.

The Arrays class provides static methods for searching through, comparing, filling, or sorting arrays. The methods are overloaded to provide implementations for all primitive datatypes as well as Objects.

The EventObject class is the super-class of all other event classes under the Java 1.1 event model. The EventListener interface is the parent interface for all listener interfaces under the Java 1.1 event model. In order for a class to serve as a listener for EventObject subclasses, it must implement the EventListener interface.

The Calendar and Date classes provide the functionality for accessing and manipulating date and calendar entities. Different types of calendars are supported along with time zones, daylight savings time, and country specific variations of dates and calendars.

Java provides classes and interfaces for handling **collections** of objects. In Java 1.1, collections were manipulated using the Dictionary, Hashtable, Stack, and Vector classes, and the Enumeration interface. Java 1.2 introduced a new series of interfaces and classes that provide a standardized way of handling collections - the interfaces are described in Section 3.2 on page 202 and the classes in Section 3.3 on page 216.

A Map is an object that stores a collection of key-value pairs. Both the keys and values are objects. Once the key-value pairs are stored in the Map object, the values can be accessed by using the keys. The map interfaces are described in Section 3.4 on page 249 and the classes in Section 3.5 on page 253.

Other classes in the java.util package include the Random class, used to generate random numbers, the StringTokenizer class, used to parse String objects (splitting a String into substrings or tokens based on a specified or default delimiter), and the ResourceBundle class represents a set of localized data.

This Chapter covers:

# 3.1 Calendar and Date Classes

The calendar and date classes provide the ability to access and manipulate dates and times. They provide the ability to use different time zones, switch between daylight and standard time, and even use different calendars. The calendar and date class hierarchy is shown in the figure below.

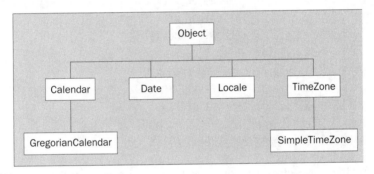

# 3.1.1 Calendar Class

```
public abstract class Calendar extends Object implements Cloneable, Serializable
```

```
Object
    Calendar
```

### Interfaces
```
Cloneable, Serializable
```

The Calendar class is used to convert a Date object, which represent a point in time, to things like months and days of the week. The Calendar class can convert a time in one time zone to another, can account for regions that observe daylight savings time, and even switch between one calendar system to another. Because it is an abstract class, a Calendar object is never instantiated. The static methods defined in the Calendar class can be accessed using the Calendar.*methodName* syntax.

## Calendar Class Field Constants

The Calendar class defines a number of field constants, which describe values that can be set. For instance Calendar.MONTH might be set to be Calendar.MAY. The field constants are:

| Constant |
| --- |
| public final static int AM_PM |
| public final static int MILLISECOND |
| public final static int SECOND |
| public final static int MINUTE |
| public final static int HOUR |
| public final static int DATE |
| public final static int MONTH |
| public final static int YEAR |
| public final static int DAY_OF_WEEK |
| public final static int DAY_OF_WEEK_IN_MONTH |
| public final static int DAY_OF_MONTH |
| public final static int DAY_OF_YEAR |
| public final static int WEEK_OF_MONTH |
| public final static int WEEK_OF_YEAR |
| public final static int DST_OFFSET |
| public final static int ERA |
| public final static int ZONE_OFFSET |

Most of these are self-explanatory. The DST_OFFSET constant is the offset due to daylight savings time. The ZONE_OFFSET constant represents the difference in milliseconds between the local time and Greenwich Mean Time (GMT).

## Calendar Class Value Constants

The Calendar class defines a number of value constants, which represent set values such as May, or Wednesday. The value constants are:

| Constant |
| --- |
| public final static int AM |
| public final static int PM |
| public final static int JANUARY |
| public final static int FEBRUARY |
| public final static int MARCH |
| public final static int APRIL |
| public final static int MAY |
| public final static int JUNE |
| public final static int JULY |
| public final static int AUGUST |
| public final static int SEPTEMBER |
| public final static int OCTOBER |

| Constant |
|---|
| public final static int NOVEMBER |
| public final static int DECEMBER |
| public final static int MONDAY |
| public final static int TUESDAY |
| public final static int WEDNESDAY |
| public final static int THURSDAY |
| public final static int FRIDAY |
| public final static int SATURDAY |
| public final static int SUNDAY |
| public final static int UNDECIMBER |

Most of these are self-explanatory. The UNDECIMBER constant is the 13th month used in lunar calendars.

# add() Method

| Method | Syntax |
|---|---|
| add() | public abstract void add(int *fieldConstant*, int *amount*) |

add() adds an amount to fieldConstant in the invoking Calendar sub-class object.

## Example: Using add()

In this example, a calendar object is created and the current day of the month is printed to the command prompt. The add() method is then used to add 10 days to the current date (which is the fieldConstant in the invoking Calendar sub-class object) and write that date to the command prompt.

```
import java.util.*;

public class TestCalAdd {
  public static void main(String args[]) {
    Calendar c = Calendar.getInstance();

    System.out.println("date is " + c.get(Calendar.DATE));

    c.add(Calendar.DATE, 10);
    System.out.println("date is now " + c.get(Calendar.DATE));
  }
}
```

**Output** *(results will vary)*
```
date is 18
date is now 28
```

## clear() Method

| Method | Syntax |
|--------|--------|
| clear() | public final void clear() |
| | public final void clear(int *fieldConstant*) |

clear() clears either all of the field constants of the invoking Calendar sub-class object (if the no-argument version is used), or the fieldconstant specified, if one is given.

### Example: Using clear()

The Calendar.DATE field constant is initially set when the Calendar object is created. The isSet() method therefore returns true when passed Calendar.DATE as an argument. When the clear() method is invoked, all of the fields are cleared and the isSet() returns false. (isSet() is covered in this section on page 176.)

```java
import java.util.*;

public class TestCalClear {
  public static void main(String args[]) {
    Calendar c = Calendar.getInstance();

    if (c.isSet(Calendar.DATE)) {
      System.out.println("date is set");

    }
    c.clear();
    if (c.isSet(Calendar.DATE)) {
      System.out.println("date is set");
    } else {
      System.out.println("date is not set");
    }
  }
}
```

**Output**
```
date is set
date is not set
```

# clone() Method

| Method | Syntax |
|--------|--------|
| clone() | public Object clone() |

clone() clones the invoking Calendar sub-class object.

## Example: Using clone()

See the following example *Comparing Calendar Objects* below.

# Methods to Compare Two Calendar Objects

| Method | Syntax |
|--------|--------|
| after() | public boolean after(Object *obj*) |
| before() | public boolean before(Object *obj*) |
| equals() | public boolean equals(Object *obj*) |

after() returns true if obj is a Calendar sub-class object whose time value is after the invoking Calendar sub-class object.

before() returns true if obj is a Calendar sub-class object whose time value is before the invoking Calendar sub-class object.

equals() returns true if obj is a Calendar sub-class object whose time value is the same as the invoking Calendar sub-class object.

## Example: Comparing Calendar Objects

In this example, three Calendar objects are created at different intervals, the before() and equals() methods are then used to compare when they were created.

```
import java.util.*;

public class TestCalCompare {
  public static void main(String args[]) {
    Calendar c1 = Calendar.getInstance();
    try {
      Thread.sleep(500);
    }
    catch (InterruptedException ie) {}
    Calendar c2 = Calendar.getInstance();
```

```
      if (c1.before(c2)) {
        System.out.println("c1 came before c2");

      }
      Calendar c3 = (Calendar) c1.clone();
      if (c1.equals(c3)) {
        System.out.println("c1 and c3 are equal");
      }
    }
  }
```

The first Calendar object created is c1. The program then sleeps for 0.5 seconds before creating Calendar c2. If c1 calls the before() method passing c2 as an argument, the method returns true. The Calendar c3 object is created as a clone of c1. If c1 calls the equals() method using c3 as the argument, the method returns true.

**Output**

```
c1 came before c2
c1 and c3 are equal
```

## get() Method

| Method | Syntax |
|--------|--------|
| get() | public final int get(int *fieldConstant*) |

get() returns the value of the fieldConstant of the invoking Calendar sub-class object.

### Example: Using get()

This example uses the get() method to return the current day of the month.

```
import java.util.*;

public class TestCalGet {
  public static void main(String args[]) {
    Calendar c = Calendar.getInstance();

    System.out.println("date is " + c.get(Calendar.DATE));
  }
}
```

> **Output** (results will vary)
>
>     date is 18

## getAvailableLocales() Method

| Method | Syntax |
|--------|--------|
| getAvailableLocales() | public static Locale[] getAvailableLocales() |

getAvailableLocales() returns an array containing the Locale objects available to the invoking Calendar object.

## getInstance() Method

| Method | Syntax |
|--------|--------|
| getInstance() | public static Calendar getInstance() |
|  | public static Calendar getInstance(Locale *loc*) |
|  | public static Calendar getInstance(TimeZone *zone*) |
|  | public static Calendar getInstance<br>(TimeZone *zone*, Locale *loc*) |

getInstance() returns a GregorianCalendar object in the Java 1.3 implementation. A Timezone and Locale can be specified. The no-argument version uses the TimeZone.getDefault() and Locale.getDefault() methods to obtain the associated TimeZone and Locale objects.

> ### Example: Using getInstance()
>
> See example *Using get()* on page 174.

## hashCode() method

| Method | Syntax |
|--------|--------|
| hashCode() | public int hashCode() |

hashCode() overrides the hashCode() method from the Object class and returns the hash code associated with the invoking Calendar object.

## isSet() Method

| Method | Syntax |
|--------|--------|
| isSet() | public final boolean isSet(int *fieldConstant*) |

isSet() returns true if fieldConstant is set for the invoking Calendar sub-class object.

### Example: Using isSet()

See example *Using clear()* on page 172.

## Leniency Methods

| Method | Syntax |
|--------|--------|
| isLenient() | public boolean isLenient() |
| setLenient() | public void setLenient(boolean *isLenient*) |

If a Calendar object is **lenient**, it will do its best to interpret bad data. For example, "February 942, 1996" would be treated as being equivalent to the 941st day after February 1, 1996.

### Example: Leniency

This example demonstrates lenient interpretation of bad data by the Calendar class.

```
import java.util.*;

public class TestCalLenient {
  public static void main(String args[]) {
    Calendar c = Calendar.getInstance();

    System.out.println("date is " + c.get(Calendar.DATE));

    c.setLenient(false);
    c.set(Calendar.DAY_OF_MONTH, 36);
    System.out.println("date is now " + c.get(Calendar.DATE));
  }
}
```

First, a Calendar object is created and its leniency set to false. Then an attempt is made to set the day of the current month to 35. Since no months have 35 days and the Calendar is not lenient, an exception is thrown. If the setLenient() statement is commented out, the program will run and the date will roll over into the next month.

*Output* (results will vary)
```
date is 4
Exception in thread "main" java.lang.IllegalArgumentException
```

If the line c.setLenient(false); is commented out, the Calendar will be lenient and the output will become:

```
date is 4
date is now 5
```

# Minimum and Maximum Methods

| Method | Syntax |
|---|---|
| getGreatestMinimum() | public abstract int getGreatestMinimum (int *fieldConstant*) |
| getLeastMaximum() | public abstract int getLeastMaximum (int *fieldConstant*) |
| getMaximum() | public abstract int getMaximum (int *fieldConstant*) |
| getMinimum() | public abstract int getMinimum (int *fieldConstant*) |
| getActualMaximum() | public int getActualMaximum(int *fieldConstant*) |
| getActualMinimum() | public int getActualMinimum(int *fieldConstant*) |

getGreatestMinimum() returns the highest minimum value for a field.

getLeastMaximum() returns the least maximum value for a field. For instance, in the Gregorian calendar, the least maximum value for DAY_OF_MONTH would be 28.

getMaximum() returns the maximum value for the specified field. For instance, in the Gregorian calendar, the maximum value for DAY_OF_MONTH would be 31.

getMinimum() returns the minimum value for the specified field.

getActualMaximum() returns the maximum value for the specified field given the current date. For example, if the current month was February, the actual maximum value for DAY_OF_MONTH would be 28.

getActualMinimum() returns the minimum value for the specified field given the current date.

**Example: Using Maximum and Minimum Methods**

In this example, a `Calendar` object is created, then the `getMaximum()` is used to retrieve the maximum number of days in a month, and the `getLeastMaximum()` method is used to get the minimum number of days in the month. The return values are then printed to the command line.

```
import java.util.*;

public class TestCalMax {
  public static void main(String args[]) {
    Calendar c1 = Calendar.getInstance();

    int max = c1.getMaximum(Calendar.DAY_OF_MONTH);
    int leastMax = c1.getLeastMaximum(Calendar.DAY_OF_MONTH);

    System.out.println("maximum days in month are " + max);
    System.out.println("least maximum days in month are " + leastMax);
  }
}
```

*Output*

```
maximum days in month are 31
least maximum days in month are 28
```

## roll() Method

| Method | Syntax |
|--------|--------|
| roll() | public abstract void roll(int *fieldConstant*, boolean *up*) |
| | public void roll(int *fieldConstant*, int amount) |

`roll()` increments or decrements `fieldConstant` by one unit. If up is `true`, `fieldConstant` is incremented; if it is `false`, `fieldConstant` is decremented. The second version allows `fieldConstant` to be changed by the specified amount.

**Example: Using roll()**

In this example, the `roll()` method is used to add one day to the current date. Note that the boolean value of `true` is passed to the method to indicate that the `fieldConstant` should be incremented.

```
import java.util.*;

public class TestCalRoll {
  public static void main(String args[]) {
    Calendar c = Calendar.getInstance();

    System.out.println("date is " + c.get(Calendar.DATE));

    c.roll(Calendar.DATE, true);
    System.out.println("date is now " + c.get(Calendar.DATE));
  }
}
```

**Output** (result will vary)
```
date is 18
date is now 19
```

## set() Method

| Method | Syntax |
|--------|--------|
| set() | public final void set(int *fieldConstant*, int *value*) |
| | public final void set(int *year*, int *month*, int *date*) |
| | public final void set(int *year*, int *month*, int *date*, int *hour*, int *minute*) |
| | public final void set(int *year*, int *month*, int *date*, int *hour*, int *minute*, int *sec*) |

set() changes one or more fields of the invoking Calendar object. The first version of set() assigns a value to a given field constant. The last three versions of set() are used to set the Calendar.YEAR, Calendar.MONTH, Calendar.DATE, Calendar.HOUR, Calendar.MINUTE, and Calendar.SECOND field constants.

### Example: Using set()

The set() method is used to specify the year, month, and date fields of a Calendar object. The month is zero-based, so January would be month 0. The date is 1-based, so dates start at 1.

```
import java.util.*;

public class TestCalSet {
  public static void main(String args[]) {
    Calendar c = Calendar.getInstance();
```

**179**

```
            c.set(1997, Calendar.JANUARY, 12);

        System.out.println("year is now " + c.get(Calendar.YEAR));
        System.out.println("month is now " + c.get(Calendar.MONTH));
        System.out.println("date is now " + c.get(Calendar.DATE));
    }
}
```

**Output**

```
year is now 1997
month is now 0
date is now 12
```

## toString() Method

| Method | Syntax |
| --- | --- |
| toString() | public String toString() |

toString() overrides the toString() method from the Object class and returns the a String representation of the invoking Calendar object. (The format of the returned string may vary between implementations.)

## Time Methods

| Method | Syntax |
| --- | --- |
| getTime() | public final Date getTime() |
| setTime() | public final void setTime(Date *date*) |

getTime() returns a Date object representing the Calendar object's current time.

setTime() sets the time contained in the invoking Calendar sub-class object.

### Example: Using the Time Methods

When a Calendar object is generated, it is initialized with the current time. The time contained in the Calendar object does not update itself. In this example, the time contained in Calendar c is updated using the setTime() method after a pause.

```
import java.util.*;

public class TestCalTime {
  public static void main(String args[]) {
    Calendar c = Calendar.getInstance();
```

```
System.out.println("hour: " + c.get(Calendar.HOUR));
System.out.println("minute: " + c.get(Calendar.MINUTE));
System.out.println("seconds: " + c.get(Calendar.SECOND));
System.out.println(" ");

try {
  Thread.sleep(5000);
} catch (Exception e) {}

Date d = new Date(System.currentTimeMillis());
c.setTime(d);
System.out.println("hour: " + c.get(Calendar.HOUR));
System.out.println("minute: " + c.get(Calendar.MINUTE));
System.out.println("seconds: " + c.get(Calendar.SECOND));
  }
}
```

The sleep() block is used to give a noticeable separation in time before and after the setTime() method is invoked. The static method currentTimeMillis() from the System class is used to provide the Date constructor with the current time.

**Output** *(results will vary)*

```
hour: 8
minute: 39
seconds: 18

hour: 8
minute: 39
seconds: 24
```

# TimeZone Methods

| Methods | Syntax |
|---------|--------|
| getTimeZone() | public TimeZone getTimeZone() |
| setTimeZone() | public void setTimeZone(TimeZone tz) |

These methods return or set the TimeZone object associated with the invoking Calendar sub-class object. See Section 3.1.6 on page 197 for a discussion of the TimeZone class.

**181**

## Weekday Methods

| Method | Syntax |
|---|---|
| getFirstDayOfWeek() | public int getFirstDayOfWeek() |
| getMinimalDaysInFirstWeek() | public int getMinimalDaysInFirstWeek() |
| setFirstDayOfWeek() | public void setFirstDayOfWeek(int *value*) |
| setMinimalDaysInFirstWeek() | public void setMinimalDaysInFirstWeek (int *value*) |

getFirstDayOfWeek() returns a Calendar class value constant (in this case Calendar.SUNDAY) corresponding to the first day of the week.

getMinimalDaysInFirstWeek() returns the number of days in the first week of the year.

setFirstDayOfWeek() is used to specify which day is the first day of the week.

setMinimalDaysInFirstWeek() specifies the number of days in the first week of the year.

# 3.1.2 Date Class

```
public class Date extends Object implements Cloneable, Serializable, Comparable
```

    Object
      Data

### Interfaces

    Cloneable, Serializable, Comparable

The Date class encapsulates the time in milliseconds since Jan 1, 1970. Most of the methods in the Date class are deprecated; their functions have been moved to the Calendar class. The Date class is still useful to provide a quick-and-dirty representation of the current time and a Date object is used in the setTime() method of the Calendar class.

## Date() Constructor

| Constructor | Syntax |
|---|---|
| Date() | public Date() |
| | public Date(long *date*) |

Date() creates a Date object. When used without any arguments, the Date object is initialized with the current date and time. If a long is provided, it should represent the number of milliseconds from January 1, 1970 to the desired time.

# Methods to Compare Two Date Objects

| Method | Syntax |
|---|---|
| after() | public boolean after(Date *d*) |
| before() | public boolean before(Date *d*) |
| equals() | public boolean equals(Object *obj*) |

after() returns true if the time associated with d is after the time associated with the invoking Date object.

before() returns true if the time associated with d is before the time associated with the invoking Date object.

equals() overrides the equals() method from the Object class and returns true if obj is a Date object and the time associated with it is the same as the time associated with the invoking Date object.

## Example: Comparing Date Objects

In this example, two Date objects generated 500 milliseconds apart are compared using the before() method.

```
import java.util.*:

public class TestDateComp {
  public static void main(String args[]) {
    Date d1 = new Date();
    try {
      Thread.sleep(500);
    }
    catch (InterruptedException ie) {}
    Date d2 = new Date();

    if ( d1.before(d2) )
      System.out.println("d1 came before d2");
  }
}
```

### Output

```
d1 came before d2
```

## hashCode() method

| Method | Syntax |
|--------|--------|
| hashCode() | public int hashCode() |

hashCode( )overrides the hashCode( ) method from the Object class and returns the hash code for the invoking Date object.

## Time Methods

| Method | Syntax |
|--------|--------|
| getTime() | public long getTime() |
| setTime() | public void setTime(long *time*) |

getTime( ) returns the time associated with the invoking Date object.

setTime( ) sets the time associated with the invoking Date object.

### Example: Using the Time Methods

The Date object is initialized with the current time, but the time is not automatically updated. The static method currentTimeMillis( ) from the System class is used to provide the current time to the setTime( ) method, and the sleep( ) method is used to provide a noticeable difference between the two times.

```
import java.util.*;

public class TestDateTime {
  public static void main(String args[]) {
    Date d = new Date();
    System.out.println("time is now " + d.toString());
    System.out.println();

    try {
      Thread.sleep(5000);
    } catch (Exception e) {}

    d.setTime(System.currentTimeMillis());
    System.out.println("time is now " + d.toString());
  }
}
```

**Output** *(results will vary)*

```
time is now Thu Nov 18 20:41:47 PST 1999

time is now Thu Nov 18 20:41:53 PST 1999
```

## toString() Method

| Method | Syntax |
|--------|--------|
| toString() | public String toString() |

toString() returns a String representation of the invoking Date object and can be used to produce a quick-and-dirty representation of the current time. The String returned is of the form "dow mon dd hh:mm:ss zzz yyyy" where dow is the day of the week, mon is the month, dd is the day of the month, hh is the hour of the day, mm is the minute within the hour, ss is the second within the minute, zzz is the time zone, and yyyy is the year.

### Example: Using toString()

This example uses the toString() method to return a string representation of the date called in the Date() method.

```
import java.util.*;

public class TestDateTS {
  public static void main(String args[]) {
    Date d = new Date();
    System.out.println("time is " + d.toString());
  }
}
```

**Output**

```
time is Thu Nov 18 20:43:10 PST 1999
```

## Deprecated Constructors and Methods from the Date Class

| Constructor or Method | Syntax |
|-----------------------|--------|
| Date() | public Date(int year, int month, int date) |
|  | public Date(int year, int month, int date, int hour, int minute) |

| Constructor or Method | Syntax |
|---|---|
| Date() | public Date(int *year*, int *month*, int *date*, int *hour*, int *minute*, int *sec*) |
| | public Date(String *s*) |
| getDate() | public int getDate() |
| getDay() | public int getDay() |
| getHours() | public int getHours() |
| getMinutes() | public int getMinutes() |
| getMonth() | public int getMonth() |
| getSeconds() | public int getSeconds() |
| getTimeZoneOffset() | public int getTimeZoneOffset() |
| getYear() | public int getYear() |
| setDate() | public void setDate(int *date*) |
| setHours() | public void setHours(int *hours*) |
| setMinutes() | public void setMinutes(int *min*) |
| setMonth() | public void setMonth(int *month*) |
| setSeconds() | public void setSeconds(int *sec*) |
| setYear() | public void setYear(int *year*) |
| toGMTString() | public String toGMTString() |
| toLocaleString() | public String toLocaleString() |

These methods were deprecated under Java 1.1 and should not be used for new code.

# 3.1.3 GregorianCalendar Class

```
public class GregorianCalendar extends Calendar
```

```
Object
  Calendar
    GregorianCalendar
```

### Interfaces
```
Cloneable, Serializable
```

GregorianCalendar is a sub-class of the Calendar class that provides an implementation of the commonly used Gregorian calendar. The calendar is divided into two eras, B.C. and A.D. The Gregorian calendar was instituted in 1582. Before this time, the Julian calendar was widely used. A GregorianCalendar object provides dates according to the Julian calendar for dates prior to 1582.

The static method `getInstance()` from the `Calendar` class returns a `GregorianCalendar` object initialized with the current date and time. The `GregorianCalendar` class also provides constructors to create a `GregorianCalendar` object.

## GregorianCalendar() Constructor

| Constructor | Syntax |
|---|---|
| GregorianCalendar() | public **GregorianCalendar**() |
| | public **GregorianCalendar**(TimeZone *timezone*) |
| | public **GregorianCalendar**(Locale *locale*) |
| | public **GregorianCalendar**(TimeZone *timezone*, Locale *locale*) |
| | public **GregorianCalendar**(int *year*, int *month*, int *date*) |
| | public **GregorianCalendar**(int *year*, int *month*, int *date*, int *hour*, int *minute*) |
| | public **GregorianCalendar**(int *year*, int *month*, int *date*, int *hour*, int *minute*, int *sec*) |

`GregorianCalendar` object constructor. A timezone and/or locale can be specified. The no-argument version uses the `TimeZone.getDefault()` and `Locale.getDefault()` methods to provide the associated `TimeZone` and `Locale` objects.

## GregorianCalendar Value Constants

| Constant |
|---|
| public final static int **AD** |
| public final static int **BC** |

In addition to the value constants defined in the `Calendar` class, two additional value constants are defined by the `GregorianCalendar` class. AD represents *Anno Domini* and BC represents *before Christ*.

## GregorianCalendar Changeover Methods

| Method | Syntax |
|---|---|
| getGregorianChange() | public final Date **getGregorianChange**() |
| setGregorianChange() | public void **setGregorianChange**(Date *date*) |

`getGregorianChange()` returns the `Date` object representing the date to switch from the Julian to Gregorian calendars. The default is October 15, 1582.

`setGregorianChange()` sets the `Date` object representing the date to switch from the Julian to Gregorian calendars.

## equals() method

| Method | Syntax |
|--------|--------|
| equals() | public boolean equals(Object obj) |

equals() overrides the equals() method from the Calendar class and and returns true if obj is a GregorianCalendar object and is the same as the invoking GregorianCalendar object.

## hashCode() method

| Method | Syntax |
|--------|--------|
| hashCode() | public int hashCode() |

hashCode()overrides the hashCode() method from the Calendar class and returns the hash code for the invoking GregorianCalendar object.

## isLeapYear() Method

| Method | Syntax |
|--------|--------|
| isLeapYear() | public boolean isLeapYear(int *year*) |

isLeapYear() returns true if the year represented by the invoking GregorianCalendar object is a leap year.

### Example: Using GregorianCalendar

In this example, a GregorianCalendar object is created, and the get() method is used to fetch the current year. The year is then checked with the isLeapYear() method, to see if the current year returned is a leap year.

```
import java.util.*;

public class TestGC {
  public static void main(String args[]) {
    GregorianCalendar gc = new GregorianCalendar();

    int year = gc.get(Calendar.YEAR);

    if (gc.isLeapYear(year)) {
      System.out.println(year + " is a leap year");
```

```
    } else {
        System.out.println(year + " is not a leap year");
    }
  }
}
```

**Output**

```
2000 is a leap year
```

## Minimum and Maximum Methods

| Method | Syntax |
|---|---|
| getGreatestMinimum() | public int getGreatestMinimum(int *fieldConstant*) |
| getLeastMaximum() | public int getLeastMaximum(int *fieldConstant*) |
| getMaximum() | public int getMaximum(int *fieldConstant*) |
| getMinimum() | public int getMinimum(int *fieldConstant*) |
| getActualMaximum() | public int getActualMaximum(int *fieldConstant*) |
| getActualMinimum() | public int getActualMinimum(int *fieldConstant*) |

getGreatestMinimum() returns the highest minimum value for a field.

getLeastMaximum() returns the least maximum value for a field. In the Gregorian calendar, the least maximum value for DAY_OF_MONTH would be 28.

getMaximum() returns the maximum value for the specified field. In the Gregorian calendar, the maximum value for DAY_OF_MONTH would be 31.

getMinimum() returns the minimum value for the specified field.

getActualMaximum() returns the maximum value for the specified field given the current date. For example, if the current month was February, the actual maximum value for DAY_OF_MONTH would be 28.

getActualMinimum() returns the minimum value for the specified field given the current date.

These methods override the methods defined in the Calendar class.

---

### Example: Using Maximum and Minimum Methods

See the *Using Maximum and Minimum Methods* example in the Calendar Class in Section 3.1.1 on page 178.

---

## roll() Method

| Method | Syntax |
|--------|--------|
| roll() | public void roll(int *fieldConstant*, boolean *up*) |
|        | public void roll(int *fieldConstant*, int *amount*) |

roll() increments or decrements fieldConstant by one unit. If up is true, fieldConstant is incremented; if it is false, fieldConstant is decremented. The second version allows fieldConstant to be changed by the specified amount. These methods override the roll() methods defined in the Calendar class.

---

### Example: Using roll()

See the *Using roll()* example from the Calendar Class in section 3.1.1 on page 178.

---

# 3.1.4 Locale Class

```
public final class Locale extends Object implements Cloneable, Serializable
```

```
Object
    Locale
```

### Implements

```
Cloneable, Serializable
```

The Locale class class is used for tailoring an application for different countries and languages. For instance, by setting the language constant to German a GUI interface can have buttons in German. It is often used in conjunction with a ResourceBundle object (See Section 3.6.4 on page 277) to provide localized text messages in a program.

## Locale Class Constants

The Locale class defines a series of constants for various languages and countries:

| Country Constants |
|---|
| public final static Locale CANADA |
| public final static Locale CANADA_FRENCH |
| public final static Locale CHINA |
| public final static Locale FRANCE |
| public final static Locale GERMANY |
| public final static Locale ITALY |
| public final static Locale JAPAN |
| public final static Locale KOREA |
| public final static Locale PRC |
| public final static Locale TAIWAN |
| public final static Locale UK |
| public final static Locale US |

| Language Constants |
|---|
| public final static Locale CHINESE |
| public final static Locale ENGLISH |
| public final static Locale FRENCH |
| public final static Locale GERMAN |
| public final static Locale ITALIAN |
| public final static Locale JAPANESE |
| public final static Locale KOREAN |
| public final static Locale SIMPLIFIED_CHINESE |
| public final static Locale TRADITIONAL_CHINESE |

## Locale() Constructor

| Constructor | Syntax |
|---|---|
| Locale() | public Locale(String *language*, String *country*) |
|  | public Locale(String *language*, String *country*, String *variant*) |

Locale() creates a Locale object based on a specified language and country. The variant is a vendor-specific String that might represent a specific dialect.

## clone() Method

| Method | Syntax |
|---|---|
| clone() | public Object clone() |

clone() returns a copy of the invoking Locale object.

## Default Locale Methods

| Method | Syntax |
|---|---|
| getDefault() | public static Locale getDefault() |
| setDefault() | public static synchronized void setDefault(<br>    Locale *defaultLocale*) |

getDefault() returns the default Locale.

setDefault() sets the default Locale.

### Example: Using Default Locale Methods

In this example, the default locale is set to France. The getDisplay() methods then return the country name and language associated with this locale in French.

```
import java.util.*;

public class TestLocale2 {
  public static void main(String args[]) {
    Locale.setDefault(Locale.FRANCE);
    Locale l = Locale.getDefault();

    System.out.println("country is " + l.getDisplayCountry());
    System.out.println("language is " + l.getDisplayLanguage());
  }
}
```

*Output*
```
country is France
language is francais
```

## equals() Method

| Method | Syntax |
|---|---|
| equals() | public boolean equals(Object *obj*) |

equals() returns true if the invoking Locale object is the same as the Locale object passed as an argument.

# Methods to Retrieve Locale Object Properties

| Method | Syntax |
|---|---|
| getCountry() | public String getCountry() |
| getDisplayCountry() | public final String getDisplayCountry() |
| | public final String getDisplayCountry<br>(Locale *locale*) |
| getDisplayLanguage() | public final String getDisplayLanguage() |
| | public final String getDisplayLanguage<br>(Locale *locale*) |
| getDisplayName() | public final String getDisplayName() |
| | public final String getDisplayName<br>(Locale *locale*) |
| getDisplayVariant() | public final String getDisplayVariant() |
| | public final String getDisplayVariant<br>(Locale *locale*) |
| getLanguage() | public String getLanguage() |
| getVariant() | public String getVariant() |
| getISOCountries() | public static String[] getISOCountries() |
| getISOLanguages() | public static String[] getISOLanguages() |
| getISO3Country() | public String getISO3Country()<br>throws MissingResourceException |
| getISO3Language() | public String getISO3Language()<br>throws MissingResourceException |

These methods return various properties of the invoking Locale object. If a Locale object is passed as an argument, the return will be in that language. For example if a Locale.FRANCE object called getDisplayLanguage() passing it Locale.GERMAN, the return String object would contain the German word for French.

getCountry() returns a two-letter country/region code for this locale.

getDisplayCountry() returns a name for the country associated with the invoking Locale object based on the language passed as an argument.

getDisplayLanguage() returns the language country associated with the invoking Locale object

getDisplayName() returns a String containing the language and/or country and/or variant country associated with the invoking Locale object.

getDisplayVariant() returns the variant, if any, associated with the invoking Locale object.

The ISO3 methods return a three letter String. The getCountry(), getLanguage(), and getVariant() methods return a two letter country or language code String.

---

## Example: Using Locale

This example illustrates how the Locale can be used to determine the language in which methods return.

```
import java.util.*;
public class TestLocale {
  public static void main(String args[]) {
    Locale l = Locale.FRANCE;
    System.out.println("country is " + l.getDisplayCountry());
    System.out.println("language is " + l.getDisplayLanguage());
    Locale.setDefault(Locale.FRANCE);
    System.out.println("language is " + l.getDisplayLanguage());
  }
}
```

The output of the getDisplay() methods depends on what the default Locale is. Initially, the language based on the default Locale will be used for the Strings returned by the getDisplayCountry() and the first getDisplayLanguage() method calls. When the default Locale object is set to Locale.FRANCE, the return String from the getDisplayLanguage() method is in French.

**Output** (results may vary between Locales)

```
country is France
language is French
language is francais
```

---

## toString() Method

| Method | Syntax |
|--------|--------|
| toString() | public final String toString() |

toString() returns a String representation of the invoking Locale object.

# 3.1.5 SimpleTimeZone Class

```
public class SimpleTimeZone extends TimeZone
```

```
Object
    TimeZone
        SimpleTimeZone
```

### Interfaces

```
Cloneable, Serializable
```

A SimpleTimeZone object is a concrete implementation of the abstract class TimeZone. Normally, a SimpleTimeZone object is not created directly but is obtained from the TimeZone.getDefault() and TimeZone.getTimeZone() methods.

## SimpleTimeZone() Constructor

| Constructor | Syntax |
|---|---|
| SimpleTimeZone() | public SimpleTimeZone(int *offset*, String *timeZoneID*) |
| | public SimpleTimeZone(int *offset*, String *timeZoneID*, int *dstMonthStart*, int *dstDayInMonthStart*, int *dstDayOfWeekStart*, int *dstTimeStart*, int *dstMonthEnd*, int *dstDayInMonthEnd*, int *dstDayOfWeekEnd*, int *dstTimeEnd*) |
| | public SimpleTimeZone(int *offset*, String *timeZoneID*, int *dstMonthStart*, int *dstDayInMonthStart*, int *dstDayOfWeekStart*, int *dstTimeStart*, int *dstMonthEnd*, int *dstDayInMonthEnd*, int *dstDayOfWeekEnd*, int *dstTimeEnd*, int *dstChange*) |

SimpleTimeZone object constructor. The offset is the time zone offset from GMT. The timeZoneID is the three letter time zone ID. The list of ID's can be obtained from the TimeZone.getAvailableIDs() method. The dst parameters define the starting and ending points of daylight savings time.

## equals() Method

| Method | Syntax |
|---|---|
| equals() | public boolean equals(Object *obj*) |

equals() returns true if obj is a SimpleTimeZone object and is the same as the invoking SimpleTimeZone object.

## Daylight Savings Time Methods

| Method | Syntax |
|--------|--------|
| getDSTSavings() | public int getDSTSavings() |
| setDSTSaving() | public void setDSTSavings(int *time*) |
| setEndRule() | public void setEndRule(int *month*, int *dayOfWeekInMonth*, int *dayOfWeek*, int *time*) |
| | public void setEndRule(int *month*, int *dayOfMonth*, int *time*) |
| setStartRule() | public void setStartRule(int *month*, int *dayOfMonth*, int *time*) |
| | public void setStartRule(int *month*, int *dayOfWeekInMonth*, int *dayOfWeek*, int *time*) |

getDSTSavings() and setDSTSavings() return or set the change in time in milliseconds due to daylight savings.

setStartRule() and setEndRule() set the starting and ending date of daylight savings time for the invoking SimpleTimeZone object. The variable time is in milliseconds.

### Example: Using SimpleTimeZone

In this example, the start date of daylight savings time for TimeZone stz is set to be the first Sunday in May at 5 a.m. The int time is the number of milliseconds from midnight. The current TimeZone and the number of hours of daylight savings are printed out.

```
import java.util.*;

public class TestSTZ {
  public static void main(String args[]) {
    SimpleTimeZone stz = (SimpleTimeZone) TimeZone.getDefault();
    System.out.println(stz.getDisplayName());

    // Convert 5 hours into milliseconds.
    int time = 5 * 3600 * 1000;
    stz.setStartRule(Calendar.MAY, 1, Calendar.SUNDAY, time);

    // Convert daylight savings from milliseconds into hours
    int dstOffset = stz.getDSTSavings() / (1000 * 3600);
    System.out.println("Daylight Savings time savings = "
                      + dstOffset);
  }
}
```

3

java.util

**Output** *(results will vary)*
```
Pacific Standard Time
Daylight Savings time savings = 1
```

# 3.1.6 TimeZone Class

```
public abstract class TimeZone extends Object implements Serializable, Cloneable
```

```
Object
  TimeZone
```

### Interfaces
```
Cloneable, Serializable
```

A TimeZone object represents a time zone. It also includes information about daylight savings time.

Because TimeZone is an abstract class, a TimeZone object is never instantiated. A TimeZone object can be obtained using the static methods getDefault() and getTimeZone().

## clone() Method

| Method | Syntax |
|--------|--------|
| clone() | public Object clone() |

clone() overrides the clone() method in class Object and returns a copy of the invoking TimeZone sub-class object.

## Daylight Savings Time Methods

| Method | Syntax |
|--------|--------|
| inDaylightTime() | public abstract boolean inDaylightTime(Date d) |
| useDaylightTime() | public abstract boolean useDaylightTime() |

inDaylightTime() returns true if the Date object represents a date in daylight saving time in the invoking TimeZone object.

useDaylightTime() returns true if the invoking TimeZone object uses daylight saving time.

---

## Example: Using Daylight Saving Time Methods

This example checks whether the user's time zone is in daylight saving time, and whether the time zone uses daylight savings time.

```java
import java.util.*;

public class TestTZdst {
  public static void main(String args[]) {
    TimeZone tz = TimeZone.getDefault();

    if (tz.inDaylightTime(new Date())) {
      System.out.println("We are in daylight savings time");
    } else {
      System.out.println("We are not in daylight savings time");
    }

    if (tz.useDaylightTime()) {
      System.out.println("This time zone uses daylight savings time");
    } else {
      System.out.println("This time zone does not use dst");
    }
  }
}
```

**Output** *(results will vary)*

```
We are not in daylight savings time
This time zone uses daylight savings time
```

## Default TimeZone Methods

| Method | Syntax |
|--------|--------|
| getDefault() | public static TimeZone getDefault() |
| setDefault() | public static void setDefault(TimeZone zone) |

getDefault() returns a default TimeZone object based on the local system.

setDefault() sets the TimeZone object returned by the getDefault() method.

## Example: Using Default Timezone Methods

This example uses the getDefault() to return the default TimeZone on the local machine, and then uses the getID() method to return the time zone that the user in in.

```
import java.util.*;

public class TestTZDef {
  public static void main(String args[]) {
    TimeZone tz = TimeZone.getDefault();

    System.out.println("The default timezone is " + tz.getID());
  }
}
```

**Output** (results will vary)

```
The default timezone is America/Los_Angeles
```

## getDisplayName() Method

| Method | Syntax |
|---|---|
| getDisplayName() | public final String getDisplayName() |
| | public final String getDisplayName (boolean *daylightSavingsTime*, int *style*) |
| | public final String getDisplayName (Locale *locale*) |
| | public String getDisplayName (boolean *daylightSavingsTime*, int *style*, Locale *locale*) |

getDisplayName() returns a descriptive String of the invoking TimeZone object. If daylightSavingsTime is true, the return String will represent the daylight savings time version of the TimeZone ID. The style is either TimeZone.LONG or TimeZone.SHORT and determines whether the long or short version of the name is returned: by default, the long version is returned. If a Locale is provided, the returned String will be in the language associated with that Locale.

---

### Example: Using getDisplayName ()

This example uses the getDisplayName() to return the display name for the default time zone.

```
import java.util.*;

public class TestTZDisplay {
  public static void main(String args[]) {
    TimeZone tz = TimeZone.getDefault();

    System.out.println(tz.getDisplayName());
  }
}
```

**Output** (results will vary)
```
GMT-08:00
```

---

## getAvailableIDs() Method

| Method | Syntax |
|---|---|
| getAvailableIDs() | public static String[] getAvailableIDs() |
| | public static String[] getAvailableIDs<br>          (int *timeOffset*) |

getAvailableIDs() returns an array of time zone IDs. The ID String objects will be things like PST, and EST. The second version returns time zone IDs that are timeOffset hours different than GMT.

### Example: Listing Available Timezone IDs

This example uses the getAvailableIDs() method to return the time zone IDs available.

```
import java.util.*;

public class TestTZIDs {
  public static void main(String args[]) {
    String[] ids = TimeZone.getAvailableIDs();

    for (int i = 0; i < ids.length; ++i) {
      System.out.println(ids[i]);
    }
```

```
    }
  }
```

*Output*
```
  Pacific/Niue
  Pacific/Apia
  MIT
  . . .
```
*(very long list follows)*

# getTimeZone() Method

| Method | Syntax |
|---|---|
| getTimeZone() | public static TimeZone getTimeZone(String *ID*) |

getTimeZone() returns a TimeZone object corresponding to the time zone specified by the argument String.

# TimeZone ID Methods

| Method | Syntax |
|---|---|
| getID() | public String getID() |
| setID() | public void setID(String *ID*) |

getID() returns the time zone ID of the invoking TimeZone sub-class object.

setID() sets the time zone ID of the invoking TimeZone sub-class object.

### Example: Using TimeZone ID Methods

See example *Using Default Timezone Methods* in this section on page 199.

# Offset Methods

| Method | Syntax |
|---|---|
| getOffset() | public abstract int getOffset(int *era*, int *year*, int *month*, int *dayOfMonth*, int *dayOfWeek*, int *milliSecond*) |
| getRawOffset() | public abstract int getRawOffset() |
| setRawOffset() | public abstract void setRawOffset(int *offset*) |

getOffset() returns the offset between GMT and local time.

getRawOffset() returns the offset between GMT and local time, without accounting for daylight saving time.

setRawOffset() sets the offset between GMT and local time, without accounting for daylight saving time.

### Example: Using TimeZone Offset Methods

This example returns the difference between GMT and local time, without accouting for daylight saving time using the getRawOffset() method. The return value is in milliseconds.

```
import java.util.*;

public class TestTZOffset {
  public static void main(String args[]) {
    TimeZone tz = TimeZone.getDefault();

    int offset = tz.getRawOffset();

    // Convert offset from milliseconds to hours
    offset = offset / (1000 * 3600);
    System.out.println("The offset from local to GMT is " + offset);
  }
}
```

**Output** *(results will vary)*

```
The offset from local to GMT is -8
```

# 3.2 Collection Interfaces

A **Collection** is a group of objects. The objects are known as the **elements of the collection**. The collection interfaces define the methods that are implemented by the collection classes. The collection interface hierarchy is shown in the following figure.

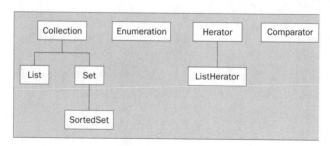

# 3.2.1 Collection Interface

```
public interface Collection
```

Collection provides the core methods that are available to all collections.

## Methods to Add Objects to a Collection

| Method | Syntax |
| --- | --- |
| add() | public boolean add(Object obj) |
| addAll() | public boolean addAll(Collection c) |

add() adds an Object to the invoking Collection object, and returns true if the operation was successful.

addAll() adds several Objects to the invoking Collection object, and returns true if the operation was successful.

## Methods to Investigate the Contents of a Collection

| Methods | Syntax |
| --- | --- |
| contains() | public boolean contains(Object obj) |
| containsAll() | public boolean containsAll(Collection c) |
| equals() | public boolean equals(Object obj) |
| isEmpty() | public boolean isEmpty() |
| size() | public int size() |

contains() returns true if the invoking Collection object contains the Object obj.

containsAll() returns true if the invoking Collection object contains all of the contains of Collection c.

equals() returns true if the invoking Collection object and obj are equal.

isEmpty() returns true if the invoking Collection object is empty.

size() returns the number of Objects contained in the invoking Collection object.

## iterator() Method

| Method | Syntax |
| --- | --- |
| iterator() | public Iterator iterator() |

iterator() returns the Iterator object that is associated with the invoking Collection object.

## hashCode() Method

| Method | Syntax |
|---|---|
| hashCode() | public int hashCode() |

hashCode() returns the hash code for the invoking Collection object.

## Methods to Remove Objects from a Collection

| Method | Syntax |
|---|---|
| clear() | public void clear() |
| remove() | public boolean remove(Object *obj*) |
| removeAll() | public boolean removeAll(Collection *c*) |
| retainAll() | public boolean retainAll(Collection *c*) |

clear() removes all of the elements from the invoking Collection object.

remove() removes obj from the invoking Collection object and returns true if the operation was successful.

removeAll() removes all of the elements contained in Collection c from the invoking Collection object and returns true if the operation was successful.

retainAll() removes all of the elements from the invoking Collection object except those contained in Collection c. It returns true if the operation was successful.

## toArray() Method

| Method | Syntax |
|---|---|
| toArray() | public Object[] toArray() |
| | public Object[] toArray(Object[] *array*) |

toArray() returns an Object array containing either all of the elements of the invoking Collection object (if the first version is used), or those elements of the invoking Collection object that match the elements in array.

# 3.2.2 Enumeration Interface

public interface Enumeration

The Enumeration interface provides two methods for cycling through a collection of objects. It was made obsolete by the other collection interfaces introduced in Java 1.2. A description of the Enumeration interface is presented here due to the common use of it in existing code and by several non-obsolete classes in java.util.

## hasMoreElements() Method

| Method | Syntax |
|---|---|
| hasMoreElements() | public boolean hasMoreElements() |

hasMoreElements() returns true if the invoking Enumeration object has more elements.

## nextElement() Method

| Method | Syntax |
|---|---|
| nextElement() | public Object nextElement() |

nextElement() returns the next Object contained in the invoking Enumeration object. The Object returned by this method must be cast to the original object (for example Button b = (Button)e.nextElement();)

# 3.2.3 Iterator Interface

public interface Iterator

The Iterator interface provides methods to cycle through elements in a Collection. An Iterator object is obtained using the iterator() method from the Collection interface.

## hasNext() Method

| Method | Syntax |
|---|---|
| hasNext() | public boolean hasNext() |

hasNext() returns true if there is another element in the Collection object.

## next() Method

| Method | Syntax |
|---|---|
| next() | public Object next() |

next() returns the next element in the invoking Collection object.

## remove( ) Method

| Method | Syntax |
|---|---|
| remove( ) | public void remove( ) |

remove( ) removes the current element.

---

### Example: Using Iterator

A HashMap object is created, and loaded with four entries. A Set object containing the entries from the HashMap object is created using the entrySet( ) method from the Map interface. The Iterator object associated with the Set object is obtained using the iterator( ) method. The Map.Entry objects contained in the Set object are then cycled through and the keys and values are printed. Because the next( ) method returns an Object object, it must be cast to a Map.Entry object.

```
import java.util.*;

public class TestIterator {
  public static void main(String args[]) {
    HashMap hm = new HashMap();

    hm.put("Jackson Palmer", new Integer(1051));
    hm.put("Lisa Reid", new Integer(5678));
    hm.put("Cheryl Spada", new Integer(2345));
    hm.put("Anne Palmer", new Integer(4567));

    Set st = hm.entrySet();

    Iterator it = st.iterator();

    while (it.hasNext()) {
      Map.Entry me = (Map.Entry) it.next();
      System.out.println("name: " + me.getKey() + " acct number: "
                          + me.getValue());
    }
  }
}
```

*Output*

```
name: Jackson Palmer acct number: 1051
name: Anne Palmer acct number: 4567
name: Cheryl Spada acct number: 2345
name: Lisa Reid acct number: 5678
```

# 3.2.4 ListIterator Interface

```
public interface ListIterator extends Iterator
```

```
Iterator
  ListIterator
```

The ListIterator interface extends the functionality of the Iterator interface to include two-way traversal of the Collection as well as the ability to modify elements.

## add() Method

| Method | Syntax |
| --- | --- |
| add() | public void add(Object *obj*) |

add() adds an element to the Collection at the current location.

## hasNext() Method

| Method | Syntax |
| --- | --- |
| hasNext() | public boolean hasNext() |

hasNext() returns true if there is a following element in the Collection.

## hasPrevious() Method

| Method | Syntax |
| --- | --- |
| hasPrevious() | public boolean hasPrevious() |

hasPrevious() returns true if there is a previous element in the Collection.

## next() Method

| Method | Syntax |
| --- | --- |
| next() | public Object next() |

next() returns the next element.

## nextIndex() Method

| Method | Syntax |
| --- | --- |
| nextIndex() | public int nextIndex() |

nextIndex() returns the index of the next element. If it is at the end of the list, it returns the size of the Collection.

## previous() Method

| Method | Syntax |
|--------|--------|
| previous() | public Object previous() |

previous() returns the previous element.

## previousIndex() Method

| Method | Syntax |
|--------|--------|
| previousIndex() | public int previousIndex() |

previousIndex() returns the index of the previous element, or -1 if it is the beginning of the list.

## remove() Method

| Method | Syntax |
|--------|--------|
| remove() | public void remove(Object *obj*) |

remove() removes from the list the last element that was returned by a call to next() or previous().

## set() Method

| Method | Syntax |
|--------|--------|
| set() | public void set(Object *obj*) |

set() sets obj to be the current element.

### Example: Using ListIterator

In this example an ArrayList object is created with four elements. A ListIterator object is used to cycle through the list, and insert to a new element between the first and second elements. The elements are then printed out in reverse order. Even though the previous method returns an Object object, it does not need to be cast to a String because the println() method will call the toString() method.

```
import java.util.*;

public class TestListIterator {
  public static void main(String args[]) {
    ArrayList al = new ArrayList();
```

```
        al.add("Jackson");
        al.add("Zachary");
        al.add("Lisa");
        al.add("Weesa");

        ListIterator li = al.listIterator();

        while (li.hasNext()) {
          if (li.nextIndex() == 1) {
            li.add("Bailey");
            li.next();
          }
        }

        while (li.hasPrevious()) {
          System.out.println(li.previous());
        }
      }
    }
```

**Output**

```
Weesa
Lisa
Zachary
Bailey
Jackson
```

# 3.2.5 Comparator Interface

```
public interface Comparator
```

The Comparator interface provides two methods to compare the elements of a sorted Collection or Map object. The default Comparator sorts elements in a "natural" way, meaning alphabetically, from lowest number to highest. To use a different sorting algorithm, the Comparator interface methods can be overridden.

## compare() Method

| Method | Syntax |
|--------|--------|
| compare() | public int compare(Object *obj1*, Object *obj2*) |

compare() returns 0 if the two objects are equal, returns a positive value if obj1 is greater than obj2, and returns a negative value if obj2 is greater than obj1.

## equals() Method

| Method | Syntax |
|--------|--------|
| equals() | public boolean **equals**(Object *obj*) |

equals() returns true if obj is a Comparator object and uses the same ordering as the invoking Comparator object.

### Example: Using Comparator

In this example, a Comparator is written that sorts peoples' names by their last name. The lastIndexOf() method from the String class determines where the last name begins. The last names are then compared using the compareTo() method from the String class. If the last names are equal, the whole names are compared.

A TreeSet is created, passing a reference to the Comparator NewComp to the constructor. Four String objects containing names are added to the TreeSet, which sorts them appropriately.

```
import java.util.*;

class NewComp implements Comparator {
  public int compare(Object obj1, Object obj2) {
    int i, j, k;

    String str1 = (String) obj1;
    String str2 = (String) obj2;

    i = str1.lastIndexOf(' ');
    j = str2.lastIndexOf(' ');

    k = str1.substring(i).compareTo(str2.substring(j));
    if (k == 0) {
      return str1.compareTo(str2);
    } else {
      return k;
    }
  }
}

public class TestComp {
  public static void main(String args[]) {
    TreeSet ts = new TreeSet(new NewComp());
```

```
        ts.add("Zachary Palmer");
        ts.add("Lisa Reid");
        ts.add("Anne Palmer");
        ts.add("Diana Davis");

        System.out.println("ts contains " + ts);
    }
}
```

**Output**

```
ts contains [Diana Davis, Anne Palmer, Zachary Palmer, Lisa Reid]
```

# 3.2.6 List Interface

```
public interface List extends Collection
```

```
Collection
    List
```

The List interface is an extension of the Collection interface and provides methods for a Collection that stores a sequence of elements. Elements of a List are given a position in the collection similar to an array element that is given an array index. A List may contain duplicate elements.

## Methods to Add Objects to a List

| Method | Syntax |
|--------|--------|
| add() | public void **add**(int *index*, Object *obj*) |
| | public void **add**(Object *obj*) |
| addAll() | public boolean **addAll**(int *index*, Collection *c*) |
| | public boolean **addAll**(Collection *c*) |

add() adds an Object to the invoking List object. If an element already exists at position index, it is shifted up. If the index is not provided, the element is placed at the end of the list.

addAll() adds the Objects in the specified Collection to the invoking List object. If an element already exists at position index, it is shifted up. addAll() returns true if the add was successful. If the index is not provided, the Collection is placed at the end of the list.

## Methods to Investigate the Contents of a List

| Methods | Syntax |
|---|---|
| contains() | public boolean contains(Object *obj*) |
| containsAll() | public boolean containsAll(Collection *c*) |
| equals() | public boolean equals(Object *obj*) |
| isEmpty() | public boolean isEmpty() |
| size() | public int size() |
| indexOf() | public int indexOf(Object *obj*) |
| lastIndexOf() | public int lastIndexOf(Object *obj*) |

contains() returns true if the invoking List object contains the Object obj.

containsAll() returns true if the invoking List object contains all of the elements of Collection c.

equals() returns true if the invoking List object and obj are equal.

isEmpty() returns true if the invoking List object is empty.

size() returns the number of Objects contained in the invoking List object.

indexOf() returns the index of the first occurrence obj in the invoking List object, or -1 if the the invoking List object does not contain obj.

lastIndexOf() returns the index of the last occurrence of of obj in the invoking List object and is typically used if there are duplicate occurrences of obj, or -1 if the the invoking List object does not contain obj.

## get() Method

| Method | Syntax |
|---|---|
| get() | public Object get(int *index*) |

get() returns the Object at position index in the invoking List object.

## hashCode() Method

| Method | Syntax |
|---|---|
| hashCode() | public int hashCode() |

hashCode() returns the hash code for the invoking List object.

# iterator() Method

| Method | Syntax |
|---|---|
| iterator() | public Iterator iterator() |

iterator() returns the Iterator object that is associated with the invoking List object.

# listIterator() Method

| Method | Syntax |
|---|---|
| listIterator() | public ListIterator listIterator() |
| | public ListIterator listIterator(int *index*) |

listIterator() returns the ListIterator object that is associated with the invoking List object. The second version returns a ListIterator object for the List starting at position index.

# Methods to Remove List Elements

| Method | Syntax |
|---|---|
| clear() | public void clear() |
| remove() | public Object remove(int *index*) |
| | public boolean remove(Object *obj*) |
| removeAll() | public boolean removeAll(Collection c) |
| retainAll() | public boolean retainAll(Collection c) |

clear() removes all of the elements from the list.

remove() removes an Object from the invoking List object based on either an index or Object argument. If an index is passed, the method returns the deleted Object. When an Object is passed, the method returns true if the element was sucessfully removed.

removeAll() method removes from the list all of the elements contained in Collection c and returns true if the operation was successful.

retainAll() method removes all of the elements from the list except those contained in Collection c. It returns true if the operation was successful.

# set() Method

| Method | Syntax |
|---|---|
| set() | public Object set(int *index*, Object *obj*) |

set() places the Object obj at position index in the invoking List object.

## subList() Method

| Method | Syntax |
|--------|--------|
| subList() | public List subList(int *start*, int *end*) |

subList() returns a sub-list of the invoking List object containing elements from index start to the element before index end.

## toArray() Method

| Method | Syntax |
|--------|--------|
| toArray() | public Object[] toArray() |
| | public Object[] toArray(Object[] *array*) |

toArray() returns an Object array containing either all of the elements of the invoking List object (if the first version is used), or those elements of the invoking List object that match the elements in array.

# 3.2.7 Set Interface

```
public interface Set extends Collection
```

```
Collection
    Set
```

A Set object is a Collection object that prohibits duplicate elements. The Set interface does not declare any new methods but the add() method will fail if it is used to add an Object that already exists in the Set.

# 3.2.8 SortedSet Interface

```
public interface SortedSet extends Set
```

```
Collection
    Set
        SortedSet
```

A SortedSet is a Set that is sorted in ascending order. A SortedSet object has access to the methods declared in the Collection interface.

## Methods to Access Elements of a SortedSet

| Method | Syntax |
|--------|--------|
| first() | public Object first() |
| last() | public Object last() |

first() and last() return the first and last Objects in the invoking SortedSet object.

## comparator() Method

| Method | Syntax |
|--------|--------|
| comparator() | public Comparator comparator() |

comparator() returns the Comparator object associated with the invoking SortedSet object .

## Methods to Extract a Subset of a SortedSet

| Method | Syntax |
|--------|--------|
| headSet() | public SortedSet headSet(Object *last*) |
| subSet() | public SortedSet subSet(Object *first*, Object *last*) |
| tailSet() | public SortedSet tailSet(Object *first*) |

headSet() returns a subset from the Object at index 0 to Object last.

subSet() returns a sub-set of the invoking SortedSet object from Object first to Object last.

tailSet() method returns a subset from Object first to the end of the invoking SortedSet.

## 3.3 Collection Classes

The Collection classes represent a group of objects. The objects that make up a collection are called the elements of the collection. The Collection classes implement the Collection interfaces. The Collection class hierarchy is shown in the following figure.

❑ The Collections class contains a large assortment of static methods for manipulating, converting, and retrieving information about Collection objects.

❑ The AbstractCollection class provides implementation of the abstract methods declared in the Collection interface. It is the parent class of the List and Set classes.

❑ The AbstractList class provides implementation of the abstract methods declared in the List interface and is the parent class of the List classes.

❑ The AbstractSet class provides implementation of the abstract methods declared in the Set interface. It is the parent class of the Set classes.

❑ The Vector and Stack classes are older collection classes that have been maintained under Java 2.

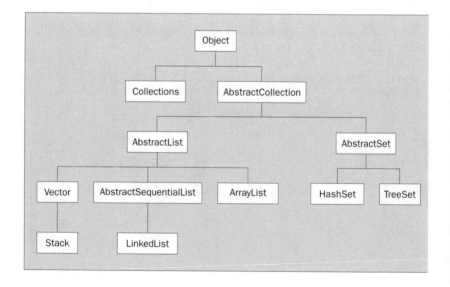

# 3.3.1 AbstractCollection Class

```
public abstract class AbstractCollection extends Object implements Collection
```

```
Object
    AbstractCollection
```

### Interfaces

```
Collection
```

The AbstractCollection class provides implementation of the abstract methods declared in the Collection interface. It is an abstract class, so an AbstractCollection object is never instantiated. A Collection object can be created by creating a class that extends AbstractCollection.

# 3.3.2 AbstractList Class

```
public abstract class AbstractList extends AbstractCollection implements List
```

```
Object
    AbstractCollection
        AbstractList
```

### Interfaces

```
Collection, List
```

The AbstractList class provides implementation of the abstract methods declared in the List interface. It is an abstract class, so an AbstractList object is never instantiated. A List object can be created by writing a class that extends AbstractList.

# 3.3.3 AbstractSequentialList Class

```
public abstract class AbstractSequentialList extends AbstractList
```

```
Object
    AbstractCollection
        AbstractList
            AbstractSequentialList
```

### Interfaces

```
Collection, List
```

The AbstractSequentialList class provides implementation of the methods from the List interface for a List that uses sequential access of its elements.

# 3.3.4 AbstractSet Class

```
public abstract class AbstractSet extends AbstractCollection implements Set
```

```
Object
  AbstractCollection
    AbstractSet
```

### Interfaces

```
Collection, Set
```

The AbstractSet class provides implementation of the abstract methods declared in the Set interface. It is an abstract class, so an AbstractSet object is never instantiated. A Set object can be created by writing a class that extends AbstractSet.

# 3.3.5 ArrayList Class

```
public class ArrayList extends AbstractList
implements List, Cloneable, Serializable
```

```
Object
  AbstractCollection
    AbstractList
      ArrayList
```

### Interfaces

```
Collection, Cloneable, List, Serializable
```

An ArrayList object is a dynamic array whose size grows and shrinks to match the number of elements it contains. Before Java 1.2 this functionality was provided by the Vector class. The ArrayList object stores objects. It cannot be used to store primitive datatypes.

## ArrayList( ) Constructor

| Constructor | Syntax |
|---|---|
| ArrayList() | public ArrayList() |
| | public ArrayList(Collection c) |
| | pubilc ArrayList(int *initialCapacity*) |

ArrayList() creates an ArrayList object. An ArrayList object can be initialized with either a Collection object or an initial size. The capacity of an ArrayList is adjusted automatically when elements are added to it.

## Methods to Add Objects to an ArrayList

| Method | Syntax |
|--------|--------|
| add() | public void add(int *index*, Object *obj*) |
|  | public void add(Object *obj*) |
| addAll() | public boolean addAll(int *index*, Collection *c*) |
|  | public boolean addAll(Collection *c*) |

add() adds an Object to the invoking ArrayList object. If an element already exists at position index, it is shifted up. If the index is not provided, the element is placed at the end of the list.

addAll() adds the Objects in the specified Collection to the invoking ArrayList object. If an element already exists at position index, it is shifted up. addAll() returns true if the add was successful. If the index is not provided, the Collection is placed at the end of the list.

## clone() Method

| Method | Syntax |
|--------|--------|
| clone() | public Object clone() |

clone() overrides the clone() method of the Object class to return a shallow copy of the invoking ArrayList object.

## Methods to Investigate the Contents to an ArrayList

| Method | Syntax |
|--------|--------|
| contains() | public boolean contains(Object *obj*) |
| indexOf() | public int indexOf(Object *obj*) |
| isEmpty() | public boolean isEmpty() |
| lastIndexOf() | public int lastIndexOf(Object *obj*) |
| size() | public int size() |

contains() returns true if the invoking ArrayList object contains the Object obj.

indexOf() returns the index of the first occurrence obj in the invoking ArrayList object or -1 if the the invoking List object does not contain obj.

isEmpty() returns true if the invoking ArrayList object is empty.

lastIndexOf() returns the index of the last occurrence of of obj in the invoking ArrayList object and is typically used if there are duplicate occurrences of obj, or -1 if the the invoking List object does not contain obj.

size() returns the number of Objects contained in the invoking ArrayList object.

## ensureCapacity() Method

| Method | Syntax |
|---|---|
| ensureCapacity() | public void ensureCapacity(int *capacity*) |

ensureCapacity() increases the capacity of the invoking ArrayList object. This is computationally more efficient that having the ArrayList increase its capacity every time an Object is added to it.

## get() Method

| Method | Syntax |
|---|---|
| get() | public Object get(int *index*) |

get() returns the Object at position index in the invoking ArrayList object.

## Methods to Remove List Elements

| Method | Syntax |
|---|---|
| clear() | public void clear() |
| remove() | public Object remove(int *index*) |
| removeRange() | protected void removeRange(int *startIndex*, int *endIndex*) |

clear() removes all of the elements from the list.

remove() removes an Object at the specified index from the invoking ArrayList object and returns the deleted Object.

removeRange() method removes the elements from startIndex to endIndex.

## set() Method

| Method | Syntax |
|---|---|
| set() | public Object set(int *index*, Object *obj*) |

set() replaces the element at position index in the invoking ArrayList object with the Object obj.

# toArray() Method

| Method | Syntax |
|--------|--------|
| toArray() | public Object[] toArray()<br>public Object[] toArray(Object[] *array*)<br>    throws ArrayStoreException |

toArray() returns an Object array containing either all of the elements of the invoking ArrayList object (if the first version is used), or those elements of the invoking ArrayList object that match the elements in array.

# trimToSize() Method

| Method | Syntax |
|--------|--------|
| trimToSize() | public void trimToSize() |

trimToSize() reduces the capacity of the invoking ArrayList object so it is equal to the number of Objects the ArrayList object contains.

## Example: Using ArrayList

This example shows how to create an ArrayList object and then manipulate it by increasing its capacity adding a new object. Finally one ArrayList element is replaced with a new element.

```
import java.util.*;

public class TestArrayList {
  public static void main(String args[]) {
    ArrayList al = new ArrayList();

    Integer three = new Integer(3);

    al.add(new Integer(0));
    al.add(new Integer(1));
    al.add(new Integer(2));
    al.add(three);
    al.add(new Integer(4));
    System.out.println("The capacity of al is " + al.size());
    System.out.println("al now contains " + al);
```

```
if (al.contains(three)) {
  System.out.println("al contains three");
  System.out.println("three is at index " + al.indexOf(three));
}

al.add(0, new Integer(5));
System.out.println("The capacity of al is now " + al.size());
System.out.println("al now contains " + al);

al.remove(1);
System.out.println("The capacity of al is now " + al.size());
System.out.println("al now contains " + al);

al.set(0, three);
System.out.println("al now contains " + al);
  }
}
```

The ArrayList object has access to the methods declared in the List and
Collection interfaces. The ArrayList object is created and five objects are
initially loaded into it. Primitive types cannot be loaded into an ArrayList object,
so the Integer wrapper class is used. The initial capacity of the ArrayList object
is five. Another Integer object is loaded into the ArrayList object at index 0 and
the capacity is increased to 6. The add() method does not overwrite elements -
the existing elements are shifted downward. The set() method does overwrite
elements. The existing Integer object at index 0 is replaced with the Integer
object three.

### Output

```
The capacity of al is 5
al now contains [0, 1, 2, 3, 4]
al contains three
three is at index 3
The capacity of al is now 6
al now contains [5, 0, 1, 2, 3, 4]
The capacity of al is now 5
al now contains [5, 1, 2, 3, 4]
al now contains [3, 1, 2, 3, 4]
```

# 3.3.6 Collections Class

```
public class Collections extends Object
```

```
Object
    Collections
```

The Collections class contains a large assortment of static methods for manipulating, converting, and retrieving information about Collection objects. The Collections class has no constructors.

## binarySearch() Method

| Method | Syntax |
|--------|--------|
| binarySearch() | public static int binarySearch(List 1, Object key) |
| | public static int binarySearch(List 1, Object key, Comparator c) |

binarySearch() searches for the Object key in the List 1. A Comparator object can also be specified. The methods return the index of the value, or -1 if the value cannot be found.

### Example: Using binarySearch()

This example creates an ArrayList object and populates it with four entries. It then uses the binarySearch() method to retrieve the index position of one of the entries.

```java
import java.util.*;

public class TestCollSearch {
   public static void main(String args[]) {
      ArrayList tmp = new ArrayList();
      tmp.add("Mark");
      tmp.add("Maria");
      tmp.add("Scott");
      tmp.add("Diana");

      String str = "Maria";
      int pos = Collections.binarySearch(tmp, str);
      System.out.println("Maria is at position " + pos);
   }
}
```

*Output*

```
Maria is at position 1
```

## copy() Method

| Method | Syntax |
|--------|--------|
| copy() | public static void copy(List *list1*, List *list2*) |

copy() copies the elements of List list1 into List list2.

## Methods to Create One-Element Collections

| Method | Syntax |
|--------|--------|
| singleton() | public static Set singleton(Object *obj*) |
| singletonList() | public static List singletonList(Object *obj*) |
| singletonMap() | public static Map singletonMap<br>(Object *key*, Object *value*) |

singleton() returns a one-object, unmodifiable Set object containing Object obj.

singletonList() returns a one-object, unmodifiable List object containing Object obj.

singletonMap() returns a one-object, unmodifiable Map object that maps only the specified key-value pair.

## enumeration() Method

| Method | Syntax |
|--------|--------|
| enumeration() | public static Enumeration enumeration(Collection *c*) |

enumeration() returns an Enumeration object containing the elements of Collection c. The Enumeration interface is considered obsolete and has been replaced by Iterator.

## fill() Method

| Method | Syntax |
|--------|--------|
| fill() | public static void fill(List *l*, Object *obj*) |

fill() assigns the Object obj to every element of List l.

## Example: Using fill()

This example creates an ArrayList object and populates it with four different values. It then assigns one Object to all of the contents of the array.

```
import java.util.*;

public class TestCollFill {
  public static void main(String args[]) {
    ArrayList tmp = new ArrayList();
    tmp.add("Mark");
    tmp.add("Maria");
    tmp.add("Scott");
    tmp.add("Diana");

    Collections.fill(tmp, "Bailey");
    System.out.println("The size of tmp is " + tmp.size());
    System.out.println("The contents of tmp are: " + tmp);
  }
}
```

*Output*

```
The size of tmp is 4
The contents of tmp are [Bailey, Bailey, Bailey, Bailey]
```

# max() and min() Methods

| Method | Syntax |
|--------|--------|
| max() | public static Object max(Collection *coll*) |
| | public static Object max(Collection *coll*, Comparator *c*) |
| min() | public static Object min(Collection *coll*) |
| | public static Object min(Collection *coll*, Comparator *c*) |

max() returns the maximum element from Collection coll based on whatever ordering scheme is being used. A Comparator object may be specified.

min() returns the minimum element from Collection coll based on whatever ordering scheme is being used. A Comparator object may be specified.

### Example: Using max() and min()

This example creates a new ArrayList object and populates it with Integers. It then uses the max() and min() methods to find the maximum and minimum elements from the ArrayList.

```
import java.util.*;

public class TestCollMax {
  public static void main(String args[]) {
    ArrayList tmp = new ArrayList();
    tmp.add(new Integer(0));
    tmp.add(new Integer(11));
    tmp.add(new Integer(-2));
    tmp.add(new Integer(3));

    Integer max = (Integer) Collections.max(tmp);
    Integer min = (Integer) Collections.min(tmp);
    System.out.println("maximum is " + max + " minimum is " + min);
  }
}
```

*Output*

```
maximum is 11 minimum is -2
```

## nCopies() Method

| Method | Syntax |
|---|---|
| nCopies() | public static List nCopies(int *numCopies*, Object *obj*) |

nCopies() returns an immutable list containing numCopies of Object obj.

## reverse() Method

| Method | Syntax |
|---|---|
| reverse() | public static void **reverse**(List *list*) |

reverse() reverses the order of the List list.

# reverseOrder() Method

| Method | Syntax |
|---|---|
| reverseOrder() | public static Comparator reverseOrder() |

reverseOrder() returns a Comparator object that compares things in the reverse order.

## Example: Using reverseOrder()

In this example a TreeSet object is populated with integers, and is then sorted from highest Integer to lowest.

```java
import java.util.*;

public class TestCollReverse {
  public static void main(String args[]) {
    Comparator c = Collections.reverseOrder();

    TreeSet ts = new TreeSet(c);

    ts.add(new Integer(0));
    ts.add(new Integer(11));
    ts.add(new Integer(-2));
    ts.add(new Integer(3));

    System.out.println("Contents of ts are " + ts);
  }
}
```

*Output*

```
Contents of ts are [11, 3, 0, -2]
```

# shuffle() Method

| Method | Syntax |
|---|---|
| shuffle() | public static void shuffle(List list) |
| | public static void shuffle(List list, Random r) |

shuffle() shuffles the order of the List list. It can be passed a Random object to increase the randomness of the shuffle.

---

### Example: Using shuffle()

In this example an `ArrayList` object is created and populated with `Integers`, which are then re-ordered using the `shuffle()` method.

```java
import java.util.*;

public class TestCollShuffle {
  public static void main(String args[]) {
    ArrayList al = new ArrayList();

    al.add(new Integer(0));
    al.add(new Integer(11));
    al.add(new Integer(-2));
    al.add(new Integer(3));

    Collections.shuffle(al);
    System.out.println("Contents of al are " + al);
  }
}
```

***Output*** *(results will vary)*
```
Contents of al are [0, 3, -2, 11]
```

## sort() Method

| Method | Syntax |
|--------|--------|
| sort() | `public static void `**`sort`**`(List list)` |
|        | `public static void `**`sort`**`(List list, Comparator c)` |

`sort()` sorts the `List list` according to the current ordering system. A `Comparator` object can be passed to this method.

### Example: Using sort()

In this example, an `ArrayList` object is created and populated with `Integers`. These are then sorted in ascending numberic order using the `sort()` method.

```java
import java.util.*;

public class TestCollSort {
  public static void main(String args[]) {
```

```
        ArrayList al = new ArrayList();

        al.add(new Integer(0));
        al.add(new Integer(11));
        al.add(new Integer(-2));
        al.add(new Integer(3));

        Collections.sort(al);
        System.out.println("Contents of al are " + al);
    }
}
```

**Output**

```
    Contents of al are [-2, 0, 3, 11]
```

## Methods to Create a Synchronized Collection

| Method | Syntax |
|---|---|
| synchronizedCollection() | public static Collection synchronizedCollection(Collection c) |
| synchronizedList() | public static List synchronizedList(List l) |
| synchronizedMap() | public static Map synchronizedMap(Map m) |
| synchronizedSet() | public static Set synchronizedSet(Set s) |
| synchronizedSortedMap() | public static SortedMap synchronizedSortedMap (SortedMap sm) |
| synchronizedSortedSet() | public static SortedSet synchronizedSortedSet (SortedSet ss) |

These methods return a synchronized version of a Collection, List, Map, Set, SortedMap or SortedSet object. None of the collection class implementations are inherently synchronized.

### Example: Creating a Synchronized Collection

In this example, a sychronized SortedSet object is created; the SortedSet object has access to the methods in the SortedSet and Collection interfaces, and sorts the elements alphabetically.

```
import java.util.*;

public class TestCollSynch {
```

```
    public static void main(String args[]) {
      SortedSet ss = Collections.synchronizedSortedSet(new TreeSet());

      ss.add("Mark");
      ss.add("Maria");
      ss.add("Scott");
      ss.add("Diana");
      System.out.println("The first element is " + (String) ss.first());
      System.out.println("The last element is " + (String) ss.last());
    }
  }
```

**Output**

```
The first element is Diana
The last element is Scott.
```

## Methods to Create an Unmodifiable Collection

| Method | Syntax |
|---|---|
| unmodifiableCollection() | public static Collection unmodifiableCollection(Collection c) |
| unmodifiableList() | public static List unmodifiableList(List l) |
| unmodifiableMap() | public static Map unmodifiableMap(Map m) |
| unmodifiableSet() | public static Set unmodifiableSet(Set s) |
| unmodifiableSortedMap() | public static SortedMap unmodifiableSortedMap (SortedMap sm) |
| unmodifiableSortedSet() | public static SortedSet unmodifiableSortedSet (SortedSet ss) |

These methods return an unmodifiable version of a Collection, List, Map, Set, SortedMap or SortedSet object.

### Example: Creating an Unmodifiable Collection

In this example, an unmodifiable List object is created and initialized with the elements of an ArrayList object; it has access to the methods from the List interface. An UnsupportedOperationException occurs when the set() method is invoked.

```
import java.util.*;

public class TestCollUnm {
  public static void main(String args[]) {
    ArrayList tmp = new ArrayList();
    tmp.add("Mark");
    tmp.add("Maria");
    tmp.add("Scott");
    tmp.add("Diana");

    List l = Collections.unmodifiableList(tmp);

    String str = (String) l.get(0);
    System.out.println("The first element is " + str);

    try {
      l.set(1, "Bailey");
    } catch (UnsupportedOperationException e) {
      System.out.println("List is unmodifiable");
    }
  }
}
```

**Output**

```
The first element is Mark
List is unmodifiable
```

# 3.3.7 HashSet Class

```
public class HashSet extends AbstractSet implements Set, Cloneable, Serializable
```

```
Object
  AbstractCollection
    AbstractSet
      HashSet
```

### Interfaces

```
Cloneable, Collection, Serializable, Set
```

A HashSet object implements the Set interface using a hash table structure. A HashSet object does not sort its elements.

## HashSet() Constructor

| Constructor | Syntax |
| --- | --- |
| HashSet() | `public HashSet()` |
| | `public HashSet(int capacity)` |
| | `public HashSet(int capacity, float loadCapacity)` |
| | `public HashSet(Collection c)` |

It is possible to provide the constructor with an initial capacity, load capacity, and initialize it with the elements from a Collection object. The load capacity is a number between 0.0 and 1.0 indicates how full the HashSet object has to be before it is re-sized. When the HashSet is to be resized, the size is doubled or increased by 11, whichever provides the largest re-size.

## add() Method

| Method | Syntax |
| --- | --- |
| add() | `public boolean add(Object o)` |

add() overrides the add() method in class AbstractCollection to add the specified Object to the invoking HashSet object if it is not already present.

## clone() Method

| Method | Syntax |
| --- | --- |
| clone() | `public Object clone()` |

clone() overrides the clone() method from the Object class to return a shallow copy of the invoking HashSet object.

## Methods to Investigate the Contents of a HashSet

| Method | Syntax |
| --- | --- |
| contains() | `public boolean contains(Object obj)` |
| isEmpty() | `public boolean isEmpty()` |
| size() | `public int size()` |

contains() returns true if the invoking HashSet object contains Object obj.

isEmpty() returns true if the invoking HashSet object is empty.

size() returns the number of elements in the invoking HashSet object.

## Methods to Remove HashSet Elements

| Method | Syntax |
|--------|--------|
| clear() | public void clear() |
| remove() | public boolean remove(Object obj) |

clear() removes all of the elements from the invoking HashSet object.

remove() removes the specified Object from the invoking HashSet object and returns true if the removal was successful.

## iterator() Method

| Method | Syntax |
|--------|--------|
| iterator() | public Iterator iterator() |

iterator() returns an Iterator object that is associated with the invoking HashSet object.

### Example: Using HashSet

This example creates a HashSet object and fills it with Integers, then prints out the capacity of the HashSet using the size() method, and its contents. Note that the elements in the HashSet object are not stored in the order that they are loaded.

```
import java.util.*;

public class TestHashSet {
  public static void main(String args[]) {
    HashSet hs = new HashSet();

    hs.add(new Integer(4));
    hs.add(new Integer(2));
    hs.add(new Integer(1));
    hs.add(new Integer(3));

    System.out.println("The capacity of hs is " + hs.size());
    System.out.println("hs contains " + hs);
  }
}
```

#### Output
```
The capacity of hs is 4
hs contains [4, 3, 2, 1]
```

# 3.3.8 LinkedList Class

```
public class LinkedList extends AbstractSequentialList
    implements List, Cloneable, Serializable
```

```
Object
  AbstractCollection
    AbstractList
      AbstractSequentialList
        LinkedList
```

### Interfaces

```
Collection, Cloneable, List, Serializable
```

A LinkedList object provides a linked-list data structure.

## LinkedList() Constructor

| Constructor | Syntax |
|---|---|
| LinkedList() | public LinkedList() |
| | public LinkedList(Collection c) |

LinkedList() creates a LinkedList object. The second version initializes the LinkedList object with the contents of Collection c.

## Methods to Add Elements to a LinkedList

| Method | Syntax |
|---|---|
| add() | public void add(int index, Object obj) |
| | public void add(Object obj) |
| addAll() | public boolean addAll(int index, Collection c) |
| | public boolean addAll(Collection c) |
| addFirst() | public void addFirst(Object obj) |
| addLast() | public void addLast(Object obj) |

add() adds an Object to the invoking LinkedList object. If an element already exists at position index, it is shifted up. If the index is not provided, the element is placed at the end of the list.

addAll() adds the Objects in the specified Collection to the invoking LinkedList object. If an element already exists at position index, it is shifted up. addAll() returns true if the add was successful. If the index is not provided, the Collection is placed at the end of the list.

addFirst() adds an Object at the beginning of the invoking LinkedList object.

addLast() adds an Object at the end of the invoking LinkedList object.

## clone() Method

| Method | Syntax |
|--------|--------|
| clone() | public Object clone() |

clone() overrides the clone() method from the Object class to return a shallow copy of the invoking LinkedList object.

## Methods to Investigate the Contents of a LinkedList

| Method | Syntax |
|--------|--------|
| contains() | public boolean contains(Object obj) |
| indexOf() | public int indexOf(Object obj) |
| lastIndexOf() | public int lastIndexOf(Object obj) |
| size() | public int size() |

contains() returns true if the invoking LinkedList object contains the Object obj.

indexOf() returns the index of the first occurrence obj in the invoking LinkedList object, or -1 if the the invoking List object does not contain obj.

lastIndexOf() returns the index of the last occurrence of of obj in the invoking LinkedList object and is typically used if there are duplicate occurrences of obj, or -1 if the the invoking LinkedList object does not contain obj.

size() returns the number of Objects contained in the invoking LinkedList object.

## listIterator() Method

| Method | Syntax |
|--------|--------|
| listIterator() | public ListIterator listIterator(int index) |

listIterator() returns the ListIterator object that is associated with the invoking LinkedList object. The index is the index of the first element that will be returned by a call to the next() method.

## Methods to Retrieve Elements from a LinkedList

| Method | Syntax |
|---|---|
| get() | public Object get(int *index*) |
| getFirst() | public Object getFirst() |
| getLast() | public Object getLast() |

get() returns the Object at position index in the invoking LinkedList object.

getFirst() retrieves the first element from the invoking LinkedList object.

getLast() retrieves the last element from the invoking LinkedList object.

## Methods to Remove Elements from a LinkedList

| Method | Syntax |
|---|---|
| clear() | public void clear() |
| remove() | public Object remove(int *index*) |
| | public boolean remove(Object *obj*) |
| removeFirst() | public Object removeFirst() |
| removeLast() | public Object removeLast() |

clear() removes all of the elements from the list.

remove() removes an Object from the invoking LinkedList object based on either an index or Object argument. The remaining elements are shifted to the left. If an index is passed, the method returns the deleted Object. If an Object is passed, the method returns true if the element was sucessfully removed.

removeFirst() removes the first element from the invoking LinkedList object and returns the removed Object.

removeLast() removes the last element from the invoking LinkedList object and returns the removed Object.

## set() Method

| Method | Syntax |
|---|---|
| set() | public Object set(int *index*, Object *obj*) |

set() replaces the element at position index in the invoking List object, with the Object obj.

# toArray() Method

| Method | Syntax |
|---|---|
| toArray() | public Object[] toArray()<br>public Object[] toArray(Object[] *array*) |

toArray() returns an Object array containing either all of the elements of the invoking LinkedList object (if the first version is used), or those elements of the invoking LinkedList object that match the elements in array.

## Example: Using LinkedList

A LinkedList object is created and loaded with Integer objects. Primitive datatypes cannot be loaded into a LinkedList, so the Integer wrapper class is used. The Integer object at index 1 is retrieved, incremented by 5, and placed back into the LinkedList. The get() method returns an Object which must be cast into an Integer object before it can be manipulated.

```
import java.util.*;

public class TestLinkedList {
  public static void main(String args[]) {
    LinkedList llist = new LinkedList();

    llist.add(new Integer(1));
    llist.add(new Integer(2));
    llist.add(new Integer(3));
    llist.add(new Integer(4));
    llist.addFirst(new Integer(0));
    System.out.println("The capacity of llist is " + llist.size());
    System.out.println("llist now contains " + llist);

    Integer iobj = (Integer) llist.get(1);
    llist.set(1, new Integer(iobj.intValue() + 5));

    llist.removeLast();

    System.out.println("llist now contains " + llist);
  }
}
```

### Output

```
The capacity of al is 5
al now contains [0, 1, 2, 3, 4]
al now contains [0, 6, 2, 3]
```

**237**

# 3.3.9 Stack Class

```
public class Stack extends Vector
```

```
Object
  AbstractCollection
    AbstractList
      Vector
        Stack
```

### Interfaces

```
Cloneable, Collection, List, Serializable
```

A Stack object is an older (Java 1.1) implementation of a dynamic array that employs a last-in-first-out model. The Stack class is not really a part of the Collection class framework. A discussion of the Stack class is included here to support older codes that may implement it.

## Stack() Constructor

| Constructor | Syntax |
|---|---|
| Stack() | public Stack() |

Initially, the Stack object is empty.

## empty() Method

| Method | Syntax |
|---|---|
| empty() | public boolean empty() |

empty() returns true if the invoking Stack object contains no elements.

## push() Method

| Method | Syntax |
|---|---|
| push() | public Object push(Object *obj*) |

push() places the Object obj on top of the invoking Stack object. The method returns obj.

# Methods to Access Stack Elements

| Method | Syntax |
|--------|--------|
| pop() | public Object pop() |
| peek() | public Object peek() |
| search() | public synchronized int search(Object *obj*) |

pop() returns the Object on top of the invoking Stack object and removes it from the Stack. It can throw an EmptyStackException if the Stack object is empty.

peek() returns the Object on top of the invoking Stack object without removing it from the Stack object.

search() returns the distance Object obj is from the top of the stack and returns -1 if the obj is not contained in the Stack object.

## Example: Using Stack

A Stack is created and three String objects are pushed onto it. The top element is popped off the stack, and the new top element is first examined without removing it and then popped off the stack itself.

```
import java.util.*;

public class TestStack {
  public static void main(String args[]) {
    Stack s = new Stack();

    s.push("first");
    s.push("second");
    s.push("third");

    String top = (String) s.pop();
    String newTop = (String) s.peek();
    String next = (String) s.pop();
    System.out.println(top + " " + newTop + " " + next);
  }
}
```

### Output
```
third second second
```

# 3.3.10 TreeSet Class

```
public class TreeSet extends AbstractSet
    implements SortedSet, Cloneable, Serializable
```

```
Object
    AbstractCollection
        AbstractSet
            TreeSet
```

### Interfaces

```
Cloneable, Collection, Serializable, Set, SortedSet
```

A TreeSet object stores objects in a sorted, ascending order tree structure.

## TreeSet() Constructor

| Constructor | Syntax |
| --- | --- |
| TreeSet() | public TreeSet() |
| | public TreeSet(Collection c) |
| | public TreeSet(Comparator cmp) |
| | public TreeSet(SortedSet s) |

TreeSet() creates a TreeSet object. The TreeSet object can be initialized with the elements from a Collection or SortedSet object or can be associated with a Comparator object.

## Methods to Add Elements to a TreeSet

| Method | Syntax |
| --- | --- |
| add() | public boolean add(Object obj) |
| addAll() | public boolean addAll(Collection c) |

add() adds the Object obj to the invoking TreeSet object if it is not already present.

addAll() adds the elements in Collection c to the invoking TreeSet object.

## Methods to Return Elements of a TreeSet

| Method | Syntax |
| --- | --- |
| first() | public Object first() |
| last() | public Object last() |

first() and last() return the first and last Objects in the invoking TreeSet object.

# clone() Method

| Method | Syntax |
|--------|--------|
| clone() | public Object clone() |

clone() overrides the clone() method from the Object class to return a shallow copy of the invoking TreeSet object.

# comparator() Method

| Method | Syntax |
|--------|--------|
| comparator() | public Comparator comparator() |

comparator() returns the Comparator object associated with the invoking TreeSet object .

# Methods to Extract a Subset of a TreeSet

| Method | Syntax |
|--------|--------|
| headSet() | public SortedSet headSet(Object *last*) |
| subSet() | public SortedSet subSet(Object *first*, Object *last*) |
| tailSet() | public SortedSet tailSet(Object *first*) |

headSet() returns a subset from the Object at index 0 to Object last.

subSet() returns a sub-set of the invoking TreeSet object from Object first to Object last.

tailSet() method returns a subset from Object first to the end of the invoking SortedSet.

# Methods to Investigate the Contents of a TreeSet

| Method | Syntax |
|--------|--------|
| contains() | public boolean contains(Object *obj*) |
| isEmpty() | public boolean isEmpty() |
| size() | public int size() |

contains() returns true if the invoking TreeSet object contains the Object obj.

isEmpty() returns true if the invoking TreeSet object has no elements.

size() returns the number of Objects contained in the invoking TreeSet object.

## Methods to Remove Elements from a TreeSet

| Method | Syntax |
| --- | --- |
| clear() | public void clear() |
| remove() | public boolean remove(Object obj) |

clear() removes all of the elements from the invoking TreeSet object.

remove() removes the Object obj from the invoking TreeSet object if it is present and returns true if the removal was successful.

### Example: Using TreeSet

In this example, a TreeSet is created and populated with Integer objects. Then the capacity of the TreeSet object is returned using the size() method. Finally the contents of the TreeSet are returned. Because the elements are stored as a tree, they are sorted according to a logical order of the elements. In this case, the contents of the tree are [1, 2, 3, 4].

```
import java.util.*;

public class TestTreeSet {
  public static void main(String args[]) {
    TreeSet ts = new TreeSet();

    ts.add(new Integer(4));
    ts.add(new Integer(2));
    ts.add(new Integer(1));
    ts.add(new Integer(3));

    System.out.println("The capacity of ts is " + ts.size());
    System.out.println("ts contains " + ts);
  }
}
```

**Output**

```
The capacity of ts is 4
ts contains [1, 2, 3, 4]
```

# 3.3.11 Vector Class

```
public class Vector extends AbstractList
  implements List, Cloneable, Serializable
```

```
Object
  AbstractCollection
    AbstractList
      Vector
```

### Interfaces
```
Cloneable, Collection, List, Serializable
```

The Vector class is an older (Java 1.1) implementation of a dynamic array. With the release of Java 1.2, the Vector class was modified to make it more compatible with newer Collection classes. Vector is now a sub-class of AbstractList and implements the List interface. A Vector object contains object references and dynamically increases or decreases in size. It cannot store primitive datatypes. Vector is the only Collection class that is inherently synchronized.

## Vector() Constructor

| Constructor | Syntax |
|---|---|
| Vector() | public **Vector**() |
| | public **Vector**(int *initialCapacity*) |
| | public **Vector**(int *initialCapacity*, int *capacityIncrement*) |
| | public **Vector**(Collection *c*) |

Vector() creates a Vector object. The Vector can be provided a capacity increment and/or an initial capacity. The default initial capacity is 10. The default capacity increment is 0. The Vector object can also be initialized with the contents of a Collection object.

## Methods to Add Elements to a Vector Object

| Method | Syntax |
|---|---|
| add() | public void **add**(int *index*, Object *obj*) |
| | public void **add**(Object *obj*) |
| addAll() | public boolean **addAll**(int *index*, Collection *c*) |
| | public boolean **addAll**(Collection *c*) |
| addElement() | public synchronized void **addElement**(Object *obj*) |

| Method | Syntax |
|---|---|
| insertElementAt() | public synchronized void insertElementAt (Object *obj*, int *index*) |
| setElementAt() | public synchronized void setElementAt (Object *obj*, int *index*) |

add() adds an Object to the invoking Vector object. If an element already exists at position index, it is shifted to the right. If the index is not provided, the element is placed at the end of the Vector.

addAll() adds the Objects in the specified Collection to the invoking Vector object. If an element already exists at position index, it is shifted to the right. addAll() returns true if the add was successful. If the index is not provided, the Collection is placed at the end of the Vector.

addElement() adds the Object argument to the end of the invoking Vector object and increases the Vector size by 1.

insertElementAt() inserts the Object argument into the invoking Vector object at position index. It shifts the existing elements at position index and above up by 1.

setElementAt() replaces the current element at position index with the Object argument.

## clone() Method

| Method | Syntax |
|---|---|
| clone() | public Object clone() |

clone() overrides the clone() method from the Object class to return a shallow copy of the invoking Vector object.

## equals() Method

| Method | Syntax |
|---|---|
| equals() | public boolean equals(Object *obj*) |

equals() returns true if Object obj is a Vector with the same elements as the invoking Vector object.

## hashCode() Method

| Method | Syntax |
|---|---|
| hashCode() | public int hashCode() |

hashCode() returns the hash code for the invoking Vector object.

## Methods to Investigate the Contents of a Vector

| Method | Syntax |
|---|---|
| contains() | public boolean contains(Object *obj*) |
| containsAll() | public boolean containsAll(Collection *c*) |
| indexOf() | public int indexOf(Object *obj*) |
| | public int indexOf(Object *obj*, int *startIndex*) |
| isEmpty() | public boolean isEmpty() |
| lastIndexOf() | public int lastIndexOf(Object *obj*) |
| | public int lastIndexOf(Object *obj*, int *startIndex*) |

contains() returns true if the invoking Vector object contains the Object obj.

containsAll() returns true if the invoking Vector object contains all of the elements in the Collection c.

indexOf() returns the index of the first occurrence of obj in the invoking Vector object, or -1 if the the invoking Vector object does not contain obj.

isEmpty() returns true if the invoking Vector object is empty.

lastIndexOf() returns the index of the last occurrence of of obj in the invoking Vector object or -1 if the the invoking Vector object does not contain obj and is typically used if there are duplicate occurrences of obj

## Methods to Remove Elements From a Vector

| Method | Syntax |
|---|---|
| clear() | public void clear() |
| remove() | public Object remove(int *index*) |
| | public boolean remove(Object *obj*) |
| removeAll() | public boolean removeAll(Collection *c*) |
| removeElement() | public boolean removeElement(Object *obj*) |
| removeElementAt() | public void removeElementAt(int *index*) |
| removeAllElements() | public void removeAllElements() |
| retainAll() | public boolean retainAll(Collection *c*) |

clear() removes all of the elements from the list.

**245**

remove() removes an Object from the invoking Vector object based on either an index or an Object argument. The remaining elements are shifted to the left. If an index is passed, the method returns the deleted Object. If an Object is passed, the method returns true if the element was sucessfully removed.

removeAll() removes the contents of the Collection c from the invoking Vector object and returns true if some elements were removed from the Vector.

removeElement() removes first occurrence of the Object obj from the invoking Vector object and returns true if the element was successfully removed.

removeElementAt() removes the element at position index and shifts all elements above it down by 1.

removeAllElements() removes all of the elements of the invoking Vector object.

retainAll() retains only the contents of the Collection c in the invoking Vector object removing all other elements. The method returns true if some elements were removed from the Vector.

## Methods to Return Elements of a Vector

| Method | Syntax |
|---|---|
| elementAt() | public Object elementAt(int index)<br>　　　throws ArrayIndexOutOfBoundsException |
| elements() | public Enumeration elements() |
| firstElement() | public Object firstElement()<br>　　　throws NoSuchElementException |
| lastElement() | public Object lastElement()<br>　　　throws NoSuchElementException |
| get() | public Object get(int index)<br>　　　throws ArrayIndexOutOfBoundsException |
| copyInto() | public void copyInto(Object[] *objArray*) |

elementAt() returns the element at position index in the invoking Vector object.

elements() returns an Enumeration object containing the elements of the invoking Vector object.

firstElement() and lastElement() return the first or last elements of the invoking Vector object.

get() returns the element at position index in the invoking Vector object.

copyInto() converts the invoking Vector object into an Object array.

## Size Methods

| Method | Syntax |
|---|---|
| capacity() | public int capacity() |
| ensureCapacity() | public sychronized void ensureCapacity (int *minimumSize*) |
| setSize() | public synchronized void setSize (int *size*) |
| size() | public int size() |
| trimToSize() | public void trimToSize() |

capacity() returns the capacity of the invoking Vector object.

ensureCapacity() adjusts the capacity of the invoking Vector object, if necessary, to ensure that it can hold at least minimumSize objects.

setSize() sets the minimum number of elements of the invoking Vector object.

size() returns the size of the invoking Vector object, that is, how many elements are in it.

trimToSize() sets the capacity equal to the size.

## set() Method

| Method | Syntax |
|---|---|
| set() | public Object set(int *index*, Object *obj*) |

set() replaces the element at position index in the invoking Vector object with the Object obj.

## toArray() Method

| Method | Syntax |
|---|---|
| toArray() | public Object[] toArray() |
| | public Object[] toArray(Object[] *array*) |

toArray() returns an Object array containing either all of the elements of the invoking Vector object (if the first version is used), or those elements of the invoking Vector object that match the elements in array.

## toString() Method

| Method | Syntax |
|---|---|
| toString() | public String toString() |

toString() returns a String representation of the invoking Vector object containing a String representation of each element.

## Example: Using Vector

This example creates a Vector object, adds four elements to it, inserts an additional element, and prints its size and contents. One element is changed and another removed, and the Vector object's size, capacity and contents are printed. The capacity of the Vector can be greater than the number of elements it contains.

```java
import java.util.*;

public class TestVector {
  public static void main(String args[]) {
    Vector v = new Vector();

    v.addElement("Lisa");
    v.addElement("Jackson");
    v.addElement("Zachary");
    v.addElement("Mark");

    v.insertElementAt("Ryan", 3);
    System.out.println("size of v is " + v.size());
    System.out.println("contents of v are " + v);

    String str = "Jackson";
    int index = v.indexOf(str);
    System.out.println(str + " is at index " + index);

    v.setElementAt("Julia", 2);
    v.removeElement("Mark");
    System.out.println("size of v is now " + v.size());
    System.out.println("the capacity of v is now " + v.capacity());
    System.out.println("contents of v are now " + v);
  }
}
```

### Output

```
size of v is 5
contents of v are [Lisa, Jackson, Zachary, Ryan, Mark]
Jackson is at index 1
size of v is now 4
the capacity of v is now 10
contents of v are now [Lisa, Jackson, Julia, Ryan]
```

# 3.4 Map Interfaces

A `Map` is an object that stores a series of key/value pairs. The map interfaces define the methods that are available to the map classes. The map interface hierarchy is shown in the following figure.

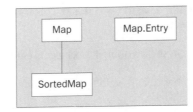

# 3.4.1 Map Interface

`public interface Map`

The `Map` interface provides the methods for assembling, modifying, and manipulating a `Map` object. The methods in the `Map` interface are declared `abstract` which means the implementation of the methods is performed by classes that implement the `Map` interface.

## Methods to Add Elements to a Map Object

| Method | Syntax |
|---|---|
| put() | public Object put(Object *key*, Object *value*) |
| putAll() | public void putAll(Map *m*) |

`put()` adds a key-value pair to the invoking `Map` object. If the `key` object already existed, the `value` passed as an argument overwrites the previous value and the previous value is returned.

`putAll()` adds the key-value entries from `Map m` into the invoking `Map` object.

## Methods to Examine the Contents of a Map Object

| Method | Syntax |
|---|---|
| containsKey() | public boolean containsKey(Object *key*) |
| containsValue() | public boolean containsValue(Object *value*) |
| equals() | public boolean equals(Object *obj*) |
| isEmpty() | public boolean isEmpty() |
| size() | public int size() |

`containsKey()` returns `true` if the invoking `Map` object contains the `key` object passed as an argument.

`containsValue()` returns `true` if the invoking `Map` object contains the `value` object passed as an argument.

`equals()` returns `true` if the `Object obj` is a `Map` object that contains the same entries as the invoking `Map` object.

`isEmpty()` returns `true` if the invoking `Map` object is empty.

`size()` returns the number of key/value pairs contained in the invoking `Map` object.

## get() Method

| Method | Syntax |
|--------|--------|
| get() | public Object get(Object *key*) |

`get()` returns the value object associated with the `key` object passed as an argument.

## hashCode() Method

| Method | Syntax |
|--------|--------|
| hashCode() | public int hashCode() |

`hashCode()` returns the hash code for the invoking `Map` object.

## Methods to Remove Elements from a Map Object

| Method | Syntax |
|--------|--------|
| clear() | public void clear() |
| remove() | public Object remove(Object key) |

`clear()` removes all of the elements of the invoking `Map` object.

`remove()` removes the element whose key is the `Object` passed as an argument and returns the removed value.

## Methods to Create a Collection or Set from a Map Object

| Method | Syntax |
|--------|--------|
| entrySet() | public Set entrySet() |
| keySet() | public Set keySet() |
| values() | public Collection values() |

entrySet() returns a Set object containing the entries from the invoking Map object. The entries are stored as Map.Entry objects.

keySet() returns a Set object containing the key objects from the invoking Map object.

values() returns a Collection object containing the value objects from the invoking Map object.

# 3.4.2 Map.Entry Interface

```
public interface Map.Entry
```

Map.Entry provides methods for manipulating Map.Entry objects. A Map.Entry object encapsulates a key-value pair used with a Map object.

## equals() Method

| Method | Syntax |
|--------|--------|
| equals() | public boolean equals(Object obj) |

equals() returns true if Object obj is a Map.Entry object with the same key-value pair as the invoking Map.Entry object.

## getKey() Method

| Method | Syntax |
|--------|--------|
| getKey() | public Object getKey() |

getKey() returns the key object for the invoking Map.Entry object.

## getValue() Method

| Method | Syntax |
|--------|--------|
| getValue() | public Object getValue() |

getValue() returns the value object for the invoking Map.Entry object.

## hashCode() Method

| Method | Syntax |
|--------|--------|
| hashCode() | public int hashCode() |

hashCode() returns the hash code for the invoking Map.Entry object.

3

java.util

## setValue() Method

| Method | Syntax |
|--------|--------|
| setValue() | public Object setValue(Object *value*) |

setValue() sets the value object for the invoking Map.Entry object and returns the previous value object.

# 3.4.3 SortedMap Interface

public interface SortedMap extends Map

    Map
       SortedMap

The SortedMap interface defines methods for a Map object where the entries are sorted in ascending key order. The entries need not be unique.

## comparator() Method

| Method | Syntax |
|--------|--------|
| comparator() | public Comparator comparator() |

comparator() returns the Comparator object associated with the invoking SortedMap object.

## firstKey() Method

| Method | Syntax |
|--------|--------|
| firstKey() | public Object firstKey() |

firstKey() returns the first key object of the invoking SortedMap object.

## lastKey() Method

| Method | Syntax |
|--------|--------|
| lastKey() | public Object lastKey() |

lastKey() returns the last key object of the invoking SortedMap object.

## Methods to Obtain a Sub-set of a SortedMap object

| Method | Syntax |
|--------|--------|
| headMap() | public SortedMap headMap(Object last) |
| subMap() | public SortedMap subMap(Object first, Object last) |
| tailMap() | public SortedMap tailMap(Object first) |

headMap() returns a sub-set of the invoking SortedMap object that starts with the first element and goes to object last.

subMap() returns a sub-set of the invoking SortedMap object that starts with object first and goes to object last.

tailMap() returns a sub-set of the invoking SortedMap object that starts object first and goes to the last element.

# 3.5 Map Classes

A Map object is used to store a series of key-value pairs. The map classes provide implementation of the map interfaces. The map class hierarchy is shown in the following figure. The AbstractMap class implements the methods declared in the Map interface. It is the super-class of the HashMap and TreeMap classes. The HashTable class represents a hash table that stores key-value pairs.

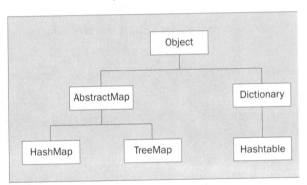

## 3.5.1 AbstractMap Class

```
public abstract class AbstractMap extends Object implements Map
```

```
Object
   AbstractMap
```

**Interfaces**

```
Map
```

The AbstractMap class implements the methods declared in the Map interface. It is the super-class of the HashMap and TreeMap classes.

## Methods to Add Elements to a Map Object

| Method | Syntax |
| --- | --- |
| put() | public Object put(Object *key*, Object *value*) |
| putAll() | public void putAll(Map *m*) |

put() adds a key-value pair to the invoking Map object. If the key object already existed, the value passed as an argument overwrites the previous value and the previous value is returned.

putAll() adds the key-value entries from Map m into the invoking Map object.

## Methods to Examine the Contents of a Map Object

| Method | Syntax |
| --- | --- |
| containsKey() | public boolean containsKey(Object *key*) |
| containsValue() | public boolean containsValue(Object *value*) |
| equals() | public boolean equals(Object *obj*) |
| isEmpty() | public boolean isEmpty() |
| size() | public int size() |

containsKey() returns true if the invoking Map object contains the key object passed as an argument.

containsValue() returns true if the invoking Map object contains the value object passed as an argument.

equals() returns true if the Object obj is a Map object that contains the same entries as the invoking Map object.

isEmpty() returns true if the invoking Map object is has no key-value pairs.

size() returns the number of key-value pairs contained in the invoking Map object .

## get() Method

| Method | Syntax |
| --- | --- |
| get() | public Object get(Object *key*) |

get() returns the value object associated with the key object passed as an argument.

## hashCode() Method

| Method | Syntax |
|--------|--------|
| hashCode() | public int hashCode() |

hashCode() returns the hash code for the invoking Map object.

## Methods to Remove Elements from a Map Object

| Method | Syntax |
|--------|--------|
| clear() | public void clear() |
| remove() | public Object remove(Object key) |

clear() removes all of the elements of the invoking Map object.

remove() removes the element whose key is the Object passed as an argument and returns the removed value.

## Methods to Create a Collection or Set from a Map Object

| Method | Syntax |
|--------|--------|
| entrySet() | public abstract Set entrySet() |
| keySet() | public Set keySet() |
| values() | public Collection values() |

entrySet() returns a Set object containing the entries from the invoking Map object. The entries are stored as Map.Entry objects.

keySet() returns a Set object containing the key objects from the invoking Map object.

values() returns a Collection object containing the value objects from the invoking Map object.

## toString() Method

| Method | Syntax |
|--------|--------|
| toString() | public String toString() |

toString() returns a String representation of the invoking Map object, consisting of a list of key-value pairs.

# 3.5.2 Dictionary Class

public abstract class **Dictionary** extends Object

```
Object
  Dictionary
```

The Dictionary class is the super-class of the Hashtable class. It has been made obsolete by the other branch of the map class hierarchy and is not discussed in detail.

# 3.5.3 HashMap Class

public class **HashMap** extends AbstractMap implements Map, Cloneable, Serializable

```
Object
  AbstractMap
    HashMap
```

### Interfaces

Cloneable, Serializable, Map

A HashMap object uses a hash table to implement the Map interface. The elements are not automatically sorted.

## HashMap() Constructor

| Constructor | Syntax |
|---|---|
| HashMap() | public HashMap() |
| | public HashMap(int *capacity*) |
| | public HashMap(int *capacity*, float *loadCapacity*) |
| | public HashMap(Map *m*) |

HashMap() creates a HashMap object. The HashMap object can be provided with an initial capacity, load capacity, and can be initialized with the elements from a Map object. The load capacity is a number between 0.0 and 1.0 indicates how full the HashMap object has to be before it is re-sized.

## Methods to Add Elements to a HashMap Object

| Method | Syntax |
|---|---|
| put() | public Object put(Object *key*, Object *value*) |
| putAll() | public void putAll(Map *m*) |

put() adds a key-value pair to the invoking HashMap object. If the key object already existed, the value passed as an argument overwrites the previous value and the previous value is returned.

putAll() adds the key-value entries from Map m into the invoking HashMap object.

# clone() Method

| Method | Syntax |
|--------|--------|
| clone() | public Object clone() |

clone() overrides the clone() method from the Object class to return a shallow copy of the invoking HashMap object.

# Methods to Examine the Contents of a HashMap Object

| Method | Syntax |
|--------|--------|
| containsKey() | public boolean containsKey(Object *key*) |
| containsValue() | public boolean containsValue(Object *value*) |
| isEmpty() | public boolean isEmpty() |
| size() | public int size() |

containsKey() returns true if the invoking HashMap object contains the key object passed as an argument.

containsValue() returns true if the invoking HashMap object contains the value object passed as an argument.

isEmpty() returns true if the invoking HashMap object has no key-value pairs.

size() returns the number of key-value pairs contained in the invoking HashMap object.

# get() Method

| Method | Syntax |
|--------|--------|
| get() | public Object get(Object *key*) |

get() returns the value object associated with the key object passed as an argument.

## Methods to Remove Elements from a HashMap Object

| Method | Syntax |
|---|---|
| clear() | public void clear() |
| remove() | public Object remove(Object *key*) |

clear() removes all of the elements of the invoking HashMap object.

remove() removes the element whose key is the Object passed as an argument and returns the removed value.

## Methods to Create a Collection or Set from a HashMap Object

| Method | Syntax |
|---|---|
| entrySet() | public Set entrySet() |
| keySet() | public Set keySet() |
| values() | public Collection values() |

entrySet() returns a Set object containing the entries from the invoking HashMap object. The entries are stored as Map.Entry objects.

keySet() returns a Set object containing the key objects from the invoking HashMap object.

values() returns a Collection object containing the value objects from the invoking HashMap object.

### Example: Using HashMap

In this example, a HashMap object is created that contains customer's account numbers. The containsKey() method is then used to retrieve details of a customer's account.

```
import java.util.*;

public class TestHashMap {
  public static void main(String args[]) {
    HashMap hm = new HashMap(5);

    hm.put("Jackson Palmer", new Integer(1051));
    hm.put("Lisa Reid", new Integer(5678));
    hm.put("Cheryl Spada", new Integer(2345));
```

```
        System.out.println("size of HashMap is " + hm.size());

        String str = "Jackson Palmer";

        if (hm.containsKey(str)) {
          System.out.println(str + "'s account number is " + hm.get(str));
        }
      }
    }
```

Another way to process the information would be with the entrySet() method and an Iterator object. The Iterator interface is discussed in Section 3.2.3.

**Output**

```
size of HashMap is 3
Jackson Palmer's account number is 1051
```

# 3.5.4 Hashtable Class

```
public class Hashtable extends Dictionary implements Map, Cloneable,
  Serializable

Object
  Dictionary
    Hashtable
```

### Interfaces

```
Cloneable, Map, Serializable
```

A Hashtable object is an earlier (Java 1.1) implementation of a hash table that stores key-value pairs. It has been updated in Java 1.2 to implement the Map interface.

## Hashtable() Constructor

| Constructor | Syntax |
|---|---|
| Hashtable() | public Hashtable() |
| | public Hashtable(int *initialSize*) |
| | public Hashtable(int *initialSize*, int *loadCapacity*) |
| | public Hashtable(Map *m*) |

Hashtable object constructor. It is possible to provide the constructor with an initial capacity, load capacity, and initialize it with the elements from a Map object. The load capacity is a number between 0.0 and 1.0 indicates how full the Hashtable object has to be before it is re-sized.

## Methods to Add Elements to a HashTable Object

| Method | Syntax |
| --- | --- |
| put() | public Object put(Object *key*, Object *value*) |
| putAll() | public void putAll(Map *m*) |

put() adds a key-value pair to the invoking HashTable object. If the key object already existed, the value passed as an argument overwrites the previous value and the previous value is returned.

putAll() adds the key-value entries from Map m into the invoking HashTable object.

## clone() Method

| Method | Syntax |
| --- | --- |
| clone() | public Object clone() |

clone() overrides the clone() method from the Object class to return a shallow copy of the invoking HashTable object.

## equals() Method

| Method | Syntax |
| --- | --- |
| equals() | public boolean equals(Object *obj*) |

equals() overrides the equals() method from the Object class and returns true if Object obj is a HashTable with the same elements as the invoking HashTable object.

## hashCode() Method

| Method | Syntax |
| --- | --- |
| hashCode() | public int hashCode() |

hashCode() returns the hash code for the invoking HashTable object.

## Methods to Examine the Contents of a HashTable Object

| Method | Syntax |
| --- | --- |
| contains() | public boolean contains(Object *value*) |
| containsKey() | public boolean containsKey(Object *key*) |
| containsValue() | public boolean containsValue(Object *value*) |
| isEmpty() | public boolean isEmpty() |
| size() | public int size() |

contains() returns true if the invoking HashTable object contains the value object passed as an argument.

containsKey() returns true if the invoking HashTable object contains the key object passed as an argument.

containsValue() returns true if the invoking HashTable object contains the value object passed as an argument.

isEmpty() returns true if the invoking HashTable object is has no key-value pairs.

size() returns the number of keys in the invoking HashTable object.

## get() Method

| Method | Syntax |
| --- | --- |
| get() | public Object get(Object *key*) |

get() returns the value object associated with the key object passed as an argument.

## Methods to Remove Elements from a HashTable Object

| Method | Syntax |
| --- | --- |
| clear() | public void clear() |
| remove() | public Object remove(Object *key*) |

clear() removes all of the elements of the invoking HashTable object.

remove() removes the element whose key is the Object passed as an argument and returns the removed value.

## Methods to Create a Collection or Set from a HashTable Object

| Method | Syntax |
|---|---|
| entrySet() | public Set entrySet() |
| keySet() | public Set keySet() |
| values() | public Collection values() |

entrySet() returns a Set object containing the entries from the invoking HashTable object. The entries are stored as Map.Entry objects.

keySet() returns a Set object containing the key objects from the invoking HashTable object.

values() returns a Collection object containing the value objects from the invoking HashTable object.

## toString() Method

| Method | Syntax |
|---|---|
| toString() | public String toString() |

toString() returns a String representation of the invoking Map object consisting of a list of keys and associated elements.

### Example: Using HashTable

In this example, a Hashtable object is created that contains customer's account numbers. The containsKey() method is used to search for a particular customer.

```
import java.util.*;

public class TestHashtable {
    public static void main(String args[]) {
        Hashtable ht = new Hashtable();

        ht.put("Jackson Palmer", new Integer(1051));
        ht.put("Lisa Reid", new Integer(5678));
        ht.put("Cheryl Spada", new Integer(2345));

        System.out.println("size of Hashtable is " + ht.size());

        String str = "Jackson Palmer";
```

```
        if (ht.containsKey(str)) {
            System.out.println(str + "'s account number is " + ht.get(str));
        }
    }
}
```

Another way to process the information would be with the entrySet() method and an Iterator object. The Iterator class is discussed in Section 3.2.3 on page 205.

**Output**

```
size of Hashtable is 3
Jackson Palmer's account number is 1051
```

# 3.5.5 TreeMap Class

```
public class TreeMap extends AbstractMap
    implements SortedMap, Cloneable, Serializable
```

```
Object
    AbstractMap
        TreeMap
```

### Interfaces

```
Cloneable, Map, Serializable, SortedMap
```

A TreeMap object implements the Map interface using a tree structure. The elements are sorted by keys according to some logical order (alphabetically, for instance).

## TreeMap() Constructor

| Constructor | Syntax |
|---|---|
| TreeMap() | public TreeMap() |
| | public TreeMap(Comparator c) |
| | public TreeMap(Map m) |
| | public TreeMap(SortedMap sm) |

TreeMap() creates a TreeMap object. The TreeMap object can be given a Comparator object or it can be initialized using the elements of a Map or SortedMap object.

## Methods to Add Elements to a TreeMap Object

| Method | Syntax |
| --- | --- |
| put() | public Object put(Object *key*, Object *value*) |
| putAll() | public void putAll(Map *m*) |

put() adds a key-value pair to the invoking TreeMap object. If the key object already existed, the value passed as an argument overwrites the previous value and the previous value is returned.

putAll() adds the key-value entries from Map m into the invoking TreeMap object.

## clone() Method

| Method | Syntax |
| --- | --- |
| clone() | public Object clone() |

clone() overrides the clone() method from the Object class to return a shallow copy of the invoking TreeMap object.

## comparator() Method

| Method | Syntax |
| --- | --- |
| comparator() | public Comparator comparator() |

comparator() returns the Comparator associated with the invoking TreeMap object.

## Methods to Examine the Contents of a TreeMap Object

| Method | Syntax |
| --- | --- |
| containsKey() | public boolean containsKey(Object *key*) |
| containsValue() | public boolean containsValue(Object *value*) |
| size() | public int size() |

containsKey() returns true if the invoking TreeMap object contains the key object passed as an argument.

containsValue() returns true if the invoking TreeMap object contains the value object passed as an argument.

size() returns the number of key-value pairs contained in the invoking TreeMap object.

## Methods to Return Elements of a TreeMap

| Method | Syntax |
|--------|--------|
| get() | public Object get(Object *key*) |
| firstKey() | public Object firstKey() |
| lastKey() | public Object lastKey() |

get() returns the value object associated with the key object passed as an argument.

firstKey() returns the first, or lowest, key from the invoking TreeMap object.

lastKey() returns the last, or highest, key from the invoking TreeMap object.

## Methods to Remove Elements from a TreeMap Object

| Method | Syntax |
|--------|--------|
| clear() | public void clear() |
| remove() | public Object remove(Object *key*) |

clear() removes all of the elements of the invoking TreeMap object.

remove() removes the element whose key is the Object passed as an argument and returns the removed value.

## Methods to Create a Collection, Set, or Map from a TreeMap Object

| Method | Syntax |
|--------|--------|
| entrySet() | public Set entrySet() |
| headMap() | public SortedMap headMap(Object *toKey*) |
| keySet() | public Set keySet() |
| subMap() | public SortedMap subMap(Object *startKey*, Object *endKey*) |
| tailMap() | public SortedMap tailMap(Object *startKey*) |
| values() | public Collection values() |

entrySet() returns a Set object containing the entries from the invoking TreeMap object. The entries are stored as Map.Entry objects.

headMap() returns a SortedMap object containing the entries from the invoking TreeMap object whose keys are less than the Object toKey.

keySet() returns a Set object containing the key objects from the invoking HashMap object.

subMap() returns a SortedMap object that is a subset of the invoking TreeMap object from startKey to endKey.

tailMap() returns a SortedMap object containing the entries from the invoking TreeMap object whose keys are greater than or equal to the Object startKey.

values() returns a Collection object containing the value objects from the invoking HashMap object.

## Example: Using TreeMap

In this example, a TreeMap object is created that contains customer's account numbers. The containsKey() method is used to search for a particular customer.

```
import java.util.*;

public class TestTreeMap {
  public static void main(String args[]) {
    TreeMap tm = new TreeMap();

    tm.put("Jackson Palmer", new Integer(1051));
    tm.put("Lisa Reid", new Integer(5678));
    tm.put("Cheryl Spada", new Integer(2345));

    System.out.println("size of TreeMap is " + tm.size());

    String str = "Jackson Palmer";

    if (tm.containsKey(str)) {
      System.out.println(str + "'s account number is " + tm.get(str));
    }
  }
}
```

Another way to process the information would be with the entrySet() method and an Iterator object. The Iterator interface is discussed in Section 3.2.3 on page 205.

### Output

```
size of TreeMap is 3
Jackson Palmer's account number is 1051
```

# 3.6 Other Classes

## 3.6.1 Arrays Class

```
public class Arrays extends Object
```

```
Object
    Arrays
```

The Arrays class provides static methods for searching through, comparing, filling, or sorting arrays. The methods are overloaded to provide implementations for all primitive datatypes as well as Objects. Since all of the methods are static, they can be accessed directly. The Arrays class has no constructors.

### asList() Method

| Method | Syntax |
| --- | --- |
| asList() | public static List asList(Object[] array) |

asList() returns a List object that points to the same reference as the Object array.

### binarySearch() Method

| Method | Syntax |
| --- | --- |
| binarySearch() | public static int binarySearch(byte[] array, byte value) |
| | public static int binarySearch(char[] array, char value) |
| | public static int binarySearch(double[] array, double value) |
| | public static int binarySearch(float[] array, float value) |
| | public static int binarySearch(int[] array, int value) |
| | public static int binarySearch(long[] array, long value) |
| | public static int binarySearch(short[] array, short value) |
| | public static int binarySearch(Object[] array, Object value) |
| | public static int binarySearch(Object[] array, Object value, Comparator c) |

binarySearch() searches an array for a given value, returning the index in the array if the value occurs, or a negative integer if the array does not contain the value. The Object versions throw a ClassCastException if the array type and value type are incompatible.

### Example: Using binarySearch()

The binarySearch() method is used to search an int array for the value 11.

```
import java.util.*;

public class TestArraysSearch {
  public static void main(String args[]) {
    int[] intArray = {
      0, 1, 2, 3, 4
    };

    int i = 11;
    int index = Arrays.binarySearch(intArray, i);
    if (index >= 0) {
      System.out.println("value " + i + " is at index " + index);
    } else {
      System.out.println("array does not contain value " + i);
    }
  }
}
```

**Output**

```
array does not contain value 11
```

## equals() Method

| Method | Syntax |
|---|---|
| equals() | public static boolean equals(byte[] *array1*, byte[] *array2*) |
| | public static boolean equals(char[] *array1*, char[] *array2*) |
| | public static boolean equals(double[] *array1*, double[] *array2*) |
| | public static boolean equals(float[] *array1*, float[] *array2*) |

| Method | Syntax |
|--------|--------|
| | public static boolean **equals**(int[] *array1*, int[] *array2*) |
| | public static boolean **equals**(long[] *array1*, long[] *array2*) |
| | public static boolean **equals**(short[] *array1*, short[] *array2*) |
| | public static boolean **equals**(Object[] *array1*, Object[] *array2*) |

equals() returns true if array1 is equal to array2.

## Example: Using equals()

The equals() method is used to compare two String arrays. The comparison is case-sensitive. In this example, the arrays are different.

```
import java.util.*;

public class TestArraysEquals {
  public static void main(String args[]) {
    String[] array1 = {
      "Jackson", "Zachary", "Ryan"
    };
    String[] array2 = {
      "jackson", "Zachary", "Ryan"
    };

    if (Arrays.equals(array1, array2)) {
      System.out.println("arrays are equal");
    } else {
      System.out.println("arrays are different");
    }
  }
}
```

*Output*

```
arrays are different
```

# fill() Method

| Method | Syntax |
|--------|--------|
| fill() | public static void fill(boolean[] *array*, boolean *value*) |
| | public static void fill(boolean[] *array*,<br>    int *startIndex*, int *endIndex*, boolean *value*) |
| | public static void fill(byte[] *array*, byte *value*) |
| | public static void fill(byte[] *array*,<br>    int *startIndex*, int *endIndex*, byte *value*) |
| | public static void fill(char[] *array*, char *value*) |
| | public static void fill(char[] *array*,<br>    int *startIndex*, int *endIndex*, char *value*) |
| | public static void fill(double[] *array*, double *value*) |
| | public static void fill(double[] *array*,<br>    int *startIndex*, int *endIndex*, double *value*) |
| | public static void fill(float[] *array*, float *value*) |
| | public static void fill(float[] *array*,<br>    int *startIndex*, int *endIndex*, float *value*) |
| | public static void fill(int[] *array*, int *value*) |
| | public static void fill(int[] *array*,<br>    int *startIndex*, int *endIndex*, int *value*) |
| | public static void fill(long[] *array*, long *value*) |
| | public static void fill(long[] *array*,<br>    int *startIndex*, int *endIndex*, long *value*) |
| | public static void fill(short[] *array*, short *value*) |
| | public static void fill(short[] *array*,<br>    int *startIndex*, int *endIndex*, short *value*) |
| | public static void fill(Object[] *array*, Object *value*) |
| | public static void fill(Object[] *array*,<br>    int *startIndex*, int *endIndex*, Object *value*) |

fill() fills a given array with a given value. They can either fill the entire array with the value, or a part between a starting and ending index. fill() is useful for initializing arrays.

## Example: Using fill()

In this example, a `double` array is initialized with the value `0.0`.

```
import java.util.*;

public class TestArraysFills {
  public static void main(String args[]) {
    double[] doubleArray = new double[5];

    Arrays.fill(doubleArray, 0.0);
    for (int i = 0; i < doubleArray.length; ++i) {
      System.out.println("index: " + i + " value: " + doubleArray[i]);
    }
  }
}
```

### Output

```
index: 0 value: 0.0
index: 1 value: 0.0
index: 2 value: 0.0
index: 3 value: 0.0
index: 4 value: 0.0
```

# sort() Method

| Method | Syntax |
|---|---|
| sort() | public static void **sort**(byte[] *array*) |
| | public static void **sort**(byte[] *array*, int *startIndex*, int *endIndex*) |
| | public static void **sort**(char[] *array*) |
| | public static void **sort**(char[] *array*, int *startIndex*, int *endIndex*) |
| | public static void **sort**(double[] *array*) |
| | public static void **sort**(double[] *array*, int *startIndex*, int *endIndex*) |
| | public static void **sort**(float[] *array*) |
| | public static void **sort**(float[] *array*, int *startIndex*, int *endIndex*) |
| | public static void **sort**(int[] *array*) |

| Method | Syntax |
|--------|--------|
| | `public static void sort(int[] array, int startIndex,`<br>`    int endIndex)` |
| | `public static void sort(long[] array)` |
| | `public static void sort(long[] array, int startIndex,`<br>`    int endIndex)` |
| | `public static void sort(short[] array)` |
| | `public static void sort(short[] array, int startIndex,`<br>`    int endIndex)` |
| | `public static void sort(Object[] array)` |
| | `public static void sort(Object[] array, Comparator c)` |
| | `public static void sort(Object[] array, int startIndex,`<br>`    int endIndex)` |
| | `public static void sort(Object[] array, int startIndex,`<br>`    int endIndex, Comparator c)` |

`sort()` sorts a given array. It can either sort the entire array, or a section between a starting and ending index. The versions to sort `Object` arrays can be given a `Comparator` object.

## Example: Using sort()

In this example, an `int` array is sorted using the `sort()` method. The default comparator sorts the elements in ascending numerical order.

```
import java.util.*;

public class TestArraysSort {
  public static void main(String args[]) {
    int[] intArray = {
      12, 0, -5, 3, 37
    };

    Arrays.sort(intArray);
    for (int i = 0; i < intArray.length; ++i) {
      System.out.println("index: " + i + " value: " + intArray[i]);
    }
  }
}
```

***Output***

```
index: 0 value: -5
index: 1 value: 0
index: 2 value: 3
index: 3 value: 12
index: 4 value: 37
```

# 3.6.2 EventListener Interface

```
public interface EventListener
```

EventListener is the parent of all event listener interfaces. It defines no methods but is used as a marker to indicate that the interface that extends EventListener is a listener interface.

# 3.6.3 EventObject Class

```
public class EventObject extends Object implements Serializable
```

```
Object
    EventObject
```

**Interfaces**

```
Serializable
```

EventObject is the super-class of all other event classes under the Java 1.1 event model, in particular the AWTEvent class. (See Section 6.4.1 on page 502.) It provides the getSource() and toString() methods that are common to all of its sub-classes.

## EventObject() Constructor

| Constructor | Syntax |
|---|---|
| EventObject() | public EventObject(Object *source*) |

EventObject constructor. The Object source is the object that generates the event.

## getSource() Method

| Method | Syntax |
|---|---|
| getSource() | public Object getSource() |

getSource() returns the Object that generated the invoking EventObject.

## toString() Method

| Method | Syntax |
|---|---|
| toString() | public String toString() |

toString() returns a String representation of the invoking EventObject.

### Example: Using EventObject

The purpose of this example is to demonstrate the use of the EventObject class methods. An EventObject is created with the String str as its source. If the programmer really wanted to have the String generate an event, an EventObject sub-class or a user-defined event object would probably be used.

```
import java.util.*;

public class TestEvent {
  public static void main(String args[]) {
    String str = "Jackson";

    EventObject evtObj = new EventObject(str);

    System.out.println("" + evtObj.getSource()
                       + " generated the event");
    System.out.println("the event is: " + evtObj.toString());
  }
}
```

#### Output

```
Jackson generated the event
the event is: java.util.EventObject[source=Jackson]
```

# 3.6.4 Random Class

```
public class Random extends Object implements Serializable
```

```
Object
  Random
```

### Interfaces

```
Serializable
```

The Random class is a generator of pseudo-random numbers. The Random object can be initialized with a 'seed' that represents the starting point for the random number sequence. Two Random objects that are given the same seed will produce the same random number sequence if the same sequence of method calls is made for each.

# Random() Constructor

| Constructor | Syntax |
|---|---|
| Random() | public Random() |
| | public Random(long *seed*) |

Random() creates a Random object. If no arguments are given, the current time is used as the seed.

# Methods That Return Random Numbers

| Method | Syntax |
|---|---|
| nextBoolean() | public boolean nextBoolean() |
| nextByte() | public void nextBytes(byte[] *bytes*) |
| nextDouble() | public double nextDouble() |
| nextFloat() | public float nextFloat() |
| nextGaussian() | public double nextGaussian() |
| nextInt() | public int nextInt() |
| | public int nextInt(int n) |
| nextLong() | public long nextLong() |

nextBoolean() returns a random boolean value.

nextByte() fills the bytes array with random bytes.

nextDouble() and nextFloat() return random double or float values between 0.0 and 1.0.

nextGaussian() method returns a double value between -1.0 and 1.0. The values returned by nextGaussian() follow a Gaussian distribution.

nextInt() and nextLong() return a random int or long value; all possible values are returned with approximately equal probability. If nextInt() is provided an int argument, the random numbers will be generated between 0 and that value.

## Example: Using Random

In this example. a Random object is created and used to generate five random double values. The double values are between 0.0 and 1.0.

```
import java.util.*;

public class TestRandom {
  public static void main(String args[]) {
    Random r = new Random();

    for (int i = 0; i < 5; ++i) {
      System.out.println("Random number: " + r.nextDouble());
    }
  }
}
```

**Output** *(results will vary)*
```
Random number: 0.220089746561387
Random number: 0.843571856141599
Random number: 0.650569810984363
Random number: 0.141231128761591
Random number: 0.875817389185762
```

## setSeed() Method

| Method | Syntax |
|--------|--------|
| setSeed() | public void setSeed(long *seed*) |

setSeed() sets the invoking Random object's seed value.

## Example: Using setSeed()

Two Random objects are created and given the same seed, so they will produce the same sequence of random numbers. Then the setSeed() method changes the seed of the r2 object. Now the two Random objects produce different numbers.

```
import java.util.*;

public class TestRandomSeed {
  public static void main(String args[]) {
    long seed = System.currentTimeMillis();
    Random r1 = new Random(seed);
```

```
        Random r2 = new Random(seed);

        r2.setSeed(seed + 2);

        for (int i = 0; i < 5; ++i) {
          System.out.println("Random number1: " + r1.nextDouble()
                          + " Random number2: " + r2.nextDouble());
        }
      }
    }
```

**Output** *(results will vary)*

```
Random number1: 0.33237567166 Random number2: 0.32891177814
Random number1: 0.12124658917 Random number2: 0.56392417667
Random number1: 0.50609482343 Random number2: 0.17739282711
Random number1: 0.46515132323 Random number2: 0.19179716252
Random number1: 0.03627161616 Random number2: 0.10427161617
```

# 3.6.4 ResourceBundle Class

```
public abstract class ResourceBundle extends Object
```

```
Object
    ResourceBundle
```

This is an abstract class that represents a set of localized data. A ResourceBundle
object contains a set of keys/values pairs that define the resources for a particular
application. It is a way of importing language specific values using language
unspecific keys. One use of a ResourceBundle is to create a flexible GUI for an
application that can easily switch the display language.

## getBundle() Method

| Method | Syntax |
|---|---|
| getBundle() | public static ResourceBundle **getBundle**(String *baseName*) throws MissingResourceException |
| | public static ResourceBundle **getBundle**(String *baseName*, Locale *l*) throws MissingResourceException |
| | public static ResourceBundle **getBundle**(String *baseName*, Locale *l*, ClassLoader *cl*) throws MissingResourceException |

getBundle() finds or constructs the appropriate ResourceBundle sub-class object. It searches for a class or property file with the base name plus whatever locale information is provided.

## getKeys() Method

| Method | Syntax |
|--------|--------|
| getKeys() | public abstract Enumeration getKeys() |

getKeys() returns an Enumeration containing the keys. This method is intended to be overridden by ResourceBundle sub-classes.

## handleGetObject() Method

| Method | Syntax |
|--------|--------|
| handleGetObject() | protected abstract Object handleGetObject (String *key*) throws MissingResourceException |

handleGetObject() returns the resource associated with the argument key as an Object. This method is called by the getObject(), getString(), and getStringArray() methods. Sub-classes of ResourceBundle must provide an implementation of this method.

## getLocale() Method

| Method | Syntax |
|--------|--------|
| getLocale() | public Locale getLocale() |

getLocale() returns the Locale object associated with the invoking ResourceBundle sub-classes.

## getObject() Method

| Method | Syntax |
|--------|--------|
| getObject() | public final Object getObject(String *key*) throws MissingResourceException |

getObject() returns the resource associated with the argument key as an Object.

## getString() Method

| Method | Syntax |
|--------|--------|
| getString() | public final String getString(String *key*) throws MissingResourceException |

getString()returns the resource associated with the argument key as an String.

# getStringArray() Method

| Method | Syntax |
|--------|--------|
| getStringArray() | public final String[] getStringArray(String *key*) throws MissingResourceException |

getStringArray() returns the resource associated with the argument key as an String array.

## Example: Using ResourceBundle

This example creates two ResourceBundle objects: one, Colors_en, that returns values in English and one, Colors_fr, that returns values in French. The two ResourceBundle objects have the same keys, "red" and "black". The ResourceBundle objects must implement the handleGetObject() and getKeys() methods and be publicly accessible to the driver program.

The driver program, TestResBundle, retrieves the English and French ResourceBundle objects, and obtains and prints the words for "red" in each language.

This example is contained in three separate source files. To run it, compile all three programs and then type javac TestResBundle.

### TestResBundle class

```
import java.util.*;

public class TestResBundle {
    public static void main(String args[]) {
        ResourceBundle rb =
            ResourceBundle.getBundle("Colors", Locale.ENGLISH);
        String str = rb.getString("red");
        System.out.println("In English, red is " + str);

        rb = ResourceBundle.getBundle("Colors", Locale.FRENCH);
        str = rb.getString("red");
        System.out.println("In French, red is " + str);
    }
}
```

### Colors_en class

```
import java.util.*;

public class Colors_en extends ResourceBundle {
    protected Object handleGetObject(String key) {
        if (key.equals("red"))
            return "Red";
        if (key.equals("black"))
            return "Black";
        return null;
    }

    public Enumeration getKeys() {
        Vector v = new Vector();
        v.addElement("red");
        v.addElement("black");
        return v.elements();
    }
}
```

### Colors_fr class

```
import java.util.*;

public class Colors_fr extends ResourceBundle {
    protected Object handleGetObject(String key) {
        if (key.equals("red"))
            return "Rouge";
        if (key.equals("black"))
            return "Noir";
        return null;
    }

    public Enumeration getKeys() {
        Vector v = new Vector();
        v.addElement("red");
        v.addElement("black");
        return v.elements();
    }
}
```

### Output

```
In English, red is Red
In French, red is Rouge
```

# 3.6.5 StringTokenizer Class

public class **StringTokenizer** extends Object implements Enumeration

```
Object
    StringTokenizer
```

### Interfaces
Enumeration

This class implements a simple string tokenizer that breaks up a String object into tokens (sub-strings) based on a delimiter. The default delimiter is whitespace. A StringTokenizer object is useful for extracting a number from a String containing both text and numbers.

A StringTokenizer object can be used to search a String for a keyword.

## StringTokenizer() Constructor

| Constructor | Syntax |
|---|---|
| StringTokenizer() | public **StringTokenizer**(String *str*) |
| | public **StringTokenizer**(String *str*, String *delim*) |
| | public **StringTokenizer**(String *str*, String *delim*, boolean *returnDelims*) |

StringTokenizer() creates a StringTokenizer object. The String str is the String object to be parsed. The constructor assigns the characters in the String delim to be the delimiters. If returnDelims is true, the delimiters are returned as tokens.

## countTokens() Method

| Method | Syntax |
|---|---|
| countTokens() | public int countTokens() |

countTokens() returns the number of tokens left in the String.

## hasMoreElements() Method

| Method | Syntax |
|---|---|
| hasMoreElements() | public boolean hasMoreElements() |

hasMoreElements() returns true if there are more tokens left in the String.

## hasMoreTokens() Method

| Method | Syntax |
|--------|--------|
| hasMoreTokens() | public boolean hasMoreTokens() |

hasMoreTokens() returns true if there are more tokens left in the String.

## nextElement() Method

| Method | Syntax |
|--------|--------|
| nextElement() | public Object nextElement()<br>    throws NoSuchElementException |

nextElement() returns the next token as an Object. This method throws a NoSuchElementException if there are no more elements.

## nextToken() Method

| Method | Syntax |
|--------|--------|
| nextToken() | public String nextToken()<br>public String nextToken(String *delimiter*) |

nextToken() returns the next token; passing a delimiter temporarily changes the delimiter. This method throws a NoSuchElementException if there are no more elements.

### Example: Using StringTokenizer

In this example a StringTokenizer object is used to parse a String and extract the substring "Halibut".

```
import java.util.*;

public class TestStrTok {
  public static void main(String args[]) {
    String request = "I want Halibut for dinner";
    String fish;

    StringTokenizer stringParse = new StringTokenizer(request);

    try {
      while (stringParse.hasMoreTokens()) {
        fish = stringParse.nextToken();
```

```
            if (fish.equals("Halibut")) {
                System.out.println(fish);
            }
        }
    } catch (NoSuchElementException e) {
        System.out.println(e);
    }
    }
}
```

**Output**

```
Halibut
```

# 3.6.6 Timer Class

```
public class Timer extends Object
```

```
Object
    Timer
```

The Timer class provides the ability for threads to schedule a task for future execution in a background thread. The task can be executed once or repeated at a specified interval.

## Timer() Constructor

| Constructor | Syntax |
|---|---|
| Timer() | public Timer() |
| | public Timer(boolean *isDaemon*) |

Timer() creates a Timer object. The associated thread may be specified to run as a daemon.

## cancel() Method

| Method | Syntax |
|---|---|
| cancel() | public void cancel() |

cancel() terminates the timer and any scheduled tasks. Once this method has been called, no more tasks may be scheduled on the invoking Timer object.

## schedule() Method

| Method | Syntax |
|--------|--------|
| schedule() | public void schedule(TimerTask task, Date time) |
| | public void schedule(TimerTask task, Date firstTime, long millisecondInterval) |
| | public void schedule(TimerTask task, long millisecondDelay) |
| | public void schedule(TimerTask task, long millisecondDelay, long millisecondInterval) |

schedule() schedules a task for execution.

❑ The first version executes the task one time at the specified Date.

❑ The second version executes the task on a fixed time interval starting at the specified Date.

❑ The third version executes the task after the specified delay.

❑ The fourth version executes the task on a fixed time interval after the specified delay.

The versions that repeat the task do so on a fixed-delay. The period between execution depends on when the previous task actually executed. The execution of the previous task may be delayed by other background activity.

## scheduleAtFixedRate() Method

| Method | Syntax |
|--------|--------|
| scheduleAtFixedRate() | public void scheduleAtFixedRate(TimerTask *task*, Date *firstTime*, long *millisecondInterval*) |
| | public void scheduleAtFixedRate(TimerTask *task*, long *millisecondDelay*, long *millisecondInterval*) |

scheduleAtFixedRate() executes a task according to a fixed-rate. Subsequent tasks are scheduled according to when the task executed for the first time.

### Example: Using Timer

See the *Using TimerTask* example on page 286.

# 3.6.7 TimerTask Class

```
public abstract class TimerTask extends Object implements Runnable
```

```
Object
    TimerTask
```

### Interfaces
```
Runnable
```

The `TimerTask` class represents a task that can be scheduled for a one-time or repeated execution, and is used in conjunction with the `Timer` class. It must be sub-classed to create a concrete class that can be used with a `Timer` object. Since the `TimerTask` class implements the `Runnable` interface, the user-defined sub-class must provide an implementation of the `run()` method.

## TimerTask() Constructor

| Method | Syntax |
|---|---|
| TimerTask() | protected TimerTask() |

`TimerTask()` creates a `TimerTask` object.

## cancel() Method

| Method | Syntax |
|---|---|
| cancel() | public boolean cancel() |

`cancel()` terminates the task. It returns `true` if it successfully prevented the `TimerTask` object from executing one or more times.

## run() Method

| Method | Syntax |
|---|---|
| run() | public abstract void run() |

`run()` contains whatever code is to be executed by the task.

## scheduledExecutionTime() Method

| Method | Syntax |
|---|---|
| scheduledExecutionTime() | public long scheduledExecutionTime() |

`scheduledExecutionTime()` returns the time of the most recent execution of the task.

## Example: Using TimerTask

In this example, a `TimerTask` object is created to execute a simple task, writing a `String` to standard output. A `Timer` object is created to execute the task every two seconds after a one second delay.

```
import java.util.*;

public class TestTimerTask {
    public static void main(String args[]) {
        Timer tmr = new Timer();
        tmr.schedule(new TimerTask(), 1000, 2000);
    }
}


class MyTask extends TimerTask {
    public MyTask() {
        super();
    }

    public void run() {
        System.out.println("Remember to walk Bailey");
    }
}
```

### Output

```
Remember to walk Bailey
Remember to walk Bailey
Remember to walk Bailey
Remember to walk Bailey
```
*(Continues until program is interrupted.)*

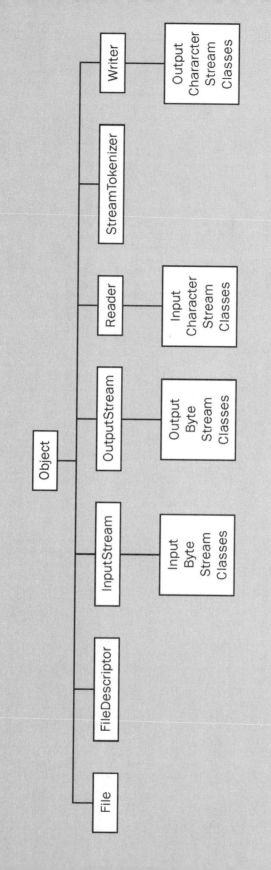

# java.io

Input and output in Java is handled through the use of streams. A stream represents a flow of data and is a logical entity that connects a data source with its destination. A stream is linked to a physical device by the Java I/O system. There are two ways to read and write data to a file in Java; the first uses **byte streams** and the second uses **character streams**.

Byte streams are based on 1 byte, or 8 bit, data. Byte streams can be used with any type of object but can not handle UNICODE characters. UNICODE is an international character set that represents the unification of dozens of charcter sets such as Latin, Greek, Cyrillic. Byte streams are generally used for byte and binary I/O. Byte streams are handled through InputStream, OutputStream, and derived classes.

Character streams are used to read and write characters. They are based on 2 byte, or 16 bit, data. Character streams are handled through Reader, Writer, and derived classes. Character streams provide the ability to handle any type of character I/O, including reading and writing UNICODE characters. Character streams are the logical choice when dealing with character or String data.

The java.io class hierarchy is shown in the figure opposite.

These I/O classes are contained in the java.io package, which must be imported.

All I/O exceptions must be caught, so I/O operations should be contained in a try block or declared using the throws keyword.

This chapter covers:

# 4.1 Byte Input Streams

The byte input stream classes are used to read byte data from an underlying stream. The byte-stream input stream class hierarchy is shown in the following figure.

InputStream is an abstract class that is the parent class of the input byte stream classes.

FileInputStream provides a mechanism for reading bytes sequentially from a file.

An ObjectInputStream object can be wrapped around an underlying InputStream object to provide the capability to read primitive datatypes, Strings, and binary data.

A BufferedInputStream object can be wrappred around an InputStream object to increase performance by allowing data to read into an intermediate buffer first.

A ByteArrayInputStream object reads a byte array from the input stream.

DataInputStream provides the ability to read primitive data from an input stream in a machine independent manner.

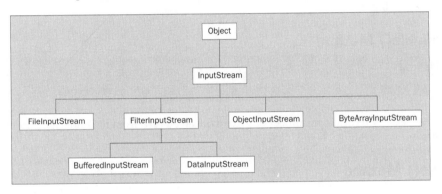

## 4.1.1 BufferedInputStream Class

```
public class BufferedInputStream extends FilterInputStream
```

```
Object
    InputStream
        FilterInputStream
            BufferedInputStream
```

A BufferedInputStream is an InputStream with a memory buffer that provides a more efficient way to read data. Instead of reading data byte by byte, a large number of bytes are first stored in an internal buffer. The higher level system functions then read the data from this buffer. This minimizes the number of times the disk must be accessed.

A BufferedInputStream object is usually wrapped around another input stream by passing a reference to the other stream to the BufferedInputStream constructor. This, in effect, turns the other input stream into a buffered stream.

## BufferedInputStream() Constructors

| Constructor | Syntax |
|---|---|
| BufferedInputStream() | public BufferedInputStream(InputStream *is*) |
|  | public BufferedInputStream(InputStream *is*, int *bufferSize*) |

BufferedInputStream() creates a BufferedInputStream object. Note that the constructor takes an InputStream object as an argument. One way to think of this is that the BufferedInputStream object is wrapped around the InputStream object to increase efficiency.

## available() Method

| Method | Syntax |
|---|---|
| available() | public int available() throws IOException |

available() returns the number of bytes that can be read from the underlying input stream.

## close() Method

| Method | Syntax |
|---|---|
| close() | public void close() throws IOException |

close() closes the invoking BufferedInputStream object and releases any resources allocated to it.

## read() Method

| Method | Syntax |
|---|---|
| read() | public int read() throws IOException |
|  | public int read(byte[] *byteBuffer*, int *offset*, int *numBytes*) throws IOException |

read() reads one or more bytes of input from input stream. The first version reads one byte of input and returns an integer representation of that byte. The second version reads numBytes bytes into the byte array byteBuffer starting at index offset and returns the number of bytes read. Both versions return -1 when the end of the stream is reached.

A BufferedInputStream object also has access to the read() method defined in the FilterInputStream class.

## Stream Position Methods

| Method | Syntax |
|---|---|
| mark() | public void **mark**(int *pastLimit*) |
| markSupported() | public boolean **markSupported**() |
| reset() | public void **reset**() throws IOException |
| skip() | public long **skip**(long *bytesToSkip*) throws IOException |

mark() sets a mark at the current position in the input stream. The pastLimit parameter is the number of bytes that can be read past the mark until the mark becomes invalid.

markSupported() returns true if the invoking BufferedInputStream object can be marked.

reset() returns the position of the BufferedInputStream object to that set by the mark() method.

skip() skips bytesToSkip bytes in the invoking BufferedInputStream object and returns the number of bytes skipped.

### Example: Reading Data From a File Using BufferedInputStream

The file jrr.txt contains the line "This is the contents of jrr.txt" followed by a line separator, and is contained in the same directory as the compiled .class file. The read() method, defined in the InputStream class, reads the data as a byte and converts it to an int. The data is printed out character by character using the print() method by casting the int to a char. The FileInputStream constructor can throw a FileNotFoundException. The read() method can throw an IOException, so the BufferedInputStream instantiation and the call to the read() method are contained in a try block.

```
        import java.io.*;

    public class TestBIS {
      public static void main(String args[]) {
        int c;

        try {
          BufferedInputStream bis =
            new BufferedInputStream(new FileInputStream("jrr.txt"));

            while ((c = bis.read()) != -1) {
            System.out.print((char) c);
            }
            bis.close();
          } catch (FileNotFoundException fnfe) {
          System.out.println(fnfe);
          } catch (IOException ioe) {
          System.out.println(ioe);
          }
        }
      }
```

**Output**

```
This is the contents of jrr.txt
```

# 4.1.2 ByteArrayInputStream Class

```
public class ByteArrayInputStream extends InputStream
```

```
Object
    InputStream
        ByteArrayInputStream
```

A ByteArrayInputStream object reads bytes from an input stream and places them in a byte array.

## ByteArrayInputStream() Constructors

| Constructor | Syntax |
|---|---|
| ByteArrayInputStream() | public ByteArrayInputStream(byte[] byteBuffer) |
| | public ByteArrayInputStream(byte[] byteBuffer, int offset, int numBytes) |

ByteArrayInputStream() creates a ByteArrayInputStream object. An initial offset and the number of bytes to be read can be specified.

# available() Method

| Method | Syntax |
|---|---|
| available() | public int available() |

available() returns the number of bytes that can be read from the input stream.

# close() Method

| Method | Syntax |
|---|---|
| close() | public void close() throws IOException |

close() closes the invoking ByteArrayInputStream object and releases any resources allocated to it.

# read() Method

| Method | Syntax |
|---|---|
| read() | public int read() |
| | public int read(byte[] byteBuffer,<br>                 int offset, int numBytes) |

read() reads one or more bytes of input from input stream. The first version reads one byte of input and returns an integer representation of that byte. The second version reads numBytes bytes into the byte array byteBuffer starting at index offset and returns the number of bytes read. Both versions return -1 when the end of the stream is reached.

A ByteArrayInputStream object also has access to the read() method defined in the InputStream class.

# Stream Position Methods

| Method | Syntax |
|---|---|
| mark() | public void mark(int pastLimit) |
| markSupported() | public boolean markSupported() |
| reset() | public void reset() |
| skip() | public long skip(long bytesToSkip) |

mark() sets a mark at the current position in the input stream. The pastLimit parameter is the number of bytes that can be read past the mark until the mark becomes invalid.

markSupported() returns true if the invoking ByteArrayInputStream object can be marked.

reset() returns the position of the ByteArrayInputStream object to that set by the mark() method.

skip() skips bytesToSkip bytes in the invoking ByteArrayInputStream object and returns the number of bytes skipped.

### Example: Using ByteArrayInputStream

See the *Using the Connectionless Protocol* example on page 375, where a ByteArrayInputStream is used in the ClientCLP class.

# 4.1.3 DataInput Interface

public abstract interface DataInput

The DataInput interface defines methods for reading primitive data types and Strings. The DataInput interface is implemented by the DataInputStream class and is the parent interface for the ObjectInput interface.

## Methods for Reading Primitive Datatypes

| Method | Syntax |
| --- | --- |
| readBoolean() | public boolean readBoolean() throws IOException |
| readByte() | public byte readByte() throws IOException |
| readChar() | public char readChar() throws IOException |
| readDouble() | public double readDouble() throws IOException |
| readFloat() | public float readFloat() throws IOException |
| readFully() | public void readFully(byte[] *byteBuffer*) throws IOException |
| | public void readFully(byte[] *byteBuffer*, int *offset*, int *length*) throws IOException |
| readInt() | public int readInt() throws IOException |
| readLong() | public long readLong() throws IOException |
| readShort() | public short readShort() throws IOException |
| readUnsignedByte() | public int readUnsignedByte() throws IOException |
| readUnsignedShort() | public int readUnsignedShort() throws IOException |

These methods read a primitive datatype from the invoking input stream. The `readFully()` method reads a number of bytes from the input stream and stores them in the byte array. The number of bytes read is equal to the length of the array.

## readLine() Method

| Method | Syntax |
|--------|--------|
| readLine() | public String readLine() throws IOException |

`readLine()` reads a line of text from the invoking input stream and returns it as a `String` object.

## skipBytes() Method

| Method | Syntax |
|--------|--------|
| skipBytes() | public int skipBytes(int *bytesToSkip*) throws IOException, EOFException |

`skipBytes()` skips over `bytesToSkip` bytes in the invoking input stream and returns the number of bytes skipped.

# 4.1.4 DataInputStream Class

public class **DataInputStream** extends FilterInputStream implements DataInput

```
Object
    InputStream
        FilterInputStream
            DataInputStream
```

### Interfaces

DataInput

A `DataInputStream` object can read primitive Java data types from an underlying input stream in a machine-independent way.

## DataInputStream() Constructor

| Constructor | Syntax |
|-------------|--------|
| DataInputStream() | public DataInputStream(InputStream *in*) |

`DataInputStream()` creates a `DataInputStream` object. The `DataInputStream` object is wrapped around another `InputStream` object. Because of this, a `DataInputStream` object can be used, for instance, to read data from a file.

## read() Method

| Method | Syntax |
|--------|--------|
| Read() | `public int read(byte[] byteBuffer)`<br>`                throws IOException` |
|  | `public int read(byte[] byteBuffer, int offset,`<br>`                int numBytes) throws IOException` |

`read()` reads one or more bytes of input from input stream. The first version reads one byte of input and returns an integer representation of that byte. The second version reads `numBytes` bytes into the byte array `byteBuffer` starting at index `offset` and returns the number of bytes read. Both versions return `-1` when the end of the stream is reached.

A `DataInputStream` object also has access to the `read()` method defined in the `FilterInputStream` class.

## Methods for Reading Primitive Datatypes

| Method | Syntax |
|--------|--------|
| readBoolean() | `public final boolean readBoolean()`<br>`    throws IOException` |
| readByte() | `public final byte readByte() throws IOException` |
| readChar() | `public final char readChar() throws IOException` |
| readDouble() | `public final double readDouble()`<br>`    throws IOException` |
| readFloat() | `public final float readFloat()`<br>`    throws IOException` |
| readFully() | `public final void readFully(byte[] byteBuffer)`<br>`    throws IOException` |
|  | `public final void readFully(byte[] byteBuffer,`<br>`    int offset, int length) throws IOException` |
| readInt() | `public final int readInt() throws IOException` |
| readLong() | `public final long readLong() throws IOException` |
| readShort() | `public final short readShort()`<br>`    throws IOException` |
| readUnsignedByte() | `public final int readUnsignedByte()`<br>`    throws IOException` |
| readUnsignedShort() | `public final int readUnsignedShort()`<br>`    throws IOException` |

These methods read a primitive datatype from the invoking input stream. The `readFully()` method reads a number of bytes from the input stream and stores them in the byte array. The number of bytes read is equal to the length of the array.

# skipBytes() Method

| Method | Syntax |
|--------|--------|
| skipBytes() | public final int **skipBytes**(int *bytesToSkip*) throws IOException |

skipBytes() skips over bytesToSkip bytes in the invoking input stream and returns the number of bytes skipped.

# Deprecated Methods

| Method | Syntax |
|--------|--------|
| readLine() | public final String **readLine**() throws IOException |

readLine() was deprecated as of Java 1.1 because it does not properly convert bytes to characters. To read a line of text, use a BufferedReader object and the readLine() method defined in the BufferedReader class.

## Example: Using DataInputStream

A DataInputStream object is wrapped around a FileInputStream object to read the contents of the file jrr.txt. The file jrr.txt contains the line "This is the contents of jrr.txt" followed by a line separator, and is contained in the same directory as the compiled .class file. A byte array is created using the number of bytes available in the input stream. The byte array is filled using the readFully(). A String object is created using the contents of the byte array and printed to standard output.

```java
import java.io.*;

public class TestDIS {
  public static void main(String args[]) {
    try {
      DataInputStream dis =
        new DataInputStream(new FileInputStream("jrr.txt"));

      byte[] data = new byte[dis.available()];
      dis.readFully(data);
      String str = new String(data);
      System.out.println(str);

      dis.close();
    } catch (FileNotFoundException fnfe) {
      System.out.println(fnfe);
      return;
    } catch (IOException ioe) {
      System.out.println(ioe);
    }
  }
}
```

> **Output**
>
> This is the contents of jrr.txt

# 4.1.5 FileInputStream Class

```
public class FileInputStream extends InputStream
```

```
Object
    InputStream
        FileInputStream
```

A FileInputStream object is used to read bytes sequentially from a file. It provides a low-level (byte) mechanism for reading data from a file. A FileInputStream object can be wrapped inside a ObjectInputStream object to read primitive datatypes, Strings, and binary data. A FileInputStream object can also be wrapped inside a BufferedInputStream object for increased performance.

## FileInputStream() Constructors

| Constructor | Syntax |
|---|---|
| FileInputStream() | public FileInputStream(File *fobj*)<br>    throws FileNotFoundException |
| | public FileInputStream(FileDescriptor *fd*) |
| | public FileInputStream(String *filePath*)<br>    throws FileNotFoundException |

FileInputStream() creates a FileInputStream object using a File object, FileDescriptor object, or String to specify the file.

## available() Method

| Method | Syntax |
|---|---|
| available() | public int available() throws IOException |

available() returns the number of bytes that can be read from the input stream.

## close() Method

| Method | Syntax |
|---|---|
| close() | public void close() throws IOException |

close() closes the invoking FileInputStream object and releases any resources allocated to it.

## getFD() Method

| Method | Syntax |
|--------|--------|
| getFD() | public final FileDescriptor getFD()<br>    throws IOException |

getFD() returns the FileDescriptor associated with the invoking FileInputStream object. If there is no FileDescriptor, this method throws an IOException. A FileDescriptor object is used to represent an open file, an open socket, or another source or sink of bytes.

## read() Method

| Method | Syntax |
|--------|--------|
| read() | public int read() throws IOException |
| | public int read(byte[] byteBuffer<br>    throws IOException |
| | public int read(byte[] byteBuffer, int offset,<br>                int numBytes) throws IOException |

read() reads one or more bytes of input from the input stream. The first version reads one byte of input and returns an integer representation of that byte. The second version tries to fill the byte array byteBuffer and returns the number of bytes successfully read. The third version attempts to read numBytes bytes into the byte array byteBuffer starting at index offset and returns the number of bytes read. All three versions return -1 when the end of the stream is reached.

## skip() Method

| Method | Syntax |
|--------|--------|
| skip() | public long skip(long bytesToSkip)<br>    throws IOException |

skip() skips bytesToSkip bytes in the input stream and returns the number of bytes skipped.

### Example: Using FileInputStream to Read Data From a File

The file jrr.txt contains the line "This is the contents of jrr.txt" followed by a line separator, and is contained in the same directory as the compiled .class file. The read() method, defined in the InputStream class, reads the data as a byte and converts it to an int. The data is printed out character by character by casting the int to a char. The FileInputStream constructor can throw a FileNotFoundException, and the read() method can throw an IOException. That is why the FileInputStream instantiation and the call to the read() method are contained in a try block. To use the print() method, the bytes are cast to chars.

```
import java.io.*;

public class TestFIS {
  public static void main(String args[]) {
    int c;

    try {
      FileInputStream fis = new FileInputStream("jrr.txt");

      while ((c = fis.read()) != -1) {
        System.out.print((char) c);
      }
      fis.close();
    } catch (FileNotFoundException fnfe) {
      System.out.println(fnfe);
    } catch (IOException ioe) {
      System.out.println(ioe);
    }
  }
}
```

**Output**

```
This is the contents of jrr.txt
```

# 4.1.6 FilterInputStream Class

```
public class FilterInputStream extends InputStream
```

```
Object
    InputStream
        FilterInputStream
```

FilterInputStream is the super-class of the filter input streams. It has no public constructors and a FilterInputStream object cannot be created directly. Sub-classes of FilterInputStream are **wrapped** around other InputStream objects to provide additional functionality. Examples of FilterInputStream sub-classes are the BufferedInputStream and ObjectInputStream classes.

## available() Method

| Method | Syntax |
|--------|--------|
| available() | public int available() throws IOException |

available() returns the number of bytes that can be read from the input stream.

# close() Method

| Method | Syntax |
|--------|--------|
| close() | public void close() throws IOException |

close() closes the invoking FilterInputStream object and releases any resources allocated to it.

# Stream Position Methods

| Method | Syntax |
|--------|--------|
| mark() | public void mark(int pastLimit) |
| markSupported() | public boolean markSupported() |
| reset() | public void reset() throws IOException |
| skip() | public long skip(long bytesToSkip) throws IOException |

mark() sets a mark at the current position in the input stream. The pastLimit parameter is the number of bytes that can read past the mark until the mark becomes invalid.

markSupported() returns true if the invoking FilterInputStream object can be marked.

reset() returns the position of the FilterInputStream object to that set by the mark() method.

skip() skips bytesToSkip bytes in the invoking FilterInputStream object and returns the number of bytes skipped.

# read() Method

| Method | Syntax |
|--------|--------|
| read() | public int read() throws IOException |
| | public int read(byte[] byteBuffer) throws IOException |
| | public int read(byte[] byteBuffer, int offset, int numBytes) throws IOException |

read() reads one or more bytes of input from the input stream. The first version reads one byte of input and returns an integer representation of that byte. The second version tries to fill the byte array byteBuffer and returns the number of bytes successfully read. The third version attempts to read numBytes bytes into the byte array byteBuffer starting at index offset and returns the number of bytes read. All three versions return -1 when the end of the stream is reached.

# 4.1.7 InputStream Class

```
public abstract class InputStream extends Object
```

```
Object
    InputStream
```

InputStream is the parent class of the input byte stream classes. It provides the methods to read bytes as well as methods to manipulate the stream. Because it is an abstract class, an InputStream object is never instantiated.

## available() Method

| Method | Syntax |
|--------|--------|
| available() | public int available() throws IOException |

available() returns the number of bytes that can be read from the input stream.

### Example: Using the available() Method

A FileInputStream object, a sub-class of InputStream, is used to read a line of data from a file. The file jrr.txt contains the line "This is the contents of jrr.txt" followed by a line separator, and is contained in the same directory as the compiled .class file. This totals 32 or 33 bytes of data, depending on the operating system.

```java
import java.io.*;

public class TestByteAvail {
    public static void main(String args[]) {
        int c;

        try {
            FileInputStream fis = new FileInputStream("jrr.txt");

            int i = fis.available();
            System.out.println("The number of bytes available is " + i);
            fis.close();
        } catch (FileNotFoundException fnfe) {}
        catch (IOException ioe) {}
    }
}
```

**Output (number of bytes varies between operating systems)**

```
The number of bytes available is 32
```

# close() Method

| Method | Syntax |
|--------|--------|
| close() | public void close() throws IOException |

close() closes the invoking InputStream object.

## Example: Using the close() Method

See *Using FileInputStream to Read Data from a File* example in section 4.1.5 on page 301.

# Stream Position Methods

| Method | Syntax |
|--------|--------|
| mark() | public void mark(int pastLimit) |
| markSupported() | public boolean markSupported() |
| reset() | public void reset() throws IOException |
| skip() | public long skip(long bytesToSkip) |
| | throws IOException |

mark() sets a mark at the current position in the input stream. The pastLimit parameter is the number of bytes that can be read past the mark until the mark becomes invalid.

markSupported() returns true if the invoking InputStream object can be marked.

reset() returns the position of the InputStream object to that set by the mark() method.

skip() skips bytesToSkip bytes in the invoking InputStream object and returns the number of bytes skipped.

## Example: Using the skip() Method

The file jrr.txt contains the line "This is the contents of jrr.txt" followed by a line separator, and is contained in the same directory as the compiled .class file. The first five characters are read and printed. The next five characters are skipped, and then the remaining characters are read.

```
import java.io.*;

public class TestBytePos {
  public static void main(String args[]) {
```

**305**

```
   int c;
     int pos = 0;

     try {
       FileInputStream fis = new FileInputStream("jrr.txt");

       while ((c = fis.read()) != -1) {
         System.out.print((char) c);
         ++pos;
         if (pos == 5) {
           fis.skip(5);
         }
       }
       fis.close();
     } catch (FileNotFoundException fnfe) {}
     catch (IOException ioe) {}
   }
 }
```

**Output**

```
This e contents of jrr.txt
```

## read() Method

| Method | Syntax |
|--------|--------|
| read() | public abstract int read() throws IOException |
|  | public int read(byte[] byteBuffer) throws IOException |
|  | public int read(byte[] byteBuffer, int offset, int numBytes) throws IOException |

read() reads one or more bytes of input from the input stream. The first version reads one byte of input and returns an integer representation of that byte. The second version tries to fill the byte array byteBuffer and returns the number of bytes successfully read. The third version attempts to read numBytes bytes into the byte array byteBuffer starting at index offset and returns the number of bytes read. All three versions return -1 when the end of the stream is reached.

### Example: Using the read() Method

See *Using the skip() Method* example in this section on page 305.

# 4.1.8 ObjectInput Interface

```
public interface ObjectInput extends DataInput
```

```
DataInput
    ObjectInput
```

The ObjectInput interface extends the DataInput interface by adding the capability to read objects and arrays of bytes.

## available() Method

| Method | Syntax |
|--------|--------|
| available() | public int available() throws IOException |

available() returns the number of bytes that can be read from the input stream.

## close() Method

| Method | Syntax |
|--------|--------|
| close() | public void close() throws IOException |

close() closes the invoking input stream.

## read() Method

| Method | Syntax |
|--------|--------|
| read() | public int read() throws IOException |
| | public int read(byte[] byteBuffer)<br>    throws IOException |
| | public int read(byte[] byteBuffer, int offset,<br>                int numBytes) throws IOException |

read() reads one or more bytes of input from the input stream. The first version reads one byte of input and returns an integer representation of that byte. The second version tries to fill the byte array byteBuffer and returns the number of bytes successfully read. The third version attempts to read numBytes bytes into the byte array byteBuffer starting at index offset and returns the number of bytes read. All three versions return -1 when the end of the stream is reached.

## readObject() Method

| Method | Syntax |
|--------|--------|
| readObject() | public Object readObject()<br>        throws ClassNotFoundException, IOException |

readObject() reads an Object from the invoking input stream.

## skip() Method

| Method | Syntax |
|--------|--------|
| skip() | public long **skip**(long *bytesToSkip*)<br>    throws IOException |

skip() skips bytesToSkip bytes in the invoking input stream.

# 4.1.9 ObjectInputStream Class

public class **ObjectInputStream** extends InputStream implements DataInput,
    ObjectInput, ObjectStreamConstants

    Object
        InputStream
            ObjectInputStream

### Interfaces

DataInput, ObjectInput, ObjectStreamConstants

An ObjectInputStream object can read both primitive datatypes and objects. It
provides implementations of the methods defined in the ObjectInput and DataInput
interfaces. An ObjectInputStream object is wrapped around an underlying
InputStream object to give the underlying InputStream object this functionality. The
data to be read must have been written by an ObjectOutputStream object.

## ObjectInputStream() Constructor

| Constructor | Syntax |
|-------------|--------|
| ObjectInputStream() | public **ObjectInputStream**(InputStream *isObj*)<br>    throws IOException, StreamCorruptedException |

ObjectInputStream() creates an ObjectInputStream object. The ObjectInputStream
object is wrapped around the InputStream object isObj to give the InputStream
object the ability to read objects and primitive datatypes.

## available() Method

| Method | Syntax |
|--------|--------|
| available() | public int **available**() throws IOException |

available() returns the number of bytes that can be read from the input stream.

## close() Method

| Method | Syntax |
|--------|--------|
| close() | public void close() throws IOException |

close() closes the invoking ObjectInputStream object and releases any resources allocated to it.

## read() Method

| Method | Syntax |
|--------|--------|
| read() | public int read() throws IOException |
| | public int read(byte[] *byteBuffer*, int *offset*, int *numBytes*) throws IOException |

read() reads one or more bytes of input from input stream. The first version reads one byte of input and returns an integer representation of that byte. The second version reads numBytes bytes into the byte array byteBuffer starting at index offset and returns the number of bytes read. Both versions return -1 when the end of the stream is reached.

A ObjectInputStream object also has access to the read() method defined in the InputStream class.

## readObject() Method

| Method | Syntax |
|--------|--------|
| readObject() | public final Object readObject() throws ClassNotFoundException, IOException, OptionalDataException |

readObject() reads an Object from the invoking input stream.

## Methods for Reading Primitive Datatypes

| Method | Syntax |
|--------|--------|
| readBoolean() | public boolean readBoolean() throws IOException, EOFException |
| readByte() | public byte readByte() throws IOException, EOFException |
| readChar() | public char readChar() throws IOException, EOFException |
| readDouble() | public double readDouble() throws IOException, EOFException |
| readFloat() | public float readFloat() throws IOException, EOFException |

| Method | Syntax |
|---|---|
| readFully() | `public void readFully(byte[] byteBuffer)`<br>`    throws IOException` |
|  | `public void readFully(byte[] byteBuffer,`<br>`    int offset, int length) throws IOException,`<br>`    EOFException` |
| readInt() | `public int readInt()`<br>`    throws IOException, EOFException` |
| readLong() | `public long readLong()`<br>`    throws IOException, EOFException` |
| readShort() | `public short readShort()`<br>`    throws IOException, EOFException` |
| readUnsignedByte() | `public int readUnsignedByte()`<br>`    throws IOException, EOFException` |
| readUnsignedShort() | `public int readUnsignedShort()`<br>`    throws IOException, EOFException` |

These methods read a primitive datatype from the input stream. The `readFully()` method reads a number of bytes from the input stream and stores them in the byte array. The number of bytes read is equal to the length of the array.

## skipBytes() Method

| Method | Syntax |
|---|---|
| skipBytes() | `public int skipBytes(int bytesToSkip)`<br>`    throws IOException` |

`skipBytes()` skips over `bytesToSkip` bytes in the invoking input stream and returns the number of bytes skipped.

## Deprecated Methods

| Method | Syntax |
|---|---|
| readLine() | `public String readLine() throws IOException` |

`readLine()` was deprecated because it does not properly convert bytes to characters. This method should not be used for new code.

### Example: Using ObjectInputStream

The file `oos.txt` was created using an `ObjectOutputStream` object. The code that created the file is shown in the *Using ObjectOutputStream* example on page 326; that example will have to be run first to create the file read by this example. The initial values in the `double` array were [1.0, 2.0, 3.0, 4.0]. An `ObjectInputStream` object is created and wrapped around a `FileInputStream` object that opens the file `oos.txt` for reading. To find out how many elements there are to be read, the return value from the `available()` method is divided by 8 (a double is 8 bytes). The `readDouble()` method reads each double and stores it in `dArray`.

```
import java.io.*;

public class TestOIS {
  public static void main(String args[]) {
    int c;
    double dArray[] = new double[5];

    try {
      ObjectInputStream ois =
        new ObjectInputStream(new FileInputStream("oos.txt"));

      int size = ois.available();

      for (int i = 0; i < size / 8; ++i) {
        dArray[i] = ois.readDouble();
        System.out.println("At index " + i + " element is "
                           + dArray[i]);
      }
      ois.close();
    } catch (FileNotFoundException fnfe) {
      System.out.println("Error: "+fnfe);
    } catch (IOException ioe) {
      System.out.println("Error: "+ioe);
    }

  }
}
```

**Output**

```
At index 0 element is 2.0
At index 1 element is 4.0
At index 2 element is 6.0
At index 3 element is 8.0
```

# 4.2 Byte Output Streams

The byte output streams are used to write bytes to an underlying output stream. The byte output stream class hierarchy is shown in the following figure.

The OutputStream class is an abstract class which is the parent of all of the output byte stream classes.

The FileOutputStream class is used to write bytes sequentially to a file.

An ObjectOutputStream object can be used to write primitive datatypes and Objects to an underlying OutputStream object.

The BufferedOutputStream class provides an intermediate buffer that increases output stream performance.

The ByteArrayOutputStream class is used to write data to an internal byte array.

A DataOutputStream object is used to write primitive data or String objects to an output stream in a machine independent manner.

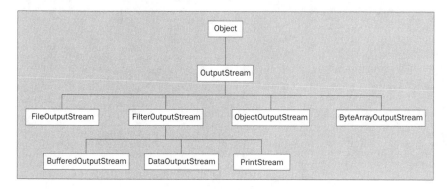

# 4.2.1 BufferedOutputStream Class

```
public class BufferedOutputStream extends FilterOutputStream
```

```
Object
    OutputStream
        FilterOutputStream
            BufferedOutputStream
```

A BufferedOutputStream object provides an associated OutputStream object with a memory buffer. The buffer increases efficiency by reducing the number of times the disk must be accessed. Data is first written into the buffer. When the buffer is full, the data is written to disk.

The BufferedOutputStream object should call the flush() method when writing is complete to ensure that the final contents of the buffer are written to disk.

## BufferedOutputStream() Constructors

| Constructor | Syntax |
|---|---|
| BufferedOutputStream() | public BufferedOutputStream(OutputStream os) |
| | public BufferedOutputStream(OutputStream os, int bufferSize) |

BufferedOutputStream() creates a BufferedOutputStream object. The BufferedOutputStream object is wrapped around another OutputStream object that is passed to the constructor as an argument.

# flush() Method

| Method | Syntax |
|--------|--------|
| flush() | public void flush() throws IOException |

flush() flushes the output buffer of the invoking BufferedOutputStream object forcing any data held in the buffer to be written to the invoking BufferedOutputStream object.

# write() Method

| Method | Syntax |
|--------|--------|
| write() | public void write(int *b*) throws IOException |
| | public void write(byte *buf*[], int *offset*, int *numBytes*) throws IOException |

write() writes either a single int or an array of bytes to output stream. The second version takes an initial offset and specifies the number of bytes to be written.

In addition to these write() methods, a BufferedOutputStream object has access to the write() method defined in the FilterOutputStream class.

## Example: Using BufferedOutputStream

A BufferedInputStream object is created to read a file named jrr.txt, which contains the line "This is the contents of jrr.txt" followed by a line separator, and is contained in the same directory as the compiled .class file. The data is read using the read() command which returns an integer representation of the byte that is read. The data is written to a file named jrr.txt.copy using a BufferedOutputStream object and the write() method from the OutputStream class. The BufferedOutputStream object is flushed to ensure that all the data is written to the file.

```
import java.io.*;

public class TestBOS {
  public static void main(String args[]) {
    int c;

    try {
      BufferedInputStream bis =
        new BufferedInputStream(new FileInputStream("jrr.txt"));

      BufferedOutputStream bos =
        new BufferedOutputStream(new FileOutputStream("jrr.txt.copy"));
```

4

java.io

```
        while ((c = bis.read()) != -1) {
          bos.write((char) c);
        }
        bos.flush();
        bos.close();
        bis.close();
      } catch (FileNotFoundException fnfe) {
        System.out.println(fnfe);
        return;
      } catch (IOException ioe) {
        System.out.println(ioe);
      }
    }
  }
}
```

**Output**

After the program is run, jrr.txt.copy will contain the line:

```
    This is the contents of jrr.txt
```

# 4.2.2 ByteArrayOutputStream Class

```
public class ByteArrayOutputStream extends OutputStream
```

```
Object
    OutputStream
        ByteArrayOutputStream
```

A ByteArrayOutputStream object writes data to an internal byte array. The byte array grows as data is written to the stream. The byte array can be accessed using the toByteArray() method. The contents of the byte array can be sent to another output stream using the writeTo() method.

## ByteArrayOutputStream() Constructors

| Constructor | Syntax |
|---|---|
| ByteArrayOutputStream() | public ByteArrayOutputStream() |
| | public ByteArrayOutputStream(int *size*) |

ByteArrayOutputStream() creates a ByteArrayOutputStream object. The initial size of the internal byte array can be specified. The default initial size is 32 bytes.

## close() Method

| Method | Syntax |
|--------|--------|
| close() | public void close() throws IOException |

close() closes the invoking output stream and releases any resources allocated to it.

## reset() Method

| Method | Syntax |
|--------|--------|
| reset() | public void reset() |

reset() discards the current contents of the internal byte array and resets the stream position to 0.

## size() Method

| Method | Syntax |
|--------|--------|
| size() | public int size() |

size() returns the number of bytes currently stored in the internal byte array of the invoking ByteArrayOutputStream object.

## toByteArray() Method

| Method | Syntax |
|--------|--------|
| toByteArray() | public byte[] toByteArray() |

toByteArray() returns a copy of the internal byte array associated with the invoking ByteArrayOutputStream object.

## toString() Method

| Method | Syntax |
|--------|--------|
| toString() | public String toString() |
| | public String toString(String *encoding*) |

toString() returns a String representation of the contents of the internal byte array. An encoding scheme may be specified, but the second version of this method has been deprecated and should not be used for new code.

## write () Method

| Method | Syntax |
|---|---|
| write() | public void **write**(int *b*)<br>public void **write**(byte *buf[]*, int *offset*,<br>    int *numBytes*) |

write() writes either a single int or an array of bytes to output stream. The second version takes an initial offset and specifies the number of bytes to be written.

In addition to these write() methods, a BufferedOutputStream object has access to the write() method defined in the FilterOutputStream class.

## writeTo() Method

| Method | Syntax |
|---|---|
| writeTo() | public void **writeTo**(OutputStream *out*)<br>    throws IOException |

writeTo() writes the contents of the internal byte array of the invoking ByteArrayOutputStream object to the specified output stream.

### Example: Using ByteArrayOutputStream

See the example *Using the Connectionless Protocol* on page 375, where a ByteArrayOutputStream is used in the ServerCLP class.

# 4.2.3 DataOutput Interface

```
public interface DataOutput
```

The DataOutput interface defines the methods that write primitive datatypes and String objects to a byte output stream.

## write() Method

| Method | Syntax |
|---|---|
| write() | public void **write**(int *b*) throws IOException<br>public void **write**(byte *buf[]*) throws IOException<br>public void **write**(byte *buf[]*, int *offset*,<br>    int *numBytes*) throws IOException |

write() writes an integer or an array of bytes to the invoking output stream. The third version takes an initial offset and specifies the number of bytes to be written.

## Methods to Write Primitive Datatypes

| Method | Syntax |
|---|---|
| writeBoolean() | public void **writeBoolean**(boolean *b*) throws IOException |
| writeByte() | public void **writeByte**(int *b*) throws IOException |
| writeChar() | public void **writeChar**(int *c*) throws IOException |
| writeDouble() | public void **writeDouble**(double *d*) throws IOException |
| writeFloat() | public void **writeFloat**(float *f*) throws IOException |
| writeInt() | public void **writeInt**(int *i*) throws IOException |
| writeLong() | public void **writeLong**(long *l*) throws IOException |
| writeShort() | public void **writeShort**(int *s*) throws IOException |

These methods convert primitive datatypes to bytes and write the bytes to the invoking output stream.

## Methods to Write Strings

| Method | Syntax |
|---|---|
| writeBytes() | public void **writeBytes**(String *s*) throws IOException |
| writeChars() | public void **writeChars**(String *s*) throws IOException |

writeBytes() writes the String s to the invoking output stream as a sequence of 8-bit bytes.

writeChars() writes the String s to the invoking output stream as a sequence of 16-bit characters.

# 4.2.4 DataOutputStream Class

```
public class DataOutputStream extends FilterOutputStream implements DataOutput
```

```
Object
    OutputStream
        FilterOutputStream
            DataOutputStream
```

### Interfaces
```
DataOutput
```

A DataOutputStream object is used to write primitive data types to an output stream in a machine independent manner.

## DataOutputStream() Constructor

| Constructor | Syntax |
| --- | --- |
| DataOutputStream() | public DataOutputStream(OutputStream out) |

DataOutputStream() creates a DataOutputStream object. The DataOutputStream object is wrapped around another OutputStream object. This permits, for instance, the DataOutputStream object to write data to a file.

## flush() Method

| Method | Syntax |
| --- | --- |
| flush() | public void flush() throws IOException |

flush() flushes the output buffer of the invoking DataOutputStream object forcing any data held in the buffer to be written to the invoking DataOutputStream object.

## 13.13.4 size() Method

| Method | Syntax |
| --- | --- |
| size() | public final int size() |

size() returns the number of bytes written to the output stream.

## write () Method

| Method | Syntax |
| --- | --- |
| write() | public void write(int b) throws IOException |
| | public void write(byte buf[], int offset, int numBytes) throws IOException |

write() writes either a single int or an array of bytes to output stream. The second version takes an initial offset and specifies the number of bytes to be written.

In addition to these write() methods, a DataOutputStream object has access to the write() method defined in the FilterOutputStream class.

## Methods to Write Primitive Datatypes

| Method | Syntax |
| --- | --- |
| writeBoolean() | public final void writeBoolean(boolean b) throws IOException |
| writeByte() | public final void writeByte(int b) throws IOException |

| Method | Syntax |
|---|---|
| writeChar() | public final void **writeChar**(int *c*) throws IOException |
| writeDouble() | public final void **writeDouble**(double *d*) throws IOException |
| writeFloat() | public final void **writeFloat**(float *f*) throws IOException |
| writeInt() | public final void **writeInt**(int *i*) throws IOException |
| writeLong() | public final void **writeLong**(long *l*) throws IOException |
| writeShort() | public final void **writeShort**(int *s*) throws IOException |

These methods convert primitive datatypes to bytes and write the bytes to the invoking output stream.

# Methods to Write Strings

| Method | Syntax |
|---|---|
| writeBytes() | public final void **writeBytes**(String *s*) throws IOException |
| writeChars() | public final void **writeChars**(String *s*) throws IOException |

writeBytes() writes the String s to the invoking output stream as a sequence of 8-bit bytes. The writeChars() method writes the String s to the invoking output stream as a sequence of 16-bit characters.

## Example: Using DataOutputStream

A DataOutputStream object is used to write a String object to a file named "dos.txt". The writeChars() methods writes the String to the file as a series of 2 byte characters.

```
import java.io.*;

public class TestDOS {
    public static void main(String args[]) {
        try {
            DataOutputStream dos =
                new DataOutputStream(new FileOutputStream("dos.txt"));

            String str = "Did this work?";

            dos.writeChars(str);
```

```
            dos.close();
        } catch (IOException ioe) {
            System.out.println(ioe);
        }
    }
}
```

**Output**

This is the contents of the dos.txt file:

```
D i d    t h i s    w o r k ?
```

# 4.2.5 FileOutputStream Class

```
public class FileOutputStream extends OutputStream
```

```
Object
    OutputStream
        FileOutputStream
```

A FileOutputStream object is an output stream that is used to write bytes sequentially to a file. The file is specified when the FileOutputStream object is instantiated.

## FileOutputStream() Constructors

| Constructors | Syntax |
|---|---|
| FileOutputStream() | public FileOutputStream(File *fobj*)<br>    throws FileNotFoundException |
| | public FileOutputStream(FileDescriptor *fd*) |
| | public FileOutputStream(String *filePath*)<br>    throws FileNotFoundException |
| | public FileOutputStream(String *filePath*,<br>    boolean *append*) throws FileNotFoundException |

The file to be written to can be passed to the constructor using a File object, a FileDescriptor object, or a String containing the file path and name. If the file name passed to the constructor does not already exist, the file will be created. If append is set to true, the file will be appended. If the directories in the file path do not exist, a FileNotFoundException is thrown.

# close() Method

| Method | Syntax |
|--------|--------|
| close() | public void close() throws IOException |

close() closes the invoking FileOutputStream object and releases any resources allocated to it.

# getFD() Method

| Method | Syntax |
|--------|--------|
| getFD() | public final FileDescriptor getFD() throws IOException |

getFD() returns the FileDescriptor object associated with the invoking FileOutputStream object. A FileDescriptor object is used to represent an open file, an open socket, or another source or sink of bytes.

# write() Method

| Method | Syntax |
|--------|--------|
| write() | public void write(int b) throws IOException |
| | public void write(byte buf[]) throws IOException |
| | public void write(byte buf[], int offset, int numBytes) throws IOException |

write() writes either a single int or an array of bytes to the output stream. The third version takes an initial offset and specifies the number of bytes to be written.

## Example: Using FileOutputStream

A BufferedInputStream object is created to read a file named jrr.txt, which contains the line "This is the contents of jrr.txt" followed by a line separator, and is contained in the same directory as the compiled .class file. The data is read using the read() command which returns an integer representation of the byte that is read. The data is written to a file named jrr.txt.copy using a FileOutputStream object and the write() method from the OutputStream class.

```
import java.io.*;

public class TestFOS {
    public static void main(String args[]) {
        int c;
```

```
      try {
        BufferedInputStream bis =
          new BufferedInputStream(new FileInputStream("jrr.txt"));

        FileOutputStream fos = new FileOutputStream("jrr.txt.copy");

        while ((c = bis.read()) != -1) {
          fos.write((char) c);
        }
        fos.close();
        bis.close();
      } catch (FileNotFoundException fnfe) {
        System.out.println(fnfe);
        return;
      } catch (IOException ioe) {
        System.out.println(ioe);
      }
    }
  }
```

**Output**

The file jrr.txt.copy contains the line:

```
This is the contents of jrr.txt
```

# 4.2.6 FilterOutputStream Class

```
public class FilterOutputStream extends OutputStream
```

```
Object
    OutputStream
        FilterOutputStream
```

FilterOuputStream is the super-class of the filter output streams. Sub-classes of FilterOutputStream are **wrapped** around other OutputStream objects to provide additional functionality. Examples of FilterOutputStream sub-classes are the BufferedOutputStream and DataOutputStream classes.

## FilterOutputStream() Constructor

| Constructor | Syntax |
|---|---|
| FilterOutputStream() | public FilterOutputStream(OutputStream os) |

FilterOutputStream() creates a FilterOutputStream object. The sub-classes of FilterOutputStream are more commonly used. A FilterOutputStream object is not usually created.

## close() Method

| Method | Syntax |
|--------|--------|
| close() | public void close() throws IOException |

close() closes the invoking FilterOutputStream object and releases any resources allocated to it.

## flush() Method

| Method | Syntax |
|--------|--------|
| flush() | public void flush() throws IOException |

flush() flushes the output buffer of the invoking FilterOutputStream object forcing any data held in the buffer to be written to the invoking FilterOutputStream object.

## write() Method

| Method | Syntax |
|--------|--------|
| write() | public void write(int *b*) throws IOException<br>public void write(byte *buf*[]) throws IOException<br>public void write(byte *buf*[], int *offset*,<br>    int *numBytes*) throws IOException |

write() writes either a single int or an array of bytes to output stream. The third version takes an initial offset and specifies the number of bytes to be written.

# 4.2.7 ObjectOutput Interface

```
public interface ObjectOutput extends DataOutput
```

```
DataOutput
    ObjectOutput
```

The ObjectOutput interface extends the DataOutput interface by adding the capability to write objects and arrays of bytes. It also provides the close() and flush() methods to those classes that implement the ObjectOutput interface.

## close() Method

| Method | Syntax |
|--------|--------|
| close() | public void close() throws IOException |

close() closes the invoking output stream and releases any resources allocated to it.

java.io

### flush() Method

| Method | Syntax |
| --- | --- |
| flush() | public void flush() throws IOException |

flush() empties any buffers associated with the invoking OutputStream object and causes any data stored there to be written to the associated physical device.

### write() Method

| Method | Syntax |
| --- | --- |
| write() | public void write(int *b*) throws IOException |
| | public void write(byte[] *byteBuffer*)<br>    throws IOException |
| | public void write(byte[] *byteBuffer*, int *offset*,<br>    int *numBytes*) throws IOException |

write() writes a single byte or an array or bytes to the invoking output stream. The third version takes an initial offset and specifies the number of bytes to be written.

### writeObject() Method

| Method | Syntax |
| --- | --- |
| writeObject() | public void writeObject(Object *obj*)<br>    throws IOException |

writeObject() writes the Object obj to the invoking output stream. The object to be written must implement the Serializable interface.

# 4.2.8 ObjectOutputStream Class

```
public class ObjectOutputStream extends OutputStream implements ObjectOutput,
  ObjectStreamConstants
```

```
Object
    OutputStream
        ObjectOutputStream
```

#### Interfaces

```
ObjectOutput,ObjectStreamConstants
```

The ObjectOutputStream class is used to add the ability to write primitive datatypes and Objects to an underlying OutputStream object. The underlying OutputStream object is passed to the ObjectOutputStream constructor. ObjectOutputStream implements the methods defined in the ObjectOutput and DataOutput interfaces.

# ObjectOutputStream() Constructor

| Constructor | Syntax |
|---|---|
| ObjectOutputStream() | public ObjectOutputStream(OutputStream osObj) throws IOException |

ObjectOutputStream() creates an ObjectOutputStream object. The ObjectOutputStream object is wrapped around the OutputStream object isObj to give the OutputStream object the ability to write objects and primitive datatypes.

# close() Method

| Method | Syntax |
|---|---|
| close() | public void close() throws IOException |

close() closes the invoking ObjectOutputStream object and releases any resources allocated to it.

# flush() Method

| Method | Syntax |
|---|---|
| flush() | public void flush() throws IOException |

flush() empties any buffers associated with the invoking ObjectOutputStream object and causes any data stored there to be written to the associated physical device.

# write() Method

| Method | Syntax |
|---|---|
| write() | public void write(int b) throws IOException |
| | public void write(byte[] byteBuffer) throws IOException |
| | public void write(byte[] byteBuffer, int offset, int numBytes) throws IOException |

write() writes a single byte or an array or bytes to the output stream. The third version takes an initial offset and specifies the number of bytes to be written.

# writeObject() Method

| Method | Syntax |
|---|---|
| writeObject() | public final void writeObject(Object obj) throws IOException |

writeObject() writes the Object obj to the output stream. The object to be written must implement the Serializable interface.

## Methods to Write Primitive Datatypes

| Method | Syntax |
|---|---|
| writeBoolean() | public void writeBoolean(boolean b) throws IOException |
| writeByte() | public void writeByte(int b) throws IOException |
| writeChar() | public void writeChar(int c) throws IOException |
| writeDouble() | public void writeDouble(double y) throws IOException |
| writeFloat() | public void writeFloat(float y) throws IOException |
| writeInt() | public void writeInt(int y) throws IOException |
| writeLong() | public void writeLong(long l) throws IOException |
| writeShort() | public void writeShort(int s) throws IOException |

These methods convert primitive datatypes to bytes and write the bytes to the output stream.

### Example: Using ObjectOutputStream

A double array is written to a file named oos.txt using an ObjectOutputStream object. The data written to the file can be read using an ObjectInputStream object.

This example is used to set up the input for the *Using ObjectInputStream* example on page 310.

```
import java.io.*;

public class TestOOS {
  public static void main(String args[]) {
    int c;
    double dArray[] = {
      1.0, 2.0, 3.0, 4.0
    };

    try {
      ObjectOutputStream oos =
        new ObjectOutputStream(new FileOutputStream("oos.txt"));

      for (int i = 0; i < dArray.length; ++i) {
        oos.writeDouble(dArray[i]);
      }
      oos.close();
    } catch (IOException ioe) {}

  }
}
```

# 4.2.9 OutputStream Class

```
public abstract class OutputStream extends Object
```

```
Object
    OutputStream
```

This is the parent class for output byte stream classes. It provides the methods to write bytes as well as methods to manipulate the stream. Because it is an abstract class, an OutputStream object is never instantiated.

## close() Method

| Method | Syntax |
|--------|--------|
| close() | public void close() throws IOException |

close() closes the invoking output stream and releases any resources allocated to it.

## flush() Method

| Method | Syntax |
|--------|--------|
| flush() | public void flush() throws IOException |

flush() flushes the output buffer of the invoking output stream forcing any data held in the buffer to be written to the invoking output stream. This method is always overridden in an OutputStream sub-class because the OutputStream class implementation does nothing.

## write() Method

| Method | Syntax |
|--------|--------|
| write() | public abstract void write(int *b*) throws IOException |
| | public void write(byte *buf[]*) throws IOException |
| | public void write(byte *buf[]*, int *offset*, int *numBytes*) throws IOException |

write() writes either a single int or an array of bytes to the invoking output stream. The third version takes an initial offset and specifies the number of bytes to be written.

# 4.2.10 PrintStream Class

```
public class PrintStream extends FilterOutputStream
```

```
Object
    OutputStream
        FilterOutputStream
            PrintStream
```

The PrintStream class provides methods for writing String object representations of primitive datatypes and objects to an output stream. This class has been made obsolete by the PrintWriter class.

## PrintStream() Constructors

| Constructor | Method |
|---|---|
| PrintStream() | public PrintStream(OutputStream *osObj*) |
| | public PrintStream(OutputStream *osObj*, boolean *autoFlush*) |

PrintStream object constructor. These constructors have been deprecated as of Java 1.1

## print() Method

| Method | Syntax |
|---|---|
| print() | public void print(boolean *b*) |
| | public void print(char *c*) |
| | public void print(char[] *c*) |
| | public void print(double *d*) |
| | public void print(float *f*) |
| | public void print(int *i*) |
| | public void print(long *l*) |
| | public void print(Object *obj*) |
| | public void print(String *str*) |

print() writes a String representation of the primitive datatype or Object to the invoking PrintStream object. The version that takes an Object as an argument calls the toString() method of that object.

## println() Method

| Method | Syntax |
|---|---|
| println() | public void println(boolean *b*) |
| | public void println(char *c*) |
| | public void println(char[] c) |
| | public void println(double *d*) |
| | public void println(float *f*) |
| | public void println(int *i*) |
| | public void println(long *l*) |
| | public void println(Object *obj*) |
| | public void println(String *str*) |
| | public void println() |

println() writes a String representation of the primitive datatype or Object followed by the default end-of-line to the invoking PrintStream object. The version that takes an Object as an argument, calls the toString() method of that object. The version that takes no arguments simply writes a default end-of-line. Because the default end-of-line character sequence varies from platform to platform, it is inadvisable to use println() for applications where data written on one platform may be read on another (socket communication, for example).

# 4.3 Character Input Streams

The character input streams are used to read character data from an underlying stream. The character input stream class hierarchy is shown in the following figure.

The Reader class is an abstract class and is the parent class of the input character stream classes.

The FileReader class provides a way to read character data from a file.

The InputStreamReader class reads character data from an underlying byte stream. This class can be used to read data input from the keyboard.

A BufferedReader object can be wrapped around a Reader sub-class object to increase efficiency by providing an intermediate buffer to store the input data.

Here is the character input stream class hierarchy:

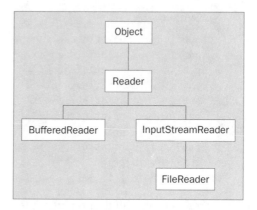

# 4.3.1 BufferedReader Class

`public class `**`BufferedReader`**` extends Reader`

```
Object
    Reader
        BufferedReader
```

A `BufferedReader` object improves the performance of an associated `Reader` object by providing a temporary storage buffer. Data is first read into the buffer before the program requests it, reducing the number of times the disk or network must be accessed.

## BufferedReader() Constructors

| Constructor | Syntax |
|---|---|
| `BufferedReader()` | `public `**`BufferedReader`**`(Reader inputStream)`<br>`public `**`BufferedReader`**`(Reader inputStream,`<br>`        int bufSize) throws IllegalArgumentException` |

`BufferReader` object constructor. Note that the constructor takes a `Reader` object as an argument. One way to think of this is that the `BufferedReader` object is wrapped around the `Reader` object to increase efficiency. The default buffer size is `8192` characters. This can be changed by providing the constructor with a buffer size.

## close() Method

| Method | Syntax |
|---|---|
| `close()` | `public void `**`close`**`() throws IOException` |

`close()` closes the invoking `BufferedReader` object and releases any resources allocate to it.

## read() Method

| Method | Syntax |
|--------|--------|
| read() | public int read() throws IOException |
| | public int read(char[] charArray,int offset, int numChars) throws IOException |

read() reads one or more characters from the input stream. The first version reads one character of data and returns the character as an int. The second version fills the char array charArray with characters read from the input stream. This methods return the number of characters read or -1 when the end of file is encountered.

In addition to the read() methods described here, a BufferedReader object has access to the read() method defined in the Reader class.

The method is fully buffered so when the no-argument read() method is used to accept input from the keyboard, nothing happens until the *Enter* key is pressed. The text can be altered using the *Backspace* or *Delete* keys. A *Ctrl-z* or *Ctrl-d* is used to indicate an end-of-file with keyboard input.

## readLine() Method

| Method | Syntax |
|--------|--------|
| readLine() | public String readLine() throws IOException |

readLine() reads a line of text from a file or keyboard input and returns the input as a String. Line terminators are not returned as part of the text. A null is returned if an end-of-file is detected.

readLine() is useful for reading in lines from an input file where only part of the line has numerical data. The String that is read can be parsed using the StringTokenizer class (see Section 3.6.5 on page 281) to extract the useful data.

## ready() Method

| Method | Syntax |
|--------|--------|
| ready() | public boolean ready() throws IOException |

ready() returns true when the invoking BufferedReader object is ready to read data.

## Stream Position Methods

| Method | Syntax |
|--------|--------|
| mark() | public void mark(int pastLimit) throws IOException |
| markSupported() | public boolean markSupported() |

| Method | Syntax |
|--------|--------|
| reset() | public void reset() throws IOException |
| skip() | public long skip(long *bytesToSkip*) throws IOException |

mark() sets a mark at the current position in the input stream. The pastLimit parameter is the number of bytes that can read past the mark until the mark becomes invalid.

markSupported() returns true if the invoking BufferedReader object can be marked.

reset() returns the position of the BufferedReader object to that set by the mark() method.

skip() skips bytesToSkip bytes in the input stream and returns the number of bytes skipped.

## Example: Using a BufferedReader to Read Data from a File

The file jrr.txt contains the line "This is the contents of jrr.txt" followed by a line separator, and is contained in the same directory as the compiled .class file. A BufferedReader object is wrapped around a FileReader object that opens the file for reading. The readLine() method reads the line of text and returns it as a String object.

```java
import java.io.*;

public class TestBR {
  public static void main(String args[]) {
    String str;

    try {
      BufferedReader br =
        new BufferedReader(new FileReader("jrr.txt"));

      while ((str = br.readLine()) != null) {
        System.out.println(str);
      }
      br.close();
    } catch (FileNotFoundException fnfe) {
      System.out.println(fnfe);
      return;
    } catch (IOException ioe) {
      System.out.println(ioe);
    }

  }
}
```

### Output

```
This is the contents of jrr.txt
```

## Example: Parsing Data Read From a File using a BufferedReader

The input file sphere.txt has one line, "radius = 4.0", followed by a line separator, and is contained in the same directory as the compiled .class file. The BufferedReader object reads this line in as a String. The StringTokenizer object breaks the input String into substrings. The last string, "4.0", is converted into a double.

This allows more informative input files to be used. The informative but extraneous text is removed from the necessary data.

```java
import java.io.*;
import java.util.*;

public class TestBR2 {
  public static void main(String args[]) {
    String str;
    double radius;
    StringTokenizer stk;

    try {
      BufferedReader br =
        new BufferedReader(new FileReader("sphere.txt"));

      while ((str = br.readLine()) != null) {
        stk = new StringTokenizer(str);
        while (stk.hasMoreTokens()) {
          str = stk.nextToken();
        }
        radius = Double.valueOf(str).doubleValue();
        System.out.println("area is " + Math.PI*radius*radius);
      }
      br.close();
    } catch (FileNotFoundException fnfe) {
      System.out.println(fnfe);
      return;
    } catch (IOException ioe) {
      System.out.println(ioe);
    }
  }
}
```

### Output
```
area is 50.26548245743669
```

# 4.3.2 FileReader Class

```
public class FileReader extends InputStreamReader
```

```
Object
    Reader
        InputStreamReader
            FileReader
```

A FileReader object represents a character input stream that can be used to read the contents of a file. A FileReader object reads data one character at a time. To increase efficiency, a BufferedReader object can be wrapped around the FileReader object.

The FileReader class inherits all of its methods from the InputStreamReader and Reader classes.

## 13.21.1 FileReader() Constructors

| Constructor | Syntax |
|---|---|
| FileReader() | public **FileReader**(File *fobj*)<br>        throws FileNotFoundException |
| | public **FileReader**(FileDescriptor *fd*)<br>public **FileReader**(String *filePath*)<br>        throws FileNotFoundException |

FileReader() creates a FileReader object. The file to be read is specified using a File object, a FileDesciptor object, or a String containing the file path.

### Example: Using a FileReader to Read Data from a File

A FileReader object is used to read the contents of a file named jrr.txt, which contains the line "This is the contents of jrr.txt" followed by a line separator, and is contained in the same directory as the compiled .class file. The read() method defined in the Reader class reads the data one character at a time.

```java
import java.io.*;

public class TestFR {
  public static void main(String args[]) {
    int c;

    try {
      FileReader fr = new FileReader("jrr.txt");

      while ((c = fr.read()) != -1) {
        System.out.print((char) c);
      }
      fr.close();
    } catch (FileNotFoundException fnfe) {
```

```
                System.out.println(fnfe);
                return;
            } catch (IOException ioe) {
                System.out.println(ioe);
            }
        }
    }
```

**Output**

```
    This is the contents of jrr.txt
```

# 4.3.3 InputStreamReader Class

```
public class InputStreamReader extends Reader
```

```
Object
    Reader
        InputStreamReader
```

The InputStreamReader class provides the ability for reading character data from an underlying byte stream. This class is often used when reading keyboard input.

A BufferedReader object may be wrapped around the InputStreamReader object to increase efficiency and allow the use of the readLine() method.

## InputStreamReader() Constructors

| Constructor | Syntax |
|---|---|
| InputStreamReader() | public InputStreamReader(InputStream *is*) |
| | public InputStreamReader(InputStream *is*, String *encodingScheme*) throws UnsupportedEncodingException |

InputStreamReader() creates an InputStreamReader object. The InputStreamReader object is wrapped around an underlying InputStream sub-class object that is passed to the InputStreamReader constructor as an argument. To set the InputStreamReader object to read input from the keyboard, pass System.in as the argument to the constructor. (Some Virtual Machines require you to set a switch to allow System.in to be read for the keyboard.)

## close() Method

| Method | Syntax |
|---|---|
| close() | public void close() throws IOException |

close() closes the invoking InputStreamReader object and releases any resources allocate to it.

## getEncoding() Method

| Method | Syntax |
|---|---|
| getEncoding() | public String getEncoding() |

getEncoding() returns the encoding scheme of the invoking InputStreamReader object.

## read() Method

| Method | Syntax |
|---|---|
| read() | public int read() throws IOException |
| | public int read(char[] *charArray*, int *offset*, |
| | int *numChars*) throws IOException |

read() reads one or more characters from the input stream. The first version reads one character of data and returns the character as an int. The second version fills the char array charArray with characters read from the input stream. This methods return the number of characters read or -1 when the end of file is encountered.

In addition to the read() methods described here, an InputStreamReader object has access to the read() method defined in the Reader class.

## ready() Method

| Method | Syntax |
|---|---|
| ready() | public boolean ready() throws IOException |

ready() returns true when the invoking InputStreamReader object is ready to read data.

### Example: Using an InputStreamReader to Read Keyboard Input

An InputStreamReader object is created and set to read keyboard input by passing System.in to the InputStreamReader constructor. The InputStreamReader object is wrapped inside a BufferedReader object for greater efficiency and to allow the use of the readLine() method from the BufferedReader class. It is the BufferedReader object that calls the readLine() method.

System.in is the standard input stream, which for UNIX and Windows machines defaults to the keyboard. If this example is run on a Mac, a preference setting may have to be changed to allow System.in to be read from the keyboard.

```
import java.io.*;

public class TestIR {
public static void main(String args[]) {
    String s;
    System.out.println("Input lines of text, CTRL-C to quit");
    try {
      BufferedReader br =
        new BufferedReader(new InputStreamReader(System.in));

      while ((s = br.readLine()) != null) {
        System.out.println(s);
      }
      br.close();
    } catch (IOException ioe) {
      System.out.println(ioe);
    }
  }
}
```

**Output**

```
Whatever is typed in.
```

# 4.3.4 Reader Class

```
public abstract class Reader extends Object
```

```
Object
    Reader
```

Reader is the super-class of the input character stream classes. Reader defines the methods that allow the Reader sub-class objects to read character data and manipulate the character stream. Because it is an abstract class, a Reader object is never created.

## close() Method

| Method | Syntax |
|--------|--------|
| close() | public abstract void close() throws IOException |

close() closes the invoking input stream and releases any resources allocate to it.

**337**

## read() Method

| Method | Syntax |
|--------|--------|
| read() | `public int read() throws IOException`<br>`public int read(char[] charArray)`<br>`    throws IOException` |
| | `public abstract int read(char[] charArray,`<br>`    int offset,int numChars) throws IOException` |

read() reads one or more characters from the invoking input stream. The first version reads one character of data and returns the character as an int. The second and third versions fill the char array charArray with characters read from the invoking input stream. These methods return the number of characters read or -1 when the end of file is encountered.

The method is fully buffered so when the read() is used to accept input from the keyboard, nothing happens until the *Enter* key is pressed. The text can be altered using the *Backspace* or *Delete* keys. A *CTRL-Z* or *CTRL-D* indicates an end of file with keyboard input (this is operating system dependent).

## Stream Position Methods

| Method | Syntax |
|--------|--------|
| mark() | `public void mark(int pastLimit)`<br>`    throws IOException` |
| markSupported() | `public boolean markSupported()` |
| reset() | `public void reset() throws IOException` |
| skip() | `public long skip(long bytesToSkip)`<br>`    throws IOException` |

mark() sets a mark at the current position in the invoking input stream. The pastLimit parameter is the number of bytes that can read past the mark until the mark becomes invalid.

markSupported() method returns true if the invoking Reader object can be marked.

reset() method returns the position of the Reader object to that set by the mark() method.

skip() method skips bytesToSkip bytes in the invoking Reader object and returns the number of bytes skipped.

## ready() Method

| Method | Syntax |
|--------|--------|
| ready() | `public boolean ready() throws IOException` |

ready() returns true when the invoking Reader object is ready to read data.

**338**

# 4.4 Character Output Streams

Character output streams are used to write character data to an underlying stream. The output character stream class hierarchy is shown in the following figure.

The `Writer` class is an abstract class and is the parent of the output character stream classes.

The `FileWriter` class provides a way to write character data to a file.

The `OutputStreamWriter` class writes character data to an underlying byte stream.

A `BufferedWriter` object can be wrapped around an underlying `Writer` sub-class object to increase efficiency by providing an intermediate buffer to store the output data.

The `PrintWriter` class allows primitive and object data to be written to an underlying output byte or character stream.

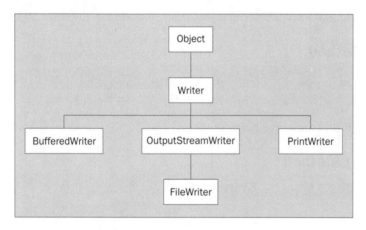

# 4.4.1 BufferedWriter Class

```
public class BufferedWriter extends Writer
```

```
Object
    Writer
        BufferedWriter
```

A `BufferedWriter` object improves the performance of an associated `Writer` object by providing a temporary storage buffer. Data is first written into the buffer. When the buffer is full, its contents are written to a file or external device. Using an intermediate buffer reduces the number of times the disk or network must be accessed.

## BufferedWriter() Constructors

| Constructor | Syntax |
|---|---|
| BufferedWriter() | public BufferedWriter(Writer outputStream) |
| | public BufferedWriter(Writer outputStream, int bufferSize) |

BufferedWriter() creates a BufferedWriter object. Note that the constructor takes a Writer object as an argument. One way to think of this is that the BufferedWriter object is wrapped around the Writer object to increase efficiency. The default buffer size is 8192 characters. This can be changed by providing the constructor with a buffer size.

## close() Method

| Method | Syntax |
|---|---|
| close() | public void close() throws IOException |

close() closes the invoking output stream and releases any resources allocated to it.

## flush() Method

| Method | Syntax |
|---|---|
| flush() | public void flush() throws IOException |

flush() flushes the output buffer of the invoking BufferedWriter object.

## newLine() Method

| Method | Syntax |
|---|---|
| newLine() | public void newLine() throws IOException |

newLine() causes a default end-of-line character sequence to be written to the invoking BufferedWriter object. output stream.

## write() Method

| Method | Syntax |
|---|---|
| write() | public void write(int c) throws IOException |
| | public void write(char buf[], int offset, int numChars) throws IOException |
| | public void write(String s, int offset, int numChars) throws IOException |

write() writes a char, an array of chars, or a String to the invoking output stream. The number of characters to be written can be specified as well as the position of the initial character to be written.

In addition to the write() methods described here, a BufferedWriter object has access to the write() methods defined in the Writer class.

## Example: Using a BufferedWriter to Write Data to a File

A BufferedWriter object is wrapped around a FileWriter object to write some data to a file named jrr.txt.copy. After the final write() method call, the flush() method is called to ensure that the buffer is emptied. The file jrr.txt contains the line "This is the contents of jrr.txt" followed by a line separator, and is contained in the same directory as the compiled .class file. The file jrr.txt.copy has the same contents.

System.getProperty("line.separator") returns the system end-of-line character sequence.

```
import java.io.*;

public class TestBW {
  public static void main(String args[]) {
    String str;
    try {
      BufferedReader br =
        new BufferedReader(new FileReader("jrr.txt"));
      BufferedWriter bw =
        new BufferedWriter(new FileWriter("jrr.txt.copy"));

      while ((str = br.readLine()) != null) {
        bw.write(str + System.getProperty("line.separator"));
      }
      bw.flush();
      br.close();
      bw.close();
    } catch (FileNotFoundException fnfe) {
      System.out.println(fnfe);
      return;
    } catch (IOException ioe) {
      System.out.println(ioe);
    }
  }
}
```

**Output**

The jrr.txt.copy file will contain the line:

```
This is the contents of jrr.txt
```

# 4.4.2 FileWriter Class

```
public class FileWriter extends OutputStreamWriter
```

```
Object
    Writer
        OutputStreamWriter
            FileWriter
```

A `FileWriter` object is an output stream that is used to write character data to a file.

The `FileWriter` class inherits all of its methods from the `OutputStreamWriter` and `Writer` classes.

## FileWriter() Constructors

| Constructor | Syntax |
|---|---|
| FileWriter() | public FileWriter(File *fobj*) throws IOException |
| | public FileWriter(FileDescriptor *fd*) |
| | public FileWriter(String *filePath*) throws IOException |
| | public FileWriter(String *filePath*, boolean *append*) throws IOException |

`FileWriter()` creates a `FileWriter` object. The file to be written to can be specified by a `File` object, a `FileDescriptor` object, or a `String` object containing the file path. If the file specified does not exist, it is created. If `append` is set to `true`, the file will be appended. The default is for the file to be overwritten.

### Example: Using a FileWriter to Write Data to a File

A `FileWriter` object is used to write character data to the file `jrr.txt.copy`. The file `jrr.txt` contains the line "This is the contents of jrr.txt" followed by a line separator, and is contained in the same directory as the compiled `.class` file. The `readLine()` method removes the carriage returns. They are added in the call to the `write()` method.

`System.getProperty("line.separator")` returns the system end-of-line character sequence.

```java
import java.io.*;

public class TestFW {
    public static void main(String args[]) {
        String str;
        try {
```

```
        BufferedReader br =
          new BufferedReader(new FileReader("jrr.txt"));

        FileWriter fw = new FileWriter("jrr.txt.copyFW");

        while ((str = br.readLine()) != null) {
          fw.write(str + System.getProperty("line.separator"));
        }
        fw.flush();
        br.close();
        fw.close();
      } catch (FileNotFoundException fnfe) {
        System.out.println(fnfe);
        return;
      } catch (IOException ioe) {
        System.out.println(ioe);
      }
    }
  }
```

**Output**

The jrr.txt.copy file will contain the line:

```
This is the contents of jrr.txt
```

# 4.4.3 OutputStreamWriter Class

```
public class OutputStreamWriter extends Writer
```

```
Object
    Writer
        OutputStreamWriter
```

An OutputStreamWriter object is a character stream that wraps around an underlying output byte stream. The characters are written as bytes to the output stream. It has an encoding scheme associated with it that translates the Unicode characters to bytes.

This class provides a bridge between the character and byte stream classes.

## OutputStreamWriter() Constructors

| Constructor | Syntax |
|---|---|
| OutputStreamWriter() | public OutputStreamWriter(OutputStream os) |
| | public OutputStreamWriter(OutputStream os, String encodingScheme) throws UnsupportedEncodingException |

**343**

OutputStreamWriter() creates an OutputStreamWriter object. The
OutputStreamWriter object is wrapped around an underlying OutputStream object
that is passed to the OutputStreamWriter constructor.

## close() Method

| Method | Syntax |
|--------|--------|
| close() | public void close() throws IOException |

close() closes the invoking output stream and releases any resources allocated to it.

## flush() Method

| Method | Syntax |
|--------|--------|
| flush() | public void flush() throws IOException |

flush() flushes the output buffer of the invoking OutputStreamWriter object.

## getEncoding() Method

| Method | Syntax |
|--------|--------|
| getEncoding() | public String getEncoding() |

getEncoding() returns a String object containing the name of the encoding scheme
associated with the invoking OutputStreamWriter object.

## write() Method

| Method | Syntax |
|--------|--------|
| write() | public void write(int c) throws IOException |
| | public void write(char buf[], int offset, int numChars) throws IOException |
| | public void write(String s, int offset, int numChars) throws IOException |

write() writes a char, an array of chars, or a String to the invoking output stream.
The number of characters to be written can be specified as well as the position of the
initial character to be written.

In addition to the write() methods described here, an OutputStreamWriter object
has access to the write() methods defined in the Writer class.

# 4.4.4 PrintWriter Class

```
public class PrintWriter extends Writer
```

```
Object
    Writer
        PrintWriter
```

The PrintWriter class provides the capability to write primitive datatypes and objects to an underlying output stream. The underlying output stream can be either a byte stream or a character stream.

## PrintWriter() Constructors

| Constructor | Syntax |
|---|---|
| PrintWriter() | public PrintWriter(OutputStream os) |
| | public PrintWriter(OutputStream os, boolean flushOnNewline) |
| | public PrintWriter(Writer w) |
| | public PrintWriter(Writer w, boolean flushOnNewline) |

PrintWriter() creates a PrintWriter object. The PrintWriter object is wrapped around an underlying output stream. The underlying output stream can be either a byte stream or character stream and is passed to the PrintWriter constructor. If flushOnNewline is true, the output buffer will be automatically flushed every time a new line is output.

## close() Method

| Method | Syntax |
|---|---|
| close() | public void close() |

close() closes the invoking output stream and releases any resources allocated to it.

## flush() Method

| Method | Syntax |
|---|---|
| flush() | public void flush() |

flush() flushes the output buffer of the invoking PrintWriter object.

## print() Method

| Method | Syntax |
|--------|--------|
| print() | public void **print**(boolean *b*) |
| | public void **print**(char *c*) |
| | public void **print**(char[] *c*) |
| | public void **print**(double *d*) |
| | public void **print**(float *f*) |
| | public void **print**(int *i*) |
| | public void **print**(long *l*) |
| | public void **print**(Object *obj*) |
| | public void **print**(String *str*) |

print() writes a String representation of the primitive datatype or Object to the invoking PrintWriter object. The version that takes an Object as an argument calls the toString() method of the object.

## println() Method

| Method | Syntax |
|--------|--------|
| println() | public void **println**(boolean *b*) |
| | public void **println**(char *c*) |
| | public void **println**(char[] *c*) |
| | public void **println**(double *d*) |
| | public void **println**(float *f*) |
| | public void **println**(int *i*) |
| | public void **println**(long *l*) |
| | public void **println**(Object *obj*) |
| | public void **println**(String *str*) |
| | public void **println**() |

println() writes a String representation of the primitive datatype or Object followed by a newline to the invoking PrintStream object. The version that takes an Object as an argument calls the toString() method of the object. The no-argument version simply writes a new line to the PrintStream.

# write() Method

| Method | Syntax |
|---|---|
| write() | public void **write**(int *c*) |
| | public void **write**(char *buf[]*) |
| | public void **write**(char *buf[]*, int *offset*, int *numChars*) |
| | public void **write**(String *s*) |
| | public void **write**(String *s*, int *offset*, int *numChars*) |

write() writes a char, an array of chars, or a String to the invoking output stream. The number of characters to be written can be specified as well as the position of the initial character to be written.

## Example: Using PrintWriter to Write Primitive Datatypes and Objects to a File

A PrintWriter object is wrapped around a FileWriter object and used to write data to a file named pw.txt. Because the println() method is overloaded, it can be used to write double, int, String, and Object data. Passing a Date object reference to the println() method calls the toString() method of the Date class.

```
import java.io.*;
import java.util.*;

public class TestPW {
   public static void main(String args[]) {
      double d = 2.0;
      int i = 3;
      Date date = new Date();

      try {
         PrintWriter pw = new PrintWriter(new FileWriter("pw.txt"),
                                          true);

         pw.println("The value of d is " + d);
         pw.println("The value of i is " + i);
         pw.println("The time is " + date);
         pw.close();
      } catch (IOException ioe) {
         System.out.println(ioe);
      }
   }
}
```

> **Output**
> The contents of file pw.txt will be:
>
> ```
> The value of d is 2.0
> The value of i is 3
> The time is Tue Nov 23 20:35:24 PST 1999
> ```

# 4.4.5 Writer Class

```
public abstract class Writer extends Object
```

```
.Object
    Writer
```

The Writer class is the superclass of all character stream output classes. It defines the methods used to write data to and manipulate output character streams.

Some of the methods defined in the Writer class are abstract, meaning that concrete sub-classes of the Writer class must provide implementations of these methods.

## close() Method

| Method | Syntax |
|--------|--------|
| close() | public abstract void close() throws IOException |

close() closes the invoking output stream and releases any resources allocated to it.

## flush() Method

| Method | Syntax |
|--------|--------|
| flush() | public abstract void flush() throws IOException |

flush() flushes the output buffer of the invoking output stream.

## write() Method

| Method | Syntax |
|--------|--------|
| write() | public void write(int c) throws IOException |
| | public void write(char buf[]) throws IOException |
| | public abstract void write(char buf[], int offset, int numChars) throws IOException |
| | public void write(String s) throws IOException |
| | public void write(String s, int offset, int numChars) throws IOException |

write() writes a char, an array of chars, or a String to the invoking output stream. The number of characters to be written can be specified as well as the position of the initial character to be written.

# 4.5 Other Classes and Pre-Defined Streams

## 4.5.1 Externalizable Interface

```
public interface Externalizable extends Serializable
```

```
Serializable
    Externalizable
```

Implementing the Externalizable interface is another way to serialize class objects. A serialized object is one that can be saved and restored. Unlike when using the Serializable interface, the Externalizable interface provides no default mechanism for saving and restoring objects. The code to save and restore the data members of the class objects must be provided inside implementations of the readExternal() and writeExternal() methods.

### readExternal() Method

| Method | Syntax |
|---|---|
| readExternal() | public void readExternal(ObjectInput *in*) throws IOException, ClassNotFoundException |

readExternal() is called when the Externalizable object is being restored and contains the code for reading the data members of the class object.

### writeExternal() Method

| Method | Syntax |
|---|---|
| writeExternal() | public void writeExternal(ObjectInput *in*) throws IOException |

writeExternal() is called when the Externalizable object is being saved and contains the code for writing the data members of the class object.

### Example: Using the Externalizable Interface

See the *Using Externalizable* example on page 1108.

## 4.5.2 File Class

public class **File** extends Object implements Serializable, Comparable

```
Object
    File
```

### Interfaces

Serializable, Comparable

A File object represents a file or directory pathname. The methods defined by the File class can be used to obtain information about and manipulate the file or directory. File objects can be used to determine the contents of a directory or to determine the path of a file or directory. Some of the Stream classes accept File objects in their constructors.

## File() Constructor

| Constructor | Syntax |
|---|---|
| File() | public **File**(String *fullPathName*) |
| | public **File**(String *directory*, String *filename*) |
| | public **File**(File *dirObj*, String *filename*) |

File() creates a File object. The file associated with the File object can be specified by its full pathname, a directory and a file name, or a File object representing the directory and a file name.

> If the file passed as an argument does not exist, the constructor will not generate the file.

There are certain situations where a file path will be ambiguous. For instance, if a Macintosh has a partitioned disk with each partition having the same name, the File object won't know which disk to access.

## Methods to Change the Attributes of a File or Directory

| Method | Syntax |
|---|---|
| renameTo() | public boolean **renameTo**(File *newFile*) |
| setLastModified() | public boolean **setLastModified**(long *time*) |
| setReadOnly() | public boolean **setReadOnly**() |

These methods are used to change the attributes of the file or directory associated with the invoking File object.

renameTo() renames the file or directory, and returns true if the change was successful. This method will only rename a file to the same logical disk, it cannot be used to move a file to another disk.

setLastModified() sets the last modification time, and returns true if the change was successful.

setReadOnly() changes the file or directory to be read-only, and returns true if the change was successful. This method only works on systems that have a read-only capability, and was introduced in JDK 1.2.

## Example: Changing the Attributes of a File or Directory

The file jrr.txt contains the line "This is the contents of jrr.txt" followed by a line separator, and is contained in the same directory as the compiled .class file. The renameTo() method is used to change the name of the file associated with the File object fobj to "jrr2.txt". The file name is changed, but the String returned when fobj invokes the getName() method is still "jrr.txt". The file is set to be read-only.

This example will only work on a system that has the read-only capability enabled.

```
import java.io.*;

public class TestFileChange {
  public static void main(String args[]) {
    File fobj = new File("jrr.txt");

    fobj.renameTo(new File("jrr2.txt"));
    fobj.setReadOnly();

    if (!fobj.canWrite()) {
      System.out.println(fobj.getName() + " is read-only");
    }
  }
}
```

### Output
```
jrr.txt is read-only
```

# Methods that Create Directories

| Method | Syntax |
|--------|--------|
| mkdir() | public boolean mkdir() |
| mkdirs() | public boolean mkdirs() |

mkdir() creates a directory according to the name associated with the invoking File object.

mkdirs() will also create any parent directories that are necessary.

## Example: Creating a Directory

The mkdir() method is used to create a directory named tmp2.

```
import java.io.*;

public class TestFileDir {
    public static void main(String args[]) {
        File fobj = new File("tmp2");

        fobj.mkdir();

        if (fobj.isDirectory()) {
            System.out.println(fobj.getName() + " is a directory");
        }
    }
}
```

*Output*
```
tmp2 is a directory
```

## Methods to Delete a File or Directory

| Method | Syntax |
|---|---|
| delete() | public boolean delete() |
| deteleOnExit() | public void deleteOnExit() |

delete() deletes the file or directory associated with the invoking File object, and returns false if the file or directory cannot be deleted. Depending on the system, the directory may have to be empty before it is deleted.

deleteOnExit() deletes the file or directory when the program terminates. Depending on the system, the directory may have to be empty before it is deleted.

## Example: Deleting a Directory

tmpDir is the name of a directory whose ownership was set such that it couldn't be deleted by the program. The use of the delete methods is somewhat risky and caution should be exercised - one some systems, the directory may be deleted even if it was set to be read-only.

```
import java.io.*;

public class TestFileDel {
  public static void main(String args[]) {
    File fobj = new File("tmpDir");

    if (!fobj.delete()) {
      System.out.println(fobj.getName() + " cannot be deleted");

    }
  }
}
```

**Output** *(may vary)*

```
tmpDir cannot be deleted
```

# Methods to Obtain the Path of the File or Directory

| Method | Syntax |
|---|---|
| getAbsoluteFile() | public File getAbsoluteFile() |
| getCanonicalFile() | public File getCanonicalFile()<br>throws IOException |
| getAbsolutePath() | public String getAbsolutePath() |
| getCanonicalPath() | public String getCanonicalPath()<br>throws IOException |
| getPath() | public String getPath() |

getAbsoluteFile() returns a File object that contains the absolute path of the invoking File object.

getCanonicalFile() returns a File object that contains the canonical path of the invoking File object.

getPath() returns the path that is provided to the File constructor.

getAbsolutePath() and getCanonicalPath() return a String object containing the absolute or canonical path of the file or directory associated with the invoking File object. An absolute path is complete, meaning that no additional information is required to find the file. The form of the canonical path is system dependent, but a canonical path will be absolute.

## Example: Using the getAbsoluteFile() Method

A File object fobj is created with no information about its path or parent directory. The getAbsoluteFile() method is used to convert fobj into a File object that contains the absolute path and information about the parent directory. The file jrr.txt is contained in the same directory as the compiled .class file.

```java
import java.io.*;

public class TestFileAbs {
  public static void main(String args[]) {
    File fobj = new File("jrr.txt");

    System.out.println("Path of " + fobj.getName() + " is "
                + fobj.getPath());
    System.out.println("Parent of " + fobj.getName() + " is "
                + fobj.getParent());

    File fobj2 = fobj.getAbsoluteFile();
    System.out.println("Path of " + fobj2.getName() + " is "
                + fobj2.getPath());
    System.out.println("Parent of " + fobj2.getName() + " is "
                + fobj2.getParent());
  }
}
```

**Output** *(will vary)*

```
Path of jrr.txt is jrr.txt
Parent of jrr.txt is null
Path of jrr.txt is /usr/palmer/Java_Book/java.io/jrr.txt
Parent of jrr.txt is /usr/palmer/Java_Book/java.io
```

## Methods to Investigate the Characteristics of a File Object

| Method | Syntax |
| --- | --- |
| canRead() | public boolean canRead() |
| canWrite() | public boolean canWrite() |
| exists() | public boolean exists() |
| isAbsolute() | public boolean isAbsolute() |
| isDirectory() | public boolean isDirectory() |
| isFile() | public boolean isFile() |
| isHidden() | public boolean isHidden() |

canRead() returns true if the file or directory associated with the invoking File object has read permission.

canWrite() returns true if the file or directory associated with the invoking File object has write permission.

exists() returns true if the file or directory exists.

isAbsolute() returns true if the File object represents an absolute path.

isDirectory() returns true if the File object represents a directory.

isFile() returns true if the File object represents a file.

isHidden() returns true if the File object represents a hidden file.

## Example: Investigating File Characteristics

A File object is created with a file name passed as an argument. The file jrr.txt contains the line "This is the contents of jrr.txt" followed by a line separator, and is contained in the same directory as the compiled .class file. Various methods described in this section are used to obtain information about the file. The isHidden() method was introduced in version 1.2 and won't work using a 1.1 JVM.

```java
import java.io.*;

public class TestFileChar {
  public static void main(String args[]) {
    File fobj = new File("jrr.txt");

    if (fobj.canRead()) {
      System.out.println(fobj + " can be read");
    }

    if (fobj.canWrite()) {
      System.out.println(fobj + " can be written to");
    }

    if (fobj.exists()) {
      System.out.println(fobj + " exists");
    }

    if (fobj.isAbsolute()) {
      System.out.println(fobj + " represents an absolute path");
    }

    if (fobj.isFile()) {
      System.out.println(fobj + " is a file");
    }
```

```
        if (fobj.isHidden()){
          System.out.println(fobj + " is a hidden file");
        }
      }
    }
```

**Output**

```
jrr.txt can be read
jrr.txt can be written to
jrr.txt exists
jrr.txt is a file
```

## list() Method

| Method | Syntax |
|--------|--------|
| list() | public String[] list() |
|        | public String[] list(FilenameFilter ff) |

list() is used with File objects representing directories, and returns a String array containing the files and directories contained within the directory represented by the invoking File object. list() can be passed a FilenameFilter object to limit the list to a subset of file names.

### Example: Listing Files in a Directory

The directory tmp should be created, containing three files, a.txt, b.txt, and c.txt. The list() method is used to return a String array containing the contents of tmp.

```java
import java.io.*;

public class TestFileList {
  public static void main(String args[]) {
    File fobj = new File("tmp");

    String[] fileList = fobj.list();
    System.out.print("Files in " + fobj.getName() + " are ");
    for (int i = 0; i < fileList.length; ++i) {
      System.out.print(fileList[i] + " ");
    }
    System.out.println("");
  }
}
```

**Output**

```
Files in tmp are a.txt b.txt c.txt
```

# listFiles() Method

| Method | Syntax |
|--------|--------|
| listFiles() | public File[] listFiles() |
| | public File[] listFiles(FilenameFilter *ff)* |
| | public File[] listFiles(FileFilter *f)* |

listFiles() is used with File objects representing directories, and returns a File array containing File objects representing the files and directories contained within the directory represented by the invoking File object. listFiles() can be passed a FilenameFilter object to limit the list to a subset of file names.

# Methods to Retrieve the Properties of a File Object

| Method | Syntax |
|--------|--------|
| getName() | public String getName() |
| getParent() | public String getParent() |
| getParentFile() | public File getParentFile() |
| lastModified() | public long lastModified() |
| length() | public long length() |

getName() returns the name of the file or directory associated with the invoking File object.

getParent() returns the name of the parent directory of the file or directory associated with the invoking File object.

getParentFile() returns a File object associated with the parent directory.

lastModified() returns the last time the file or directory was modified. The return value can be converted into a readable time using a Date or Calendar object.

length() returns the length of the file or directory in bytes.

## Example: Retrieving File Properties

The full path must be passed to the constructor in order for the getParent() method to work. The lastModified() method returns the time in milliseconds since Jan 1, 1970. It is converted into a more readable time using a Date object.

To run this example, the path will have to be changed to the correct path on your system.

```
import java.io.*;
import java.util.*;

public class TestFileProp {
    public static void main(String args[]) {
        File fobj =
            new File("/usr/people/palmer/Java_Book/java.io","jrr.txt");

        if ( fobj.exists() ) {
            System.out.println("Name of file is "+fobj.getName());
            System.out.println("Parent directory is "+fobj.getParent());
            System.out.println("File is "+fobj.length()+" bytes long");

            long time = fobj.lastModified();
            Date date = new Date(time);
            System.out.println("File was last modified "+date);
        } else {
            System.out.println("File does not exist");
        }
    }
}
```

**Output**

```
Name of file is jrr.txt
Parent directory of file is /usr/palmer/Java_Book/java.io
File is 32 bytes long
File was last modified Mon Nov 22 12:28:31 PST 1999
```

## toURL() Method

| Method | Syntax |
| --- | --- |
| toURL() | public URL toURL() throws MalformedURLException |

toURL() returns a URL object corresponding to the invoking File object.

# 4.5.3 FileDescriptor Class

```
public final class FileDescriptor extends Object
```

```
Object
    FileDescriptor
```

A FileDescriptor object represents a system-specific description of a file or socket. The FileDescriptor class has no constructor. A FileDescriptor object is obtained from the getFD() or getFileDescriptor() methods of other classes.

## FileDescriptor Class Constants

| Constant |
| --- |
| public static final FileDescriptor err |
| public static final FileDescriptor in |
| public static final FileDescriptor out |

These `FileDescriptor` objects represent standard error, standard input, and standard output.

## sync() Method

| Method | Syntax |
| --- | --- |
| sync() | public native void sync()<br>    throws SyncFailedException |

`sync()` causes the state of the underlying physical device associated with the invoking `FileDescriptor` device to be updated. This method returns after all modified data and attributes of this `FileDescriptor` have been written to the relevant device.

## valid() Method

| Method | Syntax |
| --- | --- |
| valid() | public boolean valid() |

`valid()` returns `true` if the invoking `FileDescriptor` object represents an open, valid device.

# 4.5.4 FileFilter Interface

    public interface FileFilter

A `FileFilter` is implemented by a class that wants to filter the files or directories that are included in a list of files or directories based on file paths.

## accept() Method

| Method | Syntax |
| --- | --- |
| accept() | public boolean accept(File *filePath*) |

`accept()` returns `true` if a file should be included in a list of filenames. Files are accepted if their paths match the path of the `File` object `filePath`.

# 4.5.5 FilenameFilter Interface

    public interface FilenameFilter

A `FilenameFilter` is implemented by a class that wants to filter the files or directories that are included in a list of files or directories based on file names.

## accept() Method

| Method | Syntax |
| --- | --- |
| accept() | public boolean accept(File *fileDirectory*, String *filename*) |

accept() returns true if a file should be included in a list of filenames. The File object fileDirectory represents the directory that contains the files. The String filename is the name of the file to be tested.

### Example: Using a FilenameFilter to Filter a List of Files

The directory tmp should be created, containing three files: a.java, b.txt, and c.txt. A file list is created using the list() method from the File class with a FilenameFilter to only list files that end in .java. The endsWith() method from the String class determines if the files end with .java.

```
import java.io.*;

class MyFilter implements FilenameFilter {
   String ext;

   public MyFilter(String str) {
      ext = "."+str;
   }

   public boolean accept(File fobj, String filename) {
      return filename.endsWith(ext);
   }
}

class TestFF
{
   public static void main(String args[]) {
      File fobj = new File("tmp");

      if ( fobj.exists() ) {
         String[] fileList = fobj.list( new MyFilter("java") );

         System.out.print("Files in "+fobj.getName()+" are ");
         for (int i=0; i<fileList.length; ++i) {
            System.out.print(fileList[i]+" ");
         }
         System.out.println();
      } else
            System.out.println("directory doesn't exist");

   }
}
```

***Output***

```
Files in tmp are a.java
```

# 4.5.6 Serializable Interface

```
public interface Serializable
```

The Serializable interface defines no methods but is used as a marker to indicate that the implementing class is serializable and therefore can be saved and restored.

## Example: Using the Serializable Interface

A class MyInteger is defined that contains an Integer object as its data member. The class implements the Serializable interface, so a MyInteger object can be saved and restored. The TestSerial class creates a MyInteger object and then writes it to a file. It then creates a new MyInteger instance by restoring the saved object. The Integer data member of the stored object has the same value as the original.

If MyInteger did not implement the Serializable interface, an exception would be thrown if an attempt was made to write a MyInteger object to disk.

```
import java.io.*;

public class TestSerial {
    MyInteger i1, i2;

    public TestSerial() {
        i1 = new MyInteger(2);

        try {
            ObjectOutputStream oos =
                new ObjectOutputStream(new FileOutputStream("tmp.obj"));
            oos.writeObject(i1);
        }
        catch (IOException ioe) {
            System.out.println("Error: "+ioe);
        }

        try {
            ObjectInputStream ois =
                new ObjectInputStream(new FileInputStream("tmp.obj"));
            i2 = (MyInteger)ois.readObject();
            System.out.println("value is "+i2.getValue());
        }
        catch (FileNotFoundException fnfe) {
            System.out.println("Error: "+fnfe);
        }
```

```
          catch (IOException ioe) {
            System.out.println("Error: "+ioe);
          }
          catch (ClassNotFoundException cnfe) {
            System.out.println("Error: "+cnfe);
          }
      }

    public static void main(String args[]) {
        TestSerial se = new TestSerial();
      }
  }

class MyInteger implements Serializable{
    private Integer integer;

    public MyInteger(int i) {
        integer = new Integer(i);
      }

    public int getValue() {
        return integer.intValue();
      }
  }
```

**Output**

```
value is 2
```

# 4.5.7 StreamTokenizer Class

```
public class StreamTokenizer extends Object
```

```
Object
    StreamTokenizer
```

A StreamTokenizer object can be used to break an input stream into tokens. The tokens can be numbers, words, end-of-line, or end-of-file.

## StreamTokenizer Class Constants

| Constant |
| --- |
| public static final int TT_EOF |
| public static final int TT_EOL |
| public static final int TT_NUMBER |
| public static final int TT_WORD |
| public double nval |
| public String sval |
| public int ttype |

These are the constants available to a StreamTokenizer object.

TT_EOF, TT_EOL, TT_NUMBER and TT_WORD represent end-of-file, end-of-line, number, and word token types.

nval stores the value of a TT_NUMBER token.

sval holds the String object of a TT_WORD token.

ttype is the token type and is either one of the "TT" constants or the character that was parsed from the input stream.

# StreamTokenizer() Constructors

| Constructor | Syntax |
| --- | --- |
| StreamTokenizer() | public StreamTokenizer(Reader robj) |
| | public StreamTokenizer(InputStream is) |

StreamTokenizer() creates a StreamTokenizer object. The constructor is passed a reference to a Reader object. The constructor that takes an InputStream object has been deprecated and should not be used for new code.

# Attribute Methods

| Method | Syntax |
| --- | --- |
| commentChar() | public void commentChar(int ch) |
| eolIsSignificant() | public void eolIsSignificant(boolean isSignificant) |
| lowerCaseMode() | public void lowerCaseMode(boolean lowerCase) |
| ordinaryChar() | public void ordinaryChar(int ch) |
| ordinaryChars() | public void ordinaryChars(int start, int end) |
| parseNumbers() | public void parseNumbers() |
| quoteChar() | public void quoteChar(int ch) |
| resetSyntax() | public void resetSyntax() |
| slashSlashComments() | public void slashSlashComments(boolean recognize) |
| slashStarComments() | public void slashStarComments(boolean recognize) |
| whitespaceChars() | public void whitespaceChars(int start, int end) |
| wordChars() | public void wordChars(int start, int end) |

commentChar() changes the character used at the beginning of a comment statement. The comment statement is not parsed.

eolIsSignificant() specifies whether the invoking StreamTokenizer object will return a TT_EOL token when an end-of-line is reached. If not, end-of-lines are treated as whitespace.

lowerCaseMode() specifies whether the String stored in sval will be converted to all lower case characters.

ordinaryChar() causes the invoking StreamTokenizer object to treat the character ch as an ordinary character.

ordinaryChars() causes characters within the specified range to be treated as ordinary characters.

parseNumbers() causes the invoking StreamTokenizer object to treat digits as numbers rather than characters.

quoteChar() causes the invoking StreamTokenizer object to treat the character ch as the delimiter for quoted text.

resetSyntax() resets the invoking StreamTokenizer object so all characters are treated as ordinary characters.

slashSlashComments() and slashStarComments() specify whether the invoking StreamTokenizer object will recognize and ignore double slash or slash-star comments.

whitespaceChars() causes characters within the specified range to be treated as whitespace characters.

wordChars() causes the characters within the specified range to be part of a word token. The normal range for alphabetic characters is 33 to 255.

## lineno() Method

| Method | Syntax |
| --- | --- |
| lineno() | public int lineno() |

lineno() returns the current line number.

## nextToken() Method

| Method | Syntax |
| --- | --- |
| nextToken() | public int nextToken() throws IOException |

nextToken() returns a token type constant or a character code from the invoking StreamTokenizer object.

# pushBack() Method

| Method | Syntax |
| --- | --- |
| pushBack() | public void pushBack() |

pushBack() returns the current token back to the stream. The subsequent call to the nextToken() method will return the same token.

## Example: Using StreamTokenizer to Parse a Text File

The rectangle.inp file should contain two lines of text: "width = 4.0", and "height = 3.0", and should be placed in the same directory as the compiled .class file. A StreamTokenizer object is used to parse the input file and assign the two numbers to the double variables width and height. The StreamTokenizer object is set to parse numbers and to recognize the end-of-line character.

```
import java.io.*;

public class TestST {
  public static void main(String args[]) {
    double width = 1.0;
    double height = 1.0;
    double area;

    try {
      StreamTokenizer stk =
        new StreamTokenizer(new FileReader("rectangle.inp"));

      stk.parseNumbers();
      stk.wordChars(33, 255);
      stk.eolIsSignificant(true);

      while (stk.nextToken() != stk.TT_EOL) {
        if (stk.ttype == stk.TT_NUMBER) {
          width = stk.nval;
        }
      }
      while (stk.nextToken() != stk.TT_EOF) {
        if (stk.ttype == stk.TT_NUMBER) {
          height = stk.nval;
        }
      }

      area = width * height;
      System.out.println("The area is " + area);
    } catch (FileNotFoundException fnfe) {
      System.out.println("Error: "+fnfe);
    }
```

4

java.io

```
      catch (IOException ioe) {
            System.out.println("Error: "+ioe);
         }
      }
   }
```

*Output*

```
      The area is 12.0
```

# 4.5.8 Pre-Defined Streams

The System class from the java.lang package contains the following pre-defined input, output, and error streams. On some systems, the standard input stream has to be activated before it can be used.

| Stream | Syntax |
|---|---|
| System.in | public static final InputStream in |
| System.out | public static final PrintStream out |
| System.err | public static final PrintStream err |

By default System.in refers to keyboard input and System.out refers to console output. For example, this command:

```
   System.out.println("Hello there");
```

would print "Hello there" on the screen.

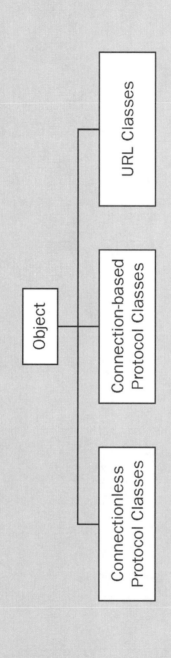

# 5

# java.net

The `java.net` package provides classes that allow programs to exchange data across a network. The programs do not have to be running on the same machine and indeed the machines can be located thousands of miles from each other. The data exchange model used by Java is based on the BSD UNIX socket library model.

There are two mechanisms, or protocols, for exchanging data. The first mechanism for transferring data between a two programs is called the **connectionless protocol**. With this protocol, a **packet** of information is sent without any guarantee that it will be delivered to the recipient, and without any way for the sender to determine whether or not it has arrived. The second basic mechanism for transfering data between a client and server is called the **connection-oriented protocol**. In this case, a connection between the client and server socket is established before data is transmitted. The connectionless protocol has a performance advantage over the connection-oriented protocol, however there is less certainty that the data will arrive as it was intended.

The `java.net` package also contains classes that implement and support connections to resources using **Uniform Resource Locators** or **URL**s.

The `java.net` class hierarchy is shown in the figure opposite.

In this Chapter we will cover:

# 5.1 Connectionless Protocol Classes

One mechanism for transferring data between a two programs is called the **connectionless protocol**. With this protocol, a given packet is sent without any guarantee that it will be delivered to the recipient, and without any way for the sender to determine whether or not it has arrived. The connectionless protocol has a performance advantage over the connection-oriented protocol and is therefore useful for applications where increased performance can be traded off against the risk of losing some data, such as when transferring video data. The connectionless protocol class hierarchy is shown in the figure below.

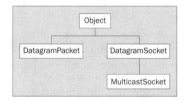

A schematic showing the mechanism for transferring data between two programs using the connectionless protocol is shown below. The sender and recipient programs each create a `DatagramPacket` object and a `DatagramSocket` object.

The sender's `DatagramPacket` object contains some data, and a destination IP address and port number. The `send()` method of the `DatagramSocket` object is then used to send the `DatagramPacket` object to its destination.

The recipient, meanwhile, has created a `DatagramSocket` object that is associated with the appropriate port number at which it wishes to listen. The `receive()` method of the `DatagramSocket` object is used to place whatever data it receives into the server's `DatagramPacket` object.

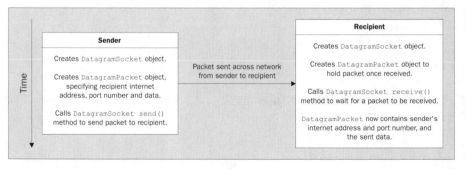

# 5.1.1 DatagramPacket Class

```
public final class DatagramPacket extends Object
```

```
Object
    DatagramPacket
```

A DatagramPacket object represents a packet of data consisting of an array of bytes. It is used to transfer data between a client machine and a server using the connectionless protocol. The DatagramPacket object also has associated with it an IP address and a port number to which it is being sent, or from which it was received.

## DatagramPacket() Constructor

| Constructor | Syntax |
|---|---|
| DatagramPacket() | public DatagramPacket(byte[] *data*, int *length*) |
| | public DatagramPacket(byte[] *data*, int *offset*, int *length*) |
| | public DatagramPacket(byte[] *data*, int *length*, InetAddress *addr*, int *port*) |
| | public DatagramPacket(byte[] data, int *offset*, int *length*, InetAddress *addr*, int *port*) |

Creates a DatagramPacket object. These constructors actually define two different types of DatagramPacket objects:

❏ The first two create DatagramPacket objects that are intended to receive data, and don't require an InetAddress object.

❏ The third and fourth versions create DatagramPacket objects that are intended to send data.

The length variable is the number of bytes to read or send and must be less than or equal to the length of the byte array. Specifying an offset allows some of the data to be skipped over when reading or sending. The port number must be between 0 and 65535. Port numbers between 1 and 511 are reserved for well-known services. For instance, port 21 is reserved for FTP and port 23 is reserved for telnet. Port numbers between 512 and 1023 are also reserved and on some systems require super-user privileges to use them. Port numbers between 1024 and 65535 are available for general use.

## Methods to Return DatagramPacket Properties

| Method | Syntax |
|---|---|
| getAddress() | public InetAddress getAddress() |
| getData() | public byte[] getData() |
| getLength() | public int getLength() |
| getOffset() | public int getOffset() |
| getPort() | public int getPort() |

getAddress() returns the IP address of the either the machine that sent the packet or the destination address, depending on whether the invoking DatagramPacket object is intended to receive or send data.

getData() returns a byte array containing the data associated with the invoking DatagramPacket object.

getLength() returns the number of bytes to be sent or received by the invoking DatagramPacket object.

getOffset() returns the offset, if any.

getPort() returns the port number of either the machine that sent the packet or the destination address, depending on whether the invoking DatagramPacket object is intended to send or receive data.

## Methods to Set DatagramPacket Properties

| Method | Syntax |
|---|---|
| setAddress() | public void setAddress(InetAddress addr) |
| setData() | public void setData(byte[] data) |
| | public void setData(byte[] data, int offset, int length) |
| setLength() | public void setLength(int length) |
| setPort() | public void setPort(int portNumber) |

setAddress() is used to set or change the destination IP address of the invoking DatagramPacket object.

setData() sets the data associated with the invoking DatagramPacket object.

setLength() specifies the number of bytes to be sent by the invoking DatagramPacket object.

setPort() sets the destination port number of the invoking DatagramPacket object.

### Example: Using DatagramPacket

See example *Using the Connectionless Protocol* on page 375, where DatagramPacket objects are used to send and receive data in a simple client-server program using the connectionless protocol.

# 5.1.2 DatagramSocket Class

```
public class DatagramSocket extends Object
```

```
Object
    DatagramSocket
```

A DatagramSocket object represents the mechanism by which packets of data are sent and received using the connectionless protocol.

## DatagramSocket() Constructor

| Constructor | Syntax |
|---|---|
| DatagramSocket() | public DatagramSocket() throws SocketException |
| | public DatagramSocket(int *port*) throws SocketException |
| | public DatagramSocket(int *port*, InetAddress *localHostMachine*) throws SocketException |

Creates a DatagramSocket object. The port number and IP address of the local machine can be specified. The port number must be between 0 and 65535. Some of the lower numbers are reserved for system use. (See *DatagramPacket() Constructor* on page 371.) If no port number is provided, the DatagramSocket object will be assigned any available port on the local machine.

## close() Method

| Method | Syntax |
|---|---|
| close() | public void close() |

close() closes the invoking DatagramSocket object and releases any resources assigned to it.

## Connection Methods

| Method | Syntax |
|---|---|
| connect() | public void connect(InetAddress *address*, int *port*) |
| disconnect() | public void disconnect() |
| getInetAddress() | public InetAddress getInetAddress() |
| getPort() | public int getPort() |

A DatagramSocket object may be connected, if desired, to a particular address and port number, so that it can only send or receive data from that address and port. (This is a completely different type of 'connection' to that of the connection-oriented protocol.) By default, a DatagramSocket object is not connected, and can send or receive data from any source.

5

java.net

connect() connects the DatagramSocket object to the specified address and port.

disconnect() disconnects the invoking DatagramSocket object. It does nothing if the DatagramSocket object is not connected.

getInetAddress() returns an InetAddress object representing the IP address of the remote machine, if the invoking DatagramSocket object is connected, or null if it object is not connected.

getPort() returns the port number to which the invoking DatagramSocket object is connected, or -1 if the DatagramSocket object is not connected.

## Methods to Return DatagramSocket Properties

| Method | Syntax |
|--------|--------|
| getLocalAddress() | public InetAddress getLocalAddress() |
| getLocalPort() | public int getLocalPort() |
| getReceiveBufferSize() | public int getReceiveBufferSize()<br>    throws SocketException |
| getSendBufferSize() | public int getSendBufferSize()<br>    throws SocketException |
| getSoTimeout() | public int getSoTimeout()<br>    throws SocketException |

getLocalAddress() returns an InetAddress object containing the local address to which the invoking DatagramSocket object is bound.

getLocalPort() returns the port number to which the invoking DatagramSocket object is bound.

getReceiveBufferSize() and getSendBufferSize() return the size of the input and output buffers used by the local machine for this socket.

getSoTimeout() returns the time in milliseconds that the invoking DatagramSocket object will wait for an incoming packet of data.

## Methods to Set DatagramSocket Properties

| Method | Syntax |
|--------|--------|
| setReceiveBufferSize() | public void setReceiveBufferSize(int *size*)<br>    throws SocketException |
| setSendBufferSize() | public void setSendBufferSize(int *size*)<br>    throws SocketException |
| setSoTimeout() | public void setSoTimeout(int *time*)<br>    throws SocketException |

setReceiveBufferSize() and setSendBufferSize() change the size of the input and output buffers used by the local machine for this socket. The local machine may or may not accept the size specified by these methods.

setSoTimeout() changes the time in milliseconds that the invoking DatagramSocket object will wait for an incoming packet of data. Setting the value to 0 indicates that the DatagramSocket object will wait indefinitely.

## receive() Method

| Method | Syntax |
|--------|--------|
| receive() | public void receive(DatagramPacket *pkt*) throws IOException |

receive() receives a DatagramPacket object from the socket. This method blocks other activity until a packet is received or until the time-out time has elapsed. Once a packet has been received, the method returns. The received packet contains a byte array containing data, the length of the byte array, the sender's IP address, and the sender's port number.

## send() Method

| Method | Syntax |
|--------|--------|
| send() | public void send(DatagramPacket *pkt*) throws IOException |

send() sends a DatagramPacket object into the socket. The DatagramPacket object must contain a byte array containing the data to be transmitted, the length of the byte array, the destination IP address, and the destination port number.

### Example: Using the Connectionless Protocol

This example sets up a simple client-server application, comprising separate client and server programs. When the user clicks on a button, the client sends a DatagramPacket to the server requesting information. The server recieves the request, and returns a DatagramPacket to the client containing a byte array representation of an Info object, which holds information about a ski resort. The client receives the DatagramPacket from the server, converts its data back into an Info object, and displays the information.

Each of the three classes is kept in a separate file. To run this example, open up two windows on the same machine. Run the server in one window and the client in the other.

#### Info Class

An Info object encapsulates some information about a ski resort. This class is used by both the client and server classes.

```
import java.io.*;

public class Info implements Serializable {
  private String name, base;
  private int runs;
```

```
    public Info(String n, int r, String b) {
       name = n;
       runs = r;
       base = b;
    }

    public String getName() {
       return name;
    }

    public int getRuns() {
       return runs;
    }

    public String getBase() {
       return base;
    }

}
```

### Server program

The ServerCLP class sets up a server to receive and transmit data using the connectionless protocol. A DatagramSocket object is created that will send and receive data packets. The listening and transmitting code is placed in an infinite loop. Thus, the server will keep listening for packets from client machines as long as the sever program keeps running.

Two separate DatagramPacket objects are created. The first, named pktReceive, is used to listen for a signal from a client machine. Once the signal is received, this DatagramPacket contains no data, but does contain the IP address and port number of the client machine. Once a signal from a client machine is received, an Info object containing information about a ski resort is sent back to the client machine.

To send the data through the socket, the Info object must be converted into a byte array. This is accomplished using ByteArrayOutputStream and ObjectOutputStream objects. The writeObject() method from the ObjectOutputStream class is used to write the Info object to an output stream. The toByteArray() method returns a byte array containing the contents of the output stream. For the writeObject() method to work properly, the Info object must implement either the Serializable or Externalizable interfaces.

Once the Info object has been written to a byte array, the outgoing DatagramPacket object can be created using the IP address and port number obtained from the incoming DatagramPacket.

```
import java.net.*;
import java.io.*;

public class ServerCLP {
  static DatagramSocket ds;
  static int portNumber = 8888;
  static DatagramPacket pktReceive, pktSend;
```

```
public static void main(String args[]) {

  // Create DatagramSocket to send and receive data packets
  try {
    ds = new DatagramSocket(portNumber);
  } catch (SocketException se) {}

  // Create a packet to receive data from the client
  pktReceive = new DatagramPacket(new byte[1], 1);

  while (true) {
    try {
      // Wait for a packet
      ds.receive(pktReceive);

      // Create ObjectOutputStream to convert Info object to
      // stream of bytes
      ByteArrayOutputStream bos = new ByteArrayOutputStream();
      ObjectOutputStream oos = new ObjectOutputStream(bos);

      // Create Info object ready to send to client
      Info info = new Info("NorthStar", 18, "72 inches");

      // Convert Info object into array of bytes
      oos.writeObject(info);
      byte[] data = bos.toByteArray();

      // Create packet and send to client
      pktSend = new DatagramPacket(data, data.length,
                                   pktReceive.getAddress(),
                                   pktReceive.getPort());
      ds.send(pktSend);
    } catch (IOException ioe) {}
  }

}
```

### Client program

The ClientCLP class creates a simple user interface by placing a JButton object and three JLabel objects in a screen window using a JFrame. When the JButton object is clicked, the actionPerformed() method is called.

Inside the actionPerformed() method, a DatagramSocket object is created to send and receive data packets. A DatagramPacket object is created and sent to the server. This object contains no data, but does contain the IP address and port number of the client machine, so that the server knows where to return its response.

The client then waits until it receives a `DatagramPacket` object from the server. Once it receives the incoming `DatagramPacket` object, it must convert the `byte` array of data to an `Info` object. It does this using a `ByteArrayInputStream` and `ObjectInputStream` object. The `readObject()` method from the `ObjectInputStream` class converts the `byte` array to an `Object` object which is then cast to an `Info` object.

The information contained in the `Info` object is then extracted and displayed in the `JLabel` components.

```java
import java.net.*;
import java.io.*;
import javax.swing.*;
import java.awt.*;
import java.awt.event.*;

public class ClientCLP extends JFrame implements ActionListener {
    DatagramSocket ds;
    int portNumber = 8888;
    DatagramPacket pktReceive, pktSend;
    JButton button;
    JLabel lblName, lblRuns, lblBase;
    Info info = null;
    JPanel p1, p2;

    public ClientCLP() {

        // Create the user interface
        button = new JButton("download");
        button.setFont(new Font("Serif", Font.PLAIN, 12));
        button.setBorder(BorderFactory.createRaisedBevelBorder());
        button.addActionListener(this);

        lblName = new JLabel("");
        lblName.setForeground(Color.black);
        lblName.setFont(new Font("Serif", Font.PLAIN, 12));

        lblRuns = new JLabel("");
        lblRuns.setForeground(Color.black);
        lblRuns.setFont(new Font("Serif", Font.PLAIN, 12));

        lblBase = new JLabel("");
        lblBase.setForeground(Color.black);
        lblBase.setFont(new Font("Serif", Font.PLAIN, 12));

        p1 = new JPanel();
        p1.setLayout(new GridLayout(3, 1));
        p1.add(lblName);
        p1.add(lblRuns);
        p1.add(lblBase);
```

```java
    p2 = new JPanel();
    p2.add(button);

    getContentPane().add(p2, BorderLayout.NORTH);
    getContentPane().add(p1, BorderLayout.CENTER);

    addWindowListener(new WinClosing());
    setBounds(100, 100, 300, 300);
    setVisible(true);
}

public void actionPerformed(ActionEvent ae) {

    // React to pressing of button on user interface
    pktReceive = new DatagramPacket(new byte[1024], 1024);

    // Create DatagramSocket to send and receive data packets
    try {
        ds = new DatagramSocket();
    } catch (SocketException se) {}

    // Create and send DatagramPacket to ask server for information
    try {
        ds.send(new DatagramPacket(new byte[1], 1,
                InetAddress.getLocalHost(), portNumber));

        // Wait for and receive response packet from server
        ds.receive(pktReceive);

        // Create ObjectInputStream to convert stream of bytes in
        // packet back into an Info object
        ByteArrayInputStream bis =
            new ByteArrayInputStream(pktReceive.getData());
        ObjectInputStream ois = new ObjectInputStream(bis);

        // Convert the packet into an Info object
        try {
            info = (Info) ois.readObject();
        } catch (ClassNotFoundException ce) {}
    } catch (IOException ioe) {}

    // If successful, display the information on the user interface
    if (info != null) {
        lblName.setText("Name: " + info.getName());
        lblRuns.setText("Number of runs open: " + info.getRuns());
        lblBase.setText("Snow Depth: " + info.getBase());
        p1.revalidate();
    }
}
```

5

java.net

```
    public static void main(String args[]) {
       ClientCLP clp = new ClientCLP();
    }
  }

  class WinClosing extends WindowAdapter {
     public void windowClosing(WindowEvent we) {
        System.exit(0);
     }
  }
```

### Output

The user interface of the client program is shown below. After pressing the download button, the information obtained from the server (the name, number of runs open and snow depth) is displayed.

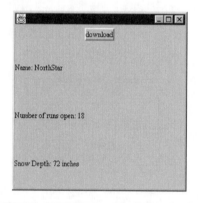

# 5.1.3 MulticastSocket Class

```
public class MulticastSocket extends DatagramSocket
```

```
Object
  DatagramSocket
    MulticastSocket
```

The MulticastSocket class is used to implement **multicast** data communication using the connectionless protocol. It can be used to send a message to multiple machines, those that are part of the sending machine's group. The MulticastSocket object can join or leave groups of other multicast hosts on the Internet. A multicast group is specified by an IP address in a particular range, and by a standard UDP port number.

When a `MulticastSocket` joins a particular multicast group, it receives `DatagramPacket` objects sent to the group by other hosts (which do not themselves need to be members of the group), as do all other members of the group.

## MulticastSocket() Constructor

| Constructor | Syntax |
|---|---|
| MulticastSocket() | public MulticastSocket() throws IOException |
| | public MulticastSocket(int *port*) throws IOException |

Creates a `MulticastSocket` object. The `MulticastSocket` object can be bound to a port on the local host machine by providing the port number to the constructor.

## joinGroup() Method

| Method | Syntax |
|---|---|
| joinGroup() | public void joinGroup(InetAddress *multicastAddress*) throws IOException |

`joinGroup()` causes the invoking `MulticastSocket` object to join a multicast group. An `IOException` is thrown if the specified address is not a multicast address.

## leaveGroup() Method

| Method | Syntax |
|---|---|
| leaveGroup() | public void leaveGroup(InetAddress *multicastAddress*) throws IOException |

`leaveGroup()` causes the invoking `MulticastSocket` object to leave a multicast group. An `IOException` is thrown if the specified address is not a multicast address.

## Methods to Return MulticastSocket Properties

| Method | Syntax |
|---|---|
| getInterface() | public InetAddress getInterface() throws SocketException |
| getTimeToLive() | public int getTimeToLive() throws IOException |

`getInterface()` returns an `InetAddress` object containing the IP address the invoking `MulticastSocket` object will use to send packets to multicast destinations.

`getTimeToLive()` returns the **time-to-live (TTL)** value of the invoking `MulticastSocket` object. The TTL value is the number of hops an outgoing packet can experience before it dies.

5

java.net

## send() Method

| Method | Syntax |
| --- | --- |
| send() | public void send(DatagramPacket *pkt*, byte *ttl*)<br>    throws IOException |

send() sends the specified DatagramPacket object from the invoking
MulticastSocket using the specified TTL value. A MulticastSocket object can use
this method in addition to the the send() method defined in the DatagramSocket
class.

## Methods to Set MulticastSocket Properties

| Method | Syntax |
| --- | --- |
| setInterface() | public void setInterface(InetAddress *addr*)<br>    throws SocketException |
| setTimeToLive() | public void setTimeToLive(int *timeToLive*)<br>    throws IOException |

setInterface() specifies the IP address the invoking MulticastSocket object will
use to send packets to multicast destinations.

setTimeToLive() changes the time-to-live (TTL) value of the invoking
MulticastSocket object.

## Deprecated Methods

| Method | Syntax |
| --- | --- |
| getTTL() | public byte getTTL() throws IOException |
| setTTL() | public void setTTL(byte *ttl*) throws IOException |

These methods have been deprecated as of Java 2 and should not be used for new
code.

getTTL() returns the time-to-live (TTL) value of the invoking MulticastSocket object
as a byte.

setTTL() method changes the TTL value of the invoking MulticastSocket object.

# 5.2 Connection-Oriented Protocol Classes

The second basic mechanism, or protocol, for transfering data between a client and server, the **connection-oriented protocol**, establishes a connection between the client and server socket before data is transmitted. The logical device used to transfer packets of data between machines is called a **socket**. A socket has an associated **port number** that is either assigned by the operating system or supplied by the program. Data is usually sent between two sockets, one associated with the client machine and one associated with the server. When the client socket sends a packet of data, the packet is accompanied with information about the client machine's network address and the port number of the client socket. The server socket specifies only the port number it is monitoring to receive data.

When one of the sockets sends a packet to the other, it waits to receive confirmation that the packet was successfully received. If the socket does not receive confirmation, it re-sends the packet. Packets are read from the receiving socket in the order that they were sent. The connection-oriented class hierarchy is shown in the figure below.

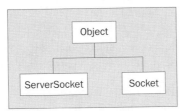

A schematic showing the mechanism for transferring data between a client and server using the connectionless protocol is shown below. The client program creates a Socket object that opens a logical connection with the server. The server program creates a ServerSocket object that will accept the connection. When the connection is made, the ServerSocket object creates a Socket object that in turn creates InputStream and OutputStream objects. The InputStream and OutputStream objects can be used to read and write byte stream data to and from the connection. It is possible for the calling application to spin off each new connection as a separate Thread, each with its own Socket object, allowing the ServerSocket to continue to listen for new connections.

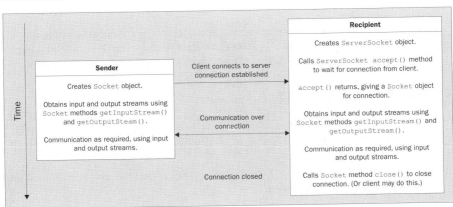

# 5.2.1 ServerSocket Class

```
public class ServerSocket extends Object
```

```
Object
    ServerSocket
```

The ServerSocket class is used to implement the connection-oriented communication protocol. A ServerSocket object is used to listen for a connection request from a client machine. When a connection is requested, the ServerSocket object can create a Socket object to receive and transmit data through the socket.

## ServerSocket() Constructor

| Constructor | Syntax |
|---|---|
| ServerSocket() | public ServerSocket(int *port*) throws IOException |
| | public ServerSocket(int *port*, int *backlog*)<br>    throws IOException |
| | public ServerSocket(int *port*, int *backlog*,<br>    InetAddress *addr*) throws IOException |

Server Socket() creates a ServerSocket object. The port that the ServerSocket object will listen to is specified. If the port is set to 0, the ServerSocket object will use any available port. The backlog is the number of connection requests that can be placed in the ServerSocket queue. The default number is 50. Once the queue is full, additional connection requests are refused and clients will receive an error. If the server machine has multiple IP addresses, the InetAddress argument can be specify which IP address will be used.

## accept() Method

| Method | Syntax |
|---|---|
| accept() | public Socket accept() throws IOException |

accept() listens for a connection request and accepts the connection. When the connection is accepted, a Socket object is returned that can be used to send and receive data through the connection. Other activity is blocked until a connection is made.

## close() method

| Method | Syntax |
|---|---|
| close() | public void close() throws IOException |

close() closes the socket used by the invoking ServerSocket object and releases any system resources associated with it.

# Methods to Return ServerSocket Properties

| Method | Syntax |
| --- | --- |
| getInetAddress() | public InetAddress getInetAddress() |
| getLocalPort() | public int getLocalPort() |
| getSoTimeout() | public int getSoTimeout() throws IOException |

getInetAddress() returns an InetAddress object representing the IP address used by the invoking ServerSocket object.

getLocalPort() returns the port number that the invoking ServerSocket object is listening to.

getSoTimeout() returns the time in milliseconds that the invoking ServerSocket object will wait for a connection. A return value of 0 means that the ServerSocket object will wait indefinitely.

# setSoTimeout() method

| Method | Syntax |
| --- | --- |
| setSoTimeout() | public void setSoTimeout(int *time*) throws SocketException |

setSoTimeout() is used to change the time in milliseconds that the ServerSocket will wait for a connection.

# toString() Method

| Method | Syntax |
| --- | --- |
| toString() | public String toString() |

toString() overrides the toString() method from the Object class and returns a String representation of the invoking Socket object.

## Example: Using ServerSocket

See example *Using the Connection-Oriented Protocol* on page 389, where a ServerSocket object is used to accept a connection from a client in a simple client-server program.

# 5.2.2 Socket Class

```
public class Socket extends Object
```

```
Object
    Socket
```

A Socket object is used to implement stream-based, connection-oriented data communication. The Socket class encapsulates a two-way communication mechanism that is connected at both ends to an IP address and port number. An InputStream and an OutputStream are associated with the Socket, to allow data to be sent to and read from the Socket using the standard methods of those classes, defined in the java.io package. (See *InputStream Class* in Section 4.1.7 on page 304 and *OutputStream Class* in Section 4.2.9 on page 327.)

## Socket() Constructor

| Constructor | Syntax |
|---|---|
| Socket() | public Socket(String *remoteHost*, int *remotePort*)<br>    throws UnknownHostException, IOException |
| | public Socket(InetAddress *remoteAddress*, int *remotePort*)<br>    throws IOException |
| | public Socket(String *remoteHost*, int *remotePort*,<br>    InetAddress *localAddress*, int *localPort*)<br>    throws IOException |
| | public Socket(InetAddress *remoteAddress*, int *remotePort*,<br>    InetAddress *localAddress*, int *localPort*)<br>    throws IOException |

Creates a Socket object. The remote port number, and remote host name or an InetAddress object, must be specified. In addition the local port number and local host name or IP address can be provided.

## Buffer Size Methods

| Method | Syntax |
|---|---|
| getReceiveBufferSize() | public int getReceiveBufferSize()<br>    throws SocketException |
| getSendBufferSize() | public int getSendBufferSize()<br>    throws SocketException |
| setRecieveBufferSize() | public void setRecieveBufferSize(int *size*)<br>    throws SocketException |
| setSendBufferSize() | public void setSendBufferSize(int *size*)<br>    throws SocketException |

getReceiveBufferSize() and getSendBufferSize() return the size of the input and output buffers for the invoking Socket object.

setRecieveBufferSize() and setSendBufferSize() suggest changes to the size of the input and output buffers. The system may or may not permit these changes.

# close() Method

| Method | Syntax |
|--------|--------|
| close() | public void close() throws IOException |

close() closes the socket associated with the invoking Socket object and releases any system resources used by the socket.

# Methods that Return Socket Properties

| Method | Syntax |
|--------|--------|
| getInetAddress() | public InetAddress getInetAddress() |
| getKeepAlive() | public boolean getKeepAlive() throws SocketException |
| getLocalAddress() | public InetAddress getLocalAddress() |
| getLocalPort() | public int getLocalPort() |
| getPort() | public int getPort() |
| getSoLinger() | public int getSoLinger() throws SocketException |
| getSoTimeout() | public int getSoTimeout() throws SocketException |
| getTcpNoDelay() | public boolean getTcpNoDelay() throws SocketException |

getInetAddress() returns an InetAddress object containing the IP address of the remote host to which the invoking Socket object is connected.

getKeepAlive() returns true if the 'keep-alive' property of the Socket is enabled.

getLocalAddress() returns an InetAddress object containing the local IP address of the invoking Socket object.

getLocalPort() returns the local port number for the invoking Socket object.

getPort() returns the port number of the remote host to which the invoking Socket object is connected.

getSoLinger() returns the delay in milliseconds between when the close() method is invoked and the socket is closed.

getSoTimeout() returns the time in milliseconds the invoking Socket object will wait for an incoming packet.

getTcpNoDelay() returns true if Nagle's algorithm is disabled for this socket. Nagle's algorithm combines smaller packets into larger packets for increased efficiency.

## Methods that Set Socket Properties

| Method | Syntax |
|---|---|
| setKeepAlive() | public void **setKeepAlive**(boolean *on*) throws SocketException |
| setSoLinger() | public void **setSoLinger**(boolean *on*, int *delay*) throws SocketException |
| setSoTimeout() | public void **setSoTimeout**(int *time*) throws SocketException |
| setTcpNoDelay() | public void **setTcpNoDelay**(boolean *on*) throws SocketException |

setKeepAlive() specifies the value of the invoking Socket object's 'keep-alive' property.

setSoLinger() sets the delay in milliseconds between when the close() method is invoked and the socket is closed. If the boolean on is set to false or the int delay is set to 0, the socket closes immediately.

setSoTimeout() specifies the time in milliseconds the invoking Socket object will wait for an incoming packet.

setTcpNoDelay() specifies if Nagle's algorithm is to be used for this socket. Nagle's algorithm combines smaller packets into larger packets for increased efficiency.

## Stream Methods

| Method | Syntax |
|---|---|
| getInputStream() | public InputStream **getInputStream**() throws IOException |
| getOutputStream() | public OutputStream **getOutputStream**() throws IOException |
| shutDownInput() | public void **shutDownInput**() throws IOException |
| shutDownOutput() | public void **shutDownOutput**() throws IOException |

getInputStream() returns an InputStream object that can be used to read data from the invoking Socket object.

getOutputStream() returns an OutputStream object that can be used to send data through the invoking Socket object.

shutDownInput() shuts down the InputStream of the invoking Socket object by placing the stream at "end of stream". Any data then received is silently discarded.

shutDownOutput() disables the OutputStream of the invoking Socket object.

# toString() Method

| Method | Syntax |
|--------|--------|
| toString() | public String toString() |

toString() overrides the toString() method from the Object class and returns a String representation of the invoking Socket object.

# Deprecated Constructors

| Constructor | Syntax |
|-------------|--------|
| Socket() | public Socket(String *remoteHost*, int *remotePort*, boolean *stream*) throws IOException |
| | public Socket(InetAddress *remoteAddress*, int *remotePort*, boolean *stream*) throws IOException |

These two constructors were deprecated as of Java 1.1. If the boolean stream is set to false, a datagram socket is created. DatagramSocket objects should be used instead to create this type of socket.

## Example: Using the Connection-Oriented Protocol

This program implements a simple client-server application. The client and server classes are contained in two separate files. When the button on the client is pressed it connects the the server, and the server returns a String object, which is then displayed on the client.

To run this example, open up two windows on the same machine. Run the server program in one window, and the client program in the other.

### Server program

The ServerCP class sets up a connection-oriented socket to transmit a String object to a client machine.

A ServerSocket object is created to listen for connection requests. The accept() method waits for a connection request and returns a Socket object when the connection is completed.

An ObjectOutputStream object is tied to the output stream of the Socket object using the getOutputStream() method. The ObjectOutputStream object is then used to write a String object to the output stream.

Placing most of the code in an infinite loop allows the server to continue to listen for connection requests as long as the program is running.

```java
import java.net.*;
import java.io.*;

public class ServerCP {
  ServerSocket serverSocket;
  int portNumber = 8888;
  Socket socket;
  String str = "Server String";

  ServerCP() {

    // Create ServerSocket to listen for connections
    try {
      serverSocket = new ServerSocket(portNumber);
    } catch (IOException se) {}

    // Enter infinite loop, waiting for connections
    while (true) {
      try {

        // Wait for client to connnect, then get Socket
        socket = serverSocket.accept();

        // Use ObjectOutputStream to send String to the client
        ObjectOutputStream oos =
          new ObjectOutputStream(socket.getOutputStream());

        oos.writeObject(str);

        oos.close();

        // Close Socket and go back to wait for next client
        socket.close();
      } catch (IOException ioe) {}
    }
  }

  public static void main(String args[]) {
    ServerCP scp = new ServerCP();
  }
}
```

### Client program

The ClientCP class creates a graphical user interface by placing a JButton and a
JLabel object on a JFrame. The JButton object is associated with an
ActionListener, so that when the JButton is pressed the actionPerformed()
method is called.

Inside the actionPerformed() method, a Socket object is created using the IP
address and port number of the server. (Since both programs will be run on the same
machine, the local host address is used.)

An ObjectInputStream object is tied to the socket input stream using the getInputStream() method. The ObjectInputStream object reads the String object from the socket stream.

The JLabel text is updated with the String transmitted from the server.

```java
import java.net.*;
import java.io.*;
import javax.swing.*;
import java.awt.*;
import java.awt.event.*;

public class ClientCP extends JFrame implements ActionListener {
    Socket socket;
    int portNumber = 8888;
    JButton button;
    JLabel lblName;
    String str = "";
    JPanel p1, p2;

    public ClientCP() {

        // Create user interface components
        button = new JButton("download");
        button.setFont(new Font("Serif", Font.PLAIN, 12));
        button.setBorder(BorderFactory.createRaisedBevelBorder());
        button.addActionListener(this);

        lblName = new JLabel("");
        lblName.setForeground(Color.black);
        lblName.setFont(new Font("Serif", Font.PLAIN, 12));

        p1 = new JPanel();
        p1.add(lblName);

        p2 = new JPanel();
        p2.add(button);

        getContentPane().add(p2, BorderLayout.NORTH);
        getContentPane().add(p1, BorderLayout.CENTER);

        addWindowListener(new WinClosing());
        setBounds(100, 100, 300, 300);
        setVisible(true);
    }

    public void actionPerformed(ActionEvent ae) {
        // Called when the button is pressed
```

```
      // Create a socket connection to the specified machine and
      // port number
      try {
        socket = new Socket(InetAddress.getLocalHost(),
                            portNumber);
      } catch (IOException se) {}

      // Use ObjectInputStream to convert input from server to a
      // String object
      try {
        ObjectInputStream ois =
          new ObjectInputStream(socket.getInputStream());
        try {
          str = (String) ois.readObject();
        } catch (ClassNotFoundException ce) {}
      } catch (IOException ioe) {}

      // Display the string on the user interface
      lblName.setText(str);
      p1.revalidate();
    }

    public static void main(String args[]) {
      ClientCP cp = new ClientCP();
    }
  }

  class WinClosing extends WindowAdapter {
    public void windowClosing(WindowEvent we) {
      System.exit(0);
    }
  }
```

### Output

The user interface of the client program is shown below. After pressing the download button, the information obtained from the server (the string Server String) is displayed.

# 5.3 Miscellaneous Classes

## 5.3.1 InetAddress Class

```
public final class InetAddress extends Object implements Serializable
```

```
Object
    InetAddress
```

### Interfaces

```
Serializable
```

An InetAddress object represents an IP address. The InetAddress class provides no public constructors. An InetAddress object is obtained from one of the static InetAddress object creation methods in this class.

### Static InetAddress Object Creation Methods

| Method | Syntax |
|--------|--------|
| getAllByName() | public static InetAddress[] getAllByName (String *hostName*) throws UnknownHostException |
| getByName() | public static InetAddress getByName(String *hostName*) throws UnknownHostException |
| getLocalHost() | public static InetAddress getLocalHost() throws UnknownHostException |

getAllByName() returns an array of InetAddress objects containing all of the IP addresses corresponding to the specified host name. The specified host name can either be a machine name, like "www.wrox.com", or an IP address such as "204.148.170.3".

getByName() returns an InetAddress object representing the primary IP address corresponding to the specified host name.

getLocalHost() returns an InetAddress object containing the IP address of the local host machine.

### equals() Method

| Method | Syntax |
|--------|--------|
| equals() | public boolean equals(Object *obj*) |

equals() overrides the equals() method from the Object class and returns true if Object obj is an InetAddress and contains the same IP address as the invoking InetAddress object.

## hashCode() Method

| Method | Syntax |
|---|---|
| hashCode() | public int hashCode() |

hashCode() overrides the hashCode() method from the Object class and returns a hash code for the invoking InetAddress object.

## Methods to Return InetAddress Properties

| Method | Syntax |
|---|---|
| getAddress() | public byte[] getAddress() |
| getHostAddress() | public String getHostAddress() |
| getHostName() | public String getHostName() |
| isMulticastAddress() | public boolean isMulticastAddress() |

getAddress() returns a byte array containing the IP address of the invoking InetAddress object.

getHostAddress() returns a String representation of the IP address of the invoking InetAddress object.

getHostName() attempts to return the host name associated with the IP address contained by the invoking InetAddress object. This method returns a String representation of the IP address if it cannot determine the host name.

isMulticastAddress() returns true if the invoking InetAddress object represents a multicast IP address.

## toString() Method

| Method | Syntax |
|---|---|
| toString() | public String toString() |

toString() overrides the toString() method from the Object class and returns a String representation of the IP address associated with the invoking InetAddress object.

### Example: Using InetAddress

See the ClientCLP class from example *Using the Connectionless Protocol* on page 375.

# 5.4 URL Classes

The URL classes provide the implementation and support of connections to resources using a **Uniform Resource Locator** or **URL**. A URL is a pointer to a resource on the network. The resource might be a file or a more complicated entity such as a database. A URL consists of a protocol type, a host name, a port number, a file name, and an optional anchor or reference. A typical URL might be:

http://www.madeupaddress.com:4567/index.html#page1

In this case the protocol is http, the host name is www.madeupaddress.com, the port number to which the TCP connection is made is 4567, the file name is "index.html" and the anchor is page1. If no port is specified, the default port for the specified protocol is used. The default HTTP port is 80, port 21 is reserved for FTP and port 23 is reserved for telnet. A relative URL contains a limited amount of information and relies on the information supplied by an absolute, or complete, URL to reach its destination.

The URL class hierarchy is shown in the figure below.

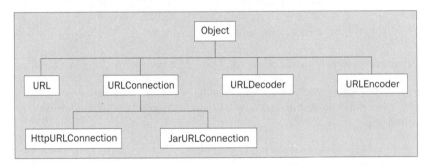

# 5.4.1 URL class

```
public final class URL extends Object implements Serializable
```

```
Object
  URL
```

### Interfaces

```
Serializable
```

A URL object represents a Uniform Resource Locator or URL.

## URL() Constructor

| Constructor | Syntax |
|---|---|
| URL() | public URL(String *absoluteURL*)<br>    throws MalformedURLException |
| | public URL(URL *contextURL*, String *url*)<br>    throws MalformedURLException |
| | public URL(URL *contextURL*, String *url*,<br>    URLStreamHandler *handler*)<br>    throws MalformedURLException |
| | public URL(String *protocol*, String *host*, String *file*)<br>    throws MalformedURLException |
| | public URL(String *protocol*, String *host*, int *port*,<br>    String *file*)<br>    throws MalformedURLException |
| | public URL(String *protocol*, String *host*, int *port*,<br>    String *file*, URLStreamHandler *handler*)<br>    throws MalformedURLException |

The first version creates a URL object using a String representation of an absolute URL.

The second version requires a URL object and a String representation of a URL. If the String does not represent an absolute URL, the URL object contextURL is used to fill in the missing pieces.

The third version is the same as the second except a URLStreamHandler object is specified to be the stream handler for the URL object.

The final three constructors create a URL object using separate arguments for the protocol, host, port number, filename, and stream handler. If the port and/or stream handler are not specified the default port and/or stream handler is used.

## equals() Method

| Method | Syntax |
|---|---|
| equals() | public boolean equals(Object *obj*) |

equals() overrides the equals() method from the Object class and returns true if Object obj is a URL and contains the same URL as the invoking URL object.

## hashCode() Method

| Method | Syntax |
|---|---|
| hashCode() | public int hashCode() |

hashCode() overrides the hashCode() method from the Object class and returns a hash code for the invoking URL object.

# openConnection() Method

| Method | Syntax |
|---|---|
| openConnection() | public URLConnection openConnection()<br>    throws IOException |

openConnection() returns a URLConnection object that represents a connection to the remote object referred to by the invoking URL object.

# openStream() Method

| Method | Syntax |
|---|---|
| openStream() | public final InputStream openStream() throws<br>IOException |

openStream() opens a connection to the URL contained by the invoking URL object and returns an InputStream object for reading from that connection.

# Methods to Return URL Properties

| Method | Syntax |
|---|---|
| getAuthority() | public String getAuthority() |
| getContent() | public final Object getContent() throws IOException |
| | public final Object getContent(Class[] *classes*)<br>    throws IOException |
| getFile() | public String getFile() |
| getHost() | public String getHost() |
| getPath() | public String getPath() |
| getPort() | public int getPort() |
| getProtocol() | public String getProtocol() |
| getQuery() | public int getQuery() |
| getRef() | public String getRef() |
| getUserInfo() | public String getUserInfo() |

getAuthority() returns the authority portion of the invoking URL object.

getContent() returns the content of the invoking URL object as an Object appropriate for the type of content. The second version allows the method to specify which classes it is looking for.

getFile() returns the filename for the invoking URL object.

getHost() returns the host for the invoking URL object.

getPath() returns the path portion of the invoking URL object.

getPort() returns the port for the invoking URL object or -1 if the port is not set.

getProtocol() returns the protocol for the invoking URL object.

getQuery() returns the query portion of the invoking URL object.

getRef() returns the anchor for the invoking URL object.

getUserInfo() returns the user info portion of the invoking URL object.

## sameFile() Method

| Method | Syntax |
| --- | --- |
| sameFile() | public boolean sameFile(URL *otherURL*) |

sameFile() returns true if the invoking URL object has the same protocol, host, port, and filename as the URL object otherURL.

## toExternalForm() Method

| Method | Syntax |
| --- | --- |
| toExternalForm() | public String toExternalForm() |

toExternalForm() returns a String representation of the invoking URL object.

## toString() Method

| Method | Syntax |
| --- | --- |
| toString() | public String toString() |

toString() overrides the toString() method from the Object class and returns a String representation of the invoking URL object.

### Example: Using URL

This program uses a URL object to access the contents of an HTML file located on the Sun Java Website. Once the URL object is created, it can be used to open a connection to the Website. Information about the HTML file can be then accessed. The URL object can open up an InputStream and download the contents of the HTML file.

The machine on which this example is run will have to be connected to the Internet. It will not work if a proxy server must be used to connect to an external web site.

```java
import java.net.*:
import java.io.*:

public class TestURL {
  int c:

  public TestURL() {
    try {

      // A URL object is created containing the URL of a Web page
      URL url =
        new URL("http://java.sun.com/products/jdk/1.3/docchanges.html");

      // A connection is made to the website
      URLConnection con = url.openConnection();

      // Information about the docchanges.html file can be accessed
      System.out.println("File name: " + url.getFile());
      System.out.println("Content type: " + con.getContentType());
      System.out.println("port: " + url.getPort());
      System.out.println("host: " + url.getHost());
      System.out.println("contents:");

      // An input stream is opened and the contents of the html page
      // are printed
      InputStream in = url.openStream();

      while ((c = in.read()) != -1) {
        System.out.print((char) c);
      }
      in.close();

    } catch (MalformedURLException me) {
      System.out.println("Error: " + me);
    } catch (IOException ioe) {
      System.out.println("Error: " + ioe);
    }
  }

  public static void main(String args[]) {
    TestURL tu = new TestURL();
  }
}
```

5

java.net

> ***Output*** *(may vary between runs)*
> ```
> File name: /products/jdk/1.3/docchanges.html
> Content type: null
> port: -1
> host: java.sun.com
> contents:
> <html>
> <head>
> <title>Java(TM) 2 SDK Documentation Changes</title>
> </head>
> ...
> ```

# 5.4.2 URLConnection Class

```
public abstract class URLConnection extends Object
```

```
Object
  URLConnection
```

The URLConnection class is the parent of all classes that represent a connection between an application and a URL and provides methods common to those sub-classes. Sub-classes of the URLConnection class support-protocol specific connections to a URL. A URLConnection sub-class object can be used to read from and write to the reference represented by the URL. URLConnection is an abstract class; a connection object is created by invoking the openConnection() method of a URL object.

## connect() Method

| Method | Syntax |
|---|---|
| connect() | public abstract void connect() throws IOException |

connect() connects a URLConnection object to the resource specified by its URL object.

## getContent() Method

| Method | Syntax |
|---|---|
| getContent() | public Object getContent() throws IOException |
| | public Object getContent(Class[] *classes*) throws IOException |

getContent() returns the content of the resource specified by the URL object that is associated with the invoking URLConnection object. The return value is an object that encapsulates the content of the connection. If a Class array is specified, the subclass of Object returned will be the first match of the contents of the Class array.

# getPermission() Method

| Method | Syntax |
|---|---|
| getPermission() | public Permission getPermission() throws IOException |

getPermission() returns a Permission object representing the permission necessary to make the connection, or null if no permission is required to make the connection.

# getURL() Method

| Method | Syntax |
|---|---|
| getURL() | public URL getURL() |

getURL() returns the URL object that is associated with the invoking URLConnection object.

# Request Property Methods

| Method | Syntax |
|---|---|
| getDefaultRequestProperty() | public static String getDefaultRequestProperty(String key) |
| getRequestProperty() | public String getRequestProperty (String key) |
| setDefaultRequestProperty() | public static void setDefaultRequestProperty (String key, String value) |
| setRequestProperty() | public void setRequestProperty (String key, String value) |

These methods allow properties associated with the URLConnection request to be queried or modified. The request properties are protocol specific. For information on the request properties for an HTTP connection, consult

http://www.ietf.org/rfc/rfc2068.txt

getRequestProperty() returns the value associated with the given key.

setRequestProperty() specifies a key-value request property pair. Both the key and value are String objects.

getDefaultRequestProperty() returns the default request property value corresponding to the specified key. This method was deprecated as of Java 2.

setDefaultRequestProperty() sets the default key-value request property pair. This method was deprecated as of Java 2.

## Resource Property Methods

| Method | Syntax |
| --- | --- |
| getContentEncoding() | public String getContentEncoding() |
| getContentLength() | public int getContentLength() |
| getContentType() | public String getContentType() |
| getDate() | public long getDate() |
| getExpiration() | public long getExpiration() |
| getHeaderField() | public String getHeaderField(int headerFieldIndex) |
| | public String getHeaderField(String headerFieldName) |
| getHeaderFieldDate() | public long getHeaderFieldDate(String headerFieldNam long defaultTime) |
| getHeaderFieldInt() | public int getHeaderFieldInt (String headerFieldName, int defaultInt) |
| getHeaderFieldKey() | public String getHeaderFieldKey (int headerFieldInde |
| getLastModified() | public long getLastModified() |
| guessContentTypeFromStream() | public static String guessContentTypeFromStream (InputStream is) throws IOException |

These methods return information about various properties of the resource specified by the URL object that is associated with the invoking URLConnection object by accessing the header fields of the resource.

getContentEncoding() returns the content encoding of the resource.

getContentLength() returns the content length of the resource, or -1 if it the length is not known.

getContentType() returns the content type of the resource.

getDate() and getExpiration() return the sending date and expiration date of the resource. The return value is the time in milliseconds since Jan 1, 1970, or 0 if the dates are not known.

getHeaderField() returns the value of a header field. Either a header field index or header field name can be passed as an argument.

getHeaderFieldDate() returns the value of a header field parsed as a time value. The return value is the time in milliseconds since Jan 1, 1970. If the header field cannot be parsed as a time, the specified defaultTime value is returned.

getHeaderFieldInt() returns the value of a header field parsed as an int. If the header field cannot be parsed as an int, the specified defaultInt value is returned.

getHeaderFieldKey() returns the name of the header field at index headerFieldIndex.

getLastModified() returns the time in milliseconds since Jan 1, 1970 when the resource was last modified.

guessContentTypeFromStream() attempts to identify the type of input stream by examining the first few bytes at the beginning of the stream. This method is useful because sometimes HTTP servers return an incorrect content type.

# Methods to Return Setup Parameters

| Method | Syntax |
|---|---|
| getAllowUserInteraction() | public boolean getAllowUserInteraction() |
| getDefaultAllowUserInteraction() | public static boolean getDefaultAllowUserInteraction() |
| getDoInput() | public boolean getDoInput() |
| getDoOutput() | public boolean getDoOutput() |
| getIfModifiedSince() | public long getIfModifiedSince() |
| getDefaultUseCaches() | public boolean getDefaultUseCaches() |
| getUseCaches() | public boolean getUseCaches() |

getAllowUserInteraction() returns true if the connection associated with the invoking URLConnection object allows user interaction.

getDefaultAllowUserInteraction() returns the default user interaction state.

getDoInput() returns true if the invoking URLConnection object is to be used for input.

getDoOutput() returns true if the invoking URLConnection object is to be used for output.

getIfModifiedSince() returns the ifModifiedSince time in milliseconds since Jan 1, 1970. This time is used to determine whether a resource should be downloaded or if a current copy of the resource exists at the local host.

getDefaultUseCaches() returns true if the use of caches is allowed by default.

getUseCaches() returns true if the invoking URLConnection object uses caches.

## Methods to Change Setup Parameters

| Method | Syntax |
|---|---|
| setAllowUserInteraction() | public void setAllowUserInteraction (boolean *interact*) |
| setDefaultAllowUserInteraction() | public static void setDefaultAllowUserInteraction (boolean *interact*) |
| setDoInput() | public void setDoInput(boolean *input*) |
| setDoOutput() | public void setDoOutput (boolean *output*) |
| setIfModifiedSince() | public void setIfModifiedSince (long *time*) |
| setDefaultUseCaches() | public void setDefaultUseCaches (boolean *useCachesByDefault*) |
| setUseCaches() | public void setUseCaches (boolean *useCaches*) |

setAllowUserInteraction() specifies if the connection associated with the invoking URLConnection object allows user interaction.

setDefaultAllowUserInteraction() sets the default user interaction mode of the invoking URLConnection object.

setDoInput() is used to specify if the invoking URLConnection object will be used for input.

setDoOutput() is used to specify if the invoking URLConnection object will be used for output.

setIfModifiedSince() changes the ifModifiedSince time. This time, in milliseconds since Jan 1, 1970 is used to determine whether a resource should be downloaded or if a current copy of the resource exists at the local host.

setDefaultUseCaches() specifies if the use of caches is allowed by default.

setUseCaches() is used to specify if the invoking URLConnection object will use caches.

## Stream Methods

| Method | Syntax |
|---|---|
| getInputStream() | public InputStream getInputStream() throws IOException |
| getOutputStream() | public OutputStream getOutputStream() throws IOException |

getInputStream() returns an InputStream object that can be used to read from the URL connection.

getOutputStream() returns an OutputStream object that can be used to write to the URL connection.

## toString() Method

| Method | Syntax |
|--------|--------|
| toString() | public String toString() |

toString() returns a String representation of the invoking URLConnection object.

### Example: Using URLConnection

See example *Using URL* on page 398 ,where a URLConnection object is created that represents a connection to an HTML file on a web site.

# 5.4.3 HttpURLConnection Class

```
public abstract class HttpURLConnection extends URLConnection
```

```
Object
  URLConnection
    HttpURLConnection
```

An HttpURLConnection object represents a connection to a resource specified by an HTTP URL and provides support for HTTP-specific features. The HttpURLConnection class provides HTTP response code constants and methods for parsing server responses. HttpURLConnection is an abstract class; a connection object is created by invoking the openConnection() method on a URL object.

## HTTP Response Code Constants

| Constant |
|----------|
| public static final int HTTP_OK |
| public static final int HTTP_CREATED |
| public static final int HTTP_ACCEPTED |
| public static final int HTTP_NOT_AUTHORITATIVE |
| public static final int HTTP_NO_CONTENT |
| public static final int HTTP_RESET |
| public static final int HTTP_PARTIAL |
| public static final int HTTP_MULT_CHOICE |
| public static final int HTTP_MOVED_PERM |
| public static final int HTTP_MOVED_TEMP |
| public static final int HTTP_SEE_OTHER |
| public static final int HTTP_NOT_MODIFIED |
| public static final int HTTP_USE_PROXY |
| public static final int HTTP_BAD_REQUEST |
| public static final int HTTP_UNAUTHORIZED |
| public static final int HTTP_PAYMENT_REQUIRED |
| public static final int HTTP_FORBIDDEN |

5

java.net

**405**

| Constant |
|---|
| `public static final int HTTP_NOT_FOUND` |
| `public static final int HTTP_BAD_METHOD` |
| `public static final int HTTP_NOT_ACCEPTABLE` |
| `public static final int HTTP_PROXY_AUTH` |
| `public static final int HTTP_CLIENT_TIMEOUT` |
| `public static final int HTTP_CONFLICT` |
| `public static final int HTTP_GONE` |
| `public static final int HTTP_LENGTH_REQUIRED` |
| `public static final int HTTP_PRECON_FAILED` |
| `public static final int HTTP_ENTITY_TOO_LARGE` |
| `public static final int HTTP_REQ_TOO_LONG` |
| `public static final int HTTP_UNSUPPORTED_TYPE` |
| `public static final int HTTP_VERSION` |
| `public static final int HTTP_INTERNAL_ERROR` |
| `public static final int HTTP_BAD_GATEWAY` |
| `public static final int HTTP_UNAVAILABLE` |
| `public static final int HTTP_GATEWAY_TIMEOUT` |

These constants represent response codes sent by the server in response to a request. See the Sun Java documentation for more details.

## disconnect() Method

| Method | Syntax |
|---|---|
| `disconnect()` | `public abstract void disconnect()` |

`disconnect()` closes the connection to the server.

## getErrorStream() Method

| Method | Syntax |
|---|---|
| `getErrorStream()` | `public InputStream getErrorStream()` |

`getErrorStream()` returns an `InputStream` object representing the error stream if the connection failed but some useful information was sent by the server. The information could then be read from the `InputStream`.

## getResponseCode() Method

| Method | Syntax |
|---|---|
| `getResponseCode()` | `public int getResponseCode() throws IOException` |

`getResponseCode()` causes the server to return one of the HTTP response codes, or -1 if none can be found.

# getResponseMessage() Method

| Method | Syntax |
|---|---|
| getResponseMessage() | public String getResponseMessage()<br>    throws IOException |

getResponseMessage() returns the message returned by the server along with the response status.

# Redirects Methods

| Method | Syntax |
|---|---|
| getFollowRedirects() | public static boolean getFollowRedirects() |
| setFollowRedirects() | public static void setFollowRedirects<br>              (boolean *redirects*) |

getFollowRedirects() returns true if the invoking HttpURLConnection object follows HTTP redirects. The default value is false.

setFollowRedirects() is used to change the redirects mode.

# Request Method Methods

| Method | Syntax |
|---|---|
| getRequestMethod() | public String getRequestMethod() |
| setRequestMethod() | public void setRequestMethod(String *method*)<br>    throws ProtocolException |

getRequestMethod() returns the current HTTP request method for the URL request. The default method is "GET".

setRequestMethod() is used to change the method for the URL request. Valid arguments are "GET", "POST", "HEAD", "OPTIONS", "PUT", "DELETE", or "TRACE".

# usingProxy() Method

| Method | Syntax |
|---|---|
| usingProxy() | public abstract boolean usingProxy() |

usingProxy() returns true if the URL connection is going through a proxy.

5

java.net

# 5.4.5 URLDecoder Class

```
public class URLDecoder extends Object
```

```
Object
  URLDecoder
```

The URLDecoder class is used to convert from a MIME format called x-www-form-urlencoded format. to a standard ASCII String object.

The x-www-form-urlencoded format is a subset of ASCII that can be read by a wide range of computer platforms. Its format is as follows: alphanumeric characters (a-z, A-Z, 0-9), the dash, the underscore, and the period are left unchanged. Spaces represented by the plus sign. All other characters are represented by the character '%' followed by a two digit hexadecimal number.

## decode() Method

| Method | Syntax |
|--------|--------|
| decode() | public static String decode(String str) |

decode() returns a standard ASCII String object that is converted from the x-www-form-urlencoded String passed as an argument.

### Example: Using URLDecoder

This example demonstrates the use of the URLDecoder class to decode a String from x-www-form-urlencoded form, and prints out the decoded form.

```
import java.net.*;

public class TestDecode {
  public static void main(String args[]) {
    String str = "Jackson%27s+bike-bell+cost+%245";

    try {
      String str2 = URLDecoder.decode(str);
      System.out.println(str2);
    } catch (Exception e) {}
  }
}
```

**Output**

```
Jackson's bike-bell cost $5
```

# 5.4.6 URLEncoder Class

```
public class URLEncoder extends Object
```

```
Object
    URLEncoder
```

The URLEncoder class is used to convert an ASCII String object into a MIME format called x-www-form-urlencoded format.

The x-www-form-urlencoded format is a subset of ASCII that can be read by a wide range of computer platforms. Its format is as follows: alphanumeric characters (a-z, A-Z, 0-9), the dash, the underscore, and the period are left unchanged. Spaces represented by the plus sign. All other characters are represented by the character '%' followed by a two digit hexadecimal number.

## encode() Method

| Method | Syntax |
|--------|--------|
| encode() | public static String encode(String *str*) |

encode() returns a String object that is a x-www-form-urlencoded version of the String passed as an argument.

### Example: Using URLEncoder

This example demonstrates the use of the URLEncoder class to encode a String into x-www-form-urlencoded form, and prints out the encoded form.

```
import java.net.*;

public class TestEncode {
  public static void main(String args[]) {
    String str = "Jackson's bike-bell cost $5";

    String str2 = URLEncoder.encode(str);
    System.out.println(str2);
  }
}
```

**Output**

```
Jackson%27s+bike-bell+cost+%245
```

5

java.net

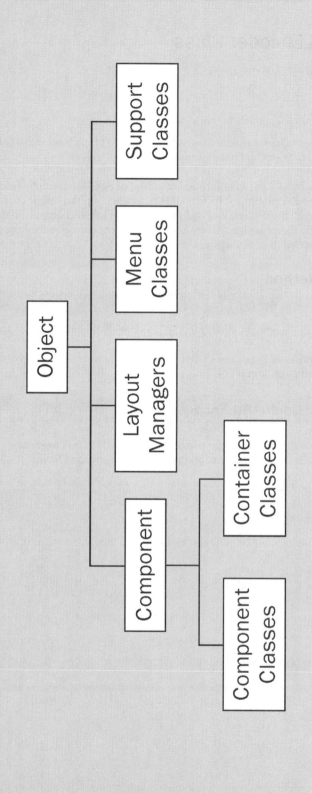

# java.awt

The **Abstract Windowing Toolkit (AWT)** was introduced in Java 1.0 and considerably enhanced in Java 1.1 as a platform-independent way to develop graphical user interfaces (GUI's). The package contains a wide assortment of containers, components, and support classes.

In this chapter we will cover:

The appearance and behavior of the AWT components mirrors that of the local environment. In other words a menu bar in a program running on a Macintosh will appear as a Macintosh menu bar normally would, butwill look different if the Java program is run on a PC under Windows. This is achieved by using peer classes that implement the components using native code. Because the actual implementation of the components is non-Java, AWT containers and components are referred to as **heavyweight** components.

Under Java 1.1, the AWT components were the only game in town. Application developers, particularly those developing large-scale enterprise applications, began to complain about the limitations of the AWT components - they wanted more functionality and a consistent look-and-feel across different platforms. This led to the development of the Swing components, which are pure Java and do not rely on native peer classes. They also add a good deal of features that are not available to the AWT components.

While some of the Swing components are updated versions of AWT components, they have not made the AWT components obsolete. The AWT components are, generally speaking, easier to use and are still valuable for applications that have simple GUI requirements. Another fact of life in the Java world is that browser compatability tends to lag behind the development of the Java language. At the time this book was written (March, 2000), no browsers currently support Java 2 SDK version 1.2, let alone version 1.3, so the AWT components are still appropriate for Web-based applications that require the use of a browser. As an alternative, the Java Plug-in can be used to allow applets to run using Sun's Java Runtime Environment instead of the web browser's default virtual machine.

The `java.awt` package class hierarchy is shown in the diagram on page 410.

❑ The **component classes** represent the GUI components provided by `java.awt` and include buttons, text components, checkboxes, lists, and scrollbars.

❑ **Containers** are rectangular components that are used to display components. Containers can also be placed inside other containers.

❑ The **menu classes** allow menus to be placed at the top of containers.

❑ **Layout managers** determine how components are positioned within a container.

❑ The **support classes** provide the tools to manipulate the appearance of the GUI including the color, what font is used, borders around components.

# 6.1 Component Class

```
public abstract class Component extends Object
    implements ImageObserver, MenuContainer, Serializable
```

```
Object
    Component
```

### Interfaces
```
ImageObserver, MenuContainer, Serializable
```

The `Component` class is the super-class of all containers and non-menu related components. Because `Component` is an abstract class, a `Component` object is never created. The class provides general purpose methods to manipulate, modify, and return information about containers and components.

## Component Class Constants

| Constant | Value |
|---|---|
| public static final float LEFT_ALIGNMENT | 0.0 |
| public static final float RIGHT_ALIGNMENT | 1.0 |
| public static final float CENTER_ALIGNMENT | 0.5 |
| public static final float TOP_ALIGNMENT | 0.0 |
| public static final float BOTTOM_ALIGNMENT | 1.0 |

**413**

These alignment constants are used by the layout manager when placing the component in its container.

## Methods to Determine the Current State of a Component

| Method | Syntax |
|---|---|
| hasFocus() | public boolean hasFocus() |
| isDisplayable() | public boolean isDisplayable() |
| isDoubleBuffered() | public boolean isDoubleBuffered() |
| isEnabled() | public boolean isEnabled() |
| isFocusTraversable() | public boolean isFocusTraversable() |
| isLightWeight() | public boolean isLightWeight() |
| isOpaque() | public boolean isOpaque() |
| isShowing() | public boolean isShowing() |
| isValid() | public boolean isValid() |
| isVisible() | public boolean isVisible() |

hasFocus() returns true if the input focus is owned by the invoking component.

isDisplayable() returns true if the invoking component can be displayed.

isDoubleBuffered() returns true if the invoking component uses double buffering. Double buffering can help reduce screen flicker at a slight performance cost. This method returns false by default and should be overridden to return true if double buffering is desired.

isEnabled() returns true if the invoking component can accept input and generate events.

isFocusTraversable() returns true if the invoking component can accept the input focus. Focus is traversed from traversable components using the *Tab* or *Shift-Tab* keyboard sequences

isLightWeight() returns true if the invoking component is pure Java (does not have a native peer). Swing components are always lightweight; AWT components are not.

isOpaque() returns true if the invoking component is opaque, meaning that it hides any features beneath it. AWT components are opaque.

isShowing() returns true if the invoking component is currently showing on the screen.

isValid() returns true if the invoking component's state is valid. A valid component is one that is correctly positioned and sized within its parent container and all of its children are valid.

isVisible() method returns true if the invoking component will be visible when the screen is painted.

## Example: Investigating the State of a Button

In this example a Button is placed on a Frame. The state of the Button is investigated using some of the methods described in this section. Because Button is a sub-class of Component, a Button object has access to Component class methods. The Button class is an AWT component, so it will be opaque and heavyweight. When it is added to the Frame and the Frame is made visible, the Button is made visible. By default the Button is enabled.

*The WinClosing class is used to terminate the program if the window is closed. See Section 7.3.8 on page 657 for more details.*

```
import java.awt.*;
import java.awt.event.*;

public class TestCompState extends Frame {
  Button b;
  public TestCompState() {
  // create a button and place it on a frame

    b = new Button("Click Me");
    setLayout(new FlowLayout());
    add(b);

    addWindowListener(new WinClosing());
    setBounds(100, 100, 200, 120);
    setVisible(true);

    // Investigate the state of the button

    if (b.isVisible()) {
      System.out.println("button is visible");
    }
    if (b.isEnabled()) {
      System.out.println("button is enabled");
    }
    if (b.isOpaque()) {
      System.out.println("button is opaque");
    }
    if (b.isLightweight()) {
      System.out.println("button is lightweight");
    } else {
      System.out.println("button is heavyweight");
    }
  }
}
```

```
    // The getInsets() method is overridden to place the button more
    // in the center of the frame

    public Insets getInsets() {
      return new Insets(30, 50, 30, 50);
    }

    public static void main(String args[]) {
      TestCompState tcs = new TestCompState();
    }
  }

  // The WinClosing class terminates the program if the window is closed

  class WinClosing extends WindowAdapter {
    public void windowClosing(WindowEvent we) {
      System.exit(0);
    }
```

***Output***

Here is the result of running the program. You can see that the Frame has been created with a Button on it.

The output on the console is:

```
button is visible
button is enabled
button is opaque
button is heavyweight
```

## addListener() Methods

| Method | Syntax |
|---|---|
| addComponentListener() | public void addComponentListener (ComponentListener cl) |
| addFocusListener() | public void addFocusListener (FocusListener fl) |
| addHierarchyBoundsListener() | public void addHierarchyBoundsListener (HierarchyBoundsListener hbl) |

| Method | Syntax |
|---|---|
| addHierarchyListener() | public void addHierarchyListener<br>(HierarchyListener *hl*) |
| addInputMethodListener() | public void addInputMethodListener<br>(InputMethodListener *il*) |
| addKeyListener() | public void addKeyListener<br>(KeyListener *kl*) |
| addMouseListener() | public void addMouseListener<br>(MouseListener *ml*) |
| addMouseMotionListener() | public void addMouseMotionListener<br>(MouseMotionListener *ml*) |
| addPropertyChangeListener() | public void addPropertyChangeListener<br>(PropertyChangeListener *pl*) |
|  | public void addPropertyChangeListener<br>(String *propertyName*,<br>PropertyChangeListener *pl*) |

The addListener() methods associate an event listener with a container or component. The event listener is activated if the registered container or component generates the appropriate event object. See Chapter 7 for more information on event listeners. The addPropertyChangeListener() method can be given a specific property name to listen in on.

## dispatchEvent() Method

| Method | Syntax |
|---|---|
| dispatchEvent() | public final void dispatchEvent(AWTEvent *evt*) |

dispatchEvent() sends the specified event to any registered listeners of the invoking component. This by-passes the normal system event queue.

## removeListener() Methods

| Method | Syntax |
|---|---|
| removeComponentListener() | public void<br>removeComponentListener<br>(ComponentListener *cl*) |
| removeFocusListener() | public void<br>removeFocusListener(FocusListener *fl*) |
| removeHierarchyBoundsListener() | public void<br>removeHierarchyBoundsListener<br>(HierarchyBoundsListener *hbl*) |

| Method | Syntax |
|---|---|
| removeHierarchyListener() | public void removeHierarchyListener (HierarchyListener *hl*) |
| removeInputMethodListener() | public void removeInputMethodListener (InputMethodListener *iml*) |
| removeKeyListener() | public void removeKeyListener (KeyListener *kl*) |
| removeMouseListener() | public void removeMouseListener (MouseListener *ml*) |
| removeMouseMotionListener() | public void removeMouseMotionListener (MouseMotionListener *ml*) |
| removePropertyChangeListener() | public void removePropertyChangeListener (PropertyChangeListener *pl*) |
| | public void removePropertyChangeListener (String *propertyName*, PropertyChangeListener *pl*) |

The removeListener() methods remove a listener from the invoking container or component. Events will no longer be reported to the listener object if they occur. See the Chapter 7 for more information on event listeners. The removePropertyChangeListener() method can removed globally or only from a specific property name.

## Image Methods

| Method | Syntax |
|---|---|
| checkImage() | public int checkImage(Image *img*, int *width*, int *height*, ImageObserver *io*) |
| | public int checkImage(Image *img*, ImageObserver *io*) |
| createImage() | public Image createImage(int *width*, int *height*) |
| | public Image createImage (ImageProducer *ip*) |
| imageUpdate() | public boolean imageUpdate(Image *img*, int *flags*, int *x*, int *y*, int *width*, int *height*) |

| Method | Syntax |
|---|---|
| prepareImage() | public boolean prepareImage<br>(Image *i*, ImageObserver *io*) |
| | public boolean prepareImage<br>(Image *i*, int *width*,<br>int *height*, ImageObserver *io*) |

checkImage() returns the status of the Image object being loaded. The return value will be one or more ImageObserver class constants.

createImage() create either a blank image or an off-screen image from an image producer.

imageUpdate() repaints the invoking component when an associated image has changed. It returns false when the image has completely loaded. This method is generally not called by the user.

prepareImage() methods trigger the loading of image data.

## Layout and Validity Methods

| Method | Syntax |
|---|---|
| addNotify() | public void addNotify() |
| doLayout() | public void doLayout() |
| invalidate() | public void invalidate() |
| validate() | public void validate() |

addNotify() creates the peer of the invoking component and the component is invalidated. This method is normally called only by the system.

doLayout() invokes the layout manager on the invoking container. The doLayout() method is not called explicitly in the program but is instead called by the validate() method.

invalidate() invalidates the invoking container and all of its ancestors. This method is called when one or more components in a container have been altered. After the invalidate() method is called, the validate() method should be called. If an invalid component is contained in a valid container, the container must be invalidated and then validated for the layout manager to update the modified (invalid) component.

validate() validates the invoking container by again laying out its components. The validate() method calls the doLayout() method that invokes the layout manager. If a container calls invalidate(), validate() must be explicitly called. The only time the system will call validate() is if the window is resized.

## Example: Updating a Label Display

In this example, a Label is created and placed within a Frame. After waiting 5 seconds, the Label text is changed to a longer String. The Frame must then call invalidate() and validate() to properly update the Label display.

*The WinClosing class is used to terminate the program if the window is closed. See Section 7.3.8 on page 657 for more details.*

```java
import java.awt.*;
import java.awt.event.*;

public class TestCompL extends Frame {
  Label lbl;
  public TestCompL() {
    lbl = new Label("first String");

    setLayout(new FlowLayout());
    add(lbl);
    addWindowListener(new WinClosing());
    setBounds(100, 100, 250, 100);
    setVisible(true);

    try {
      Thread.sleep(5000);
    } catch (Exception e) {}

    // when the Label text is changed to a longer String, the Frame
    // calls invalidate() and then validate() to update the Label
    // display. If these calls aren't made, the new String will be
    // truncated.
    lbl.setText("second much longer String");
    invalidate();    // Try commenting out
    validate();      // these lines
  }

  public static void main(String args[]) {
    TestCompL tcl = new TestCompL();
  }
}


// The WinClosing class terminates the program if the window is closed

class WinClosing extends WindowAdapter {
  public void windowClosing(WindowEvent we) {
    System.exit(0);
  }
}
```

If the container is not invalidated and then validated, the updated text will be truncated. Comment out those two lines and try it for yourself.

### Output

Here are the two Labels that are created:

followed by:

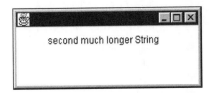

## list() method

| Method | Syntax |
|--------|--------|
| list() | public void list() |
| | public void list(PrintStream *ps*) |
| | public void list(PrintStream *ps*, int *indent*) |
| | public void list(PrintWriter *pw*) |
| | public void list(PrintWriter *pw*, int *indent*) |

list() sends a String representation of the invoking component to an output stream. The no-argument version sends the String to System.out. The value indent is the number of spaces to indent during printing.

### Example: Using list() to Obtain Information about a Button

In this example, a Frame is created and a Button is positioned upon it with the text **Click Me**. The list() method is used to write out information on the position and properties of the Button.

*The WinClosing class is used to terminate the program if the window is closed. See Section 7.3.8 on page 657 for more details.*

```
import java.awt.*;
import java.awt.event.*;
```

```
public class TestCompList extends Frame {
  Button b;

  public TestCompList() {
    b = new Button("Click Me");

    setLayout(new FlowLayout());
    add(b);
    addWindowListener(new WinClosing());
    setBounds(100, 100, 200, 120);
    setVisible(true);

    // The list() method call sends information about the
    // Button to System.out
    b.list();
  }

  // The getInsets() method is overridden to place the button more
  // in the center of the frame
  public Insets getInsets() {
    return new Insets(30, 50, 30, 50);
  }
  public static void main(String args[]) {
    TestCompList tcl = new TestCompList();
  }
}

// The WinClosing class terminates the program if the window is closed

class WinClosing extends WindowAdapter {
  public void windowClosing(WindowEvent we) {
    System.exit(0);
  }
}
```

In this case the list() method provides the Button name, x location, y location, bounding box dimensions, and label. Here is the result:

### Output

Here is the result:

Here is the command-line output:

```
java.awt.Button[button0, 162 ,30 ,75x27 , label=Click Me]
```

## Location Methods

| Method | Syntax |
|---|---|
| contains() | public boolean contains(int *x*, int *y*) |
| | public boolean contains(Point *p*) |
| getAlignmentX() | public float getAlignmentX() |
| getAlignmentY() | public float getAlignmentY() |
| getBounds() | public Rectangle getBounds() |
| | public Rectangle getBounds(Rectangle *rect*) |
| getComponentAt() | public Component getComponentAt(int *x*, int *y*) |
| | public Component getComponentAt(Point *p*) |
| getLocation() | public Point getLocation() |
| | public Point getLocation(Point *p*) |
| getLocationOnScreen() | public Point getLocationOnScreen() |
| getX() | public int getX() |
| getY() | public int getY() |
| setBounds() | public void setBounds(int *x*, int *y*, int *width*, int *height*) |
| | public void setBounds(Rectangle *r*) |
| setLocation() | public void setLocation(int x, int *y*) |
| | public void setLocation(Point *p*) |

contains() returns true if the location passed as an argument lies within the bounding box of the invoking component.

getAlignmentX() and getAlignmentY() return the x and y alignments of the invoking component. They will be float values between 0.0 and 1.0.

getBounds() returns a Rectangle object that encompasses the outer boundary of the invoking component. If a Rectangle object is passed as an argument, its values will be set to the outer boundary of the invoking component and the modified Rectangle object is returned.

getComponentAt() returns the component, if any, at the given location.

getLocation() returns a Point object containing the x and y locations of the upper left hand corner of the bounding area of the invoking component. The x and y coordinates are relative to the parent container. If a Point object is passed as an argument, its values will be set to the previously described x and y locations and the modified Point object is returned.

getLocationOnScreen() returns a Point object containing the x and y locations of the upper left hand corner of the bounding area of the invoking component. The x and y coordinates are relative to the screen.

getX() and getY() methods return the x and y locations in pixels of the origin of the invoking component.

setBounds() is a combination of the setLocation() and setSize() methods. It sets the location and size of the invoking component.

setLocation() places the upper left hand corner of the invoking component at the designated location.

## Example: Finding the Location of a Component

This example uses the getBounds() method to obtain the location and dimensions of the Button object.

*The WinClosing class is used to terminate the program if the window is closed. See Section 7.3.8 on page 657 for more details.*

```
import java.awt.*;
import java.awt.event.*;

public class TestCompLoc extends Frame {
  Button b;

  public TestCompLoc() {
    b = new Button("Click Me");

    setLayout(new FlowLayout());
    add(b);

    addWindowListener(new WinClosing());
    setBounds(100, 100, 200, 120);
    setVisible(true);

    // The getBounds() method returns a Rectangle object containing
    // the button's location and size.  The println() method calls
    // the toString() method from the Rectangle class to print out
    // the values.

    System.out.println(b.getName() + " bounds are " + b.getBounds());
  }
  // The getInsets() method is overridden to place the button more
  // in the center of the frame

  public Insets getInsets() {
    return new Insets(30, 50, 30, 50);
  }
```

```
public static void main(String args[]) {
    TestCompLoc tcl = new TestCompLoc();
}
}

// The WinClosing class terminates the program if the window is closed
class WinClosing extends WindowAdapter {
    public void windowClosing(WindowEvent we) {
        System.exit(0);
    }
}
```

### Output

The location is returned at the command prompt, like so:

```
button0 bounds are java.awt.Rectangle[x=70,y=35,width=60,height=23]
```

Note that the location is the number of pixels from the upper left hand corner of the frame. The getBounds() method returns a Rectangle object which when passed to the println() method is converted into a String by the toString() method.

## Painting Methods

| Method | Syntax |
|---|---|
| paint() | public void paint(Graphics g) |
| paintAll() | public void paintAll(Graphics g) |
| repaint() | public void repaint() |
| | public void repaint(long millisecondsDelay) |
| | public void repaint(int x, int y, int width, int height) |
| | public void repaint(long millisecondsDelay, int x, int y, int width, int height) |
| update() | public void update(Graphics g) |

These methods are usually used to refresh the display area of an applet.

repaint() is the only method called explicitly.

update() is called by AWT when the user calls the repaint() method. It clears the background and calls the paint() method. The repaint() method can be given a time delay and repaint() can be executed over a subset of the display area.

paint() re-displays the window, and is called by update().

> Excessive clearing of the background can cause window flickering. To reduce the flickering, override the update() method to call paint() without clearing the background.

## Example: Repainting

See the *Rotating Images* example on page 669 where repaint() is used to create a slideshow applet.

## Pop-up Menu Methods

| Method | Syntax |
|--------|--------|
| add() | public void add(PopupMenu p) |
| remove() | public void remove(MenuComponent popup) |

add() and remove() add or remove a PopupMenu object from the invoking component. See Section 6.6.6 on page 544 for more information on popup menus.

## Methods to Retrieve Component Properties

| Method | Syntax |
|--------|--------|
| getBackground() | public Color getBackground() |
| getColorModel() | public ColorModel getColorModel() |
| getCursor() | public Cursor getCursor() |
| getFont() | public Font getFont() |
| getFontMetrics() | public FontMetrics getFontMetrics(Font font) |
| getForeground() | public Color getForeground() |
| getGraphics() | public Graphics getGraphics() |
| getLocale() | public Locale getLocale() |
| getName() | public String getName() |
| getParent() | public Container getParent() |
| getToolkit() | public Toolkit getToolkit() |
| getTreeLock() | public final Object getTreeLock() |

getBackground() and getForeground() return the Color object representing the background and foreground color.

getColorModel() returns the ColorModel object used to display the invoking component.

getCursor() returns the Cursor associated with the invoking component.

getFont() returns the Font object associated with the invoking component.

getFontMetrics() returns the FontMetrics object associated with the specified Font object.

getGraphics() returns the Graphics object associated with the invoking component. This method is usually only called by containers.

getLocale() returns the Locale object associated with the invoking component. A Locale object is used to internationalize programs. See Section 3.1.4 on page 190 for more details.

getName() returns the name of the invoking component.

getParent() returns the parent container of the invoking component.

getToolkit() returns the current Toolkit object associated with the invoking component. A component's toolkit can, among other things, indicate which fonts are available.

getTreeLock() retrieves the invoking component's treelock for the entire AWT component tree. The tree lock is used to synchronize access to a given component. It prevents inconsistent actions being attempted on a component simultaneously, for example counting a component while trying to remove it.

## Example: Retrieving Component Properties

This example creates a Frame object and adds a Label to it. It then prints the Label's the font, parent container and locale information.

*The WinClosing class is used to terminate the program if the window is closed. See Section 7.3.8 on page 657 for more details.*

```
import java.awt.*;
import java.awt.event.*;

public class TestCompGetP extends Frame {
  Label lbl;

  public TestCompGetP() {
    lbl = new Label("Zack-a-boo");

    setLayout(new FlowLayout());
    add(lbl);

    addWindowListener(new WinClosing());
    setBounds(100, 100, 200, 120);
    setVisible(true);

    // The name, parent, and locale of the Label object are printed out
```

6

java.awt

**427**

```
         System.out.println("Font is " + lbl.getFont().getName());
         System.out.println("Parent is " + lbl.getParent().getName());
         System.out.println("Locale is " + lbl.getLocale());
      }

   // The getInsets() method is overridden to place the button more
   // in the center of the frame

   public Insets getInsets() {
      return new Insets(30, 50, 30, 50);
   }

   public static void main(String args[]) {
      TestCompGetP tcp = new TestCompGetP();
   }
}
// The WinClosing class terminates the program if the window is closed

class WinClosing extends WindowAdapter {
   public void windowClosing(WindowEvent we) {
      System.exit(0);
   }
}
```

***Output***

Here is the result:

The Font, parent Frame object and Locale object are returned at the command line.
The results will vary.

```
Font is Dialog
Parent is frame0
Locale is en
```

## Methods to Set Component Properties

| Method | Syntax |
|--------|--------|
| requestFocus() | public void requestFocus() |
| setBackground() | public void setBackground (Color backgroundColor) |

| Method | Syntax |
|---|---|
| setComponentOrientation() | public void setComponentOrientation (ComponentOrientation *co*) |
| setCursor() | public void setCursor(Cursor *c*) |
| setEnabled() | public void setEnabled(boolean *enabled*) |
| setFont() | public void setFont(Font *f*) |
| setForeground() | public void setForeground (Color *foregroundColor*) |
| setLocale() | public void setLocale(Locale *l*) |
| setName() | public void setName(String *name*) |
| setVisible() | public void setVisible(boolean *visible*) |
| transferFocus() | public void transferFocus() |

requestFocus() attempts to bring the focus to the invoking component. If the component is not focus traversable, the attempt will fail. A focus traversable component is one that can obtain focus using a *Tab* or *Shift-Tab* keyboard sequence.

setBackground() and setForeground() set the background and foreground color of the invoking component. Some platforms may not allow this.

setComponentOrientation() is used to set the language-sensitive orientation that layout managers will use for arranging the elements or text that make up the invoking component.

setCursor() changes the cursor of the invoking component.

setEnabled() enables or disables the invoking component. A disabled component will not respond to user interactions and will not generate events.

setFont() changes or sets the font displayed by the invoking component.

setLocale() sets the Locale object associated with the invoking component. The Locale object allows for the internationalization of a Java program. See Section 3.1.4 on page 190 for more details.

setName() sets the name associated with the invoking component.

setVisible() determines whether the invoking component is visible on the screen.

transferFocus() moves the focus away from the invoking component to the next focus traversable component.

6

java.awt

## Example: Changing Component Properties

In this example, a Label and Button object are placed on a Frame. The font for the Label and the background color of the Frame are specified, and the Button is disabled.

*The WinClosing class is used to terminate the program if the window is closed. See Section 7.3.8 on page 657 for more details.*

```java
import java.awt.*;
import java.awt.event.*;

public class TestCompSet extends Frame {
    Label lbl;
    Button b;

    public TestCompSet() {

        // A Label is created and its font is specified

        lbl = new Label("Zack-a-boo");
        lbl.setFont(new Font("SansSerif", Font.PLAIN, 12));

        // A Button is created and then disabled

        Button b = new Button("click me");
        b.setEnabled(false);

        setLayout(new FlowLayout());
        add(lbl);
        add(b);

        addWindowListener(new WinClosing());
        setBounds(100, 100, 300, 120);
        setBackground(Color.red);
        setVisible(true);

    }

    // The getInsets() method is overridden to place the button more
    // in the center of the frame

    public Insets getInsets() {
        return new Insets(30, 30, 30, 30);
    }

    public static void main(String args[]) {
        TestCompSet tcs = new TestCompSet();
    }
}
```

```
// The WinClosing class terminates the program if the window is closed

class WinClosing extends WindowAdapter {
  public void windowClosing(WindowEvent we) {
    System.exit(0);
  }
}
```

The font of the Button is set using the setFont() method. The Button is disabled using the setEnabled() method. The background color of the Frame is set to be red using the setBackground() method and the frame is made visible using the setVisible() method.

### Output

Here is the result:

## Size Methods

| Method | Syntax |
|---|---|
| getHeight() | public int getHeight() |
| getMaximumSize() | public Dimension getMaximumSize() |
| getMinimumSize() | public Dimension getMinimumSize() |
| getPreferredSize() | public Dimension getPreferredSize() |
| getSize() | public Dimension getSize() |
| | public Dimension getSize(Dimension d) |
| getWidth() | public int getWidth() |
| setSize() | public void setSize(int width, int height) |
| | public void setSize(Dimension d) |

getHeight() and getWidth() return the current width and height of the invoking component.

getMaximumSize(), getMinimumSize(), and getPreferredSize() return the maximum, minimum, and preferred size. These quantities are determined by the component's peer class.

getSize() returns a Dimension object containing the current width and height of the invoking component. If a Dimension object is specified, its values are set to the size of the invoking component and the modified Dimension object is returned.

setSize() method changes the size, if possible, of the invoking component to the specified size.

## Example: Size Methods

This example creates a Frame with a Button object on it. It then checks the maximum and preferred sizes of the Button, returning them at the command line.

*The WinClosing class is used to terminate the program if the window is closed. See Section 7.3.8 on page 657 for more details.*

```java
import java.awt.*;
import java.awt.event.*;

public class TestCompSize extends Frame {
  Button b;

  public TestCompSize() {
    Button b = new Button("click me");

    setLayout(new FlowLayout());
    add(b);

    addWindowListener(new WinClosing());
    setBounds(100, 100, 200, 120);
    setVisible(true);

    // print out the maximum and preferred size of the Button

    Dimension d = b.getMaximumSize();
    System.out.println("Maximum size of " + b.getName() + " is "
                    + d.getWidth() + " by " + d.getHeight());
    d = b.getPreferredSize();
    System.out.println("Preferred size of " + b.getName() + " is "
                    + d.getWidth() + " by " + d.getHeight());
  }

  // The getInsets() method is overridden to place the button more
  // in the center of the frame

  public Insets getInsets() {
    return new Insets(30, 50, 30, 50);
  }
```

```
    public static void main(String args[]) {
        TestCompSize tcs = new TestCompSize();
    }
}

// The WinClosing class terminates the program if the window is closed

class WinClosing extends WindowAdapter {
    public void windowClosing(WindowEvent we) {
        System.exit(0);
    }
}
```

### Output

Here's the result:

The maximum size of the Button object and its preferred size are returned at the command line:

```
Maximum size of button0 is 32767.0 by 32767.0
Preferred size of button0 is 59.0 by 23.0
```

## toString() Method

| Method | Syntax |
|---|---|
| toString() | public String toString() |

toString() overrides the toString() method from the Object class and returns a String representation of the invoking component.

## Deprecated Methods

| Method | Syntax |
|---|---|
| action() | public boolean action(Event evt, Object obj) |
| bounds() | public Rectangle bounds() |
| deliverEvent() | public void deliverEvent(Event evt) |
| disable() | public void disable() |

| Method | Syntax |
|---|---|
| enable() | public void enable() |
| | public void enable(boolean state) |
| getPeer() | public ComponentPeer getPeer() |
| gotFocus() | public boolean gotFocus(Event evt, Object obj) |
| handleEvent() | public boolean handleEvent(Event evt) |
| hide() | public void hide() |
| inside() | public boolean inside(int x, int y) |
| keyDown() | public boolean keyDown(Event evt, int key) |
| keyUp() | public boolean keyUp(Event evt, int key) |
| layout() | public void layout() |
| locate() | public Component locate(int x, int y) |
| location() | public Point location() |
| lostFocus() | public boolean lostFocus(Event evt, Object obj) |
| minimumSize() | public Dimension minimumSize() |
| mouseDown() | public boolean mouseDown(Event evt, int x, int y) |
| mouseDrag() | public boolean mouseDrag(Event evt, int x, int y) |
| mouseEnter() | public boolean mouseEnter(Event evt, int x, int y) |
| mouseExit() | public boolean mouseExit(Event evt, int x, int y) |
| mouseMove() | public boolean mouseMove(Event evt, int x, int y) |
| mouseUp() | public boolean mouseUp(Event evt, int x, int y) |
| move() | public void move(int x, int y) |
| nextFocus() | public void nextFocus() |
| postEvent() | public boolean postEvent(Event evt) |
| preferredSize() | public Dimension preferredSize() |
| reshape() | public void reshape(int x, int y, int width, int height) |
| resize() | public void resize(int width, int height) |
| | public void resize(Dimension d) |
| show() | public void show() |
| | public void show(boolean state) |
| size() | public Dimension size() |

These Component class methods were deprecated as of Java 1.1. They should not be used for new code.

# 6.2 Component Classes

A **GUI component** is an object that resides in a container and is visible to the user. They can be used to provide information, initiate some action, or store data. For the purposes of this book, a GUI component is defined as a sub-class of Component that is not a Container. It could be a button that can be clicked, a list of item from which to select, or simply a label that provides some information. GUI components placed inside a container make up the user interface.

GUI components have various properties associated with them:

❑ **A component is either enabled or disabled**. Only an enabled component can generate events. For example, clicking on a disabled button will have no effect.

❑ **A component can be in or out of focus.** There can only be one component with focus at any one time. A component will fire a FocusEvent object when it gains or loses focus. If components are focus traversable, the user can move the focus from one component to another in a container using the *Tab* and *Shift-Tab* keys.

❑ **A component is either visible or invisible.**

    ❑ Most containers are by default invisible.

    ❑ Most GUI components are by default visible.

❑ **Every component has an internal name** that is used by the program to identify the component. This name is accessed by the getName() and setName() methods and can be different from the label that appears on the component.

❑ **A component can have one or more pop-up menus associated with it.** The pop-up menus contain menu items that are specific to the component.

The component class hierarchy is shown in the following diagram:

❑ The Button class implements a rectangular button that can be clicked.

❑ The Canvas class implements a blank, rectangular drawing area.

❑ The Checkbox provides a label with a small box beside it that can be checked.

❑ Several Checkbox objects can be grouped together using a CheckboxGroup object.

❑ The Choice and List classes represent a list of choices from which one or more selections can be made.

❑ The Scrollbar class provides a vertical or horizontal scrollbar.

❑ The TextArea and TextField classes allow an area to input one or more lines of text.

6

java.awt

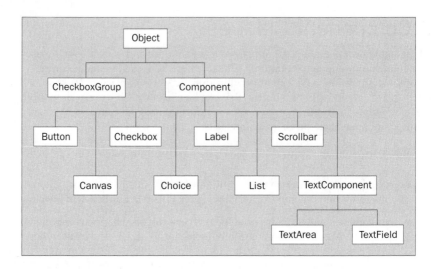

# 6.2.1 Button Class

```
public class Button extends Component implements Accessible
```

```
Object
  Component
    Button
```

### Interfaces

```
Accessible, ImageObserver, MenuContainer, Serializable
```

A Button object represents a labelled button that can be clicked. It is used to initiate an action. Every Button has an action command associated with it that can be used to identify the Button.

A Button object will generate an ActionEvent object when pressed.

## Button() Constructor

| Constructor | Syntax |
|---|---|
| Button() | public Button() |
| | public Button(String label) |

Creates a Button object. Passing the constructor a String gives the Button object a label.

## Action Command Methods

| Method | Syntax |
|---|---|
| getActionCommand() | public String getActionCommand() |
| setActionCommand() | public void setActionCommand<br>    (String *actionCommand*) |

Every Button object has an **action command** associated with it. These methods return or set the action command for the invoking Button object. If no action command is set, it returns the Button label. The getActionCommand() method can also be used by the ActionListener interface to determine which button has been selected.

## ActionListener Methods

| Method | Syntax |
|---|---|
| addActionListener() | public void addActionListener<br>    (ActionListener *al*) |
| removeActionListener() | public void removeActionListener<br>    (ActionListener *al*) |

addActionListener() registers the invoking Button object with an ActionListener object. The ActionListener is notified if the Button generates an action event.

removeActionListener() removes an ActionListener object from the invoking Button object. ActionEvent objects generated by the Button will no longer be received by the ActionListener.

## getListeners() Method

| Method | Syntax |
|---|---|
| getListeners() | public EventListener[] getListeners<br>    (Class *listenerClass*) |

getListeners() returns any listeners of the specified type registered to the invoking Button object as an EventListener array.

## Label Methods

| Method | Syntax |
|---|---|
| getLabel() | public String getLabel() |
| setLabel() | public void setLabel(String *label*) |

getLabel() returns the label of the invoking Button object.

setLabel() sets the label of the invoking Button object.

## Example: Using Button

In this example, two Button objects are created and placed on a Frame. The font and label are changed on the first Button, while the second one is disabled and the background color is changed to red. A TextField is also placed on the Frame. The two buttons are registered with an ActionListener. If either button is pressed, an ActionEvent is generated and sent to the actionPerformed() method. If the **disable** button was pressed, the TextField is disabled. If the **enable** button was pressed, the TextField is enabled.

*The WinClosing class is used to terminate the program if the window is closed. See Section 7.3.8 on page 657 for more details.*

```java
import java.awt.*;
import java.awt.event.*;

public class TestButton extends Frame implements ActionListener {
    Button b1, b2;
    TextField tf;

    public TestButton() {

        // two Button objects are created.  Several of their properties
        // are changed using the appropriate set() method

        b1 = new Button();
        b1.setFont(new Font("Serif", Font.BOLD, 12));
        b1.setLabel("enable");

        b2 = new Button("disable");
        b2.setBackground(Color.red);

        // register the buttons with an action listener.  In this case
        // the Frame itself serves as the action listener

        b1.addActionListener(this);
        b2.addActionListener(this);

        tf = new TextField(20);
        tf.setText("this is some text");

        setLayout(new FlowLayout());
        add(b1);
        add(b2);
        add(tf);
```

```
    addWindowListener(new WinClosing());
    setBounds(100, 100, 400, 120);
    setVisible(true);
  }

  // The actionPerformed() method is implemented by the ActionListener,
  // so it is included in the TestButton class

  public void actionPerformed(ActionEvent ae) {

    // If the "enable" button is pressed, the textfield is enabled
    // If the "disable" button is pressed, the textfield is disabled.
    // The actionPerformed() method determines which button generated
    // the ActionEvent, and therefore which button was pressed, by
    // examining the action command.

    if (ae.getActionCommand().equals("enable")) {
      tf.setEnabled(true);
    }
    if (ae.getActionCommand().equals("disable")) {
      tf.setEnabled(false);
    }
  }
  public static void main(String args[]) {
    TestButton tb = new TestButton();
  }
}

// The WinClosing class terminates the program when the window is closed

class WinClosing extends WindowAdapter {
  public void windowClosing(WindowEvent we) {
    System.exit(0);
  }
}
```

Note that the setFont(), setEnabled(), and setForeground() methods are
Component class methods.

### Output

Here is the result:

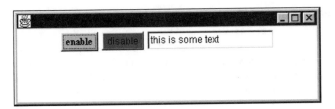

# 6.2.2 Canvas Class

```
public class Canvas extends Component implements Accessible
```

```
Object
   Component
      Canvas
```

### Interfaces
```
Accessible, ImageObserver, MenuContainer, Serializable
```

A Canvas object is a rectangular drawing area.

## Canvas() Constructor

| Constructor | Syntax |
|---|---|
| Canvas() | Canvas() |
| | Canvas(GraphicsConfiguration gc) |

Creates a Canvas object constructor. If a GraphicsConfiguration object is provided, it is used to describe the characteristics of a graphics destination such as a printer or monitor.

## paint() method

| Method | Syntax |
|---|---|
| paint() | public void paint(Graphics g) |

This is an empty method that is overridden to draw something on the invoking Canvas object using the methods provided in the Graphics class. See Section 6.7.5 on page 561.

# 6.2.3 Checkbox Class

```
public class Checkbox extends Component implements ItemSelectable, Accessible
```

```
Object
   Component
      Checkbox
```

### Interfaces
```
Accessible, ImageObserver, ItemSelectable, MenuContainer, Serializable
```

A Checkbox object is a box with a label that can either be checked or unchecked, similar to an on/off switch. Two or more Checkboxes can be grouped together, and made mutually exclusive, by using a CheckboxGroup object.

A Checkbox object generates an ItemEvent object when it is selected or de-selected.

# Checkbox() Constructor

| Constructor | Syntax |
|---|---|
| Checkbox() | public Checkbox() |
| | public Checkbox(String *label*) |
| | public Checkbox(String *label*, boolean *checked*) |
| | public Checkbox(String *label*, boolean *checked*, CheckboxGroup *cg*) |
| | public Checkbox(String *label*, CheckboxGroup *cg*, boolean *checked*) |

Creates a Checkbox object. The Checkbox can be set to initially be checked or unchecked. The default state is unchecked. The Checkbox object can be associated with a group of Checkbox objects by specifying a CheckboxGroup argument. Assigning the CheckboxGroup to null makes the Checkbox initially independent.

# Label Methods

| Method | Syntax |
|---|---|
| getLabel() | public String getLabel() |
| setLabel() | public void setLabel(String *label*) |

getLabel() returns the Label displayed by the invoking Checkbox object.

setLabel() sets the Label displayed by the invoking Checkbox object.

# Checked State Methods

| Method | Syntax |
|---|---|
| getState() | public boolean getState() |
| setState() | public void setState(boolean *checked*) |

getState() returns true if the invoking Checkbox object is checked.

setState() checks or unchecks the invoking Checkbox object.

# CheckboxGroup Methods

| Method | Syntax |
|---|---|
| getCheckboxGroup() | public CheckboxGroup getCheckboxGroup() |
| setCheckboxGroup() | public void setCheckboxGroup(CheckboxGroup *cbg*) |

A CheckboxGroup object is used to group two or more Checkbox objects together so they are mutually exclusive, only one of them can be checked.

getCheckboxGroup() returns the `CheckboxGroup` associated with the invoking `Checkbox` object.

setCheckboxGroup( ) sets the `CheckboxGroup` associated with the invoking `Checkbox` object. If `null` is passed to the `setCheckboxGroup( )` method, the invoking `Checkbox` object becomes independent.

## getListeners() Method

| Method | Syntax |
|---|---|
| getListeners() | public EventListener[] getListeners (Class *listenerClass*) |

getListeners( ) returns any listeners of the specified type registered to the invoking `Checkbox` object as an `EventListener` array.

## ItemListener Methods

| Method | Syntax |
|---|---|
| addItemListener() | public void addItemListener(ItemListener *il*) |
| removeItemListener() | public void removeItemListener(ItemListener *il*) |

addItemListener( )registers the invoking `Checkbox` object with an `ItemListener` object. The `ItemListener` is notified if the `Checkbox` generates an `ItemEvent` object.

removeItemListener( )removes an `ItemListener` object from the invoking `Checkbox` object. `ItemEvent` objects generated by the `Checkbox` will no longer be received by the `ItemListener`.

### Example: Using Checkbox

In this example, a `Checkbox` object is created and placed on a `Frame`. The `Checkbox` is given the label **Bold**. A `TextField` is also placed on the `Frame`. The `Checkbox` is registered with an `ItemListener`. If the `Checkbox` is checked, an `ItemEvent` is generated and the font style of the `TextField` is set to bold. If the `Checkbox` is unchecked, the style is changed to plain.

*The WinClosing class is used to terminate the program if the window is closed. See Section 7.3.8 on page 657 for more details.*

```
import java.awt.*;
import java.awt.event.*;

public class TestCheckbox extends Frame implements ItemListener {
    Checkbox cb;
    TextField tf;
```

```
public TestCheckbox() {

  cb = new Checkbox("Bold");
  cb.setFont(new Font("Serif", Font.BOLD, 12));
  cb.setState(true);

  // The Checkbox is registered with an ItemListener.  In this case
  // the Frame acts as the ItemListener

  cb.addItemListener(this);

  tf = new TextField(15);
  tf.setFont(new Font("Serif", Font.BOLD, 12));
  tf.setText("JavaJavaJava");

  setLayout(new FlowLayout());
  add(cb);
  add(tf);

  addWindowListener(new WinClosing());
  setBounds(100, 100, 300, 120);
  setVisible(true);
}

// The itemStateChanged() method must be implemented by the
// ItemListener.  Since the Frame is acting as the ItemListener in
// this example, the method is contained in the TestCheckbox class.

public void itemStateChanged(ItemEvent ie) {

  // The Checkbox generates ItemEvent objects when its selected state
  // changes. The checked state of the Checkbox is determined.  If the
  // Checkbox is currently checked, the font style is set to bold.
  // If unchecked, the style is set to plain.

  Checkbox cbox = (Checkbox) ie.getItemSelectable();
  if (cbox.getState()) {
    tf.setFont(new Font("Serif", Font.BOLD, 12));
  } else {
    tf.setFont(new Font("Serif", Font.PLAIN, 12));
  }
}

public static void main(String args[]) {
  TestCheckbox tc = new TestCheckbox();
}
}

// The WinClosing class terminates the program when the window is closed
```

```
  class WinClosing extends WindowAdapter {
    public void windowClosing(WindowEvent we) {
      System.exit(0);
    }
  }
```

**Output**

Here is the result:

# 6.2.4 CheckboxGroup Class

```
public class CheckboxGroup extends Object implements Serializable
```

```
Object
    CheckboxGroup
```

### Interfaces
```
Serializable
```

A CheckboxGroup object groups a number of Checkbox objects together making them mutually exclusive, so that only one of the member Checkbox objects may be selected. A CheckboxGroup object is not really a GUI component, as it is not a sub-class of Component. All the Checkbox components associated with a CheckboxGroup are normally placed into their own panel.

## CheckboxGroup() Constructor

| Constructor | Syntax |
|---|---|
| CheckboxGroup() | public CheckboxGroup() |

Creates a CheckboxGroup object. The constructor takes no arguments. Checkbox objects are associated with a CheckboxGroup by passing a reference to the CheckboxGroup to the Checkbox constructor when the Checkbox object is instantiated.

## Checkbox Selection Methods

| Method | Syntax |
|---|---|
| getSelectedCheckbox() | public Checkbox getSelectedCheckbox() |
| setSelectedCheckbox() | public void setSelectedCheckbox(Checkbox cb) |

getSelectedCheckbox() returns the selected Checkbox from the invoking CheckboxGroup object.

setSelectedCheckbox() sets the selected Checkbox from the invoking CheckboxGroup object.

## toString() Method

| Method | Syntax |
|---|---|
| toString() | public String toString() |

toString() overrides the toString() method from the Object class and returns a String representation of the invoking CheckboxGroup object.

## Deprecated Methods

| Method | Syntax |
|---|---|
| getCurrent() | public Checkbox getCurrent() |
| setCurrent() | public void setCurrent(Checkbox cbx) |

These methods have been deprecated as of Java 1.1 and should not be used for new code.

### Example: Using CheckboxGroup

In this example, three Checkbox objects are created and grouped together using a CheckboxGroup object. Only one of the three can be selected. The TextField is updated to reflect the current selection.

*The WinClosing class is used to terminate the program if the window is closed. See Section 7.3.8 on page 657 for more details.*

```
import java.awt.*;
import java.awt.event.*;

public class TestCBG extends Frame implements ItemListener {
    Checkbox cb1, cb2, cb3;
    CheckboxGroup cbg;
    TextField tf;

    TestCBG() {

        // Three Checkbox objects are created.  They are assigned to a
        // CheckboxGroup when they are instantiated.  Initially, none of
        // the Checkbox objects are selected.
```

```java
      cbg = new CheckboxGroup();
      cb1 = new Checkbox("London", cbg, false);
      cb2 = new Checkbox("Tokyo", cbg, false);
      cb3 = new Checkbox("Ottawa", cbg, false);

      // The Checkbox objects are registered with an ItemListener.
      // In this case the Frame acts as the ItemListener

      cb1.addItemListener(this);
      cb2.addItemListener(this);
      cb3.addItemListener(this);

      tf = new TextField(15);
      tf.setEditable(false);

      Panel p = new Panel();
      p.add(cb1);
      p.add(cb2);
      p.add(cb3);

      add(p, BorderLayout.CENTER);
      add(tf, BorderLayout.SOUTH);

      addWindowListener(new WinClosing());
      setBounds(100, 100, 300, 120);
      setVisible(true);
   }
   // The itemStateChanged() method must be implemented by the
   // ItemListener.  Since the Frame is acting as the ItemListener in
   // this example, the method is contained in the TestCheckbox class.
   public void itemStateChanged(ItemEvent ie) {

      // The TextField is updated to reflect the currently selected
      // Checkbox.

      Checkbox cbox = (Checkbox) ie.getItemSelectable();
      tf.setText("city selected is " + cbox.getLabel());
   }

   public static void main(String args[]) {
      TestCBG tcbg = new TestCBG();
   }
}

// The WinClosing class terminates the program if the window when closed
```

```
class WinClosing extends WindowAdapter {
  public void windowClosing(WindowEvent we) {
    System.exit(0);
  }
}
```

### Output
Here is the result:

---

# 6.2.5 Choice Class

```
public class Choice extends Component implements ItemSelectable, Accessible
```

```
Object
   Component
      Choice
```

### Interfaces
```
Accessible, ImageObserver, ItemSelectable, MenuContainer, Serializable
```

A Choice object is a pull-down list. When the component is selected, a list of choices appears on the screen. When the selection is made, only the selected item remains visible.

A Choice object generates ItemEvent objects when an item is selected.

## Choice() Constructor

| Constructor | Syntax |
|---|---|
| Choice() | public Choice() |

Creates a Choice object. Initially, the Choice object is empty. The add() method is used to add elements.

## Methods that Add or Remove Elements

| Method | Syntax |
|---|---|
| add() | public void add(String *item*) |
| addItem() | public void addItem(String *item*) |
| insert() | public void insert(String *item*, int *index*) |
| remove() | public void remove(String *item*) |
| | public void remove(int *index*) |
| removeAll() | public void removeAll() |

add() and addItem() add an item to the end of the invoking Choice object.

insert() adds an item to the invoking Choice object at the index provided. The Choice list index starts at 0.

remove() removes an item from the invoking Choice object based on either a String or index argument.

removeAll() removes all of the items from the invoking Choice object.

## getItemCount() Method

| Method | Syntax |
|---|---|
| getItemCount() | public int getItemCount() |

getItemCount() returns the number of selectable items in the invoking Choice object.

## getItem() Method

| Method | Syntax |
|---|---|
| getItem() | public String getItem(int *index*) |

getItem() returns the item at position index of the invoking Choice object as a String.

## getListeners() Method

| Method | Syntax |
|---|---|
| getListeners() | public EventListener[] getListeners (Class *listenerClass*) |

getListeners() returns any listeners of the specified type registered to the invoking Choice object as an EventListener array.

## ItemListener Methods

| Method | Syntax |
|---|---|
| addItemListener() | public void addItemListener(ItemListener *il*) |
| removeItemListener() | public void removeItemListener(ItemListener *il*) |

addItemListener() registers the invoking Choice object with an ItemListener object. The ItemListener is notified if the Choice object generates an ItemEvent object.

removeItemListener() removes an ItemListener object from the invoking Choice object. ItemEvent objects generated by the Choice object will no longer be received by the ItemListener.

## Methods that Select or Return Selected Elements

| Method | Syntax |
|---|---|
| select() | public void select(int *index*) |
| | public void select(String *item*) |
| getSelectedItem() | public String getSelectedItem() |
| getSelectedIndex() | public int getSelectedIndex() |
| getSelectedObjects() | public Object[] getSelectedObjects() |

select() selects an item of the invoking Choice object based on either a String or index argument.

getSelectedItem() returns the selected item of the invoking Choice object as a String.

getSelectedIndex() returns the index of the currently selected item.

getSelectedObjects() returns the currently selected item, if any, as an Object array.

## Deprecated Methods

| Method | Syntax |
|---|---|
| countItems() | public int countItems() |

This method has been deprecated as of Java 1.1 and should not be used for new code.

## Example: Using Choice

In this example, a Choice object is added to the Frame, creating a drop-down list of available foods. A TextField is also placed on the Frame. The Choice object is registered with an ItemListener. When the selection is changed, an ItemEvent is generated, and the TextField is updated to reflect the new selection.

*The WinClosing class is used to terminate the program if the window is closed. See Section 7.3.8 on page 657 for more details.*

```java
import java.awt.*;
import java.awt.event.*;

public class TestChoice extends Frame implements ItemListener {
  Choice c;
  TextField tf;

  TestChoice() {

    // A Choice object is created and four selections are added to it.

    c = new Choice();
    c.add("Fish");
    c.add("Rice");
    c.add("Beans");
    c.add("Cheese");
    c.select("Rice");

    // The Choice object is registered with an ItemListener.
    // In this case, the TestChoice class acts as the ItemListener

    c.addItemListener(this);

    tf = new TextField(15);
    tf.setEditable(false);
    tf.setText("food selected is " + c.getSelectedItem());

    Panel p = new Panel();
    p.add(c);
    add(p, BorderLayout.CENTER);
    add(tf, BorderLayout.SOUTH);

    addWindowListener(new WinClosing());
    setBounds(100, 100, 200, 120);
    setVisible(true);
  }
```

```
      // The itemStateChanged() method must be implemented by the
      // ItemListener.  Since the TestChoice class is acting as the
      // ItemListener in this example, the method is contained in
      // the TestChoice class.

      public void itemStateChanged(ItemEvent ie) {

        // The TextField is updated to reflect the currently selected item.

        Choice choice = (Choice) ie.getItemSelectable();
        tf.setText("food selected is " + choice.getSelectedItem());
      }

      public static void main(String args[]) {
        TestChoice tc = new TestChoice();
      }
    }

    // The WinClosing class terminates the program when the window is closed

    class WinClosing extends WindowAdapter {
      public void windowClosing(WindowEvent we) {
        System.exit(0);
      }
    }
```

**6**

java.awt

### Output

The result of this program should be as follows:

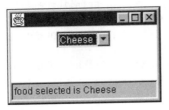

## 6.2.6 Label Class

```
public class Label extends Component implements Accessible
```

```
Object
  Component
    Label
```

### Interfaces

```
Accessible, ImageObserver, MenuContainer, Serializable
```

A Label is a component that displays a single line of text. A Label object is often used for putting a title or message next to another component.

Label objects do not generate events.

## Label() Constructor

| Constructor | Syntax |
|---|---|
| Label() | public Label() |
| | public Label(String s) |
| | public Label(String s, int alignment) |

Creates a Label object. If a String is not provided, the Label is initialized with the empty String, "". The default alignment is LEFT. The alignment can be passed to the constructor with one of these three constants:

- ❑ Label.LEFT
- ❑ Label.RIGHT
- ❑ Label.CENTER

## Alignment Methods

| Method | Syntax |
|---|---|
| getAlignment() | public int getAlignment() |
| setAlignment() | public void setAlignment(int align) |

getAlignment() returns the current alignment of the invoking Label object.

setAlignment() sets the alignment of the invoking Label object. The argument must be either Label.LEFT, Label.RIGHT, or Label.CENTER.

## Text Methods

| Method | Syntax |
|---|---|
| getText() | public String getText() |
| setText() | public void setText(String text) |

getText() returns a String object containing the text of the invoking Label object.

setText() sets the text of the invoking Label object.

## Example: Using Label

In this example, a `Label` object is created and placed on a `Frame`. The `Label` object font is set using the `setFont()` method from the `Component` class.

*The `WinClosing` class is used to terminate the program if the window is closed. See Section 7.3.8 on page 657 for more details.*

```java
import java.awt.*;
import java.awt.event.*;

public class TestLabel extends Frame {
  Label lbl;

  TestLabel() {
    lbl = new Label("Test Label");
    lbl.setFont(new Font("Serif", Font.BOLD, 14));
    lbl.setAlignment(Label.CENTER);

    add(lbl);

    addWindowListener(new WinClosing());
    setBounds(100, 100, 200, 100);
    setVisible(true);
  }

  public static void main(String args[]) {
    TestLabel tl = new TestLabel();
  }
}

// The WinClosing class terminates the program when the window is closed

class WinClosing extends WindowAdapter {
  public void windowClosing(WindowEvent we) {
    System.exit(0);
  }
}
```

### *Output*

Here is the result:

# 6.2.7 List Class

```
public class List extends Component implements ItemSelectable, Accessible
```

```
Object
   Component
      List
```

### Interfaces

```
Accessible, ImageObserver, ItemSelectable, MenuContainer, Serializable
```

A List object implements a list. More than one item can be shown on the screen and more than one item can be selected. A scrollbar is often associated with a List to allow the user to move to items that do not fit on the screen.

A List object generates an ItemEvent object when an item is single-clicked, and an ActionEvent object when an item is double-clicked.

## List() Constructor

| Constructor | Syntax |
|---|---|
| List() | public List() |
| | public List(int *visibleRows*) |
| | public List(int *visibleRows*, boolean *multipleSelections*) |

Creates a List object. The no-argument constructor creates an empty List object with four visible lines. The default selection mode is single selection. Setting multipleSelections to true allows multiple selections.

## ActionListener Methods

| Method | Syntax |
|---|---|
| addActionListener() | public void addActionListener (ActionListener *al*) |
| removeActionListener() | public void removeActionListener (ActionListener *al*) |

addActionListener() registers the invoking List object with an ActionListener object. The ActionListener is notified if the List generates an action event.

removeActionListener() removes an ActionListener object from the invoking List object. ActionEvent objects generated by the List will no longer be received by the ActionListener.

## Methods that Add or Remove Elements

| Method | Syntax |
|---|---|
| add() | public void add(String *item*) |
| | public void add(String *item*, int *index*) |
| replaceItem() | public void replaceItem(String *item*, int *index*) |
| remove() | public void remove(String *item*) |
| | public void remove(int *index*) |
| removeAll() | public void removeAll() |

add() adds an item to the invoking List object. If no index is specified, the item is added to the bottom of the List.

replaceItem() replaces the current element at position index in the invoking List object with the item passed as an argument.

remove() removes an item from the invoking List object. A String object or index can be passed as an argument.

removeAll() removes all of the items from the invoking List object.

## getItemCount() Method

| Method | Syntax |
|---|---|
| getItemCount() | public int getItemCount() |

getItemCount() returns the number of items in the invoking List object.

## getListeners() Method

| Method | Syntax |
|---|---|
| getListeners() | public EventListener[] getListeners (Class *listenerClass*) |

getListeners() returns any listeners of the specified type registered to the invoking List object as an EventListener array.

## ItemListener Methods

| Method | Syntax |
|---|---|
| addItemListener() | public void addItemListener(ItemListener *il*) |
| removeItemListener() | public void removeItemListener(ItemListener *il*) |

6

java.awt

addItemListener() registers the invoking List object with an ItemListener object. The ItemListener is notified if the List generates an ItemEvent object.

removeItemListener() removes an ItemListener object from the invoking List object. ItemEvent objects generated by the List will no longer be received by the ItemListener.

## Multiple Mode and Visible Property Methods

| Method | Syntax |
|---|---|
| isMultipleMode() | public boolean isMultipleMode() |
| setMultipleMode() | public void setMultipleMode(boolean b) |
| makeVisible() | public void makeVisible(int index) |
| getRows() | public int getRows() |
| getVisibleIndex() | public int getVisibleIndex() |

isMultipleMode() returns true if the invoking List object allows multiple selections.

setMultipleMode() sets the selection state of the invoking List object.

makeVisible() causes the item at position index to be displayed on the screen.

getRows() returns the number of visible rows.

getVisibleIndex() returns the index from the last call to makeVisible(), or -1 if the makeVisible() method has not been called.

## Methods that Return an Element

| Method | Syntax |
|---|---|
| getItem() | public String getItem(int index) |
| getItems() | public String[] getItems() |

getItem() returns the item at the specified index from the invoking List object.

getItems() returns all the items from the invoking List object as a String array.

## Selection Methods

| Method | Syntax |
|---|---|
| getSelectedItem() | public String getSelectedItem() |
| getSelectedItems() | public String[] getSelectedItems() |
| getSelectedIndex() | public int getSelectedIndex() |
| getSelectedIndexes() | public int[] getSelectedIndexes() |

| Method | Syntax |
|---|---|
| getSelectedObjects() | public Object[] getSelectedObjects() |
| select() | public void select(int *index*) |
| deselect() | public void deselect(int *index*) |
| isIndexSelected() | public boolean isIndexSelected(int *index*) |

getSelectedItem() and getSelectedItems() return the item or items of the invoking List object that are currently selected.

getSelectedIndex() and getSelectedIndexes() return the index or indices of the currently selected items.

getSelectedObjects() return the currently selected items as an List array.

select() causes the element at position index of the invoking List object to be selected.

deselect() deselects the item at position index.

isIndexSelected() returns true if the element at index is selected.

## Sizing Methods

| Method | Syntax |
|---|---|
| getPreferredSize() | public Dimension getPreferredSize(int *rows*) |
|  | public Dimension getPreferredSize() |
| getMinimumSize() | public Dimension getMinimumSize(int *rows*) |
|  | public Dimension getMinimumSize() |

getPreferredSize() returns a Dimension object containing the preferred size of the invoking List object.

getMinimumSize() returns the minimum size of the invoking List object. If the number of rows is not passed to the getPerferredSize() and getMinimumSize() methods, the number of rows passed to the constructor is used to calculate these properties.

## Deprecated Methods

| Method | Syntax |
|---|---|
| addItem() | public void addItem(String *str*) |
|  | public void addItem(String *str*, int *index*) |
| allowsMultipleSelections() | public boolean allowsMultipleSelections() |

6

java.awt

| Method | Syntax |
|---|---|
| clear() | public void clear() |
| countItems() | public int countItems() |
| delItems() | public void delItems(int *start*, int *end*) |
| isSelected() | public boolean isSelected(int *index*) |
| minimumSize() | public Dimension minimumSize() |
| | public Dimension minimumSize(int *rows*) |
| preferredSize() | public Dimension preferredSize() |
| | public Dimension preferredSize(int *rows*) |
| setMultipleSelections() | public void setMultipleSelections (boolean *b*) |

These methods have been deprecated as of Java 1.1 and should not be used for new code.

## Example: Using List

In this example, a List object is created and placed on a Frame. Four elements are added to the List object. A TextField is also placed on the Frame. The List object is registered with an ItemListener. When the selection is changed, an ItemEvent is generated, and the TextField is updated to reflect the new selection.

*The WinClosing class is used to terminate the program if the window is closed. See Section 7.3.8 on page 657 for more details.*

```
import java.awt.*;
import java.awt.event.*;

public class TestList extends Frame implements ItemListener {
  List lst;
  TextField tf;

  TestList() {

    // A List object is created and four selections are added to it.

    lst = new List(5);
    lst.add("Fish");
    lst.add("Rice");
    lst.add("Beans");
    lst.add("Cheese");
    lst.setFont(new Font("Serif", Font.BOLD, 12));

    // The List object is registered with an ItemListener.
    // In this case, the TestList class acts as the ItemListener
```

```
      lst.addItemListener(this);

   tf = new TextField(15);
   tf.setEditable(false);
   tf.setText("food selected is " + lst.getSelectedItem());

   Panel p = new Panel();
   p.add(lst);
   add(p, BorderLayout.CENTER);
   add(tf, BorderLayout.SOUTH);

   addWindowListener(new WinClosing());
   setBounds(100, 100, 200, 200);
   setVisible(true);
   }

// The itemStateChanged() method must be implemented by the
// ItemListener.  Since the TestList class is acting as the
// ItemListener in this example, the method is contained in
// the TestList class.

public void itemStateChanged(ItemEvent ie) {

   // The TextField is updated to reflect the currently selected item.

   List l = (List) ie.getItemSelectable();
   tf.setText("food selected is " + l.getSelectedItem());
   }

   public static void main(String args[]) {
     TestList tl = new TestList();
   }
}

// The WinClosing class terminates the program when the window is closed

class WinClosing extends WindowAdapter {
   public void windowClosing(WindowEvent we) {
     System.exit(0);
   }
}
```

The font that is displayed is set using the setFont() method from the Component class.

### Output

Here is the result:

# 6.2.8 Scrollbar Class

```
public class Scrollbar extends Component implements Adjustable, Accessible
```

```
Object
   Component
      Scrollbar
```

### Interfaces

```
Accessible, Adjustable, ImageObserver, MenuContainer, Serializable
```

A Scrollbar object is used to set an integer value within a pre-determined range. It is displayed as a horizontal or vertical bar with arrow buttons at either end and a slider bar that can be moved back and forth. The user can change the value of the Scrollbar by clicking on the arrows, moving the slider bar, or clicking in the scrollbar area itself.

A Scrollbar object generates AdjustmentEvent objects when the Scrollbar is moved.

## Scrollbar() Constructor

| Constructor | Syntax |
|---|---|
| Scrollbar() | public Scrollbar() |
| | public Scrollbar(int *orientation*) |
| | public Scrollbar(int *orientation*, int *value*, int *visible*, int *minimum*, int *maximum*) |

Creates a Scrollbar object. The value is initial value of the Scrollbar. The minimum and maximum are the range of values the Scrollbar can have. The visible quantity is the range of values represented by the width of the slider. Note that the maximum value that the Scrollbar can reach by moving the slider is equal to maximum – visible. The orientation is set using one of the following two constants:

❑ Scrollbar.HORIZONTAL

❑ Scrollbar.VERTICAL

If they are not provided to the constructor, the orientation is set to vertical and the value, visible, minimum, and maximum parameters are set to 0.

## AdjustmentListener Methods

| Method | Syntax |
|---|---|
| addAdjustmentListener() | public void addAdjustmentListener (AdjustmentListener *al*) |
| removeAdjustmentListener() | public void removeAdjustmentListener (AdjustmentListener *al*) |

addAdjustmentListener() registers the invoking Scrollbar object with an AdjustmentListener object. The AdjustmentListener is notified if the Scrollbar generates an AdjustmentEvent object.

removeAdjustmentListener() removes an AdjustmentListener object from the invoking Scrollbar object. AdjustmentEvent objects generated by the Scrollbar will no longer be received by the AdjustmentListener.

## Appearance Methods

| Method | Syntax |
|---|---|
| getVisibleAmount() | public int getVisibleAmount() |
| setVisibleAmount() | public void setVisibleAmount(int *amount*) |

getVisibleAmount() returns the visible amount of the invoking Scrollbar object. The visible amount is the range of values represented by the width of the slider.

setVisibleAmount() sets the visible amount of the invoking Scrollbar object.

## getListeners() Method

| Method | Syntax |
|---|---|
| getListeners() | public EventListener[] getListeners (Class *listenerClass*) |

6

java.awt

getListeners() returns any listeners of the specified type registered to the invoking Scrollbar object as an EventListener array.

## Orientation Methods

| Method | Syntax |
| --- | --- |
| getOrientation() | public int getOrientation() |
| setOrientation() | public void setOrientation(int *orientation*) |

getOrientation() returns the orientation of the invoking Scrollbar object. The return value will be either Scrollbar.HORIZONTAL or Scrollbar.VERTICAL.

setOrientation() sets the orientation of the invoking Scrollbar object. The argument passed to the setOrientation() method must be either Scrollbar.HORIZONTAL or Scrollbar.VERTICAL.

## Range and Increment Methods

| Method | Syntax |
| --- | --- |
| getBlockIncrement() | public int getBlockIncrement() |
| getMaximum() | public int getMaximum() |
| getMinimum() | public int getMinimum() |
| getUnitIncrement() | public int getUnitIncrement() |
| setBlockIncrement() | public void setBlockIncrement(int *increment*) |
| setMaximum() | public void setMaximum(int *max*) |
| setMinimum() | public void setMinimum(int *min*) |
| setUnitIncrement() | public void setUnitIncrement(int *increment*) |

getBlockIncrement() returns the block increment, the amount the value changes if the user clicks inside the Scrollbar area, of the invoking Scrollbar object.

getMaximum() and getMinimum() return the maximum and minimum values of the invoking Scrollbar object.

getUnitIncrement() returns the unit increment, the amount the value changes if the user clicks on one of the Scrollbar object's arrows.

setBlockIncrement(), setMaximum(), setMinimum(), and setUnitIncrement() methods set the block increment, maximum, minimum, or unit increment values.

# Methods that Return or Set the Scrollbar Value

| Method | Syntax |
|---|---|
| getValue() | public int getValue() |
| setValue() | public void setValue(int *value*) |

getValue() returns the current value of the invoking Scrollbar object.

setValue() sets the value of the invoking Scrollbar object. The slider bar will move to reflect the new value.

# setValues() method

| Method | Syntax |
|---|---|
| setValues() | public void setValues(int *value*, int *visible*, int *minimum*, int *maximum*) |

setValues() sets the value, visible range, minimum value, and maximum value of the invoking Scrollbar object. The visible amount is the range of values represented by the width of the slider.

# Deprecated Methods

| Method | Syntax |
|---|---|
| getLineIncrement() | public int getLineIncrement() |
| getPageIncrement() | public int getPageIncrement() |
| getVisible() | public int getVisible() |
| setLineIncrement() | public void setLineIncrement(int *inc*) |
| setPageIncrement() | public void setPageIncrement(int *inc*) |

These methods have been deprecated as of Java 1.1 and should not be used for new code.

## Example: Using Scrollbar

In this example, a Scrollbar object is created and placed on a Frame. A TextField object is provided that displays the current value of the Scrollbar object.

*The WinClosing class is used to terminate the program if the window is closed.*
*See Section 7.3.8 on page 657 for more details.*

6

java.awt

```
import java.awt.*;
import java.awt.event.*;

public class TestScrollbar extends Frame
  implements AdjustmentListener {
  Scrollbar sb;
  TextField tf;

  TestScrollbar() {

    // a Scrollbar object is created and its properties set.

    sb = new Scrollbar(Scrollbar.VERTICAL);
    sb.setMinimum(1);
    sb.setMaximum(100);
    sb.setValue(50);
    sb.setUnitIncrement(1);
    sb.setBlockIncrement(10);
    sb.setVisibleAmount(1);

    // The Scrollbar object is registered with an AdjustmentListener.
    // In this case, the TestScrollbar class acts as the
    // AdjustmentListener

    sb.addAdjustmentListener(this);

    tf = new TextField(3);
    tf.setEditable(false);
    tf.setText("" + sb.getValue());

    Panel p = new Panel();
    p.add(tf);
    p.add(sb);

    add(p);

    addWindowListener(new WinClosing());
    setBounds(100, 100, 200, 120);
    setVisible(true);
  }

  // The adjustmentValueChanged() method must be implemented by the
  // AdjustmentListener.  Since the TestScrollbar class is acting as the
  // AdjustmentListener in this example, the method is contained in
  // the TestScrollbar class.

  public void adjustmentValueChanged(AdjustmentEvent ae) {
```

```
        // The TextField is updated to reflect the value of the Scrollbar.

        tf.setText("" + sb.getValue());
    }

    public static void main(String args[]) {
        TestScrollbar ts = new TestScrollbar();
    }
}

// The WinClosing class terminates the program when the window is closed

class WinClosing extends WindowAdapter {
    public void windowClosing(WindowEvent we) {
        System.exit(0);
    }
}
```

An AdjustmentListener object is added to the Scrollbar object to update the TextField text when the Scrollbar value is changed. The minimum value of the Scrollbar object occurs at the top of the Scrollbar. The maximum value is at the bottom. The more standard convention is to have the minimum value at the bottom. The way that the TextField text is updated can be modified to make it appear that the minimum value is at the bottom.

### Output

Here is the result:

Note that it is not possible to reach the maximum value by clicking on the arrow or Scrollbar area. The largest value that can be reached is equal to the maximum value minus the visible amount.

# 6.2.9 TextArea Class

```
public class TextArea extends TextComponent
```

```
Object
  Component
    TextComponent
      TextArea
```

### Interfaces

```
Accessible, ImageObserver, MenuContainer, Serializable
```

A TextArea object provides a rectangular display area for multi-line text input. It can be set to be editable or read-only.

A TextArea can generate KeyEvent and TextEvent objects. A TextEvent is generated if the text inside the TextArea changes. Because a carriage return is treated as just another character by the TextArea object, a carriage return does not generate an ActionEvent.

## TextArea() Constructor

| Constructor | Syntax |
| --- | --- |
| TextArea() | `public TextArea()` |
| | `public TextArea(int rows, int columns)` |
| | `public TextArea(String s)` |
| | `public TextArea(String s, int rows, int columns)` |
| | `public TextArea(String s, int rows, int columns, int scrollbarPolicy)` |

Creates a TextArea object . An initial String to be displayed and the number of rows and columns in the TextArea can be passed to the constructor. The default scrollbar policy is to show scrollbars on both the vertical and horizontal axes. To specify the scrollbar policy, use one of the following constants:

❑  TextArea.SCROLLBARS_BOTH

❑  TextArea.SCROLLBARS_HORIZONTAL_ONLY

❑  TextArea.SCROLLBARS_NONE

❑  TextArea.SCROLLBARS_VERTICAL_ONLY

## Methods to Add Text

| Method | Syntax |
|--------|--------|
| append() | public void append(String *str*) |
| insert() | public void insert(String *str*, int *pos*) |
| replaceRange() | public void replaceRange(String *str*, <br> int *start*, <br> int *end*) |

These methods are used to add text to the invoking TextArea object.

append() adds the String str to the end of the existing text.

insert() adds the String str starting at position pos. Any existing text is shifted to the right.

replaceRange() replaces some part of the existing text with String str.

## getScrollbarVisibility() method

| Method | Syntax |
|--------|--------|
| getScrollbarVisibility() | public int getScrollbarVisibility() |

getScrollbarVisibility() returns the current scrollbar policy. The return value will be one of the four constants listed above.

## Sizing Methods

| Method | Syntax |
|--------|--------|
| getRows() | public int getRows() |
| setRows() | public void setRows(int *rows*) |
| getColumns() | public int getColumns() |
| setColumns() | public void setColumns(int *columns*) |
| getPreferredSize() | public Dimension getPreferredSize <br> (int *rows*, int *columns*) |
| | public Dimension getPreferredSize() |
| getMinimumSize() | public Dimension getMinimumSize <br> (int *rows*, int *columns*) |
| | public Dimension getMinimumSize() |

getRows() and getColumns() return the number of rows and columns in the invoking TextArea object.

setRows() and setColumns() set the number of rows and columns of the invoking TextArea object.

**467**

getPreferredSize() and getMinimumSize() return the preferred or minimum size of a TextArea object with a specified number of rows and columns. If the number of rows and columns is not passed to the getPreferredSize() and getMinimumSize() methods, the number of rows and columns passed to the constructor is used to calculate these properties.

## Deprecated Methods

| Method | Syntax |
|---|---|
| appendText() | public void appendText(String *str*) |
| insertText() | public void insertText(String *str*, int *pos*) |
| minimumSize() | public Dimension minimumSize() |
| | public Dimension minimumSize(int *rows*, int *columns*) |
| preferredSize() | public Dimension preferredSize() |
| | public Dimension preferredSize(int *rows*, int *columns*) |
| replaceText() | public void replaceText(String *str*, int *startIndex*, int *endIndex*) |

These methods have been deprecated as of Java 1.1 and should not be used for new code.

### Example: Using TextArea

In this example, a TextArea object is created with 5 rows and 25 columns and placed on a Frame. A String is then appended to the TextArea object. Another String is inserted at position 0, pushing the original String to the right.

The TextArea is registered with a TextListener. When the contents of the TextArea changes, a TextEvent is generated and the contents of a TextField are updated to indicate the time that the change took place.

*The WinClosing class is used to terminate the program if the window is closed. See Section 7.3.8 on page 657 for more details.*

```java
import java.awt.*;
import java.awt.event.*;
import java.util.*;

public class TestTA extends Frame implements TextListener {
   TextArea ta;
   TextField tf;
   Date date;

   TestTA() {
```

```
    // A TextArea object is created with 5 rows and 25 columns.
    // A String is added to the TextArea. Another String is
    // inserted at position 0, pushing the original String to the
    // right.

    ta = new TextArea(5, 25);
    ta.append("Filling Santa's Shelves");
    ta.insert("We are Santa's Elves \n", 0);

    // The TextArea object is registered with a TextListener.
    // In this case, the TestTA class acts as the TextListener

    ta.addTextListener(this);

    tf = new TextField(20);
    tf.setEditable(false);

    Panel p = new Panel();
    p.add(ta);

    add(p, BorderLayout.CENTER);
    add(tf, BorderLayout.SOUTH);

    addWindowListener(new WinClosing());
    setBounds(100, 100, 400, 200);
    setVisible(true);
  }

  // The textValueChanged() method must be implemented by the
  // TextListener. Since the TestTA class is acting as the
  // TextListener in this example, the method is contained in
  // the TestTA class.

  public void textValueChanged(TextEvent te) {

    // If the contents of the TextArea are changed,
    // The TextField indicates when the text in the TextArea was changed.

    date = new Date();
    tf.setText("text changed at " + date.toString());
  }

  public static void main(String args[]) {
    TestTA tta = new TestTA();
  }
}
// The WinClosing class terminates the program when the window is closed

class WinClosing extends WindowAdapter {
  public void windowClosing(WindowEvent we) {
    System.exit(0);
  }
}
```

***Output***

Here is the result. When running this example, make some changes to the contents of the TextArea and watch the TextField display change.

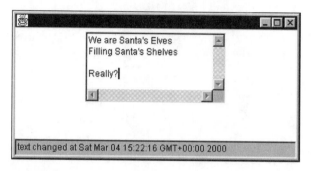

# 6.2.10 TextComponent Class

```
public class TextComponent extends Component implements Accessible
```

```
Object
   Component
      TextComponent
```

### Interfaces

```
Accessible, ImageObserver, MenuContainer, Serializable
```

The TextComponent class is the parent class of the TextArea and TextField classes, and provides methods used by both of these classes. The TextComponent class does not provide a public or protected constructor, so a TextComponent object is never created.

## Caret Methods

| Method | Syntax |
|--------|--------|
| getCaretPosition() | public int getCaretPosition() |
| setCaretPosition() | public void setCaretPosition(int *pos*) |

The **caret** is another name for the text cursor. The caret position begins at index 0.

getCaretPosition() returns the current caret position.

setCaretPosition() changes the caret position.

# Color Methods

| Method | Syntax |
|---|---|
| getBackground() | public Color getBackground() |
| setBackground() | public void setBackground(Color backgroundColor) |

getBackground() returns the current background color of the invoking text component.

setBackground() changes the background color of the invoking text component

# Editable Property Methods

| Method | Syntax |
|---|---|
| isEditable() | public boolean isEditable() |
| setEditable() | public void setEditable(boolean editable) |

isEditable() returns true if the invoking TextComponent sub-class object can be edited.

setEditable() changes the editable state of the invoking TextComponent sub-class object. Setting the editable property to be false means the TextComponent sub-class object is read-only.

# getListeners() Method

| Method | Syntax |
|---|---|
| getListeners() | public EventListener[] getListeners (Class listenerClass) |

getListeners() returns any listeners of the specified type registered to the invoking text component as an EventListener array.

# Selection Methods

| Method | Syntax |
|---|---|
| getSelectionEnd() | public int getSelectionEnd() |
| getSelectionStart() | public int getSelectionStart() |
| select() | public void select(int startIndex, int endIndex) |
| selectAll() | public void selectAll() |
| setSelectionStart() | public void setSelectionStart(int startIndex) |
| setSelectionEnd() | public void setSelectionEnd(int endIndex) |

**6**

java.awt

getSelectionStart() and getSelectionEnd() return the starting and ending position of the selected text.

setSelectionStart() and setSelectionEnd() change the the beginning or end position of the selected text.

select() selects text starting at startIndex and ending at endIndex.

selectAll() method selects all of the text.

Text can also be selected by pressing the mouse button and dragging the cursor across the text.

## Text Methods

| Method | Syntax |
| --- | --- |
| getText() | public String getText() |
| setText() | public void setText(String *text*) |
| getSelectedText() | public String getSelectedText() |

getText() returns the text contained by the invoking TextComponent sub-class object.

getSelectedText() returns only the selected text.

setText() changes the text contained by the invoking TextComponent sub-class object.

## TextListener Methods

| Method | Syntax |
| --- | --- |
| addTextListener() | public synchronized void addTextListener (TextListener *tl*) |
| removeTextListener() | public synchronized void removeTextListener (TextListener *tl*) |

TextEvent objects are generated when the text inside a text component changes.

addTextListener() registers the invoking text component with an TextListener object. The TextListener is notified if the text component generates a TextEvent object.

removeTextListener() removes a TextListener object from the invoking text component. TextEvent objects generated by the text component will no longer be received by the TextListener.

# 6.2.11 TextField Class

```
public class TextField extends TextComponent
```

```
Object
  Component
    TextComponent
      TextField
```

### Interfaces

```
Accessible, ImageObserver, MenuContainer, Serializable
```

A TextField is an object that permits a single line of input. The text in a TextField object is left-justified. A TextField can be made to be editable or read-only. The font and size of the text in a TextField can be modified using the appropriate Component class methods.

A TextField object generates an ActionEvent object when the *Return* key is hit, and a TextEvent object when the the text inside the TextField is changed.

## TextField() Constructor

| Constructor | Syntax |
| --- | --- |
| TextField() | public TextField() |
| | public TextField(int *columns*) |
| | public TextField(String *s*) |
| | public TextField(String *s*, int *columns*) |

Creates a TextField object. The TextField object may be given an initial String and the number of columns may be specified.

## ActionListener Methods

| Method | Syntax |
| --- | --- |
| addActionListener() | public void addActionListener (ActionListener *al*) |
| removeActionListener() | public void removeActionListener (ActionListener *al*) |

addActionListener() registers the invoking TextField object with an ActionListener object. The ActionListener is notified if the TextField generates an action event.

removeActionListener() removes an ActionListener object from the invoking TextField object. ActionEvent objects generated by the TextField will no longer be received by the ActionListener.

## Echo Character Methods

| Method | Syntax |
|---|---|
| echoCharIsSet() | public boolean echoCharIsSet() |
| getEchoChar() | public char getEchoChar() |
| setEchoChar() | public void setEchoChar(char echoChar) |

The echo character is a character that replaces the characters entered into the TextField object. It is often used in TextField objects that accept passwords.

echoCharIsSet() returns true if the echo character has been set for the invoking TextField object.

getEchoChar() returns the echo character.

setEchoChar() sets the echo character for the invoking TextField object. If (char)0 is passed to the setEchoChar() method, the echo mode is turned off.

## getListeners() Method

| Method | Syntax |
|---|---|
| getListeners() | public EventListener[] getListeners (Class listenerClass) |

getListeners() returns any listeners of the specified type registered to the invoking TextField object as an EventListener array.

## Sizing Methods

| Method | Syntax |
|---|---|
| getColumns() | public int getColumns() |
| setColumns() | public synchronized void setColumns (int columns) |
| getPreferredSize() | public Dimension getPreferredSize(int columns) |
| | public Dimension getPreferredSize() |
| getMinimumSize() | public Dimension getMinimumSize(int columns) |
| | public Dimension getMinimumSize() |

getColumns() returns the number of columns in the invoking TextField object.

setColumns() changes the number of columns for the invoking TextArea object.

getPreferredSize() and getMinimumSize() return the preferred or minimum size of a TextField object with a specified number of columns. If the columns argument is not passed to the getPerferredSize() and getMinimumSize() methods, the number of columns passed to the constructor is used to calculate these properties.

# setText() Method

| Method | Syntax |
|--------|--------|
| setText() | public void setText(String *text*) |

setText() overrides the setText() method from the TextComponent class and changes the text contained in the invoking TextArea object.

# Deprecated Methods

| Method | Syntax |
|--------|--------|
| minimumSize() | public Dimension minimumSize() |
| | public Dimension minimumSize(int *columns*) |
| preferredSize() | public Dimension preferredSize() |
| | public Dimension preferredSize(int *columns*) |
| setEchoCharacter() | public void setEchoCharacter(char *c*) |

These methods have been deprecated as of Java 1.1 and should not be used for new code.

## Example: Using TextField

In this example. two TextField objects are created and placed on a Frame. The first TextField object is given an initial String and made to be read-only. The second TextField object is given an echo character.

*The WinClosing class is used to terminate the program if the window is closed.
See Section 7.3.8 on page 657 for more details.*

```
import java.awt.*;
import java.awt.event.*;

public class TestTextField extends Frame {
  TextField tf1, tf2;

  TestTextField() {

    // two TextField objects are created.  The first is made
    // read-only.  The second uses an echo character to replace
    // whatever text is inserted.
    tf1 = new TextField("This text is read only", 20);
    tf1.setFont(new Font("Serif", Font.PLAIN, 12));
    tf1.setEditable(false);
    tf1.select(5, 10);
```

6

java.awt

```
        tf2 = new TextField(10);
        tf2.setEchoChar('*');

        Panel p = new Panel();
        p.add(tf1);
        p.add(tf2);

        add(p);

        addWindowListener(new WinClosing());
        setBounds(100, 100, 400, 120);
        setVisible(true);
    }

    public static void main(String args[]) {
        TestTextField ttf = new TestTextField();
    }
}

// The WinClosing class terminates the program when the window is closed

class WinClosing extends WindowAdapter {
    public void windowClosing(WindowEvent we) {
        System.exit(0);
    }
}
```

### Output

Here is the result:

# 6.3 Container Classes

A Container object is a sub-class of Component that provides a rectangular display area on the screen. GUI components and other containers can be placed inside a Container object. All Container classes inherit from the Component class and therefore have access to Component class methods. Container objects also possess properties associated with Component sub-class objects such as visiblity, focus, enablement. Most containers are, by default, invisible.

Every container has a layout manager, either default or specified, that controls the placement and size of components that have been placed in the container. If the contents of a container are changed, the container must be re-validated by first calling the invalidate() method and then calling the validate() method.

The Container class hierarchy is shown in the following diagram. The Container class provides common methods used by the other container classes:

❑ A Panel object is a generic container without window properties such as frames or titles. It is often used as a container-within-a-container.

❑ A ScrollPane object is a container that can add scrollbars to the vertical and horizontal edges.

❑ The Window class represents a top-level display area with no title, menubar, or border.

❑ A Frame object is a container with window-like features such as a title, menubar, and border.

❑ The Dialog class represents a top-level window that is normally used for pop-up messages or to accept input from the user.

❑ FileDialog is a sub-class of Dialog that can be used to access files.

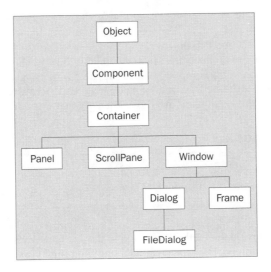

# 6.3.1 Container Class

```
public class Container extends Component
```

```
Object
    Component
        Container
```

### *Interfaces*

```
ImageObserver, MenuContainer, Serializable
```

The Container class provides common methods used by its sub-classes Dialog, FileDialog, Frame, Panel, ScrollPane, and Window. Although the Container class does provide a no-argument constructor, a Container object is rarely created.

## Container() Constructor

| Method | Syntax |
| --- | --- |
| Container() | public Container() |

Creates a Container object.

## add() Method

| Method | Syntax |
| --- | --- |
| add | public Component add(Component c) |
| | public Component add(Component c, int index) |
| | public void add(Component c, Object constraints) |
| | public void add(Component c, Object constraints, int index) |
| | public Component add(String name, Component c) |

add() adds the Component c to the invoking Container. The constraints Object could be an alignment variable such as BorderLayout.NORTH. The index refers to the component's position in the component stack-up, or Z-order. The default is 0, meaning the last component added will be on top. Adding a component always invalidates the container. Some of the versions return the Component that was added.

## Alignment Methods

| Method | Syntax |
| --- | --- |
| getAlignmentX() | public float getAlignmentX() |
| getAlignmentY() | public float getAlignmentY() |

These methods override the methods defined in the Component class. They return the alignment of the invoking Container object along the x- and y-axis, that is, how the invoking Container object would like to be aligned relative to other components.

## ContainerListener Methods

| Method | Syntax |
| --- | --- |
| addContainerListener() | public void addContainerListener (ContainerListener c) |
| removeContainerListener() | public void removeContainerListener (ContainerListener c) |

addContainerListener() registers the invoking Container object with an ContainerListener object. The ContainerListener is notified if the Container generates any ContainerEvent objects. A ContainerEvent is generated when a component is added or removed from a Container.

removeContainerListener() removes an ContainerListener object from the invoking Container object. ContainerEvent objects generated by the Container will no longer be received by the ContainerListener.

## getComponentCount() Method

| Method | Syntax |
|---|---|
| getComponentCount() | public int getComponentCount() |

getComponentCount() returns the number of components contained by the invoking Container object.

## getInsets() Method

| Method | Syntax |
|---|---|
| getInsets() | public Insets getInsets() |

getInsets() returns the Insets object associated with the invoking Container object. This method can be overridden to provide a user-specified inset.

## getListeners() Method

| Method | Syntax |
|---|---|
| getListeners() | public EventListener[] getListeners<br>(Class listenerClass) |

getListeners() returns any listeners of the specified type registered to the invoking Container object as an EventListener array.

## isAncestorOf() Method

| Method | Syntax |
|---|---|
| isAncestorOf() | public boolean isAncestorOf(Component comp) |

isAncestorOf() returns true if the Component comp is contained in the component hierarchy of the invoking Container object.

## Layout and Validity Methods

| Method | Syntax |
|---|---|
| addNotify() | public void addNotify() |
| doLayout() | public void doLayout() |
| invalidate() | public void invalidate() |
| validate() | public void validate() |

6

java.awt

These methods override the methods defined in the Component class.

addNotify() creates the peer of the invoking Container object and the Container is invalidated. This method is normally called only by the system.

doLayout() invokes the layout manager on the invoking Container object. The doLayout() method is not called explicitly in the program but is instead called by the validate() method.

invalidate() invalidates the invoking Container object and all of its ancestors. This method is called when one or more components in a container have been altered. After the invalidate() method is called, the validate() method is called. If an invalid component is contained in a valid container, the container must be invalidated and then validated for the layout manager to update the modified (invalid) component.

validate() validates the invoking Container object by again laying out its components. The validate() method calls the doLayout() method that invokes the layout manager. If a container calls invalidate(), validate() must be explicitly called. The only time the system will call validate() is if the window is resized.

## Layout Manager Methods

| Method | Syntax |
|---|---|
| getLayout() | public LayoutManager getLayout() |
| setLayout() | public void setLayout(LayoutManager lm) |

getLayout() returns the layout manager associated with the invoking Container object.

setLayout() changes the layout manager associated with the invoking Container object.

## Methods to Remove Components from a Container

| Method | Syntax |
|---|---|
| remove() | public void remove(Component c) |
|  | public void remove(int index) |
| removeAll() | public void removeAll() |

remove() removes a component from the invoking Container object. Either a Component object or an index can be used as an argument. The container should be invalidated and then validated after a component is removed.

removeAll() removes all components from the invoking container.

# Methods to Retrieve Components from a Container

| Method | Syntax |
|---|---|
| findComponentAt() | public Component findComponentAt(int x, int y) |
| | public Component findComponentAt(Point p) |
| getComponent() | public Component getComponent(int index) |
| getComponentAt() | public Component getComponentAt(int x, int y) |
| | public Component getComponentAt(Point p) |
| getComponents() | public Component[] getComponents() |

getComponent() returns the Component at the specified index.

getComponentAt() returns the Component at the specified location in the invoking Container object, or null if there is no Component at the location.

findComponentAt() returns the visible Component at the specified location in the invoking Container object, or null if there is no visible Component at the location.

getComponents() returns all of the Component objects inside the invoking Container object in a Component object array.

## setFont() Method

| Method | Syntax |
|---|---|
| setFont() | public void setFont(Font f) |

setFont() overrides the setFont() method from the Component class and changes the font associated with the invoking Container object.

## Size Methods

| Method | Syntax |
|---|---|
| getMaximumSize() | public Dimension getMaximumSize() |
| getMinimumSize() | public Dimension getMinimumSize() |
| getPreferredSize() | public Dimension getPreferredSize() |

These methods override the methods defined in the Component class and return the maximum, minimum, or preferred size of the invoking Container object.

6

java.awt

## Deprecated Methods

| Method | Syntax |
|---|---|
| countComponents() | public int countComponents() |
| deliverEvent() | public void deliverEvent() |
| insets() | public Insets insets() |
| layout() | public void layout() |
| locate() | public Component locate(int x, int y) |
| minimumSize() | public Dimension minimumSize() |
| preferredSize() | public Dimension preferredSize() |

These methods were deprecated as of Java 1.1 and should not be used for new code.

# 6.3.2 Dialog Class

```
public class Dialog extends Window
```

```
Object
    Component
        Container
            Window
                Dialog
```

### Interfaces

```
Accessible, ImageObserver, MenuContainer, Serializable
```

Dialog objects are top-level windows that are normally used for pop-up messages or to accept input from the user. A Dialog object resembles a Frame object but does not have all the Frame object properties. It may either be **modal**, meaning the Dialog locks out other processes until the dialog is closed, or **modeless**, meaning the user can interact with other things while the Dialog is open. The default layout manager for dialogs is BorderLayout.

A Dialog is not a standalone container but is always the child of another top-level window component, usually a Frame or another Dialog. A top-level window is one that does not have to be contained within another object but can sit directly on the desktop.

A Dialog object fires window events when the state of its window is changed.

## Dialog() Constructor

| Constructor | Syntax |
|---|---|
| Dialog() | public Dialog(Frame *parent*) |
| | public Dialog(Frame *parent*, boolean *modal*) |

| Constructor | Syntax |
|---|---|
| | public Dialog(Frame *parent*, String *title*) |
| | public Dialog(Frame *parent*, String *title*, boolean *modal*) |
| | public Dialog(Dialog *parent*) |
| | public Dialog(Dialog *parent*, String *title*) |
| | public Dialog(Dialog *parent*, String *title*, boolean *modal*) |

Creates a Dialog object. Dialogs are always the children of another top-level window, either a Frame or another Dialog. A title and modal state can also be passed to the Dialog constructor. The defaults are a modeless Dialog that is initially resizable.

# dispose() Method

| Method | Syntax |
|---|---|
| dispose() | public void dispose() |

dispose() closes the invoking Dialog object and releases any resources associated with it.

# hide() Method

| Method | Syntax |
|---|---|
| hide() | public void hide() |

hide() hides the invoking Dialog object, making it no longer visible.

# Modal Property Methods

| Method | Syntax |
|---|---|
| isModal() | public boolean isModal() |
| setModal() | public void setModal(boolean *modal*) |

isModal() returns true if the invoking Dialog object is modal.

setModal() is used to change the modal state of the invoking Dialog object.

# Resizing Methods

| Method | Syntax |
|---|---|
| isResizable() | public boolean isResizable() |
| setResizable() | public void setResizable(boolean *b*) |

isResizable() returns true if the invoking Dialog object is resizable.

setResizable() is used to change the resizable state of the invoking Dialog object.

## show() Method

| Method | Syntax |
|--------|--------|
| show() | public void show() |

show() brings the invoking Dialog object to the front and displays it.

## Title Methods

| Method | Syntax |
|--------|--------|
| getTitle() | public String getTitle() |
| setTitle() | public void setTitle(String *title*) |

getTitle() returns the title for the invoking Dialog object. It returns null if the invoking Dialog object has no title.

setTitle() is used to set or change the title of the invoking Dialog object.

### Example: Using Dialog

In this example, a Dialog is used to confirm whether a user wants to quit a program. When the quit button is pressed, the Dialog is made visible. If the yes button in the Dialog is pressed, the program terminates. If the no button in the Dialog is pressed, the dialog is made invisible.

*The WinClosing class is used to terminate the program if the window is closed. See Section 7.3.8 on page 657 for more details.*

```
import java.awt.*;
import java.awt.event.*;

public class TestDialog extends Frame implements ActionListener {
    Button quitButton, yesButton, noButton;
    Dialog d;

    public TestDialog() {
        quitButton = new Button("quit");
        quitButton.addActionListener(this);

        setLayout(new FlowLayout());
        add(quitButton);

        createDialog();
```

```
    addWindowListener(new WinClosing());
    setBounds(150, 150, 200, 200);
    setVisible(true);
}

// createDialog() creates a dialog that confirms the quit command.
// Dialog objects are always the child of a parent object.  A
// reference to the parent object, in this case the TestDialog class,
// is passed to the Dialog constructor.

public void createDialog() {
  d = new Dialog(this);
  d.setResizable(false);

  yesButton = new Button("yes");
  yesButton.addActionListener(this);

  noButton = new Button("no");
  noButton.addActionListener(this);

  d.setLayout(new FlowLayout());
  d.add(yesButton);
  d.add(noButton);
  d.setSize(200, 100);
}

public void actionPerformed(ActionEvent ae) {

  // If the "quit" button is pressed, the confirm dialog is made
  // visible. If the "yes" button in the dialog is pressed, the
  // program terminates.  If the "no" button in the dialog is
  // pressed, the dialog is made invisible
if (ae.getActionCommand().equals("quit")) {
    d.show();
  }
  if (ae.getActionCommand().equals("yes")) {
    System.exit(0);
  }
  if (ae.getActionCommand().equals("no")) {
    d.setVisible(false);
  }
}

public static void main(String args[]) {
  TestDialog td = new TestDialog();
}
}

// The WinClosing class terminates the program when the window is closed
```

```
class WinClosing extends WindowAdapter {
  public void windowClosing(WindowEvent we) {
    System.exit(0);
  }
}
```

### Output

The result looks like this:

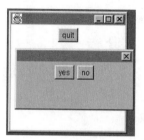

A Dialog is used to confirm that a user wants to quit the program. If the quit button is pushed, the Dialog is made visible. If the no button in the Dialog is pushed, the Dialog is made invisible. If the yes button in the Dialog is pushed, the program terminates.

# 6.3.3 FileDialog Class

```
public class FileDialog extends Dialog
```

```
Object
  Component
    Container
      Window
        Dialog
          FileDialog
```

### Interfaces

```
Accessible, ImageObserver, MenuContainer, Serializable
```

A FileDialog is a sub-class of Dialog that allows the user to select files for opening or saving. It is always modal, meaning the FileDialog must be closed before other operations are performed.

A FileDialog is not a standalone container but is always the child of another top-level window component, usually a Frame.

# FileDialog() Constructor

| Constructor | Syntax |
|---|---|
| FileDialog() | public FileDialog(Frame *parent*) |
| | public FileDialog(Frame *parent*, String *title*) |
| | public FileDialog(Frame *parent*, String *title*, int *mode*) |

Creates a FileDialog object. FileDialogs are always child windows to another high-level window such as a Frame. A title or file mode can also be passed to the constructor. There are two FileDialog constants that are used to specify the mode:

❑ FileDialog.LOAD

❑ FileDialog.SAVE

The default mode is to load, or read, a file.

## Directory Methods

| Method | Syntax |
|---|---|
| getDirectory() | public String getDirectory() |
| setDirectory() | public void setDirectory(String *directory*) |

getDirectory() returns the directory currently being accessed by the invoking FileDialog object.

setDirectory() sets the directory that is displayed by the invoking FileDialog object.

## File Methods

| Method | Syntax |
|---|---|
| getFile() | public String getFile() |
| setFile() | public void setFile(String *file*) |

getFile() returns the current file selection from the invoking FileDialog as a String object. If the cancel button is pushed, getFile() returns null. Note that on many platforms it is possible to select more than one file in the FileDialog but getFile() will return only one of the selected file names.

setFile() changes the default file for the invoking FileDialog object. The String may contain a filename filter like "*.java" to show a preliminary list of files from which to select.

## FilenameFilter Methods

| Method | Syntax |
|---|---|
| getFilenameFilter() | public FilenameFilter getFilenameFilter() |
| setFileNameFilter() | public void setFileNameFilter<br>    (FilenameFilter *ff*) |

getFilenameFilter() returns the FilenameFilter object associated with the invoking FileDialog object.

setFileNameFilter() sets the FilenameFilter object associated with the invoking FileDialog object. The FilenameFilter class is part of the java.io package; see Section 4.5.5 on page 359. A FilenameFilter object can be used to limit selections to files with certain extensions, but filename filters do not function under Windows.

## Mode Methods

| Method | Syntax |
|---|---|
| getMode() | public int getMode() |
| setMode() | public void setMode(int *mode*) |

getMode() returns the current mode for the invoking FileDialog object.

setMode() changes the mode for the invoking FileDialog object. The argument passed to the setMode() method must be either FileDialog.LOAD or FileDialog.SAVE.

### Example: Using FileDialog

A FileDialog object is created that displays the contents of the current directory. Once a file is selected, the FileDialog disappears and the name of the file selected is sent to System.out.

*The WinClosing class is used to terminate the program if the window is closed. See Section 7.3.8 on page 657 for more details.*

```
import java.awt.*;
import java.awt.event.*;

public class TestFD extends Frame {
    FileDialog fd;

    TestFD() {
        addWindowListener(new WinClosing());
        setBounds(100, 100, 400, 400);
```

```
    setVisible(true);
      createFileDialog();
    }

    // createFileDialog() creates a FileDialog object that lists the
    // contents of the current directory.  The FileDialog object remains
    // visible until a file is selected.

    public void createFileDialog() {
      fd = new FileDialog(this, "Pick a File");
      fd.show();
    }

    // getString() is used to return the name of the selected file

    public String getString() {
      return fd.getFile();
    }

    public static void main(String args[]) {
      TestFD tfd = new TestFD();
      System.out.println("File selected was " + tfd.getString());
    }
    }

// The WinClosing class terminates the program when the window is closed

class WinClosing extends WindowAdapter {
  public void windowClosing(WindowEvent we) {
    System.exit(0);
  }
  }
```

*Output*

The result should look like this:

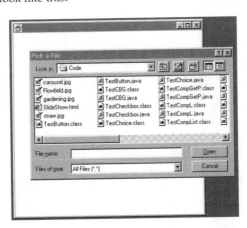

# 6.3.4 Frame Class

```
public class Frame extends Window implements MenuContainer
```

```
Object
  Component
    Container
      Window
        Frame
```

### Interfaces

```
Accessible, ImageObserver, MenuContainer, Serializable
```

A Frame is a window with window-manager type features such as a title, borders, and menubar. Its default layout manager is BorderLayout. Frames provide the basic building block for screen-oriented applications.

Frame objects fire window events when the state of their window is changed.

## Frame() Constructor

| Constructor | Syntax |
|---|---|
| Frame() | public Frame() |
| | public Frame(String title) |
| | public Frame(GraphicConfiguration gc) |
| | public Frame(String title, GraphicConfiguration gc) |

Creates a Frame object. A title can be provided. The third and fourth versions were introduced in version 1.3. A GraphicsConfiguration object describes the characteristics of a graphics destination such as a printer or monitor.

## IconImage Methods

| Method | Syntax |
|---|---|
| getIconImage() | public Image getIconImage() |
| setIconImage() | public void setIconImage(Image image) |

getIconImage() returns the Image that is used when the Frame object is iconified (minimized).

setIconImage() sets the Image displayed when the invoking Frame object is iconified. Not all platforms support this.

# MenuBar Methods

| Method | Syntax |
|---|---|
| getMenuBar() | public MenuBar getMenuBar() |
| remove() | public void remove(MenuComponent *menubar*) |
| setMenuBar() | public void setMenuBar(MenuBar *mb*) |

getMenuBar() returns the MenuBar object associated with the invoking Frame object.

setMenuBar() changes the MenuBar object associated with the invoking Frame object. If the argument to the setMenuBar() method is null, the MenuBar object is removed.

remove() removes a MenuBar from the invoking Frame object. If null is sent to this method, a NullPointerException is thrown and no action is taken.

# Resizing Methods

| Method | Syntax |
|---|---|
| isResizable() | public boolean isResizable() |
| setResizable() | public void setResizable(boolean *resizable*) |

isResizable() returns true if the invoking Frame object is resizable.

setResizable() is used to set the resizable state of the invoking Frame object.

# State Methods

| Method | Syntax |
|---|---|
| getState() | public int getState() |
| setState() | public void setState(int *state*) |

getState() returns the current state of the invoking Frame object.

setState() changes the state of the invoking Frame object. The argument passed to the setState() method must be one of:

- ❑ Frame.NORMAL
- ❑ Frame.ICONIFIED

# Title Methods

| Method | Syntax |
|---|---|
| getTitle() | public String getTitle() |
| setTitle() | public void setTitle(String *title*) |

getTitle() returns the title of the invoking Frame and returns null if the invoking Frame object has no title.

setTitle() is used to set or change the title of the invoking Frame object.

## Deprecated Methods

| Method | Syntax |
|---|---|
| getCursorType() | public int getCursorType() |
| setCursor() | public void setCursor(int *cursor*) |

These methods were deprecated as of Java 1.1. They should not be used in new code. The Frame class version of setCursor() has been superceded by the version defined in the Component class.

### Example: Using Frame

This example creates and displays a Frame. The Frame is given a title and is set so it cannot be resized.

*The WinClosing class is used to terminate the program if the window is closed. See Section 7.3.8 on page 657 for more details.*

```
import java.awt.*;
import java.awt.event.*;

public class TestFrame extends Frame {
  TestFrame() {
    addWindowListener(new WinClosing());
    setTitle("Simple Frame");
    setResizable(false);
    setBounds(100, 100, 200, 200);
    setVisible(true);
  }

  public static void main(String args[]) {
    TestFrame tf = new TestFrame();
  }
}

// The WinClosing class terminates the program when the window is closed

class WinClosing extends WindowAdapter {
  public void windowClosing(WindowEvent we) {
    System.exit(0);
  }
}
```

*Output*

The result is a simple frame that looks like this:

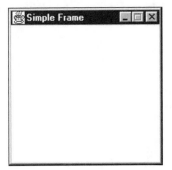

Many other examples of using Frame objects can be found in this chapter.

# 6.3.5 Panel Class

```
public class Panel extends Container implements Accessible
```

```
Object
  Component
    Container
      Panel
```

### Interfaces

```
Accessible, ImageObserver, MenuContainer, Serializable
```

A Panel object is a generic container without window properties (frames, title). The default layout manager for Panel objects is FlowLayout.

Panels are often used as a container-within-a-container to group components together.

## Panel() Constructor

| Constructor | Syntax |
|-------------|--------|
| Panel() | public Panel() |
| | public Panel(LayoutManager *lm*) |

Panel object constructor. A LayoutManager can be specified when the Panel object is created.

6

java.awt

## Example: Using Panel

In this example, a `Panel` is used to group two `Button` objects together. The `Buttons` are placed in the `Panel` and then the `Panel` is placed on a `Frame`.

*The `WinClosing` class is used to terminate the program if the window is closed. See Section 7.3.8 on page 657 for more details.*

```java
import java.awt.*;
import java.awt.event.*;

public class TestPanel extends Frame {
  Button b1, b2;

  TestPanel() {
    b1 = new Button("Button 1");
    b2 = new Button("Button 2");
    Panel p = new Panel();
    p.add(b1);
    p.add(b2);
add(p);

    addWindowListener(new WinClosing());
    setBounds(100, 100, 200, 120);
    setVisible(true);
  }

  public static void main(String args[]) {
    TestPanel f = new TestPanel();
  }
}

// The WinClosing class terminates the program when the window is closed

class WinClosing extends WindowAdapter {
  public void windowClosing(WindowEvent we) {
    System.exit(0);
  }
}
```

### Output

Here is the result:

# 6.3.6 ScrollPane Class

public class ScrollPane extends Container implements Accessible

```
Object
   Component
      Container
         ScrollPane
```

### Interfaces

Accessible, ImageObserver, MenuContainer, Serializable

A ScrollPane is a container that contains a single child component. Scrollbars can be added to scroll the ScrollPane both horizontally and vertically. To get multiple components into a ScrollPane, place the components on a Panel and place the Panel inside the ScrollPane.

Since the ScrollPane class only contains one component, it has no layout manager. Any attempt by a ScrollPane object to call the setLayout() method will result in a AWTError being thrown.

## ScrollPane() Constructor

| Constructor | Syntax |
|---|---|
| ScrollPane() | public ScrollPane() |
| | public ScrollPane(int *scrollbarDisplay*) |

ScrollPane object constructor. The value of scrollbarDisplay must be one of the following:

❑   ScrollPane.SCROLLBARS_AS_NEEDED

❑   ScrollPane.SCROLLBARS_ALWAYS

❑   ScrollPane.SCROLLBARS_NEVER

The default ScrollPane constant is SCROLLBARS_AS_NEEDED.

## Scroll Position Methods

| Method | Syntax |
|---|---|
| getScrollPosition() | public Point getScrollPosition() |
| setScrollPosition() | public void setScrollPosition(int *x*, int *y*) |
| | public void setScrollPosition(Point *p*) |

getScrollPosition() returns the position of the scrollbars or other adjustable objects used by the invoking ScrollPane object.

6

java.awt

setScrollPosition() changes the position of the scrollbars. The Point object contains the x and y positions corresponding to values on the horizontal and vertical scrollbars.

## Scrollbar Property Methods

| Method | Syntax |
|---|---|
| getHScrollbarHeight() | public int getHScrollbarHeight() |
| getScrollbarDisplayPolicy() | public int getScrollbarDisplayPolicy() |
| getVScrollbarWidth() | public int getVScrollbarWidth() |

getHScrollbarHeight() returns the height of the horizontal scrollbar associated with the invoking ScrollPane object whether the scrollbar is displayed or not.

getScrollbarDisplayPolicy() returns the scrollbar display policy. The return value will be one of the ScrollPane constants.

getVScrollbarWidth() returns the width of the vertical scrollbar associated with the invoking ScrollPane object whether the scrollbar is displayed or not.

### Example: Using ScrollPane

In this example 10 Buttons are placed on a Panel, which is placed in a ScrollPane, which is placed on a Frame. The scroll bars appear when all the buttons do not fit on the Frame.

*The WinClosing class is used to terminate the program if the window is closed. See Section 7.3.8 on page 657 for more details.*

```
import java.awt.*;
import java.awt.event.*;

public class TestSP extends Frame {
  ScrollPane sp;

  TestSP() {
    sp = new ScrollPane();

    Panel p = new Panel();
    for (int i = 0; i < 10; ++i) {
      p.add(new Button("button " + i));
    }

    // The Panel containing the Button objects is placed within a
    // ScrollPane and the ScrollPane is placed in the Frame.
    // The Button objects must be placed in a Panel first, because
    // a ScrollPane can only contain one component.
```

```
      sp.add(p);
      add(sp);

      addWindowListener(new WinClosing());
      setBounds(100, 100, 200, 120);
      setVisible(true);
   }

   public static void main(String args[]) {
      TestSP tsp = new TestSP();
   }
}

// The WinClosing class terminates the program when the window is closed

class WinClosing extends WindowAdapter {
   public void windowClosing(WindowEvent we) {
      System.exit(0);
   }
}
```

**Output**

Here is the result:

# 6.3.7 Window Class

```
public class Window extends Container implements Accessible
```

```
Object
   Component
      Container
         Window
```

### Interfaces

```
Accessible, ImageObserver, MenuContainer, Serializable
```

A Window is a top level display area, meaning it does not need to be contained within another object. A Window has no title, menubar, or border. Window is the super-class of the Frame and Dialog classes. A Window is sometimes used to implement a pop-up menu. A Window object can generate WindowEvent objects.

A Window generates a WindowEvent when it is opened, closed, iconified, deiconified, activated, or deactivated.

**497**

## Window() Constructor

| Constructor | Syntax |
|---|---|
| Window() | public Window(Frame *parent*) |
| | public Window(Window *parent*) |
| | public Window(Window *parent*,<br>                GraphicsConfiguration gc) |

Creates a Window object. Windows are always created as the child-object of a Frame or another Window object. The third version was introduced in version 1.3. A GraphicsConfiguration object describes the characteristics of a graphics destination such as a printer or monitor.

## dispose() Method

| Method | Syntax |
|---|---|
| dispose() | public void dispose() |

dispose() closes the invoking Window object and releases any resources associated with it.

## getListeners() Method

| Method | Syntax |
|---|---|
| getListeners() | public EventListener[] getListeners<br>     (Class *listenerClass*) |

getListeners() returns any listeners of the specified type registered to the invoking Window object as an EventListener array.

## hide() Method

| Method | Syntax |
|---|---|
| hide() | public void hide() |

hide() hides the invoking Window object from view.

## pack() Method

| Method | Syntax |
|---|---|
| pack() | public void pack() |

pack() resizes the Window to the preferred size of the components it contains and validates the Window.

# Window Property Methods

| Method | Syntax |
|---|---|
| getFocusOwner() | public Component getFocusOwner() |
| getLocale() | public Locale getLocale() |
| getOwnedWindows() | public Window[] getOwnedWindows() |
| getOwner() | public Window getOwner() |
| getToolkit() | public Toolkit getToolkit() |
| isShowing() | public boolean isShowing() |
| setCursor() | public void setCursor(Cursor cursor) |

getFocusOwner() returns the child component of the invoking Window object that has focus if the Window is active.

getLocale() returns the Locale object associated with the invoking Window object . A Locale object is used to internationalize programs. See Section 3.1.4 on page 190 for more details.

getOwnedWindows() returns any windows owned by the invoking Window object as a Window array.

getOwner() returns the owner of the invoking Window object.

getTookit() returns the Toolkit object associated with the invoking Window object.

isShowing() returns true if the invoking Window object is showing on the screen.

setCursor() overrides the setCursor() method from the Component class and changes the Cursor associated with the invoking Window object.

# show() Method

| Method | Syntax |
|---|---|
| show() | public void show() |

show() makes the invoking Window object visible. When a Window object is created, by default it is invisible. If the invoking Window object is already visible, the show() method calls the toFront() method to bring the Window to the foreground.

# toBack() Method

| Method | Syntax |
|---|---|
| toBack() | public void toBack() |

toBack() sends the invoking Window object to the background of the display.

## toFront() Method

| Method | Syntax |
|--------|--------|
| toFront() | public void toFront() |

toFront() brings the window to the foreground of the display.

## WindowListener Methods

| Method | Syntax |
|--------|--------|
| addWindowListener() | public void addWindowListener<br>(WindowListener wl) |
| removeWindowListener() | public void removeWindowListener<br>(WindowListener wl) |

addWindowListener() registers the invoking Window object with an WindowListener object. The WindowListener is notified if the Window generates any WindowEvent objects. A WindowEvent is generated when a window is opened, closed, iconified, deiconified, activated, or deactivated.

removeContainerListener() removes an ContainerListener object from the invoking Container object. ContainerEvent objects generated by the Container will no longer be received by the ContainerListener.

### Example: Using Window

In this example, a small Window object is created and displayed. It is the small, white box that appears with the Frame. A Window can't exist on its own, it is always the child component of another container.

*The WinClosing class is used to terminate the program if the window is closed.*
*See Section 7.3.8 on page 657 for more details.*

```
import java.awt.*;
import java.awt.event.*;

public class TestWind extends Frame {
  public TestWind() {
    addWindowListener(new WinClosing());
    setBounds(100, 100, 250, 250);
    setVisible(true);
    createWindow();
  }

  // The createWindow() method creates and displays a Window object.
  // Window objects are always the child of a parent object. A reference
  // to the parent object, in this case the TestWind class, is passed
  // to the Window constructor.
```

```
    public void createWindow() {
      Window w = new Window(this);
      w.setSize(100, 100);
      w.setBackground(Color.yellow);
      w.add(new Label("Jackson"));
      w.show();
    }

    public static void main(String args[]) {
      TestWind tw = new TestWind();
    }
  }

// The WinClosing class terminates the program when the window is closed

class WinClosing extends WindowAdapter {
  public void windowClosing(WindowEvent we) {
    System.exit(0);
  }
}
```

**Output**

The output should look like this:

# 6.4 Event and Exception Classes

The AWTEvent class is the parent class for the Events defined in the java.awt.event package. The AWTException class represents a generic exception that can be thrown when an exceptional condition occurs under AWT. The Event and Exception class hierarchy is shown in the following diagram; the EventObject class is from the java.util package. The Exception and Throwable classes are from the java.lang package.

The main discussion of exception handling can be found in Section 1.7 on page 36 and the main discussion of event handling, and the specific AWTEvent sub-classes, is found in Chapter 7.

The AWTEvent and AWTException classes are contained in the java.awt package and are therefore discussed here.

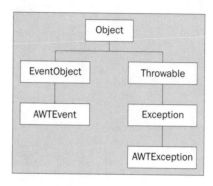

# 6.4.1 AWTEvent Class

```
public abstract class AWTEvent extends EventObject
```

```
Object
    EventObject
        AWTEvent
```

### Interfaces

```
Serializable
```

AWTEvent is the parent class for the Event classes defined in the java.awt.event package and defines methods common to the event sub-classes. It is an abstract class, so an AWTEvent object is never created directly.

## getID() method

| Method | Syntax |
|--------|--------|
| getID() | public int getID() |

getID() returns an int that characterizes the type of event.

## paramString() method

| Method | Syntax |
|--------|--------|
| paramString() | public String paramString() |

paramString() returns an String representing the state of the event and is intended for debugging purposes.

## toString() method

| Method | Syntax |
|---|---|
| toString() | public String toString() |

toString() returns an String representation of the event object.

# 6.4.2 AWTException Class

```
public class AWTException extends Exception
```

```
Object
  Throwable
    Exception
      AWTException
```

### Interfaces
```
Serializable
```

The AWTException class represents a generic exception that can be thrown when an exceptional condition occurs under AWT. Like any other exception it must be caught in a catch block or declared in the throws clause of the method.

## AWTException() Constructor

| Method | Syntax |
|---|---|
| AWTException() | public AWTException(String *message*) |

AWTException object constructor. A message can be associated with the AWTExcepton object.

# 6.5 Layout Managers

A **layout manager** is an object that is responsible for the positioning and dimensioning of the components contained inside a Container object. It does this automatically based on its own criteria. Under other programming environments, such as Windows, GUI components are sized and positioned by hand. While this does give the programmer absolute control over the layout of the components, the developers of Java tried to avoid this for several reasons. First, it is tedious to manually lay out a large number of components. This also does not lend itself nicely to a dynamic GUI environment. If the window is resized or if components are added or removed from the window, it would be a difficult programming task to re-configure the layout every time this happened by hand. Furthermore, sometimes the width and height of a component might not be available because the native components have not been realized.

It is for these reasons that, while it is possible to lay out Java components by hand, it is standard practice to use a layout manager. Every Container object has a default layout manager associated with it and can change its layout manager using the Container class method setLayout(). Every layout manager class implements either the LayoutManager or LayoutManager2 interface.

The layout manager class hierarchy is shown in the diagram below.

❑   The BorderLayout class separates the Container into five regions: NORTH, SOUTH, EAST, WEST, and CENTER. BorderLayout is the default layout manager for the Dialog, Frame, and Window classes.

❑   The CardLayout class stacks components on top of each other such that only one component is visible at any one time

❑   With the FlowLayout class, components are laid out such that they flow from left to right and from top to bottom. FlowLayout is the default layout manager for the Panel and Applet class.

❑   The GridLayout arranges the components in a two-dimensional grid. Each component is given the same amount of space.

❑   The GridBagLayout class, in conjunction with the GridBagConstraints class, allows the most flexibility in arranging components.

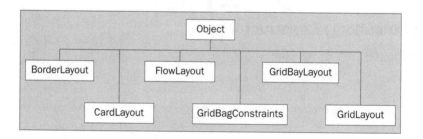

# 6.5.1 BorderLayout Class

```
public class BorderLayout extends Object implements LayoutManager2, Serializable
```

```
Object
   BorderLayout
```

### Interfaces

```
LayoutManager, LayoutManager2, Serializable
```

The BorderLayout class divides the Container into 5 regions: NORTH, SOUTH, EAST, WEST, and CENTER. BorderLayout is the default layout manager for Windows, Frames, and Dialogs. There can only be one component placed in any one region. To put more than one component in a region, first place them into a Container and add the Container to the region.

When components are added with the BorderLayout layout manager, the region where they are to be placed must be specified. The version of the add() method used is:

```
public void add(Component c, Object constraints)
```

where the constraints object is one of these five constants:

- ❏ BorderLayout.NORTH
- ❏ BorderLayout.SOUTH
- ❏ BorderLayout.WEST
- ❏ BorderLayout.EAST
- ❏ BorderLayout.CENTER

## BorderLayout() Constructor

| Constructor | Syntax |
|---|---|
| BorderLayout() | public BorderLayout() |
| | public BorderLayout(int hgap, int vgap) |

BorderLayout object constructor. hgap and vgap specify the space in pixels between the components. If they are set to negative values, the components will overlap.

## addLayoutComponent() Method

| Method | Syntax |
|---|---|
| addLayoutComponent() | public void addLayoutComponent (Component comp, Object constraints) |

addLayoutComponent() adds the Component comp to the Container object associated with the invoking BorderLayout object. The Object constraints will be one of the BorderLayout region constants described above. This method is usually not called directly.

## Gap Methods

| Method | Syntax |
|---|---|
| getHgap() | public int getHgap() |
| getVgap() | public int getVgap() |
| setHgap() | public void setHgap(int hgap) |
| setVgap() | public void setVgap(int vgap) |

getHgap() and getVgap() return the values of the horizontal or vertical gaps of the invoking BorderLayout object.

setHgap() and setVgap() set or change values of the horizontal or vertical gaps of the invoking BorderLayout object.

## layoutContainer() method

| Method | Syntax |
| --- | --- |
| layoutContainer() | public void layoutContainer(Container *cont*) |

layoutContainer() causes the components contained in Container cont to be redrawn.

## removeLayoutComponent() method

| Method | Syntax |
| --- | --- |
| removeLayoutComponent() | public void removeLayoutComponent (Component *c*) |

removeLayoutComponent() removes the Component c from the Container associated with the invoking BorderLayout object. This method is usually not called directly.

## Sizing Methods

| Method | Syntax |
| --- | --- |
| maximumLayoutSize() | public Dimension maximumLayoutSize (Container *cont*) |
| minimumLayoutSize() | public Dimension minimumLayoutSize (Container *cont*) |
| preferredLayoutSize() | public Dimension preferredLayoutSize (Container *cont*) |

maximumLayoutSize() returns the maximum size of the Container cont.

minimumLayoutSize() returns the minimum size of the Container cont.

preferredLayoutSize() returns the preferred size of the Container cont.

## toString() Method

| Method | Syntax |
| --- | --- |
| toString() | public String toString() |

toString() returns a String representation of the invoking CardLayout object.

## Example: Using BorderLayout

In this example, Button and Label objects are placed in a Frame using a BorderLayout object as the layout manager.

*The WinClosing class is used to terminate the program if the window is closed. See Section 7.3.8 on page 657 for more details.*

```
import java.awt.*;
import java.awt.event.*;

public class TestBL extends Frame {
  Button northButton, eastButton, westButton, southButton;
  Label nameLabel, secondLabel;

  public TestBL() {
    northButton = new Button("north");
    eastButton = new Button("east");
    westButton = new Button("west");
    southButton = new Button("south");

    nameLabel = new Label("The Center");
    secondLabel = new Label("Region");

    // The Button objects are placed in Panels before being
    // placed on the Frame.  If the Buttons were placed on
    // the BorderLayout regions directly, they would be sized
    // to fill the entire region.  Placing them in Panels,
    // maintains the preferred size of the Button.

    Panel pN = new Panel();
    pN.add(northButton);

    Panel pE = new Panel();
    pE.add(eastButton);
    Panel pW = new Panel();
    pW.add(westButton);

    Panel pS = new Panel();
    pS.add(southButton);

    Panel pc = new Panel();
    pc.setBackground(Color.yellow);
    pc.add(nameLabel);
    pc.add(secondLabel);
    add(pN, BorderLayout.NORTH);
    add(pE, BorderLayout.EAST);
    add(pW, BorderLayout.WEST);
    add(pS, BorderLayout.SOUTH);
    add(pc, BorderLayout.CENTER);
```

```
      addWindowListener(new WinClosing());
      setBounds(100, 100, 300, 150);
      setVisible(true);
    }

  public static void main(String args[]) {
    TestBL tbl = new TestBL();
    }
  }


  // The WinClosing class terminates the program when the window is closed

  class WinClosing extends WindowAdapter {
    public void windowClosing(WindowEvent we) {
      System.exit(0);
    }
  }
```

Button and Label objects are placed in a Frame using a BorderLayout object as the layout manager. The Button objects are placed in the NORTH, EAST, WEST, and SOUTH regions. The two Label objects are placed in the CENTER region by first placing them inside a Panel. The Buttons are placed in a Panel first because if they are placed directly onto the Frame it fills up the entire region. The resulting wide and tall Buttons look funny. Placing the Button into a Panel (which has a default layout manager of FlowLayout) results in a normal looking Button.

### Output

The result should look like this:

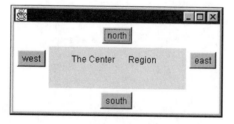

# 6.5.2 CardLayout Class

```
public class CardLayout extends Object implements LayoutManager2, Serializable
```

```
Object
  CardLayout
```

### Interfaces

```
LayoutManager, LayoutManager2, Serializable
```

A `CardLayout` object is a layout manager that stacks the components like a deck of cards, with only one component visible at any one time. Because the `CardLayout` class has a number of member functions, it is usually desirable to instantiate an instance of it.

`Button` components can be used to select which component to show.

To add components to a `Container` using the `CardLayout` class as its layout manager, the `Container` object would invoke the following version of the `add()` method:

```
public void add(Component c, Object constraints)
```

where the `constraints` in this case is a name given to the component. The name is required to use the `CardLayout` class method `show()`.

## CardLayout() Constructor

| Constructor | Syntax |
|---|---|
| CardLayout() | public CardLayout() |
| | public CardLayout(int hgap, int vgap) |

Creates a `CardLayout` object. `hgap` and `vgap` specify the space around the edges of the `Container`.

## addLayoutComponent() Method

| Method | Syntax |
|---|---|
| addLayoutComponent() | public void addLayoutComponent(Component comp, Object constraints) |

`addLayoutComponent()` adds the `Component` comp to the layout. The `Object` constraints is a `String` containing a name associated with the `Component`.

## Methods to Display Components

| Method | Syntax |
|---|---|
| first() | public void first(Container cont) |
| last() | public void last(Container cont) |
| next() | public void next(Container cont) |
| previous() | public void previous(Container cont) |
| show() | public void show(Container cont, String compName) |

`first()` causes the first component in the stack contained by `Container` cont to be displayed.

last() causes the last component in the stack contained by Container cont to be displayed.

next() causes the next component in the stack contained by Container cont to be displayed.

previous() causes the previous component in the stack contained by Container cont to be displayed.

show() causes the component whose name is compName to be displayed.

## Gap Methods

| Method | Syntax |
|--------|--------|
| getHgap() | public int getHgap() |
| getVgap() | public int getVgap() |
| setHgap() | public void setHgap(int hgap) |
| setVgap() | public void setVgap(int vgap) |

getHgap() and getVgap() return the values of the horizontal or vertical gaps of the invoking CardLayout object.

setHgap() and setVgap() set or change values of the horizontal or vertical gaps of the invoking CardLayout object.

## layoutContainer() method

| Method | Syntax |
|--------|--------|
| layoutContainer() | public void layoutContainer(Container cont) |

layoutContainer() lays out the Components in Container cont using the invoking CardLayout object.

## removeLayoutComponent() method

| Method | Syntax |
|--------|--------|
| removeLayoutContainer() | public void removeLayoutComponent (Component comp) |

removeLayoutComponent() removes the Component comp from the layout.

## Sizing Methods

| Method | Syntax |
|--------|--------|
| maximumLayoutSize() | public Dimension maximumLayoutSize (Container cont) |

| Method | Syntax |
|--------|--------|
| minimumLayoutSize() | public Dimension minimumLayoutSize (Container *cont*) |
| preferredLayoutSize() | public Dimension preferredLayoutSize (Container *cont*) |

maximumLayoutSize() returns the maximum size of the Container cont.

minimumLayoutSize() returns the minimum size of the Container cont.

preferredLayoutSize() returns the preferred size of the Container cont.

# toString() Method

| Method | Syntax |
|--------|--------|
| toString() | public String toString() |

toString() returns a String representation of the invoking CardLayout object.

## Example: Using CardLayout

In this example, ten Label objects are created and stacked in a Panel using a CardLayout layout manager. Three Button objects are used to determine which Label is displayed.

*The WinClosing class is used to terminate the program if the window is closed.*
*See Section 7.3.8 on page 657 for more details.*

```
import java.awt.*;
import java.awt.event.*;

public class TestCard extends Frame implements ActionListener {
    Button nextButton, prevButton, firstButton;
    Panel centerPanel, southPanel;
    String name;
    CardLayout cl;

    public TestCard() {
        cl = new CardLayout();

        nextButton = new Button("next");
        prevButton = new Button("previous");
        firstButton = new Button("first");

        nextButton.addActionListener(this);
        prevButton.addActionListener(this);
        firstButton.addActionListener(this);
```

```
      southPanel = new Panel();
      southPanel.add(nextButton);
      southPanel.add(prevButton);
      southPanel.add(firstButton);

      // 10 Label objects are added to a Panel using a CardLayout
      // layout manager.

      centerPanel = new Panel();
      centerPanel.setLayout(cl);
      for (int i = 0; i < 10; ++i) {
        name = "Label " + i;
        centerPanel.add(new Label("Label " + i, Label.CENTER), name);
      }

      add(southPanel, BorderLayout.SOUTH);
      add(centerPanel, BorderLayout.CENTER);

      addWindowListener(new WinClosing());
      setBounds(100, 100, 200, 120);
      setVisible(true);
    }

  public void actionPerformed(ActionEvent ae) {

      // depending on which Button is pressed, the CardLayout object
      // calls the next(), previous(), or first() methods

      if (ae.getActionCommand().equals("next")) {
        cl.next(centerPanel);
      }
      if (ae.getActionCommand().equals("previous")) {
        cl.previous(centerPanel);
      }
      if (ae.getActionCommand().equals("first")) {
        cl.first(centerPanel);
      }
    }

  public static void main(String args[]) {
      TestCard tc = new TestCard();
    }
  }

// The WinClosing class terminates the program when the window is closed

class WinClosing extends WindowAdapter {
  public void windowClosing(WindowEvent we) {
    System.exit(0);
  }
}
```

*Output*

Here is the result:

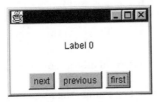

# 6.5.3 FlowLayout Class

```
public class FlowLayout extends Object implements, LayoutManager, Serializable
```

```
Object
    FlowLayout
```

**Interfaces**

```
LayoutManager, Serializable
```

A FlowLayout layout manager positions the components so they flow from left to right. When the right border is reached, the next component is placed on left border of the next row. When the Container is resized, the components are re-laid out according to the same guidelines.

FlowLayout is the default layout manager of Panel and Applet objects.

## FlowLayout() Constructor

| Constructor | Syntax |
|---|---|
| FlowLayout() | public FlowLayout() |
| | public FlowLayout(int *alignment*) |
| | public FlowLayout(int *alignment*, int *hgap*, int *vgap*) |

Creates a FlowLayout. The alignment argument must be one of these three constants

- ❏ FlowLayout.LEFT
- ❏ FlowLayout.CENTER
- ❏ FlowLayout.RIGHT

Setting the alignment to FlowLayout.LEFT means the components will be added in a left-justified manner (starting from the left hand side of the Container). The default alignment is FlowLayout.CENTER. The gaps specify the spacings between components. The units are in pixels. A negative gap can be used to place components on top of each other.

**513**

## Alignment Methods

| Method | Syntax |
|---|---|
| getAlignment() | public int getAlignment() |
| setAlignment() | public void setAlignment(int *align*) |

getAlignment() returns the current alignment of the invoking FlowLayout object.

setAlignment() is used to set or change the alignment of the invoking FlowLayout object.

## Gap Methods

| Method | Syntax |
|---|---|
| getHgap | public int getHgap() |
| getVgap | public int getVgap() |
| setHgap | public void setHgap(int *hgap*) |
| setVgap | public void setVgap(int *vgap*) |

getHgap() and getVgap() return the values of the horizontal or vertical gaps of the invoking FlowLayout object.

setHgap() and setVgap() methods set or change values of the horizontal or vertical gaps of the invoking FlowLayout object.

## layoutContainer() method

| Method | Syntax |
|---|---|
| layoutContainer() | public void layoutContainer(Container *cont*) |

layoutContainer() causes the components contained in Container cont to be redrawn.

## Sizing Methods

| Method | Syntax |
|---|---|
| minimumLayoutSize() | public Dimension minimumLayoutSize (Container *cont*) |
| preferredLayoutSize() | public Dimension preferredLayoutSize (Container *cont*) |

minimumLayoutSize() returns the minimum size of the Container cont.

preferredLayoutSize() returns the preferred size of the Container cont.

# toString() Method

| Method | Syntax |
|--------|--------|
| toString() | public String toString() |

toString() returns a String representation of the invoking FlowLayout object.

## Example: Using FlowLayout

In this example, 6 Button objects are placed on a Frame using a FlowLayout layout manager. They are placed from left to right in a center-justified manner. The Frame can only contain four Button objects on a row. The fifth and sixth Button objects are placed on the second row.

*The WinClosing class is used to terminate the program if the window is closed. See Section 7.3.8 on page 657 for more details.*

```java
import java.awt.*;
import java.awt.event.*;

public class TestFL extends Frame {
   public TestFL() {

      // 10 buttons are added to the Frame using a FlowLayout
      // layout manager.
   setLayout(new FlowLayout(FlowLayout.CENTER));
      for (int i = 0; i < 6; ++i) {
         add(new Button("button" + i));
      }

      addWindowListener(new WinClosing());
      setBounds(100, 100, 300, 120);
      setVisible(true);
   }

   public static void main(String args[]) {
      TestFL tfl = new TestFL();
   }
}

// The WinClosing class terminates the program when the window is closed

class WinClosing extends WindowAdapter {
   public void windowClosing(WindowEvent we) {
      System.exit(0);
   }
}
```

### Output

Here is the result:

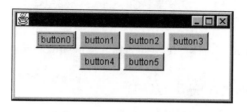

# 6.5.4 GridBagConstraints Class

```
public class GridBagConstraints extends Object
  implements Cloneable, Serializable
```

```
Object
  GridBagConstraints
```

### Interfaces

```
Cloneable, Serializable
```

A GridBagConstraints object stores the layout constraints for a given component for use with the GridBagLayout layout manager.

## GridBagConstraints() Constructor

| Constructor | Syntax |
|---|---|
| GridBagConstraints() | public GridBagConstraints() |
| | public GridBagContstrains(int *gridx*, int *gridy*, int *gridwidth*, int *gridheight*, double *weightx*, double *weighty*, int *anchor*, int *fill*, Insets *insets*, int *ipadx*, int *ipady*) |

Creates a GridBagConstraints object. The second version passes all of the GridBagConstraint constants to the constructor.

## anchor Field

| Field |
|---|
| public int anchor |

anchor specifies the anchor point for the component if the Container is resized. Valid options are:

- ❏   GridBagConstraints.CENTER (default)
- ❏   GridBagConstraints.NORTH
- ❏   GridBagConstraints.NORTHWEST
- ❏   GridBagConstraints.NORTHEAST
- ❏   GridBagConstraints.SOUTH
- ❏   GridBagConstraints.SOUTHWEST
- ❏   GridBagConstraints.SOUTHEAST
- ❏   GridBagConstraints.EAST
- ❏   GridBagConstraints.WEST

## fill Field

**Field**

public int fill

fill determines how a component is stretched if the Container is resized larger. Valid settings are:

- ❏   GridBagConstraints.NONE (default)
- ❏   GridBagConstraints.VERTICAL
- ❏   GridBagConstraints.HORIZONTAL
- ❏   GridBagConstraints.BOTH

## gridx Field

**Field**

public int gridx

gridx specifies the column the component will be placed. For components that take up more than one column, gridx specifies the left-most column. gridx can also be assigned the value GridBagConstraints.RELATIVE, which places the component to the right of the last component added.

## gridy Field

**Field**

public int gridy

6

java.awt

gridy specifies the row the component will be placed. For components that take up more than one row, gridy specifies the top-most row. gridy can also be assigned the value GridBagConstraints.RELATIVE, which places the component below the last component added.

## gridwidth Field

| Field |
| --- |
| public int gridwidth |

gridwidth sets the number of columns a component occupies. Components in the last column can have gridwidth of GridBagConstraints.REMAINDER, which cause the component to fill up the remainder of the row. Assigning gridwidth to GridBagConstraints.RELATIVE forces that component to be the next-to-last in the row.

## gridheight Field

| Field |
| --- |
| public int gridheight |

gridheight sets the number of rows a component occupies. Components in the last row can have gridheight of GridBagConstraints.REMAINDER, which cause the component to fill up the remainder of the column. Assigning gridheight to GridBagConstraints.RELATIVE forces that component to be the next-to-last in the column.

## insets Field

| Field |
| --- |
| public Insets insets |

insets sets the Insets object associated with the component. The Insets object specifies the space between the component and the edge of its display area.

## ipadx Field

| Field |
| --- |
| public int ipadx |

ipadx sets the internal padding in pixels to the minimum width of the component. The width of the component will be set to at least its minimum width + (2*ipadx).

# ipady Field

**Field**

```
public int ipady
```

ipady sets the internal padding in pixels to the minimum height of the component. The height of the component will be set to at least its minimum height + (2*ipadx).

# weightx Field

**Field**

```
public double weightx
```

weightx determines how any additional space within the row is distributed. This controls how components are allowed to grow or shrink if the Container is re-sized. A weightx value of 0.0 means the component will not grow or shrink. Non-zero values provide a relative scale. A component with a weightx value of 2.0 will get twice as much of the available row space as a component with a weightx value of 1.0.

# weighty Field

**Field**

```
public double weighty
```

wieghty behaves similar to weightx but controls how extra column space is allocated.

# 6.5.5 GridBagLayout Class

```
public class GridBagLayout extends Object
    implements LayoutManager2, Serializable
```

```
Object
    GridBagLayout
```

### Interfaces

```
LayoutManager, LayoutManager2, Serializable
```

A GridBagLayout object is a layout manager that is similar to the GridLayout class in that components are placed in rows and columns. The difference is that with the GridBagLayout manager there is much more flexibility in how components are sized and placed. Components can be of different sizes and can take up more than one row or column. The anchor point and fill-policy of the components can also be set.

The attributes of each component are set by assigning the values to a GridBagConstraints object. Connecting a component to a set of constraints is done via the setConstraints() method, or when adding the component to the Container using the method:

```
add(Component c, GridBagConstraints gbc)
```

## GridBagLayout() Constructor

| Constructor | Syntax |
| --- | --- |
| GridBagLayout() | GridBagLayout() |

Creates a GridBagLayout object.

## addLayoutComponent() Method

| Method | Syntax |
| --- | --- |
| addLayoutComponent() | public void addLayoutComponent<br>(Component *comp*, Object *constraints*) |
| | public void addLayoutComponent<br>(String *name*, Component *comp*) |

addLayoutComponent() adds the Component *comp* to the layout. In the first version, the Object constraints is the GridBagConstraints object associated with the Component. The second version adds the specified Component with the specified name to the layout. This method is usually not called directly.

## getConstraints() Method

| Method | Syntax |
| --- | --- |
| getConstraints() | public GridBagConstraints getConstraints<br>(Component *c*) |

getConstraints() returns a clone of the current constraints for Component c. It is useful if you want to duplicate the constraints of an existing component.

## layoutContainer() method

| Method | Syntax |
| --- | --- |
| layoutContainer() | public void layoutContainer(Container *cont*) |

layoutContainer() causes the components contained in Container cont to be redrawn.

## removeLayoutComponent() method

| Method | Syntax |
| --- | --- |
| removeLayoutComponent() | public void removeLayoutComponent<br>(Component *comp*) |

removeLayoutComponent() removes the Component comp from the layout. This method is usually not called directly.

# setConstraints() Method

| Method | Syntax |
|---|---|
| setConstraints() | public void setConstraints<br>(Component *c*, GridBagConstraints *gbc*) |

setConstraints() assigns a set of constraints to a Component. This method is called by a GridBagLayout object.

# Sizing Methods

| Method | Syntax |
|---|---|
| maximumLayoutSize() | public Dimension maximumLayoutSize<br>(Container *cont*) |
| minimumLayoutSize() | public Dimension minimumLayoutSize<br>(Container *cont*) |
| preferredLayoutSize() | public Dimension preferredLayoutSize<br>(Container *cont*) |

maximumLayoutSize() returns the maximum size of the Container cont.

minimumLayoutSize() returns the minimum size of the Container cont.

preferredLayoutSize() returns the preferred size of the Container cont.

# toString() Method

| Method | Syntax |
|---|---|
| toString() | public String toString() |

toString() returns a String representation of the invoking GridBagLayout object.

## Example: Using GridBagLayout

In this example, a Button, Label, and TextField object are added to a Frame using a GrigBagLayout layout manager to position them.

*The WinClosing class is used to terminate the program if the window is closed. See Section 7.3.8 on page 657 for more details.*

```
import java.awt.*;
import java.awt.event.*;

public class TestGBL extends Frame {
```

6

java.awt

```
Button goButton;
  Label nameLabel;
  TextField nameTF;
  GridBagConstraints gbc;

  public TestGBL() {
    Insets i = new Insets(0, 0, 0, 0);

    goButton = new Button("Go");
    goButton.setFont(new Font("Times", Font.BOLD, 14));

    nameLabel = new Label("Name");

    nameTF = new TextField(20);

    // A GridBagLayout object is created and it is set to be
    // the layout manager for the Frame.  An instance of
    // GridBagLayout is needed later to call the setConstraints()
    // method.

    GridBagLayout gbl = new GridBagLayout();
    setLayout(gbl);

    // The constraints are set for the Label object.  All of the
    // constraint values are passed to the GridBagConstraints
    // constructor.  The setConstraints() method is used to associate.
    // the GridBagConstraints object with the Label.

    gbc = new GridBagConstraints(0, 0, 1, 1, 0.0, 0.0,
                                 GridBagConstraints.EAST,
                                 GridBagConstraints.NONE, i, 0, 0);
    gbl.setConstraints(nameLabel, gbc);

    // The constraints are similarly set for the TextField
    gbc = new GridBagConstraints(1, 0, 1, 1, 0.0, 0.0,
                                 GridBagConstraints.WEST,
                                 GridBagConstraints.NONE, i, 0, 0);
    gbl.setConstraints(nameTF, gbc);

    // The constraints are similarly set for the Button

    gbc = new GridBagConstraints(0, 1, 2, 1, 0.0, 0.0,
                                 GridBagConstraints.CENTER,
                                 GridBagConstraints.HORIZONTAL, i, 0,
                                 0);
    gbl.setConstraints(goButton, gbc);

    add(nameLabel);
    add(nameTF);
    add(goButton);
```

```
        addWindowListener(new WinClosing());
        setBounds(100, 100, 300, 120);
        setVisible(true);
    }

    public static void main(String args[]) {
        TestGBL tgbl = new TestGBL();
    }
}

// The WinClosing class terminates the program when the window is closed

class WinClosing extends WindowAdapter {
    public void windowClosing(WindowEvent we) {
        System.exit(0);
    }
}
```

The Label and TextField objects are placed on the first row. The Button is sized to take up two columns. The weightx and weighty constants are set to 0.0 so the components will not re-size if the Frame is re-sized.

### Output

Here is the result:

# 6.5.6 GridLayout Class

```
public class GridLayout extends Object implements LayoutManager, Serializable
```

```
Object
    GridLayout
```

### Interfaces

```
LayoutManager, Serializable
```

The GridLayout layout manager arranges the components in rows and columns. Each cell in the layout has the same size. Components are added to the Container left to right, top to bottom.

The actual number of rows and columns depends on the number of components. Only one component is placed in each cell. If the grid fills up and additional components are added, the number of columns is increased unless the number of rows is set to 0 in which case the number of rows is increased.

## GridLayout() Method

| Method | Syntax |
|---|---|
| GridLayout() | public GridLayout() |
| | public GridLayout(int *rows*, int *columns*) |
| | public GridLayout(int *rows*, int *columns*, int *hgap*, int *vgap*) |

GridLayout object constructor. If the no-argument version is used, a one row layout is used. The quantity hgap is the horizontal spacing between components. The vgap quantity is the vertical spacing between rows. The default setting for the horizontal and vertical gaps is 0.

## addLayoutComponent() Method

| Method | Syntax |
|---|---|
| addLayoutComponent() | public void addLayoutComponent (String *name*, Component *comp*) |

addLayoutComponent() adds the specified Component with the specified name to the layout.

## Gap Methods

| Method | Syntax |
|---|---|
| getHgap() | public int getHgap() |
| getVgap() | public int getVgap() |
| setHgap() | public void setHgap(int *hgap*) |
| setVgap() | public void setVgap(int *vgap*) |

getHgap() and getVgap() return the values of the horizontal or vertical gaps of the invoking GridLayout object.

setHgap() and setVgap() set or change values of the horizontal or vertical gaps of the invoking GridLayout object.

# layoutContainer() method

| Method | Syntax |
|--------|--------|
| layoutContainer() | public void layoutContainer(Container *cont*) |

layoutContainer() causes the components contained in Container cont to be redrawn.

# removeLayoutComponent() method

| Method | Syntax |
|--------|--------|
| removeLayoutComponent() | public void removeLayoutComponent (Component *comp*) |

removeLayoutComponent() removes the Component comp from the layout

# Row and Column Methods

| Method | Syntax |
|--------|--------|
| getColumns() | public int getColumns() |
| getRows() | public int getRows() |
| setColumns() | public void setColumns(int *numColumns*) |
| setRows() | public void setRows(int *numRows*) |

getColumns() and getRows() return the current number of rows or columns of the invoking GridLayout object.

setColumns() and setRows() change the number of rows or columns of the invoking GridLayout object.

# Sizing Methods

| Method | Syntax |
|--------|--------|
| minimumLayoutSize() | public Dimension minimumLayoutSize (Container *cont*) |
| preferredLayoutSize() | public Dimension preferredLayoutSize (Container *cont*) |

minimumLayoutSize() returns the minimum size of the Container cont.

preferredLayoutSize() returns the preferred size of the Container cont.

6

java.awt

## toString() Method

| Method | Syntax |
|---|---|
| toString() | public String toString() |

toString() returns a String representation of the invoking GridLayout object.

### Example: Using GridLayout

In this example, a Button, Label, and TextField object are placed on a Frame using a GridLayout layout manager.

*The WinClosing class is used to terminate the program if the window is closed. See Section 7.3.8 on page 657 for more details.*

```java
import java.awt.*;
import java.awt.event.*;

public class TestGL extends Frame {
   Button goButton;
   Label nameLabel;
   TextField nameTF;

   public TestGL() {
      goButton = new Button("Go");
      goButton.setFont(new Font("Times", Font.BOLD, 14));

      nameLabel = new Label("Name");
      nameTF = new TextField(20);

      // setting the number of rows to 0 means the number of rows
      // will be increased to match the number of components added
      // to the layout

      setLayout(new GridLayout(0, 1));

      Panel p1 = new Panel();
      p1.add(nameLabel);
      add(p1);

      Panel p2 = new Panel();
      p2.add(nameTF);
      add(p2);

      Panel p3 = new Panel();
      p3.add(goButton);
      add(p3);
```

```
        addWindowListener(new WinClosing());
        setBounds(100, 100, 200, 200);
        setVisible(true);
    }

    public static void main(String args[]) {
        TestGL tf1 = new TestGL();
    }
}

// The WinClosing class terminates the program when the window is closed

class WinClosing extends WindowAdapter {
    public void windowClosing(WindowEvent we) {
        System.exit(0);
    }
}
```

The number of rows is set to 0 in the GridLayout constructor meaning the number of columns will remain fixed at 1 and the number of rows increased to match the number of components. The components are first placed in Panel objects because if they are placed directly on the Frame the size of the components will be increased to match the size of the Frame. Placing the components in Panels preserves a more natural component size.

### Output

Here is the result:

## 6.6 Menu Classes

**Menus** are pull-downs that are attached to a Frame object or pop-ups that are attached to a GUI component. The Menu class hierarchy is shown in the following diagram.

❑ The MenuComponent class is an abstract class that is the parent class of most of the other menu classes.

❑ A MenuBar object is used to hold Menu objects and appears at the top of the Frame object.

- ❏ Menu objects are the pull down lists that contain MenuItem object. Because Menu is a sub-class of MenuItem, a Menu object can be added to another Menu.

- ❏ A CheckboxItem object is a MenuItem that provides a checkbox that can be toggled on or off.

- ❏ A PopupMenu object is a menu that is associated with another GUI component.

- ❏ A MenuShortcut Object represents a keyboard sequence, such as *Ctrl-Q*, that will select a MenuItem object.

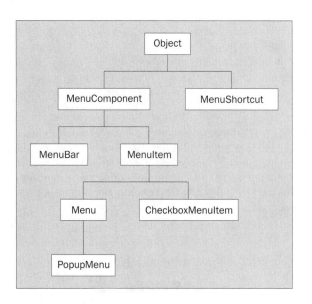

## 6.6.1 CheckboxMenuItem Class

```
public class CheckboxMenuItem extends MenuItem
    implements ItemSelectable, Accessible
```

```
Object
  MenuComponent
    MenuItem
      CheckboxMenuItem
```

### Interfaces

```
Accessible, ItemSelectable, Serializable
```

A CheckboxMenuItem is a MenuItem that provides a checkbox that can be toggled on or off. It is often used to set up the user environment for an application.

A CheckboxMenuItem object generates an ItemEvent object when it is selected or de-selected.

# CheckboxMenuItem() Constructor

| Constructor | Syntax |
|---|---|
| CheckboxMenuItem() | public CheckboxMenuItem() |
| | public CheckboxMenuItem(String *label*) |
| | public CheckboxMenuItem(String *label*, boolean *checked*) |

Creates a CheckboxMenuItem object. The CheckboxMenuItem object can be provided a label and an intial checked state. The default checked state is false or unchecked.

# Checked State Methods

| Method | Syntax |
|---|---|
| getState() | public boolean getState() |
| setState() | public void setState(boolean *checked*) |

getState() returns true if the invoking CheckboxMenuItem object is checked.

setState() is used to changed the checked state of the invoking CheckboxMenuItem object.

# getListeners() Method

| Method | Syntax |
|---|---|
| getListeners() | public EventListener[] getListeners (Class *listenerClass*) |

getListeners() returns any listeners of the specified type registered to the invoking CheckboxMenuItem object as an EventListener array.

# getSelectedObjects() Method

| Method | Syntax |
|---|---|
| getSelectedObjects() | public Object[] getSelectedObjects() |

getSelectedObjects() returns a one element array containing the label of the invoking CheckboxMenuItem object if it is checked or null if it is not checked.

# ItemListener Methods

| Method | Syntax |
|---|---|
| addItemListener() | public void addItemListener(ItemListener *il*) |
| removeItemListener() | public void removeItemListener(ItemListener *il*) |

6

java.awt

addItemListener() registers the invoking CheckboxMenuItem object with an ItemListener object. The ItemListener is notified if the CheckboxMenuItem generates an ItemEvent.

removeItemListener() removes an ItemListener object from the invoking CheckboxMenuItem object. ItemEvent objects generated by the CheckboxMenuItem will no longer be received by the ItemListener.

## paramString() Method

| Method | Syntax |
|---|---|
| paramString() | public String paramString() |

paramString() returns a String representing the checked state of the invoking CheckboxMenuItem object. This method is usually used for de-bugging purposes.

### Example: Using CheckboxMenuItem

In this example, a CheckboxMenuItem object is created and added to a Menu object.

*The WinClosing class is used to terminate the program if the window is closed. See Section 7.3.8 on page 657 for more details.*

```java
import java.awt.*;
import java.awt.event.*;

public class TestCBM extends Frame implements ItemListener {
  MenuBar mb;
  Menu styleMenu;
  CheckboxMenuItem italic;
  TextField tf;

  public TestCBM() {
    tf = new TextField(15);
    tf.setFont(new Font("Serif", Font.PLAIN, 12));
    tf.setText("Style is plain");
    tf.setEditable(false);

    Panel p = new Panel();
    p.add(tf);
    add(p);
    // create a CheckboxMenuItem and add it to a menu named
    // "Style" and add the menu to a menu bar.  The CheckboxMenuItem
    // is registered with an ItemListener.

    italic = new CheckboxMenuItem("italic");
    italic.addItemListener(this);
```

```
      styleMenu = new Menu("Style");
      styleMenu.add(italic);

      mb = new MenuBar();
      mb.add(styleMenu);

      setMenuBar(mb);

      addWindowListener(new WinClosing());
      setBounds(100, 100, 200, 150);
      setVisible(true);
   }

// When the CheckboxMenuItem is toggled on or off, an ItemEvent
// is generated and the itemStateChanged() method is called.
// Inside the method, the style and text of the TextField is
// updated to reflect the checked state of the CheckboxMenuItem

   public void itemStateChanged(ItemEvent ie) {
     if (italic.getState()) {
       tf.setFont(new Font("Serif", Font.ITALIC, 12));
       tf.setText("Style is italic");
     } else {
       tf.setFont(new Font("Serif", Font.PLAIN, 12));
       tf.setText("Style is plain");
     }
   }

// The getInsets() method is overridden to place the TextField more
// in the center of the frame

   public Insets getInsets() {
     return new Insets(60, 30, 0, 30);
   }

   public static void main(String args[]) {
     TestCBM tcb = new TestCBM();
   }
}

// The WinClosing class terminates the program when the window is closed
class WinClosing extends WindowAdapter {
   public void windowClosing(WindowEvent we) {
     System.exit(0);
   }
}
```

When the CheckboxMenuItem object is toggled on or off, an ItemEvent event is
generated and processed by the itemStateChanged() method. The style and
text of a TextField object is changed to reflect the checked state of the
CheckboxMenuItem

> **Output**
>
> Here is the result:
>
>

# 6.6.2 Menu Class

```
public class Menu extends MenuItem implements MenuContainer, Accessible
```

```
Object
   MenuComponent
      MenuItem
         Menu
```

### Interfaces
```
Accessible, MenuContainer, Serializable
```

A Menu object is a pull-down list that appears on the MenuBar of a Frame or within other menus. It contains MenuItem objects, CheckboxMenuItem objects, or other Menu objects. Tear-off menus are menus that can be dragged to different locations on the screen.

## Menu() Constructor

| Constructor | Syntax |
|---|---|
| Menu() | public Menu() |
| | public Menu(String *title*) |
| | public Menu(String *title*, boolean *tearOff*) |

Creates a Menu object. The Menu object can be given a title. The default tearOff mode is false. Tear-off menus are menus that can be dragged to different locations on the screen.

## Methods to Add MenuItems to a Menu

| Method | Syntax |
|---|---|
| add() | public MenuItem add(MenuItem *item*) |
| | public void add(String *label*) |

| Method | Syntax |
|---|---|
| addSeparator() | public void addSeparator() |
| insert() | public void insert(MenuItem *item*, int *index*) |
| | public void insert(String *label*, int *index*) |
| insertSeparator() | public void insertSeparator(int *index*) |

add() adds a MenuItem object to the bottom of the invoking Menu object. If a String is passed to the add() method, a MenuItem object is created with label as the text. The first version returns the MenuItem that was added.

insert() inserts a MenuItem object at position index in the invoking Menu object.

addSeparator() adds a horizontal line to the invoking Menu object.

insertSeparator() inserts a horizontal line at position index in the invoking Menu object.

# getItem() Method

| Method | Syntax |
|---|---|
| getItem() | public MenuItem getItem(int *index*) |

getItem() returns the MenuItem object at position index in the invoking Menu object.

# getItemCount() Method

| Method | Syntax |
|---|---|
| getItemCount() | public int getItemCount() |

getItemCount() returns the number of items within the invoking Menu object.

# isTearOff() Method

| Method | Syntax |
|---|---|
| isTearOff() | public boolean isTearOff() |

isTearOff() returns true if the invoking Menu object is a tear-off menu. Tear-off menus are menus that can be dragged to different locations on the screen.

# paramString() Method

| Method | Syntax |
|---|---|
| paramString() | public String paramString() |

paramString() returns a String representing the state of the invoking Menu object. This method is usually used for de-bugging purposes.

## Methods to Remove Menu Items from a Menu

| Method | Syntax |
|---|---|
| remove() | public void remove(int *index*) |
| | public void remove(MenuComponent *mc*) |
| removeAll() | public void removeAll() |

remove() removes a MenuItem object from the invoking Menu object based on either the index of the MenuItem object or a reference to the MenuItem object.

removeAll() removes all of the MenuItem objects from the invoking Menu object.

## Deprecated Methods

| Method | Syntax |
|---|---|
| countItems() | public int countItems() |

countItems() has been replaced by the getItemCount() method and should not be used for new code.

---

### Example: Using Menu

See the *Using CheckboxMenuItem* example on page 530 and the *Using MenuItem* example on page 541 that create menus, add menu items to them, and place them on the menu bar.

---

# 6.6.3 MenuBar Class

```
public class MenuBar extends MenuComponent implements MenuContainer, Accessible
```

```
Object
    MenuComponent
        MenuBar
```

### Interfaces

```
Accessible, MenuContainer, Serializable
```

A MenuBar object contains Menu objects. It is attached to the top of a Frame object, or on some platforms it is attached to the main menubar at the top of the screen. A Frame can display only one MenuBar at a time. A MenuBar object is added to a Frame using the Frame class method setMenuBar().

# MenuBar() Constructor

| Constructor | Syntax |
|---|---|
| MenuBar() | public MenuBar() |

Creates an empty MenuBar object.

# add() Method

| Method | Syntax |
|---|---|
| add() | public Menu add(Menu *m*) |

add() adds a Menu object to the invoking MenuBar object. A reference to the Menu object added is returned.

# getMenu() Method

| Method | Syntax |
|---|---|
| getMenu() | public Menu getMenu(int *index*) |

getMenu() returns the Menu object at position index from the invoking MenuBar object.

# getMenuCount() Method

| Method | Syntax |
|---|---|
| getMenuCount() | public int getMenuCount() |

getMenuCount() returns the number of top-level menus in the invoking MenuBar object.

# Help Menu Methods

| Method | Syntax |
|---|---|
| getHelpMenu() | public Menu getHelpMenu() |
| setHelpMenu() | public void setHelpMenu(Menu *helpMenu*) |

getHelpMenu() returns the Menu object that has been designated as the help menu for the invoking MenuBar object.

setHelpMenu() sets the specified Menu as the help Menu for the invoking MenuBar object and places it as the right-most Menu on the MenuBar.

## remove() Method

| Method | Syntax |
|---|---|
| remove() | public void remove(int *index*) |
| | public void remove(MenuComponent *mc*) |

remove() removes a Menu object from the invoking MenuBar object based on either an index or a MenuComponent reference.

## Shortcut Methods

| Method | Syntax |
|---|---|
| deleteShortcut() | public void deleteShortcut(MenuShortcut *ms*) |
| getShortcutMenuItem() | public MenuItem getShortcutMenuItem<br>(MenuShortcut *ms*) |
| shortcuts() | public Enumeration shortcuts() |

deleteShortcut() removes a MenuShortcut object from the invoking Menubar object.

getShortcutMenuItem() returns the MenuItem associated with the specified MenuShortcut Item.

shortcuts() returns an Enumeration of all of the MenuShortcut items associated with the invoking MenuBar object.

## Deprecated Methods

| Method | Syntax |
|---|---|
| countMenus() | public int countMenus() |

countMenus() has been replaced by the getMenuCount() method and should not be used for new code.

### Example: Using MenuBar

In this example, a MenuBar object containing two Menu objects is created and placed on a Frame. One of the Menu objects is designated as the help menu and appears on the far right of the MenuBar.

*The WinClosing class is used to terminate the program if the window is closed. See Section 7.3.8 on page 657 for more details.*

```
import java.awt.*;
import java.awt.event.*;
```

```java
public class TestMenuBar extends Frame {
  MenuBar mb;
  Menu helpMenu, fileMenu;
  TestMenuBar() {

    // two Menu objects are created and placed on a MenuBar
    helpMenu = new Menu("Help");
    helpMenu.add("help");

    fileMenu = new Menu("File");
    fileMenu.add("save");

    mb = new MenuBar();
    mb.add(fileMenu);

    // One of the Menu objects is designated as the help
    // menu and is placed at the far right of the MenuBar.
    // It is not added to the MenuBar using add() in the
    // normal way.

    mb.setHelpMenu(helpMenu);

    setMenuBar(mb);

    addWindowListener(new WinClosing());
    setBounds(100, 100, 200, 120);
    setVisible(true);
  }

  public static void main(String args[]) {
    TestMenuBar tmb = new TestMenuBar();
  }
}

// The WinClosing class terminates the program when the window is closed

class WinClosing extends WindowAdapter {
  public void windowClosing(WindowEvent we) {
    System.exit(0);
  }
}
```

**Output**

Here's the result:

# 6.6.4 MenuComponent Class

```
public abstract class MenuComponent extends Object implements Serializable
```

```
Object
   MenuComponent
```

### Interfaces
```
Serializable
```

The MenuComponent class is the parent class of all menu-related classes. It provides methods common to all of its sub-classes. Because this is an abstract class, a MenuComponent object is never created.

## MenuComponent() Constructor

| Constructor | Syntax |
|---|---|
| MenuComponent() | public MenuComponent() |

Because MenuComponent is an abstract class, a MenuComponent object is never created. The MenuComponent constructor can be used by MenuComponent sub-classes.

## Font Methods

| Method | Syntax |
|---|---|
| getFont() | public Font getFont() |
| setFont() | public void setFont(Font f) |

getFont() returns the Font object associated with the invoking MenuComponent object.

setFont() is used to change the Font object associated with the invoking MenuComponent object.

## getParent() method

| Method | Syntax |
|---|---|
| getParent() | public MenuContainer getParent() |

getParent() returns the parent container for the invoking MenuComponent object or null if a MenuBar object calls this method. (MenuBar is the top-level MenuComponent.)

## Name Methods

| Method | Syntax |
|---|---|
| getName() | public String getName() |
| setName() | public void setName(String name) |

getName() returns the internal name associated with the invoking MenuComponent object.

setName() changes or sets the internal name associated with the invoking MenuComponent object.

## toString() method

| Method | Syntax |
|---|---|
| toString() | public String toString() |

toString() returns a String representation of the invoking MenuComponent object.

# 6.6.5 MenuItem Class

```
public class MenuItem extends MenuComponent implements Accessible
```

```
Object
    MenuComponent
        MenuItem
```

### Interfaces
```
Accessible, Serializable
```

A MenuItem object is an item that goes on a Menu. A MenuItem is represented by a String object that is displayed when the Menu is clicked. Menu is itself a MenuItem subclass, allowing Menus to be nested inside other Menus.

A MenuItem object generates an ActionEvent when it is selected.

## MenuItem() Constructor

| Constructor | Syntax |
|---|---|
| MenuItem() | public MenuItem() |
| | public MenuItem(String label) |
| | public MenuItem(String label, MenuShortcut ms) |

Creates a MenuItem object. A label and MenuShortcut object can be passed to the constructor. If the character '-' is passed as the label, a separator (horizontal line) is placed on the menu. A MenuShortcut is a keyboard sequence that will select the associated MenuItem.

## ActionCommand Methods

| Method | Syntax |
|---|---|
| getActionCommand() | public String getActionCommand() |
| setActionCommand() | public void setActionCommand(String command) |

**539**

Every MenuItem object has an associated action command that can be used by an event handler to determine which MenuItem object generated the event.

getActionCommand() returns the action command of the invoking MenuItem object.

setActionCommand() changes the action command of the invoking MenuItem object.

## ActionListener Methods

| Method | Syntax |
| --- | --- |
| addActionListener() | public void addActionListener<br>(ActionListener al) |
| removeActionListener() | public void removeActionListener<br>(ActionListener al) |

addActionListener() registers the invoking MenuItem object with an ActionListener object. The ActionListener is notified if the MenuItem generates an action event.

removeActionListener() removes an ActionListener object from the invoking MenuItem object. ActionEvent objects generated by the MenuItem will no longer be received by the ActionListener.

## getListeners() Method

| Method | Syntax |
| --- | --- |
| getListeners() | public EventListener[] getListeners<br>(Class listenerClass) |

getListeners() returns any listeners of the specified type registered to the invoking MenuItem object as an EventListener array.

## Methods to Enable or Disable a MenuItem

| Method | Syntax |
| --- | --- |
| isEnabled() | public boolean isEnabled() |
| setEnabled() | public void setEnabled(boolean state) |

isEnabled() returns true if the invoking MenuItem object is enabled. An enabled MenuItem object can be selected by the user.

setEnabled() method is used to change the enabled state of the invoking MenuItem object.

## Label Methods

| Method | Syntax |
|---|---|
| getLabel() | public String getLabel() |
| setLabel() | public void setLabel(String *label*) |

getLabel() returns the label displayed by the invoking MenuItem object.

setLabel() changes the label displayed by the invoking MenuItem object.

## MenuShortcut Methods

| Method | Syntax |
|---|---|
| deleteShortcut() | public void deleteShortcut() |
| getShortcut() | public MenuShortcut getShortcut() |
| setShortcut() | public void setShortcut(MenuShortcut *msc*) |

A MenuShortCut object represents a keyboard sequence that selects a MenuItem object.

deleteShortcut() removes the MenuShortcut object associated with the invoking MenuItem object.

getShortcut() returns the MenuShortcut object associated with the invoking MenuItem object.

setShortCut() is used to set the MenuShortcut object associated with the invoking MenuItem object.

## Deprecated Methods

| Method | Syntax |
|---|---|
| disable() | public synchronized void disable() |
| enable() | public synchronized void enable() |
| | public void enable(boolean *b*) |

These methods have been deprecated and should not be used for new code.

### Example: Using MenuItem

In this example, a Menu object is created and added to a Frame. The Menu contains one MenuItem called quit that is used to terminate the program.

*The WinClosing class is used to terminate the program if the window is closed. See Section 7.3.8 on page 657 for more details.*

```java
import java.awt.*;
import java.awt.event.*;

public class TestMenuItem extends Frame implements ActionListener {
  MenuBar mb;
  Menu fileMenu;
  MenuItem quit;

  public TestMenuItem() {

    // A MenuItem object is created with an associated MenuShortcut
    // of CTRL-Q

    quit = new MenuItem("quit", new MenuShortcut(KeyEvent.VK_Q));

    // The MenuItem object is registered with an ActionListener

    quit.addActionListener(this);

    fileMenu = new Menu("File");
    fileMenu.add(quit);

    mb = new MenuBar();
    mb.add(fileMenu);

    setMenuBar(mb);

    addWindowListener(new WinClosing());
    setBounds(100, 100, 200, 120);
    setVisible(true);
  }

  // When the MenuItem object is selected, the actionPerformed()
  // method is called and the program terminates

  public void actionPerformed(ActionEvent ae) {
    System.exit(0);
  }
  public static void main(String args[]) {
    TestMenuItem tmi = new TestMenuItem();
  }
}

// The WinClosing class terminates the program when the window is closed

class WinClosing extends WindowAdapter {
  public void windowClosing(WindowEvent we) {
    System.exit(0);
  }
}
```

The MenuItem object is given an associated MenuShortcut object when it is created. If the quit MenuItem is selected or if the MenuShortcut keyboard sequence *Ctrl-Q* is typed, the actionPerformed() method is called and terminates the program.

### Output

Here is the result:

## 6.6.6 MenuShortcut Class

```
public class MenuShortcut extends Object implements Serializable
```

```
Object
    MenuShortcut
```

### Interfaces

```
Serializable
```

A MenuShortcut object is a keyboard sequence that selects a MenuItem object. A MenuShortcut object can be associated with a MenuItem object either through the MenuItem object constructor or by using the setShortcut() method from the MenuItem class.

To select the associated MenuItem object, the user must type in a modifier key and the key code. On Macs, the modifier key is the **Command**, or **Apple**, key. On Windows, the modifier key is the **Ctrl** key.

### MenuShortcut() Constructor

| Constructor | Syntax |
|---|---|
| MenuShortcut() | public MenuShortcut(int *key*) |
| | public MenuShortcut(int *key*, boolean *useShiftModifier*) |

MenuShortcut object constructor. If useShiftModifier is true, the **Shift** key must be pressed to access the associated MenuItem. The integer key is a virtual key code from the KeyEvent class. Examples of virtual key codes are:

- ❑ KeyEvent.VK_Q
- ❑ KeyEvent.VK_S
- ❑ KeyEvent.VK_SHIFT

## equals() Method

| Method | Syntax |
|---|---|
| equals() | public boolean equals(MenuShortcut *msc*) |
| | public boolean equals(Object *obj*) |

equals() returns true if the argument passed to the method is a MenuShortcut object that is the same as the invoking MenuShortcut object.

## getKey() Method

| Method | Syntax |
|---|---|
| getKey() | public int getKey() |

getKey() returns the virtual key code for the invoking MenuShortcut object.

## usesShiftModifier() Method

| Method | Syntax |
|---|---|
| usesShiftModifier() | public boolean usesShiftModifier() |

usesShiftModifier() returns true if the shift modifier must be used to select the associated MenuItem object.

## toString() method

| Method | Syntax |
|---|---|
| toString() | public String toString() |

toString() returns a String representation of the invoking MenuShortcut object.

### Example: Using MenuShortcut

See the *Using MenuItem* example on page 541 where a MenuShortcut object can be used to select the quit MenuItem.

# 6.6.6 PopupMenu Class

public class PopupMenu extends Menu

```
Object
    MenuComponent
        MenuItem
            Menu
                PopupMenu
```

### Interfaces

```
Accessible, MenuContainer, Serializable
```

A PopupMenu object represents a pop-up menu that can be assigned to a component. A PopupMenu object adds MenuItem objects to itself by calling the Menu class method add(). To add a PopupMenu object to a component, the component must call the Component class method add(PopupMenu).

# PopupMenu() Constructor

| Constructor | Syntax |
| --- | --- |
| PopupMenu() | public PopupMenu() |
| | public PopupMenu(String *name*) |

Creates a PopupMenu object. The PopupMenu can be given a name

# show() Method

| Method | Syntax |
| --- | --- |
| show() | public void show(Component *origin*, int *x*, int *y*) |

show() displays the invoking PopupMenu object. The Component argument sets the origin used to place the PopupMenu object. The values x and y are the horizontal and vertical distances away from upper left corner of the Component.

## Example: Using PopupMenu

In this example, a PopupMenu object is created and associated with a TextField object. A CheckboxMenuItem is added to the PopupMenu object. The PopupMenu object is made visible every time the mouse is pressed while over the TextField. The style and text of the TextField is changed to reflect the checked state of the CheckboxMenuItem.

*The WinClosing class is used to terminate the program if the window is closed. See Section 7.3.8 on page 657 for more details.*

```
import java.awt.*;
import java.awt.event.*;

public class TestPopup extends Frame implements ItemListener {
    TextField tf;
    PopupMenu pm;
    CheckboxMenuItem italic;

    public TestPopup() {
```

```
    // A PopupMenu object is created.  One MenuItem is added to the
    // PopupMenu.  The MenuItem is associated with an ItemListener

    pm = new PopupMenu("Style");
    italic = new CheckboxMenuItem("italic");
    italic.addItemListener(this);
    pm.add(italic);

    // A TextField is created and registered with a MouseListener.
    // The previously created PopupMenu is associated with the
    // TextField.

    tf = new TextField(20);
    tf.setText("Style is plain");
    tf.setEditable(false);
    tf.addMouseListener(new MouseHandler());
    tf.add(pm);

    setLayout(new FlowLayout());
    add(tf);

    addWindowListener(new WinClosing());
    setBounds(100, 100, 200, 120);
    setVisible(true);
  }
// When the CheckboxMenuItem inside the PopupMenu is toggled on or
// off, an ItemEvent is generated and the itemStateChanged()
// method is called. Inside the method, the style of the TextField is
// updated to reflect the checked state of the CheckboxMenuItem

public void itemStateChanged(ItemEvent ie) {
  if (italic.getState()) {
    tf.setFont(new Font("Serif", Font.ITALIC, 12));
    tf.setText("Style is italic");
  } else {
    tf.setFont(new Font("Serif", Font.PLAIN, 12));
    tf.setText("Style is plain");
  }
}

// When the mouse is pressed while over the TextField, a MouseEvent
// is generated. The mousePressed() method is called and the
// PopupMenu is made to appear at the coordinates at which the
// MouseEvent occurred.

class MouseHandler extends MouseAdapter {
  public void mousePressed(MouseEvent me) {
    pm.show(tf, me.getX(), me.getY());
  }
}
```

```
    public static void main(String args[]) {
      TestPopup tp = new TestPopup();
    }
  }


// The WinClosing class terminates the program when the window is closed

class WinClosing extends WindowAdapter {
  public void windowClosing(WindowEvent we) {
    System.exit(0);
  }
}
```

**Output**

Here's the result:

## 6.7 Support Classes

The **support classes** provide access to properties that are used by the other classes in the java.awt package. The support class hierarchy is shown in the diagram below.

- ❑ The Color class represents a color.

- ❑ The Cursor class provides the ability to access and modify the mouse pointer.

- ❑ The Dimension class encapsulates a width and height in a single object.

- ❑ The Font class allows the font to be manipulated.

- ❑ The Graphics class provides methods to draw objects and images on the screen.

- ❑ The Insets class specifies borders that can placed inside a Container object.

- ❑ The MediaTracker class monitors the loading of an arbitrary number of images.

- ❑ The Point class encapsulates an x and y location into a single object.

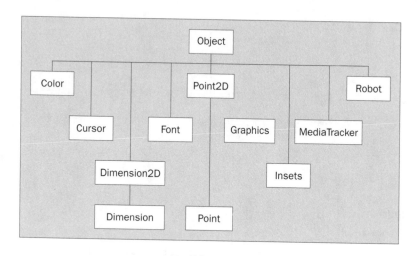

# 6.7.1 Color Class

public class **Color** extends Object implements Paint, Serializable

    Object
      Color

### Interfaces

Paint, Serializable, Transparency

A Color object defines a particular color.

## Color() Constructor

| Constructor | Syntax |
|---|---|
| Color() | public Color(int *red*, int *green*, int *blue*) |
| | public Color(int *red*, int *green*, int *blue*, int *alpha*) |
| | public Color(int *rgb*) |
| | public Color(float *red*, float *green*, float *blue*) |
| | public Color(float *red*, float *green*, float *blue*, int *alpha*) |

Creates a Color object. The levels of red, green, and blue are provided to the constructor. For the constructor that takes three int values, the int values range between 0 and 255. For the constructor that takes three float values, the float values range between 0.0 and 1.0. The rgb parameter combines the red, green, and blue levels into a single int. With this parameter, the blue component is stored in bits 0-7, the green component is stored in bits 8-15, and the red component is stored in bits 16-23. The alpha paramter defines the transparency level of the color. It ranges from 0.0 to 1.0 when using a float value or 0 to 255 when using an int value. An alpha value of 1.0 or 255 means the color is completely opaque. An alpha value of 0.0 or 0 means that the color is completely transparent.

## Pre-Defined Color Objects

| Color Object |
| --- |
| public static final Color white |
| public static final Color lightGray |
| public static final Color gray |
| public static final Color DarkGray |
| public static final Color black |
| public static final Color red |
| public static final Color pink |
| public static final Color orange |
| public static final Color yellow |
| public static final Color green |
| public static final Color magenta |
| public static final Color cyan |
| public static final Color blue |

These Color objects are defined by the Color class. Because they are static objects, they can be accessed using the class name (for example, Color.red).

## brighter() Method

| Method | Syntax |
| --- | --- |
| brighter() | public Color brighter() |

brighter() returns a Color object somewhat brighter than the invoking Color object.

## darker() method

| Method | Syntax |
| --- | --- |
| darker() | public Color darker() |

darker() returns a Color object somewhat darker than the invoking Color object.

## Static Methods to Create Color Objects

| Method | Syntax |
| --- | --- |
| decode() | public static Color decode(String *colorName*) throws NumberFormatException |
| getColor() | public static Color getColor(String *sysPropName*) |

6

java.awt

| Method | Syntax |
|---|---|
| | `public static Color getColor(String sysPropName, Color defaultColor)` |
| | `public static Color getColor(String sysPropName, int defaultColor)` |
| getHSBColor() | `public static Color getHSBColor(float hue, float saturation, float brightness)` |

`decode()` attempts to create a `Color` object based on the `colorName` `String` passed as an argument. The `String` must be a decimal, octal, or hexadecimal representation of a 24-bit integer.

`getColor()` returns the `Color` object associated with the system property name. Valid system properties are:

❏ `myPackage.myClass.foreground`

❏ `myPackage.myClass.background`

❏ `myPackage.myClass.inactive`

❏ `myPackage.myClass.highlight`

If an invalid system property name is passed as an argument, a default `Color` object can be specified.

`getHSBColor()` returns a `Color` object based on hue, saturation, and brightness parameters.

## equals() Method

| Method | Syntax |
|---|---|
| equals() | `public boolean equals(Object obj)` |

`equals()` returns `true` if the `Object` `obj` is a `Color` object and represents the same color as the invoking `Color` object.

## hashCode() Method

| Method | Syntax |
|---|---|
| hashCode() | `public int hashCode()` |

`hashCode()` converts the invoking `Color` object to a hashcode.

# Methods that Return Color Properties

| Method | Syntax |
|---|---|
| getBlue() | public int getBlue() |
| getGreen() | public int getGreen() |
| getRed() | public int getRed() |
| getRGB() | public int getRGB() |

getBlue(), getGreen(), and getRed() methods return the level of blue, green, and red in the invoking Color object.

getRGB() returns the level of red, green, blue, and alpha as a single integer value. The blue component is stored in bits 0-7, the green component is stored in bits 8-15, the red component is stored in bits 16-23, and alpha is stored in bits 24-31.

## Example: Using Color

In this example, a pre-defined Color object is used to create a yellow Frame.

*The WinClosing class is used to terminate the program if the window is closed. See Section 7.3.8 on page 657 for more details.*

```
import java.awt.*;
import java.awt.event.*;

public class TestColor extends Frame {
  public TestColor() {
    setBackground(Color.yellow);

    addWindowListener(new WinClosing());
    setBounds(100, 100, 200, 120);
    setVisible(true);
  }

  public static void main(String args[]) {
    TestColor tc = new TestColor();
  }
}
// The WinClosing class terminates the program when the window is closed

class WinClosing extends WindowAdapter {
  public void windowClosing(WindowEvent we) {
    System.exit(0);
  }
}
```

> **Output**
>
> Here's the result:
>
>

# 6.7.2 Cursor Class

```
public class Cursor extends Object implements Serializable
```

```
Object
    Cursor
```

### Interfaces

```
Serializable
```

The Cursor class defines the appearance of the mouse pointer. A Cursor object can be associated with a GUI component or container. To change the Cursor object associated with a component, the component must invoke the setCursor() method.

## Cursor() Constructor

| Constructor | Syntax |
|---|---|
| Cursor() | public Cursor(int *cursorType*) |

Creates a Cursor object. The cursorType argument must be one of the Cursor class constants.

## Cursor Class Constants

| Constant | Description |
|---|---|
| public static final int DEFAULT_CURSOR | The system default cursor |
| public static final int CROSSHAIR_CURSOR | Defines a cursor that looks like a crosshair |
| public static final int TEXT_CURSOR | Represents the cursor that appears over a text component |
| public static final int WAIT_CURSOR | The cursor that appears when the system is busy |

| Constant | Description |
|----------|-------------|
| `public static final int SW_RESIZE_CURSOR` | The RESIZE cursors are seen when |
| `public static final int SE_RESIZE_CURSOR` | the window is being re-sized |
| `public static final int NW_RESIZE_CURSOR` | |
| `public static final int NE_RESIZE_CURSOR` | |
| `public static final int N_RESIZE_CURSOR` | |
| `public static final int S_RESIZE_CURSOR` | |
| `public static final int E_RESIZE_CURSOR` | |
| `public static final int W_RESIZE_CURSOR` | |
| `public static final int HAND_CURSOR` | Represents a cursor that looks like a hand |
| `public static final int MOVE_CURSOR` | A cursor that appears when something is moved |

## Static Methods that Create Cursor Objects

| Method | Syntax |
|--------|--------|
| `getDefaultCursor()` | `public static Cursor getDefaultCursor()` |
| `getPredefinedCursor()` | `public static Cursor getPredefinedCursor (int cursorType)` |

`getDefaultCursor()` returns the default Cursor object.

`getPredefinedCursor()` returns a Cursor object corresponding to the int cursorType. The parameter cursorType must be one of the Cursor class constants defined above.

## getName() Method

| Method | Syntax |
|--------|--------|
| `getName()` | `public String getName()` |

`getName()` returns the name of the invoking Cursor object.

## getType() Method

| Method | Syntax |
|--------|--------|
| `getType()` | `public int getType()` |

`getType()` returns the Cursor class constant corresponding to the invoking Cursor object.

## toString() method

| Method | Syntax |
|--------|--------|
| toString() | public String toString() |

toString() returns a String representation of the invoking Cursor object.

### Example: Using Cursor

In this example, a Button object is created and placed on a Frame. The cursor associated with the Button object is changed so that whenever the mouse pointer is over the Button object a crosshair cursor appears.

*The WinClosing class is used to terminate the program if the window is closed. See Section 7.3.8 on page 657 for more details.*

```
import java.awt.*;
import java.awt.event.*;

public class TestCursor extends Frame {
  Button b1;

  public TestCursor() {

    // A Button is created.  The cursor that appears when the mouse
    // is over the Button is changed using the setCursor() method

    b1 = new Button("Fire");
    b1.setCursor(Cursor.getPredefinedCursor(Cursor.CROSSHAIR_CURSOR));

    setLayout(new FlowLayout());
    add(b1);

    addWindowListener(new WinClosing());
    setBounds(100, 100, 200, 120);
    setVisible(true);
  }
    public static void main(String args[]) {
    TestCursor tc = new TestCursor();
    }
}

// The WinClosing class terminates the program when the window is closed

class WinClosing extends WindowAdapter {
  public void windowClosing(WindowEvent we) {
    System.exit(0);
  }
}
```

### Output

Here's the result:

# 6.7.3 Dimension Class

```
public class Dimension extends Dimension2D implements Serializable
```

```
Object
  Dimension2D
    Dimension
```

### Interfaces

```
Cloneable, Serializable
```

A Dimension object encapsulates a width and a height in a single object in pixels. Dimension objects are the return types or arguments of several Component and Container class methods.

## Dimension() Constructor

| Constructor | Syntax |
|---|---|
| Dimension() | public Dimension() |
| | public Dimension(int *width*, int *height*) |
| | public Dimension(Dimension *dim*) |

Creates a Dimension object. The Dimension object can be initialized with a width and height or with another Dimension object.

## Dimension Class Variables

| Class Variable |
|---|
| public int width |
| public int height |

These variables contain the values of the width and height contained by the associated Dimension object.

6

java.awt

## equals() Method

| Method | Syntax |
|---|---|
| equals() | public boolean equals(Object *obj*) |

equals() returns true if the Object obj is a Dimension object and has the same width and height values as the invoking Dimension object.

## hashCode() Method

| Method | Syntax |
|---|---|
| hashCode() | public int hashCode() |

hashCode() returns a hashcode for the invoking Dimension object.

## Methods to Return the Width and Height

| Method | Syntax |
|---|---|
| getHeight() | public double getHeight() |
| getWidth() | public double getWidth() |

getHeight() and getWidth() return the width and height contained by the invoking Dimension object.

## toString() method

| Method | Syntax |
|---|---|
| toString() | public String toString() |

toString() returns a String representation of the height and width fields of the invoking Dimension object.

### Example: Using Dimension

In this example, the Component class method getSize() returns the size of the invoking component as a Dimension object.

*The WinClosing class is used to terminate the program if the window is closed. See Section 7.3.8 on page 657 for more details.*

```
import java.awt.*;
import java.awt.event.*;
```

```
public class TestDim extends Frame {
  Button b1;

  public TestDim() {
    b1 = new Button("Fire");

    setLayout(new FlowLayout());
    add(b1);

    addWindowListener(new WinClosing());
    setBounds(100, 100, 200, 120);
    setVisible(true);

    Dimension d = b1.getSize();
    System.out.println("The width of b1 is " + d.getWidth()
                  + "  The height of b1 is " + d.getHeight());
  }

  public static void main(String args[]) {
    TestDim td = new TestDim();
  }
}

// The WinClosing class terminates the program when the window is closed

class WinClosing extends WindowAdapter {
  public void windowClosing(WindowEvent we) {
    System.exit(0);
  }
}
```

The width and height of the component can be accessed throught the
getWidth() and getHeight() methods of the Dimension class.

### Output

The result should look like this:

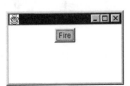

The output written to the command prompt is:

```
The width of b1 is 35  The height of b1 is 23
```

# 6.7.4 Font Class

public class **Font** extends Object implements Serializable

```
Object
  Font
```

### Interfaces

Serializable

A Font object represents a font type. A Font object is specified by its name, style, and size.

## Font() Constructor

| Constructor | Syntax |
|---|---|
| Font() | public **Font**(String *name*, int *style*, int *size*) |

Creates a Font object. The size is the font size in points. The style is either:

| Font Style Constants |
|---|
| Font.BOLD |
| Font.PLAIN |
| Font.ITALIC |
| Font.BOLD \| Font.ITALIC |

## Determining Available Fonts

To determine which fonts are available on a given system, use the getAvailableFontFamilyNames() method from the GraphicsEnvironment Class. This method returns a String array containing all the available Fonts.

### Example: Determining Available Fonts

This example uses the getAvailableFontFamilyNames() method of the GraphicsEnvironment Class, and prints the available fonts on the local machine at the command prompt.

```
import java.awt.*;
import java.awt.event.*;

public class GetFonts extends Frame {
  public static void main(String args[]) {

    // A GraphicsEnvironment object is created using a static method
    // from the GraphicsEnvironment class
```

```
GraphicsEnvironment ge =
  GraphicsEnvironment.getLocalGraphicsEnvironment();

// The GraphicsEnvironment object is used to access the available
// fonts on the local system.

String[] fontNames = ge.getAvailableFontFamilyNames();

for (int i = 0; i < fontNames.length; ++i) {
  System.out.println("font " + i + ": " + fontNames[i]);
}
  }
}
```

*Output*

```
font 0: Abadi MT Condensed
font 1: Abadi MT Condensed Extra Bold
font 2: Abadi MT Condensed Light
font 3: Algerian
font 4: American Uncial
font 5: Andy
font 6: Arial
```

*Long output follows.*

## equals() Method

| Method | Syntax |
| --- | --- |
| equals() | public boolean equals(Object *obj*) |

equals() returns true if the Object obj is a Font object and that is the same as the invoking Font object.

## getFont() Method

| Method | Syntax |
| --- | --- |
| getFont() | public static Font getFont(String *name*) |
|  | public static Font getFont(String *name*, Font *defaultFont*) |

getFont() returns the Font object corresponding to name. The second version provides a default Font object in case there is no Font corresponding to the String name. These are static methods that can be called without using a Font object.

## hashCode() Method

| Method | Syntax |
|--------|--------|
| hashCode() | public int hashCode() |

hashCode() returns a hashcode for the invoking Font object.

## Font Property Methods

| Method | Syntax |
|--------|--------|
| getName() | public String getName() |
| getStyle() | public int getStyle() |
| getSize() | public int getSize() |
| isPlain() | public boolean isPlain() |
| isBold() | public boolean isBold() |
| isItalic() | public boolean isItalic() |

getName() returns the name of the invoking Font object.

getStyle() returns an int representing the style of the invoking Font object. The int will be one of the Font style constants described at the top of this section.

getSize() method returns the size of the invoking Font object.

isPlain(), isBold(), and isItalic() methods return true if the style of the invoking Font object is plain, bold, or italic.

## toString() method

| Method | Syntax |
|--------|--------|
| toString() | public String toString() |

toString() returns a String representation of the invoking Font object.

### Example: Using Font

In this example, a String using SansSerif font is placed on a Frame.

*The WinClosing class is used to terminate the program if the window is closed. See Section 7.3.8 on page 657 for more details.*

```
import java.awt.*;
import java.awt.event.*;
```

```
public class TestFont extends Frame {
  public TestFont() {

    // The setFont() method is used to change the font
    // displayed by the Frame

    setFont(new Font("SansSerif", Font.BOLD, 14));

    addWindowListener(new WinClosing());
    setBounds(100, 100, 300, 120);
    setVisible(true);
  }

  // The paint method draws a String on the Frame

  public void paint(Graphics g) {
    g.drawString("This is " + getFont().getName() + " font", 50, 50);
  }

  public static void main(String args[]) {
    TestFont tf = new TestFont();
    tf.repaint();
  }
}

// The WinClosing class terminates the program when the window is closed

class WinClosing extends WindowAdapter {
  public void windowClosing(WindowEvent we) {
    System.exit(0);
  }
}
```

*}*

**Output**

Here's the result:

# 6.7.5 Graphics Class

```
public abstract class Graphics extends Object
```

```
Object
  Graphics
```

The Graphics class provides access to various graphics devices, drawing on the screen, displaying images, etc.

Because it is an abstract class, a Graphics object is never created directly. A Graphics object is always available to the paint() and update() methods when they are overridden. This Graphics object is then used to call the graphical methods.

The Graphics class contains a large number of methods. Two of the most important ones are discussed here.

## drawString() Method

| Method | Syntax |
|---|---|
| drawString() | public abstract void drawString(String s, int x, int y) |

drawString() writes a String object on the screen beginning at x, y.

### Example: Using drawString()

See the *Using Font* example on page 560, where the drawString() method is used to draw a String on a Frame.

## drawImage() Method

| Method | Syntax |
|---|---|
| drawImage() | public abstract boolean drawImage(Image *img*, int *x*, int *y*, ImageObserver *io*) |
| | public abstract boolean drawImage(Image *img*, int *x*, int *y*, Color *backgroundColor*, ImageObserver *io*) |
| | public abstract boolean drawImage(Image *img*, int *x*, int *y*, int *width*, int *height*, ImageObserver *io*) |
| | public abstract boolean drawImage(Image *img*, int *x*, int *y*, int *width*, int height, Color *backgroundColor*, ImageObserver *io*) |

drawImage() draws an image to the screen starting at position (x, y). This method returns immediately even if the image hasn't finished being drawn yet.

A Color object can be provided to specify the color that is copied to transparent pixels in the original image.

If a width and height are specified, the image will be scaled to those dimensions.

The ImageObserver object monitors the loading of the image. The "this" reference is almost always used for the ImageObserver object.

# 6.7.6 Image Class

```
public abstract class Image extends Object
```

```
Object
    Image
```

The Image class is an abstract class that is the super-class of all classes that represent graphical images. The methods declared in this class are mostly abstract, meaning the implementation of them is left to sub-classes of the Image class.

## Insets() Constructor

| Constructor | Syntax |
|---|---|
| Image() | public Image() |

An Image object is never created but its constructor can be accessed by its sub-classes.

## flush() Method

| Method | Syntax |
|---|---|
| flush() | public abstract void flush() |

flush() disposes of all resources being used by the invoking Image object.

## getScaledInstance() Method

| Method | Syntax |
|---|---|
| getScaledInstance() | public Image getScaledInstance(int *height*, int *width*, int *flags*) |

getScaledInstance() returns a scaled version of the invoking Image object. The flags parameter determines the type of image scaling algorithm to be used. Valid choices are

- ❏ Image.SCALE_DEFAULT
- ❏ Image.SCALE_FAST
- ❏ Image.SCALE_SMOOTH
- ❏ Image.SCALE_REPLICATE
- ❏ Image.SCALE_AREA_AVERAGING

6

java.awt

## Image Property Methods

| Method | Syntax |
|---|---|
| getHeight() | public abstract int getHeight (ImageObserver *observer*) |
| getSource() | public abstract ImageProducer getSource() |
| getWidth() | public abstract int getWidth (ImageObserver *observer*) |

getHeight() returns the height of the invoking Insets object in pixels. The ImageObserver observer is the object waiting for the Image to be loaded, usually a Container.

getSource() returns the object that produces the pixels for the image.

getHeight() returns the width of the invoking Insets object in pixels. The ImageObserver observer is the object waiting for the Image to be loaded, usually a Container.

### Example: Using Image

See the *Creating a Slideshow Using a MediaTracker* example on page 570, where the getImage() method from the Applet class returns an Image object.

# 6.7.7 Insets Class

public class Insets extends Object implements Serializable, Cloneable

```
Object
    Insets
```

### Interfaces

Cloneable, Serializable

An Inset object provides a way to implement margins for a Container object. Any child components are placed within the inner area specified by the Insets. All Container objects automatically have an Inset object associated with them. To provide a different Insets object from the default, override the Container class method getInsets() to return an Insets object with the desired margins.

# Insets() Constructor

| Constructor | Syntax |
|---|---|
| Insets() | public Insets(int *top*, int *left*, int *bottom*, int *right*) |

Insets object constructor. The arguments are the margins in pixels along each of the four edges.

# Insets Class Variables

| Class Variable |
|---|
| public int bottom |
| public int left |
| public int right |
| public int top |

These int variables contain the size in pixels of the bottom, left, right, and top margins.

# clone() Method

| Method | Syntax |
|---|---|
| clone() | public Object clone() |

clone() returns a copy of the invoking Insets object.

# equals() Method

| Method | Syntax |
|---|---|
| equals() | public boolean equals(Object *obj*) |

equals() returns true if the Object obj is an Insets object and has the bottom, left, right, and top values as the invoking Insets object.

# hashCode() Method

| Method | Syntax |
|---|---|
| hashCode() | public int hashCode() |

hashCode() returns a hashcode for the invoking Insets object.

## toString() method

| Method | Syntax |
|--------|--------|
| toString() | `public String toString()` |

toString() returns a String representation of the invoking Insets object.

### Example: Using Insets

In this example, a Button object is created and placed on a Frame. The getInsets() is overridden to provide a margin around the Frame.

*The WinClosing class is used to terminate the program if the window is closed. See Section 7.3.8 on page 657 for more details.*

```
import java.awt.*;
import java.awt.event.*;

public class TestInsets extends Frame {
  public TestInsets() {

    // A Button object is added to a Frame

    setLayout(new FlowLayout());
    add(new Button("button"));

    addWindowListener(new WinClosing());
    setBounds(100, 100, 200, 120);
    setVisible(true);
  }
  // The getInsets() method is overridden to return a
  // user-defined Insets object.  This centers the
  // Button in the frame.  If default Insets object, that has
  // zero margins on all four edges, is used, the Button is
  // placed at the top of the Frame.

  public Insets getInsets() {
    return new Insets(30, 50, 30, 50);
  }

  public static void main(String args[]) {
    TestInsets ti = new TestInsets();
  }
}

// The WinClosing class terminates the program when the window is closed
```

```
class WinClosing extends WindowAdapter {
public void windowClosing(WindowEvent we) {
  System.exit(0);
 }
}
```

The default Insets object has zero margins on all four sides. If the getInsets()
method is not overridden, the Button is placed at the top of the Frame. Overridding
the getInsets() method is used to center the Button in the Frame.

### Output

Here's the result:

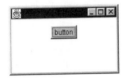

## 6.7.8 MediaTracker Class

```
public class MediaTracker extends Object implements Serializable
```

```
Object
  MediaTracker
```

### Interfaces

```
Serializable
```

A MediaTracker object is used to monitor the status of an arbitrary number of loading
images.

## MediaTracker() Constructor

| Constructor | Syntax |
| --- | --- |
| MediaTracker() | public MediaTracker(Component comp) |

Creates a MediaTracker object. The Component comp is the component the images are
being loaded into, usually a Container.

## MediaTracker Status Constants

| Constant |
| --- |
| public static final int ABORTED |
| public static final int COMPLETED |

java.awt

6

| Constant |
|---|
| public static final int ERRORED |
| public static final int LOADING |

These constants are used to indicate the status of a loading process.

## addImage() Method

| Method | Syntax |
|---|---|
| addImage() | public void addImage(Image *img*, int *imageID*) |
| | public void addImage(Image *img*, int *imageID*, int *width*, int *height*) |

addImage() adds an Image object to the invoking MediaTracker object's list of images to track. The imageID parameter is used to identify an individual Image object from the group. If a width and height are specified, the Image object will be scaled to fit those dimensions. Multiple Image objects can be grouped together by giving them the same imageID tag.

## Error Methods

| Method | Syntax |
|---|---|
| getErrorsAny() | public synchronized Object[] getErrorsAny() |
| getErrorsID() | public synchronized Object[] getErrorsID (int *imageID*) |
| isErrorAny() | public synchronized boolean isErrorAny() |
| isErrorID() | public synchronized boolean isErrorID(int *imageID*) |

isErrorAny() returns true if any of the Image objects associated with the invoking MediaTracker object experienced an error while loading.

isErrorID() returns true if any of the Image objects associated with imageID tag experienced an error while loading.

getErrorsAny() returns any of the Image objects that experienced an error while loading.

getErrorsID() returns any of the Image objects associated with the imageID tag that experienced an error while loading.

# removeImage() Method

| Method | Syntax |
|---|---|
| removeImage() | public void removeImage(Image *img*) |
| | public void removeImage(Image *img*, int *imageID*) |
| | public void removeImage(Image *img*, int *imageID*, int *width*, int *height*) |

removeImage() removes an Image object from the group of Image objects the invoking MediaTracker object is tracking. An imageID, and width and height parameters can be used to further identify the image to be removed.

## Status Methods

| Method | Syntax |
|---|---|
| checkAll() | public boolean checkAll() |
| | public boolean checkAll(boolean *startLoading*) |
| checkID() | public boolean checkID(int *imageID*) |
| | public boolean checkID(int *imageID*, boolean *startLoading*) |
| statusAll() | public int statusAll(boolean *startLoading*) |
| statusID() | public int statusID(int *imageID*, boolean *startLoading*) |

checkAll() returns true if all of the images monitored by the invoking MediaTracker object have finished loading.

checkID() returns true if the images associated with the imageID tag have finished loading.

statusAll() returns a MediaTracker status constant for the current state of all of the Images associated with the invoking MediaTracker object.

statusID() returns a MediaTracker status constant reflecting the status of the images associated with the imageID tag.

If startLoading is set to be true, any image that has not started loading will start.

## Waiting Methods

| Method | Syntax |
|---|---|
| waitForAll() | public void waitForAll() throws InterruptedException |
| | public boolean waitForAll(long *millisecondTimeLimit*) throws InterruptedException |

| Method | Syntax |
|---|---|
| waitForID() | public void **waitForID**(int *imageID*)<br>    throws InterruptedException |
| | public boolean **waitForID**(int *imageID*,<br>    long *millisecondTimeLimit*)<br>    throws InterruptedException |

waitForAll() stops the current thread from continuing until all of the Image objects monitored by the invoking MediaTracker object have finished loading. The second version returns true if all of the images were successfully loaded.

waitForID() stops the current Thread from continuing until the Image designated by imageID finishes loading. The second version returns true if all of the images were successfully loaded.

If a time limit parameter is given, the Thread will be blocked until the loading is finished or until the specified time limit has passed.

## Example: Creating a Slideshow Using a MediaTracker

This program creates a slideshow applet. Four pictures are loaded using a MediaTracker object to monitor the loading progress.

This example works better when viewed using Netscape Navigator than it does with Internet Explorer.

```
import java.awt.*;
import java.awt.event.*;
import java.applet.*;

public class SlideShow extends Applet implements ActionListener {
  int numImages = 4;
  Button startButton;
  boolean display;
  MediaTracker mt;
  Image[] img = new Image[4];
  String[] imageNames = {
    "Flowfield.jpg", "straw.jpg", "carousel.jpg", "gardening.jpg"
  };

  public void init() {
    display = false;
    startButton = new Button("start");
    startButton.addActionListener(this);
    add(startButton);

    // A MediaTracker object is used to load the four images.
    // The waitForAll() method blocks other activity until the images
    // have finished loading
```

```
    mt = new MediaTracker(this);
    for (int i = 0; i < numImages; ++i) {
      img[i] = getImage(getCodeBase(), imageNames[i]);
      mt.addImage(img[i], i);
    }
    try {
      mt.waitForAll();
    } catch (InterruptedException ie) {}
}

// If the display flag is set to true, this method displays
// each of the four methods for three seconds

public void paint(Graphics g) {
  if (display) {
    for (int i = 0; i < numImages; ++i) {
      g.drawImage(img[i], 100, 200, this);
      try {
        Thread.sleep(3000);
      } catch (InterruptedException ie) {}
    }
  }
  display = false;
}

// When the "start" Button is pressed, this method is called.
// The display flag is set to true, and the slideshow is begun

public void actionPerformed(ActionEvent ae) {
  display = true;
  repaint();
}
}
```

The waitForAll() method suspends other activities until all of the images are loaded. When the start button is clicked, the paint() method is called and each picture is displayed for three seconds. It was desired to only start the slideshow when the start button is clicked, but the paint() method is always called when the applet begins execution. To avoid this, the boolean flag display is used to only display the pictures if the start button is clicked.

The HTML code that was used to run the SlideShow.class code was

```
<HTML>
<HEAD><TITLE> Hello World </TITLE>
</HEAD><BODY>
<APPLET CODE="SlideShow.class" WIDTH=500 HEIGHT=500>
</APPLET>
</BODY>
</HTML>
```

**571**

**Output**

Here's the result:

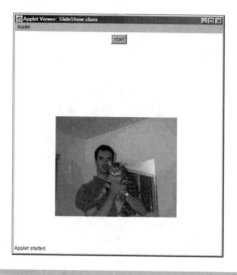

# 6.7.9 Point Class

`public class `**`Point`**` extends Point2D implements Serializable`

```
Object
    Point2D
        Point
```

### Interfaces

`Cloneable, Serializable`

A `Point` object encapsulates an x- and y-coordinate into a single object. A `Point` object is the return type or the argument for several `Component` class methods.

## Point() Constructor

| Constructor | Syntax |
|---|---|
| Point() | `public `**`Point`**`()` |
| | `public `**`Point`**`(int x, int y)` |
| | `public `**`Point`**`(Point p)` |

Creates a `Point` object . The `Point` object can be given an initial x and y values or it can take these values from another `Point` object passed to the constructor.

## Class Variables

| Class Variable |
| --- |
| public int x |
| public int y |

These variables are the *x* and *y* values encapsulated by the Point object.

## getX() method

| Method | Syntax |
| --- | --- |
| getX() | public double getX() |

getX() returns the *x* value of the invoking Point object. Note that this method returns a double whereas the class variable and constructor argument is an int.

## getY() method

| Method | Syntax |
| --- | --- |
| getY() | public double getY() |

getX() returns the *y* value of the invoking Point object. Note that this method returns a double whereas the class variable and constructor argument is an int.

# 6.7.10 Robot Class

    public class Robot extends Object

        Object
          Robot

The Robot class was introduced in Java 2 version 1.3. It is used to generate mouse and keyboard input events automatically for the purposes of automatic testing, self-running demos, and other applications that require automated control of the mouse and keyboard.

Generating an event using the Robot class is different from posting an event to the standard event queue in that the Robot class will simulate the action that caused the event. In other words, the mouse will be pressed when the mousePressed() method is called.

Some platforms will not allow the low-level input control used by the Robot class. If a platform does not allow this input control, an AWTEvent object will be thrown by the Robot constructor.

## Robot() Constructor

| Constructor | Syntax |
|---|---|
| Robot() | public Robot() throws AWTException |
| | public Robot(GraphicsDevice *screen*) throws AWTException |

Creates a Robot object. The no-argument version creates a Robot object in the coordinate system of the primary screen. A GraphicsDevice can be provided to specify an alternative graphics device to the primary screen.

## createScreenCapture() method

| Method | Syntax |
|---|---|
| createScreenCapture() | public BufferedImage createScreenCapture (Rectangle *rect*) |

createScreenCapture() creates an image containing pixels read from the screen. The Rectangle object specifies the area to be read from.

## Delay Methods

| Method | Syntax |
|---|---|
| delay() | public void delay(int *milliseconds*) |
| getAutoDelay() | public int getAutoDelay() |
| setAutoDelay() | public void setAutoDelay(int *milliseconds*) |

delay() sleeps for the specified amount of time. The argument passed to this method must be an int between 0 and 60,000.

getAutoDelay() returns the number of milliseconds the invoking Robot object will sleep after generating an event.

setAutoDelay() sets the number of milliseconds the invoking Robot object will sleep after generating an event. The argument passed to this method must be an int between 0 and 60,000.

## Idle Methods

| Method | Syntax |
|---|---|
| isAutoWaitForIdle() | public boolean isAutoWaitForIdle() |
| setAutoWaitForIdle() | public int setAutoWaitForIdle(boolean *idle*) |
| waitForIdle() | public void waitForIdle() |

`isAutoWaitForIdle()` returns true if the invoking Robot object will invoke the `waitForIdle()` method after generating an event.

`setAutoWaitForIdle()`specifies if the invoking Robot object will invoke the `waitForIdle()` method after generating an event.

`waitForIdle()` waits until all events currently on the event have been processed.

## Keyboard Event Methods

| Method | Syntax |
| --- | --- |
| keyPress() | public void **keyPress**(int *keyCode*) |
| keyRelease() | public void **keyRelease**(int *keyCode*) |

`keyPress()` presses the key associated with the specified *keyCode*. The keycodes are defined in the KeyEvent class. An example of a keycode syntax is VK_A.

`keyRelease()` releases the key associated with the specified *keyCode*.

## Mouse Event Methods

| Method | Syntax |
| --- | --- |
| mouseMove() | public void **mouseMove**(int *x*, int *y*) |
| mousePress() | public void **mousePress**(int *mouseButton*)<br>        throws IllegalArgumentException |
| mouseRelease() | public void **mouseRelease**(int *mouseButton*)<br>        throws IllegalArgumentException |

`mouseMove()` moves the mouse to the specified x and y location.

`mousePress()` presses the specified mouse. The argument must be one of the following masks

❑   InputEvent.BUTTON1_MASK

❑   InputEvent.BUTTON2_MASK

❑   InputEvent.BUTTON3_MASK

`mouseRelease()` releases the specified mouse.

## toString() method

| Method | Syntax |
| --- | --- |
| toString() | public String **toString**() |

`toString()` returns a `String` representation of the invoking `Robot` object.

## Example: Using A Robot to Generate Mouse Events

In this example, a `Robot` object is used to move the mouse around a `Frame`. The `Robot` object is set to delay for 1 second after each mouse move. A `TextField` is used to indicate the current position of the mouse.

*The `WinClosing` class is used to terminate the program if the window is closed. See Section 7.3.8 on page 657 for more details.*

```java
import java.awt.*;
import java.awt.event.*;

public class TestRobot extends Frame {
    TextField tf;
    Robot robbie;

    public TestRobot() {
        tf = new TextField(20);
        tf.setEditable(false);

        // A Robot object is created.  It is set to wait for 1 second
        // after generating an event

        robbie = new Robot();
        robbie.setAutoDelay(1000);

        addMouseMotionListener(new MouseHandler());

        add(tf, BorderLayout.SOUTH);

        addWindowListener(new WinClosing());
        setBounds(100, 100, 300, 300);
        setVisible(true);

        // After the Frame is made visible, the Robot object starts moving
        // the mouse.

        robbie.moveMouse(20, 20);
        robbie.moveMouse(200, 20);
        robbie.moveMouse(200, 200);
    }
    class MouseHandler extends MouseMotionAdapter {
        public void mouseMoved(MouseEvent me) {
            tf.setText("Mouse Moved to position " + me.getX() + ","
                    + me.getY());
        }
    }
}
```

```
    public static void main(String args[]) {
      TestRobot tr = new TestRobot();
    }
  }

// The WinClosing class terminates the program when the window is closed

class WinClosing extends WindowAdapter {
  public void windowClosing(WindowEvent we) {
    System.exit(0);
  }
}
```

### Output

The result should look like this:

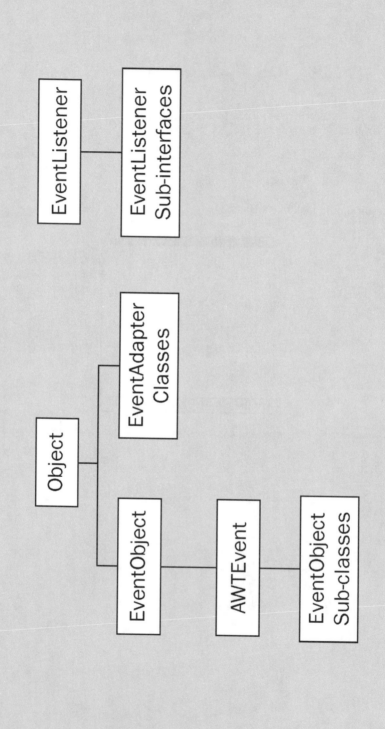

# java.awt.event

The containers and GUI components defined in the java.awt and javax.swing packages are all very nice to look at, but they don't become useful unless there is some mechanism to detect when the container or GUI component has been interacted with. The java.awt.event package defines many of the classes and interfaces that provide this functionality.

When a container or GUI component is interacted with, the container or component generates, or **fires**, an Event object. If an EventListener object is associated the container or GUI component, the appropriate method defined by the EventListener is then called to respond to the event.

For instance, an object that implements the ActionListener interface can be registered with a Button object. When the Button object is clicked, an ActionEvent object is generated and sent to the actionPerformed() method of the ActionListener object. Inside the actionPerformed() method is the code that is to be executed if the Button object is clicked.

A GUI component or container can generate many different types of Event objects. If desired some or all of the Event objects can be ignored. For instance, a Button object can generate MouseEvent objects when the mouse is moved over the Button and ActionEvent and MouseEvents if the Button is clicked. If the MouseEvent objects are irrelevant for the current application, they may simply be ignored.

The EventListener interfaces define the signatures of the methods that are called when a particular type of event is generated by an associated container or GUI component. Some of the listener interfaces provide multiple methods to handle different types of events within the same interface.

A class that implements a multiple-method listener interface must implement every method declared by the interface, and this can be inconvenient if the programmer has no intention of using some of the methods. The java.awt.event package therefore provides **adapter classes** for the multiple-method interfaces. These adapter classes implement the corresponding interface and provide stubs (methods with empty bodies) for each method declared by the interface. Only the methods that are to be used then need to be overridden within the user-defined listener class. Adapter classes are sometimes implemented as an inner class that extends the adapter class.

This chapter covers:

# 7.1 Event Classes

The `java.awt.event` package event class hierarchy is shown in the following figure. All of the event classes defined in the `java.awt.event` package are sub-classes of the abstract class `AWTEvent`, which is contained in the `java.awt` package. (See Section 6.4.1 on page 502.)

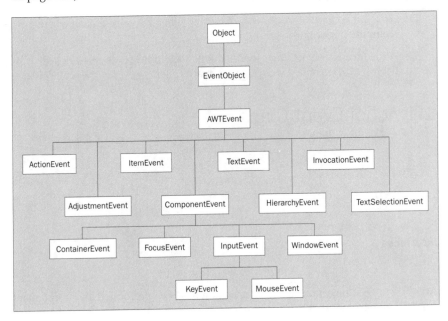

- ❏ `ActionEvent` objects are generated when a button is clicked, a list or menu item is selected, or the _Return_ key is pressed with a text field or `JPasswordField`.

- ❏ `AdjustmentEvent` objects are created by an object that implements the `Adjustable` interface, a `Scrollbar` or `ScrollPane`, when the slider is moved.

- ❏ `ComponentEvent` objects are generated when a component is moved, resized, hidden, or made visible.

- ❏ `ContainerEvent` objects are created when a component is added to or removed from a container.

- ❏ `FocusEvent` objects are fired when a component gains or loses focus.

- ❏ `HierarchyEvent` objects are generated by a `Container` when a change is made to its component hierarchy.

- ❏ `InputEvent` is the super-class of the `KeyEvent` and `MouseEvent` classes.

- ❏ `InvocationEvent` objects can be used to execute the `run()` method of an object that implements the `Runnable` interface.

- ❏ ItemEvent objects are generated when an item is selected.

- ❏ KeyEvent objects are fired when a key is pressed and/or released.

- ❏ MouseEvent objects are created when the mouse is moved, clicked, or dragged.

- ❏ TextEvent objects are generated when the contents of a TextField or TextArea object have been modified.

- ❏ TextSelectionEvent objects are created when the selected text of a text component changes.

- ❏ WindowEvent objects are generated when a window is opened, closed, iconified, deiconified, activated, or deactivated.

# 7.1.1 ActionEvent Class

```
public class ActionEvent extends AWTEvent
```

```
Object
  EventObject
    AWTEvent
      ActionEvent
```

### Interfaces

```
Serializable
```

An ActionEvent object signifies that an action has been performed on a component. An ActionEvent object is generated when:

- ❏ a button is pushed

- ❏ a list item is double-clicked

- ❏ a menu item is selected

- ❏ the *Return* key is pressed in a text or password field.

Every ActionEvent object has an action command associated with it. The action command is a String that is used to identify the action. The action command can be obtained using the getActionCommnand() method.

## ActionEvent() Constructors

| Constructor | Syntax |
|---|---|
| ActionEvent() | public ActionEvent(Object *source*, int *id*, String *command*) |
| | public ActionEvent(Object *source*, int *id*, String *command*, int *modifiers*) |

ActionEvent() creates an ActionEvent object. The source is the object generating the event. The event id will normally be ACTION_PERFORMED. The String command is the action command associated with the ActionEvent source. The modifiers are the modifier keys held down during the action.

## ActionEvent Class Constants

| Constant |
| --- |
| public static final int ACTION_FIRST |
| public static final int ACTION_LAST |
| public static final int ACTION_PERFORMED |
| public static final int ALT_MASK |
| public static final int CTRL_MASK |
| public static final int META_MASK |
| public static final int SHIFT_MASK |

The ACTION_PERFORMED constant is used as an identification of the action event.

ACTION_FIRST and ACTION_LAST are the first and last number in the range of ID's used for action events.

The final four constants can be used as modifiers in the ActionEvent class constructor, to indicate that the *Alt, Ctrl, Meta* or *Shift* key was held down.

## getActionCommand() Method

| Method | Syntax |
| --- | --- |
| getActionCommand() | public String getActionCommmand() |

getActionCommnand() returns the action command of the component that generated the invoking ActionEvent object.

## getModifiers() method

| Method | Syntax |
| --- | --- |
| getModifiers() | public int getModifiers() |

getModifiers() returns the integer sum of the modifiers associated with the invoking ActionEvent object. The modifiers correspond to the modifier keys (*Alt, Ctrl, Meta, Shift*) that were held down during the event.

## paramString() method

| Method | Syntax |
| --- | --- |
| paramString() | public String paramString() |

paramString() returns a String identifying the event. This method is usually used for event-logging and de-bugging purposes.

**583**

# 7.1.2 AdjustmentEvent Class

```
public class AdjustmentEvent extends AWTEvent
```

```
Object
  EventObject
    AWTEvent
      AdjustmentEvent
```

### Interfaces

```
Serializable
```

AdjustmentEvent objects are generated by components that implement the Adjustable interface. For instance, a scrollbar will generate an AdjustmentEvent when its slider is moved.

## AdjustmentEvent() Constructor

| Constructor | Syntax |
|---|---|
| AdjustmentEvent() | public AdjustmentEvent(Adjustable *source*, int *id*, int *type*, int *value*) |

AdjustmentEvent() creates an AdjustmentEvent object. The source is the object generating the event. The event id will normally be ADJUSTMENT_VALUE_CHANGED. The type will be one of UNIT_DECREMENT, UNIT_INCREMENT, BLOCK_DECREMENT, BLOCK_INCREMENT, or TRACK. The value is usually the current value of the slider.

## AdjustmentEvent Constants

| Constant |
|---|
| public static final int ADJUSTMENT_FIRST |
| public static final int ADJUSTMENT_LAST |
| public static final int ADJUSTMENT_VALUE_CHANGED |
| public static final int BLOCK_DECREMENT |
| public static final int BLOCK_INCREMENT |
| public static final int UNIT_DECREMENT |
| public static final int UNIT_INCREMENT |
| public static final int TRACK |

ADJUSTMENT_FIRST and ADJUSTMENT_LAST are the first and last number in the range of ID's used for adjustment events.

ADJUSTMENT_VALUE_CHANGED is used as an identification of the adjustment event.

BLOCK_DECREMENT and BLOCK_INCREMENT indicate that the slider value was changed by clicking inside the scrollbar area.

UNIT_DECREMENT and UNIT_INCREMENT indicate that the slider value was changed by clicking on the down or up arrow.

TRACK indicates that the slider value was changed by dragging the slider.

## getAdjustable() Method

| Method | Syntax |
|--------|--------|
| getAdjustable() | public Adjustable getAdjustable() |

getAdjustable() returns the Adjustable object that generated the invoking AdjustmentEvent object. An Adjustable object is an object that implements the Adjustable interface.

## getAdjustmentType() Method

| Method | Syntax |
|--------|--------|
| getAdjustmentType() | public int getAdjustmentType() |

getAdjustmentType() returns one of the AdjustmentEvent constants representing the type of adjustment.

## getValue() Method

| Method | Syntax |
|--------|--------|
| getValue() | public int getValue() |

getValue() returns the current setting of the Adjustable object that generated the invoking AdjustmentEvent object.

## paramString() method

| Method | Syntax |
|--------|--------|
| paramString() | public String paramString() |

paramString() returns a String identifying the event. This method is usually used for event-logging and de-bugging purposes.

# 7.1.3 ComponentEvent Class

```
public class ComponentEvent extends AWTEvent
```

```
Object
    EventObject
        AWTEvent
            ComponentEvent
```

7

java.awt.event

# java.awt.event

### Interfaces

```
Serializable
```

A `ComponentEvent` object is generated whenever a `Component` is shown, hidden, moved or resized. This event is for notification purposes only. The Abstract Windowing Toolkit (AWT) handles component moves and resizes automatically whether these events are listened to or not.

# ComponentEvent() Constructor

| Constructor | Syntax |
| --- | --- |
| ComponentEvent() | public ComponentEvent(Component *source*, int *id*) |

`ComponentEvent()` creates a `ComponentEvent` object. The `source` is the `Component` that generated the event. The `id` is used to identify the `ComponentEvent` and will be one of the `ComponentEvent` class constants described below.

# ComponentEvent Class Constants

| Constant |
| --- |
| public static final int COMPONENT_FIRST |
| public static final int COMPONENT_LAST |
| public static final int COMPONENT_HIDDEN |
| public static final int COMPONENT_MOVED |
| public static final int COMPONENT_RESIZED |
| public static final int COMPONENT_SHOWN |

`COMPONENT_FIRST` and `COMPONENT_LAST` are the first and last number in the range of ID's used for component events.

The other constants identify various `ComponentEvent` types.

# getComponent() Method

| Method | Syntax |
| --- | --- |
| getComponent() | public Component getComponent() |

`getComponent()` returns the source of the invoking `ComponentEvent`.

# paramString() method

| Method | Syntax |
| --- | --- |
| paramString() | public String paramString() |

`paramString()` returns a `String` identifying the event. This method is usually used for event-logging and de-bugging purposes.

# 7.1.4 ContainerEvent Class

```
public class ContainerEvent extends ComponentEvent
```

```
Object
  EventObject
    AWTEvent
      ComponentEvent
        ContainerEvent
```

### Interfaces

```
Serializable
```

ContainerEvent objects are generated whenever a component is added or removed from a container. This event is for notification purposes only; the AWT handles changes to a container automatically whether these events are listened to or not.

## ContainerEvent() Constructor

| Constructor | Syntax |
|---|---|
| ContainerEvent() | public ContainerEvent(Component *source*, int *id*, Component *child*) |

ContainerEvent() creates a ContainerEvent object. The source is the Component generating the event. The id identifies the ContainerEvent and will either be COMPONENT_ADDED or COMPONENT_REMOVED. The child is the component that has been added or removed.

## ContainerEvent Class Constants

| Constant |
|---|
| public static final int COMPONENT_ADDED |
| public static final int COMPONENT_FIRST |
| public static final int COMPONENT_LAST |
| public static final int COMPONENT_REMOVED |

COMPONENT_ADDED and COMPONENT_REMOVED indicate whether the event was generated as a consequence of a component being added or removed.

COMPONENT_FIRST and COMPONENT_LAST are the first and last number in the range of ID's used for component events.

7

java.awt.event

**587**

## getChild() Method

| Method | Syntax |
|---|---|
| getChild() | public Component getChild() |

getChild() returns the Component object that caused the event, the object that was added or removed from the Container.

## getContainer() Method

| Method | Syntax |
|---|---|
| getContainer() | public Container getContainer() |

getContainer() returns the Container object that generated the ContainerEvent.

## paramString() method

| Method | Syntax |
|---|---|
| paramString() | public String paramString() |

paramString() returns a String identifying the event. This method is usually used for event-logging and de-bugging purposes.

# 7.1.5 FocusEvent Class

public class FocusEvent extends ComponentEvent

```
Object
  EventObject
    AWTEvent
      ComponentEvent
        FocusEvent
```

### Interfaces
Serializable

A FocusEvent is generated when a component gains or loses focus.

## FocusEvent() Constructors

| Constructor | Syntax |
|---|---|
| FocusEvent() | public FocusEvent(Component *source*, int *id*, boolean *temporary*) |
| | public FocusEvent(Component *source*, int *id*) |

FocusEvent() creates a FocusEvent object. The source is the Component generating the event. The id identifies the FocusEvent and will either be FOCUS_GAINED or FOCUS_LOST. The temporary parameter is set to true if this is a temporary focus change. A temporary focus change occurs if focus is temporarily gained or lost due to an operation such as a window activation or scrollbar drag. The focus returns when the operation is finished.

## FocusEvent Class Constants

| Constant |
| --- |
| public static final int FOCUS_FIRST |
| public static final int FOCUS_GAINED |
| public static final int FOCUS_LAST |
| public static final int FOCUS_LOST |

FOCUS_FIRST and FOCUS_LAST are the first and last number in the range of ID's used for focus events.

FOCUS_GAINED and FOCUS_LOST indicate whether the event was generated as a consequence of a gain or loss of focus.

## isTemporary() Method

| Method | Syntax |
| --- | --- |
| isTemporary() | public boolean isTemporary() |

isTemporary() returns true if the invoking FocusEvent object represents a temporary change of focus.

## paramString() method

| Method | Syntax |
| --- | --- |
| paramString() | public String paramString() |

paramString() returns a String identifying the event. This method is usually used for event-logging and de-bugging purposes.

# 7.1.6 HierarchyEvent Class

```
public class HierarchyEvent extends AWTEvent
```

```
Object
   EventObject
      AWTEvent
         HierarchyEvent
```

### Interfaces

Serializable

A HierarchyEvent is generated by a Container when a change is made to its component hierarchy, adding or removing an ancestor component, moving or resizing an ancestor component, making its hierarchy visible or invisible. This event is for notification purposes only. The AWT handles changes to a hierarchy automatically whether these events are listened to or not.

## HierarchyEvent() Constructors

| Constructor | Syntax |
|---|---|
| HeirarchyEvent() | public **HierarchyEvent**(Component *source*, int *id*, Component *componentTop*, Component *changedParent*) |
| | public **HierarchyEvent**(Component *source*, int *id*, Component *componentTop*, Component *changedParent*, long *changeFlags*) |

HeirarchyEvent() creates a HierarchyEvent object. The source is the Component generating the event. The id identifies the HierarchyEvent and will be one of the HierarchyEvent class constants described below. The componentTop is the component at the top of the hierarchy. The changedParent is the parent of the changed component. The changeFlags is a bitmask representing the type or types of hierarchy events.

## HierarchyEvent Class Constants

| Constant |
|---|
| public static final int ANCESTOR_MOVED |
| public static final int ANCESTOR_RESIZED |
| public static final int DISPLAYABILITY_CHANGED |
| public static final int HIERARCHY_CHANGED |
| public static final int HIERARCHY_FIRST |
| public static final int HIERARCHY_LAST |
| public static final int PARENT_CHANGED |
| public static final int SHOWING_CHANGED |

HIERARCHY_FIRST and HIERARCHY_LAST are the first and last number in the range of ID's used for hierarchy events.

The other constants indicate the type of hierarchy event.

## getChanged() Method

| Method | Syntax |
|--------|--------|
| getChanged() | public Component getChanged() |

getChanged() returns the Component that was changed.

## getChangedFlags() Method

| Method | Syntax |
|--------|--------|
| getChangedFlags() | public long getChangedFlags() |

getChangedFlags() returns a bitmask representing the type or types of hierarchy events.

## getChangedParent() Method

| Method | Syntax |
|--------|--------|
| getChangedParent() | public Container getChangedParent() |

getChangedParent() returns the parent of the Component that was changed.

## getComponent() Method

| Method | Syntax |
|--------|--------|
| getComponent() | public Component getComponent() |

getComponent() returns the source of the invoking HierarchyEvent

## paramString() method

| Method | Syntax |
|--------|--------|
| paramString() | public String paramString() |

paramString() returns a String identifying the event. This method is usually used for event-logging and de-bugging purposes.

# 7.1.7 InputEvent Class

```
public abstract class InputEvent extends ComponentEvent
```

```
Object
  EventObject
    AWTEvent
      ComponentEvent
        InputEvent
```

### Interfaces

```
Serializable
```

InputEvent is the parent class for keyboard and mouse event classes. Because it is an abstract class, an InputEvent object is never created.

## InputEvent Class Constants

| Constant |
| --- |
| public static final int ALT_GRAPH_MASK |
| public static final int ALT_MASK |
| public static final int CTRL_MASK |
| public static final int META_MASK |
| public static final int SHIFT_MASK |
| public static final int BUTTON1_MASK |
| public static final int BUTTON2_MASK |
| public static final int BUTTON3_MASK |

These contants are used to indicate which keyboard or mouse button has been pressed.

## Methods that Check if Keys are Pressed

| Method | Syntax |
| --- | --- |
| isAltDown() | public boolean isAltDown() |
| isAltGraphDown() | public boolean isAltGraphDown() |
| isControlDown() | public boolean isControlDown() |
| isMetaDown() | public boolean isMetaDown() |
| isShiftDown() | public boolean isShiftDown() |

isAltDown(), isAltGraphDown(), isControlDown(), isMetaDown(), and isShiftDown() return true if the *Alt, Alt-Graph, Ctrl, Meta,* or *Shift* keys were pressed.

## consume() method

| Method | Syntax |
| --- | --- |
| consume() | public void consume() |

consume() is used to indicate to any listeners that the invoking InputEvent object has been handled and may be ignored.

## getModifiers() method

| Method | Syntax |
| --- | --- |
| getModifiers() | public int getModifiers() |

getModifiers() returns the modifiers associated with the invoking InputEvent subclass object. The modifiers are any modifier keys that are pressed when the event occurs.

## getWhen() method

| Method | Syntax |
|--------|--------|
| getWhen() | public long getWhen() |

getWhen() returns the time in milliseconds that the InputEvent object was generated. This can be converted into a more readable date using a Date object.

## isConsumed() method

| Method | Syntax |
|--------|--------|
| isConsumed() | public boolean isConsumed() |

isConsumed() returns true if the invoking InputEvent object has been marked as being consumed meaning it may be ignored by any registered listeners.

# 7.1.8 InvocationEvent Class

```
public class InvocationEvent extends AWTEvent implements ActiveEvent
```

```
Object
    EventObject
        AWTEvent
            InvocationEvent
```

### Interfaces
```
ActiveEvent, Serializable
```

An InvocationEvent can be used to execute the run() method of an object that implements the Runnable interface.

## InvocationEvent() Constructors

| Constructor | Syntax |
|-------------|--------|
| InvocationEvent() | public InvocationEvent(Object *source*, Runnable *runnable)* |
| | public InvocationEvent(Object *source*, Runnable *runnable*, Object *notifier*, boolean *catchExceptions)* |

InvocationEvent() creates an InvocationEvent object. The source is the Component generating the event. The Runnable object is the whose run() method is called when the event is dispatched. If a notifier object is specified, that object will call its

7

java.awt.event

notifyAll() method after the run() method returns. If catchExceptions is true, the dispatch() method will catch any exceptions that occur during the execution of the run() method.

## dispatch() method

| Method | Syntax |
|--------|--------|
| dispatch() | public void dispatch() |

dispatch() calls the Runnable object's run() method and, if specified, notifies the notifier object once the run() method returns.

## getException() method

| Method | Syntax |
|--------|--------|
| getException() | public Exception getException() |

getException() returns any exception caught during the execution of the run() method.

## paramString() method

| Method | Syntax |
|--------|--------|
| paramString() | public String paramString() |

paramString() returns a String identifying the event. This method is usually used for event-logging and de-bugging purposes.

### Example: Using an InvocationEvent

In this example, an InvocationEvent object is used to call the run() method of the Blah class.

```
import java.awt.event.*;

public class TestInvoc {
  TestInvoc() {
    InvocationEvent ie = new InvocationEvent(this, new Blah());
    ie.dispatch();
  }

  public static void main(String args[]) {
    TestInvoc ti = new TestInvoc();
  }
}
```

```
class Blah implements Runnable {
  public void run() {
    System.out.println("Blah");
  }
}
```

**Output**

```
Blah
```

# 7.1.9 ItemEvent Class

```
public class ItemEvent extends AWTEvent
```

```
Object
  EventObject
    AWTEvent
      ItemEvent
```

### Interfaces

```
Serializable
```

ItemEvent objects are generated by components that implement the ItemSelectable interface. Actions that can generate an ItemEvent are:

❏ selecting an element from a Choice or JComboBox component

❏ selecting or de-selecting a Checkbox, JCheckBox, JRadioButton, or JToggleButton

❏ single-clicking a List item

❏ toggling a CheckboxMenuItem, JCheckBoxMenuItem, or JRadioButtonMenuItem on or off.

## ItemEvent() Constructor

| Constructor | Syntax |
|---|---|
| ItemEvent() | public ItemEvent(ItemSelectable *source*, int *id*, Object *item*, int *state*) |

ItemEvent() creates an ItemEvent object. The source is the object that generated the event. The id is used to identify the ItemEvent object and will generally be ITEM_STATE_CHANGED. The item represents the text of the item that was selected. The state is generally either ItemEvent.SELECTED or ItemEvent.DESELECTED.

## ItemEvent Class Constants

| Constant |
| --- |
| public static final int ITEM_FIRST |
| public static final int ITEM_LAST |
| public static final int ITEM_STATE_CHANGED |
| public static final int SELECTED |
| public static final int DESELECTED |

ITEM_FIRST and ITEM_LAST are the first and last number in the range of ID's used for item events.

ITEM_STATE_CHANGED identifies the Event as an ItemEvent.

SELECTED and DESELECTED indicate whether the item that generated the event is selected or deselected.

## getItem() Method

| Method | Syntax |
| --- | --- |
| getItem() | public Object getItem() |

getItem() returns the selected item from the object that generated the ItemEvent. Usually a String is returned.

## getItemSelectable() Method

| Method | Syntax |
| --- | --- |
| getItemSelectable() | public ItemSelectable getItemSelectable() |

getItemSelectable() returns the ItemSelectable object that generated the invoking ItemEvent object.

## getStateChange() Method

| Method | Syntax |
| --- | --- |
| getStateChange() | public int getStateChange() |

getStateChange() returns the state of the item that generated the ItemEvent, either ItemEvent.SELECTED or ItemEvent.DESELECTED.

## paramString() method

| Method | Syntax |
| --- | --- |
| paramString() | public String paramString() |

paramString() returns a String identifying the event. This method is usually used for event-logging and de-bugging purposes.

# 7.1.10 KeyEvent Class

```
public class KeyEvent extends InputEvent
```

```
Object
    EventObject
      AWTEvent
        ComponentEvent
          InputEvent
            KeyEvent
```

### Interfaces

```
Serializable
```

A KeyEvent is generated when the user types on the keyboard.

## KeyEvent() Constructor

| Constructor | Syntax |
|---|---|
| KeyEvent() | public KeyEvent(Component *source*, int *id*, long *when*, int *modifiers*, int *keyCode*) |
| | public KeyEvent(Component *source*, int *id*, long *when*, int *modifiers*, int *keyCode*, int *keyChar* |

KeyEvent() creates an KeyEvent object. The source is the object that generated the event. The id is used to identify the KeyEvent object and will be one of the KeyEvent class constants described below. The when represents the time that the event occurred. A Date object can be used to convert the long into a recognizable time. The modifiers represent any modifier keys that were pressed when the event was generated. The keyCode is one of the keyboard constants described below. The keyChar is the Unicode character generated by this event.

## KeyEvent Class Constants

| Constant |
|---|
| public static final int KEY_FIRST |
| public static final int KEY_LAST |
| public static final int KEY_PRESSED |
| public static final int KEY_RELEASED |
| public static final int KEY_TYPED |

KEY_FIRST and KEY_LAST are the first and last number in the range of ID's used for key events.

The other constants identify the type of KeyEvent. KEY_TYPED is a combination of a key press followed by a key release.

java.awt.event

**7**

## KeyEvent Class Keyboard Constants

The keyboard constants are used to represent the keys on a keyboard. They are all `public static final int`.

| Type | Constants |
|------|-----------|
| letters | `VK_A - VK_Z` |
| numbers | `VK_0 - VK_9` |
| keypad numbers | `VK_NUMPAD0 - VK_NUMPAD9` |
| modifiers | `VK_SHIFT, VK_ALT, VK_CTRL, VK_META` |
| actions | `VK ENTER, VK BACK SPACE, VK TAB, VK_CANCEL, VK_CLEAR, VK_CAPS_LOCK, VK_SPACE, VK_ESCAPE, VK_DELETE, VK_PAGE_UP, VK_PAGE_DOWN, VK_NUM_LOCK, VK_SCROLL_LOCK, VK_PRINTSCREEN, VK_INSERT` |
| punctuation | `VK COMMA, VK PERIOD, VK SLASH, VK SEMICOLON, VK BACK SLASH, VK COLON, VK_QUOTE, VK_BACKQUOTE` |
| math | `VK EQUALS, VK MULTIPLY, VK ADD, VK_SUBTRACT, VK_DECIMAL, VK_DIVIDE` |
| miscellaneous | `VK END, VK HOME, VK LEFT, VK RIGHT, VK UP, VK DOWN, VK SEPARATER, VK HELP, VK_OPEN_BRACKET, VK_CLOSE_BRACKET` |

## getKeyChar() Method

| Method | Syntax |
|--------|--------|
| **getKeyChar()** | **public char getKeyChar()** |

`getKeyChar()` returns the Unicode character of the key that generated the `KeyEvent`.

## getKeyCode() Method

| Method | Syntax |
|--------|--------|
| getKeyCode() | `public int getKeyCode()` |

`getKeyCode()` returns the virtual keycode of the key that generated the `KeyEvent`.

## getKeyModifiersText() Method

| Method | Syntax |
|--------|--------|
| getKeyModifiersText() | `public static String getKeyModifiersText(int modifiers)` |

`getKeyModifiersText()` returns a `String` describing the specified modifier keys.

## getKeyText() Method

| Method | Syntax |
|---|---|
| getKeyText() | public static String getKeyText(int *keyCode*) |

getKeyText() returns a String representation of a given keycode. The keycodes are the keyboard constants described above.

## isActionKey() Method

| Method | Syntax |
|---|---|
| isActionKey() | public boolean isActionKey() |

isActionKey() determines if the KeyEvent was generated by an action key (arrow, keypad, or function).

## setKeyChar() Method

| Method | Syntax |
|---|---|
| setKeyChar() | public void setKeyChar(char *keyChar*) |

setKeyChar() changes the keyChar value for the KeyEvent. The keyChar is the Unicode character of the key that generated the KeyEvent.

## setKeyCode() Method

| Method | Syntax |
|---|---|
| setKeyCode() | public void setKeyCode(int *keyCode*) |

setKeyCode() changes the keycode for the KeyEvent.

## setKeyModifiers() Method

| Method | Syntax |
|---|---|
| setKeyModifiers() | public void setKeyModifiers(int *modifiers*) |

setKeyModifiers() changes the modifier keys associated with the KeyEvent.

## paramString() method

| Method | Syntax |
|---|---|
| paramString() | public String paramString() |

paramString() returns a String identifying the event. This method is usually used for event-logging and de-bugging purposes.

7

java.awt.event

# 7.1.11 MouseEvent Class

```
public class MouseEvent extends InputEvent
```

```
Object
   EventObject
      AWTEvent
         ComponentEvent
            InputEvent
               MouseEvent
```

### Interfaces

```
Serializable
```

MouseEvent objects are generated when the user moves or clicks the mouse.

## MouseEvent() Constructor

| Constructor | Syntax |
|---|---|
| MouseEvent() | public MouseEvent(Component *source*, int *id*, long *time*, int *modifiers*, int *x*, int *y*, int *clickCount*, boolean *isPopupTrigger*) |

MouseEvent object constructor. The source is the component that generated the MouseEvent object. The id identifies the MouseEvent and will be one of the MouseEvent class constants described below. The time represents the time the MouseEvent ocurred. The x and y parameters represent the mouse location relative to the origin of source. The clickCount is the number of consecutive times the mouse was clicked. The isPopupTrigger is true if the MouseEvent object will make any PopupMenu items associated with the Component source visible.

## MouseEvent Class Constants

| Constant |
|---|
| public static final int MOUSE_CLICKED |
| public static final int MOUSE_DRAGGED |
| public static final int MOUSE_ENTERED |
| public static final int MOUSE_EXITED |
| public static final int MOUSE_FIRST |
| public static final int MOUSE_LAST |
| public static final int MOUSE_MOVED |
| public static final int MOUSE_PRESSED |
| public static final int MOUSE_RELEASED |

MOUSE_FIRST and MOUSE_LAST are the first and last number in the range of ID's used for mouse events.

The other constants identify the type of MouseEvent. They are for the most part self-explanatory.

A MOUSE_ENTERED event is generated when the mouse cursor enters the space occupied by a component.

A MOUSE_EXITED event is generated when the mouse cursor leaves the space occupied by a component.

## getClickCount() Method

| Method | Syntax |
|---|---|
| getClickCount() | public int getClickCount() |

getClickCount() retrieves the number of mouse clicks associated with the invoking MouseEvent object.

## isPopupTrigger() Method

| Method | Syntax |
|---|---|
| isPopupTrigger() | public boolean isPopupTrigger() |

isPopupTrigger() returns true if the invoking invoking MouseEvent object is the popup menu trigger. Each platform designates a MouseEvent as the popup menu trigger. When this event occurs, it indicates that the popup menu should be displayed.

## Location Methods

| Method | Syntax |
|---|---|
| getPoint() | public Point getPoint() |
| getX() | public int getX() |
| getY() | public int getY() |
| translatePoint() | public void translatePoint(int x, int y) |

getPoint(), getX(), and getY() return the location of the Event relative to its source.

translatePoint() moves the location of the event to a new position by adding the specified x and y values to the current location.

## paramString() method

| Method | Syntax |
|---|---|
| paramString() | public String paramString() |

paramString() returns a String identifying the event. This method is usually used for event-logging and de-bugging purposes.

7

java.awt.event

# 7.1.12 TextEvent Class

```
public class TextEvent extends AWTEvent
```

```
Object
  EventObject
    AWTEvent
      TextEvent
```

### Interfaces
```
Serializable
```

`TextEvent` objects are generated by text components (`TextField`, `TextArea`, `JTextField`, `JTextArea`, `JPasswordField`) when their contents change.

## TextEvent() Constructor

| Constructor | Syntax |
|---|---|
| TextEvent() | public TextEvent(Object *source*, int *id*) |

`TextEvent()` creates a `TextEvent` object. The source is the `TextComponent` object that generated the event. The `id` identifies the `TextEvent` object and will generally be `TEXT_VALUE_CHANGED`.

## TextEvent Class Constants

| Constant |
|---|
| public static final int TEXT_FIRST |
| public static final int TEXT_LAST |
| public static final int TEXT_VALUE_CHANGED |

`TEXT_FIRST` and `TEXT_LAST` are the first and last number in the range of ID's used for text events.

`TEXT_VALUE_CHANGED` is the ID for a `TextEvent`.

## paramString() method

| Method | Syntax |
|---|---|
| paramString() | public String paramString() |

`paramString()` returns a `String` identifying the event. This method is usually used for event-logging and de-bugging purposes.

# 7.1.13 TextSelectionEvent Class

```
public class TextSelectionEvent extends AWTEvent
```

```
Object
  EventObject
    AWTEvent
      TextSelectionEvent
```

### Interfaces
```
Serializable
```

TextSelectionEvent objects are generated by text components (TextField, TextArea, JTextField, JTextArea, JPasswordField) when their selected text changes.

## TextSelectionEvent() Constructor

| Constructor | Syntax |
|---|---|
| TextSelectionEvent() | public TextSelectionEvent(Object *source*, int *id*, int *startIndex*, int *endIndex*) |

TextSelectionEvent() creates a TextSelectionEvent object. The source is the object that generated the event. The id identifies the TextSelectionEvent object and will generally be TEXT_SELECTION_CHANGED. The parameters startIndex and endIndex represent the extent of the selected text.

## TextSelectionEvent Class Constants

| Constant |
|---|
| public static final int TEXT_SELECTION_CHANGED |
| public static final int TEXT_SELECTION_FIRST |
| public static final int TEXT_SELECTION_LAST |

TEXT_SELECTION_FIRST and TEXT_SELECTION_LAST are the first and last number in the range of ID's used for text selection events.

TEXT_SELECTION_CHANGED is the ID for a TextSelectionEvent.

## getEnd() method

| Method | Syntax |
|---|---|
| getEnd() | public int getEnd() |

getEnd() returns the index of the end of the selected text.

java.awt.event

7

**603**

## getStart() method

| Method | Syntax |
|---|---|
| getStart() | public int getStart() |

getStart() returns the index of the start of the selected text.

## paramString() method

| Method | Syntax |
|---|---|
| paramString() | public String paramString() |

paramString() returns a String identifying the event. This method is usually used for event-logging and de-bugging purposes.

# 7.1.14 WindowEvent Class

```
public class WindowEvent extends ComponentEvent
```

```
Object
    EventObject
      AWTEvent
        ComponentEvent
          WindowEvent
```

### Interfaces

```
Serializable
```

A WindowEvent is generated when a window is opened, closed, iconified, deiconified, activated, or deactivated.

## WindowEvent() Constructor

| Constructor | Syntax |
|---|---|
| WindowEvent() | public WindowEvent(Object source, int id) |

WindowEvent() creates a WindowEvent object. The source is the Window object that generated the WindowEvent object. The id identifies the WindowEvent object and will be one of the WindowEvent class constants described below.

## WindowEvent Class Constants

| Constant |
| --- |
| public static final int WINDOW_ICONIFIED |
| public static final int WINDOW_DEICONIFIED |
| public static final int WINDOW_OPENED |
| public static final int WINDOW_CLOSING |
| public static final int WINDOW_CLOSED |
| public static final int WINDOW_ACTIVATED |
| public static final int WINDOW_DEACTIVATED |
| public static final int WINDOW_FIRST |
| public static final int WINDOW_LAST |

WINDOW_FIRST and WINDOW_LAST are the first and last number in the range of ID's used for window events.

The other constants identify the type of WindowEvent. A window that is activated is one that has been brought to the front. A window that is closing is in the process of being closed. A window that is closed is already closed.

## getWindow() Method

| Method | Syntax |
| --- | --- |
| getWindow() | public Window getWindow() |

getWindow() returns the Window object that generated the invoking WindowEvent object.

## paramString() method

| Method | Syntax |
| --- | --- |
| paramString() | public String paramString() |

paramString() returns a String identifying the event. This method is usually used for event-logging and de-bugging purposes.

7

java.awt.event

# 7.2 Listener Interfaces

Listener interfaces provide the methods to receive and process events. Some interfaces only have one method; others have multiple methods. The multiple method interfaces usually have an adapter class associated with them. An adapter class provides stubs (methods with empty bodies) for the interface methods; this prevents the user from having to overwrite methods that aren't needed.

There are three ways to implement a listener interface. The Component or Container class itself may implement the interface, the interface may be implemented in a separate class, or it may be implemented in an inner class.

❑   If the Component or Container class implements the listener interface, then the corresponding listener interface methods are implemented within the class. All event objects generated by Components that have registered with the listener will be sent to the corresponding listener interface method. For instance, ActionEvent objects generated by registered Button, MenuItem, and TextField objects will all be sent to the actionPerformed() method defined within the class. Logic must be built into the actionPerformed() method to determine which object generated the event.

❑   If the listener interface is implemented by a separate class, the resulting code is highly portable. A separate listener object can be provided for each component, or for a group of components of the same type. This helps reduce the amount of logic required in the listener interface method implementations. The disadvantage of this method is that the private data members of the Component or Container class are not readily accessible by the listener class object.

❑   If the listener interface is implemented as an inner class, a separate listener object can be provided for each component, or for a group of components of the same type, and the private data members of the Component or Container class are available to the listener class.

The java.awt.event package listener interface hierarchy is shown in the following figure. All of the Listener interfaces defined in the java.awt.event package extend the EventListener interface defined in the java.util package.

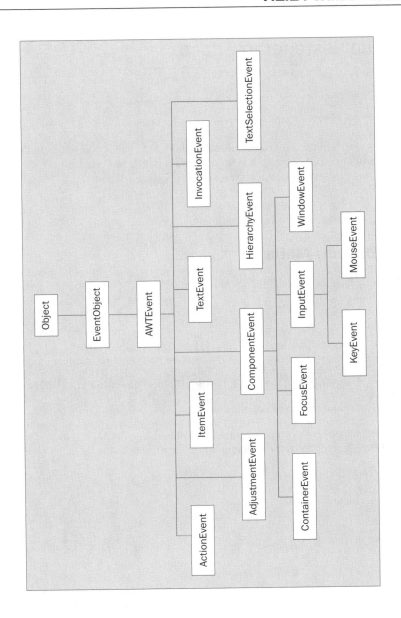

java.awt.event

7

# 7.2.1 ActionListener Interface

```
public interface ActionListener extends EventListener
```

```
EventListener
    ActionListener
```

The ActionListener interface contains one method, actionPerformed(), that is called when an ActionEvent object is fired. Because it only has one method, the ActionListener interface does not have a corresponding adaptor class.

For an ActionListener to be registered with a Component, the Component's addActionListener() method must be called.

## actionPerformed() Method

| Method | Syntax |
|---|---|
| actionPerformed() | public void actionPerformed(ActionEvent ae) |

actionPerformed() is called when an ActionEvent object is generated. The ActionEvent object can be used to determine the source of the event.

### Example: Having a Container implement the ActionListener Interface

In this example, a Button object is created and placed in a Frame. It is intended that when the Button is clicked, the program would terminate.

```
import java.awt.*;
import java.awt.event.*;

public class TestAction extends Frame implements ActionListener {
  Button quitButton;

  public TestAction() {
    quitButton = new Button("quit");
    quitButton.addActionListener(this);  // registers quitButton with an
                                          // ActionListener
    Panel p = new Panel();
    p.add(quitButton);

    add(p);

    setBounds(100, 100, 200, 200);
    setVisible(true);
  }
```

```
  public void actionPerformed(ActionEvent ae) {
    if (ae.getActionCommand().equals("quit")) {
      System.exit(0);
    }
  }

  public static void main(String args[]) {
    TestAction ta = new TestAction();
  }
}
```

An `ActionListener` is associated with the `Button` object. Because the `Frame` itself implements the `ActionListener` interface, the argument passed to the `addActionListener()` method is `this`, meaning the `Frame` object. When the `Button` is clicked, an `ActionEvent` is generated and sent to the `actionPerformed()` method. The program tests to see if the action command of the object that generated the event was `quit`. If it is, the program is terminated.

In this case, the `TestAction` class itself acts as the `ActionListener`. It implements the `ActionListener` interface and provides the `actionPerformed()` method within the class.

### Output

The user interface of the program is shown below. When the quit button is clicked, the `ActionListener` (the `TestAction` object) will terminate.

## Example: Implementing an ActionListener Using an Inner Class

In this more complicated example, two Button objects and a TextField object are placed in a Frame. Each of the components can generate an ActionEvent object. If the Frame implements ActionListener, logic will have to be built in to the actionPerformed() method to determine if a Button or TextField generated the event. To avoid this, the Button and TextField objects are given separate ActionListeners contained in two inner classes.

```java
import java.awt.*;
import java.awt.event.*;

public class TestAction2 extends Frame {
  Button enableButton, disableButton;
  TextField tf;

  public TestAction2() {
    enableButton = new Button("enable");
    enableButton.addActionListener(new ButtonHandler());

    disableButton = new Button("disable");
    disableButton.addActionListener(new ButtonHandler());

    tf = new TextField(20);
    tf.addActionListener(new TextFieldHandler());

    Panel p = new Panel();
    p.add(tf);
    p.add(enableButton);
    p.add(disableButton);

    add(p);

    addWindowListener(new WinClosing());
    setBounds(100, 100, 200, 200);
    setVisible(true);
  }

  // This ActionListener handles ActionEvents generated by the Buttons

  class ButtonHandler implements ActionListener {
    public void actionPerformed(ActionEvent ae) {
      if (ae.getActionCommand().equals("enable")) {
        tf.setEnabled(true);
    }
```

```
      if (ae.getActionCommand().equals("disable")) {
           tf.setEnabled(false);
        }
      }
    }

    // This ActionListener handles ActionEvents generated by the TextField

    class TextFieldHandler implements ActionListener {
      public void actionPerformed(ActionEvent ae) {
        System.out.println("Text is :" + tf.getText());
      }
    }

    public static void main(String args[]) {
      TestAction2 ta = new TestAction2();
    }
  }

  class WinClosing extends WindowAdapter {
    public void windowClosing(WindowEvent we) {
      System.exit(0);
    }
  }
```

If the **enable** Button is clicked, the actionPerformed() method of the
ButtonHandler class is called and the TextField is enabled. If the **disable** Button is
clicked, the actionPerformed() method of the ButtonHandler class is called and the
TextField is disabled. If the *Return* key is pressed while the mouse is over the
TextField, the actionPerformed() method of the TextFieldHandler class is called
and the contents of the TextField are printed to standard output.

The use of inner classes is beneficial if a lot of different components are generating a
certain type of event. The logic that needs to built-in to a single listener interface
method to differentiate between a large number of components capable of firing a
given event can become quite cumbersome. Inner classes can be used to divide the
components up into more manageable groups.

*The WinClosing() class is used to terminate the program if the window is
closed; see Section 7.3.8 on page 657 for more details.*

7

java.awt.event

> **Output**
>
> The user interface of the program is shown below. The **disable** button has been clicked, causing the ActionListener (the TextFieldHandler object) to disable the TextField.
>
>

# 7.2.2 AdjustmentListener Interface

```
public interface AdjustmentListener extends EventListener
```

```
EventListener
   AdjustmentListener
```

The AdjustmentListener interface contains one method that is called when an AdjustmentEvent is generated. Because it only has one method, the AdjustmentListener interface does not have an adapter class.

For a component to register itself with an AdjustmentListener, it must call the addAdjustmentListener() method.

## adjustmentValueChanged() Method

| Method | Syntax |
|---|---|
| adjustmentValueChanged() | public void adjustmentValueChanged (AdjustmentEvent *ae*) |

adjustmentValueChanged() is called when an AdjustmentEvent object is generated. The AdjustmentEvent object can be used to obtain information about the object that generated the event.

**612**

## Example: Using AdjustmentListener

In this example, Scrollbar, TextField, and Label objects are placed in a Frame. The Scrollbar object is associated with an AdjustmentListener. Because the Frame implements the AdjustmentListener interface, the this argument, meaning the Frame, is passed to the addAdjustmentListener() method. When the Scrollbar slider is moved, the TextField is changed to display the new slider value in the adjustmentValueChanged() method. In the default implementation of the Scrollbar object, the minimum value is at the top of the Scrollbar.

*The WinClosing object terminates the program when the window is closed; see Section 7.3.8 on page 657 for more details.*

```
import java.awt.*;
import java.awt.event.*;

public class TestAL extends Frame implements AdjustmentListener {
  TextField tf;
  Scrollbar s;
  Label lbl;

  public TestAL() {
    tf = new TextField("1", 3);
    tf.setEditable(false);
    lbl = new Label("Current value:");

    s = new Scrollbar(Scrollbar.VERTICAL, 1, 1, 1, 100);
    s.addAdjustmentListener(this); // registers the Scrollbar with
                                   //  an AdjustmentListener
    Panel p = new Panel();
    p.add(lbl);
    p.add(tf);
    p.add(s);

    add(p);

    addWindowListener(new WinClosing());
    setBounds(100, 100, 300, 200);
    setVisible(true);
  }
```

java.awt.event

7

```
      public void adjustmentValueChanged(AdjustmentEvent ae) {
        tf.setText("" + ae.getValue());
        invalidate();
      }

      public static void main(String args[]) {
        TestAL al = new TestAL();
      }
    }

class WinClosing extends WindowAdapter {
  public void windowClosing(WindowEvent we) {
    System.exit(0);
  }
}
```

### Output

The user interface of the program is shown below. The Scrollbar has been dragged, causing the AdjustmentListener (the TestAL object) to set the value shown in the TextField to 7.

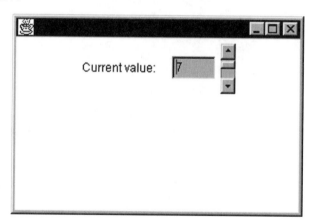

## 7.2.3 AWTEventListener Interface

```
public interface AWTEventListener extends EventListener
```

```
EventListener
  AWTEventListener
```

The AWTEventListener interface is used to passively monitor events that are dispatched in the AWT.

## eventDispatched() Method

| Method | Syntax |
|---|---|
| eventDispatched() | public void eventDispatched(AWTEvent *ae*) |

eventDispatched() is called whenever an event is dispatched in the AWT.

# 7.2.4 ComponentListener Interface

```
public interface ComponentListener extends EventListener
```

```
EventListener
    ComponentListener
```

The ComponentListener interface contains four methods that are called whenever a registered component is hidden, moved, resized, or made visible. It has an associated adapter class, ComponentAdapter. Component events are for notification purposes only. The AWT handles component moves and resizes automatically whether these events are listened to or not.

To register a component with a ComponentListener object, the component must call the addComponentListener() method.

## componentHidden() Method

| Method | Syntax |
|---|---|
| componentHidden() | public void componentHidden(ComponentEvent *ce*) |

componentHidden() is called when a component is hidden, for example by using setVisible(false).

## componentMoved() Method

| Method | Syntax |
|---|---|
| componentMoved() | public void componentMoved(ComponentEvent *ce*) |

componentMoved() is called when a component is moved.

## componentResized() Method

| Method | Syntax |
|---|---|
| componentResized() | public void componentResized(ComponentEvent *ce*) |

componentResized() is called when a component is resized.

## componentShown() Method

| Method | Syntax |
|---|---|
| componentShown() | public void componentShown(ComponentEvent *ce*) |

componentShown() is called when a component is shown, for example by sending true to the setVisible() method.

---

### Example: Using ComponentListener

A ComponentListener is associated with a Frame. If the Frame is re-sized by the user, the componentResized() method is called to set the size back to its original dimensions and move it back to its original location. If the ComponentListener interface is implemented directly, implementations of every method defined in the ComponentListener interface must be provided even if they are written as stub (empty body) methods. This could have been avoided by using the ComponentAdapter class described in Section 7.3.1 on page 642.

*The WinClosing object terminates the program when the window is closed; see Section 7.3.8 on page 657 for more details.*

```
import java.awt.*;
import java.awt.event.*;

public class TestCompL extends Frame implements ComponentListener {
    Label lbl;

    public TestCompL() {
        lbl = new Label("Jackson and Zachary");

        Panel p = new Panel();
        p.add(lbl);

        add(p);

        addComponentListener(this);   // the Frame is registered with a
                                      // ComponentListener

        addWindowListener(new WinClosing());
        setBounds(100, 100, 200, 200);
        setVisible(true);
    }
```

```
  public void componentResized(ComponentEvent ce) {
    setBounds(100, 100, 200, 200);     // if an attempt is made to resize
  }                                    // the Frame, it is re-set to its
                                       // original size and location.

  public void componentHidden(ComponentEvent ce) {}
  public void componentMoved(ComponentEvent ce) {}
  public void componentShown(ComponentEvent ce) {}

  public static void main(String args[]) {
    TestCompL cl = new TestCompL();
  }
}

class WinClosing extends WindowAdapter {
  public void windowClosing(WindowEvent we) {
    System.exit(0);
  }
}
```

### Output

The user interface of the program is shown below, with the window being resized. When this is done, the ComponentListener (the TestCompL object) will change its size and location back to the original values.

# 7.2.5 ContainerListener Interface

```
public interface ContainerListener extends EventListener
```

```
EventListener
    ContainerListener
```

The ContainerListener interface contains two methods that are called whenever a component is added to or removed from a registered Container. It has an associated adapter class, ContainerAdapter. Container events are for notification purposes only. The AWT handles changes to a container automatically whether these events are listened to or not.

To register a Container with a ContainerListener object, the Container object must call the addContainerListener() method.

## componentAdded() Method

| Method | Syntax |
|---|---|
| componentAdded() | public void componentAdded(ContainerEvent ce) |

componentAdded() is called when a component is added to a registered container.

## componentRemoved() Method

| Method | Syntax |
|---|---|
| componentRemoved() | public void componentRemoved(ContainerEvent ce) |

componentRemoved() is called when a component is removed from a registered container.

### Example: Using ContainerListener

In this example, a Button object is created and placed in a Frame. The Frame object is registered with a ContainerListener. Every time the Button is clicked, a new Button object is placed on the Frame. When this happens, the componentAdded() method is called and "button added" is written to standard output. Because the Frame implements the ContainerListener interface directly, an implementation of the componentRemoved() method must be included even though in this example it is implemented as a stub (empty) method. This can be avoided by using the ContainerAdapter class described in Section 7.3.2 on page 644. The Frame must call invalidate() and validate() every time a Button is added or the new Button will not be displayed.

*The WinClosing object terminates the program when the window is closed; see Section 7.3.8 on page 657 for more details.*

```java
import java.awt.*;
import java.awt.event.*;

public class TestContL extends Frame implements ContainerListener,
        ActionListener {
  Button addButton;
  int count = 0;

  public TestContL() {
    addButton = new Button("add");
    addButton.addActionListener(this);

    setLayout(new FlowLayout());
    add(addButton);

    addContainerListener(this);  // the Frame is registered with a
                                 // ContainerListener
    addWindowListener(new WinClosing());
    setBounds(100, 100, 300, 200);
    setVisible(true);
  }

  public void actionPerformed(ActionEvent ae) {
    add(new Button("button " + count));
    ++count;
    invalidate();
    validate();
  }

  // when a Button is added to the Frame, a ContainerEvent object is
  // generated and the componentAdded() method is called

  public void componentAdded(ContainerEvent ce) {
    System.out.println("button added");
  }

  public void componentRemoved(ContainerEvent ce) {}

  public static void main(String args[]) {
    TestContL cl = new TestContL();
  }
}
```

```
class WinClosing extends WindowAdapter {
  public void windowClosing(WindowEvent we) {
    System.exit(0);
  }
}
```

### Output

The user interface of the program is shown below. The **add** button has been clicked four times, adding an extra button each time; when this is done, the ContainerListener (the TestContL object) prints a message to System.out.

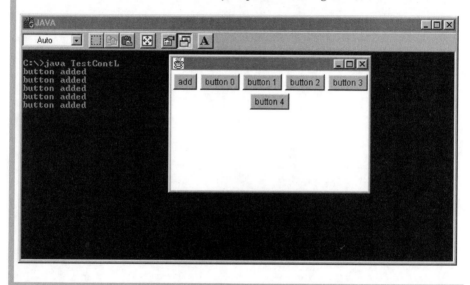

## 7.2.6 FocusListener Interface

```
public interface FocusListener extends EventListener
```

```
EventListener
  FocusListener
```

The FocusListener interface contains two methods that are called whenever a registered component gains or loses focus. It has an associated adapter class, FocusAdapter.

To register a component with a FocusListener object, the component must call the addFocusListener() method.

# focusGained() Method

| Method | Syntax |
|---|---|
| focusGained() | public void focusGained(FocusEvent *fe*) |

focusGained() is called when a registered component gains focus.

# focusLost() Method

| Method | Syntax |
|---|---|
| focusLost() | public void focusLost(FocusEvent *fe*) |

focusLost() is called when a registered component loses focus.

## Example: Using FocusListener

Two TextField objects are created and placed in a Frame. The TextField objects are registered with a FocusListener. Because the Frame implements the FocusListener interface, the this argument is passed to the addFocusListener() method. When either of the TextField objects gains or loses focus, the focusGained() or focusLost() methods are called. The getComponent() method defined in the ComponentEvent class returns the Component that generated the event.

*The WinClosing object terminates the program when the window is closed; see Section 7.3.8 on page 657 for more details.*

```
import java.awt.*;
import java.awt.event.*;

public class TestFocus extends Frame implements FocusListener {
  TextField tf1, tf2;

  public TestFocus() {
    tf1 = new TextField(10);
    tf1.setName("textfield 1");
    tf1.addFocusListener(this);   // the TextField is registered with
                                  // FocusListener
    tf2 = new TextField(10);
    tf2.setName("textfield 2");
    tf2.addFocusListener(this);

    Panel p = new Panel();
    p.add(tf1);
    p.add(tf2);
```

7

java.awt.event

**621**

```
     add(p);

     addWindowListener(new WinClosing());
     setBounds(100, 100, 300, 200);
     setVisible(true);
   }

   // focusGained() and focusLost() are the methods from the FocusListener
   // interface.  They are called when one of the TextFields gains or loses
   // focus

   public void focusGained(FocusEvent fe) {
     TextField tf = (TextField)fe.getComponent();
     System.out.println( tf.getName()+" gained focus");
   }

   public void focusLost(FocusEvent fe) {
     TextField tf = (TextField)fe.getComponent();
     System.out.println( tf.getName()+" lost focus");
   }

   public static void main(String args[]) {
     TestFocus f = new TestFocus();
   }
}

class WinClosing extends WindowAdapter {
  public void windowClosing(WindowEvent we) {
    System.exit(0);
  }
}
```

### Output

The user interface of the program is shown below. Each time a `TextField` gains or loses focus, the `FocusListener` (the `TestF` object) prints a message to `System.out`.

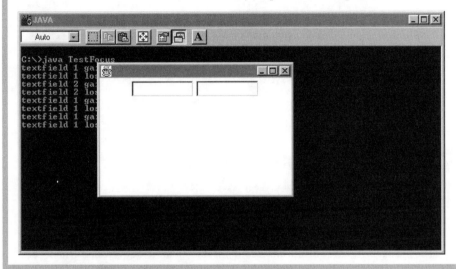

# 7.2.7 HierarchyBoundsListener Interface

```
public interface HierarchyBoundsListener extends EventListener
```

```
EventListener
    HierarchyBoundsListener
```

The `HierarchyBoundsListener` interface contains two methods that are called whenever an ancestor of the object registered with a `HierarchyBoundsListener` is moved or resized. It has an associated adapter class, `HierarchyBoundsAdapter`. `HierarchyEvent` objects are for notification purposes only. The AWT handles changes to a hierarchy automatically whether these events are listened to or not.

To register a component with a `HierarchyBoundsListener` object, the component must call the `addHierarchyBoundsListener()` method.

java.awt.event

### ancestorMoved() Method

| Method | Syntax |
|--------|--------|
| ancestorMoved() | public void ancestorMoved(HierarchyEvent *he*) |

ancestorMoved() is called when an ancestor of the event source is moved.

### ancestorResized() Method

| Method | Syntax |
|--------|--------|
| ancestorResized() | public void ancestorResized(HierarchyEvent *he*) |

ancestorResized() is called when an ancestor of the event source is resized.

## 7.2.8 HierarchyListener Interface

```
public interface HierarchyListener extends EventListener
```

```
EventListener
    HierarchyListener
```

The HierarchyListener interface contains one method that is called whenever the hierarchy of the object registered with a HierarchyListener is changed. The change might mean that an ancestor has been added or removed. HierarchyEvent objects are for notification purposes only. The AWT handles changes to a hierarchy automatically whether these events are listened to or not.

To register a component with a HierarchyListener object, the component must call the addHierarchyListener() method.

### hierarchyChanged() Method

| Method | Syntax |
|--------|--------|
| hierarchyChanged() | public void hierarchyChanged(HierarchyEvent *he*) |

hierarchyChanged() is called when the hierarchy of the event source is changed.

## 7.2.9 ItemListener Interface

```
public interface ItemListener extends EventListener
```

```
EventListener
    ItemListener
```

The ItemListener interface contains one method that is called when an ItemEvent occurs. Because it only has one method, ItemListener interface does not have an adapter class.

A component registers itself with an ItemListener by calling the addItemListener() method.

## itemStateChanged() Method

| Method | Syntax |
|---|---|
| itemStateChanged() | public void itemStateChanged(ItemEvent e) |

itemStateChanged() is called whenever an ItemEvent object is generated. The ItemEvent can be used to obtain information about the object that generated the event.

### Example: Using ItemListener

In this example, a List object is created and placed in a Frame. The List object is registered with an ItemListener to detect if one of the List elements is selected. Because the Frame implements the ItemListener interface, the this reference, meaning the Frame, is passed to the addItemListener() method. When a List element is selected, the itemStateChanged() method is called and the TextField object text is updated to reflect the selection.

*The WinClosing object terminates the program when the window is closed; see Section 7.3.8 on page 657 for more details.*

```java
import java.awt.*;
import java.awt.event.*;

public class TestIL extends Frame implements ItemListener {
  List l;
  TextField tf;

  public TestIL() {
    l = new List();
    l.add("Tokyo");
    l.add("London");
    l.add("Cairo");
    l.addItemListener(this);  // registers the List with an
                              // ItemListener
    tf = new TextField(25);
    tf.setText("None selected");
    tf.setEditable(false);

    Panel p = new Panel();
    p.add(l);
    p.add(tf);

    add(p);
```

java.awt.event

7

```
    addWindowListener(new WinClosing());
    setBounds(100, 100, 300, 200);
    setVisible(true);
  }

  // itemStateChanged() is the method declared in the ItemListener
  // interface

  public void itemStateChanged(ItemEvent ie) {
    List l = (List)ie.getItemSelectable();
    if ( l.getSelectedIndex() != -1 ) {
      tf.setText("City selected is "+l.getSelectedItem());
    } else {
      tf.setText("None selected");
    }
  }

  public static void main(String args[]) {
    TestIL il = new TestIL();
  }
}

class WinClosing extends WindowAdapter {
  public void windowClosing(WindowEvent we) {
    System.exit(0);
  }
}
```

### Output

The user interface of the program is shown below. When the item London was selected from the List, the TextField was updated accordingly by the ItemListener (the TestIL object).

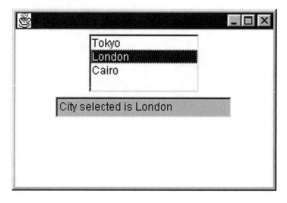

# 7.2.10 KeyListener Interface

```
public interface KeyListener extends EventListener
```

```
EventListener
    KeyListener
```

The KeyListener interface contains three methods, one of which is called whenever a KeyEvent is generated. It has an associated adapter class, KeyAdapter.

To register a component with a KeyListener object, the component must call the addKeyListener() method.

## keyPressed() Method

| Method | Syntax |
| --- | --- |
| keyPressed() | public void keyPressed(KeyEvent ke) |

keyPressed() is called when a user presses a key.

## keyReleased() Method

| Method | Syntax |
| --- | --- |
| keyReleased() | public void keyReleased(KeyEvent ke) |

keyReleased() is called when a user releases a key.

## keyTyped() Method

| Method | Syntax |
| --- | --- |
| keyTyped() | public void keyTyped(KeyEvent ke) |

keyTyped() is called when a user types (presses and releases) a key.

### Example: Using KeyListener

In this example, a Panel is created and registered with a KeyListener to process keyboard events. Because the Frame implements the KeyListener interface, the this argument, meaning the Frame, is passed to the addKeyListener() method. All of the methods from the KeyListener interface must be implemented, even if some of the methods are implemented only as stub (empty body) methods. To avoid having to implement KeyListener methods that aren't needed, the KeyAdapter class can be used. See Section 7.3.5 on page 650 for more details. Before the Panel can generate any KeyEvent objects, it must have focus. The Panel may gain focus if the mouse arrow is placed over it, or the user may have to click on the Panel.

7

java.awt.event

The *WinClosing* object terminates the program when the window is closed; see Section 7.3.8 on page 657 for more details.

```java
import java.awt.*;
import java.awt.event.*;

public class TestKey extends Frame implements KeyListener {
  Label lbl;

  public TestKey() {
    lbl = new Label("Character: ");

    Panel p = new Panel();
    p.setBackground(Color.gray);
    p.addKeyListener(this);    //  the Panel is registered with a
                               //  KeyListener
    add(p, BorderLayout.CENTER);
    add(lbl, BorderLayout.SOUTH);

    addWindowListener(new WinClosing());
    setBounds(100, 100, 200, 200);
    setVisible(true);
  }

  // when the mouse is over the Panel and a key is typed, the keyTyped()
  // method is called and the character printed in the TextField.

  public void keyTyped(KeyEvent ke) {
    lbl.setText("Character: " + ke.getKeyChar());
    invalidate();
    validate();
  }

  public void keyPressed(KeyEvent ke) {}
  public void keyReleased(KeyEvent ke) {}

  public static void main(String args[]) {
    TestKey tk = new TestKey();
  }
}
```

```
class WinClosing extends WindowAdapter {
  public void windowClosing(WindowEvent we) {
    System.exit(0);
  }
}
```

### Output

The user interface of the program is shown below. The character *s* was typed when the Panel had focus, and the KeyListener (the TestKey object) updated the Label at the bottom.

# 7.2.11 MouseListener Interface

```
public interface MouseListener extends EventListener
```

```
EventListener
  MouseListener
```

The MouseListener interface contains five methods that are called whenever a non-motion oriented MouseEvent is generated. There is an associated adapter class, MouseAdapter.

To register a MouseListener for a Component, the Component must call the addMouseListener() method.

## mouseEntered() Method

| Method | Syntax |
|---|---|
| mouseEntered() | public void mouseEntered(MouseEvent *me*) |

mouseEntered() is called whenever the mouse first enters the bounding area of the component.

## mouseExited() Method

| Method | Syntax |
|---|---|
| mouseExited() | public void **mouseExited**(MouseEvent *me*) |

mouseExited() is called whenever the mouse leaves the bounding area of the component.

## mousePressed() Method

| Method | Syntax |
|---|---|
| mousePressed() | public void **mousePressed**(MouseEvent *me*) |

mousePressed() is called each time the mouse button is pressed within the component's space.

## mouseReleased() Method

| Method | Syntax |
|---|---|
| mouseReleased() | public void **mouseReleased**(MouseEvent *me*) |

mouseReleased() is called whenever the mouse is released.

## mouseClicked() Method

| Method | Syntax |
|---|---|
| mouseClicked() | public void **mouseClicked**(MouseEvent *me*) |

mouseClicked() is called whenever the mouse is clicked.

### Example: Using MouseListener

Two Button objects are created and placed in a Frame. The Button objects are registered with a MouseListener to process mouse events. Because the Frame implements the MouseListener interface, the this argument, meaning the Frame, is passed to the addMouseListener() method. All of the methods from the MouseListener interface must be implemented, even if some of the methods are implemented only as stub (empty body) methods. To avoid having to implement MouseListener methods that aren't needed, the MouseAdapter class can be used. See Section 7.3.6 on page 652 for more details. Whenever the mouse pointer enters or leaves the space occupied by one of the Button objects, the text of the TextField object is updated to report this fact.

*The WinClosing object terminates the program when the window is closed; see Section 7.3.8 on page 657 for more details.*

```
import java.awt.*;
import java.awt.event.*;

public class TestML extends Frame implements MouseListener {
  Button b1, b2;
  TextField tf;

  public TestML() {
    tf = new TextField(27);
    tf.setEditable(false);

    b1 = new Button("Button 1");
    b1.setName("Button 1");
    b1.addMouseListener(this);  // the Button is registered with a
                                // MouseListener
    b2 = new Button("Button 2");
    b2.setName("Button 2");
    b2.addMouseListener(this);

    Panel p1 = new Panel();
    p1.add(b1);
    p1.add(b2);

    Panel p2 = new Panel();
    p2.add(tf);

    setLayout(new BorderLayout());
    add(p1, BorderLayout.NORTH);
    add(p2, BorderLayout.SOUTH);

    addWindowListener(new WinClosing());
    setBounds(100, 100, 300, 200);
    setVisible(true);
  }

// whenever the mouse enters or exits the display space of one of
// Buttons, a MouseEvent is generated and sent to either the
// mouseEntered() or MouseExited() methods.

  public void mouseEntered(MouseEvent me) {
    tf.setText("mouse is over "+me.getComponent().getName());
  }
```

7

java.awt.event

```
      public void mouseExited(MouseEvent me) {
        tf.setText("mouse is no longer over "+ me.getComponent().getName());
      }

    public void mousePressed(MouseEvent me) {}
    public void mouseReleased(MouseEvent me) {}
    public void mouseClicked(MouseEvent me) {}

    public static void main(String args[]) {
      TestML tml = new TestML();
    }
  }

  class WinClosing extends WindowAdapter {
    public void windowClosing(WindowEvent we) {
      System.exit(0);
    }
  }
```

### Output

The user interface of the program is shown below. The MouseListener (the TestML object) has updated the TextField to show that the mouse is over **Button 2**.

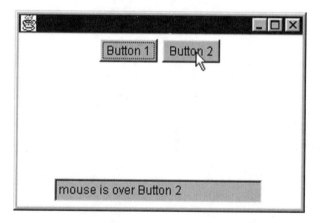

## 7.2.12 MouseMotionListener Interface

```
public interface MouseMotionListener extends EventListener
```

```
    EventListener
      MouseMotionListener
```

The MouseMotionListener interface contains two methods that are called when a motion-oriented MouseEvent object is generated. There is also an associated adapter class, MouseMotionAdapter.

To register a Component with a MouseMotionListener, the Component must call the addMouseMotionListener() method.

## mouseMoved() Method

| Method | Syntax |
|---|---|
| mouseMoved() | public void mouseMoved(MouseEvent me) |

mouseMoved() is called every time the mouse is moved within the bounding area of the component and no mouse button is pressed.

## mouseDragged() Method

| Method | Syntax |
|---|---|
| mouseDragged() | public void mouseDragged(MouseEvent me) |

mouseDragged() is called every time the mouse is moved within the bounding area of the component while a mouse button is pressed.

### Example: Using MouseMotionListener

In this example, a Panel is created and registered with a MouseMotionListener to process motion-oriented mouse events. Because the Frame implements the MouseMotionListener interface, the this argument, meaning the Frame, is passed to the addMouseMotionListener() method. All of the methods from the MouseMotionListener interface must be implemented, even if some of the methods are implemented only as stub (empty body) methods. To avoid having to implement MouseMotionListener methods that aren't needed, the MouseMotionAdapter class can be used. See Section 7.3.7 on page 654 for more details. When the mouse pointer is moved or dragged across the Panel, the TextField text is updated to reflect this fact and the mouse's new location.

The WinClosing object terminates the program when the window is closed; see Section 7.3.8 on page 657 for more details.

```
import java.awt.*;
import java.awt.event.*;

public class TestMML extends Frame implements MouseMotionListener {
    TextField tf;

    public TestMML() {
```

java.awt.event

7

```
      tf = new TextField(20);
      tf.setEditable(false);

      Panel p = new Panel();
      p.setBackground(Color.gray);
      p.addMouseMotionListener(this);   // registers the Panel with a
                                        // MouseMotionListener
      add(p, BorderLayout.CENTER);
      add(tf, BorderLayout.SOUTH);

      addWindowListener(new WinClosing());
      setBounds(100, 100, 300, 300);
      setVisible(true);
   }

   // whenever the mouse is moved or dragged over the display area of the
   // Panel, a MouseEvent is generated and sent to either the mouseMoved()
   // or mouseDragged() method.  The methods print out whether the mouse was
   // moved or dragged and the current position of the mouse.

   public void mouseMoved(MouseEvent me) {
      tf.setText("Mouse Moved to position "+me.getX()+","+me.getY());
   }

   public void mouseDragged(MouseEvent me) {
      tf.setText("Mouse Dragged to position "+me.getX()+","+me.getY());
   }

   public static void main(String args[]) {
      TestMML mml = new TestMML();
   }
}

class WinClosing extends WindowAdapter {
   public void windowClosing(WindowEvent we) {
      System.exit(0);
   }
}
```

### Output

The user interface of the program is shown below. The mouse is being dragged over the `Panel`, and the `MouseMotionListener` (the `TestMML` object) has updated the `TextField` at the bottom accordingly.

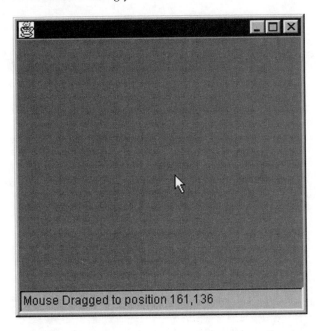

Mouse Dragged to position 161,136

# 7.2.13 TextListener Interface

```
public interface TextListener extends EventListener
```

```
EventListener
   TextListener
```

The `TextListener` interface contains one method that is called whenever a `TextEvent` is generated. `TextEvent` objects are generated by text components when their contents change. Because it only has one method, `TextListener` interface does not have an adapter class.

A component registers itself with an `TextListener` by calling the `addTextListener()` method.

## textValueChanged() Method

| Method | Syntax |
|---|---|
| textValueChanged() | public void textValueChanged(TextEvent *te*) |

textValueChanged() is called whenever a TextEvent is generated.

### Example: Using TextListener

In this example, a TextField object is created and placed at the top of a Frame. The TextField object is registered with a TextListener. Because the Frame implements the TextListener interface, the this argument, meaning the Frame, is passed to the addTextListener() method. Whenever the text inside the TextField at the top of the Frame is changed, the textValueChanged() method is called and the text inside the TextField at the bottom of the Frame is updated to reflect this fact. The getSource() method from the EventObject class returns the source of the TextEvent.

*The WinClosing object terminates the program when the window is closed; see Section 7.3.8 on page 657 for more details.*

```java
import java.awt.*;
import java.awt.event.*;

public class TestTL extends Frame implements TextListener {
  TextField tf, tf2;

  public TestTL() {
    tf = new TextField(20);
    tf.addTextListener(this);  // registers the TextField with a
                               // TextListener
    tf2 = new TextField(20);
    tf2.setText("Text is now: ");
    tf2.setEditable(false);

    Panel p = new Panel();
    p.add(tf);

    add(p, BorderLayout.CENTER);
    add(tf2, BorderLayout.SOUTH);

    addWindowListener(new WinClosing());
    setBounds(100, 100, 300, 300);
    setVisible(true);
  }
```

```
// Whenever the text in the TextField at the top of the Frame is changed,
// a TextEvent is generated.  The textValueChanged() method is called and
// updates the TextField at the bottom of the Frame with the modified
// text.

public void textValueChanged(TextEvent te) {
   TextField tmp = (TextField)te.getSource();

   tf2.setText("Text is now: "+tmp.getText());
}

public static void main(String args[]) {
   TestTL t1 = new TestTL();
}
}

class WinClosing extends WindowAdapter {
   public void windowClosing(WindowEvent we) {
      System.exit(0);
   }
}
```

### Output

The user interface of the program is shown below. When the contents of the
TextField at the top of the Frame changed, the TextListener (the TestTL object)
updated the text in the TextField at the bottom.

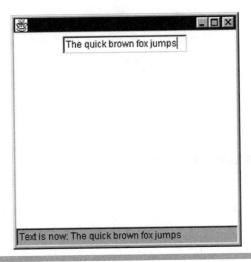

java.awt.event

# 7.2.14 TextSelectionListener Interface

```
public interface TextSelectionListener extends EventListener
```

```
EventListener
    TextSelectionListener
```

The TextSelectionListener interface contains one method that is called whenever a TextSelectionEvent is generated. TextSelectionEvent objects are generated by text components when their selected text changes. Because it only has one method, TextSelectionListener interface does not have an adapter class.

## textSelectionChanged() Method

| Method | Syntax |
|--------|--------|
| textSelectionChanged() | public void textSelectionChanged (TextSelectionEvent *tse*) |

textSelectionChanged() is called whenever the selected text of a text component is changed.

# 7.2.15 WindowListener Interface

```
public interface WindowListener extends EventListener
```

```
EventListener
    WindowListener
```

The WindowListener interface provides methods for handling the seven types of WindowEvents that are defined by the constants in the WindowEvent class. There is an adapter class, WindowAdapter, which can be used if an application doesn't need all seven methods.

A Window object registers itself with a WindowListener object by calling the addWindowListener() method.

## windowActivated() Method

| Method | Syntax |
|--------|--------|
| windowActivated() | public void windowActivated(WindowEvent *we*) |

windowActivated() is called when a WindowEvent is generated due to a window being brought to the front.

# windowClosed() Method

| Method | Syntax |
|---|---|
| windowClosed() | public void windowClosed(WindowEvent we) |

windowClosed() is called when a WindowEvent is generated after a window has closed.

# windowClosing() Method

| Method | Syntax |
|---|---|
| windowClosing() | public void windowClosing(WindowEvent we) |

windowClosing() is called whenever a WindowEvent object is generated because a window is being closed.

Sometimes, it is desirable to exit the program when the window is closed, but Java does not automatically do this.

To terminate the program when the window is closed, the windowClosing() method is implemented within a class and a System.exit(0) call is placed within the method body. Note that this is done in the windowClosing() method and not the windowClosed() method.

# windowDeactivated() Method

| Method | Syntax |
|---|---|
| windowDeactivated() | public void windowDeactivated(WindowEvent we) |

windowDeactivated() is called whenever a WindowEvent object is generated because a window has lost focus. It is implemented within a class to handle the needs of the individual program.

# windowDeiconified() Method

| Method | Syntax |
|---|---|
| windowDeiconified() | public void windowDeiconified(WindowEvent we) |

windowDeiconified() is called whenever a WindowEvent object is generated because a window has been de-iconified. A de-iconified window is one that has been restored from an iconified state.

7

java.awt.event

## windowIconified() Method

| Method | Syntax |
|---|---|
| windowIconified() | public void **windowIconified**(WindowEvent *we*) |

windowIconified() is called whenever a WindowEvent object is generated because a window has been iconified. An iconified window is one that is minimized, and appears on the screen as a small icon.

## windowOpened() Method

| Method | Syntax |
|---|---|
| windowOpened() | public void **windowOpened**(WindowEvent *we*) |

windowOpened() is called whenever a WindowEvent object is generated because a window has been opened.

### Example: Using WindowListener

In this example, a Frame is registered with a WindowListener. If the Frame window is closed, the program terminates. The WindowListener is implemented by a separate class. The WinClosing2 class does not need access to the data members of class TestW and placing the code in a separate class makes it completely portable. The windowActivated(),windowDeactivated(), and windowClosed() methods are left as stub methods. Because WinClosing2 implements the WindowListener interface, every method defined in the WindowListener interface must be implemented even if the implementation is only a stub (empty body) method. To avoid this, the WindowAdapter class can be used; see Section 7.3.8 on page 657 for details.

```
import java.awt.*;
import java.awt.event.*;

public class TestWindowL extends Frame {
  public TestWindowL() {
    addWindowListener(new WinClosing2());  // the Frame is registered
                                           // with a WindowListener

    setBounds(100, 100, 200, 200);
    setVisible(true);
  }

  public static void main(String args[]) {
    TestWindowL tw = new TestWindowL();
  }
}
```

```
// when the window is closing, a WindowEvent is generated.  The
// windowClosing() method is called and the program is terminated.

class WinClosing2 implements WindowListener {
  public void windowClosing(WindowEvent we) {
    System.exit(0);
  }

  public void windowDeiconified(WindowEvent we) {
    System.out.println("window de-iconified");
  }

  public void windowIconified(WindowEvent we) {
    System.out.println("window iconified");
  }

  public void windowOpened(WindowEvent we) {
    System.out.println("window opened");
  }

  public void windowActivated(WindowEvent we) {}
  public void windowClosed(WindowEvent we) {}
  public void windowDeactivated(WindowEvent we) {}
}
```

### Output

The user interface of the program is shown below. Clicking the close button (top right) will cause the WindowListener (the WinClosing2 object) to terminate the program.

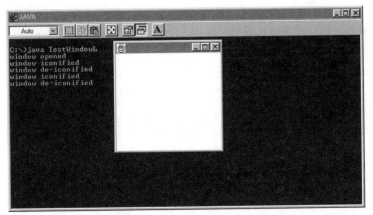

# 7.3 Listener Interface Adapter Classes

Often, only some of the methods defined in the listener interfaces are necessary for a given application. However, all of the methods must be implemented in a class that implements the listener interface. To avoid having to implement unnecessary methods, the java.awt.event package provides listener interface adapter classes. The adapter classes provide stub, or empty-body, implementations for the methods defined in the listener interfaces. A class that extends an adapter class need only override the methods that will actually be used.

The adapter class hierarchy is shown in the following figure. All of the adapter classes defined in the java.awt.event class are sub-classes of Object.

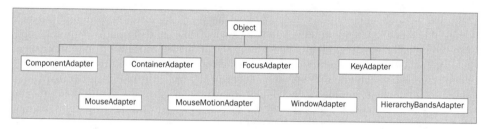

# 7.3.1 ComponentAdapter Class

```
public abstract class ComponentAdapter extends Object
    implements ComponentListener
```

```
Object
   ComponentAdapter
```

### Interfaces

```
ComponentListener
```

The ComponentAdapter class provides stub methods for the ComponentListener interface methods. A user-defined sub-class of ComponentAdapter overrides only those ComponentListener interface methods that are needed.

If the adapter class is not used, if a Container implements the ComponentListener interface directly or if an inner class implements the interface, every ComponentListener method must be included, even if it is implemented as a stub, or empty, method.

## Example: Using ComponentAdapter

This is a revision of the *Using ComponentListener* example on page 616. A
ComponentListener is associated with a Frame using an inner class that extends the
ComponentAdapter class. The ComponentAdapter class implements the
ComponentListener interface. If the Frame is re-sized, the componentResized()
method is called and sets the size back to its original dimensions and moves it back
to its default location.

*The WinClosing object terminates the program when the window is closed; see
Section 7.3.8 on page 657 for more details.*

```java
import java.awt.*;
import java.awt.event.*;

public class TestCompAdapter extends Frame {
  Label lbl;

  public TestCompAdapter() {
    lbl = new Label("Jackson and Zachary");

    Panel p = new Panel();
    p.add(lbl);

    add(p);

    addComponentListener(new CompListener());  // the Frame is registered
                                               // with a ComponentListener

    addWindowListener(new WinClosing());
    setBounds(100, 100, 400, 400);
    setVisible(true);
  }

  // if an attempt is made to resize the Frame, the componentResized()
  // method is called and the Frame is returned to its original size and
  // location

  class CompListener extends ComponentAdapter {
    public void componentResized(ComponentEvent ce) {
      setBounds(100, 100, 200, 200);
    }
  }
}
```

```
        public static void main(String args[]) {
          TestCompAdapter tca = new TestCompAdapter();
        }
      }

    class WinClosing extends WindowAdapter {
      public void windowClosing(WindowEvent we) {
        System.exit(0);
      }
    }
```

### Output

The user interface of the program is shown below, with the window being resized.
When this is done, the ComponentAdapter will change its size and location back to
the original values.

# 7.3.2 ContainerAdapter Class

```
public abstract class ContainerAdapter extends Object
  implements ContainerListener
```

```
Object
  ContainerAdapter
```

### Interfaces

```
ContainerListener
```

The ContainerAdapter class provides stub methods for the ContainerListener
interface methods. A user-defined sub-class of ContainerAdapter overrides only those
ContainerListener interface methods that are needed.

If the adapter class is not used, if a `Container` implements the `ContainerListener` interface directly or if an inner class implements the interface, every `ContainerListener` method must be included, even if it is implemented as a stub, or empty, method.

## Example: Using ContainerAdapter

This is a revision of the *Using ContainerListener* example on page 618. A `Button` object is created and placed in a `Frame`. The `Frame` object is registered with a `ContainerListener` using an inner class that extends the `ContainerAdapter` class. The `ContainerAdapter` class implements the `ContainerListener` interface. Every time the `Button` is clicked, a new `Button` object is placed on the `Frame`. When this happens, the `componentAdded()` method is called and "button added" is written to standard output. The `Frame` must call `invalidate()` and `validate()` every time a `Button` is added or the new `Button` will not be displayed.

*The `WinClosing` object terminates the program when the window is closed; see Section 7.3.8 on page 657 for more details.*

```
import java.awt.*;
import java.awt.event.*;

public class TestContAdapter extends Frame implements ActionListener {
  Button addButton;
  int count = 0;

  public TestContAdapter() {
    addButton = new Button("add");
    addButton.addActionListener(this);

    setLayout(new FlowLayout());
    add(addButton);

    addContainerListener(new ContListener());  // the Frame is registered
                                               // with a ContainerListener
    addWindowListener(new WinClosing());
    setBounds(100, 100, 300, 200);
    setVisible(true);
  }

  public void actionPerformed(ActionEvent ae) {
    add(new Button("button " + count));
    ++count;
```

```
   invalidate();
   validate();
}

// when a Button is added to the Frame, a ContainerEvent object is
// generated and the componentAdded() method is called

class ContListener extends ContainerAdapter {
  public void componentAdded(ContainerEvent ce) {
    System.out.println("button added");
  }
}

public static void main(String args[]) {
  TestContAdapter cl = new TestContAdapter();
}
}

class WinClosing extends WindowAdapter {
  public void windowClosing(WindowEvent we) {
    System.exit(0);
  }
}
```

### Output

The user interface of the program is shown below.

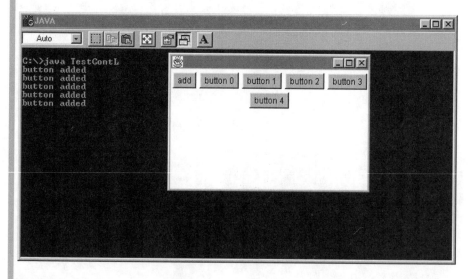

# 7.3.3 FocusAdapter Class

```
public abstract class FocusAdapter extends Object implements FocusListener
```

```
Object
  FocusAdapter
```

### Interfaces

```
FocusListener
```

The `FocusAdapter` class provides stub methods for the `FocusListener` interface methods. A user-defined sub-class of `FocusAdapter` overrides only those `FocusListener` interface methods that are needed.

If the adapter class is not used, if a `Container` implements the `FocusListener` interface directly or if an inner class implements the interface, every `FocusListener` method must be included, even if it is implemented as a stub, or empty, method.

## Example: Using FocusAdapter

This is a revision of the *Using FocusListener* example on page 621. Two `TextField` objects are created and placed in a `Frame`. The `TextField` objects are registered with a `FocusListener` using an inner class that extends the `FocusAdapter` class. The `FocusAdapter` class implements the `FocusListener` interface. When either of the `TextField` objects gains focus, the `focusGained()` method is called. The `getComponent()` method defined in the `ComponentEvent` class returns the `Component` that generated the event.

*The WinClosing object terminates the program when the window is closed; see Section 7.3.8 on page 657 for more details.*

```
import java.awt.*;
import java.awt.event.*;

public class TestFocusAdapter extends Frame {
  TextField tf1, tf2;

  public TestFocusAdapter() {
    tf1 = new TextField(10);
    tf1.setName("textfield 1");
    tf1.addFocusListener(new FocListener());  // registers the TextField
                                              // with a FocusListener

    tf2 = new TextField(10);
    tf2.setName("textfield 2");
    tf2.addFocusListener(new FocListener());
```

7

java.awt.event

```
      Panel p = new Panel();
      p.add(tf1);
      p.add(tf2);

      add(p);

      addWindowListener(new WinClosing());
      setBounds(100, 100, 300, 300);
      setVisible(true);
    }

    // When one of the TextFields gains focus, a FocusEvent is generated and
    // the focusGained() method is called.

    class FocListener extends FocusAdapter {
      public void focusGained(FocusEvent fe) {
        TextField tf = (TextField)fe.getComponent();
        System.out.println( tf.getName()+" gained focus");
      }
    }

    public static void main(String args[]) {
      TestFocusAdapter f = new TestFocusAdapter();
    }
  }

class WinClosing extends WindowAdapter {
  public void windowClosing(WindowEvent we) {
    System.exit(0);
  }
}
```

### Output

The user interface of the program is shown below. Each time a `TextField` gains or loses focus, the `FocusAdapter` prints a message to `System.out`.

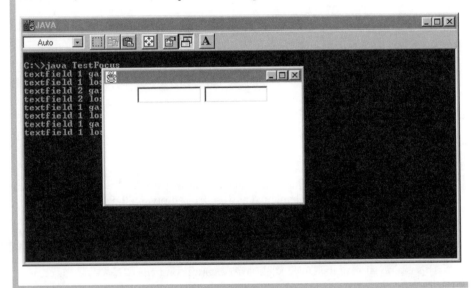

# 7.3.4 HierarchyBoundsAdapter Class

```
public abstract class HierarchyBoundsAdapter extends Object
  implements HierarchyBoundsListener
```

```
Object
  HierarchyBoundsAdapter
```

### Interfaces
```
HierarchyBoundsListener
```

The `HierarchyBoundsAdapter` class provides stub methods for the `HierarchyBoundsListener` interface methods. A user-defined sub-class of `HierarchyBoundsAdapter` overrides only those `HierarchyBoundsListener` interface methods that are needed.

If the adapter class is not used, if a `Container` implements the `HierarchyBoundsListener` interface directly or if an inner class implements the interface, then every `HierarchyBoundsListener` method must be included, even if it is implemented as a stub, or empty, method.

java.awt.event

7

# 7.3.5 KeyAdapter Class

```
public abstract class KeyAdapter extends Object implements KeyListener
```

```
Object
   KeyAdapter
```

### Interfaces
```
KeyListener
```

The KeyAdapter class provides stub methods for the KeyListener interface methods. A user-defined sub-class of KeyAdapter overrides only those KeyListener interface methods that are needed.

If the adapter class is not used, if a Container implements the KeyListener interface directly or if an inner class implements the interface, every KeyListener method must be included, even if it is implemented as a stub, or empty, method.

## Example: Using KeyAdapter

This is a revision of the *Using KeyListener* example on page 627. A Panel is created and registered with a KeyListener to process keyboard events using an inner class that extends the KeyAdapter class. The KeyAdapter class implements the KeyListener interface. Before the Panel can generate any KeyEvent objects, it must have focus. The Panel gains focus by clicking on it.

*The WinClosing object terminates the program when the window is closed; see Section 7.3.8 on page 657 for more details.*

```java
import java.awt.*;
import java.awt.event.*;

public class TestKeyAdapt extends Frame {
  Label lbl;

  public TestKeyAdapt() {
    lbl = new Label("Character: ");

    Panel p = new Panel();
    p.setBackground(Color.gray);
    p.addKeyListener(new KeyHandler());  // the Panel is registered with
                                         // a KeyListener
    add(p, BorderLayout.CENTER);
    add(lbl, BorderLayout.SOUTH);
```

```
    addWindowListener(new WinClosing());
    setBounds(100, 100, 200, 200);
    setVisible(true);
  }

  // when the mouse is over the Panel and a key is typed, the keyTyped()
  // method is called and the character printed in the TextField.

  class KeyHandler extends KeyAdapter {
    public void keyTyped(KeyEvent ke) {
      lbl.setText("Character: " + ke.getKeyChar());
      lbl.invalidate();
      invalidate();
      validate();
    }
  }

  public static void main(String args[]) {
    TestKeyAdapt tk = new TestKeyAdapt();
  }
}

class WinClosing extends WindowAdapter {
  public void windowClosing(WindowEvent we) {
    System.exit(0);
  }
}
```

## Output

The user interface of the program is shown below. The character **g** was typed when the `Panel` had focus, and the `KeyAdapter` updated the `Label` at the bottom.

## 7.3.6 MouseAdapter Class

```
public abstract class MouseAdapter extends Object implements MouseListener
```

```
Object
  MouseAdapter
```

### Interfaces
```
MouseListener
```

The MouseAdapter class provides stub methods for all of the MouseListener interface methods. A user-defined sub-class of MouseAdapter implements only those MouseListener interface methods that are needed.

If the adapter class is not used, if a Container implements the MouseListener interface directly or if an inner class implements the interface, every MouseListener method must be included, even if it is implemented as a stub, or empty, method.

### Example: Using MouseAdapter

This is a revision of the *Using MouseListener* example on page 630. Two Button objects are created and placed in a Frame. The Button objects are registered with a MouseListener to process mouse events using an inner class that extends the MouseAdapter class. The MouseAdapter class implements the MouseListener interface. Whenever the mouse pointer enters or leaves the space occupied by one of the Button objects, the text of the TextField object is updated to report this fact.

*The WinClosing object terminates the program when the window is closed; see Section 7.3.8 on page 657 for more details.*

```
import java.awt.*;
import java.awt.event.*;

public class TestMouseAdapter extends Frame {
   Button b1, b2;
   TextField tf;

   public TestMouseAdapter() {
      tf = new TextField(27);
      tf.setEditable(false);

      b1 = new Button("Button 1");
      b1.setName("Button 1");
```

```
        b1.addMouseListener(new MouseHandler());  // the Button is registered
                                                  // with a MouseListener
      b2 = new Button("Button 2");
      b2.setName("Button 2");
      b2.addMouseListener(new MouseHandler());

      Panel p1 = new Panel();
      p1.add(b1);
      p1.add(b2);

      Panel p2 = new Panel();
      p2.add(tf);

      setLayout(new BorderLayout());
      add(p1, BorderLayout.NORTH);
      add(p2, BorderLayout.SOUTH);

      addWindowListener(new WinClosing());
      setBounds(100, 100, 300, 200);
      setVisible(true);
   }

   // whenever the mouse enters or exits the display space of one of
   // Buttons, a MouseEvent is generated and sent to either the
   // mouseEntered() or mouseExited() methods.

   class MouseHandler extends MouseAdapter {
     public void mouseEntered(MouseEvent me) {
       tf.setText("mouse is over "+me.getComponent().getName());
     }
     public void mouseExited(MouseEvent me) {
       tf.setText("");
     }
   }
   public static void main(String args[]) {
     TestMouseAdapter tma = new TestMouseAdapter();
   }
}
class WinClosing extends WindowAdapter {
  public void windowClosing(WindowEvent we) {
    System.exit(0);
  }
}
```

7

java.awt.event

**653**

### *Output*

The user interface of the program is shown below. The `MouseAdapter` has updated the `Label` to show that the mouse is over **Button 2**.

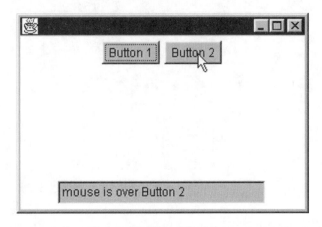

# 7.3.7 MouseMotionAdapter Class

```
public abstract class MouseMotionAdapter extends Object
  implements MouseMotionListener
```

```
Object
  MouseMotionAdapter
```

### *Interfaces*

```
MouseMotionListener
```

The `MouseMotionAdapter` class provides stub methods for the `MouseMotionListener` interface methods. A user-defined sub-class of `MouseMotionAdapter` overrides only those `MouseMotionListener` interface methods that are needed.

If the adapter class is not used, if a `Container` implements the `MouseMotionListener` interface directly or if an inner class implements the interface, every `MouseMotionListener` method must be included, even if it is implemented as a stub, or empty, method.

## Example: Using MouseMotionAdapter

This is a revision of the *Using MouseMotionListener* example on page 633. A Panel is created and registered with a MouseMotionListener to process motion-oriented Mouse events using an inner class that extends the MouseMotionAdapter class. The MouseMotionAdapter class implements the MouseMotionListener interface. When the mouse pointer is moved across the Panel, the TextField text is updated to indicate whether the mouse was moved or dragged as well as the current position of the mouse.

*The WinClosing object terminates the program when the window is closed; see Section 7.3.8 on page 657 for more details.*

```
import java.awt.*;
import java.awt.event.*;

public class TestMMAdapter extends Frame {
  TextField tf;

  public TestMMAdapter() {
    tf = new TextField(20);
    tf.setEditable(false);

    Panel p = new Panel();
    p.setBackground(Color.gray);
    p.addMouseMotionListener(new MouseHandler());

    add(p, BorderLayout.CENTER);
    add(tf, BorderLayout.SOUTH);

    addWindowListener(new WinClosing());
    setBounds(100, 100, 300, 300);
    setVisible(true);
  }

  class MouseHandler extends MouseMotionAdapter {
    public void mouseMoved(MouseEvent me) {
      tf.setText("Mouse Moved to position " + me.getX() + ","
              + me.getY());
    }
```

7

java.awt.event

```
      public void mouseDragged(MouseEvent me) {
         tf.setText("Mouse Dragged to position " + me.getX() + ","
               + me.getY());
       }
     }


   public static void main(String args[]) {
     TestMMAdapter mm1 = new TestMMAdapter();
     }
   }

class WinClosing extends WindowAdapter {
   public void windowClosing(WindowEvent we) {
     System.exit(0);
     }
   }
```

### Output

The user interface of the program is shown below. The mouse is being dragged over the Panel, and the MouseMotionAdapter has updated the TextField at the bottom accordingly.

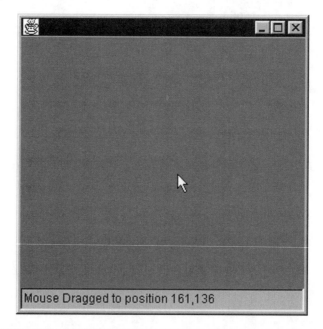

# 7.3.8 WindowAdapter Class

```
public abstract class WindowAdapter extends Object implements WindowListener
```

```
Object
   WindowAdapter
```

### Interfaces
```
WindowListener
```

The WindowAdapter class provides stub methods for all of the WindowListener interface methods. A user-defined sub-class of WindowAdapter overrides only those WindowListener interface methods that are needed.

If the adapter class is not used, if a Container implements the WindowListener interface directly or if an inner class implements the interface, every WindowListener method must be included, even if it is implemented as a stub, or empty, method.

## Example: Using WindowAdapter

A Frame is registered with a WindowListener using an inner class that extends the WindowAdapter class. The WindowAdapter class implements the WindowListener interface. If the Frame window is closed, the program terminates. The WindowListener is implemented by a separate class. The WinClosing class does not need access to the data members of class TestW and, placing the code in a separate class makes it completely portable.

```
import java.awt.*;
import java.awt.event.*;

public class TestWindowAdapter extends Frame {
  public TestWindowAdapter() {
    addWindowListener(new WinClosing());  // the Frame is registered with
    setBounds(100, 100, 200, 200);        // a WindowListener
    setVisible(true);
  }

  public static void main(String args[]) {
    TestW2 tw = new TestW2();
  }
}

// when the window is closing, a WindowEvent is generated.  The
// windowClosing() method is called and the program is terminated.
```

7

```
class WinClosing extends WindowAdapter {
  public void windowClosing(WindowEvent we) {
    System.exit(0);
  }
}
```

### Output

The user interface of the program is shown below. The close button (top right) is about to be clicked and will cause the WindowAdapter to terminate the program.

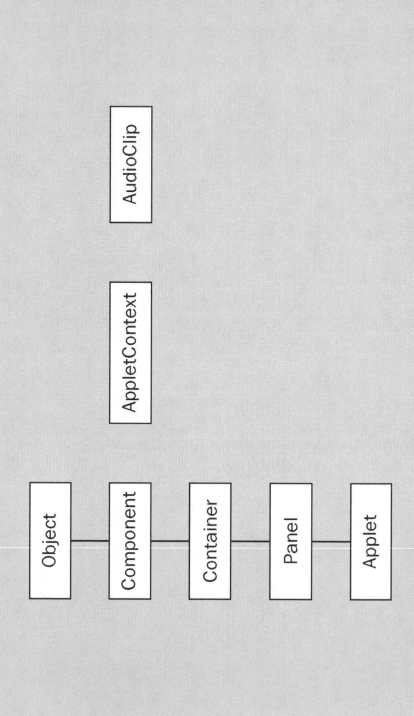

# 8

# java.applet

An **applet** is a special type of Java container that can be embedded in HTML code and viewed using a web browser. When a web browser on a client machine accesses an HTML page containing an applet across the Internet, the applet is downloaded from the web server and executed on the client system.

The Applet classes and interfaces are shown in the figure opposite.

In this Chapter we will cover:

## 8.1 Applets

This section covers the basics of creating applets, and the `Applet` class, which must be extended by all applets.

## 8.1.1 Applet Fundamentals

The `Applet` class is one of the Container classes, and an `Applet` can therefore be used to hold GUI components such as buttons, textfields, and labels, or it can display messages or images. An `Applet` is different from the other container classes in that it is intended to run through a Web browser. Applets can also be viewed using the `appletviewer` utility that comes with the JDK. Applets do not need a `main()` method.

A difficulty with applet programming is that some web browsers only support Java 1.0; if an applet is intended for the widest possible audience, it is necessary to restrict yourself to using only Java 1.0 facilities.

Because an applet may originate from an unknown source, certain restrictions are placed on them for security reasons – to prevent such things as viruses from being introduced to the local machine. These restrictions may be modified, for example to allow greater access to digitally signed applets. By default,

❏ applets cannot read from or write to local files.

❏ applets cannot communicate with any servers other than the one that stores the applet.

❏ applets cannot run programs on the local system.

Both images and audio files can be loaded into an applet. To load these files, the applet must know where they are located. This information is supplied by creating an instance of class URL, from the java.net package (see Section 5.4.1 on page 395). A URL object containing the location of the file is obtained using one of two methods:

❏ getCodeBase(), which returns the URL address where the .class files are located

❏ getDocumentBase(), which returns the URL address of the HTML file that started the applet is running.

An Image object representing the image file can then be created using the URL object containing the location of the image file. The image is displayed on the applet using the drawImage() method from the Graphics class. The Graphics class is contained in the java.awt package.

An AudioClip object representing the audio file is created using the getAudioClip() or newAudioClip() methods. The audio file can then be played using either the play() and loop() methods defined in the AudioClip interface, or the audio file can be loaded and played in one step using the play() method defined in the Applet class.

The Applet class is a sub-class of the Panel class defined in the java.awt package (see Chapter 6). All applets import the java.applet package (which contains the Applet class). If the applet is intended to use the support classes defined in the java.awt package, the java.awt package must also be imported.

# 8.1.2 HTML Code and Applets

HTML is the basic language of web browsers. A Java applet is not loaded directly into a web browser but can only be executed within an HTML file. A reference to the Java class is built into the HTML code and the HTML code is loaded into the browser. HTML is a relatively simple language consisting of tags that convey information to the browser. Each tag is enclosed with angle brackets (<>); the tags are not case sensitive. The information to load and view an applet is placed inside an <APPLET> tag.

The following attributes are mandatory on the `<APPLET>` element:

| Attribute | Usage |
| --- | --- |
| CODE | Name of applet `.class` file |
| WIDTH | Width of display window in pixels |
| HEIGHT | Height of display window in pixels |

The following attributes are optional:

| Attribute | Usage |
| --- | --- |
| CODEBASE | Base URL of the applet code |
| ARCHIVE | Used to specify a Java Archive (JAR) file containing classes for the applet |
| ALT | Text message to be displayed if the browser cannot run the applet |
| NAME | Name of the applet |
| ALIGN | Alignment of the applet. Valid choices are LEFT, RIGHT, TOP, BOTTOM, MIDDLE, BASELINE, TEXTTOP, ABSMIDDLE, ABSBOTTOM |
| VSPACE | Space, in pixels, above and below the applet |
| HSPACE | Space, in pixels, on each side of the applet |

CLASS, ID, STYLE, and TITLE attributes may also be specified.

## Example: Using an Applet in an HTML Page

```
<HTML>
  <HEAD>
    <TITLE> Test Program </TITLE>
  </HEAD>
  <BODY>
    <APPLET CODE="TestAudio.class" WIDTH=400 HEIGHT=400>
    </APPLET>
  </BODY>
</HTML>
```

This is a simple HTML file that is used to load an applet contained in a class called `TestAudio` into a browser. This file is used to load the applet examples presented in this chapter. The name of the applet `.class` file will have to be changed for each different example. For a description of the `<HTML>`, `<HEAD>`, `<TITLE>`, and `<BODY>` tags, consult an HTML reference such as *Instant HTML* from Wrox Press, ISBN 1-861001-56-8.

8

java.applet

Parameters can be passed into the applet from the HTML code, using <PARAM> tags between the <APPLET> and </APPLET> tags:

```
<APPLET CODE="TestAudio.class" WIDTH=400 HEIGHT=400>
    <PARAM NAME=identifierName VALUE=value>
</APPLET>
```

specifying the NAME and VALUE for the parameter. The getParameter() method from the Applet class can be used to retrieve the parameter values.

## 8.1.3 Loading an Applet into a Web Browser

To view an applet using a web browser, an HTML file must be created. This file must contain the <APPLET> tag, which in turn must contain the name of the .class file in the CODE attribute, as well as HEIGHT and WIDTH attributes. See Section 8.1.2 on page 662 for more details. The HTML file is loaded into the browser either by specifying the URL location of the file. If a local file is to be loaded the URL might be:

```
file:///path/filename.html
```

in Netscape or:

```
c:/path/filename.html
```

in Internet Explorer. If the HTML file resides on another machine, the URL might be

```
http://www.siteName.com/filename.html
```

An alternative to viewing a Java applet using a Web browser is to use the appletviewer utility, which is included with the JDK. This utility simulates what the applet would look like if loaded into a web browser.

## 8.1.4 Applet Class

```
public class Applet extends Panel
```

```
Object
  Component
    Container
      Panel
        Applet
```

### Interfaces

```
Accessible, ImageObserver, MenuContainer, Serializable
```

An Applet object is a container that can be embedded within an HTML page and executed by a web browser.

# Applet() Constructor

| Constructor | Syntax |
|---|---|
| Applet() | public Applet() |

Creates an Applet object. The Applet constructor is generally not used in program code, but it is used by the browser to instantiate an Applet object. The init() method is then called to initialize the applet.

# AudioClip Methods

| Method | Syntax |
|---|---|
| getAudioClip() | public AudioClip getAudioClip(URL *u*) |
| | public AudioClip getAudioClip(URL *u*, String *filename*) |
| newAudioClip() | public static final AudioClip newAudioClip(URL *u*) |
| play() | public void play(URL *u*) |
| | public void play(URL *u*, String *filename*) |

getAudioClip() and newAudioClip() return an AudioClip object that represents the audio file located at URL u. The name of the audio file can be built into the URL object or passed as a separate argument. These methods return immediately whether or not the audio clip file exists. The data is loaded when the applet attempts to play the audio clip using the play() method defined in the AudioClip interface.

The play() method defined in the Applet class loads an audio file located at URL u and plays it once. It does not save the audio file as an AudioClip object.

Under Java 1.1 and Java 2 SDK version 1.2, the only audio format that was guaranteed to work on every Java platform was the AU format. The Java 2 SDK version 1.3 adds the capability to handle AIFF and WAV formats.

## Example: Playing an Audio Clip

This example creates an applet that plays back an audio file called outent.au. It consists of the applet code in a class called TestAudio, and an HTML file called TestAudio.html. When the browser opens the file, or the applet is viewed in the applet viewer, a window with a **start** and **stop** buttons is created, which allow the user to control playback. Text is also provided to show the status of the clip.

Here is the code for the TestAudio class:

```
import java.awt.*;
import java.applet.*;
import java.awt.event.*;
```

8

java.applet

```
public class TestAudio extends Applet implements ActionListener {
  AudioClip ac;
  Button startButton, stopButton;
  String msg = "";

  public void init() {
    ac = getAudioClip(getCodeBase(), "outend.au");

    startButton = new Button("start");
    startButton.addActionListener(this);

    stopButton = new Button("stop");
    stopButton.addActionListener(this);

    add(startButton);
    add(stopButton);
  }

  public void stop() {
    ac.stop();
  }

  public void paint(Graphics g) {
    g.drawString(msg, 100, 300);
  }

  public void actionPerformed(ActionEvent ae) {
    if (ae.getActionCommand().equals("start")) {
      ac.loop();
      msg = "playing sounds";
      repaint();
    }

    if (ae.getActionCommand().equals("stop")) {
      ac.stop();
      msg = "sounds stopped";
      repaint();
    }
  }
}
```

An applet is created that plays an audio clip. A reference to an AudioClip object is obtained using the getAudioClip() method. Two Button objects are provided to start and stop the audio clip. When the **start** button is clicked, the loop() method defined in the AudioClip interface loads the sound data and continuously plays the audio file.

Testing if the `AudioClip` is not equal to `null` confirms that the audio file loaded successfully. If the **stop** button is clicked the audio file stops playing.

Here is the HTML file, `TestAudio.html` that is used with the example:

```
<HTML>
  <HEAD>
    <TITLE> Test Program </TITLE>
  </HEAD>
  <BODY>
    <APPLET CODE="TestAudio.class" WIDTH=400 HEIGHT=400>
    </APPLET>
  </BODY>
</HTML>
```

The file `outend.au` is also required to be in the same directory.

### *Output*

The end result should look like this in `appletviewer`:

## init() Method

| Method | Syntax |
|--------|--------|
| init() | public void init() |

init() is the first method called for any applet; it is only called once by the browser when the applet is first loaded. It used for tasks that are only done once – initializing variables, loading images or sound files, and creating and positioning GUI components. It does things that would otherwise be done by a constructor.

## start() Method

| Method | Syntax |
|--------|--------|
| start() | public void start() |

start() is called every time the browser displays the web page containing the applet. The start() method is automatically called after init() is run. If the applet is to run in its own thread (see example *Running an Applet as a Thread* on page 675), the start() method performs the task of turning the applet into a thread.

## stop() Method

| Method | Syntax |
|--------|--------|
| stop() | public void stop() |

stop() is called whenever the browser leaves the web page. It stops or suspends anything the applet was doing – stopping threads or suspending an audio play, for instance.

## destroy() Method

| Method | Syntax |
|--------|--------|
| destroy() | public void destroy() |

destroy() releases any resources the init() method allocated.

## getImage() Method

| Method | Syntax |
|--------|--------|
| getImage() | public Image getImage(URL *u*) |
|  | public Image getImage(URL *u*, String *filename*) |

getImage() is used to load an image into an applet and returns an Image object that represents the image file located at the URL u. The name of the image file can be built in to the URL object or passed as a separate argument. The URL object can be obtained by calling the getCodeBase() or getDocumentBase() methods. The Image class is defined in the java.awt package and supports both GIF and JPEG image formats.

## Example: Rotating Images

This program creates a slideshow applet that rotates four images. It consists of the applet code in a class called `SlideShow`, and an HTML file called `SlideShow.html`. When the browser opens the file, or the applet is viewed in `appletviewer`, a window with a **start** button is created, which allow the user to start the slide presentation. Text is also provided to show the status of the images. Here is the `SlideShow` class:

```java
import java.awt.*;
import java.awt.event.*;
import java.applet.*;

public class SlideShow extends Applet implements ActionListener {
    int numImages = 4;
    Button startButton;
    String msg = "";
    boolean display;
    MediaTracker mt;
    Image[] img = new Image[4];
    String[] imageNames = {
        "Flowfield.jpg", "straw.jpg", "carousel.jpg", "gardening.jpg"
    };

    public void init() {
        display = false;

        startButton = new Button("start");
        startButton.addActionListener(this);
        add(startButton);

        mt = new MediaTracker(this);
        for (int i = 0; i < numImages; ++i) {
            img[i] = getImage(getCodeBase(), imageNames[i]);
            mt.addImage(img[i], i);
        }
        try {
            mt.waitForAll();
            if (mt.isErrorAny()) {
                msg = "Error loading images";
                repaint();
            }
        } catch (InterruptedException ie) {}
    }
```

java.applet

8

```
public void paint(Graphics g) {
  if (display) {
    for (int i = 0; i < numImages; ++i) {
      g.drawImage(img[i], 40, 50, this);
      try {
        Thread.sleep(3000);
      } catch (InterruptedException ie) {}
    }
  }
  g.drawString(msg, 100, 400);
}

public void actionPerformed(ActionEvent ae) {
  display = true;
  repaint();
}
}
```

Four pictures are loaded using the getImage() method. A MediaTracker object is used to monitor the loading progress. The MediaTracker class is contained in the java.awt package. The waitForAll() method suspends other activities until all of the images are loaded. If there is an error in loading the images, a message stating that fact is displayed on the screen. When the **start** button is clicked, the repaint() method is called which calls the paint() method and each picture is displayed for three seconds. It was desired to only start the slideshow when the **start** button is clicked, but the paint() method is always called when the applet begins execution. To avoid this, the boolean flag display is used to only display the pictures if the **start** button has been clicked.

The HTML file used with the applet is the same as the one used in the previous example, although the .class file name has been changed to SlideShow.class:

```
<HTML>
  <HEAD>
    <TITLE> Test Program </TITLE>
  </HEAD>
  <BODY>
    <APPLET CODE="SlideShow.class" WIDTH=400 HEIGHT=400>
    </APPLET>
  </BODY>
</HTML>
```

The files Flowfield.jpg, straw.jpg, carousel.jpg, and gardening.jpg are also required to be in the same directory.

### Output

The end result should look like this:

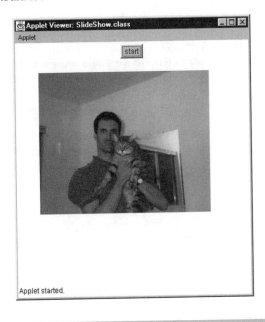

## Parameter Methods

| Method | Syntax |
|---|---|
| getParameter() | public String getParameter(String *name*) |
| getParameterInfo() | public String[][] getParameterInfo() |

It is possible to pass parameters to an applet through the HTML file (See Section 8.1.2, on page 662). These methods are used to access those parameters.

getParameter() returns a value corresponding to a name in a <PARAM> tag of an HTML file.

getParameterInfo() returns information about the parameters passed to the applet in an HTML file. The implementation provided by the Applet class returns null. If desired, the method may overridden to provide information about the name, type, and description of each parameter.

This example is the same as the preceding "Rotating Images" example on page 669 except that it uses HTML parameters to specify the number and names of the images to be loaded into the slideshow. The getParameter() method is used to retrieve the parameters. This method returns a String. The parseInt() method from the Integer class is used to convert the String to an int.

The program creates a slideshow applet that rotates four images. It consists of the applet code in a class called TestParam, and an HTML file called TestParam.html. When the browser opens the file, or the applet is viewed in appletviewer, a window with a start button is created, which allow the user to start the slide presentation. Text is also provided to show the status of the images. Here is the TestParam class:

```
import java.awt.*;
import java.awt.event.*;
import java.applet.*;

public class TestParam extends Applet implements ActionListener {
    int numImages;
    Button startButton;
    boolean display;
    String msg = "";
    MediaTracker mt;
    Image[] img = new Image[4];
    String[] imageNames = new String[10];

    public void init() {
        display = false;

        numImages = Integer.parseInt(getParameter("number"));

        for(int i=0; i<numImages; ++i) {
            imageNames[i] = getParameter("image"+i);
        }

        startButton = new Button("start");
        startButton.addActionListener(this);
        add(startButton);

        mt = new MediaTracker(this);
        for (int i=0; i<numImages; ++i) {
            img[i] = getImage(getCodeBase(), imageNames[i]);
            mt.addImage(img[i], i);
        } try {
```

```
          mt.waitForAll();
          if (mt.isErrorAny()) {
              msg = "Error loading images";
              repaint();
          }
      } catch(InterruptedException ie) {}
  }

  public void paint(Graphics g) {
      if (display) {
          for(int i = 0; i<numImages; ++i) {
              g.drawImage(img[i], 40, 50, this);
              try {
                  Thread.sleep(3000);
              } catch(InterruptedException ie) {}
          }
      }
      g.drawString(msg, 100, 400);
  }

  public void actionPerformed(ActionEvent ae) {
      display = true;
      repaint();
  }
}
```

Four pictures are loaded using the getImage() method. A MediaTracker object
is used to monitor the loading progress. The MediaTracker class is contained in
the java.awt package. The waitForAll() method suspends other activities
until all of the images are loaded. If there is an error in loading the images, a
message stating that fact is displayed on the screen. When the start button is
clicked, the repaint() method is called which calls the paint() method and
each picture is displayed for three seconds. It was desired to only start the
slideshow when the start button is clicked, but the paint() method is always
called when the applet begins execution. To avoid this, the boolean flag display
is used to only display the pictures if the start button is clicked.

The HTML file used with the applet, titled TestParam.html, has <PARAM> tags to
pass the number and names of the images to the applet.

```
<HTML>
  <HEAD>
    <TITLE> Test Program </TITLE>
  </HEAD>
  <BODY>
<APPLET CODE="TestParam.class" WIDTH=400 HEIGHT=400>
```

```
        <PARAM NAME=number VALUE=4>
        <PARAM NAME=image0 VALUE=Flowfield.jpg>
        <PARAM NAME=image1 VALUE=straw.jpg>
        <PARAM NAME=image2 VALUE=carousel.jpg>
        <PARAM NAME=image3 VALUE=gardening.jpg>
      </APPLET>
    </BODY>
  </HTML>
```

The files `Flowfield.jpg`, `straw.jpg`, `carousel.jpg`, and `gardening.jpg` are also required to be in the same directory.

### Output

The end result will be the same as that shown on page 671 for the *Rotating Images* example.

## Applet Property Methods

| Method | Syntax |
|---|---|
| getAppletContext() | public AppletContext getAppletContext() |
| getAppletInfo() | public String getAppletInfo() |
| isActive() | public boolean isActive() |
| setStub() | public final void setStub(AppletStub *stub*) |
| getLocale() | public Locale getLocale() |

getAppletContext() returns the AppletContext object associated with the applet. An AppletContext object can be used by the applet to obtain information about the environment in which it is running.

getAppletInfo() is often overwritten to provide a description of the applet.

isActive() returns true if the applet has finished initializing and is active.

setStub() sets the stub of the applet. It is called by the web browser when the applet is loaded.

getLocale() returns the Locale object associated with the applet.

## resize() Method

| Method | Syntax |
|---|---|
| resize() | public void resize(int *width*, int *height*) |
| | public void resize(Dimension *d*) |

resize() requests that the applet be re-sized to the dimensions passed as an argument. Not all web browsers will allow the applet to be resized.

# showStatus() Method

| Method | Syntax |
|---|---|
| showStatus() | public void showStatus(String s) |

showStatus() displays the passed String on the browser's status line, which appears at the bottom of the web browser window.

# URL Methods

| Method | Syntax |
|---|---|
| getDocumentBase() | public URL getDocumentBase() |
| getCodeBase() | public URL getCodeBase() |

getDocumentBase() returns a URL object containing the location of the .html file that loaded the applet.

getCodeBase() returns a URL object containing the location of the .class file that contains the applet.

## Example: Using getCodeBase()

See examples *Playing an Audio Clip* on page 665 and *Rotating Images* on page 669.

# Running an Applet as a Thread

Often it is desirable to place certain actions performed by an applet into a separate thread. (Threads are discussed in Section 2.3 on page 93.) For instance, if a continuously updating clock is placed in an applet and not placed in its own thread, it might prevent other applets in the same web page from executing.

Because a user-defined applet will always be a sub-class of Applet, it cannot also extend the Thread class because Java prohibits multiple inheritance. The user-defined applet must therefore implement the Runnable interface or define the thread as an inner Thread class.

## Example: Moving Message Banner Thread

This program creates a moving banner applet with scrolling text, and also a text box to illustrate that the scrolling text is running in a separate thread. It consists of the applet code in a class called TestThread, and an HTML file called TestThread.html. When the browser opens the file, or the applet is viewed in appletviewer, a window appears with a text box and the scrolling text. Here is the TestThread class:

8

java.applet

```
import java.applet.*;
import java.awt.*;

public class TestThread extends Applet implements Runnable {
  String message = "Jackson and Zachary";
  TextField tf;
  Thread thread;
  boolean running;

  public void init() {
    Font fnt = new Font("Serif", Font.BOLD, 24);
    setFont(fnt);

    FontMetrics fm = getFontMetrics(fnt);
    int spaceWidth = fm.charWidth(' ');
    int panelWidth = getSize().width;
    int numSpaces = panelWidth / spaceWidth + 1;

    // Pad message with spaces to required length
    for (int i = 0; i < numSpaces; ++i) {
      message = message + ' ';
    }

    tf = new TextField(30);
    tf.setFont(new Font("Serif", Font.PLAIN, 12));
    add(tf);
  }

  public void start() {
    if (thread == null) {
      thread = new Thread(this);
      running = true;
      thread.start();
    }
  }

  public void run() {
    while (running) {
      message = message.substring(1, message.length())
                  + message.charAt(0);
      repaint();

      try {
        Thread.sleep(100);
      } catch (InterruptedException e) {}
    }
```

```
    }

  public void stop() {
    if (thread != null) {
      running = false;
      thread = null;
    }
  }

  public void paint(Graphics g) {
    g.drawString(message, 0, 350);
  }
}
```

A moving message banner and a TextField object are placed on an Applet. The message banner is spun off as a separate thread. If this was not done, the message banner would take all of the CPU and it would not be possible to add any input to the TextField. The message banner is configured so it takes up the entire width of the applet. When the last character runs off the left hand side, the first character appears on the right hand side.

The start() method of the Applet class is overridden to instantiate the banner thread object, if it does not already exist, and start the thread. A boolean flag called running tracks the active state of the thread. The message is modified in the run() method. The call to the sleep() method slows the movement of the message banner down and allows other processes to grab hold of the CPU. The stop() method stops the message banner thread if it exists.

The HTML file used with this example is the same as the one used in the other examples, with the class name changed, this time it is called TestThread.html:

```
<HTML>
  <HEAD>
    <TITLE> Test Program </TITLE>
  </HEAD>
  <BODY>
    <APPLET CODE="TestThread.class" WIDTH=400 HEIGHT=400>
    </APPLET>
  </BODY>
</HTML>
```

8

java.applet

**677**

*Output*

The result should look like this:

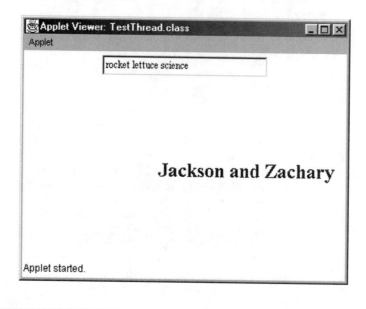

## 8.2 Applet Interfaces

The `AppletContext` and `AudioClip` interfaces are also contained in the `java.applet` package.

## 8.2.1 AppletContext Interface

```
public interface AppletContext
```

The `AppletContext` interface defines methods such as `getAudioClip()`, `getImage()`, and `showStatus()` that are also provided in the `Applet` class. It also defines a method `showDocument()` that can be used to load and display another page from within the currently running applet, and methods that can be used to find out what other applets are running in the same HTML document.

An `AppletContext` object can be obtained from the `getAppletContext()` method defined in the `Applet` class.

### showDocument() Method

| Method | Syntax |
|---|---|
| showDocument() | `public void showDocument(URL url)` |
| | `public void showDocument(URL url, String where)` |

showDocument() causes the HTML document located at URL url to be loaded and displayed. This method may be ignored by some applet viewers or browsers, such as appletviewer. The String where defines how the new document is displayed. It can have the following values:

| String | Usage |
|---|---|
| _blank | Use a new, unnamed window |
| _parent | Display inside the current window |
| _self | Replace the current window |
| _top | Use the top-most frame |
| frameName | Use the frame titled frameName or a new window with that title if there is no such frame |

## Example: Using showDocument()

This program loads one applet created using the TestCont class first, and presents the user with a button that says new frame. When the user clicks on this button a second HTML file containing an applet is loaded – in this case it is the example *Passing in Parameters through an HTML file* on page 672. Here is the TestCont class:

```java
import java.applet.*;
import java.awt.*;
import java.awt.event.*;
import java.net.*;

public class TestCont extends Applet implements ActionListener {
  String message;
  Button newButton;

  public void init() {
    message = "This is the original";

    newButton = new Button("new frame");
    newButton.addActionListener(this);
    add(newButton);
  }

  public void actionPerformed(ActionEvent ae) {
    AppletContext ac = getAppletContext();

    String filename = "TestParam.html";
    try {
      ac.showDocument(new URL(getCodeBase() + filename));
```

```
        } catch (MalformedURLException me) {}
    }

    public void paint(Graphics g) {
      g.drawString(message, 0, 350);
    }
}
```

A `Button` is placed on an `Applet`. When the button is selected, another HTML document containing an applet is loaded into the web browser and displayed using the `showDocument()` method. The `getCodeBase()` method returns a URL object containing the location of the `.class` file that contains the applet. A URL object is created using this location and the name of the HTML file to be loaded.

Here is the `TestCont.html` file that loads the first applet:

```
<HTML>
  <HEAD>
    <TITLE> Test Program </TITLE>
  </HEAD>
  <BODY>
    <APPLET CODE="TestCont.class" WIDTH=400 HEIGHT=400>
    </APPLET>
  </BODY>
</HTML>
```

### Output

The result of loading the `TestCont.html` file is shown here. Internet Explorer has been used rather than `appletviewer`, because `appletviewer` ignores the `showDocument()` method.

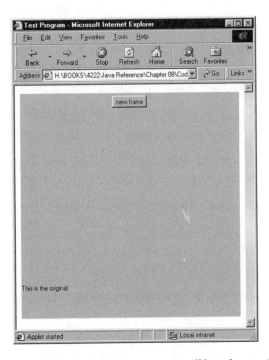

Then when you click on the new frame button you will be taken to the new page, which looks like this:

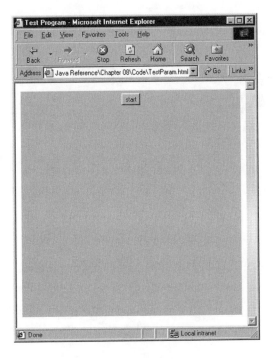

## Methods to Find other Applets

| Method | Syntax |
|---|---|
| getApplet() | public Applet getApplet(String *name*) |
| getApplets() | public Enumeration getApplets() |

getApplet() finds and returns an applet in the current HTML document with the specified name. (The name is set using the NAME attribute of the <APPLET> tag.)

getApplets() finds all the applets in the current HTML document and returns an Enumeration containing them.

# 8.2.2 AudioClip Interface

    public interface AudioClip

The AudioClip interface provides methods to play or stop the sound contained by an AudioClip object. Any AudioClip object created using the getAudioClip() or newAudioClip() methods will have access to the methods defined in the AudioClip interface.

## loop() method

| Method | Syntax |
|---|---|
| loop() | public void loop() |

loop() runs the audio file represented by the invoking AudioClip object continously. When the end of the audio file is reached, it is reset to the beginning.

## play() method

| Method | Syntax |
|---|---|
| play() | public void play() |

play() plays the audio file represented by the invoking AudioClip object once.

## stop() method

| Method | Syntax |
|---|---|
| stop() | public void stop() |

stop() stops the play of the audio file represented by the invoking AudioClip object.

## Example: Using AudioClip

See example *Playing an Audio Clip* on page 665.

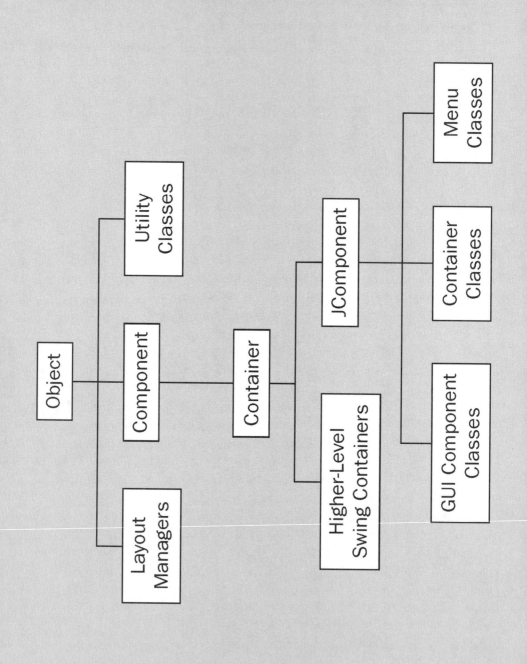

# javax.swing

The classes contained in the `java.awt` package provide a basic capability to create graphical user interfaces, but the scope of the tools contained in `java.awt` is limited. Furthermore, the actual implementation of the components is done in a language other than Java, and the look and behavior of the components is somewhat dependent on the runtime platform's native environment. AWT components might act slightly differently on a UNIX system than they would on a PC.

The Swing classes are the next-generation (Java 2) Graphical User Interface classes. Swing and AWT are now part of what is called the Java Foundation Classes. The Swing classes provide a number of new components including trees, tables, and tooltips (oh my). The containers defined by the `javax.swing` package contain different layers, or panes, on which components can be placed. A new set of classes containing borders that can be placed around components is introduced.

Swing components are written entirely in Java, so their look and behavior is not dependent on the runtime platform's native environment. Swing also offers the programmer more control of how the components look on the screen by the use of various built-in look-and-feel models. User-defined look-and-feel models can also be created. Swing components employ a model-view-controller (MVC) architecture that gives the components a great deal of flexibility in specifying the behavior of the component.

A somewhat simplified overall class hierarchy is shown in the figure opposite. The layout manager and utility classes are sub-classes of `Object`. The higher-level Swing container classes, `JFrame`, `JDialog`, `JWindow`, and `JApplet`, are sub-classes of their AWT counterparts `Frame`, `Dialog`, `Window`, and `Applet`, which are in turn sub-classes of `Container`. The higher-level container classes are characterized by their having access to a root pane object and its sub-elements. The other container classes, GUI component classes, and menu classes derive from the `JComponent` class, which is similar to the `Component` class in that it provides methods that are common to its sub-classes. More detailed class hierarchy diagrams are provided at the beginning of each section.

This chapter covers:

# Model-View-Controller Architecture

Swing components use a variation of the **model-view-controller** design architecture. The characteristics of a component are separated into three categories:

❑ The **model** contains the quantitative aspects of the component. The minimum and maximum values of a `JScrollBar` or the list of objects contained in a `JList` would be examples of information encompassed by the model.

❑ The **view** takes care of how the component is actually displayed on the screen. The appearance and width of a slider, the configuration of the title bar, and the way a label is positioned on a button are examples of activities handled by the view.

❑ The **controller** defines the manner that the component can be interacted with. The controller would define, for instance, that clicking on a button is an acceptable way to interact with the button.

All three design elements, the model, view, and controller, interact with each other. The view receives the necessary information to render the component from the model. The view determines if the component has been interacted with, if the mouse pointer was over a button when the mouse was clicked for instance, and sends this information to the controller. The controller decides if this action requires the information contianed in the model to be updated, for example if the value associated with a scrollbar needs to be changed.

9

javax.swing

**687**

The Swing components combine the view and controller elements into a single entity called the **UI-delegate**: Sun calls this the **Separable Model Architecture**. The UI delegate thus controls how the component is displayed on the screen as well as how to deal with any interactions with the component. Separating the model from the view and controller allows different UI delegate objects to be assigned to a single set of data contained by a model. The Separable Model Architecture is illustrated in the figure below:

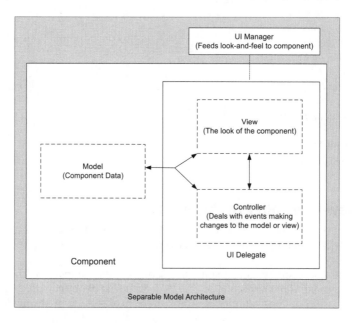

## 9.1 Swing GUI Components

The `javax.swing` package GUI component class hierarchy is shown in the figure below. Some of the classes, like `JLabel`, `JButton`, and `JTextField`, are enhanced versions of AWT GUI components. Others, such as the `JPasswordField`, `ProgressMonitor`, and `JSlider` classes, represent new types of components. The `javax.swing` components are lightweight in nature, meaning they are written in pure Java and don't rely on native peers to render themselves. Lightweight components are faster and less resource-intensive than their heavyweight counterparts. Even though the Swing components themselves are lightweight, the majority of them inherit from the heavyweight `Container` and `Component`. The enhanced funtionality of the Swing components is built on the core functionality provided by the earlier AWT component classes.

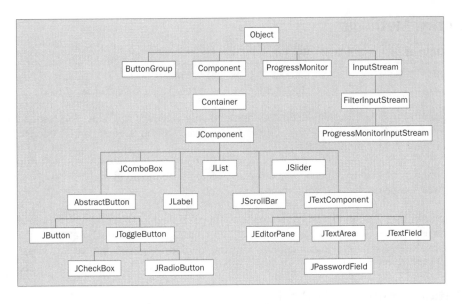

# 9.1.1 AbstractButton Class

```
public abstract class AbstractButton extends JComponent
   implements SwingConstants, ItemSelectable
```

```
Object
   Component
      Container
         JComponent
            AbstractButton
```

### Interfaces

```
ImageObserver, ItemSelectable, MenuContainer, Serializable SwingConstants
```

The AbstractButton class is the parent class for all Swing button components and many menu components as well.. It provides methods that are common to all of its sub-classes. Because it is an abstract class, an AbstractButton object is never created.

One big difference between Swing button components and those found in the java.awt package is that the surfaces of AbstractButton sub-class objects can display icons as well as text. An AbstractButton object can also display a different icon depending on its current state. Separate icons can be provided to indicate that the button is disabled, selected, disabled and selected, pressed, to indicate that the cursor has passed over (rolled over) the button, and to indicate that the cursor has passed over a selected button. Not all of these icons need be provided.

9

javax.swing

## Action Methods

| Method | Syntax |
|---|---|
| getAction() | public Action **getAction**() |
| setAction() | public void **setAction**(Action *action*) |

An Action object implements the ActionListener interface and is used to respond to events from one or more event sources. See Section 9.5.1 on page 911 and Section 9.5.2 on page 915 for more details

getAction() returns the Action object associated with the invoking AbstractButton sub-class object or null if there is no Action object.

setAction() associates an Action object with the invoking AbstractButton sub-class object. The Action passed as an argument will replace any previously set Action. null can also be used as an argument to set the the invoking AbstractButton sub-class object to have no action.

## ActionCommand Methods

| Method | Syntax |
|---|---|
| getActionCommand() | public String **getActionCommand**() |
| setActionCommand() | public void **setActionCommand**(String *actionCommand*) |

Every AbstractButton sub-class object can have an action command String associated with it that can be used to identify the button.

getActionCommand() returns the action command associated with the invoking AbstractButton sub-class object.

setActionCommand() is used to change the action command associated with the invoking AbstractButton sub-class object.

### Example: Using setActionCommand()

A JButton object is created and placed on a JFrame. The JButton is intended to terminate the program when clicked. Because a label was not provided to the constructor, the JButton object does not have a default action command. An action command is provided using the setActionCommand() method that can be used by actionPerformed() to identify the source of the ActionEvent.

*The WinClosing class is used to terminate the program if the window is closed. See Section 7.3.8 on page 657 for more details.*

```java
import javax.swing.*;
import java.awt.event.*;
import java.awt.*;

public class TestActCmd extends JFrame implements ActionListener {
  JButton b1;

  public TestActCmd() {

    // A JButton is created and registered with an ActionListener

    b1 = new JButton(new ImageIcon("StopSign.jpg"));
    b1.setBorder(BorderFactory.createRaisedBevelBorder());
    b1.addActionListener(this);

    // The action command of the JButton is set.

    b1.setActionCommand("stop");

    JPanel p = new JPanel();
    p.setLayout(new FlowLayout(FlowLayout.CENTER, 20, 20));
    p.add(b1);

    getContentPane().add(p);

    // The WindowListener is used to terminate the program when the window
    // is closed.  Under Java 2 version 1.3, the addWindowListener() syntax
    // can be replaced by
    //
    // setDefaultCloseOperation(JFrame.EXIT_ON_CLOSE);

    addWindowListener(new WinClosing());
    setBounds(100, 100, 200, 120);
    setVisible(true);
  }

  // When the JButton is pressed, the actionPerformed() method is called.
  // If the action command of the event source is "stop" the program
  // terminates.

  public void actionPerformed(ActionEvent ae) {
    if (ae.getActionCommand().equals("stop")) {
      System.exit(0);
    }
  }

  public static void main(String args[]) {
    TestActCmd tac = new TestActCmd();
  }
}
```

```
    // The WinClosing class terminates the program when the window is closed

    class WinClosing extends WindowAdapter {
      public void windowClosing(WindowEvent we) {
        System.exit(0);
      }
    }
```

**Output**

The user interface of the program is shown below.

## ActionListener Methods

| Method | Syntax |
| --- | --- |
| addActionListener() | public void **addActionListener** (ActionListener *al*) |
| removeActionListener() | public void **removeActionListener** (ActionListener *al*) |

ActionEvent objects are generated when a JButton object is pressed, a menu item is selected, or a JToggleButton object is clicked.

addActionListener() registers the invoking AbstractButton sub-class object with an ActionListener object. The ActionListener is notified if the invoking AbstractButton sub-class object generates an ActionEvent object.

removeActionListener() disconnects the ActionListener object from the invoking AbstractButton sub-class object.

### Example: Using ActionListeners

See the *Using setActionCommand()* example on page 690 where the actionPerformed() method of an ActionListener is used to terminate the program.

## Alignment Methods

| Method | Syntax |
|---|---|
| getHorizontalAlignment() | public int getHorizontalAlignment() |
| getHorizontalTextPosition() | public int getHorizontalTextPosition() |
| getVerticalAlignment() | public int getVerticalAlignment() |
| getVerticalTextPosition() | public int getVerticalTextPosition() |
| setHorizontalAlignment() | public void setHorizontalAlignment<br>(int *horizAlign*) |
| setHorizontalTextPosition() | public void setHorizontalTextPosition<br>(int *horizAlign*)<br>throws IllegalArgumentException |
| setVerticalAlignment() | public void setVerticalAlignment<br>(int *vertAlign*) |
| setVerticalTextPosition() | public void setVerticalTextPosition<br>(int *vertAlign*) |

These methods return or set the horizontal or vertical alignment of the invoking AbstractButton sub-class object. Values for the horizontal alignment must be one of the following:

- ❏ SwingConstants.LEFT

- ❏ SwingConstants.CENTER

- ❏ SwingConstants.RIGHT (this is the default)

- ❏ SwingConstants.LEADING

- ❏ SwingConstants.TRAILING

Values for the vertical alignment must be one of the following:

- ❏ SwingConstants.TOP

- ❏ SwingConstants.CENTER (this is the default)

- ❏ SwingConstants.BOTTOM

The text position methods align the String object relative to the Icon. They use the same constants as the alignment methods.

### Example: Using Alignment Methods

A JButton object is created and placed on a JFrame. The JButton is given an icon and some text. The text is positioned so that it appears below the icon.

*The WinClosing class is used to terminate the program if the window is closed.*
*See Section 7.3.8 on page 657 for more details.*

9

javax.swing

```
import javax.swing.*;
import java.awt.event.*;
import java.awt.*;

public class TestTextPos extends JFrame {
  JButton b1;

  public TestTextPos() {

    // A JButton is created that displays both text and an icon

    b1 = new JButton("stop", new ImageIcon("StopSign.jpg"));
    b1.setBorder(BorderFactory.createRaisedBevelBorder());
    b1.setFont(new Font("Serif", Font.BOLD, 14));
    b1.setBackground(Color.white);

    // The text is aligned to be centered below the icon.

    b1.setHorizontalTextPosition(SwingConstants.CENTER);
    b1.setVerticalTextPosition(SwingConstants.BOTTOM);

    JPanel p = new JPanel();
    p.setLayout(new FlowLayout(FlowLayout.CENTER, 20, 20));
    p.add(b1);

    getContentPane().add(p);

    // The WindowListener is used to terminate the program when the window
    // is closed.  Under Java 2 version 1.3, the addWindowListener() syntax
    // can be replaced by
    //
    // setDefaultCloseOperation(JFrame.EXIT_ON_CLOSE);

    addWindowListener(new WinClosing());
    setBounds(100, 100, 200, 150);
    setVisible(true);
  }

  public static void main(String args[]) {
    TestTextPos ttp = new TestTextPos();
  }
}

// The WinClosing class terminates the program when the window is closed

class WinClosing extends WindowAdapter {
  public void windowClosing(WindowEvent we) {
    System.exit(0);
  }
}
```

***Output***

The user interface of the program is shown below.

## ChangeListener Methods

| Method | Syntax |
|---|---|
| addChangeListener() | public void addChangeListener<br>(ChangeListener *cl*) |
| removeChangeListener() | public void removeChangeListener<br>(ChangeListener *cl*) |

Change events occur when any of the button properties are changed. Typical button properties are such things as the action command, the display label, the display icons, the alignments, or the state properties (enabled, selected, etc.).

addChangeListener() registers the invoking AbstractButton sub-class object with a ChangeListener object. The ChangeListener is notified if the invoking AbstractButton sub-class object generates a ChangeEvent object.

removeChangeListener() disconnects the ChangeListener object from the invoking AbstractButton sub-class object.

## doClick() Method

| Method | Syntax |
|---|---|
| doClick() | public void doClick()<br>public void doClick(int *milliseconds*) |

doClick() simulates the invoking AbstractButton sub-class object being pressed both visually and by issuing an ActionEvent. A time can be provided that specifies how long the button will appear to be pressed.

### Example: Using doClick()

A JButton is created that terminates the program when pressed. Five seconds after the program begins execution, the doClick() method is called which "presses" the JButton and the program terminates.

*The WinClosing class is used to terminate the program if the window is closed.*
*See Section 7.3.8 on page 657 for more details.*

9

javax.swing

```java
import javax.swing.*;
import java.awt.event.*;
import java.awt.*;

public class TestDoClick extends JFrame implements ActionListener {
  JButton b1;

  public TestDoClick() {

    // A JButton object is created and registered with an ActionListener

    b1 = new JButton("quit");
    b1.setBorder(BorderFactory.createRaisedBevelBorder());
    b1.addActionListener(this);

    JPanel p = new JPanel();
    p.setLayout(new FlowLayout(FlowLayout.CENTER, 20, 20));
    p.add(b1);

    getContentPane().add(p);

    // The WindowListener is used to terminate the program when the window
    // is closed.  Under Java 2 version 1.3, the addWindowListener() syntax
    // can be replaced by
    //
    // setDefaultCloseOperation(JFrame.EXIT_ON_CLOSE);

    addWindowListener(new WinClosing());
    setBounds(100, 100, 200, 120);
    setVisible(true);
  }

  // The click() method sleeps for 5 seconds and then calls the
  // doClick() method which simulates the button being pressed.
  // This causes an ActionEvent to be sent to the actionPerformed()
  // method terminating the program.

  public void click() {
    try {
      Thread.sleep(5000);
    } catch (InterruptedException ie) {}

    b1.doClick();
  }

  public void actionPerformed(ActionEvent ae) {
    if (ae.getActionCommand().equals("quit")) {
      System.exit(0);
    }
  }
```

```
    public static void main(String args[]) {
      TestDoClick tdc = new TestDoClick();
      tdc.click();
    }
  }

  // The WinClosing class terminates the program when the window is closed

  class WinClosing extends WindowAdapter {
    public void windowClosing(WindowEvent we) {
      System.exit(0);
    }
  }
```

## Icon Methods

| Method | Syntax |
|---|---|
| getDisabledIcon | public Icon getDisabledIcon() |
| getDisabledSelectedIcon | public Icon getDisabledSelectedIcon() |
| getIcon | public Icon getIcon() |
| getPressedIcon() | public Icon getPressedIcon() |
| getRolloverIcon() | public Icon getRolloverIcon() |
| getRolloverSelectedIcon() | public Icon getRolloverSelectedIcon() |
| getSelectedIcon() | public Icon getSelectedIcon() |
| setDisabledIcon() | public void setDisabledIcon (Icon *icon*) |
| setDisabledSelectedIcon() | public void setDisabledSelectedIcon(Icon *icon*) |
| setIcon() | public void setIcon(Icon *icon*) |
| setPressedIcon() | public void setPressedIcon(Icon *icon*) |
| setRolloverIcon() | public void setRolloverIcon(Icon *icon*) |
| setRolloverSelectedIcon() | public void setRolloverSelectedIcon (Icon *icon*) |
| setSelectedIcon() | public void setSelectedIcon(Icon *icon*) |

AbstractButton sub-class objects can display up to seven different Icon objects depending on their state. "Rollover" happens when the cursor passes over the button. These methods are used to return or set the Icon object associated with each state of the invoking AbstractButton sub-class object.

### Example: Using Icon Methods

A JButton object is created and given different icons to be displayed when the mouse pointer is over the JButton or when the JButton is pressed. The icons weren't all the same size, so the preferred size of the JButton was set to accomadate the largest icon.

*The WinClosing class is used to terminate the program if the window is closed.*
*See Section 7.3.8 on page 657 for more details.*

9

javax.swing

**697**

```
import javax.swing.*;
import java.awt.event.*;
import java.awt.*;

public class TestIcons extends JFrame {
   JButton b1;

   public TestIcons() {

// A JButton object is created.  The preferred size is
// increased somewhat to accomodate the icons that will
// be displayed.  The default icon is set.

      b1 = new JButton(new ImageIcon("dollar.jpg"));
      b1.setBorder( BorderFactory.createRaisedBevelBorder() );
      b1.setPreferredSize(new Dimension(70,100));

// Icons are specified to be displayed for two other JButton
// states; when the button is pressed and when the mouse is
// over the button.

      b1.setPressedIcon(new ImageIcon("pounds.jpg"));
      b1.setRolloverEnabled(true);
      b1.setRolloverIcon(new ImageIcon("yen.jpg"));

      JPanel p = new JPanel();
      p.setLayout(new FlowLayout(FlowLayout.CENTER, 20, 20));
      p.add(b1);

      getContentPane().add(p);

// The WindowListener is used to terminate the program when the window
// is closed.  Under Java 2 version 1.3, the addWindowListener() syntax
// can be replaced by
//
//    setDefaultCloseOperation(JFrame.EXIT_ON_CLOSE);

      addWindowListener(new WinClosing());
      setBounds(100, 100, 200, 150);
      setVisible(true);
   }

   public static void main(String args[]) {
      TestIcons tdc = new TestIcons();
   }
}

// The WinClosing class terminates the program when the window is closed
```

```
class WinClosing extends WindowAdapter {
   public void windowClosing(WindowEvent we) {
      System.exit(0);
   }
}
```

### Output

The user interface of the program is shown below. The icon displayed on the
JButton will change as the mouse passes over the button or it is clicked.

## ItemListener Methods

| Method | Syntax |
|---|---|
| addItemListener() | public void addItemListener(ItemListener il) |
| removeItemListener() | public void removeItemListener(ItemListener il) |

ItemEvents are generated when a JToggleButton object is toggled on or off or when a
JCheckBox or JRadioButton object is selected or deselected.

addItemListener() registers the invoking AbstractButton sub-class object with an
ItemListener object. The ItemListener is notified if the invoking AbstractButton
sub-class object generates an ItemEvent object.

removeItemListener() method disconnects the ItemListener object from the
invoking AbstractButton sub-class object.

### Example: Using ItemListeners

A JToggleButton is created and placed on a JFrame. The JToggleButton is
registered with an ItemListener to detect ItemEvents. The ItemListener interface
defines the itemStateChanged() method which must be implemented.

When the JToggleButton is toggled on or off, an ItemEvent object is generated and
sent to the itemStateChanged() method. The text of a JTextField is changed to
reflect the selected state of the JToggleButton.

*The WinClosing class is used to terminate the program if the window is closed.*
*See Section 7.3.8 on page 657 for more details.*

9

javax.swing

```java
import javax.swing.*;
import java.awt.event.*;
import java.awt.*;

public class TestItemLis extends JFrame implements ItemListener {
  JToggleButton b1;
  JTextField jtf;

  public TestItemLis() {
    jtf = new JTextField(15);

    // A JToggleButton is created and registered with an ItemListener.
    // The itemStateChanged() method is called when the JToggleButton
    // generates an ItemEvent.

    b1 = new JToggleButton("fish");
    b1.setBorder(BorderFactory.createRaisedBevelBorder());
    b1.addItemListener(this);

    JPanel p = new JPanel();
    p.setLayout(new FlowLayout(FlowLayout.CENTER, 20, 20));
    p.add(b1);

    getContentPane().add(p, BorderLayout.CENTER);
    getContentPane().add(jtf, BorderLayout.SOUTH);

    // The WindowListener is used to terminate the program when the window
    // is closed.  Under Java 2 version 1.3, the addWindowListener() syntax
    // can be replaced by
    //
    // setDefaultCloseOperation(JFrame.EXIT_ON_CLOSE);

    addWindowListener(new WinClosing());
    setBounds(100, 100, 200, 150);
    setVisible(true);
  }

  // The itemStateChanged() method updates the text of the JTextField
  // to reflect the checked state of the JToggleButton.

  public void itemStateChanged(ItemEvent ie) {
    if (b1.isSelected()) {
      jtf.setText("fish is selected");
    }
    if (!b1.isSelected()) {
      jtf.setText("fish is de-selected");
    }
  }
```

```
    public static void main(String args[]) {
      TestItemLis til = new TestItemLis();
    }
  }

  // The WinClosing class terminates the program when the window is closed

  class WinClosing extends WindowAdapter {
    public void windowClosing(WindowEvent we) {
      System.exit(0);
    }
  }
```

### Output

The user interface of the program is shown below.

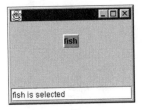

## Mnemonic Methods

| Method | Syntax |
|---|---|
| getMnemonic() | public int getMnemonic() |
| setMnemonic() | public void setMnemonic(char c) |
| | public void setMnemonic(int keyCode) |

A mnemonic is a key that when pressed along with a control key (the *Alt* key) produces the same effect as clicking the button with the mouse. If a key code is passed to the setMnemonic() function it should be one of the KeyEvent class keyboard constants described in Section 7.1.10 on page 598.

### Example: Using Mnemonics

A JButton that terminates the program when pressed. The JButton is given a mnemonic such that if *Alt-Q* is pressed the actionPerformed() method is called to terminate the program.

This is an example of where Java cannot implement the write once/run everywhere philosophy and at the same time preserve the native user experience a user on a particular platform would expect. The mnemonic is set up to use the *Alt* key, whereas a Mac user would be more accustomed to pressing the *Apple* key.

9

javax.swing

*The* WinClosing *class is used to terminate the program if the window is closed.*
*See Section 7.3.8 on page 657 for more details.*

```java
import javax.swing.*;
import java.awt.event.*;
import java.awt.*;

public class TestMnem extends JFrame implements ActionListener {
  JButton b1;

  public TestMnem() {

    // A JButton is created and registered with an ActionListener

    b1 = new JButton("quit");
    b1.setBorder(BorderFactory.createRaisedBevelBorder());
    b1.addActionListener(this);

    // A mnemonic is set up such that when Alt-Q is pressed it simulates
    // the button being pressed.

    b1.setMnemonic(KeyEvent.VK_Q);

    JPanel p = new JPanel();
    p.setLayout(new FlowLayout(FlowLayout.CENTER, 20, 20));
    p.add(b1);

    getContentPane().add(p);

    // The WindowListener is used to terminate the program when the window
    // is closed.  Under Java 2 version 1.3, the addWindowListener() syntax
    // can be replaced by
    //
    // setDefaultCloseOperation(JFrame.EXIT_ON_CLOSE);

    addWindowListener(new WinClosing());
    setBounds(100, 100, 200, 120);
    setVisible(true);
  }

  // When the JButton is pressed, the actionPerformed() method is called.
  // If the action command of the event source is "stop" the program
  // terminates.

  public void actionPerformed(ActionEvent ae) {
    if (ae.getActionCommand().equals("quit")) {
      System.exit(0);
    }
  }
}
```

```
public static void main(String args[]) {
    TestMnem tm = new TestMnem();
  }
}

// The WinClosing class terminates the program when the window is closed

class WinClosing extends WindowAdapter {
  public void windowClosing(WindowEvent we) {
    System.exit(0);
  }
}
```

**Output**

The user interface of the program is shown below.

# Methods to Return or Set AbstractButton Properties

| Method | Syntax |
|---|---|
| getMargin() | public Insets getMargin() |
| getModel() | public ButtonModel getModel() |
| getSelectedObjects() | public Object[] getSelectedObjects() |
| getText() | public String getText() |
| setMargin() | public void setMargin(Insets insets) |
| setModel() | public void setModel(ButtonModel bm) |
| setText() | public void setText(String label) |

getMargin() returns the distance between the borders of the AbstractButton sub-class object and its contents.

getModel() returns the ButtonModel used by the invoking AbstractButton sub-class object.

getSelectedObjects() returns an Object array of length 1 containing the label of the invoking AbstractButton sub-class object if the button is selected, or null if the button is not selected.

getText() returns the label displayed by the AbstractButton sub-class object. This method takes the place of the deprecated getLabel() method.

setMargin() changes the distance between the borders of the AbstractButton sub-class object and its contents.

setModel() sets the ButtonModel used by the invoking AbstractButton sub-class object.

setText() changes the label displayed by the AbstractButton sub-class object. This method takes the place of the deprecated setLabel() method.

## Example: Using AbstractButton Properties

A JButton is created and added to a JFrame. When the JButton is pressed, the label and button model associated with the JButton are printed to standard output.

*The WinClosing class is used to terminate the program if the window is closed. See Section 7.3.8 on page 657 for more details.*

```
import javax.swing.*;
import java.awt.event.*;
import java.awt.*;

public class TestButProp extends JFrame implements ActionListener {
   JButton b1;

   public TestButProp() {

      // A JButton is created and registered with an ActionListener

      b1 = new JButton();
      b1.setBorder(BorderFactory.createRaisedBevelBorder());
      b1.setText("blah");
      b1.addActionListener(this);

      JPanel p = new JPanel();
      p.setLayout(new FlowLayout(FlowLayout.CENTER, 20, 20));
      p.add(b1);

      getContentPane().add(p);

      // The WindowListener is used to terminate the program when the window
      // is closed.  Under Java 2 version 1.3, the addWindowListener() syntax
      // can be replaced by
      //
      // setDefaultCloseOperation(JFrame.EXIT_ON_CLOSE);
```

```
  addWindowListener(new WinClosing());
    setBounds(100, 100, 200, 120);
    setVisible(true);
  }

  // When the JButton is pressed, the actionPerformed() method is called
  // and information on the label and button model is printed out.

  public void actionPerformed(ActionEvent ae) {
    System.out.println("label is " + b1.getText());
    System.out.println("button model is " + b1.getModel());
  }

  public static void main(String args[]) {
    TestButProp tbp = new TestButProp();
  }
}

// The WinClosing class terminates the program when the window is closed

class WinClosing extends WindowAdapter {
  public void windowClosing(WindowEvent we) {
    System.exit(0);
  }
}
```

**Output** *(will vary)*

The output produced when the JButton is clicked is:

```
label is blah
button model is javax.swing.DefaultButtonModel@60ff2f
```

9

javax.swing

# Methods to Return or Change the State of an AbstractButton

| Method | Syntax |
|---|---|
| isBorderPainted() | public boolean isBorderPainted() |
| isContentAreaFilled() | public boolean isContentAreaFilled() |
| isFocusPainted() | public boolean isFocusPainted() |
| isFocusTraversable() | public boolean isFocusTraversable() |
| isRolloverEnabled() | public boolean isRolloverEnabled() |
| isSelected() | public boolean isSelected() |
| setBorderPainted() | public void setBorderPainted (boolean *borderPainted*) |
| setContentAreaFilled() | public void setContentAreaFilled (boolean *filled*) |
| setEnabled() | public void setEnabled(boolean *enabled*) |
| setFocusPainted() | public void setFocusPainted(boolean *painted*) |
| setRolloverEnabled() | public void setRolloverEnabled(boolean *enabled*) |
| setSelected() | public void setSelected(boolean *selected*) |

isBorderPainted() returns true if a border is to be painted around the invoking AbstractButton sub-class object.

isContentAreaFilled() returns true if the area bounded by the invoking AbstractButton sub-class object should be filled.

isFocusPainted() returns true if the invoking AbstractButton sub-class object is to be displayed differently if it has focus.

isFocusTraversable() returns true if the invoking AbstractButton sub-class object can receive focus by pressing the *Tab* or *Shift-Tab* keyboard sequences.

isRolloverEnabled() returns true if the invoking AbstractButton sub-class object is to be displayed differently if the mouse pointer travels over it.

isSelected() returns true if the invoking AbstractButton sub-class object is selected.

setBorderPainted() specifies whether a border should be painted around the invoking AbstractButton sub-class object.

setContentAreaFilled() determines whether the area bounded by the invoking AbstractButton sub-class object should be filled. Its function is similar to the setOpaque() method defined in the Component class.

setEnabled() changes the enabled state of the invoking AbstractButton sub-class object.

setFocusPainted() indicates whether the invoking AbstractButton sub-class object should be displayed differently if it has focus.

setRolloverEnabled() determines if the invoking AbstractButton sub-class object can be displayed differently if the mouse pointer travels over it.

setSelected() is used to select or de-select the invoking AbstractButton sub-class object.

## Example: Changing AbstractButton State

A JCheckBox object is created and placed on a JFrame. The border is specified to be painted and the JCheckBox is initially selected. When the JCheckBox is checked or unchecked, an ItemEvent is generated and the itemStateChanged() method updates the JTextField to reflect the checked state of the JCheckBox.

*The WinClosing class is used to terminate the program if the window is closed. See Section 7.3.8 on page 657 for more details.*

```
import javax.swing.*;
import java.awt.event.*;
import java.awt.*;

public class TestState extends JFrame implements ItemListener {
  JCheckBox b1;
  JTextField jtf;

  public TestState() {
    jtf = new JTextField(15);

    // A JCheckBox is created and registered with an ItemListener.
    // The itemStateChanged() method is called when the JCheckBox
    // generates an ItemEvent.

    b1 = new JCheckBox("fish");
    b1.setBorder(BorderFactory.createRaisedBevelBorder());
    b1.setPreferredSize(new Dimension(70, 50));
    b1.addItemListener(this);

    // The JCheckBox is set to be selected and have its border drawn.

    b1.setBorderPainted(true);
    b1.setSelected(true);

    JPanel p = new JPanel();
    p.setLayout(new FlowLayout(FlowLayout.CENTER, 20, 20));
    p.add(b1);

    getContentPane().add(p, BorderLayout.CENTER);
    getContentPane().add(jtf, BorderLayout.SOUTH);

    // The WindowListener is used to terminate the program when the window
    // is closed.  Under Java 2 version 1.3, the addWindowListener() syntax
    // can be replaced by
    //
    // setDefaultCloseOperation(JFrame.EXIT_ON_CLOSE);

    addWindowListener(new WinClosing());
    setBounds(100, 100, 200, 150);
    setVisible(true);
  }

  // The itemStateChanged() method updates the text of the JTextField
  // to reflect the checked state of the JCheckBox.

  public void itemStateChanged(ItemEvent ie) {
    if (b1.isSelected()) {
      jtf.setText("fish is selected");
    }
```

```
          if (!b1.isSelected()) {
             jtf.setText("fish is de-selected");
          }
      }

      public static void main(String args[]) {
         TestState ts = new TestState();
      }
   }

   // The WinClosing class terminates the program when the window is closed

   class WinClosing extends WindowAdapter {
      public void windowClosing(WindowEvent we) {
         System.exit(0);
      }
   }
```

**Output**

The user interface of the program is shown below.

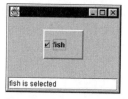

## UI Delegate Methods

| Method | Syntax |
|---|---|
| getUI() | public ButtonUI getUI() |
| setUI() | public void setUI(ButtonUI bui) |
| updateUI() | public void updateUI() |

getUI() returns the ButtonUI object associated with the invoking AbstractButton sub-class object.

setUI() is used to change the ButtonUI object associated the invoking AbstractButton sub-class object.

updateUI() is called to update the way the invoking component is displayed if the look-and-feel has been changed.

**708**

# 9.1.2 ButtonGroup Class

```
public class ButtonGroup extends Object implements Serializable
```

```
Object
    ButtonGroup
```

### Interfaces
```
Serializable
```

A ButtonGroup object associates a group of AbstractButton objects with each other such that only one of the group may be selected. They are normally used to group JRadioButton objects together but may be used with any AbstractButton sub-class object.

Once an button is selected, the ButtonGroup object will ensure that one button is always selected. It is not possible to un-select all of the associated buttons.

## ButtonGroup() Constructor

| Method | Syntax |
| --- | --- |
| ButtonGroup() | public ButtonGroup() |

## Methods that Add or Remove Buttons

| Method | Syntax |
| --- | --- |
| add() | public void add(AbstractButton b) |
| remove() | public void remove(AbstractButton b) |

add() and remove() add or remove the AbstractButton b from the invoking ButtonGroup object.

## getButtonCount() Method

| Method | Syntax |
| --- | --- |
| getButtonCount() | public int getButtonCount() |

getButtonCount() contains the number of buttons managed by the invoking ButtonGroup object.

## getElements() Method

| Method | Syntax |
| --- | --- |
| getElements() | public Enumeration getElements() |

getElements() returns an Enumeration containing the buttons managed by the invoking ButtonGroup object.

9

javax.swing

## Selection Methods

| Method | Syntax |
|---|---|
| getSelection() | public ButtonModel getSelection() |
| setSelected() | public void setSelected(ButtonModel *m*, boolean *b*) |
| isSelected() | public boolean isSelected(ButtonModel *m*) |

getSelection() returns the currently selected button of the invoking ButtonGroup object.

setSelected() selects the button m if the boolean argument is true.

isSelected() returns true if button m is selected.

### Example: Using ButtonGroup

A ButtonGroup object is used to make three JRadioButton objects mutually exclusive. The JRadioButton objects are associated with an ItemListener using an inner class. When one of the JRadioButton objects is selected, a JTextField object is updated to indicate the selected object.

*The WinClosing class is used to terminate the program if the window is closed. See Section 7.3.8 on page 657 for more details.*

```
import javax.swing.*;
import java.awt.*;
import java.awt.event.*;

public class TestBG extends JFrame {
  JRadioButton jrb1, jrb2, jrb3;
  ButtonGroup bg;
  JTextField jtf;

  public TestBG() {
    jtf = new JTextField(15);
    jtf.setEditable(false);

    // Three JRadioButton objects are created.

    jrb1 = new JRadioButton("flounder");
    jrb1.setBorder(BorderFactory.createRaisedBevelBorder());
    jrb1.setBorderPainted(true);
    jrb1.setFont(new Font("Serif", Font.BOLD, 12));
    jrb1.setPreferredSize(new Dimension(90, 50));
    jrb1.setHorizontalAlignment(SwingConstants.CENTER);
    jrb1.addItemListener(new RadioButtonListener());
```

```
jrb2 = new JRadioButton("sole");
jrb2.setBorder(BorderFactory.createRaisedBevelBorder());
jrb2.setBorderPainted(true);
jrb2.setFont(new Font("Serif", Font.BOLD, 12));
jrb2.setPreferredSize(new Dimension(90, 50));
jrb2.setHorizontalAlignment(SwingConstants.CENTER);
jrb2.addItemListener(new RadioButtonListener());

jrb3 = new JRadioButton("halibut");
jrb3.setBorder(BorderFactory.createRaisedBevelBorder());
jrb3.setBorderPainted(true);
jrb3.setFont(new Font("Serif", Font.BOLD, 12));
jrb3.setPreferredSize(new Dimension(90, 50));
jrb3.setHorizontalAlignment(SwingConstants.CENTER);
jrb3.addItemListener(new RadioButtonListener());

// create a ButtonGroup object that permits only one of the
// JRadioButton objects to be selected.

bg = new ButtonGroup();
bg.add(jrb1);
bg.add(jrb2);
bg.add(jrb3);

JPanel p = new JPanel();
p.setLayout(new FlowLayout(FlowLayout.CENTER, 20, 20));
p.add(jrb1);
p.add(jrb2);
p.add(jrb3);

getContentPane().add(p, BorderLayout.CENTER);
getContentPane().add(jtf, BorderLayout.SOUTH);

// The WindowListener is used to terminate the program when the window
// is closed.  Under Java 2 version 1.3, the addWindowListener() syntax
// can be replaced by
//
// setDefaultCloseOperation(JFrame.EXIT_ON_CLOSE);

addWindowListener(new WinClosing());
setBounds(100, 100, 400, 200);
setVisible(true);
}

// The RadioButtonListener class serves as the ItemListener.  When the
// selection is changed, the JTextField is updated to reflect the
// selected item.
```

9

javax.swing

```
class RadioButtonListener implements ItemListener {
    public void itemStateChanged(ItemEvent ie) {
       JRadioButton b = (JRadioButton) ie.getItemSelectable();
       jtf.setText("The selection is: " + b.getText());
    }
  }

  public static void main(String args[]) {
    TestBG tbg = new TestBG();
  }
}

// The WinClosing class terminates the program when the window is closed

class WinClosing extends WindowAdapter {
  public void windowClosing(WindowEvent we) {
    System.exit(0);
  }
}
```

### Output

The user interface of the program is shown below.

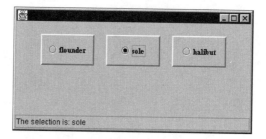

## 9.1.3 JButton Class

```
public class JButton extends AbstractButton implements Accessible
```

```
Object
  Component
    Container
      JComponent
        AbstractButton
          JButton
```

#### Interfaces

```
Accessible, ImageObserver, ItemSelectable, MenuContainer, Serializable,
SwingConstants
```

A JButton object is a rectangular button. The surface of the button can display text, an icon, or both. When clicked, a JButton object generates an ActionEvent object.

## JButton() Constructors

| Method | Syntax |
|---|---|
| JButton() | public JButton() |
| | public JButton(Action *action*) |
| | public JButton(Icon *icon*) |
| | public JButton(String *text*) |
| | public JButton(String *text*, Icon *icon*) |

Creates a JButton object. The JButton object can display a label, an icon, both, or neither.

## Default Button Methods

| Method | Syntax |
|---|---|
| isDefaultButton() | public boolean isDefaultButton() |
| isDefaultCapable() | public boolean isDefaultCapable() |
| setDefaultCapable() | public void setDefaultCapable (boolean *capable*) |

The default button is one that is activated when a certain event occurs inside the JRootPane object containing the JButton object. Generally, the pressing the *Enter* key will activate the default button. The default button is set by having the associated JRootPane object invoke the setDefaultButton() method.

isDefaultButton() returns true if the invoking JButton object is the default button.

isDefaultCapable() returns true if the invoking JButton object is capable of becoming the default button.

setDefaultCapable() is used to change the default-capable state of the invoking JButton object.

## UI Delegate Methods

| Method | Syntax |
|---|---|
| getUIClassID() | public String getUIClassID() |
| updateUI() | public void updateUI() |

getUIClassID() returns the String "ButtonUI" which is the suffix of the look-and-feel class that renders a JButton object.

updateUI() is called to update the way the invoking component is displayed if the look-and-feel has been changed.

## Example: Using JButton

A JButton is created and placed on a JFrame. The JButton object is registered with an ActionListener to monitor ActionEvents, When the JButton is pressed, an ActionEvent is generated. The actionPerformed() method is called terminating the program. The JButton is made the default button so if the *Enter* key is pressed, the JButton is activated.

*The WinClosing class is used to terminate the program if the window is closed. See Section 7.3.8 on page 657 for more details.*

```
import javax.swing.*;
import java.awt.event.*;
import java.awt.*;

public class TestJButton extends JFrame implements ActionListener {
  JButton b1;

  public TestJButton() {

    // A JButton is created and registered with an ActionListener

    b1 = new JButton("quit");
    b1.setBorder(BorderFactory.createRaisedBevelBorder());
    b1.setFont(new Font("Serif", Font.BOLD, 14));
    b1.addActionListener(this);

    JPanel p = new JPanel();
    p.setLayout(new FlowLayout(FlowLayout.CENTER, 20, 20));
    p.add(b1);

    getContentPane().add(p);

    JRootPane rootPane = getRootPane();
    rootPane.setDefaultButton(b1);

    // The WindowListener is used to terminate the program when the window
    // is closed.  Under Java 2 version 1.3, the addWindowListener() syntax
    // can be replaced by
    //
    // setDefaultCloseOperation(JFrame.EXIT_ON_CLOSE);

    addWindowListener(new WinClosing());
    setBounds(100, 100, 200, 120);
    setVisible(true);
  }
```

```
// When the JButton is pressed, an ActionEvent is generated and sent
// to the actionPerformed() method which terminates the program

public void actionPerformed(ActionEvent ae) {
  if (ae.getActionCommand().equals("quit")) {
    System.exit(0);
  }
}

public static void main(String args[]) {
  TestJButton tdc = new TestJButton();
}
}

// The WinClosing class terminates the program when the window is closed

class WinClosing extends WindowAdapter {
  public void windowClosing(WindowEvent we) {
    System.exit(0);
  }
}
```

**Output**

The user interface of the program is shown below.

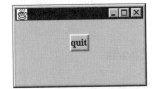

# 9.1.4 JCheckBox Class

```
public class JCheckBox extends JToggleButton implements Accessible
```

```
Object
  Component
    Container
      JComponent
        AbstractButton
          JToggleButton
            JCheckBox
```

**Interface**

Accessible, ImageObserver, ItemSelectable, MenuContainer, Serializable, SwingConstants

A JCheckBox object is a box with a label and a box that appears to one side; a check is displayed in the box when the JCheckBox object is selected. JCheckBox objects can display different icons depending on their selected state.

A JCheckBox object fires an ItemEvent when selected or de-selected.

Except for its constructors, the JCheckBox class does not define any new methods.

## JCheckBox() Constructors

| Method | Syntax |
|---|---|
| JCheckBox() | public JCheckBox() |
| | public JCheckBox(Action *action*) |
| | public JCheckBox(Icon *icon*) |
| | public JCheckBox(Icon *icon*, boolean *selected*) |
| | public JCheckBox(String *text*) |
| | public JCheckBox(String *text*, boolean *selected*) |
| | public JCheckBox(String *text*, Icon *icon*) |
| | public JCheckBox(String *text*, Icon *icon*, boolean *selected*) |

Creates a JCheckBox object. The JCheckBox object can be initialized with a label, an icon, and the selected state. The default selected state is unselected. If an icon is provided, it is displayed in place of the default box. A selected icon should then also be set, using the icon methods defined in the AbstractButton class, to differentiate between the selected and unselected states.

## Border Painting Methods

| Method | Syntax |
|---|---|
| isBorderPaintedFlat() | public boolean isBorderPaintedFlat() |
| setBorderPaintedFlat() | public void setBorderPaintedFlat(boolean b) |

It is customary when a JCheckBox is used as a renderer for a JTable or JTree to have its border painted flat

isBorderPaintedFlat() returns true if the JCheckBox border will be painted flat.

setBorderPaintedFlat() specifies whether the border of the invoking JCheckBox object will be painted flat.

## UI Delegate Methods

| Method | Syntax |
|---|---|
| getUIClassID() | public String getUIClassID() |
| updateUI() | public void updateUI() |

getUIClassID() returns the String "CheckBoxUI" which is the suffix of the look-and-feel class that renders a JCheckBox object.

updateUI() is called to update the way the invoking component is displayed if the look-and-feel has been changed.

## Example: Using JCheckBox

A JCheckBox object is created and placed on a JFrame. The JCheckBox is registered with an ItemListener to detect when the JCheckBox is selected or deselected. A JTextField object is used to display the selected state of the JCheckBox.

*The WinClosing class is used to terminate the program if the window is closed. See Section 7.3.8 on page 657 for more details.*

```
import javax.swing.*;
import java.awt.event.*;
import java.awt.*;

public class TestJCB extends JFrame implements ItemListener {
  JCheckBox b1;
  JTextField jtf;

  public TestJCB() {
    jtf = new JTextField(20);
    jtf.setEditable(false);

    // A JCheckBox object is created and configured.

    b1 = new JCheckBox("Zachary");
    b1.setName("Zachary");
    b1.setBorder(BorderFactory.createRaisedBevelBorder());
    b1.setBorderPainted(true);
    b1.setPreferredSize(new Dimension(100, 40));
    b1.setHorizontalAlignment(SwingConstants.CENTER);
    b1.setVerticalAlignment(SwingConstants.CENTER);
    b1.addItemListener(this);

    JPanel p = new JPanel();
    p.setLayout(new FlowLayout(FlowLayout.CENTER, 20, 20));
    p.add(b1);

    getContentPane().add(p, BorderLayout.CENTER);
    getContentPane().add(jtf, BorderLayout.SOUTH);

    // The WindowListener is used to terminate the program when the window
    // is closed.  Under Java 2 version 1.3, the addWindowListener() syntax
    // can be replaced by
```

9

javax.swing

```
        // setDefaultCloseOperation(JFrame.EXIT_ON_CLOSE);

        addWindowListener(new WinClosing());
        setBounds(100, 100, 200, 120);
        setVisible(true);
    }

    // When the JCheckBox is checked or unchecked, an ItemEvent is generated
    // and sent to the itemStateChanged() method.  The text of the JTextField
    // is updated to reflect the checked state of the JCheckBox

    public void itemStateChanged(ItemEvent ie) {
        JCheckBox jtb = (JCheckBox) ie.getItemSelectable();

        if (jtb.isSelected()) {
            jtf.setText(jtb.getName() + " is selected");
        }
        if (!jtb.isSelected()) {
            jtf.setText(jtb.getName() + " is de-selected");
        }
    }

    public static void main(String args[]) {
        TestJCB jcbox = new TestJCB();
    }
}

// The WinClosing class terminates the program when the window is closed

class WinClosing extends WindowAdapter {
    public void windowClosing(WindowEvent we) {
        System.exit(0);
    }
}
```

### Output

The user interface of the program is shown below.

# 9.1.5 JComboBox Class

```
public class JComboBox extends JComponent
   implements ItemSelectable, ListDataListener, ActionListener, Accessible
```

```
Object
   Component
      Container
         JComponent
            JComboBox
```

### *Interfaces*

```
Accessible, ActionListener, EventListener, ImageObserver, ItemSelectable,
ListDataListener, MenuContainer, Serializable
```

A JComboBox object is a combination of a JList and a JTextField. The JTextField is displayed at the top of the JComboBox. To the right of the JTextField is an arrow and. when the arrow is pressed, a list of choices appear. If a selection is made from the list, the selection appears in the JTextField. Only one element of the list may be selected at a time, and the contents of the JTextField can be set to be editable or not.

A JComboBox object uses a ListCellRenderer object to determine how the elements are displayed. It also uses a ComboBoxModel object to provide methods to access the combo box elements.

A JComboBox object fires an ItemEvent when the selected item changes for any reason, and an ActionEvent when the user explicitly makes a selection. The JComboBox class implements the ActionListener interface so it can serve as its own ActionListener.

## JComboBox() Constructors

| Method | Syntax |
|---|---|
| JComboBox() | public JComboBox() |
| | public JComboBox(ComboBoxModel c) |
| | public JComboBox(Object[] *items*) |
| | public JComboBox(Vector *items*) |

Creates a JComboBox object. The no-argument version creates an empty JComboBox object using a DefaultComboBoxModel object as its ComboBoxModel. The JComboBox can be initialized with a list of elements from either an Object array or a Vector object.

## Action Methods

| Method | Syntax |
|---|---|
| getAction() | public Action getAction() |
| setAction() | public void setAction(Action *action*) |

9

javax.swing

geAction() returns the Action object associated with the invoking JComboBox object or null if there is no Action object.

setAction() associates an Action object with the invoking JComboBox object. The Action passed as an argument will replace any previously set Action. null can also be used as an argument to set the the invoking JComboBox object to have no action.

## ActionCommand Methods

| Method | Syntax |
|--------|--------|
| getActionCommand() | public String getActionCommand() |
| setActionCommand() | public void setActionCommand<br>(String *actionCommand*) |

The action command can be used by the actionPerformed() method defined in the ActionListener interface to identify the source of an ActionEvent.

getActionCommand() returns the action command associated with the invoking JComboBox object.

setActionCommand() is used to change the action command associated with the invoking JComboBox object.

## ActionListener Methods

| Method | Syntax |
|--------|--------|
| addActionListener() | public void addActionListener<br>(ActionListener *al*) |
| removeActionListener() | public void removeActionListener<br>(ActionListener *al*) |

addActionListener() registers the invoking JComboBox object with an ActionListener object. The ActionListener is notified if the invoking JComboBox object generates an ActionEvent object.

removeActionListener() disconnects the ActionListener object from the invoking JComboBox object.

## Methods that Add or Remove Elements

| Method | Syntax |
|--------|--------|
| addItem() | public void addItem(Object *obj*) |
| insertItemAt() | public void insertItemAt(Object *obj*,<br>int *index*) |
| removeItem() | public void removeItem(Object *obj*) |
| removeItemAt() | public void removeItemAt(int *index*) |
| removeAllItems() | public void removeAllItems() |

`addItem()` adds an element to the end of the list of the invoking JComboBox object.

`insertItemAt()` adds an element at position index.

`removeItem()` removes Object obj from the list of the invoking JComboBox object.

`removeItemAt()` removes the element at position index.

`removeAllItems()` removes all of the elements from the list.

## ItemListener Methods

| Method | Syntax |
|---|---|
| addItemListener() | public void addItemListener(ItemListener *il*) |
| removeItemListener() | public void removeItemListener(ItemListener *il*) |

`addItemListener()` registers the invoking JComboBox object with an ItemListener object. The ItemListener is notified if the invoking JComboBox object generates an ItemEvent object.

`removeItemListener()` disconnects the ItemListener object from the invoking JComboBox object.

## Popup List Methods

| Method | Syntax |
|---|---|
| hidePopup() | public void hidePopup() |
| setPopupVisible() | public void setPopupVisible(boolean *isVisible*) |
| showPopup() | public void showPopup() |
| isPopupVisible() | public boolean isPopupVisible() |

`hidePopup()` causes the invoking JComboBox list to close its popup window

`showPopup()` causes the list to be made visible.

`setPopupVisible()` method sets whether the list is visible.

`isPopupVisible()` returns true if the list is visible.

## Methods that Return the Properties of a JComboBox

| Method | Syntax |
|---|---|
| getEditor() | public ComboBoxEditor getEditor() |
| getItemCount() | public int getItemCount() |
| getMaximumRowCount() | public int getMaximumRowCount() |

9

javax.swing

| Method | Syntax |
|--------|--------|
| getModel() | public ComboBoxModel getModel() |
| getRenderer() | public ListCellRenderer getRenderer() |
| isEditable() | public boolean isEditable() |
| isFocusTraversable() | public boolean isFocusTraversable() |
| isLightWeightPopupEnabled() | public boolean isLightWeightPopupEnabled() |

getEditor(), getModel(), and getRenderer() return the ComboBoxEditor, ComboBoxModel, and ListCellRenderer objects associated with the invoking JComboBox object.

getItemCount() returns the number of elements contained in with the invoking JComboBox object.

getMaximumRowCount() returns the maximum number of rows that can be displayed in the list without using a scrollbar.

isEditable() returns true if the invoking JComboBox object is editable.

isFocusTraversable() returns true if the invoking JComboBox object can accept focus using the *Tab* or *Shift-Tab* keyboard sequences.

isLightWeightPopupEnabled() returns true if a lightweight component is used to draw the list.

# Methods that Set the Properties of a JComboBox

| Method | Syntax |
|--------|--------|
| setEditable() | public void setEditable (boolean *editable*) |
| setEditor() | public void setEditor (ComboBoxEditor *cbe*) |
| setEnabled() | public boolean setEnabled (boolean *enabled*) |
| setLightWeightPopupEnabled() | public void setLightWeightPopupEnabled (boolean *isEnabled*) |
| setMaximumRowCount() | public void setMaximumRowCount (int *maxRows*) |
| setModel() | public void setModel(ComboBoxModel *cbm*) |
| setRenderer() | public void setRenderer (ListCellRenderer *lcr*) |

setEditable() determines if the invoking JComboBox object is editable.

setEnabled() sets the enabled state of the invoking JComboBox object is editable.

`setEditor()`, `setModel()`, and `setRenderer()` are used to change the `ComboBoxEditor`, `ComboBoxModel`, and `ListCellRenderer` objects associated with the invoking `JComboBox` object.

`setMaximumRowCount()` sets the maximum number of rows that can be displayed in the list.

`setLightWeightPopupEnabled()` determines if a lightweight component will be used to draw the list. This must be set to `false` if an application mixes lightweight and heavyweight components (although mixing of lightweight and heavyweight components is strongly discouraged).

## Selection Methods

| Method | Syntax |
|---|---|
| getItemAt() | public Object getItemAt(int *index*) |
| getSelectedIndex() | public int getSelectedIndex() |
| getSelectedItem() | public Object getSelectedItem() |
| getSelectedObjects() | public Object[] getSelectedObjects() |
| setSelectedIndex() | public void setSelectedIndex(int *index*) throws IllegalArgumentException |
| setSelectedItem() | public void setSelectedItem(Object *obj*) |

`getItemAt()` returns the element at position index in the list of the invoking `JComboBox` object.

`getSelectedIndex()` returns the index of the currently selected item.

`getSelectedItem()` returns the currently selected item.

`getSelectedObjects()` returns an `Object` array 1 element long containing the selected item. This method is included for compatibility with the `ItemSelectable` interface.

`setSelectedIndex()` changes the index of the selected item.

`setSelectedItem()` selects `Object obj`.

## UI Delegate Methods

| Method | Syntax |
|---|---|
| getUI() | public ComboBoxUI getUI() |
| getUIClassID() | public String getUIClassID() |
| setUI() | public void setUI(ComboBoxUI *cbui*) |
| updateUI() | public void updateUI() |

`getUI()` returns the `ComboBoxUI` object associated with the invoking `JComboBox` object.

9

javax.swing

getUIClassID() returns the String "ComboBoxUI" which is the suffix of the look-and-feel class that renders a JComboBox object.

setUI() is used to change the ComboBoxUI object associated the invoking JComboBox object.

updateUI() is called to update the way the invoking component is displayed if the look-and-feel has been changed.

## Example: Using JComboBox

A JComboBox is created and initialized with a String array. An additional String is added to the end of the list. The number of rows that are visible in the list is set to 5. The JComboBox is registered with an ActionListener. When a selection is made, the actionPerformed() method is called and the selection is indicated by a JTextField object.

*The WinClosing class is used to terminate the program if the window is closed. See Section 7.3.8 on page 657 for more details.*

```
import javax.swing.*;
import java.awt.*;
import java.awt.event.*;

public class TestJCmbBox extends JFrame implements ActionListener {
  JComboBox jcb;
  JTextField jtf;

  public TestJCmbBox() {
    jtf = new JTextField(20);

    // A JComboBox object is created and initialized with the contents
    // of a String array.

    String[] names = {
      "Allison", "Ellen", "Marguerite", "Deena", "DeShon", "Austin",
      "Nathan", "Kelsen", "Alex", "Lucas"
    };
    jcb = new JComboBox(names);

    String name2 = "Shane";
    jcb.addItem(name2);
    jcb.setMaximumRowCount(5);
    jcb.addActionListener(this);

    JPanel p = new JPanel();
    p.add(jcb);
```

```
        getContentPane().add(p, BorderLayout.CENTER);
        getContentPane().add(jtf, BorderLayout.SOUTH);

        // The WindowListener is used to terminate the program when the window
        // is closed.  Under Java 2 version 1.3, the addWindowListener() syntax
        // can be replaced by
        //
        // setDefaultCloseOperation(JFrame.EXIT_ON_CLOSE);

        addWindowListener(new WinClosing());
        setBounds(100, 100, 200, 200);
        setVisible(true);
    }

    // When a selection is made by the user, an ActionEvent is generated
    // and sent to the actionPerformed() method.  The text of the
    // JTextField object is updated to reflect the selection.

    public void actionPerformed(ActionEvent ae) {
        String s = (String) jcb.getSelectedItem();
        jtf.setText("Selection is: " + s);
    }

    public static void main(String args[]) {
        TestJCmbBox tjcb = new TestJCmbBox();
    }
}

// The WinClosing class terminates the program when the window is closed

class WinClosing extends WindowAdapter {
    public void windowClosing(WindowEvent we) {
        System.exit(0);
    }
}
```

### Output

The user interface of the program is shown below.

# 9.1.6 JComponent Class

```
public abstract class JComponent extends Container implements Serializable
```

```
Object
  Component
    Container
      JComponent
```

### Interfaces

```
ImageObserver, MenuContainer, Serializable
```

The parent class of all Swing GUI components and some of the Swing container classes. It provides methods that are common to its sub-classes. Because it is an abstract class a JComponent object is never instantiated.

## Alignment Methods

| Method | Syntax |
|---|---|
| getAlignmentX() | public float getAlignmentX() |
| getAlignmentY() | public float getAlignmentY() |
| setAlignmentX() | public void setAlignmentX(float *align*) |
| setAlignmentY() | public void setAlignmentY(float *align*) |

setAlignmentX() and setAlignmentY() change the x (horizontal) or y (vertical) alignment of the invoking Swing component with respect to the left-hand corner of the display. The alignment influences how the components are positioned by the BoxLayout and OverlayLayout layout managers. These layout managers are the only ones that use these methods - other layout managers will ignore them.

The argument can either be one of the alignment constants defined in the Component class, or a number between 0.0 and 1.0.

getAlignmentX() and getAlignmentY() return the current x and y alignment of the invoking Swing component.

### Example: Using Alignment Methods

Two JButton objects are placed on a JFrame. One of the JButton objects is placed higher than the other using the setAlignmentY() method. This method requires a float argument, but the number 1.0 is interpreted to be a double. It must be explicitly cast to a float. Alternatively, the syntax 1.0F could have been used.

*The WinClosing class is used to terminate the program if the window is closed. See Section 7.3.8 on page 657 for more details.*

```
import javax.swing.*;
import java.awt.event.*;
import java.awt.*;

public class TestAlign extends JFrame {
  JButton b1, b2;

  public TestAlign() {
    b1 = new JButton("top alignment");
    b1.setFont(new Font("Serif", Font.BOLD, 12));
    b1.setAlignmentY((float) 1.0);

    b2 = new JButton("middle alignment");
    b2.setFont(new Font("Serif", Font.BOLD, 12));

    JPanel p = new JPanel();
    p.setLayout(new BoxLayout(p, BoxLayout.X_AXIS));
    p.add(b1);
    p.add(b2);

    getContentPane().add(p);

    addWindowListener(new WinClosing());
    setBounds(100, 100, 300, 120);
    setVisible(true);
  }

  public static void main(String args[]) {
    TestAlign tal = new TestAlign();
  }
}

// The WinClosing class terminates the program when the window is closed

class WinClosing extends WindowAdapter {
  public void windowClosing(WindowEvent we) {
    System.exit(0);
  }
}
```

### Output

The user interface of the program is shown below.

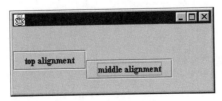

## Border Methods

| Method | Syntax |
|--------|--------|
| getBorder() | public Border getBorder() |
| setBorder() | public void setBorder(Border b) |

getBorder() returns the Border object associated with the invoking Swing component.

setBorder() changes the Border object associated with the invoking Swing component. Java provides eight border classes, and it is possible to create additional user-defined borders. See the Chapter 10 for more details.

### Example: Using Border Methods

Two JButton objects are created and placed on a JFrame. The first JButton gets the default border which is EtchedBorder, and the second is given a bevel border using the static method createRaisedBevelBorder() from the BorderFactory class.

*The WinClosing class is used to terminate the program if the window is closed. See Section 7.3.8 on page 657 for more details.*

```
import javax.swing.*;
import java.awt.event.*;
import java.awt.*;

public class TestBor extends JFrame {
  JButton b1, b2;

  public TestBor() {

    // The first JButton uses the default border class, which is
    // EtchedBorder

    b1 = new JButton("default border");
    b1.setFont(new Font("Serif", Font.BOLD, 12));

    // The second JButton uses the setBorder() method to change
    // its border type to BevelBorder

    b2 = new JButton("bevel border");
    b2.setFont(new Font("Serif", Font.BOLD, 12));
    b2.setBorder(BorderFactory.createRaisedBevelBorder());

    JPanel p = new JPanel();
    p.setLayout(new FlowLayout(FlowLayout.CENTER, 20, 20));
    p.add(b1);
    p.add(b2);
```

```
      getContentPane().add(p);

      addWindowListener(new WinClosing());
      setBounds(100, 100, 200, 120);
      setVisible(true);
   }

   public static void main(String args[]) {
      TestBor tb = new TestBor();
   }
}

// The WinClosing class terminates the program when the window is closed

class WinClosing extends WindowAdapter {
   public void windowClosing(WindowEvent we) {
      System.exit(0);
   }
}
```

**Output**

The user interface of the program is shown below.

## Color Methods

| Method | Syntax |
|---|---|
| setBackground() | public void **setBackground**(Color *color*) |
| setForeground() | public void **setForeground**(Color *color*) |

setBackground() changes the background color of the invoking Swing component.

setForeground() changes the foreground color of the invoking Swing component.

A Swing component also has access to the getBackground() and getForeground() methods from the Component class.

## Methods to Determine the Current State of a Component

| Method | Syntax |
| --- | --- |
| isDoubleBuffered() | public boolean isDoubleBuffered() |
| isOpaque() | public boolean isOpaque() |
| isOptimizedDrawingEnabled() | public boolean<br>    isOptimizedDrawingEnabled() |
| isPaintingTile() | public boolean isPaintingTile() |
| isValidateRoot() | public boolean isValidateRoot() |

isDoubleBuffered() returns true if the invoking Swing component uses double buffering.

isOpaque() returns true if the invoking Swing component is opaque.

isOptimizedDrawingEnabled() should be overridden to return false if child components will overlap; by default, Swing will optimize the repainting process by not computing the hidden portion of a component.

isPaintingTile() returns true if the invoking component is painting a child component that does not overlap any other child components.

isValidateRoot() returns true if the invoking Swing component is the root component in a validation tree. The only components for which this will be true are JRootPane, JScrollPane, and JTextField objects.

Swing components also have access to the state methods defined in the Component and Container classes.

## Event and EventListener Methods

| Method | Syntax |
| --- | --- |
| addAncestorListener() | public void addAncestorListener<br>    (AncestorListener al) |
| addProperyChangeListener() | public void addPropertyChangeListener<br>    (PropertyChangeListener pcl) |
|  | public void addPropertyChangeListener<br>    (String propertyName,<br>    PropertyChangeListener pcl) |
| addVetoableChangeListener() | public void addVetoableChangeListener<br>    (VetoableChangeListener vcl) |
| firePropertyChange() | public void firePropertyChange<br>    (String property, byte oldValue,<br>    byte newValue) |
|  | public void firePropertyChange<br>    (String property, char oldValue,<br>    char newValue) |
|  | public void firePropertyChange<br>    (String property, double oldValue,<br>    double newValue) |

| Method | Syntax |
|---|---|
| | `public void firePropertyChange` `(String property, float oldValue,` `float newValue)` |
| | `public void firePropertyChange` `(String property, int oldValue,` `int newValue)` |
| | `public void firePropertyChange` `(String property, long oldValue,` `long newValue)` |
| | `public void firePropertyChange` `(String property, short oldValue,` `short newValue)` |
| | `public void firePropertyChange` `(String property, boolean oldValue,` `boolean newValue)` |
| `getListeners()` | `public EventListener[] getListeners` `(Class listenerClass)` |
| `removeAncestorListener()` | `public void removeAncestorListener` `(AncestorListener al)` |
| `removeProperyChangeListener()` | `public void` `removePropertyChangeListener` `(PropertyChangeListener pcl)` |
| | `public void` `removePropertyChangeListener` `(String propertyName,` `PropertyChangeListener pcl)` |
| `removeVetoableChangeListener()` | `public void` `removeVetoableChangeListener` `(VetoableChangeListener vil)` |

`addAncestorListener()` registers the invoking Swing component with an `AncestorListener` object. The `AncestorListener` is notified if the component generates an `AncestorEvent`. An `AncestorEvent` is generated if an ancestor (super-class, super-super-class, etc) of a Swing component has moved or changed its visible state.

`addPropertyChangeListener()` registers the invoking Swing component with a `PropertyChangeListener` object. The `PropertyChangeListener` is notified if the component generates an `PropertyChangeEvent`. A `PropertyChangeEvent` is generated if the value of the associated property changes. A specific property to be monitored can be specified.

`addVetoableChangeListener()` registers the invoking Swing component with a `VetoableChangeListener` object. The `VetoableChangeListener` is notified if the component generates a `VetoablePropertyChangeEvent`. A `VetoablePropertyChangeEvent` is generated if a vetoable change has occurred in a Swing component.

`firePropertyChange()` issues a `PropertyChangeEvent` if newValue differs from oldValue.

`getListeners()` returns any listeners of the specified type registered to the invoking Swing component as an `EventListener` array.

9

javax.swing

removeAncestorListener() removes an AncestorListener object from the invoking Swing component. AncestorEvent objects generated by the component will no longer be received by the AncestorListener.

removePropertyChangeListener() removes a PropertyChangeListener object from the invoking Swing component. PropertyChangeEvent objects generated by the component will no longer be received by the PropertyChangeListener. If a property is specified, the listener is removed only from that property.

removeVetoableChangeListener() removes a VetoableChangeListener object from the invoking Swing component. VetoableChangePropertyEvent objects generated by the component will no longer be received by the VetoableChangeListener.

## Focus Methods

| Method | Syntax |
| --- | --- |
| getNextFocusableComponent | public Component getNextFocusableComponent() |
| grabFocus() | public void grabFocus() |
| hasFocus() | public boolean hasFocus() |
| isFocusCycleRoot() | public boolean isFocusCycleRoot() |
| isFocusTraversable() | public boolean isFocusTraversable() |
| isManagingFocus() | public boolean isManagingFocus() |
| isRequestFocusEnabled() | public boolean isRequestFocusEnabled() |
| requestDefaultFocus() | public boolean requestDefaultFocus() |
| requestFocus() | public void requestFocus() |
| setNextFocusableComponent() | public void setNextFocusableComponent (Component next) |
| setRequestFocusEnabled() | public void setRequestFocusEnabled (boolean enabled) |

getNextFocusableComponent() returns the component that is next in line to receive the focus.

grabFocus() sets the focus to the invoking Swing component regardless of the requestFocusEnabled state. This method is generally called by the system: an application should usually call the requestFocus() method instead.

hasFocus() returns true if the invoking Swing component currently has focus.

isFocusCycleRoot() is overridden to return true if the invoking Swing container wishes to be the root of a component tree with its own focus cycle.

isFocusTraversable() returns true if the invoking component can accept the input focus. Focus is traversed from traversable components using the *Tab* or *Shift-Tab* keyboard sequences.

isManagingFocus() can be overridden to return true if a Swing container wishes to disable the default focus manager.

`isRequestFocusEnabled()` returns `true` if the invoking Swing component is able to request the focus.

`requestDefaultFocus()` returns the focus to a default component, usually the first focus-traversable component. The method returns `false` if it is unable to shift the focus.

`requestFocus()` moves the focus to the invoking Swing component if the component is able to receive focus.

`setNextFocusableComponent()` is used to set the component that will receive focus next.

`setRequestFocusEnabled()` changes the `requestFocusEnabled` state of the invoking component.

Swing components also have access to the focus methods defined in the `Component` class.

## KeyStroke Constants

| Syntax |
| --- |
| `public static final int WHEN_FOCUSED` |
| `public static final int WHEN_ANCESTOR_OF_FOCUSED_COMPONENT` |
| `public static final int WHEN_IN_FOCUSED_WINDOW` |

These constants are used as conditions to register keyboard actions.

## Keyboard and Keystroke Methods

| Method | Syntax |
| --- | --- |
| `getActionForKeyStroke()` | `public ActionListener getActionForKeyStroke(KeyStroke ks)` |
| `getConditionForKeyStroke()` | `public int getConditionForKeyStroke (KeyStroke ks)` |
| `getRegisteredKeyStrokes()` | `public KeyStroke[] getRegisteredKeyStrokes()` |
| `registerKeyboardAction()` | `public void registerKeyboardAction (ActionListener action, String command, KeyStroke ks, int condition)` |
| | `public void registerKeyboardAction (ActionListener action, KeyStroke ks, int condition)` |
| `resetKeyboardActions()` | `public void resetKeyboardActions()` |
| `unregisterKeyboardAction()` | `public void unregisterKeyboardAction (KeyStroke ks)` |

A `KeyStroke` object represents a keyboard sequence that, when entered, will call the `actionPerformed()` method of an associated `ActionListener` object.

9

javax.swing

getActionForKeyStroke() returns the ActionListener object associated with a given KeyStroke object.

getConditionForKeyStroke() returns the condition, one of the KeyStroke constants defined above, associated with the given KeyStroke object. As of Java 2 version 1.3, a KeyStroke object can be associated with more than one condition.

getRegisteredKeyStrokes() returns an array containing all of the registered keystrokes.

registerKeyboardAction() associates an Action object and a KeyStroke object to a Swing component. When the keystroke is peformed, the Action object is generated subject to the Swing component meeting a condition. The condition is set to one of the KeyStroke constants defined above. As of Java 2 version 1.3, this method is considered obsolete. The replacement syntax for this command is:

```
getInputMap().put(KeyStroke ks, String aCommand);
getActionMap().put(String aCommand, ActionListener action);
```

resetKeyboardActions() clears all of the registered keyboard actions.

unregisterKeyboardAction() removes the keyboard action associated with the given KeyStroke object.

## Example: Using Keyboard and Keystroke Methods

A JButton object is created and placed on a JFrame. When the JButton is clicked, the actionPerformed() method is called and the program terminates. A keyboard action is set up such that when *Ctrl-Q* is typed, the actionPerformed() method will also be called.

The modifier key can be changed to suit the needs of a particular platform. For instance, the Alt key could be used instead of the *Ctrl* key.

*The WinClosing class is used to terminate the program if the window is closed. See Section 7.3.8 on page 657 for more details.*

```
import java.awt.*;

public class TestKey extends JFrame {
   JButton quitButton;

   public TestKey() {
      QuitHandler qh = new QuitHandler();
      KeyStroke ks = KeyStroke.getKeyStroke(KeyEvent.VK_Q,
                                   KeyEvent.CTRL_MASK, true);
```

```java
      quitButton = new JButton("quit");
      quitButton.setFont(new Font("Serif", Font.BOLD, 12));
      quitButton.setBorder(BorderFactory.createRaisedBevelBorder());
      quitButton.addActionListener(qh);

      // The KeyStroke object is associated with an ActionListener.
      // When the keyboard sequence represented by the KeyStroke (CTRL-Q)
      // is performed, the actionPerformed() method is called

      int condition = JComponent.WHEN_IN_FOCUSED_WINDOW;
      quitButton.getInputMap(condition).put(ks, "quit");
      quitButton.getActionMap().put("quit", qh);

      // If running under Java 2 version 1.2, this is the command to
      // associate the keyboard sequence to the ActionListener
      //
      // quitButton.registerKeyboardAction(qh, ks,
      // JComponent.WHEN_IN_FOCUSED_WINDOW);

      JPanel p = new JPanel();
      p.setLayout(new FlowLayout(FlowLayout.CENTER));
      p.add(quitButton);

      getContentPane().add(p);

      addWindowListener(new WinClosing());
      setBounds(100, 100, 200, 120);
      setVisible(true);
   }

class QuitHandler extends AbstractAction {
   public void actionPerformed(ActionEvent ae) {
      System.exit(0);
   }
}

// If running under Java 2 version 1.2, QuitHandler can implement
// ActionListener rather than extending AbstractAction
//
// class QuitHandler implements ActionListener {
//    public void actionPerformed(ActionEvent ae) {
//       System.exit(0);
//    }
// }

public static void main(String args[]) {
   TestKey tk = new TestKey();
   }
}
```

9

javax.swing

```
// The WinClosing class terminates the program when the window is closed

class WinClosing extends WindowAdapter {
  public void windowClosing(WindowEvent we) {
    System.exit(0);
  }
}
```

## Location Methods

| Method | Syntax |
|---|---|
| contains() | public boolean contains(int x, int y) |
| getLocation() | public Point getLocation(Point p) |
| getX() | public int getX() |
| getY() | public int getY() |

contains() returns true if the location passed as an argument lies within the bounding box of the invoking component.

getLocation() stores the x and y locations of the upper left hand corner of the bounding the invoking Swing component in Point p and returns the modified Point object.

getX() and getY() methods return the x and y locations in pixels of the origin (upper left hand corner) of the invoking component.

A Swing component also has access to the location methods defined in the Component class.

## Mapping Methods

| Method | Syntax |
|---|---|
| getActionMap() | public final ActionMap getActionMap() |
| getInputMap() | public final InputMap getInputMap() |
| | public final InputMap getInputMap (int condition) |
| setActionMap() | public final void setActionMap(ActionMap map) |
| setInputMap() | public final void setInputMap (int condition, InputMap map) |

An ActionMap object provides a mapping between an Object key (oftentimes a String) and an Action. An InputMap object provides a mapping between an input event and an Object key. Currently the only input event supported is a KeyStroke. Used together, the ActionMap and InputMap objects can be used to associate a KeyStroke object with an Action object.

getActionMap() returns an ActionMap object that can be used to map an an Object key and an Action.

getInputMap() returns an InputMap object that can be used to map an an Object key and a KeyStroke. The condition is one of the KeyStroke constants defined in the *KeyStroke Constants* section on page 733.

setActionMap() changes the ActionMap object associated with the invoking Swing component.

setInputMap() changes the InputMap object associated with the invoking Swing component. The condition is one of the KeyStroke constants defined in the *KeyStroke Constants* section on page 733.

## repaint() Method

| Method | Syntax |
|--------|--------|
| repaint() | public void repaint(Rectangle r) |
| | public void repaint(long timeWithin, int x, int y, int width, int height) |

repaint() takes a Rectangle object as an argument. The timeWithin parameter in the second version is the maximum time in milliseconds before the display is updated. Swing components also have access to the paint() and repaint() methods defined in the Component class.

## Methods that Return Related Objects or Components

| Method | Syntax |
|--------|--------|
| getClientProperty() | public final Object getClientProperty (Object keyName) |
| getAutoscrolls() | public boolean getAutoscrolls() |
| getInsets() | public Insets getInsets() |
| | public Insets getInsets(Insets insets) |
| getRootPane() | public JRootPane getRootPane() |
| getTopLevelAncestor() | public Container getTopLevelAncestor() |

getClientProperty() searches the client property list and returns the Object associated with keyName. It returns null if keyName does not exist.

getAutoScrolls() returns true if the invoking component automatically scrolls its contents when the mouse is dragged.

getInsets() returns the Insets object associated with the invoking Swing component. If an Insets object is provided, the margins from the invoking Swing component will be written to the Insets object, which will then be returned.

javax.swing

9

getRootPane() returns the JRootPane object associated with the invoking Swing component.

getTopLevelAncestor() returns a reference to the top-level ancestor that contains the invoking component. This will generally be a Window, Frame, or Applet.

## revalidate() Method

| Method | Syntax |
|---|---|
| revalidate() | public void revalidate() |

revalidate() is a combination of invalidate() followed by validate(). It causes the layout manager to lay out the child components again.

## Methods to Set Component Properties

| Method | Syntax |
|---|---|
| setAutoscrolls() | public void setAutoscrolls(boolean b) |
| setDoubleBuffered() | public void setDoubleBuffered(boolean b) |
| setEnabled() | public void setEnabled(boolean enabled) |
| setFont() | public void setFont(Font font) |
| setOpaque() | public void setOpaque(boolean b) |
| setVisible() | public void setVisible(boolean visible) |

setAutoscrolls() specifies if the invoking component will automatically scroll its contents when the mouse is dragged.

setDoubleBuffered() specifies if the invoking component will use double buffering. Double buffering can help to reduce screen flicker and is useful for components that will updated frequently.

setEnabled() sets whether the invoking Swing component is enabled. A component that has been disabled will not respond to user input.

setFont() changes the font used by the invoking Swing component.

setOpaque() specifies whether the invoking component will be opaque, meaning the underlying pixels will not be shown. Setting this to false allows some of the underlying pixels to show through.

setVisible() changes the visible state of the invoking Swing component.

Swing components also have access to the property methods defined in the Component and Container classes.

## Example: Setting Component Properties

Two JButton objects are placed on a JFrame. The opaque property of the first JButton object is set to be true. The background of the first JButton is gray, the default background color. The background of the second JButton is green (the background color of the JPanel), because the second JButton is transparent.

*The WinClosing class is used to terminate the program if the window is closed. See Section 7.3.8 on page 657 for more details.*

```
import javax.swing.*;
import java.awt.event.*;
import java.awt.*;

public class TestProp extends JFrame {
  JButton b1, b2;

  public TestProp() {

    // Two JButton objects are created.  The first JButton is
    // set to be opaque.  The second is set to be transparent.

    b1 = new JButton("opaque");
    b1.setFont(new Font("Serif", Font.BOLD, 12));
    b1.setBorder(BorderFactory.createRaisedBevelBorder());
    b1.setOpaque(true);

    b2 = new JButton("not opaque");
    b2.setFont(new Font("Serif", Font.BOLD, 12));
    b2.setBorder(BorderFactory.createRaisedBevelBorder());
    b2.setOpaque(false);

    JPanel p = new JPanel();
    p.setBackground(Color.green);
    p.setLayout(new FlowLayout(FlowLayout.CENTER, 20, 20));
    p.add(b1);
    p.add(b2);

    getContentPane().add(p);

    addWindowListener(new WinClosing());
    setBounds(100, 100, 200, 120);
    setVisible(true);
  }

  public static void main(String args[]) {
    TestProp tp = new TestProp();
  }
}
```

```
// The WinClosing class terminates the program when the window is closed

class WinClosing extends WindowAdapter {
  public void windowClosing(WindowEvent we) {
    System.exit(0);
  }
}
```

**Output**

The user interface of the program is shown below.

## Size Methods

| Method | Syntax |
|---|---|
| getBounds() | public Rectangle getBounds(Rectangle rect) |
| getHeight() | public int getHeight() |
| getMaximumSize() | public Dimension getMaximumSize() |
| getMinimumSize() | public Dimension getMinimumSize() |
| getPreferredSize() | public Dimension getPreferredSize() |
| getSize() | public Dimension getSize(Dimension dim) |
| getVisibleRect() | public Rectangle getVisibleRect() |
| getWidth() | public int getWidth() |
| setMaximumSize() | public void setMaximumSize(Dimension d) |
| setMinimumSize() | public void setMinimumSize(Dimension d) |
| setPreferredSize() | public void setPreferredSize(Dimension d) |

getBounds() stores the size and location of the invoking JComponent in Rectangle rect and returns the modified Rectangle.

getHeight() returns the height of the invoking Swing component in pixels.

getMaximumSize() returns the maximum size of the invoking Swing component.

getMinimumSize() returns the minimum size of the invoking Swing component.

getPreferredSize() returns the preferred size of the invoking Swing component.

getSize() stores the width and height of the invoking JComponent in Dimension dim and returns the modified Dimension.

`getWidth()` returns the width of the invoking Swing component in pixels.

`setMaximumSize()` changes the maximum size of the invoking Swing component.

`setMinimumSize()` changes the minimum size of the invoking Swing component.

`setPreferredSize()` changes the preferred size of the invoking Swing component.

`getVisibleRect()` returns a `Rectangle` object containing the location and size of the invoking Swing component.

Swing components also have access to the sizing methods defined in the `Component` and `Container` classes.

## Example: Using Size Methods

Two `JButton` objects are created and placed on a `JFrame`. The `setPreferredSize()` method is used to change the size of the objects.

*The `WinClosing` class is used to terminate the program if the window is closed. See Section 7.3.8 on page 657 for more details.*

```
import javax.swing.*;
import java.awt.event.*;
import java.awt.*;

public class TestSize extends JFrame {
    JButton b1, b2;

    public TestSize() {

        // Two JButton objects are created.  The preferred size of
        // the second JButton is changed using the setPreferredSize()
        // method.

        b1 = new JButton("small");
        b1.setFont(new Font("Serif", Font.BOLD, 12));
        b1.setBorder(BorderFactory.createRaisedBevelBorder());
        b1.setPreferredSize(new Dimension(50, 30));

        b2 = new JButton("big");
        b2.setFont(new Font("Serif", Font.BOLD, 12));
        b2.setBorder(BorderFactory.createRaisedBevelBorder());
        b2.setPreferredSize(new Dimension(70, 70));

        JPanel p = new JPanel();
        p.add(b1);
        p.add(b2);
```

9

javax.swing

```
      getContentPane().add(p);

      addWindowListener(new WinClosing());
      setBounds(100, 100, 200, 120);
      setVisible(true);
   }

   public static void main(String args[]) {
     TestSize ts = new TestSize();
   }
 }

 // The WinClosing class terminates the program when the window is closed

 class WinClosing extends WindowAdapter {
   public void windowClosing(WindowEvent we) {
     System.exit(0);
   }
 }
```

***Output***

The user interface of the program is shown below.

## ToolTip Methods

| Method | Syntax |
|---|---|
| createToolTip() | public JToolTip createToolTip() |
| getToolTipLocation() | public Point getToolTipLocation(MouseEvent *me*) |
| getToolTipText() | public String getToolTipText() |
| | public String getToolTipText(MouseEvent *me*) |
| setToolTipText() | public void setToolTipText(String *text*) |

A ToolTip is a small text box that pops up when the mouse pointer is over an associated component.

createToolTip() returns a system default tooltip.

getToolTipLocation() returns the location the tooltip is displayed in the coordinate system of the associated component. The MouseEvent is the event that triggered the tooltip display. This method can be overwritten to specify where the tooltip will appear.

getToolTipText() returns the text displayed by the tooltip. The MouseEvent is the event that triggered the tooltip display.

setToolTipText() is used to change the text displayed by the tooltip.

## Example: Using ToolTips

A ToolTip is attached to a JButton that terminates the program when clicked. The ToolTip appears when the mouse is placed over the JButton.

*The WinClosing class is used to terminate the program if the window is closed. See Section 7.3.8 on page 657 for more details.*

```
import javax.swing.*;
import java.awt.event.*;
import java.awt.*;

public class TestTip extends JFrame {
  JButton quitButton;

  public TestTip() {
    quitButton = new JButton("quit");
    quitButton.setFont(new Font("Serif", Font.BOLD, 12));
    quitButton.setBorder(BorderFactory.createRaisedBevelBorder());
    quitButton.addActionListener(new QuitHandler());

    // A ToolTip is attached to the JButton. The ToolTip text appears
    // when the mouse is placed over the JButton.

    quitButton.createToolTip();
    quitButton.setToolTipText("terminates program");

    JPanel p = new JPanel();
    p.setLayout(new FlowLayout(FlowLayout.CENTER, 50, 50));
    p.add(quitButton);

    getContentPane().add(p);

    addWindowListener(new WinClosing());
    setBounds(100, 100, 200, 120);
    setVisible(true);
  }

  class QuitHandler implements ActionListener {
    public void actionPerformed(ActionEvent ae) {
      System.exit(0);
    }
  }
}
```

```
      public static void main(String args[]) {
        TestTip tt = new TestTip();
      }
    }

    // The WinClosing class terminates the program when the window is closed

    class WinClosing extends WindowAdapter {
      public void windowClosing(WindowEvent we) {
        System.exit(0);
      }
    }
```

*Output*

The user interface of the program is shown below.

## UI Delegate Methods

| Method | Syntax |
|---|---|
| getUIClassID() | public String getUIClassID() |
| updateUI() | public void updateUI() |

getUIClassID() returns a String that describes the generic UI class of the invoking object. A JButton object, for instance, would return the String "ButtonUI".

updateUI() is called to update the way the invoking component is displayed if the look-and-feel has been changed.

### Example: Using UI Delegate Methods

Two JButton objects are created with the default Metal look-and-feel. The look-and-feel model is changed to Motif, but the appearance of the JButton objects doesn't change unless the updateUI() method is called. The second JButton calls the updateUI() method and is displayed using the Motif look.

Some look-and-feels do not work on some platforms due to the desires of the companies that "own" the look-and-feel. The UIManager and UIManager.LookAndFeelInfo classes can be used to determine the available look-and-feels for a given system

**744**

The *WinClosing* class is used to terminate the program if the window is closed.
See Section 7.3.8 on page 657 for more details.

```java
import javax.swing.*;
import java.awt.event.*;
import java.awt.*;
import javax.swing.plaf.metal.*;
import com.sun.java.swing.plaf.motif.*;

public class TestUI extends JFrame {
  JButton metalButton, motifButton;
  String LandF;

  public TestUI() {
    metalButton = new JButton("metal");
    metalButton.setFont(new Font("Serif", Font.BOLD, 14));

    motifButton = new JButton("motif");
    motifButton.setFont(new Font("Serif", Font.BOLD, 14));

    LandF = "com.sun.java.swing.plaf.motif.MotifLookAndFeel";
    try {
      UIManager.setLookAndFeel(LandF);
    } catch (Exception e) {}

    // The second JButton changes its look-and-feel to Motif

    motifButton.updateUI();

    JPanel p = new JPanel();

    // p.setLayout(new FlowLayout(FlowLayout.CENTER, 50, 50));
    p.add(metalButton);
    p.add(motifButton);

    getContentPane().add(p);

    addWindowListener(new WinClosing());
    setBounds(100, 100, 300, 120);
    setVisible(true);
  }

  public static void main(String args[]) {
    TestUI tui = new TestUI();
  }
}

// The WinClosing class terminates the program when the window is closed
```

9

javax.swing

```
class WinClosing extends WindowAdapter {
  public void windowClosing(WindowEvent we) {
    System.exit(0);
  }
}
```

**Output**

The user interface of the program is shown below.

# 9.1.7 JEditorPane Class

```
public class JEditorPane extends JTextComponent
```

```
Object
  Component
    Container
      JComponent
        JTextComponent
          JEditorPane
```

### Interfaces

Accessible, ImageObserver, MenuContainer, Scrollable, Serializable

A JEditorPane object is capable of displaying html and rtf format files. It is often used as a way to display on-line help information for applications. A JEditorPane object has an EditorKit object associated with it to provide the JEditorPane object with information on how to display a particular format.

A JEditorPane object can generate a HyperlinkEvent object if the user clicks on a hyperlink in the currently displayed document.

## JEditorPane() Constructors

| Method | Syntax |
|--------|--------|
| JEditorPane() | public JEditorPane() |
| | public JEditorPane(String url) throws IOException |
| | public JEditorPane(URL url) throws IOException |
| | public JEditorPane<br>(String mimeType, String intialText) |

Creates a `JEditorPane` object. The `JEditorPane` object can be initialized with a URL object or a `String` representation of a URL address. The fourth version initializes the `JEditorPane` with a given initial text and mime type. Valid mime types are `"text/plain"`, `"text/html"`, or `"text/rtf"`.

## Content Type Methods

| Method | Syntax |
|---|---|
| getContentType() | public String getContentType() |
| setContentType() | public void setContentType<br>   (String *contentType*) |

`getContentType()` and `setContentType()` return and set the content type of the `EditorKit` object associated with the invoking `JEditorPane` object. Typical values are `"text/plain"`, `"text/html"`, and `"text/rtf"`.

## EditorKit Methods

| Method | Syntax |
|---|---|
| createEditorKitForContentType() | public static EditorKit<br>createEditorKitForContentType<br>   (String *contentType*) |
| getEditorKit | public EditorKit getEditorKit() |
| getEditorKitForContentType() | public EditorKit<br>getEditorKitForContentType<br>   (String *contentType*) |
| registerEditorKitForContentType() | public static void<br>registerEditorKitForContentType<br>   (String *contentType*,<br>    String *classname*) |
| setEditorKit() | public void setEditorKit<br>   (EditorKit *e*) |
| setEditorKitForContentType() | public void<br>setEditorKitForContentType<br>   (String *contentType*, EditorKit *ek*) |

These methods return or set an `EditorKit` object associated with the invoking `JEditorPane` object.

## HyperlinkListener Methods

| Method | Syntax |
|---|---|
| addHyperlinkListener() | public void addHyperlinkListener<br>   (HyperlinkListener *h*) |
| removeHyperlinkListener() | public void removeHyperlinkListener<br>   (HyperlinkListener *h*) |

A `HyperlinkEvent` object is generated if the user clicks on a hyperlink inside the contents of the `JEditorPane` object.

9

javax.swing

addHyperlinkListener() registers the invoking JEditorPane component with a HyperlinkListener. The HyperlinkListener is notified if the JEditorPane generates any HyperlinkEvent objects.

removeHyperlinkListener() removes an HyperlinkListener from the invoking JEditorPane component.

# Page Methods

| Method | Syntax |
|---|---|
| getPage() | public URL getPage() |
| setPage() | public void setPage(URL *page*) throws IOException |
| | public void setPage(String *url*) <br> throws IOException |

getPage() returns the URL object associated with the page displayed by the invoking JEditorPane object.

setPage() sets or changes the URL object representing the page to be displayed by the invoking JEditorPane object.

## Example: Using JEditorPane for a Pop-up Help Window

A JButton object is created and placed on a JFrame. When the JButton is pressed, a dialog appears containing information about the JEditorPane class. The information is contained inside an HTML file that is placed inside a JEditorPane object, and the JEditorPane is itself placed inside the JDialog. To provide scrollbars for the HTML file, the JEditorPane object is bundled into a JScrollPane object before being added to the JDialog object. The HTML file, "help.html", is listed below.

To run this example on your own machine, change the directory location of the HTML file to correspond to your local system.

*The WinClosing class is used to terminate the program if the window is closed.* *See Section 7.3.8 on page 657 for more details.*

```
import javax.swing.*;
import java.awt.*;
import java.awt.event.*;
import java.io.*;

public class TestJEP extends JFrame {
  JEditorPane jep = null;
  JButton helpButton;
  JDialog helpDialog;

  public TestJEP() {
    helpDialog = new JDialog(this, "Help");
```

```
        helpButton = new JButton("Help");
        helpButton.addActionListener(new HelpButtonHandler());

        JPanel p = new JPanel();
        p.add(helpButton);

        getContentPane().add(p, BorderLayout.SOUTH);

        // The WindowListener is used to terminate the program when the window
        // is closed.  Under Java 2 version 1.3, the addWindowListener() syntax
        // can be replaced by
        //
        // setDefaultCloseOperation(JFrame.EXIT_ON_CLOSE);

        addWindowListener(new WinClosing());
        setBounds(100, 100, 400, 400);
        setVisible(true);
    }

// When the "Help" button is pressed, the actionPerformed() method
// is called and the JEditorPane() object is created and displayed.

class HelpButtonHandler implements ActionListener {
    public void actionPerformed(ActionEvent ae) {
        jep = new JEditorPane();

        // The location of the HTML file will have to be changed to
        // correspond to its location on your system.

        String file =
          "file:/usr/people/palmer/Java_Book/javax.swing/help.html";

        try {
          jep.setPage(file);
        } catch (IOException ioe) {
          System.out.println(ioe);
        }

        helpDialog.getContentPane().add(new JScrollPane(jep));
        helpDialog.setBounds(200, 200, 400, 300);
        helpDialog.show();
    }
  }

public static void main(String args[]) {
    TestJEP tjep = new TestJEP();
  }
}

// The WinClosing class terminates the program when the window is closed
```

```
class WinClosing extends WindowAdapter {
  public void windowClosing(WindowEvent we) {
    System.exit(0);
  }
}
```

### help.html

```
<HTML>
<BODY>
<H1 ALIGN=CENTER>Help with JEditorPanes</H1>
<BR><BR>
<P>syntax: public class JEditorPane extends JTextComponent
<BR><BR>
A JEditorPane object is capable of displaying html
and rtf format files. It is often used as a way to
display on-line help information for applications.
<BR><BR>
A JEditorPane object needs an EditorKit object associated
with it to provide the JEditorPane object with information
on how to display a particular format.
</BODY>
</HTML>
```

### Output

The user interface of the program is shown below.

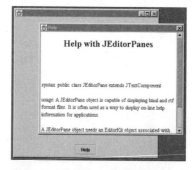

# 9.1.8 JLabel Class

```
public class JLabel extends JComponent implements SwingConstants, Accessible
```

```
Object
  Component
    Container
      JComponent
        JLabel
```

### Interfaces

    Accessible, ImageObserver, MenuContainer, Serializable, SwingConstants

A `JLabel` object is an object that contains a `String`, an image, or both. They are used for informational or display purposes. `JLabel` objects do not generate events.

# JLabel() Constructors

| Method | Syntax |
|--------|--------|
| JLabel() | public **JLabel**() |
| | public **JLabel**(Icon *image*) |
| | public **JLabel**(Icon *image*, int *horizontalAlignment*) |
| | public **JLabel**(String *text*) |
| | public **JLabel**(String *text*, int *horizontalAlignment*) |
| | public **JLabel**(String *text*, Icon *image*, int *horizontalAlignment*) |

Creates a `JLabel` object. A `JLabel` object can consist of text, an image, or both. The horizontal alignment of the `JLabel` object can also be specified. The values for `horizontalAlignment` must be one of:

❑   SwingConstants.LEFT

❑   SwingConstants.CENTER

❑   SwingConstants.RIGHT

❑   SwingConstants.LEADING

❑   SwingConstants.TRAILING

# Alignment Methods

| Method | Syntax |
|--------|--------|
| getHorizontalAlignment() | public int **getHorizontalAlignment**() |
| getHorizontalTextPosition() | public int **getHorizontalTextPosition**() |
| getVerticalAlignment() | public int **getVerticalAlignment**() |
| getVerticalTextPosition() | public int **getVerticalTextPosition**() |
| setHorizontalAlignment() | public void **setHorizontalAlignment** (int *horizAlign*) |
| setHorizontalTextPosition() | public void **setHorizontalTextPosition** (int *horizAlign*) |
| setVerticalAlignment() | public void **setVerticalAlignment** (int *vertAlign*) |
| setVerticalTextPosition() | public void **setVerticalTextPosition** (int *vertAlign*) |

9

javax.swing

These methods return or set the values of the horizontal or vertical alignment of the invoking JLabel object. Values for the horizontal alignment must be one of the following:

- ❏   SwingConstants.LEFT
- ❏   SwingConstants.CENTER
- ❏   SwingConstants.RIGHT
- ❏   SwingConstants.LEADING
- ❏   SwingConstants.TRAILING

Values for the vertical alignment must be one of the following:

- ❏   SwingConstants.TOP
- ❏   SwingConstants.CENTER
- ❏   SwingConstants.BOTTOM

The text position methods align the text relative to the Icon. They use the same constants as the alignment methods.

## Icon Methods

| Method | Syntax |
| --- | --- |
| getDisabledIcon() | public Icon getDisabledIcon() |
| getIcon() | public Icon getIcon() |
| getIconTextGap() | public int getIconTextGap() |
| setDisabledIcon() | public void setDisabledIcon (Icon disabledIcon) |
| setIcon() | public void setIcon(Icon i) |
| setIconTextGap() | public void setIconTextGap(int gap) |

getDisabledIcon() returns the disabled icon associated with the invoking JLabel object. If no disabled Icon is set, a greyscale version of the default icon is returned.

getIcon() returns the default icon associated with the invoking JLabel object.

getIconTextGap() returns the space in pixels between the icon and text.

setDisabledIcon() and setIcon() set or change the disabled and default icons associated with the invoking JLabel object.

setIconTextGap() sets the spacing between the text and icon for the invoking JLabel object.

## Mnemonic and Component Association Methods

| Method | Syntax |
|---|---|
| getDisplayedMnemonic() | public int getDisplayedMnemonic() |
| getLabelFor() | public Component getLabelFor() |
| setDisplayedMnemonic() | public void setDisplayedMnemonic(char *key*) |
| | public void setDisplayedMnemonic(int *key*) |
| setLabelFor() | public void setLabelFor(Component *c*) |

A mnemonic is a keyboard sequence, generally the *Alt* key and another character, that when pressed initiates an action.

getDisplayedMnemonic() returns the keycode for the mnemonic, if any, associated with the invoking JLabel object.

getLabelFor() returns the Component associated with the invoking JLabel object.

setDisplayedMnemonic() associates a mnemonic, or control key, with the invoking JLabel object.

setLabelFor() associates the JLabel object with another component. If the JLabel is associated with another component and the mnemonic is pressed, the associated component gains focus.

## Text Methods

| Method | Syntax |
|---|---|
| getText() | public String getText() |
| setText() | public void setText(String *text*) |

getText() returns the text displayed by the invoking JLabel object.

setText() method is used to change the text displayed by the invoking JLabel object.

## UI Delegate Methods

| Method | Syntax |
|---|---|
| getUI() | public LabelUI getUI() |
| getUIClassID() | public String getUIClassID() |
| setUI() | public void setUI(LabelUI *ui*) |
| updateUI() | public void updateUI() |

getUI() returns the LabelUI object associated with the invoking JLabel object.

getUIClassID() returns the String "LabelUI" which is the suffix of the look-and-feel class that renders a JLabel object.

9

javax.swing

setUI() is used to change the LabelUI object associated the invoking JLabel object.

updateUI() is called to update the way the invoking component is displayed if the look-and-feel has been changed.

## Example: Using JLabel

Two JLabel objects are created, one containing text and one containing an image. The text JLabel is used to describe the funtion of a JButton object. The image JLabel is placed on a JPanel that is initially not visible. When the JButton is pressed, the JPanel is made visible and the image appears on the screen. Using JLabel objects is the easiest way to incorporate images into an application.

*The WinClosing class is used to terminate the program if the window is closed. See Section 7.3.8 on page 657 for more details.*

```
import javax.swing.*;
import java.awt.event.*;
import java.awt.*;

public class TestJLabel extends JFrame implements ActionListener {
    JButton b1;
    JLabel lbl, lbl2;
    JPanel northPanel, southPanel;

    public TestJLabel() {
        lbl = new JLabel("Click here to see the boys");
        lbl.setFont(new Font("Serif", Font.PLAIN, 12));
        lbl.setHorizontalAlignment(SwingConstants.RIGHT);
        lbl.setForeground(Color.black);

        // This JLabel object contains an image.

        lbl2 = new JLabel(new ImageIcon("Halloween.jpg"));

        b1 = new JButton(" X ");
        b1.setBorder(BorderFactory.createRaisedBevelBorder());
        b1.addActionListener(this);

        southPanel = new JPanel();
        southPanel.setLayout(new FlowLayout(FlowLayout.CENTER));
        southPanel.add(lbl);
        southPanel.add(b1);

        // The JPanel northPanel contains the JLabel object containing
        // the image.  It is initally made invisible
```

```
        northPanel = new JPanel();
        northPanel.add(lbl2);
        northPanel.setVisible(false);

        getContentPane().add(northPanel, BorderLayout.CENTER);
        getContentPane().add(southPanel, BorderLayout.SOUTH);

        // The WindowListener is used to terminate the program when the window
        // is closed.  Under Java 2 version 1.3, the addWindowListener() syntax
        // can be replaced by
        //
        // setDefaultCloseOperation(JFrame.EXIT_ON_CLOSE);

        addWindowListener(new WinClosing());
        setBounds(100, 100, 400, 400);
        setVisible(true);
    }

    // When the button is pressed, the actionPerformed() method is
    // called and the JPanel northPanel is made visible

    public void actionPerformed(ActionEvent ae) {
        northPanel.setVisible(true);
        northPanel.revalidate();
    }

    public static void main(String args[]) {
        TestJLabel jl = new TestJLabel();
    }
}

// The WinClosing class terminates the program when the window is closed

class WinClosing extends WindowAdapter {
    public void windowClosing(WindowEvent we) {
        System.exit(0);
    }
}
```

### Output

The user interface of the program is shown below.

# 9.1.9 JList Class

```
public class JList extends JComponent implements Scrollable, Accessible
```

```
Object
  Component
    Container
      JComponent
        JList
```

### Interfaces

Accessible, ImageObserver, MenuContainer, Serializable, Scrollable

A JList object is a list of elements from which the user can make one or more selections. Generally, more than one selection is displayed.

A JList object does not automatically implement scrollbars. It should be contained in a JScrollPane container if scrollbars are desired.

A JList object uses a ListCellRenderer object to determine how the list elements will be displayed, and a JListModel object that holds the elements contained in the list, provides methods to access elements of the list, and provides listener interfaces. A ListSelectionModel object manages the currently selected items in the list.

## JList() Constructors

| Method | Syntax |
|--------|--------|
| JList() | public JList() |
| | public JList(ListModel lm) |
| | public JList(Object[] objects) |
| | public JList(Vector vector) |

Creates a JList object. The JList object can be initialized with an Object array or a Vector object. The default list model is the DefaultListModel class. The default cell renderer is the DefaultListCellRenderer class. If the no-argument constructor is used, an empty JList object that cannot be added to is created.

Any object type can be stored in the JList. The DefaultListCellRenderer will display a String representation of the list elements

## Color Methods

| Method | Syntax |
|--------|--------|
| getSelectionBackground() | public Color getSelectionBackground() |
| getSelectionForeground() | public Color getSelectionForeground() |
| setSelectionBackground() | public void setSelectionBackground (Color backgroundColor) |
| setSelectionForeground() | public void setSelectionForeground (Color foregroundColor) |

These methods return or change the foreground and background color of the selected elements of the invoking JList object. The ability to change the foreground and background color of components is one of the advantages of using Swing components - some platforms will not allow AWT heavyweight components to change color.

## ListSelectionListener Methods

| Method | Syntax |
|--------|--------|
| addListSelectionListener() | public void addListSelectionListener (ListSelectionListener *ll*) |
| removeListSelectionListener() | public void removeListSelectionListener (ListSelectionListener *ll*) |

A ListSelectionEvent is generated when any of the selections in a JList change.

addListSelectionListener() registers a ListSelectionListener with the invoking JList component.

removeListSelectionListener() removes a ListSelectionListener from the invoking JList component.

## Methods to Return JList Properties

| Method | Syntax |
|--------|--------|
| getCellRenderer() | public ListCellRenderer getCellRenderer() |
| getFirstVisibleIndex() | public int getFirstVisibleIndex() |
| getFixedCellHeight() | public int getFixedCellHeight() |
| getFixedCellWidth() | public int getFixedCellWidth() |
| getLastVisibleIndex() | public int getLastVisibleIndex() |
| getModel() | public ListModel getModel() |
| getPrototypeCellValue() | public Object getPrototypeCellValue() |
| getSelectionModel() | public ListSelectionModel getSelectionModel() |
| getValueIsAdjusting() | public boolean getValueIsAdjusting() |
| getVisibleRowCount() | public int getVisibleRowCount() |

getCellRenderer(), getModel(), and getSelectionModel() return the ListCellRenderer, ListModel, and ListSelectionModel objects associated with the invoking JList component.

getFirstVisibleIndex() and getLastVisibleIndex() return the indices of the topmost and bottommost elements visible in the JList display.

getFixedCellWidth() and getFixedCellHeight() return the widths and heights of each cell if they have been given fixed values using the setFixedCellWidth() and setFixedCellHeight() methods.

getPrototypeCellValue() returns the object that was used to set the minimum width of each cell in the invoking JList component.

9

javax.swing

`getValueIsAdjusting()` returns `true` if a series of selections is being made, for instance by dragging the mouse down the list.

`getVisibleRowCount()` returns the number of rows visible in the `JList` display.

## Methods to Set JList Properties

| Method | Syntax |
|---|---|
| ensureIndexIsVisible() | public void ensureIndexIsVisible(int *index*) |
| setCellRenderer() | public void setCellRenderer<br>(ListCellRenderer *lcr*) |
| setFixedCellHeight() | public void setFixedCellHeight(int *height*) |
| setFixedCellWidth() | public void setFixedCellWidth(int *width*) |
| setListData() | public void setListData(Vector *v*) |
| | public void setListData(Object[] *obj*) |
| setModel() | public void setModel(ListModel *lm*) |
| setPrototypeCellValue() | public void setPrototypeCellValue<br>(Object *prototype*) |
| setSelectionModel() | public void setSelectionModel<br>(ListSelectionModel *lsm*) |
| setValueIsAdjusting() | public void setValueIsAdjusting<br>(boolean *adjusting*) |
| setVisibleRowCount() | public void setVisibleRowCount(int *row*) |

`ensureIndexIsVisible()` scrolls the viewport to make the specified cell completely visible. The `JList` must be displayed within a `JViewport` for this method to work.

When the `JList` object is created, default renderers and models are used. The `setCellRenderer()`, `setModel()`, and `setSelectionModel()` methods are used to change the `ListCellRenderer`, `ListModel`, and `ListSelectionModel` objects associated with the invoking `JList` component.

`setListData()` is used to re-populate the list of the invoking `JList` object with either the elements contained in an `Object` array or in a `Vector` object.

`setFixedCellWidth()` and `setFixedCellHeight()` set a fixed width or height for each cell in the list.

`setPrototypeCellValue()` specifies an object that is used to set the minimum width of each cell in the invoking `JList` component. The `Object` passed to the method might be the `String` "123456789" if a 9 column cell was desired.

`setValueIsAdjusting()` method indicates if the selections of the invoking `JList` object are changing.

`setVisibleRowCount()` specifies the number of rows that will be visible in the `JList` display.

# Methods to Return Information on Selected Items

| Method | Syntax |
|--------|--------|
| getAnchorSelectionIndex | public int getAnchorSelectionIndex() |
| getLeadSelectionIndex() | public int getLeadSelectionIndex() |
| getMaxSelectionIndex() | public int getMaxSelectionIndex() |
| getMinSelectionIndex() | public int getMinSelectionIndex() |
| getSelectedIndex() | public int getSelectedIndex() |
| getSelectedIndices() | public int[] getSelectedIndices() |
| getSelectedValue() | public Object getSelectedValue () |
| getSelectedValues() | public Object[] getSelectedValues() |
| getSelectionMode() | public int getSelectionMode() |
| isSelectedIndex() | public boolean isSelectedIndex(int *index*) |
| isSelectionEmpty() | public boolean isSelectionEmpty() |

getAnchorSelectionIndex() and getLeadSelectionIndex() return the anchor and lead position for the most recently selected item.

getSelectedIndex() returns the index of the first selected item in the invoking JList object list.

getSelectedIndices() returns an array containing the indices of all selected items.

getMaxSelectionIndex() and getMinSelectionIndex() return the largest and smallest indices of the selected items.

getSelectedValue() returns the first selected element of the list.

getSelectedValues() returns an array containing all selected values.

isSelectedIndex() returns true if the element at position index is selected.

isSelectionEmpty() returns true if there are no elements currently selected.

getSelectionMode() returns the selection mode of the invoking JList object. The selection mode will be one of these constants

- ❏ ListSelectionModel.MULTIPLE_INTERVAL_SELECTION
- ❏ ListSelectionModel.SINGLE_INTERVAL_SELECTION
- ❏ ListSelectionModel.SINGLE_SELECTION

A single interval selection means that one range of elements can be selected, and a multiple interval selection means that two or more selection ranges are possible.

9

javax.swing

## Methods to Set Selected Items

| Method | Syntax |
|---|---|
| addSelectionInterval() | public void addSelectionInterval<br>(int *startIndex*, int *endIndex*) |
| clearSelection() | public void clearSelection() |
| removeSelectionInterval() | public void removeSelectionInterval<br>(int *startIndex*, int *endIndex*) |
| setSelectedIndex() | public void setSelectedIndex(int *index*) |
| setSelectedIndices() | public void setSelectedIndices<br>(int[] *indices*) |
| setSelectedValue() | public void setSelectedValue<br>(Object *obj*, boolean *makeVisible*) |
| setSelectionInterval() | public void setSelectionInterval<br>(int *startIndex*, int *endIndex*) |
| setSelectionMode() | public void setSelectionMode<br>(int *selectionMode*) |

addSelectionInterval() selects the elements from position startIndex to position endIndex in addition to any previously selected items.

removeSelectionInterval() de-selects the elements between startIndex and endIndex.

clearSelection() de-selects every element in the list.

setSelectedIndex() selects the element at position index in the list.

setSelectedIndices() selects the elements corresponding to the contents of the specified integer array.

setSelectedValue() selects the Object obj as the only selected item in the list.

setSelectionInterval() selects the elements from position startIndex to position endIndex.

setSelectionMode() changes the selection mode of the invoking JList object. The selection mode must be one of these constants

- ❑  ListSelectionModel.MULTIPLE_INTERVAL_SELECTION

- ❑  ListSelectionModel.SINGLE_INTERVAL_SELECTION

- ❑  ListSelectionModel.SINGLE_SELECTION

A single interval selection means that one range of elements can be selected.

# UI Delegate Methods

| Method | Syntax |
|--------|--------|
| getUI() | public ListUI getUI() |
| setUI() | public void setUI(ListUI *lui*) |

getUI() returns the ListUI object associated with the invoking JList object.

setUI() is used to change the ListUI object associated the invoking JList object.

---

### Example: Using JList

A JList object is created and initialized with the contents of a String array. The foreground color of selected items is set to red. The JList object is registered with a ListSelectionListener. When the selection state of any list element changes, the valueChanged() method is called. The selected items are returned using the getElementAt() method defined in the DefaultListModel class. A reference to the DefaultListModel object associated with the JList object is obtained using the getModel() method. The call to the getValueIsAdjusting() method ignores the ListSelectionEvent objects that are generated when the mouse is pressed and only listens for ListSelectionEvent objects that are generated when the mouse is released.

*The WinClosing class is used to terminate the program if the window is closed.*
*See Section 7.3.8 on page 657 for more details.*

```
import javax.swing.*;
import javax.swing.event.*;
import java.awt.*;
import java.awt.event.*;

public class TestJL extends JFrame implements ListSelectionListener {
  JList list;
  JTextField jtf;

  public TestJL() {
    jtf = new JTextField(15);
    jtf.setEditable(false);

    // A JList object is created and initialized with the contents
    // of a String array.  The JList is registered with a
    // ListSelectionListener.

    String[] names = {
      "Allison", "Ellen", "Marguerite", "Deena", "DeShon", "Austin",
      "Nathan", "Kelsen", "Alex", "Lucas"
```

9

javax.swing

```
      };
      list = new JList(names);
      list.setSelectionForeground(Color.red);
      list.addListSelectionListener(this);

      JPanel p = new JPanel();
      p.add(new JScrollPane(list));

      getContentPane().add(p, BorderLayout.CENTER);
      getContentPane().add(jtf, BorderLayout.SOUTH);

      // The WindowListener is used to terminate the program when the window
      // is closed.  Under Java 2 version 1.3, the addWindowListener() syntax
      // can be replaced by
      //
      // setDefaultCloseOperation(JFrame.EXIT_ON_CLOSE);

      addWindowListener(new WinClosing());
      setBounds(100, 100, 300, 300);
      setVisible(true);
    }

    // When a list selection is made, the valueChanged() method is called.
    // The method ignores events generated when the mouse is pressed.

    public void valueChanged(ListSelectionEvent le) {
      if (le.getValueIsAdjusting()) {
        return;
      }

      int[] index = list.getSelectedIndices();
      for (int i = 0; i < index.length; ++i) {
        String s = (String) list.getModel().getElementAt(index[i]);
        jtf.setText("Selection is: " + s);
      }
    }

    public static void main(String args[]) {
      TestJL tjl = new TestJL();
    }
  }

// The WinClosing class terminates the program when the window is closed

class WinClosing extends WindowAdapter {
  public void windowClosing(WindowEvent we) {
    System.exit(0);
  }
}
```

*Output*

The user interface of the program is shown below.

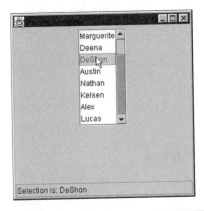

# 9.1.10 JPasswordField Class

```
public JPasswordField extends JTextField
```

```
Object
  Component
    Container
      JComponent
        JTextComponent
          JTextField
            JPasswordField
```

### Interfaces

```
Accessible, Scrollable, ImageObserver, MenuContainer, Serializable,
SwingConstants
```

A JPasswordField object is the same as a JTextField object except the text entered into the input area is replaced by an echo character. A JPasswordField is normally used for accepting passwords.

A JPasswordField object generates an ActionEvent when the *Enter* key is hit.

## JPasswordField() Constructors

| Method | Syntax |
|---|---|
| JPasswordField() | public JPasswordField() |
| | public JPasswordField(String *text*) |
| | public JPasswordField(int *columns*) |

9

javax.swing

| Method | Syntax |
|---|---|
| | `public JPasswordField`<br>    `(String text, int columns)` |
| | `public JPasswordField`<br>    `(Document doc, String text, int columns)` |

Creates a `JPasswordField` object. The number of columns, initial text (which is masked by the echo character), and a `Document` model can be specified. A `Document` object is a container for text that implements the `Document` interface, and is found in the `javax.swing.text` package. If no `Document` object is specified, a default `Document` object is used.

## Cut and Copy Methods

| Method | Syntax |
|---|---|
| `copy()` | `public void copy()` |
| `cut()` | `public void cut()` |

`copy()` and `cut()`, as they are defined in the `JTextComponent` class, would place the contents of the invoking `JPasswordField` object into the system clipboard. This is undesirable with passwords, so the methods have been overridden to simply beep.

## Echo Character Methods

| Method | Syntax |
|---|---|
| `echoCharIsSet()` | `public boolean echoCharIsSet()` |
| `getEchoChar()` | `public char getEchoChar()` |
| `setEchoChar()` | `public void setEchoChar(char echoCharacter)` |

`echoCharIsSet()` returns `true` if the echo character of the invoking `JPasswordField` object has been set. The echo character is set if it has not been assigned to the char `'0'`.

`getEchoChar()` returns the echo character of the invoking `JPasswordField` object.

`setEchoChar()` changes the echo character of the invoking `JPasswordField` object. The default echo character is `'*'`. Setting the character to `'0'` disables the echo character.

## getPassword() Method

| Method | Syntax |
|---|---|
| `getPassword()` | `public char[] getPassword()` |

`getPassword()` returns the text in the `JPasswordField` input field. Each character in the char array can be cleared after the password is read. This provides better security than if a password `String` is returned using the `getText()` method.

## Example: Using JPasswordField

A JPasswordField is created and placed on a JFrame. The echo character is set to be
'$'. The JPasswordField is registered with an ActionListener. When the *Enter* key
is pressed, the actionPerformed() method is called. The contents of the
JPasswordField is compared to the String "Oh-Man"; if it matches, the String
"Password accepted" is displayed at the bottom of the frame. If the password is
entered incorrectly three times, the program terminates.

This is example is meant only to show some features of the JPasswordField class. In
a real-life application, additional security measures would probably be taken to
protect the passwords.

*The WinClosing class is used to terminate the program if the window is closed.*
*See Section 7.3.8 on page 657 for more details.*

```java
import javax.swing.*;
import java.awt.event.*;
import java.awt.*;

public class TestJPF extends JFrame implements ActionListener {
  JPasswordField jpf;
  String pwd = "Oh-Man";
  int count;
  JTextField jtf;

  public TestJPF() {
    count = 0;

    jtf = new JTextField(15);
    jtf.setEditable(false);

    // A JPasswordField object is created.  The echo character is
    // set to '$' and the JPasswordField object is registered with
    // an ActionListener.

    jpf = new JPasswordField(20);
    jpf.setEchoChar('$');
    jpf.addActionListener(this);

    JPanel p = new JPanel();
    p.setLayout(new FlowLayout(FlowLayout.CENTER, 20, 20));
    p.add(jpf);

    getContentPane().add(p, BorderLayout.CENTER);
    getContentPane().add(jtf, BorderLayout.SOUTH);
```

```
      // The WindowListener is used to terminate the program when the window
      // is closed.  Under Java 2 version 1.3, the addWindowListener() syntax
      // can be replaced by
      //
      // setDefaultCloseOperation(JFrame.EXIT_ON_CLOSE);

      addWindowListener(new WinClosing());
      setBounds(100, 100, 300, 150);
      setVisible(true);
    }

    // When the JPasswordField has focus and the enter key is pressed,
    // an ActionEvent is generated and the actionPerformed() method is
    // called.  The entered text is compared against the password
    // "Oh-Man".  After 3 unsuccessful tries, the program terminates.

    public void actionPerformed(ActionEvent ae) {
      String enteredPwd = new String(jpf.getPassword());

      if (pwd.equals(enteredPwd)) {
        jtf.setText("Password accepted");
      } else {
        if (count > 2) {
          System.exit(0);
        }

        jtf.setText("Wrong Password");
        ++count;
      }
    }

    public static void main(String args[]) {
      TestJPF tjp = new TestJPF();
    }
}

// The WinClosing class terminates the program when the window is closed

class WinClosing extends WindowAdapter {
  public void windowClosing(WindowEvent we) {
    System.exit(0);
  }
}
```

*javax.swing*

9

### Output

The user interface of the program is shown below.

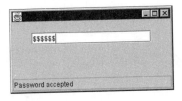

# 9.1.11 JRadioButton Class

```
public class JRadioButton extends JToggleButton implements Accessible
```

```
Object
  Component
    Container
      JComponent
        AbstractButton
          JToggleButton
            JRadioButton
```

### Interfaces

```
Accessible, ImageObserver, ItemSelectable, MenuContainer, Serializable,
SwingConstants
```

A JRadioButton object provides a radio button that can be selected or unselected. Its behavior is very similar to a JCheckBox object.

Several JRadioButton objects are often grouped together (made mutually exclusive) using a ButtonGroup object. See Section 9.1.2 on page 709 for more details.

A JRadioButton object fires an ItemEvent when selected or de-selected.

## JRadioButton() Constructors

| Method | Syntax |
|---|---|
| JRadioButton() | public JRadioButton() |
| | public JRadioButton(Action *act*) |
| | public JRadioButton(Icon *icon*) |
| | public JRadioButton(Icon *icon*, boolean *selected*) |
| | public JRadioButton(String *text*) |
| | public JRadioButton(String *text*, boolean *selected*) |
| | public JRadioButton(String *text*, Icon *icon*) |
| | public JRadioButton(String *text*, Icon *icon*, boolean *selected*) |

Creates a JRadioButton object. The JRadioButton object can be initialized with a label, an icon, and the selected state. The default selected state is unselected. If an Icon is provided, it is displayed in place of the default radio button. A selected icon should then also be set to differentiate between the selected and unselected states. If an Action is provided, the JRadioButton properties are taken from the Action.

## Example: Using JRadioButton

Two JRadioButton objects are created and placed on a JFrame. The JRadioButton objects are registered with an ItemListener to detect when one of the JRadioButton is selected. The JRadioButton objects are associated with a ButtonGroup object so that only one of the JRadioButton objects may be selected. A JTextField object is used to indicate which JRadioButton is selected.

*The WinClosing class is used to terminate the program if the window is closed. See Section 7.3.8 on page 657 for more details.*

```
import javax.swing.*;
import java.awt.event.*;
import java.awt.*;

public class TestJRB extends JFrame implements ItemListener {
  JRadioButton b1, b2;
  JTextField jtf;
  ButtonGroup bg;

  public TestJRB() {
    jtf = new JTextField(20);
    jtf.setEditable(false);

    // Two JRadioButton objects are created and registered with an
    // ItemListener

    b1 = new JRadioButton("Jackson");
    b1.setName("Jackson");
    b1.setBorder(BorderFactory.createRaisedBevelBorder());
    b1.setBorderPainted(true);
    b1.setPreferredSize(new Dimension(100, 40));
    b1.setHorizontalAlignment(SwingConstants.CENTER);
    b1.setVerticalAlignment(SwingConstants.CENTER);
    b1.addItemListener(this);

    b2 = new JRadioButton("Zachary");
    b2.setName("Zachary");
    b2.setBorder(BorderFactory.createRaisedBevelBorder());
    b2.setBorderPainted(true);
    b2.setPreferredSize(new Dimension(100, 40));
```

```
      b2.setHorizontalAlignment(SwingConstants.CENTER);
      b2.setVerticalAlignment(SwingConstants.CENTER);
      b2.addItemListener(this);

      // The JRadioButton objects are associated with a ButtonGroup so
      // that only one of them may be selected

      bg = new ButtonGroup();
      bg.add(b1);
      bg.add(b2);

      JPanel p = new JPanel();
      p.setLayout(new FlowLayout(FlowLayout.CENTER, 20, 20));
      p.add(b1);
      p.add(b2);

      getContentPane().add(p, BorderLayout.CENTER);
      getContentPane().add(jtf, BorderLayout.SOUTH);

      // The WindowListener is used to terminate the program when the window
      // is closed.  Under Java 2 version 1.3, the addWindowListener() syntax
      // can be replaced by
      //
      // setDefaultCloseOperation(JFrame.EXIT_ON_CLOSE);

      addWindowListener(new WinClosing());
      setBounds(100, 100, 300, 120);
      setVisible(true);
   }

   // When one of the JRadioButton objects is selected, an ItemEvent
   // is generated and the itemStateChanged() method is called.  The
   // text inside a JTextField object is updated to reflect the new
   // selection

   public void itemStateChanged(ItemEvent ie) {
      JRadioButton jrb = (JRadioButton) ie.getItemSelectable();
      jtf.setText(jrb.getName() + " is selected");
   }

   public static void main(String args[]) {
      TestJRB jrbn = new TestJRB();
   }
}

// The WinClosing class terminates the program when the window is closed
```

```
class WinClosing extends WindowAdapter {
  public void windowClosing(WindowEvent we) {
    System.exit(0);
  }
}
```

**Output**

The user interface of the program is shown below.

# 9.1.12 JScrollBar Class

```
public class JScrollBar extends JComponent implements Adjustable, Accessible
```

```
Object
  Component
    Container
      JComponent
        JScrollBar
```

### Interfaces

```
Accessible, Adjustable, ImageObserver, MenuContainer, Serializable
```

A JScrollBar object is a horizontal or vertical scrollbar, and is used for selecting an int between a minimum and maximum value. The value of the JScrollBar object can be changed by moving the slider bar, clicking on the up or down arrows, or by clicking anywhere within the paging area of the JScrollBar object.

A JScrollBar object fires an AdjustmentEvent when its value is changed.

## JScrollBar() Constructors

| Method | Syntax |
|---|---|
| JScrollBar() | public JScrollBar() |
| | public JScrollBar(int *orientation*) |
| | public JScrollBar(int *orientation*, int *value*, int *extent*, int *minimum*, int *maximum*) |

Creates a `JScrollBar` object. The `extent` is the width of the slider bar. The `orientation` must be one of these two constants:

- `JScrollBar.VERTICAL`
- `JScrollBar.HORIZONTAL`

## AdjustmentListener Methods

| Method | Syntax |
|---|---|
| addAdjustmentListener() | public void addAdjustmentListener<br>(AdjustmentListener al) |
| removeAdjustmentListener() | public void removeAdjustmentListener<br>(AdjustmentListener al) |

An `AdjustmentEvent` is generated when value of the `JScrollBar` changes.

`addAdjustmentListener()` registers the invoking `JScrollBar` component with a `AdjustmentListener`. The `AdjustmentListener` is notified if the `JScrollBar` generates an `AdjustmentEvent` object.

`removeAdjustmentListener()` removes an `AdjustmentListener` from the invoking `JScrollBar` component.

## Methods to Return JScrollBar Properties

| Method | Syntax |
|---|---|
| getBlockIncrement() | public int getBlockIncrement() |
| getMaximum() | public int getMaximum() |
| getMinimum() | public int getMinimum() |
| getModel() | public BoundedRangeModel getModel() |
| getOrientation() | public int getOrientation() |
| getUnitIncrement() | public int getUnitIncrement() |
|  | public int getUnitIncrement(int direction) |
| getVisibleAmount() | public int getVisibleAmount() |

`getBlockIncrement()` returns the amount the value changes if the paging area is clicked.

`getUnitIncrement()` returns the amount the value changes if one of the arrows is clicked. A direction can be specified, 1 for the unit increment in the up or right direction and -1 for the unit increment in the down or left direction.

`getMaximum()` and `getMinimum()` return the maximum and minimum values of the invoking `JScrollBar` object.

`getModel()` returns a reference to the `BoundedRangeModel` object associated with the invoking `JScrollBar` object.

9

javax.swing

getOrientation() returns the orientation of the invoking JScrollBar object. The return value will be either JScrollBar.VERTICAL or JScrollBar.HORIZONTAL.

getVisibleAmount() returns the extent of the scrollbar, how many units the slider represents. The display size of slider bar will usually be proportional to the extent.

## Methods to Set JScrollBar Properties

| Method | Syntax |
|---|---|
| setBlockIncrement() | public void setBlockIncrement(int *increment*) |
| setEnabled() | public void setEnabled(boolean *enabled*) |
| setMaximum() | public void setMaximum(int *maxValue*) |
| setMinimum() | public void setMinimum(int *minValue*) |
| setModel() | public void setModel(BoundedRangeModel *brm*) |
| setOrientation() | public void setOrientation(int *orientation*) throws IllegalArgumentException |
| setUnitIncrement() | public void setUnitIncrement(int *increment*) |
| setVisibleAmount() | public void setVisibleAmount(int *size*) |

setBlockIncrement() sets the amount the value changes if the paging area is clicked.

setEnabled() sets the enabled state of the invoking JScrollBar object.

setUnitIncrement() sets the amount the value changes if one of the arrows is clicked.

setMaximum() and setMinimum() change the maximum and minimum values of the invoking JScrollBar object.

setModel() sets the BoundedRangeModel object associated with the invoking JScrollBar object.

setVisibleAmount() is used to change the extent of the slider bar. The extent is how many units the slider bar represents.

setOrientation() defines the orientation of the invoking JScrollBar object. The argument passed to this method must be one of the following:

❑   JScrollBar.VERTICAL

❑   JScrollBar.HORIZONTAL

## Value Methods

| Method | Syntax |
|---|---|
| getValue() | public int getValue() |
| getValueIsAdjusting() | public boolean getValueIsAdjusting() |
| setValue() | public void setValue(int *value*) |

| Method | Syntax |
|---|---|
| setValueIsAdjusting() | public void setValueIsAdjusting (boolean *adjusting*) |
| setValues() | public void setValues(int *value*, int *extent*, int *minimum*, int *maximum*) |

getValue() returns the current value of the invoking JScrollBar object.

setValue() changes the value of the invoking JScrollBar object.

getValueIsAdjusting() method returns true if the value of the invoking JScrollBar object is changing. This means that the slider bar is being dragged.

setValues() can used to change the value, extent, minimum, and maximum properties.

## UI Delegate Methods

| Method | Syntax |
|---|---|
| getUI() | public ScrollBarUI getUI() |
| getUIClassID() | public String getUIClassID() |
| updateUI() | public void updateUI() |

getUI() returns the ScrollBarUI object associated with the invoking JScrollBar object.

getUIClassID() returns the String "ScrollBarUI" which is the suffix of the object used to render a JScrollBar object.

updateUI() is called when the look-and-feel of the invoking JScrollBar object has changed.

### Example: Using JScrollBar

A JScrollBar and a JTextField object are coupled together such that if the value of the JScrollBar object is changed, the text shown in the JTextField object is changed to the same value and vice versa. The implementation of the JScrollBar is that the minimum value corresponds to the top of the scrollbar. Logic is built in to the program so the value 1 corresponds to the bottom of the JScrollBar and 100 corresponds to the top.

It was desired that the JScrollBar range be from 1 to 100. The maximum value was set to 105 because the largest value that can be reached by clicking on the up arrow is the maximum value minus the extent value, in this case $105 - 5 = 100$.

*The WinClosing class is used to terminate the program if the window is closed. See Section 7.3.8 on page 657 for more details.*

9

javax.swing

```
import javax.swing.*;
import java.awt.*;
import java.awt.event.*;

public class TestJSB extends JFrame {
  JScrollBar jsb;
  JTextField jtf;
  int i, maxValue, extentValue;

  public TestJSB() {
    maxValue = 100;
    extentValue = 5;

    // A JScrollBar object is created.

    jsb = new JScrollBar(JScrollBar.VERTICAL, 1, extentValue, 1,
                         maxValue + extentValue);
    jsb.setPreferredSize(new Dimension(20, 85));
    jsb.addAdjustmentListener(new JScrollBarHandler());

    // A JTextField is created.

    jtf = new JTextField(3);
    jtf.addActionListener(new JTextFieldHandler());
    i = maxValue + 1 - jsb.getValue();
    jtf.setText("" + i);

    JPanel p = new JPanel();
    p.add(jtf);
    p.add(jsb);

    getContentPane().add(p);

    // The WindowListener is used to terminate the program when the window
    // is closed.  Under Java 2 version 1.3, the addWindowListener() syntax
    // can be replaced by
    //
    // setDefaultCloseOperation(JFrame.EXIT_ON_CLOSE);

    addWindowListener(new WinClosing());
    setBounds(100, 100, 300, 150);
    setVisible(true);
  }

// The JScrollBar and JTextField are linked together by the
// AdjustmentListener and ActionListener classes.  If the value
// of the JScrollBar is changed, the text in the JTextField is
// updated.  If the text in the JTextField is changed, the value
// of the JScrollBar is updated.
```

```
class JScrollBarHandler implements AdjustmentListener {
  public void adjustmentValueChanged(AdjustmentEvent ae) {
    i = maxValue + 1 - jsb.getValue();
    jtf.setText("" + i);
  }
}

class JTextFieldHandler implements ActionListener {
  public void actionPerformed(ActionEvent ae) {
    i = maxValue + 1 - Integer.parseInt(jtf.getText());
    jsb.setValue(i);
  }
}

  public static void main(String args[]) {
    TestJSB tjsb = new TestJSB();
  }
}

// The WinClosing class terminates the program when the window is closed

class WinClosing extends WindowAdapter {
  public void windowClosing(WindowEvent we) {
    System.exit(0);
  }
}
```

**Output**

The user interface of the program is shown below.

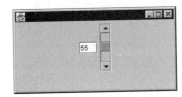

# 9.1.13 JSlider Class

```
public class JSlider extends JComponent implements SwingConstants, Accessible
```

```
Object
  Component
    Container
      JComponent
        JSlider
```

### Interfaces

Accessible, ImageObserver, MenuContainer, Serializable, SwingConstants

A JSlider object provides a slider bar with both tick marks and labels. There can be both major and minor tick marks.

A JSlider object fires a ChangeEvent when its value is changed.

# JSlider() Constructors

| Method | Syntax |
|--------|--------|
| JSlider() | public JSlider() |
| | public JSlider(int *orientation*) |
| | public JSlider(int *min*, int *max*) |
| | public JSlider(int *min*, int *max*, int *value*) |
| | public JSlider(int *orientation*, int *min*, int *max*, int *value*) |
| | public JSlider(BoundedRangeModel *brm*) |

Creates a JSlider object. The orientation must be one of these two constants:

- ❏   JSlider.VERTICAL
- ❏   JSlider.HORIZONTAL

# Appearance Methods

| Method | Syntax |
|--------|--------|
| getPaintLabels() | public boolean getPaintLabels() |
| getPaintTicks() | public boolean getPaintTicks() |
| getPaintTrack () | public boolean getPaintTrack () |
| setPaintLabels() | public void setPaintLabels(boolean *b*) |
| setPaintTicks() | public void setPaintTicks(boolean *b*) |
| setPaintTrack() | public void setPaintTrack(boolean *b*) |

getPaintLabels(), getPaintTicks(), and getPaintTrack() return true if the labels, ticks, or the track on the slider are to be painted.

setPaintLabels(), setPaintTicks(), and setPaintTrack() are used to specify if these elements are to be painted.

# ChangeListener Methods

| Method | Syntax |
|--------|--------|
| addChangeListener() | public void addChangeListener (ChangeListener *cl*) |
| removeChangeListener() | public void removeChangeListener (ChangeListener *cl*) |

A `ChangeEvent` is generated when any of the properties of the `JSlider` changes.

`addChangeListener()` registers the invoking `JSlider` component with a `ChangeListener` object. The `ChangeListener` is notified if the `JSlider` generates a `ChangeEvent` object.

`removeChangeListener()` removes a `ChangeListener` from the invoking `JSlider` component.

## Increment and Range Methods

| Method | Syntax |
|---|---|
| getExtent() | public int getExtent() |
| getMajorTickSpacing() | public int getMajorTickSpacing() |
| getMaximum() | public int getMaximum() |
| getMinimum() | public int getMinimum() |
| getMinorTickSpacing() | public int getMinorTickSpacing() |
| setExtent() | public void setExtent(int *width*) |
| setMajorTickSpacing() | public void setMajorTickSpacing(int *spacing*) |
| setMaximum() | public void setMaximum(int *minValue*) |
| setMinimum() | public void setMinimum(int *maxValue*) |
| setMinorTickSpacing() | public void setMinorTickSpacing(int *spacing*) |

These methods are used to change various increment and range properties of the invoking `JSlider` object. The `extent` is the width of the thumb of the `JSlider` object. The `maximum` and `minimum` properties refer to the maximum and minimum values of the `JSlider`.

## isFilled Property

The `javax.swing.plaf.metal.MetalSliderUI` class, which provides the UI Delegate for the `JSlider` class in the Metal look-and-feel, provides a `String` property, `JSlider.isFilled`, which can be set using the `putClientProperty()` method defined in the `JComponent` class. If it is set to `true`, the descending portion of the slider will be filled.

This only works with the Metal Look-and-Feel. See the *Using JSlider* example on page 779 for an example of how this is done.

## Label Methods

| Method | Syntax |
|---|---|
| createStandardLabels() | public Hashtable createStandardLabels(int *increment*) |
| createStandardLabels() | public Hashtable createStandardLabels(int *increment*, int *startValue*) |
| getLabelTable() | public Dictionary getLabelTable() |
| setLabelTable() | public void setLabelTable(Dictionary *d*) |

9

javax.swing

createStandardLabels() creates a Hashtable of numeric labels. This Hashtable can be passed to the setLabelTable() to change the labels that are displayed by the invoking JSlider object.

getLabelTable() returns a Dictionary object containing a collection of labels and numeric values.

## JSlider Property Methods

| Method | Syntax |
|--------|--------|
| getInverted() | public boolean getInverted() |
| getModel() | public BoundedRangeModel getModel() |
| getOrientation() | public int getOrientation() |
| getSnapToTicks() | public boolean getSnapToTicks() |
| setInverted() | public void setInverted(boolean *direction*) |
| setModel() | public void setModel(BoundedRangeModel *brm*) |
| setOrientation() | public void setOrientation(int *orientationConstant*) |
| setSnapToTicks() | public void setSnapToTicks(boolean *snap*) |

getInverted() returns true if the invoking JSlider object increments from right-to-left or top-to-bottom.

getModel() returns the BoundedRangeModel object associated with the invoking JSlider object.

getOrientation() returns the orientation of the invoking JSlider object. The return value will be either JSlider.VERTICAL or JSlider.HORIZONTAL

getSnapToTicks() returns true if the slider arrow is constrained to always be directly over one of the ticks.

setInverted(), setModel(), setOrientation(), and setSnapToTicks() methods are used to change the corresponding properties.

## Value Methods

| Method | Syntax |
|--------|--------|
| getValue | public int getValue() |
| getValueIsAdjusting() | public boolean getValueIsAdjusting() |
| setValue() | public void setValue(int *value*) |
| setValueIsAdjusting() | public void setValueIsAdjusting (boolean *adjusting*) |

getValue() returns the current value of the invoking JSlider object.

setValue() changes the value of the invoking JSlider object.

getValueIsAdjusting() returns true if the value of the invoking JSlider object is changing. This means the slider bar is being dragged.

# UI Delegate Methods

| Method | Syntax |
|---|---|
| getUI() | public SliderUI getUI() |
| getUIClassID() | public String getUIClassID() |
| setUI() | public void setUI(SliderUI sui) |
| updateUI() | public void updateUI() |

getUI() returns the SliderUI object associated with the invoking JSlider object.

getUIClassID() returns the String "SliderUI" which is the suffix of the object used to render a JSlider object.

setUI() is used to change the SliderUI object associated the invoking JSlider object.

updateUI() is called when the look-and-feel of the invoking JSlider object has changed.

## Example: Using JSlider

A horizontal JSlider is created with an initial range from 0 to 100. Major and minor ticks are set up in increments of 20 and 5 respectively. The ticks and labels are painted. The JSlider object is registered with a ChangeListener, and the isFilled property is set to be true.

When the slider value is changed, the stateChanged() method is called and the text of a JTextField object is update to reflect the change.

*The WinClosing class is used to terminate the program if the window is closed. See Section 7.3.8 on page 657 for more details.*

```java
import javax.swing.*;
import java.awt.*;
import java.awt.event.*;
import javax.swing.event.*;

public class TestJS extends JFrame {
    JSlider js;
    JTextField jtf;

    public TestJS() {

        // A JSlider object is created, various properties are set, and
        // the JSlider is registered with a ChangeListener
```

9

javax.swing

```
        js = new JSlider(JSlider.HORIZONTAL, 0, 100, 50);
        js.setMajorTickSpacing(20);
        js.setMinorTickSpacing(5);
        js.setPaintTicks(true);
        js.setPaintLabels(true);
        js.putClientProperty("JSlider.isFilled", Boolean.TRUE);
        js.setForeground(Color.black);
        js.setBorder(BorderFactory.createEtchedBorder());
        js.addChangeListener(new JSliderHandler());

        // A JTextField object is used to display the JSlider value

        jtf = new JTextField(15);
        jtf.setEditable(false);
        jtf.setText("JSlider value is " + js.getValue());

        JPanel p = new JPanel();
        p.add(js);

        getContentPane().add(p, BorderLayout.CENTER);
        getContentPane().add(jtf, BorderLayout.SOUTH);

        // The WindowListener is used to terminate the program when the window
        // is closed.  Under Java 2 version 1.3, the addWindowListener() syntax
        // can be replaced by
        //
        // setDefaultCloseOperation(JFrame.EXIT_ON_CLOSE);

        addWindowListener(new WinClosing());
        setBounds(100, 100, 300, 120);
        setVisible(true);
    }

    // When the value of the JSlider is changed, a ChangeEvent is
    // generated and the stateChanged() method is called.  The text
    // of the JTextField is updated to the new JSlider value.

    class JSliderHandler implements ChangeListener {
        public void stateChanged(ChangeEvent ce) {
            jtf.setText("JSlider value is " + js.getValue());
        }
    }

    public static void main(String args[]) {
        TestJS tjs = new TestJS();
    }
}

// The WinClosing class terminates the program when the window is closed
```

```
class WinClosing extends WindowAdapter {
  public void windowClosing(WindowEvent we) {
    System.exit(0);
  }
}
```

**Output**

The user interface of the program is shown below.

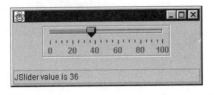

# 9.1.14 JTextArea Class

```
public class JTextArea extends JTextComponent
```

```
Object
  Component
    Container
      JComponent
        JTextComponent
          JTextArea
```

### Interfaces

```
Accessible, ImageObserver, Scrollable, MenuContainer, Serializable
```

A JTextArea object is a multi-line area for user input or text display. The JTextArea class has methods to enable line-wrapping. JTextArea objects are often placed inside a JScrollPane object if the size of the JTextArea is expected to exceed the size of the display window.

## JTextArea() Constructors

| Method | Syntax |
|---|---|
| JTextArea() | public JTextArea() |
| | public JTextArea(int *rows*, int *columns*) throws IllegalArgumentException |
| | public JTextArea(String *text*) |
| | public JTextArea(String *text*, int *rows*, int *columns*) throws IllegalArgumentException |
| | public JTextArea(Document *doc*) |
| | public JTextArea(Document *doc*, String *text*, int *rows*, int *columns*) throws IllegalArgumentException |

**781**

The number or rows and columns, an initial `String` of text, and a `Document` model can be specified. A `Document` object is a container for text that implements the `Document` interface, which is found in the `javax.swing.text` package. If no `Document` object is specified, a default `Document` object is used.

## Methods to Add or Replace Text

| Method | Syntax |
|---|---|
| `append()` | `public void append(String str)` |
| `insert()` | `public void insert(String str, int index)`<br>`        throws IllegalArgumentException` |
| `replaceRange()` | `public void replaceRange(String str,`<br>`    int startIndex, int endIndex)`<br>`        throws IllegalArgumentException` |

`append()` appends `String str` to the text contained by the invoking `JTextArea` object at the end of the text.

`insert()` inserts `String str` into the invoking `JTextArea` object starting at the specified `index`.

`replaceRange()` replaces the current text in the invoking `JTextArea` object from position `startIndex` to position `endIndex` with `String str`.

## Line Wrap Methods

| Method | Syntax |
|---|---|
| `getLineWrap()` | `public boolean getLineWrap()` |
| `getWrapStyleWord()` | `public boolean getWrapStyleWord()` |
| `setLineWrap()` | `public void setLineWrap(boolean lineWrapMode)` |
| `setWrapStyleWord()` | `public void setWrapStyleWord`<br>`        (boolean wrapStyleWordMode)` |

`getLineWrap()` returns the current line wrap mode of the invoking `JTextArea` object.

`setLineWrap()` sets the line wrap mode. If the line wrap mode is set to `false`, any entered text will be placed on one row with the number of columns adjusted to fit the size of the `String`. If the line wrap mode is set to `true`, the text will be placed on the next line once the end of the line, specified by the number of columns, is reached.

`getWrapStyleWord()` returns the current wrap style mode of the invoking `JTextArea` object are to be broken at word boundaries. If the wrap style word mode is set to `true`, lines are broken at word boundaries, otherwise lines are broken at character boundaries.

`setWrapStyleWord()` is used to set the wrap style word mode.

## Line count and Line Offset Methods

| Method | Syntax |
|---|---|
| getLineCount() | public int getLineCount() |
| getLineEndOffset() | public int getLineEndOffset(int *line*)<br>    throws BadLocationException |
| getLineOfOffset() | public int getLineOfOffset(int *offset*)<br>    throws BadLocationException |
| getLineStartOffset() | public int getLineStartOffset(int *line*)<br>    throws BadLocationException |

getLineCount() returns the number of lines of text in the invoking JTextArea object.

getLineEndOffset() returns the number of characters from the beginning of the text to the end of the specified line.

getLineOfOffset() the line that contains the specified character offset.

getLineStartOffset() returns the number of characters from the beginning of the text to the beginning of the specified line.

## Miscellaneous Property Methods

| Method | Syntax |
|---|---|
| getPreferredSize() | public Dimension getPreferredSize() |
| getUIClassID() | public String getUIClassID() |
| setFont() | public void setFont(Font *font*) |

These methods override the versions defined in the JComponent class.

getPreferredSize() returns the preferred size of the invoking JTextArea object.

getUIClassID() returns the String "TextAreaUI" which is the suffix of the class that renders a JTextArea object.

setFont() changes the font displayed by the invoking JTextArea object.

## Row and Column Methods

| Method | Syntax |
|---|---|
| getColumns() | public int getColumns() |
| getRows() | public int getRows() |
| setColumns() | public void setColumns(int *columns*)<br>    throws IllegalArgumentException |
| setRows() | public void setRows(int *rows*)<br>    throws IllegalArgumentException |

9

javax.swing

getColumns() and getRows() return the number of columns and rows of the invoking JTextArea object. The number of rows refers to the number of rows displayed.

setColumns() and setRows() are used to change the number of columns and rows of the invoking JTextArea object.

## Tab Size Methods

| Method | Syntax |
|---|---|
| getTabSize() | public int getTabSize() |
| setTabSize() | public void setTabSize(int tabSize) |

getTabSize() returns the tab size of the invoking JTextArea object.

setTabSize() is used to change the tab size.

### Example: Using JTextArea

A JTextArea object is created and placed in a JFrame. The JTextArea is set to have 15 columns and to display 10 rows of text. The JTextArea object is set to line wrap and to break lines at word boundaries. Some text is added to the JTextArea. JTextArea objects do not automatically implement scrollbars. A scrollbar can be added by wrapping a JScrollPane object around the JTextArea and placing the JScrollPane object on the content pane.

*The WinClosing class is used to terminate the program if the window is closed. See Section 7.3.8 on page 74 for more details.*

```java
import javax.swing.*;
import java.awt.event.*;
import java.awt.*;

public class TestJTA extends JFrame {
  JTextArea jta;

  public TestJTA() {

    // A JTextArea object is created. Some text is added and the
    // JTextArea is set to line wrap and break lines at word boundaries

    jta = new JTextArea(10, 15);
    jta.setFont(new Font("Serif", Font.PLAIN, 12));
    jta.append("Jackson and Zachary are my boys");
    jta.setLineWrap(true);
    jta.setWrapStyleWord(true);
```

```
    // The JTextArea object is added to a JScrollPane before being added
    // to the JFrame.  This way if the contents of the JTextArea exceed its
    // display size, scrollbars will be automatically added.

    JPanel p = new JPanel();
    p.add(new JScrollPane(jta));

    getContentPane().add(p, BorderLayout.CENTER);

    // The WindowListener is used to terminate the program when the window
    // is closed.  Under Java 2 version 1.3, the addWindowListener() syntax
    // can be replaced by
    //
    // setDefaultCloseOperation(JFrame.EXIT_ON_CLOSE);

    addWindowListener(new WinClosing());
    setBounds(100, 100, 300, 300);
    setVisible(true);
  }

  public static void main(String args[]) {
    TestJTA tjta = new TestJTA();
  }
}

// The WinClosing class terminates the program when the window is closed

class WinClosing extends WindowAdapter {
  public void windowClosing(WindowEvent we) {
    System.exit(0);
  }
}
```

### Output

The user interface of the program is shown below.

# 9.1.15 JTextComponent Class

```
public abstract class JTextComponent extends JComponent
    implements Scrollable, Accessible
```

```
Object
  Component
    Container
      JComponent
        JTextComponent
```

### Interfaces

Accessible, ImageObserver, MenuContainer, Serializable, Scrollable

JTextComponent is the parent class of the Swing text component classes. The JTextComponent class defines methods that are common to JTextComponent sub-classes. Since it is an abstract class, a JTextComponent object is not normally created.

Unlike the other Swing text component classes which are contained in the javax.swing package, the JTextComponent class is found in the javax.swing.text package, but is included here for completeness.

## Caret Methods

| Method | Syntax |
|---|---|
| addCaretListener() | public void addCaretListener(CaretListener *cl*) |
| getCaret() | public Caret getCaret() |
| getCaretColor() | public Color getCaretColor() |
| getCaretPosition() | public int getCaretPosition() |
| moveCaretPosition() | public void moveCaretPosition(int *newPosition*) |
| removeCaretListener() | public void removeCaretListener(CaretListener *cl*) |
| setCaret() | public void setCaret(Caret *c*) |
| setCaretColor() | public void setCaretColor(Color *caretColor*) |
| setCaretPosition() | public void setCaretPosition(int *position*) |

The caret is the cursor that appears inside a JTextComponent sub-class object that indicates the location that text will inserted. CaretEvent objects are generated when the state of the caret changes. The CaretEvent class and the CaretListener interface are defined in the javax.swing.event package.

getCaret() returns the Caret object associated with the invoking JTextComponent sub-class object.

setCaret() is used to set or change the Caret object associated with the invoking JTextComponent sub-class object.

getCaretColor() and setCaretColor() return or change the Color object associated with the invoking JTextComponent sub-class object.

getCaretPosition() and setCaretPosition() return or change the caret position.

moveCaretPosition() selects a section of text by moving the caret from its current position to newPosition.

addCaretListener() associates a CaretListener object to the invoking JTextComponent sub-class object to listen for CaretEvents.

removeCaretListener() disconnects the CaretListener object from the invoking JTextComponent sub-class object.

## Example: Using Caret Methods

A JTextField object is created and placed on a JFrame. The color of the caret associated with the JTextField is set to be red, and the position of the caret is set to be between the first and second characters. The caret only appears if the JTextField has focus. The grabFocus() methods places the focus on the JTextField object when the JFrame becomes visible. The JTextField object is associated with a CaretListener. The caretUpdate() method is called every time the caret position is changed, and the contents of a second JTextField are updated to reflect the move.

*The WinClosing class is used to terminate the program if the window is closed. See Section 7.3.8 on page 657 for more details.*

```
import javax.swing.*;
import javax.swing.event.*;
import java.awt.event.*;
import java.awt.*;

public class TestCaret extends JFrame implements CaretListener {
    JTextField jtf, jtf2;

    public TestCaret() {

        // A JTextField object is created, some caret properties are set,
        // and the JTextField object is registered with a CaretListener

        jtf = new JTextField(20);
        jtf.setText("Jackson and Zachary");
        jtf.setFont(new Font("Serif", Font.BOLD, 12));

        jtf.setCaretPosition(2);
        jtf.setCaretColor(Color.red);
        jtf.addCaretListener(this);

        // A second JTextField is created to display the output from the
        // caretUpdate() method
```

9

javax.swing

```
        jtf2 = new JTextField(20);
        jtf2.setText("Caret is at index " + jtf.getCaretPosition());
        jtf2.setEditable(false);

        JPanel p = new JPanel();
        p.setLayout(new FlowLayout(FlowLayout.CENTER, 20, 20));
        p.add(jtf);

        getContentPane().add(p, BorderLayout.CENTER);
        getContentPane().add(jtf2, BorderLayout.SOUTH);

        // The WindowListener is used to terminate the program when the window
        // is closed.  Under Java 2 version 1.3, the addWindowListener() syntax
        // can be replaced by
        //
        // setDefaultCloseOperation(JFrame.EXIT_ON_CLOSE);

        addWindowListener(new WinClosing());
        setBounds(100, 100, 300, 150);
        setVisible(true);
        jtf.grabFocus();
    }

    // The caretMoved() method is called when a CaretEvent is generated
    // due to the caret moving.

    public void caretUpdate(CaretEvent ce) {
        jtf2.setText("Caret is at index " + jtf.getCaretPosition());
    }

    public static void main(String args[]) {
        TestCaret tc = new TestCaret();
    }
}

// The WinClosing class terminates the program when the window is closed

class WinClosing extends WindowAdapter {
    public void windowClosing(WindowEvent we) {
        System.exit(0);
    }
}
```

*Output*

The user interface of the program is shown below.

## Copy, Cut, and Paste Methods

| Method | Syntax |
|--------|--------|
| copy() | public void copy() |
| cut() | public void cut() |
| paste() | public void paste() |

copy() copies the currently selected text of the invoking JTextComponent sub-class object into the system clipboard.

cut() deletes the currently selected text of the invoking JTextComponent sub-class object and places the deleted text into the system clipboard.

paste() inserts the contents of the system clipboard into the invoking JTextComponent sub-class object.

### Example: Using Cut, and Paste

A JTextField object is created and placed on a JFrame. The Keymap associated with the JTextField is acquired using the getKeymap() method. Two KeyStroke-Action pairs are added to the Keymap. If *Ctrl-X* is pressed, the actionPerformed() method of the CutAction class is called and the selected text is cut and placed in the system clipboard. If *Ctrl-V* is pressed, the actionPerformed() method of the PasteAction class is called and the text contained in the system clipboard is inserted into the JTextField.

To see the cut and paste features in action, type some text into the JTextField, select some of the text, and then use *Ctrl-X* and *Ctrl-V* to cut and paste the text.

*The WinClosing class is used to terminate the program if the window is closed. See Section 7.3.8 on page 657 for more details.*

9

javax.swing

```
import javax.swing.*;
import javax.swing.text.*;
import java.awt.event.*;
import java.awt.*;

public class TestCutPaste extends JFrame {
  JTextField jtf;

  public TestCutPaste() {
    jtf = new JTextField(20);
    jtf.setFont(new Font("Serif", Font.PLAIN, 12));

    Keymap km = jtf.getKeymap();

    // The keyboard sequence Ctrl-X is mapped to a CutAction object

    KeyStroke cut = KeyStroke.getKeyStroke(KeyEvent.VK_X,
                                        InputEvent.CTRL_MASK,
                                        false);
    km.addActionForKeyStroke(cut, new CutAction());

    // The keyboard sequence Ctrl-V is mapped to a PasteAction object

    KeyStroke paste = KeyStroke.getKeyStroke(KeyEvent.VK_V,
                                        InputEvent.CTRL_MASK,
                                        false);
    km.addActionForKeyStroke(paste, new PasteAction());

    JPanel p = new JPanel();
    p.setLayout(new FlowLayout(FlowLayout.CENTER, 20, 20));
    p.add(jtf);

    getContentPane().add(p, BorderLayout.CENTER);

    // The WindowListener is used to terminate the program when the window
    // is closed.  Under Java 2 version 1.3, the addWindowListener() syntax
    // can be replaced by
    //
    // setDefaultCloseOperation(JFrame.EXIT_ON_CLOSE);

    addWindowListener(new WinClosing());
    setBounds(100, 100, 300, 120);
    setVisible(true);
  }

  // When Ctrl-X is typed, the actionPerformed() method from the CutAction
  // class is called and the selected text is cut
```

```
   class CutAction extends AbstractAction {
   public void actionPerformed(ActionEvent ae) {
     jtf.cut();
   }
 }

// When Ctrl-V is typed, the actionPerformed() method from the
// PasteAction class is called and the text contained in the system
// clipboard is pasted.

class PasteAction extends AbstractAction {
  public void actionPerformed(ActionEvent ae) {
    jtf.paste();
  }
}

 public static void main(String args[]) {
   TestCutPaste tc = new TestCutPaste();
 }
}

// The WinClosing class terminates the program when the window is closed

class WinClosing extends WindowAdapter {
  public void windowClosing(WindowEvent we) {
    System.exit(0);
  }
}
```

### Output

The user interface of the program is shown below.

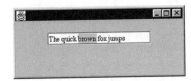

## I/O Methods

| Method | Syntax |
|--------|--------|
| read() | public void **read**(Reader *inputStream*, Object *description*) throws IOException |
| write() | public void **write**(Writer *outputStream*) throws IOException |

read( ) intializes the invoking JTextComponent sub-class object from data read from inputStream. The Object description is typically a String used to describe some information about the input stream; if no description is desired, null can be passed as an argument.

write( ) writes the contents of the invoking JTextComponent sub-class object to outputStream.

## Example: Using JTextComponent I/O Methods

A JTextField and a JButton object are placed on a JFrame. When the JButton is pressed, the actionPerformed( ) method is called and the contents of the JTextField are written to a file named TestIO.txt.

*The WinClosing class is used to terminate the program if the window is closed. See Section 7.3.8 on page 657 for more details.*

```
import javax.swing.*;
import java.awt.event.*;
import java.awt.*;
import java.io.*;

public class TestIO extends JFrame implements ActionListener {
  JTextField jtf;
  JButton b1;

  public TestIO() {
    b1 = new JButton("Write");
    b1.setBorder(BorderFactory.createRaisedBevelBorder());
    b1.addActionListener(this);

    jtf = new JTextField(20);
    jtf.setFont(new Font("Serif", Font.PLAIN, 12));
    jtf.addActionListener(this);

    JPanel p = new JPanel();
    p.setLayout(new FlowLayout(FlowLayout.CENTER, 20, 20));
    p.add(jtf);
    p.add(b1);

    getContentPane().add(p, BorderLayout.CENTER);

    // The WindowListener is used to terminate the program when the window
    // is closed.  Under Java 2 version 1.3, the addWindowListener() syntax
    // can be replaced by
    //
    // setDefaultCloseOperation(JFrame.EXIT_ON_CLOSE);
```

```
   addWindowListener(new WinClosing());
    setBounds(100, 100, 300, 120);
    setVisible(true);
  }

  // When the "Write" button is pressed, an ActionEvent is generated
  // and sent to the actionPerformed() method.  The contents of the
  // JTextField are written to a file named "TestIO.txt"

  public void actionPerformed(ActionEvent ae) {
    try {
      FileWriter fw = new FileWriter("TestIO.txt");
      jtf.write(fw);
    } catch (IOException ioe) {
      System.out.println("Error: " + ioe);
    }
  }

  public static void main(String args[]) {
    TestIO tio = new TestIO();
  }
}

// The WinClosing class terminates the program when the window is closed

class WinClosing extends WindowAdapter {
  public void windowClosing(WindowEvent we) {
    System.exit(0);
  }
}
```

### Output
The user interface of the program is shown below.

## Keymap Methods

| Method | Syntax |
| --- | --- |
| addKeymap() | public static Keymap addKeymap(String keymapName, KeyMap parent) |
| getKeymap() | public Keymap getKeymap() |
| | public static Keymap getKeymap(String keymapName) |
| removeKeyMap() | public static Keymap removeKeymap(String keymapName) |
| setKeymap() | public void setKeymap(Keymap km) |

A `Keymap` object relates a keyboard sequence to an action. For instance, *Ctrl-C* could be typed to copy text. A `Keymap` object can contain more than one keyboard sequence – action pair.

`addKeymap()` adds a `Keymap` into a keymap hierarchy. The `Keymap` name and its parent must be specified.

`getKeymap()` returns the currently active `Keymap` obect associated with the invoking `JTextComponent` sub-class object. The static version returns a named `Keymap` that was previously added to the invoking `JTextComponent` sub-class object.

`removeKeymap()` removes a named `Keymap` that was previously added to the invoking `JTextComponent` sub-class object.

`setKeymap()` sets or changes the `Keymap` obect associated with the invoking `JTextComponent` sub-class object.

## Example: Using Keymaps

See *Using Cut and Paste* example on page 789, where a `Keymap` obect is used to map the cut and paste functions to keyboard sequences.

## Methods to Return or Set JTextComponent Properties

| Method | Syntax |
|---|---|
| getActions() | public Action[] getActions() |
| getFocusAccelerator() | public char getFocusAccelerator() |
| getMargin() | public Insets getMargin() |
| isEditable() | public boolean isEditable() |
| isFocusTraversable() | public boolean isFocusTraversable() |
| setEditable | public void setEditable(boolean *editable*) |
| setFocusAccelerator() | public void setFocusAccelerator(char *key*) |
| setMargin() | public void setMargin(Insets *i*) |

`getActions()` returns an array containing the `Action` objects associated with the invoking `JTextComponent` sub-class object.

`getFocusAccelerator()` returns the key character which when pressed along with the *Alt* key moves the focus to the invoking `JTextComponent` sub-class object.

`getMargin()` returns the distance from the invoking `JTextComponent` sub-class object's outer boundaries to the element it displays.

`isEditable()` returns `true` if the text contained by the invoking `JTextComponent` sub-class object can be changed.

isFocusTraversable() returns true if the invoking JTextComponent sub-class object can receive focus by typing the *Tab* or *Shift-Tab* keyboard sequences.

setEditable() changes the editable state of the invoking JTextComponent sub-class object.

setFocusAccelerator() sets or changes the key character which when pressed along with the *Alt* key moves the focus to the invoking JTextComponent sub-class object.

setMargin() changes the margin maintained by the invoking JTextComponent sub-class object.

## Example: Setting JTextComponent Properties

A JTextField object is created and placed on a JFrame. The margins between the boundary of the JTextField and the text it contains is increased using the setMargin() method. The JTextField object is also given a focus accelerator. A JButton is also added to the JFrame. If the focus is placed on the JButton and the focus accelerator, *Alt*-F, is pressed, the focus will shift to the JTextField.

*The WinClosing class is used to terminate the program if the window is closed. See Section 7.3.8 on page 657 for more details.*

```java
import javax.swing.*;
import java.awt.event.*;
import java.awt.*;

public class TestTCProp extends JFrame {
  JTextField jtf;
  JButton b1;

  public TestTCProp() {
    b1 = new JButton("focus me");
    b1.setBorder(BorderFactory.createRaisedBevelBorder());

    // A JTextField object is created and given some text

    jtf = new JTextField(20);
    jtf.setText("Jackson and Zachary");
    jtf.setFont(new Font("Serif", Font.BOLD, 12));

    // The JTextField object is given a margin and a focus accelerator

    jtf.setMargin(new Insets(20, 20, 20, 20));
    jtf.setFocusAccelerator('F');

    JPanel p = new JPanel();
    p.setLayout(new FlowLayout(FlowLayout.CENTER, 20, 20));
    p.add(jtf);
    p.add(b1);
```

9

javax.swing

```
        getContentPane().add(p);

    // The WindowListener is used to terminate the program when the window
    // is closed. Under Java 2 version 1.3, the addWindowListener() syntax
    // can be replaced by
    //
    // setDefaultCloseOperation(JFrame.EXIT_ON_CLOSE);

    addWindowListener(new WinClosing());
    setBounds(100, 100, 300, 200);
    setVisible(true);
  }

  public static void main(String args[]) {
    TestTCProp tcp = new TestTCProp();
  }
}

// The WinClosing class terminates the program when the window is closed

class WinClosing extends WindowAdapter {
  public void windowClosing(WindowEvent we) {
    System.exit(0);
  }
}
```

*Output*

The user interface of the program is shown below.

## Text Methods

| Method | Syntax |
|---|---|
| getText() | `public String getText()` |
| | `public String getText(int offset, int length)` <br> `   throws BadLocationException` |
| setText() | `public void setText(String text)` |

getText() returns the text contained by the invoking JTextComponent sub-class object. The second version returns a sub-set of the text.

setText() is used to change the text contained by the invoking JTextComponent sub-class object.

## Example: Using JTextComponent Text Methods

A JTextField and a JButton object are created and placed on a JFrame. The JTextField and JButton objects are registered with an ActionListener to monitor ActionEvents. If the JButton is pressed or the *Enter* key pressed while the JTextField object is in focus, an ActionEvent is generated and the actionPerformed() method is called updating the JTextField displayed at the bottom of the window.

*The WinClosing class is used to terminate the program if the window is closed. See Section 7.3.8 on page 657 for more details.*

```java
import javax.swing.*;
import java.awt.event.*;
import java.awt.*;

public class TestText extends JFrame implements ActionListener {
    JTextField jtf, jtf2;
    JButton b1;
    JLabel lbl;

    public TestText() {
        lbl = new JLabel("Name");
        lbl.setFont(new Font("Serif", Font.PLAIN, 12));
        lbl.setForeground(Color.black);

        b1 = new JButton("Enter");
        b1.setBorder(BorderFactory.createRaisedBevelBorder());
        b1.addActionListener(this);

        jtf = new JTextField(15);
        jtf.setFont(new Font("Serif", Font.PLAIN, 12));
        jtf.addActionListener(this);

        jtf2 = new JTextField(20);
        jtf2.setText("Name is: ");

        JPanel p = new JPanel();
        p.setLayout(new FlowLayout(FlowLayout.CENTER, 20, 20));
        p.add(lbl);
        p.add(jtf);
        p.add(b1);
```

9

javax.swing

**797**

```
    getContentPane().add(p, BorderLayout.CENTER);
      getContentPane().add(jtf2, BorderLayout.SOUTH);

      // The WindowListener is used to terminate the program when the window
      // is closed.  Under Java 2 version 1.3, the addWindowListener() syntax
      // can be replaced by
      //
      // setDefaultCloseOperation(JFrame.EXIT_ON_CLOSE);

      addWindowListener(new WinClosing());
      setBounds(100, 100, 400, 150);
      setVisible(true);
    }

    // if the JButton is pressed, an ActionEvent is generated and the
    // actionPerformed() method is called.  The text in the JTextField
    // at the bottom of the display is updated using the setText() and
    // getText() methods.

    public void actionPerformed(ActionEvent ae) {
      jtf2.setText("Name is " + jtf.getText());
    }

    public static void main(String args[]) {
      TestText tt = new TestText();
    }
  }

// The WinClosing class terminates the program when the window is closed

class WinClosing extends WindowAdapter {
  public void windowClosing(WindowEvent we) {
    System.exit(0);
  }
}
```

### Output

The user interface of the program is shown below.

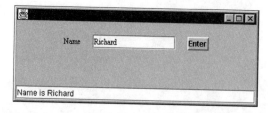

## Text Color Methods

| Method | Syntax |
|---|---|
| getDisabledTextColor() | public Color getDisabledTextColor() |
| getSelectedTextColor() | public Color getSelectedTextColor() |
| getSelectionColor() | public Color getSelectionColor() |
| setDisabledTextColor() | public void setDisabledTextColor (Color *disabledColor*) |
| setSelectedTextColor() | public void setSelectedTextColor (Color *selectedColor*) |
| setSelectionColor() | public void setSelectionColor (Color *selectionColor*) |

getDisabledTextColor() returns the color that is used to display the text of a disabled text component.

getSelectedTextColor() returns the color that is used to display the selected text of a text component.

getSelectionColor() returns the background color that is used to display the region of selected text in the text component.

setDisabledTextColor() changes the color that is used to display the text of a disabled text component.

setSelectedTextColor() changes the color that is used to display the selected text of a text component.

setSelectionColor() changes the background color that is used to display the region of selected text in the text component.

### Example: Using Text Color Methods

A JTextField object is created and given a String of text. Part of the text is selected using the select() method. The color of the selected text and the background color of the selected text are changed.

*The WinClosing class is used to terminate the program if the window is closed. See Section 7.3.8 on page 657 for more details.*

```
import javax.swing.*;
import java.awt.event.*;
import java.awt.*;

public class TestTextColor extends JFrame {
   JTextField jtf;
```

9

javax.swing

```
    public TestTextColor() {
      jtf = new JTextField(15);
      jtf.setText("Jackson and Zachary");
      jtf.setFont(new Font("Serif", Font.PLAIN, 12));

      // A region of selected text is created.  The color of the
      // selected text and the background color of the selected region
      // are specified.

      jtf.select(3, 7);
      jtf.setSelectedTextColor(Color.red);
      jtf.setSelectionColor(Color.yellow);

      JPanel p = new JPanel();
      p.setLayout(new FlowLayout(FlowLayout.CENTER, 20, 20));
      p.add(jtf);

      getContentPane().add(p, BorderLayout.CENTER);

      // The WindowListener is used to terminate the program when the window
      // is closed.  Under Java 2 version 1.3, the addWindowListener() syntax
      // can be replaced by
      //
      // setDefaultCloseOperation(JFrame.EXIT_ON_CLOSE);

      addWindowListener(new WinClosing());
      setBounds(100, 100, 300, 120);
      setVisible(true);
    }

    public static void main(String args[]) {
      TestTextColor ttc = new TestTextColor();
    }
}

// The WinClosing class terminates the program when the window is closed

class WinClosing extends WindowAdapter {
  public void windowClosing(WindowEvent we) {
    System.exit(0);
  }
}
```

**Output**

The user interface of the program is shown below.

## Text Selection Methods

| Method | Syntax |
|---|---|
| getSelectedText() | public String getSelectedText() |
| getSelectionEnd() | public int getSelectionEnd() |
| getSelectionStart() | public int getSelectionStart() |
| replaceSelection() | public void replaceSelection(String replaceString) |
| select() | public void select(int startIndex, int endIndex) |
| selectAll() | public void selectAll() |
| setSelectionEnd() | public void setSelectionEnd(int startIndex) |
| setSelectionStart() | public void setSelectionStart(int endIndex) |

getSelectedText() returns the selected text of the invoking JTextComponent sub-class object.

getSelectionStart() and getSelectionEnd() return the starting and ending indices of the selected text.

setSelectionStart() and setSelectionEnd() set the starting and ending indices of the selected text.

replaceSelection() replaces the selected text with replaceString. If there is no selected text, replaceString is appended to the end of the text.

select() and selectAll() are used to select part or all of the text.

### Example: Using Text Selection Methods

See the *Using Text Color Methods* example on page 799, where the select() method is used to select a portion of the text contained in a JTextField.

## UI Delegate Methods

| Method | Syntax |
|--------|--------|
| getUI() | public TextUI getUI() |
| setUI() | public void setUI(TextUI *tui*) |
| updateUI() | public void updateUI() |

getUI() returns the TextUI object associated with the invoking JTextComponent sub-class object.

setUI() is used to change the TextUI object associated the invoking JTextComponent sub-class object.

updateUI() is called to indicate that the look-and-feel of the invoking JTextComponent sub-class object has changed.

# 9.1.16 JTextField Class

```
public class JTextField extends JTextComponent implements SwingConstants
```

```
Object
  Component
    Container
      JComponent
        JTextComponent
          JTextField
```

### Interfaces

```
Accessible, ImageObserver, MenuContainer, Scrollable, Serializable,
SwingConstants
```

A JTextField object provides a single line for text input. It fires an ActionEvent when the *Enter* key is pressed. The text can be aligned using the constants contained in the SwingConstants interface.

## JTextField() Constructors

| Method | Syntax |
|--------|--------|
| JTextField() | public JTextField() |
| | public JTextField(String *text*) |
| | public JTextField(int *columns*) |
| | public JTextField(String *text*, int *columns*) |
| | public JTextField(Document *doc*, String *text*, int *columns*) |

Creates a JTextField object. The JTextField can be initialized to a specified width and contain an initial String of text. It also can be provided a Document model. A Document object is a container for text that implements the Document interface, which is found in the javax.swing.text package. If no Document object is specified, a default Document object is used.

## Action Methods

| Method | Syntax |
|---|---|
| getAction() | public Action getAction() |
| setAction() | public void setAction(Action *action*) |

An Action object implements the ActionListener interface and is used to respond to events from one or more event sources. See Section 9.5.1 on page on page 911 and Section 9.5.2 on page 915 for more details

geAction() returns the Action object associated with the invoking JTextField object or null if there is no Action object.

setAction() associates an Action object with the invoking JTextField object. The Action passed as an argument will replace any previously set Action. null can also be used as an argument to set the invoking JTextField object to have no action.

## ActionListener Methods

| Method | Syntax |
|---|---|
| addActionListener() | public void addActionListener(ActionListener *al*) |
| removeActionListener() | public void removeActionListener (ActionListener *al*) |

ActionEvent objects are generated when the *Enter* key is pressed.

addActionListener() registers the invoking JTextField object with an ActionListener object. The ActionListener is notified if the JTextField generates any ActionEvent objects.

removeActionListener() disconnects the ActionListener object from the invoking TextField object.

## Alignment Methods

| Method | Syntax |
|---|---|
| getHorizontalAlignment() | public int getHorizontalAlignment() |
| setHorizontalAlignment() | public void setHorizontalAlignment(int *align*) throws IllegalArgumentException |

getHorizontalAlignment() returns the horizontal alignment of the text in the invoking JTextField object. The return value will be one of these constants

9

javax.swing

- ❏ JTextField.LEFT
- ❏ JTextField.CENTER
- ❏ JTextField.RIGHT
- ❏ JTextField.LEADING
- ❏ JTextField.TRAILING

setHorizontalAlignment() changes the horizontal alignment of the text in the invoking JTextField object.

## postActionEvent() Method

| Method | Syntax |
|---|---|
| postActionEvent() | public void postActionEvent() |

postActionEvent() causes an ActionEvent to be fired by the invoking JTextField object

## Methods to Return or Set JTextField Properties

| Method | Syntax |
|---|---|
| getColumns() | public int getColumns() |
| getHorizontalVisibility() | public BoundedRangeModel getHorizontalVisibility() |
| getPreferredSize() | public Dimension getPreferredSize() |
| getScrollOffset() | public int getScrollOffset() |
| setActionCommand() | public void setActionCommand (String actionCommand) |
| setColumns() | public void setColumns(int cols) throws IllegalArgumentException |
| setFont() | public void setFont(Font font) |
| setScrollOffset() | public void setScrollOffset(int offset) |

getColumns() returns the number of columns the invoking JTextField object.

getHorizontalVisibility() returns the BoundedRangeModel that determines which part of the text is displayed if the text is longer than the width of the JTextField.

getPreferredSize() returns the preferred size of the invoking JTextField.

getScrollOffset() returns the index of the first character of the text displayed by the JTextField. This value may or may not be 0 depending on the length of the text and the current horizontal visibility property.

setActionCommand() sets or changes the action command associated with the invoking JTextField object.

setColumns() is used to change the number of columns of the invoking JTextField object.

setFont() changes the font displayed by the invoking JTextField object.

setScrollOffset() specifies the index of the first character of the text displayed by the JTextField.

## Example: Using JTextField

A JTextField object is created and placed on a JFrame. The JTextField is given an initial column width of 20. Methods defined in the JTextComponent and Component classes are used to set the text and font displayed by the JTextField. The JTextField object is registered with an ActionListener. When the *Enter* key is pressed, the actionPerformed() method is called and a JLabel object is updated to display the contents of the JTextField.

*The WinClosing class is used to terminate the program if the window is closed. See Section 7.3.8 on page 657 for more details.*

```
import javax.swing.*;
import java.awt.event.*;
import java.awt.*;

public class TestJTF extends JFrame implements ActionListener {
  JTextField jtf;
  JLabel lbl;

  public TestJTF() {
    lbl = new JLabel("Text is: ");
    lbl.setFont(new Font("Serif", Font.PLAIN, 12));
    lbl.setHorizontalAlignment(SwingConstants.CENTER);
    lbl.setForeground(Color.black);

    // A JTextField object is created, given some text, and registered
    // with an ActionListener.  The postActionEvent() method sends an
    // ActionEvent to the actionPerformed() method to set the JLabel
    // text to the initial String.

    jtf = new JTextField(15);
    jtf.setText("Initial Text");
    jtf.setFont(new Font("Serif", Font.PLAIN, 12));
    jtf.addActionListener(this);
    jtf.postActionEvent();

    JPanel p = new JPanel();
    p.setLayout(new FlowLayout(FlowLayout.CENTER, 20, 20));
    p.add(jtf);
```

9

javax.swing

```
        getContentPane().add(p, BorderLayout.CENTER);
        getContentPane().add(lbl, BorderLayout.SOUTH);

        // The WindowListener is used to terminate the program when the window
        // is closed.  Under Java 2 version 1.3, the addWindowListener() syntax
        // can be replaced by
        //
        // setDefaultCloseOperation(JFrame.EXIT_ON_CLOSE);

        addWindowListener(new WinClosing());
        setBounds(100, 100, 300, 120);
        setVisible(true);
    }

    // The actionPerformed() method changes the JLabel text to match
    // the text in the JTextField.

    public void actionPerformed(ActionEvent ae) {
        lbl.setText("Text is: " + jtf.getText());
        lbl.revalidate();
    }

    public static void main(String args[]) {
        TestJTF tj = new TestJTF();
    }
}

// The WinClosing class terminates the program when the window is closed

class WinClosing extends WindowAdapter {
    public void windowClosing(WindowEvent we) {
        System.exit(0);
    }
}
```

### Output

The user interface of the program is shown below.

# 9.1.17 JToggleButton Class

```
public class JToggleButton extends AbstractButton implments Accessible
```

```
Object
  Component
    Container
      JComponent
        AbstractButton
          JToggleButton
```

### Interfaces

```
Accessible ImageObserver ItemSelectable MenuContainer Serializable
SwingConstants
```

A JToggleButton object is a button that maintains a selected or unselected state. When a JToggleButton object is pressed, it stays pressed (selected) until it is pressed again. It generates an ItemEvent when selected or deselected and an ActionEvent when the JToggleButton object is clicked.

## JToggleButton() Constructors

| Method | Syntax |
|---|---|
| JToggleButton() | public JToggleButton() |
| | public JToggleButton(Action action) |
| | public JToggleButton(Icon icon) |
| | public JToggleButton(Icon icon, boolean selected) |
| | public JToggleButton(String text) |
| | public JToggleButton(String text, boolean selected) |
| | public JToggleButton(String text, Icon icon) |
| | public JToggleButton(String text, Icon icon, boolean selected) |

Creates a JToggleButton object. An Icon, label, and the intial selected state can be provided. The default selected state is unselected.

## Example: Using JToggleButton

A JToggleButton object is created using both an icon and a label and placed on a JFrame. The label is positioned so it is beneath the icon. The JToggleButton is registered with an ItemListener to detect when the JToggleButton is selected or deselected. A JTextField object is used to display the selected state of the JToggleButton.

*The WinClosing class is used to terminate the program if the window is closed. See Section 7.3.8 on page 657 for more details.*

9

javax.swing

```
import javax.swing.*;
import java.awt.event.*;
import java.awt.*;

public class TestJTB extends JFrame implements ItemListener {
  JToggleButton b1;
  JTextField jtf;

  public TestJTB() {

    // A JToggleButton object is created that displays both text
    // and an icon.  The JToggleButton is registered with a
    // ChangeListener

    b1 = new JToggleButton("yen", new ImageIcon("yen.jpg"));
    b1.setName("Yen button");
    b1.setHorizontalTextPosition(SwingConstants.CENTER);
    b1.setVerticalTextPosition(SwingConstants.BOTTOM);
    b1.setBorder(BorderFactory.createRaisedBevelBorder());
    b1.setPreferredSize(new Dimension(90, 90));
    b1.addItemListener(this);

    jtf = new JTextField(15);
    jtf.setEditable(false);

    JPanel p = new JPanel();
    p.setLayout(new FlowLayout(FlowLayout.CENTER, 20, 20));
    p.add(b1);

    getContentPane().add(p, BorderLayout.CENTER);
    getContentPane().add(jtf, BorderLayout.SOUTH);

    // The WindowListener is used to terminate the program when the window
    // is closed.  Under Java 2 version 1.3, the addWindowListener() syntax
    // can be replaced by
    //
    // setDefaultCloseOperation(JFrame.EXIT_ON_CLOSE);

    addWindowListener(new WinClosing());
    setBounds(100, 100, 200, 160);
    setVisible(true);
  }

  // When the JToggleButton is toggled on or off, an ItemEvent object
  // is generated and sent to the itemStateChanged() method.  The
  // text of the JTextField object is updated to reflect the selected
  // state of the JToggleButton.

  public void itemStateChanged(ItemEvent ie) {
    JToggleButton jtb = (JToggleButton) ie.getItemSelectable();
```

```
    if (jtb.isSelected()) {
      jtf.setText(jtb.getName() + " is selected");
    }
    if (!jtb.isSelected()) {
      jtf.setText(jtb.getName() + " is de-selected");
    }
  }

  public static void main(String args[]) {
    TestJTB jtb = new TestJTB();
  }
}

// The WinClosing class terminates the program when the window is closed

class WinClosing extends WindowAdapter {
  public void windowClosing(WindowEvent we) {
    System.exit(0);
  }
}
```

**Output**

The user interface of the program is shown below.

## 9.1.18 ProgressMonitor Class

```
public class ProgressMonitor extends Object
```

```
Object
  ProgressMonitor
```

A `ProgressMonitor` object provides a `JProgressBar` object inside a dialog that is used to track the progress of some action. A `ProgressMonitor` object also has a label, called the note, that can provide information.

A `ProgressMonitor` tracks the execution of a block of code. If a `ProgressMonitor` is placed in an event handler method, it and the code it is monitoring must be placed in a separate thread. Once an event is fired and is caught by the event listener, it locks out other processes within that thread until the event method is finished executing. The `ProgressMonitor` will not be updated until after the code finishes at which point it is removed from the display.

9

javax.swing

**809**

## ProgressMonitor() Constructor

| Method | Syntax |
|---|---|
| ProgressMonitor() | public ProgressMonitor(Component *parent*, Object *message*, String *note*, int *min*, int *max*) |

Creates a ProgressMonitor object. The message is an internal title and cannot be changed. The note is a short note that can be displayed to provide information on the progress of the operation. The min and max values bound the range of the ProgressMonitor status bar.

## close() Method

| Method | Syntax |
|---|---|
| close() | public void close() |

close() causes the invoking ProgressMonitor object to shut down. This will happen automatically when the max value is reached.

## Display Delay Methods

| Method | Syntax |
|---|---|
| getMillisToDecideToPopup() | public int getMillisToDecideToPopup() |
| getMillisToPopup() | public int getMillisToPopup() |
| setMillisToDecideToPopup() | public void setMillisToDecideToPopup (int *delay*) |
| setMillisToPopup() | public void setMillisToPopup(int *delay*) |

By default, the ProgressMonitor object is not displayed immediately: the system first determines if the process will take long enough to warrant displaying the dialog.

getMillisToDecideToPopup() returns the time the system waits before deciding if the dialog should be shown.

getMillisToPopup() returns the minimum time the operation must take before ProgressMonitor object will be shown.

setMillisToDecideToPopup() and setMillisToPopup() methods are used to change these properties.

## isCanceled() Method

| Method | Syntax |
|---|---|
| isCanceled() | public boolean isCanceled() |

isCanceled() returns true if the cancel button in the ProgressMonitor dialog has been clicked.

# JProgressBar Property Methods

| Method | Syntax |
|---|---|
| getMaximum() | public int getMaximum() |
| getMinimum() | public int getMinimum() |
| getNote() | public String getNote() |
| setMaximum() | public void setMaximum(int *max*) |
| setMinimum() | public void setMinimum(int *min*) |
| setNote() | public void setNote(String *note*) |
| setProgress() | public void setProgress(int *progress*) |

getMaximum() and getMinimum() return the range of the invoking ProgressMonitor object.

getNote() returns the note attached to the invoking ProgressMonitor object.

setMaximum(), setMinimum(), setNote(), and setProgress() methods are used to change the maximum value, minimum value, note, and current value of the invoking ProgressMonitor object.

## Example: Using ProgressMonitor

A ProgressMonitor object is used to monitor the progress of an operation, in this case counting from 1 to 100 with a 0.1 second delay between each number. When the JButton is pressed the count begins. For proper operation of the ProgressMonitor, the operation it is montioring is placed in its own thread. The note is updated to reflect the current state of the operation.

*The WinClosing class is used to terminate the program if the window is closed. See Section 7.3.8 on page 657 for more details.*

```java
import javax.swing.*;
import java.awt.*;
import java.awt.event.*;
import java.io.*;

public class TestPM extends JFrame implements ActionListener {
    JButton runButton;
    ProgressMonitor pm;
    MyThread mt = null;
    int maxCount = 100;

    public TestPM() {
        runButton = new JButton("run");
        runButton.addActionListener(this);
```

```
      JPanel p = new JPanel();
      p.add(runButton);

      getContentPane().add(p, BorderLayout.CENTER);

      // The WindowListener is used to terminate the program when the window
      // is closed.  Under Java 2 version 1.3, the addWindowListener() syntax
      // can be replaced by
      //
      // setDefaultCloseOperation(JFrame.EXIT_ON_CLOSE);

      addWindowListener(new WinClosing());
      setBounds(0, 100, 300, 300);
      setVisible(true);
   }

   public void actionPerformed(ActionEvent ae) {
      mt = new MyThread();
      mt.start();
   }

   // The MyThread class uses a ProgressMonitor object to monitor
   // a count between 0 and 99.

   class MyThread extends Thread {
      public void run() {
         pm = new ProgressMonitor(runButton, "Process Running",
                                  "process is 0% complete", 0, maxCount);

         for (int count = 0; count < maxCount; ++count) {
            pm.setProgress(count + 1);
            double percent = 100.0 * (count + 1) / maxCount;
            pm.setNote("process is " + (int) percent + "% complete");
            try {
               java.lang.Thread.sleep(100);
            } catch (InterruptedException e) {}

            // If the "Cancel" button is hit in the ProgressMonitor dialog,
            // the count is cancelled and the thread returns

            if (pm.isCanceled()) {
               return;
            }
         }
      }
   }

   public static void main(String args[]) {
      TestPM tpm = new TestPM();
   }
}
```

```
// The WinClosing class terminates the program when the window is closed

class WinClosing extends WindowAdapter {
  public void windowClosing(WindowEvent we) {
    System.exit(0);
  }
}
```

*Output*

The user interface of the program is shown below.

# 9.1.19 ProgressMonitorInputStream Class

```
public class ProgressMonitorInputStream extends FilterInputStream
```

```
Object
  InputStream
    FilterInputStream
      ProgressMonitorInputStream
```

A `ProgressMonitorInputStream` object is a dialog that pops up when a file is being read. A `JProgressBar` in the dialog indicates the progress of the read operation.

A `ProgressMonitorInputStream` object has a `ProgressMonitor` object associated with it that can be manipulated using `ProgressMonitor` class methods to change the appearance of the dialog.

A `ProgressMonitorInputStream` requires an `InputStream` object in its constructor. Therefore it is used with byte-stream input.

## ProgressMonitorInputStream() Constructor

| Method | Syntax |
|---|---|
| ProgressMonitorInputStream() | public ProgressMonitorInputStream (Component *parent*, Object *message*, InputStream *in*) |

9

javax.swing

Creates a `ProgressMonitorInputStream` object. A parent `Component`, a `message` providing descriptive text, and an `InputStream` must be provided.

## close() Method

| Method | Syntax |
|---|---|
| close() | public void close() throws IOException |

`close()` closes the invoking `ProgressMonitorInputStream` object.

## getProgressMonitor() Method

| Method | Syntax |
|---|---|
| getProgressMonitor() | public ProgressMonitor getProgressMonitor() |

`getProgressMonitor()` returns the `ProgressMonitor` object associated with the invoking `ProgressMonitorInputStream` object.

## read() Method

| Method | Syntax |
|---|---|
| read() | public int read() throws IOException |
| | public int read(byte[] *ba*) throws IOException |
| | public int read(byte[] *ba*, int *off*, int *len*) throws IOException |

`read()` reads a `byte` or an array of `bytes` from the invoking `ProgressMonitorInputStream` object. The third version reads `bytes` into a subset of a `byte` array.

### Example: Using ProgressMonitorInputStream

A `JButton` is created and placed on a `JFrame`. When the `JButton` is pressed, a file is read using a `ProgressMonitorInputStream`. A `ProgressMonitor` display pops up and tracks the read operation. As with the `ProgressMonitor` example, the read operation is placed in its own thread. If it were placed in the `actionPerformed()` method without being placed in its own thread, it would block out all other actions and the `ProgressMonitor` dialog would never get updated. The 1 millisecond delay put in after each line is read gives the display a smoother look.

In order for the read operation to require enough time for the `ProgressMonitor` display to be shown, a fairly large file must be read.

*The `WinClosing` class is used to terminate the program if the window is closed. See Section 7.3.8 on page 657 for more details.*

```
import javax.swing.*;
import java.awt.*;
import java.awt.event.*;
import java.io.*;

public class TestJPIS extends JFrame implements ActionListener {
  JTextArea ta;
  JButton readButton;
  ProgressMonitorInputStream pmis;
  ProgressMonitor pm;
  String s;

  public TestJPIS() {
    ta = new JTextArea(10, 50);

    readButton = new JButton("read");
    readButton.addActionListener(this);

    JPanel pc = new JPanel();
    pc.add(new JScrollPane(ta));

    JPanel ps = new JPanel();
    ps.add(readButton);

    JPanel cp = (JPanel) getContentPane();
    cp.setLayout(new BorderLayout());
    cp.add(pc, BorderLayout.CENTER);
    cp.add(ps, BorderLayout.SOUTH);

    // The WindowListener is used to terminate the program when the window
    // is closed.  Under Java 2 version 1.3, the addWindowListener() syntax
    // can be replaced by
    //
    // setDefaultCloseOperation(JFrame.EXIT_ON_CLOSE);

    addWindowListener(new WinClosing());
    setBounds(100, 100, 700, 300);
    setVisible(true);
  }

  // When the "read" button is pressed, the actionPerformed() method
  // creates a thread that reads a file.

  public void actionPerformed(ActionEvent ae) {
    ReadThread rt = new ReadThread();
    rt.start();
  }

  // The ReadThread class reads the contents of a file into a
  // JTextArea using a ProgressMonitorInputStream object.
```

```
class ReadThread extends Thread {
  public void run() {
    try {
      pmis =
        new ProgressMonitorInputStream(ta, "Reading",
                                    new FileInputStream("reference.txt"));
      pm = pmis.getProgressMonitor();
      pm.setMillisToDecideToPopup(1);
      pm.setMillisToPopup(1);

      BufferedReader br =
        new BufferedReader(new InputStreamReader(pmis));

      while ((s = br.readLine()) != null) {
        ta.append(s + "\n");
        try {
          java.lang.Thread.sleep(1);
        } catch (Exception e) {}
      }
      br.close();
    } catch (FileNotFoundException fnfe) {}
    catch (IOException ioe) {}
  }
}

  public static void main(String args[]) {
    TestJPIS tjp = new TestJPIS();
  }
}

// The WinClosing class terminates the program when the window is closed

class WinClosing extends WindowAdapter {
  public void windowClosing(WindowEvent we) {
    System.exit(0);
  }
}
```

### Output

The user interface of the program is shown below.

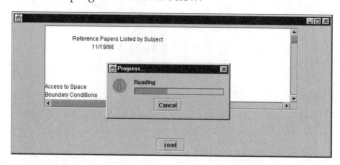

# 9.2 Swing Containers

The `javax.swing` package provides a new collection of container classes. The container class hierarchy is shown in the following figure. The container classes are divided into two main categories:

❑ The higher level Swing containers, `JApplet`, `JDialog`, `JFrame`, and `JWindow`, which are extensions of their AWT counterparts. They contain a root pane and its sub-elements and inherit some heavyweight features such as native AWT peer objects.

❑ Most of the other Swing containers, which are sub-classes of `JComponent`.

One of the major differences between the higher level Swing containers and their AWT counterparts is the existence of the root pane. In Swing, components are not directly placed on the higher level Swing containers (such as `JApplet`, `JDialog`, `JFrame`, and `JWindow`), rather they are held by a sub-element called a `JRootPane`. A `JRootPane` contains a fixed number of child components: the content pane, menu bar, layered pane, and glass pane. So, when components are added to a higher level Swing container, they are actually added to one of the `JRootPane` sub-elements, generally the content pane, which is a sub-element of the `JLayeredPane`.

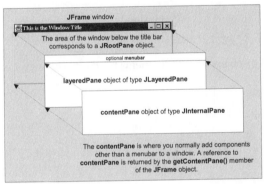

The `JRootPane` and its sub-elements provide a good deal of flexibility in determining the appearance of an application.

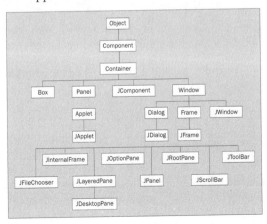

9

javax.swing

# 9.2.1 Box Class

```
public class Box extends Container implements Accessible
```

```
Object
  Component
    Container
      Box
```

### Interfaces

```
ImageObserver, MenuContainer, Serializable, Accessible
```

A Box object is a simple container that uses the BoxLayout layout manager. The Box object can have either a horizontal or vertical alignment meaning that components are added to the Box object either left to right or top to bottom.

A Box object can be created either by using the constructor or through static creation methods.

## Box() Constructor

| Method | Syntax |
|---|---|
| Box() | public Box(int *alignment*) |

Box() creates a Box object. Valid arguments for the alignment are:

❏ BoxLayout.X_AXIS
❏ BoxLayout.Y_AXIS

The alignment specifies how components will be added to the Box, either along the x-axis or the y-axis

## Static Box Object Creation Methods

| Method | Syntax |
|---|---|
| createHorizontalBox() | public static Box createHorizontalBox() |
| createVerticalBox() | public static Box createVerticalBox() |

createHorizonalBox() and createVerticalBox() create a horizontal or vertical Box object.

## Glue Methods

| Method | Syntax |
|---|---|
| createGlue() | public static Component createGlue() |
| createHorizontalGlue() | public static Component createHorizontalGlue() |
| createVerticalGlue() | public static Component createVerticalGlue() |

createHorizontalGlue() and createVerticalGlue() create invisible **glue** components that can be added to the Box object. If the window is re-sized, the glue components help preserve preferred sizes of GUI components by stretching to their maximum size before other components are re-sized. Horizontal glue stretches along the x-axis and vertical glue stretches along the y-axis.

createGlue() creates glue in both directions.

## Rigid Space Methods

| Method | Syntax |
|---|---|
| createHorizontalStrut() | public static Component createHorizontalStrut (int *width*) |
| createRigidArea() | public static Component createRigidArea (Dimension *d*) |
| createVerticalStrut() | public static Component createVerticalStrut (int *height*) |

These methods create fixed size invisible components that are used to create spaces between other GUI components. A horizontal strut provides a fixed width, variable height component. A vertical strut is a fixed height, variable width component.

createHorizontalStrut() creates a fixed width, variable height component.

createRigidArea() creates an invisible component of fixed width and height.

createVerticalStrut() creates a variable width, fixed height component.

### Example: Using Box

In this example, three JButton objects are placed on a Box. A horizontal space is added between the second and third JButtons, and glue is added to stretch in the vertical direction.

*The WinClosing class is used to terminate the program if the window is closed.*
*See Section 7.3.8 on page 657 for more details.*

```
import javax.swing.*;
import java.awt.*;
import java.awt.event.*;

public class TestB extends JFrame {
    Box box;
    JButton b1, b2, b3;

    public TestB() {
```

```
        b1 = new JButton("button 1");
        b2 = new JButton("button 2");
        b3 = new JButton("button 3");

        // A Box object with vertical alignment is created and set to
        // be the content pane of the JFrame.  Three JButtons are added
        // to the Box with a vertical strut placed between the second
        // and third JButton.

        box = Box.createVerticalBox();

        // setContentPane(box);

        box.add(Box.createVerticalGlue());
        box.add(b1);
        box.add(b2);
        box.add(Box.createVerticalStrut(20));
        box.add(b3);

        getContentPane().add(box);

        // The WindowListener is used to terminate the program when the window
        // is closed.  Under Java 2 version 1.3, the addWindowListener() syntax
        // can be replaced by
        //
        // setDefaultCloseOperation(JFrame.EXIT_ON_CLOSE);
        //
        // The ComponentListener redoes the component layout if the window
        // is re-sized.

        addWindowListener(new WinClosing());
        addComponentListener(new CompAdapt());
        setBounds(100, 100, 200, 200);
        setVisible(true);
    }

    class CompAdapt extends ComponentAdapter {
        public void componentResized(ComponentEvent ce) {
            System.out.println("window re-sized");
            doLayout();
        }
    }

    // The getInsets() method is overridden to provide a margin around
    // the JFrame

    public Insets getInsets() {
        return new Insets(20, 20, 20, 20);
    }
```

```
   public static void main(String args[]) {
     TestB tb = new TestB();
   }
 }

 // The WinClosing class terminates the program when the window is closed

 class WinClosing extends WindowAdapter {
   public void windowClosing(WindowEvent we) {
     System.exit(0);
   }
 }
```

### Output

Here is the user interface that this program generates:

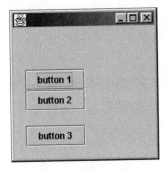

## 9.2.2 JApplet Class

```
public class JApplet extends Applet implements RootContainer, Accessible
```

```
Object
  Component
    Container
      Panel
        Applet
          JApplet
```

### Interfaces

```
ImageObserver, MenuContainer, Serializable, RootPaneContainer, Accessible
```

A JApplet object is a special type of Swing container that can be embedded in HTML code and viewed using a Web browser. It is similar to an Applet object except that a JApplet contains a JRootPane and the associated JRootPane sub-elements. See Chapter 8 for a more complete description of applets.

To avoid any thread complications, the adding or manipulating of components should be done in the init() method.

## JApplet() Constructor

| Method | Syntax |
|--------|--------|
| JApplet() | public JApplet() |

JApplet() creates a JApplet object. The JApplet constructor is generally not used in program code, but it is used by the browser to instantiate an JApplet object

## Methods to Return the JRootPane and its Sub-Elements

| Method | Syntax |
|--------|--------|
| getContentPane() | public Container getContentPane() |
| getGlassPane() | public Component getGlassPane() |
| getJMenuBar() | public JMenuBar getJMenuBar() |
| getLayeredPane() | public JLayeredPane getLayeredPane() |
| getRootPane() | public JRootPane getRootPane() |

These methods return a reference to the content pane, glass pane, layered pane, menu bar, or JRootPane associated with the invoking JApplet object.

## Methods to Set the JRootPane Sub-Elements

| Method | Syntax |
|--------|--------|
| setContentPane() | public void setContentPane (Container contentPane) |
| setGlassPane() | public void setGlassPane(Component glassPane) |
| setJMenuBar() | public void setJMenuBar(JMenuBar menuBar) |
| setLayeredPane() | public void setLayeredPane (JLayeredPane layeredPane) |

These methods are used to change the content pane, glass pane, layered pane, or menu bar associated with the invoking JApplet object.

### Example: Using JApplet

In this simple applet example, a JButton is placed on a JApplet. When the JButton is pressed, a message is displayed.

*For more detailed applet examples, see Chapter 8.*

```
import java.awt.*;
import java.awt.event.*;
import javax.swing.*;

public class TestJApplet extends JApplet implements ActionListener {
  JButton b1;
  String msg;
```

```
public void init() {
  msg = "";

  b1 = new JButton("Click Me");
  b1.setFont(new Font("Serif", Font.BOLD, 12));
  b1.addActionListener(this);

  getContentPane().add(b1);
}

public void actionPerformed(ActionEvent ae) {
  msg = "Don't touch the button";
  repaint();
}

public void paint(Graphics g) {
  g.drawString(msg, 100, 200);
}
}
```

Here is the HTML file used to test the applet:

```
<HTML>
  <HEAD>
    <TITLE> Test Program </TITLE>
  </HEAD>
  <BODY>
    <APPLET CODE="TestJApplet.class" WIDTH=400 HEIGHT=400 >
      <PARAM NAME=string VALUE=Applet>
    </APPLET>
  </BODY>
</HTML>
```

### Output

The user interface of the program is shown below.

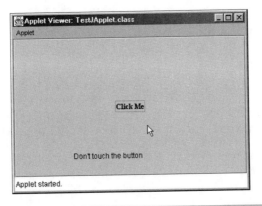

# 9.2.3 JDesktopPane Class

```
public class JDesktopPane extends JLayeredPane implements Accessible
```

```
Object
  Component
    Container
      JComponent
        JLayeredPane
          JDesktopPane
```

### Interfaces

ImageObserver, MenuContainer, Serializable, Accessible

A JDesktopPane object is a container that uses a DesktopManager object to control the placement and movement of frames. It has no layout manager. Components placed on a JDesktopPane object object must be placed at absolute locations with absolute sizes.

## JDesktopPane() Constructor

| Method | Syntax |
|---|---|
| JDesktopPane() | public JDesktopPane() |

JDesktopPane() creates a JDesktopPane object. The constructor calls the method updateUI() which results in the installation of a DesktopManager.

## DesktopManager Methods

| Method | Syntax |
|---|---|
| getDesktopManager() | public DesktopManager getDesktopManager() |
| setDesktopManager() | public void setDesktopManager(DesktopManager d) |

getDesktopManager() returns the DesktopManager object associated with the invoking JDesktopPane object.

setDesktopManager() specifies the DesktopManager object that will be associated with the invoking JDesktopPane object.

## Frame Methods

| Method | Syntax |
|---|---|
| getAllFrames() | public JInternalFrame[] getAllFrames() |
| getAllFramesInLayer() | public JInternalFrame[] getAllFramesInLayer (int *layer*) |
| getSelectedFrame() | public JInternalFrame getSelectedFrame() |
| setSelectedFrame() | public void setSelectedFrame (JInternalFrame *frame*) |

getAllFrames() returns an array containing all the JInternalFrame objects contained in the JDesktopPane object.

getAllFramesInLayer() returns an array containing all the JInternalFrame objects contained in the specified layer of the JDesktopPane object.

getSelectedFrame() returns the currently active JInternalFrame object in the invoking JDesktopPane object or null if there are no active frames.

setSelectedFrame() changes the currently active JInternalFrame in the invoking JDesktopPane object.

## UI Delegate Methods

| Method | Syntax |
|---|---|
| getUI() | public DesktopPaneUI getUI() |
| getUIClassID() | public String getUIClassID() |
| setUI() | public void setUI(DesktopPaneUI ui) |
| updateUI() | public void updateUI() |

getUI() returns the DesktopPaneUI object associated with the invoking JDesktopPane object.

getUIClassID() returns the String "DesktopPaneUI" which is the suffix of the object used to render a JDesktopPane object.

setUI() is used to change the DesktopPaneUI object associated the invoking JDesktopPane object.

updateUI() is called when the look-and-feel of the invoking JDesktopPane object has changed.

### Example: Building a Desktop Using JDesktopPane and JInternalFrame

In this example, a JDesktopPane object is created and assigned to be the content pane of a JFrame. A JInternalFrame is added to the JDesktopPane. There is no layout manager associated with a JDesktopPane object. Components placed onto a JDesktopPane object must be given an upper left hand corner origin and a width and height. This is done using the setBounds() method. TheWindowListener is used to terminate the program if the window is closed.

When components are added to the JDesktopPane object, their layer position must be specified using an Integer object. The picture is meant to be a background scene with the JInternalFrame appearing on top of it. Using Integer.MIN_VALUE ensures it will be placed at the bottom of the stack.

9

javax.swing

```
import javax.swing.*;
import java.awt.event.*;

public class TestJDP extends JFrame {
  JDesktopPane jdp;

  public TestJDP() {

    // The content pane of the JFrame is set to be a JDesktopPane

    jdp = new JDesktopPane();
    setContentPane(jdp);

    // A Label and JInternalFrame object are added to the default layer
    // of the JDesktopPane. Because the JDesktopPane does not use a
    // layout manager, the JLabel and JInternalFrame must be given an
    // absolute position and size with the setBounds() method.
    // The JInternalFrame is given a higher position number and is
    // placed above the JLabel

    ImageIcon icon = new ImageIcon("Halloween.jpg");
    JLabel l = new JLabel(icon);
    l.setBounds(0, 0, icon.getIconWidth(), icon.getIconHeight());
    jdp.add(l, new Integer(Integer.MIN_VALUE));

    JInternalFrame jif = new JInternalFrame("Internal Frame");
    jif.setClosable(true);
    jif.setResizable(true);
    jif.setBounds(20, 20, 150, 150);
    jdp.add(jif, new Integer(1));

    // In Java 2 version 1.3, JInternalFrame objects are invisible by
    // default, whereas under version 1.2 they were by default visible.
    // The following line is not needed in Java 2 version 1.2.
    jif.setVisible(true);

    // The WindowListener is used to terminate the program when the window
    // is closed.  Under Java 2 version 1.3, the addWindowListener() syntax
    // can be replaced by
    //
    // setDefaultCloseOperation(JFrame.EXIT_ON_CLOSE);

    addWindowListener(new WinClosing());
    setBounds(100, 100, 300, 300);
    setVisible(true);
  }

  public static void main(String args[]) {
    TestJDP tjdp = new TestJDP();
  }
}
```

```
// The WinClosing class terminates the program when the window is closed

class WinClosing extends WindowAdapter {
  public void windowClosing(WindowEvent we) {
    System.exit(0);
  }
}
```

### Output
The user interface of the program is shown below.

## 9.2.4 JDialog Class

```
public class JDialog extends Dialog
    implements RootPaneContainer, WindowConstants, Accessible
```

```
Object
  Component
    Container
      Window
        Dialog
          JDialog
```

### Interfaces
```
ImageObserver, MenuContainer, Serializable, WindowConstants, Accesible,
RootPaneContainer
```

A JDialog object is similar to the AWT Dialog object. It is a top-level window that is often used to get confirmation from the user for a particular action.

Components are not added to the JDialog directly, but instead are added to one of the sub-panes of the JRootPane object associated with the JDialog object. Generally, objects are added to the content pane.

## JDialog() Constructors

| Method | Syntax |
|--------|--------|
| JDialog() | public JDialog() |
| | public JDialog(Dialog *parent*) |
| | public JDialog(Dialog *parent*, boolean *isModal*) |
| | public JDialog(Dialog *parent*, String *title*) |
| | public JDialog(Dialog *parent*, String *title*, boolean *isModal*) |
| | public JDialog(Frame *parent*) |
| | public JDialog(Frame *parent*, boolean *isModal*) |
| | public JDialog(Frame *parent*, String *title*) |
| | public JDialog(Frame *parent*, String *title*, boolean *isModal*) |

JDialog() creates a JDialog object. The JDialog object can be associated with a parent container, either a JFrame or another JDialog. If isModal is set to true, the JDialog object will lock out any other activity while it is displayed. The no argument constructor creates a non-modal JDialog object without a parent Frame.

## Default Close Operation Methods

| Method | Syntax |
|--------|--------|
| getDefaultCloseOperation() | public int getDefaultCloseOperation() |
| setDefaultCloseOperation() | public void setDefaultCloseOperation (int *operation*) |

getDefaultCloseOperation() returns a value from the WindowConstants class that defines what the invoking JDialog object does when its window is closed. The default operation is for the JDialog to hide.

setDefaultCloseOperation() sets the closing mode for the invoking JDialog object. Valid arguments are:

- ❑   DISPOSE_ON_CLOSE
- ❑   DO_NOTHING_ON_CLOSE
- ❑   HIDE_ON_CLOSE

When the JDialog object is closed or closing, a WindowEvent object is generated. If the default close operation is set to JDialog.DO_NOTHING_ON_CLOSE, any action that is to be performed when the JDialog is closed will have to be done in windowClosing() method of a registered WindowListener.

# Methods to Return the JRootPane and its Sub-Elements

| Method | Syntax |
|---|---|
| getContentPane() | public Container getContentPane() |
| getGlassPane() | public Component getGlassPane() |
| getJMenuBar() | public JMenuBar getJMenuBar() |
| getLayeredPane() | public JLayeredPane getLayeredPane() |
| getRootPane() | public JRootPane getRootPane() |

These methods return a reference to the content pane, glass pane, layered pane, menu bar, or JRootPane associated with the invoking JDialog object.

# Methods to Set the JRootPane Sub-Elements

| Method | Syntax |
|---|---|
| setContentPane() | public void setContentPane (Container contentPane) |
| setGlassPane() | public void setGlassPane(Component glassPane) |
| setJMenuBar() | public void setJMenuBar(JMenuBar menuBar) |
| setLayeredPane() | public void setLayeredPane (JLayeredPane layeredPane) |

These methods are used to change the content pane, glass pane, layered pane, or menu bar associated with the invoking JDialog object.

# setLocationRelativeTo() Method

| Method | Syntax |
|---|---|
| setLocationRelativeTo() | public void setLocationRelativeTo (Component target) |

setLocationRelativeTo() centers the invoking JDialog object in the middle of Component target or in the middle of the screen if target is not currently displayed.

## Example: Using JDialog

In this example, a JDialog is placed over a JLabel. The JDialog contains a JButton. When the JButton is pressed, the JDialog is hidden.

It is not possible to change the layout manager of a JDialog object directly, and an error is thrown if the JDialog object invokes the setLayout() method. To change the layout manager of the elements contained in a JDialog, the content pane of the JDialog must call the setLayout() method.

JDialogs, like Dialogs, are not added to a Container. They are made visible by the JDialog object calling the show() method. The call to setLocationRelativeTo() has to be made after the Frame is made visible to properly place the JDialog object over the JLabel object.

9

javax.swing

*The WinClosing class is used to terminate the program if the window is closed. See Section 7.3.8 on page 74 for more details.*

```java
import javax.swing.*;
import java.awt.*;
import java.awt.event.*;

public class TestJD extends JFrame implements ActionListener {
    JLabel lbl;
    JDialog d;
    JButton okButton;

    public TestJD() {
        lbl = new JLabel("Hello There");
        lbl.setForeground(Color.black);

        // A JDialog object is created.  A JButton is placed inside
        // the JDialog

        okButton = new JButton("OK");
        okButton.addActionListener(this);

        d = new JDialog(this, "JDialog");
        d.setSize(200, 100);
        d.getContentPane().setLayout(new FlowLayout());
        d.getContentPane().add(okButton);

        JPanel jp = new JPanel();
        jp.add(lbl);

        getContentPane().add(jp, BorderLayout.CENTER);

        // The WindowListener is used to terminate the program when the window
        // is closed.  Under Java 2 version 1.3, the addWindowListener() syntax
        // can be replaced by
        //
        // setDefaultCloseOperation(JFrame.EXIT_ON_CLOSE);

        addWindowListener(new WinClosing());
        setBounds(100, 100, 200, 200);
        setVisible(true);

        // The JDialog is made visible

        d.setLocationRelativeTo(lbl);
        d.show();
    }

    // The JDialog remains visible until the "OK" button is pressed.
    // This calls the actionPerformed() method which disposes of the
    // JDialog
```

```
    public void actionPerformed(ActionEvent ae) {
      d.dispose();
    }

    public static void main(String args[]) {
      TestJD tjd = new TestJD();
    }
  }

  // The WinClosing class terminates the program when the window is closed

  class WinClosing extends WindowAdapter {
    public void windowClosing(WindowEvent we) {
      System.exit(0);
    }
  }
```

### Output

The user interface of the program is shown below.

## 9.2.5 JFileChooser Class

```
public class JFileChooser extends JComponent implements Accessible
```

```
Object
  Component
    Container
      JComponent
        JFileChooser
```

### Interfaces

```
ImageObserver, MenuContainer, Serializable, Accessible
```

A JFileChooser object bundles a directory pane with selection buttons into one interface. It provides a simple mechanism for the user to read or save a file. The JFileChooser object consists of a dialog that contains a file list, a text field, an approve button (save, open, or user-specified), a cancel button, and various other file selection buttons. The types of files displayed can be restricted by using a FileFilter object.

A JFileChooser object fires an ActionEvent object when the user clicks the open, save or cancel buttons.

9

javax.swing

## JFileChooser() Constructors

| Method | Syntax |
| --- | --- |
| JFileChooser() | public JFileChooser() |
| | public JFileChooser(File *directory*) |
| | public JFileChooser(String *path*) |

JFileChooser() object constructor. If a directory or path is provided, the initial directory is set there. The file chooser type is not set by the constructor: this property is set using the setDialogType() method.

## Methods to Display the Dialog

| Method | Syntax |
| --- | --- |
| showDialog() | public int showDialog(Component *parent*, String *approveButtonText*) |
| showOpenDialog() | public int showOpenDialog(Component *parent*) |
| showSaveDialog() | public int showSaveDialog(Component *parent*) |

These methods make the JFileChooser object dialog visible.

showDialog() creates a custom file chooser with a user-specified approve button text. This method returns JFileChooser.APPROVE_OPTION if the user clicks the approve button, JFileChooser.CANCEL_OPTION if the user clicks the cancel button, or JFileChooser.ERROR_OPTION if an error occurs or the dialog is dismissed.

showOpenDialog() and showSaveDialog() create an Open or Save dialog. These methods return JFileChooser.APPROVE_OPTION if the user clicks the approve button, JFileChooser.CANCEL_OPTION if the user clicks the cancel button, or JFileChooser.ERROR_OPTION if an error occurs or the dialog is dismissed.

## File Selection Methods

| Method | Syntax |
| --- | --- |
| getFileSelectionMode() | public int getFileSelectionMode() |
| getSelectedFile() | public File getSelectedFile() |
| getSelectedFiles() | public File[] getSelectedFiles() |
| setFileSelectionMode() | public void setFileSelectionMode(int *mode*) |
| setSelectedFile() | public void setSelectedFile(File *selectedFile*) |
| setSelectedFiles() | public void setSelectedFiles (File[] *selectedFiles*) |

getFileSelectionMode() returns the file selection mode of the invoking JFileChooser object.

setFileSelectionMode() changes the selection mode. Valid choices for the selection mode are:

- ❑ JFileChooser.FILES_ONLY
- ❑ JFileChooser.DIRECTORIES_ONLY
- ❑ JFileChooser.FILES_AND_DIRECTORIES

getSelectedFile() and getSelectedFiles() return a File object or an array of File objects representing the selected files.

setSelectedFile() and setSelectedFiles() methods are used to specify which files are selected.

## FileFilter Methods

| Method | Syntax |
|---|---|
| addChoosableFileFilter() | public void addChoosableFileFilter(FileFilter f) |
| getFileFilter() | public FileFilter getFileFilter() |
| removeChoosableFileFilter() | public void removeChoosableFileFilter(FileFilter f) |
| resetChoosableFileFilters() | public void resetChoosableFileFilters() |
| setFileFilter() | public void setFileFilter(FileFilter f) |

These methods are used to return, set, or remove a FileFilter object from the invoking JFileChooser object.

## Other JFileChooser Property Methods

| Method | Syntax |
|---|---|
| getApproveButtonText | public String getApproveButtonText() |
| getApproveButtonToolTipText() | public String getApproveButtonToolTipText() |
| getChoosableFileFilters() | public FileFilter[] getChoosableFileFilters() |
| getCurrentDirectory() | public File getCurrentDirectory() |
| getDialogTitle() | public String getDialogTitle() |
| isFileHidingEnabled() | public boolean isFileHidingEnabled() |
| isMultiSelectionEnabled() | public boolean isMultiSelectionEnabled() |
| setApproveButtonText() | public void setApproveButtonText(String text) |
| setApproveButtonToolTipText() | public void setApproveButtonToolTipText(String text) |
| setCurrentDirectory() | public void setCurrentDirectory(File dir) |
| setDialogTitle() | public void setDialogTitle(String title) |
| setFileHidingEnabled() | public void setFileHidingEnabled(boolean b) |
| setMultiSelectionEnabled() | public void setMultiSelectionEnabled(boolean b) |

9

javax.swing

**833**

These methods are used to access or change various properties of the invoking JFileChooser object.

## setDialogType() Method

| Method | Syntax |
|---|---|
| setDialogType() | public void setDialogType(int *dialogType*) |

setDialogType() sets the display type of the invoking JFileChooser object. Valid arguments are:

- ❑ JFileChooser.OPEN_DIALOG
- ❑ JFileChooser.CUSTOM_DIALOG
- ❑ JFileChooser.SAVE_DIALOG

A custom dialog is one that contains a user-defined file operation.

### Example: Using JFileChooser

In this example, a JFileChooser object is used to save the contents of a JTextArea to a file. When the **Save** JButton is pressed, a save-mode JFileChooser object is created and displayed. If the user selects a file and presses the **Save** button in the JFileChooser dialog, the contents of the JTextArea are written to that file. The WindowListener is used to terminate the program if the window is closed.

```
import javax.swing.*;
import java.awt.*;
import java.awt.event.*;
import java.io.*;

public class TestJFC extends JFrame implements ActionListener {
  JButton saveButton;
  JTextArea ta;

  public TestJFC() {
    ta = new JTextArea(8, 30);
    ta.setText("Head and Shoulders Knees and Toes");
    JPanel pn = new JPanel();
    pn.add(ta);

    saveButton = new JButton("Save");
    saveButton.setFont(new Font("Serif", Font.BOLD, 14));
    saveButton.addActionListener(this);
    JPanel ps = new JPanel();
    ps.add(saveButton);

    getContentPane().add(pn, BorderLayout.NORTH);
    getContentPane().add(ps, BorderLayout.SOUTH);
```

```
   // The WindowListener is used to terminate the program when the window
   // is closed.  Under Java 2 version 1.3, the addWindowListener() syntax
   // can be replaced by
   //
   // setDefaultCloseOperation(JFrame.EXIT_ON_CLOSE);

   addWindowListener(new WinClosing());
   setBounds(100, 100, 400, 300);
   setVisible(true);
}

// When the "Save" button is pressed, a JFileChooser object is
// created and displayed.

public void actionPerformed(ActionEvent ae) {
   JFileChooser jfc = new JFileChooser();
   jfc.setSize(400, 300);
   Container parent = saveButton.getParent();

   // The showSaveDialog() method blocks other activity until the
   // user presses either the "Save" or "Cancel" buttons

   int choice = jfc.showSaveDialog(parent);

   if (choice == JFileChooser.APPROVE_OPTION) {
     String filename = jfc.getSelectedFile().getAbsolutePath();

     try {
       FileWriter fw = new FileWriter(filename);
       fw.write(ta.getText());
       fw.flush();
     } catch (IOException ioe) {}
     :
   }
 }

 public static void main(String args[]) {
   TestJFC tjfc = new TestJFC();
 }
}

// The WinClosing class terminates the program when the window is closed

class WinClosing extends WindowAdapter {
 public void windowClosing(WindowEvent we) {
   System.exit(0);
 }
}
```

9

javax.swing

### Output

Here is the user interface of the program shown below:

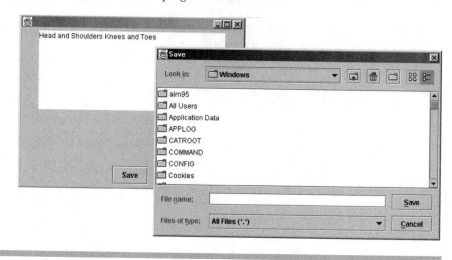

## 9.2.6 JFrame Class

```
public class JFrame extends Frame
    implements RootPaneContainer, WindowConstants, Accessible
```

```
Object
    Component
        Container
            Window
                Frame
                    JFrame
```

### Interfaces

```
ImageObserver, MenuContainer, WindowConstants, Accessible, RootPaneContainer
```

A JFrame is a top-level window with a title, border, and other platform specific buttons, such as minimize, maximize, and close buttons.

Components are not added to the JFrame directly, but instead are added to one of the sub-panes of the JRootPane object associated with the JFrame object. Generally, components are added to the content pane.

An error is thrown if an attempt is made to change the layout manager associated with the JFrame object. Changes to the layout manager should be made to the content, layered, or glass pane.

# JFrame() Constructors

| Method | Syntax |
|---|---|
| JFrame() | public JFrame()<br>public JFrame(String *title*)<br>public JFrame(GraphicsConfiguration *gc*)<br>public JFrame(String *title*, GraphicsConfiguration *gc*) |

The no-argument constructor creates an unnamed, invisible JFrame object with a close operation set to HIDE_ON_CLOSE. If a GraphicsConfiguration object is provided, it is used to describe the characteristics of a graphics destination such as a printer or monitor.

# Default Close Operation Methods

| Method | Syntax |
|---|---|
| getDefaultCloseOperation() | public int getDefaultCloseOperation() |
| setDefaultCloseOperation() | public void setDefaultCloseOperation<br>(int *operation*) |

getDefaultCloseOperation() returns a value from the WindowConstants class that defines what the invoking JFrame object does when its window is closed. The default operation is for the JFrame to hide.

setDefaultCloseOperation() sets the closing mode for the invoking JFrame object. Valid arguments are:

❑ DISPOSE_ON_CLOSE

❑ DO_NOTHING_ON_CLOSE

❑ EXIT_ON_CLOSE

❑ HIDE_ON_CLOSE.

The EXIT_ON_CLOSE option was introduced in Java 2 vesion 1.3 and can be used to terminate the program if the JFrame window is closed. Using this option with the setDefaultCloseOperation() method is an alternative to terminating the program in the windowClosing()method of an associated WindowListener object.

# Methods to Return the JRootPane and its Sub-Elements

| Method | Syntax |
|---|---|
| getContentPane() | public Container getContentPane() |
| getGlassPane() | public Component getGlassPane() |
| getJMenuBar() | public JMenuBar getJMenuBar() |
| getLayeredPane() | public JLayeredPane getLayeredPane() |
| getRootPane() | public JRootPane getRootPane() |

9

javax.swing

**837**

These methods return a reference to the content pane, glass pane, layered pane, menu bar, or JRootPane associated with the invoking JFrame object.

## Methods to Set the JRootPane Sub-Elements

| Method | Syntax |
|---|---|
| setContentPane() | public void setContentPane(Container *contentPane*) |
| setGlassPane() | public void setGlassPane(Component *glassPane*) |
| setJMenuBar() | public void setJMenuBar(JMenuBar *menuBar*) |
| setLayeredPane() | public void setLayeredPane(JLayeredPane *layeredPane*) |

These methods are used to change the content pane, glass pane, layered pane, or menu bar associated with the invoking JFrame object

### Example: Using JFrame

In this example, a JLabel object is created and placed on the content pane of a JFrame. The size and location of the JFrame is specified using the setBounds() method, and it is made visible using the setVisible() method. The WindowListener is used to terminate the program if the window is closed.

```
import javax.swing.*;
import java.awt.event.*;
import java.awt.*;

public class TestJFrame extends JFrame {
  JLabel lbl;

  public TestJFrame() {
    lbl = new JLabel("  This is a JFrame");
    lbl.setFont(new Font("Serif", Font.BOLD, 14));
    lbl.setForeground(Color.black);

    // The JLabel object is placed in the content pane of the
    // JFrame.

    getContentPane().add(lbl, BorderLayout.CENTER);

    // The WindowListener is used to terminate the program when the window
    // is closed.  Under Java 2 version 1.3, the addWindowListener() syntax
    // can be replaced by
    //
    // setDefaultCloseOperation(JFrame.EXIT_ON_CLOSE);

    addWindowListener(new WinClosing());
    setBounds(100, 100, 300, 200);
    setVisible(true);
  }
```

```
    public static void main(String args[]) {
      TestJFrame tjf = new TestJFrame();
    }
}

// The WinClosing class terminates the program when the window is closed

class WinClosing extends WindowAdapter {
  public void windowClosing(WindowEvent we) {
    System.exit(0);
  }
}
```

**Output**

The user interface of the program is shown below.

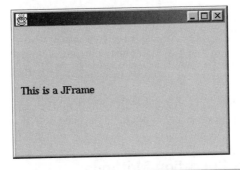

# 9.2.7 JInternalFrame Class

```
public class JInternalFrame extends JComponent
  implements RootPaneContainer, WindowConstants, Accessible
```

```
Object
  Component
    Container
      JComponent
        JInternalFrame
```

**Interfaces**

```
ImageObserver, MenuContainer, Serializable, RootPaneContainer,
WindowConstants, Accessible
```

A JInternalFrame object is a lightweight frame that is contained inside another Java Container. The JInternalFrame object is managed by its parent container like a child component would be.

Each JInternalFrame object keeps a reference to a static inner class called JDesktopIcon, which takes the place of the JInternalFrame when it is iconified.

JInternalFrames fire InternalFrameEvents when the state of the frame changes.

> Note that the default visibility of JInternalFrame objects has changed
> in Java 2 version 1.3. In previous versions they were visible by
> default, but now they are initially invisible.

## JInternalFrame() Constructors

| Method | Syntax |
|---|---|
| JInternalFrame() | public JInternalFrame() |
| | public JInternalFrame(String *title*) |
| | public JInternalFrame(String *title*,<br>                                  boolean *resizable*) |
| | public JInternalFrame(String *title*,<br>       boolean *resizable*, boolean *closable*) |
| | public JInternalFrame(String *title*,<br>       boolean *resizable*, boolean *closable*,<br>       boolean *maximizable*) |
| | public JInternalFrame(String *title*,<br>       boolean *resizable*, boolean *closable*,<br>       boolean *maximizable*, boolean *iconifiable*) |

JInternalFrame object constructor. By default all the resizable, closable, maximizable, and iconifiable properties are all set to false. The default close operation is HIDE_ON_CLOSE.

## Default Close Operation Methods

| Method | Syntax |
|---|---|
| getDefaultCloseOperation() | public int getDefaultCloseOperation() |
| setDefaultCloseOperation() | public void setDefaultCloseOperation<br>                    (int *operation*) |

getDefaultCloseOperation() returns a value from the WindowConstants class that defines what the invoking JInternalFrame object does when its window is closed. The default operation is for the JInternalFrame to hide.

setDefaultCloseOperation() sets the closing mode for the invoking JInternalFrame object. Valid WindowConstants class arguments are:

❑   DISPOSE_ON_CLOSE

❑   DO_NOTHING_ON_CLOSE

❑   HIDE_ON_CLOSE.

## Display Methods

| Method | Syntax |
|--------|--------|
| dispose() | public void dispose() |
| pack() | public void pack() |
| reshape() | public void reshape(int *x*, int *y*, int *width*, int *height*) |
| show() | public void show() |

dispose() makes the frame invisible, unselected, and closed.

pack() resizes the JInternalFrame to just fit the components it contains.

reshape() resizes and repositions the invoking JInternalFrame object.

show() makes the invoking JInternalFrame object visible, selected, and brings it to the front.

## InternalFrameListener Methods

| Method | Syntax |
|--------|--------|
| addInternalFrameListener() | public void addInternalFrameListener (InternalFrameListener *ifl*) |
| removeInternalFrameListener() | public void removeInternalFrameListener (InternalFrameListener *ifl*) |

InternalFrameEvent objects are generated when the state of the JInternalFrame changes.

addInternalFrameListener() associates an InternalFrameListener object to the invoking JInternalFrame object to listen for InternalFrameEvents.

removeInternalFrameListener() disconnects the InternalFrameListener object from the invoking JInternalFrame object.

## JLayeredPane Positioning Methods

| Method | Syntax |
|--------|--------|
| getLayer() | public int getLayer() |
| moveToBack() | public void moveToBack() |
| moveToFront() | public void moveToFront() |
| setLayer() | public void setLayer(int *layer*) |
| | public void setLayer(Integer *layer*) |
| toBack() | public void toBack() |
| toFront() | public void toFront() |

These methods position invoking JInternalFrame object within a JLayeredPane. If the invoking JInternalFrame object is not contained in a JLayeredPane, the methods do nothing.

9

javax.swing

getLayer() returns the layer that contains the invoking JInternalFrame object.

setLayer() is used to change the layer.

moveToBack() and toBack() move the invoking JInternalFrame object to the bottom of the JLayeredPane.

moveToFront() and toFront() move move the invoking JInternalFrame object to the top of the JLayeredPane.

## Methods to Return the JRootPane Sub-Elements

| Method | Syntax |
|---|---|
| getContentPane() | public Container getContentPane() |
| getGlassPane() | public Component getGlassPane() |
| getJMenuBar() | public JMenuBar getJMenuBar() |
| getLayeredPane() | public JLayeredPane getLayeredPane() |

These methods return a reference to the content pane, glass pane, layered pane, or menu bar associated with the invoking JInternalFrame object.

## Methods to Set the JRootPane Sub-Elements

| Method | Syntax |
|---|---|
| setContentPane() | public void setContentPane(Container contentPane) |
| setGlassPane() | public void setGlassPane(Component glassPane) |
| setJMenuBar() | public void setJMenuBar(JMenuBar menuBar) |
| setLayeredPane() | public void setLayeredPane(JLayeredPane layeredPane) |

These methods are used to change the content pane, glass pane, layered pane, or menu bar associated with the invoking JInternalFrame object

## Methods to Return JInternalFrame Properties

| Method | Syntax |
|---|---|
| getDesktopIcon | public JInternalFrame.JDesktopIcon getDesktopIcon() |
| getDesktopPane() | public JDesktopPane getDesktopPane() |
| getFrameIcon() | public Icon getFrameIcon() |
| getTitle() | public String getTitle() |
| isClosable() | public boolean isClosable() |
| isClosed() | public boolean isClosed() |
| isIcon() | public boolean isIcon() |
| isIconifiable() | public boolean isIconifiable() |
| isMaximizable() | public boolean isMaximizable() |
| isMaximum() | public boolean isMaximum() |
| isResizable() | public boolean isResizable() |
| isSelected() | public boolean isSelected() |

getDesktopIcon() returns the icon that is displayed if the invoking JInternalFrame object is iconified.

getDesktopPane() returns a reference to the JDesktopPane, if any, containing the invoking JInternalFrame object.

getFrameIcon() returns the icon, if any, painted on the left-hand corner of the frame titlebar.

getTitle() returns the title displayed on the frame titlebar.

isCloseable() returns true if the JInternalFrame can be closed.

isClosed() returns true if the JInternalFrame is currently closed.

isIconifiable() returns true if the JInternalFrame can be iconified.

isIcon() returns true if the JInternalFrame is currently iconified.

isMaximizable() returns true if the JInternalFrame can be maximized.

isMaximum() returns true if the JInternalFrame is currently maximized.

isResizable() returns true if the JInternalFrame can be resized.

isSelected() returns true if the JInternalFrame is currently selected.

## Methods to Set JInternalFrame Properties

| Method | Syntax |
| --- | --- |
| setClosable() | public void setClosable(boolean b) |
| setClosed() | public void setClosed(boolean b) throws PropertyVetoException |
| setDesktopIcon() | public void setDesktopIcon (JInternalFrame.JDesktopIcon icon) |
| setFrameIcon() | public void setFrameIcon(Icon frameIcon) |
| setIcon() | public void setIcon(boolean b) throws PropertyVetoException |
| setIconifiable() | public void setIconifiable(boolean b) |
| setMaximizable() | public void setMaximizable(boolean b) |
| setMaximum() | public void setMaximum(boolean b) throws PropertyVetoException |
| setResizable() | public void setResizable(boolean b) |
| setSelected() | public void setSelected(boolean b) throws PropertyVetoException |
| setTitle() | public void setTitle(String s) |

9

javax.swing

setClosable() is used to specify if the invoking JInternalFrame can be closed.

setClosed() is used to open or close the JInternalFrame.

setDesktopIcon() changes that icon that is displayed if the invoking JInternalFrame object is iconified.

setFrameIcon() sets the icon to be painted on the left-hand corner of the frame titlebar.

setIconifiable() specifies whether the JInternalFrame can be iconified.

setIcon() is used to iconify or deiconify the invoking JInternalFrame object.

setMaximizable() specifies whether the JInternalFrame can be maximized.

setMaximum() sets the maximized state of the JInternalFrame.

setResizable() specifies whether the JInternalFrame can be resized.

setSelected() changes the selected state of the JInternalFrame.

setTitle() sets or changes the title displayed on the frame titlebar.

---

### Example: Using JInternalFrame

See the *Building a Desktop Using JDesktopPane and JInternalFrame* example on page 825 where a JInternalFrame object is placed within a JDesktopPane.

---

# 9.2.8 JLayeredPane Class

```
public class JLayeredPane extends JComponent implements Accessible
```

```
Object
   Component
      Container
         JComponent
            JLayeredPane
```

### Interfaces

```
ImageObserver, MenuContainer, Serializable, Accessible
```

The JLayeredPane class is one of the sub-element classes of JRootPane. A JLayeredPane object is a container that can add its components on different layers. It can be thought of as a three-dimensional container. Components can be added to the JLayeredPane using:

```
public void add(Component c, Object constraints)
```

where `constraints` is an `Integer` object that indicates a component's position within the layer. The `JLayeredPane` class by default has no assigned layout manager. If GUI components are added to the `JLayeredPane`, they are done so without a layout manager.

The `JLayeredPane` layer stack-up is shown in the following diagram:

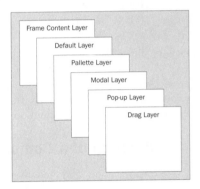

❑   The frame content layer is used to position the content pane and menu bar. It is the bottommost layer.

❑   The default layer is where components are most often placed.

❑   The palette layer is positioned above the default layer and is used for floating toolbars and palettes.

❑   The modal layer is used to place modal dialogs that are intended to appear on top of toolbars, palettes, or other components.

❑   The pop-up layer is used for pop-up displays.

❑   The drag layer is where components that are being dragged are re-positioned so that they will appear on top of everything else.

Components contained in a given layer also have a property called their `position`, that determines the order in which they are drawn. Components with the lowest position numbers are drawn last.

## JLayeredPane() Constructor

| Method | Syntax |
|---|---|
| JLayeredPane() | public JLayeredPane() |

`JLayeredPane()` creates a `JLayeredPane` object.

## Layer Constants

| Syntax |
| --- |
| `public static final Integer FRAME_CONTENT_LAYER` |
| `public static final Integer DEFAULT_LAYER` |
| `public static final Integer PALETTE_LAYER` |
| `public static final Integer MODAL_LAYER` |
| `public static final Integer POPUP_LAYER` |
| `public static final Integer DRAG_LAYER` |

The `JLayeredPane` class provides these constants to define the layers available to the user. They are listed from bottommost to topmost layer. These constants can be used as an argument to the `add()` method to place a component on a desired layer.

## Methods to Change the Position of a Component

| Method | Syntax |
| --- | --- |
| `moveToBack()` | `public void moveToBack(Component c)` |
| `moveToFront()` | `public void moveToFront(Component c)` |
| `setLayer()` | `public void setLayer(Component c, int layer)` |
| | `public void setLayer`<br>`(Component c, int layer, int position)` |
| `setPosition()` | `public void setPosition`<br>`(Component c, int position)` |

`moveToBack()` moves `Component c` to the back (highest position number) of its layer.

`moveToFront()` moves `Component c` to the front of its layer.

`setLayer()` is used to change the position and/or layer of `Component c`. This method will not add `Component c` to the `JLayeredPane` but is used to change its layer and position once it has already been added.

`setPosition()` changes the position of `Component c` within its layer.

## Methods to Return the Position of a Component

| Method | Syntax |
| --- | --- |
| `getIndexOf()` | `public int getIndexOf(Component c)` |
| `getLayer()` | `public int getLayer(Component c)` |
| `getPosition()` | `public int getPosition(Component c)` |

`getIndexOf()` returns the index of `Component c` within the invoking `JLayeredPane` object. This is an absolute index ignoring layers whereas a component's position refers to its position (or index) within a given layer.

`getLayer()` and `getPosition()` return the layer or position of `Component c` within the invoking `JLayeredPane` object.

## JLayeredPane Property Methods

| Method | Syntax |
|---|---|
| getComponentCountInLayer() | public int getComponentCountInLayer<br>(int *layer*) |
| getComponentsInLayer() | public Component[] getComponentsInLayer<br>(int *layer*) |
| highestLayer() | public int highestLayer() |
| lowestLayer() | public int lowestLayer() |

getComponentCountInLayer() returns the number of components in the specified layer.

getComponentsinLayer() returns a Component array containing the components in the specified layer.

highestLayer() and lowestLayer() return the number corresponding to the highest and lowest layers of the invoking JLayeredPane object.

### Example: Using JLayeredPane

In this example, three JButton objects are placed on the JLayeredPane of a JFrame. The first two JButtons are added to the default layer. The third button is added to the drag layer, which is painted above the default layer.

The first two JButton objects are registered with an ActionListener, so that when either of the JButtons are pressed, that JButton is brought to the front. The third JButton will always be painted on top of the other two.

*The WinClosing class is used to terminate the program if the window is closed. See Section 7.3.8 on page 657 for more details.*

```
import javax.swing.*;
import java.awt.*;
import java.awt.event.*;

public class TestJLP extends JFrame implements ActionListener {
   JButton b1, b2, b3;
   JLayeredPane jlp;

   public TestJLP() {

      // Three JButton objects are created.  Because they are to be
      // placed on a JLayerPane that uses no layout manager, they
      // are given an absolute position and size with the setBounds()
      // method
```

9

javax.swing

```
         b1 = new JButton();
         b1.setBackground(Color.yellow);
         b1.setBounds(10, 10, 60, 60);
         b1.addActionListener(this);

         b2 = new JButton();
         b2.setBackground(Color.green);
         b2.setBounds(40, 40, 60, 60);
         b2.addActionListener(this);

         b3 = new JButton();
         b3.setBackground(Color.black);
         b3.setBounds(70, 70, 60, 60);

         // The three JButton objects are placed within the layered pane
         // of the JFrame.  The first two JButton objects are placed on
         // the default layer.  The third is placed in the drag layer.

         jlp = getLayeredPane();
         jlp.add(b1, JLayeredPane.DEFAULT_LAYER);
         jlp.add(b2, JLayeredPane.DEFAULT_LAYER);
         jlp.add(b3, JLayeredPane.DRAG_LAYER);

         // The WindowListener is used to terminate the program when the window
         // is closed.  Under Java 2 version 1.3, the addWindowListener() syntax
         // can be replaced by
         //
         // setDefaultCloseOperation(JFrame.EXIT_ON_CLOSE);

         addWindowListener(new WinClosing());
         setBounds(100, 100, 200, 200);
         setVisible(true);
      }

   // When either of the first two JButton objects are pressed, it
   // is moved on top of the other.  Since the third JButton is in
   // the drag layer, it will always be displayed on top of the
   // other two.

   public void actionPerformed(ActionEvent ae) {
      JButton btn = (JButton) ae.getSource();
      jlp.moveToFront(btn);
   }

   public static void main(String args[]) {
      TestJLP tjlp = new TestJLP();
   }
}

// The WinClosing class terminates the program when the window is closed
```

```
class WinClosing extends WindowAdapter {
  public void windowClosing(WindowEvent we) {
    System.exit(0);
  }
}
```

### Output

Here are the resulting layers:

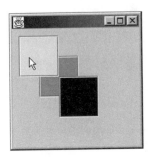

## 9.2.9 JOptionPane Class

```
public class JOptionPane extends JComponent implements Accessible
```

```
Object
  Component
    Container
      JComponent
        JOptionPane
```

### Interfaces

```
ImageObserver, MenuContainer, Serializable, Accessible
```

A JOptionPane object provides a way to create common pop-up dialog boxes directly without having to build one up from its individual components. There are four basic types of JOptionPanes.

❑ An **Input Dialog** provides a way for the user to enter data. It includes two buttons, OK and Cancel:

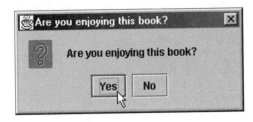

❏ A **Confirm Dialog** asks the user to confirm some information. It also has two buttons, Yes and No, or OK and Cancel:

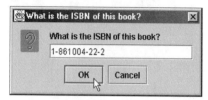

❏ A **Message Dialog** displays information to the user and has a single OK button:

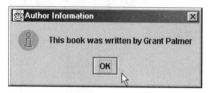

❏ An **Option Dialog** displays arbitrary data to the user and may contain any number of buttons:

JOptionPane objects can be created in one of two ways. The first is by using a constructor which creates a permanent JOptionPane object. The second is using one of the static dialog display methods provided by the class. These create a temporary instance of a JOptionPane object that goes away when the JOptionPane is closed.

JOptionPanes are not standalone containers but exist inside a JDialog or JInternalFrame object. The associated JDialog or JInternalFrame that contains the JOptionPane can be created using the createDialog() or createInternalFrame() methods. The static JOptionPane display methods create the associated JDialog or JInternalFrame object automatically.

## JOptionPane() Constructors

| Constructor | Syntax |
| --- | --- |
| JOptionPane() | public JOptionPane() |
| | public JOptionPane(Object *message*) |
| | public JOptionPane(Object *message*, int *messageType*) |
| | public JOptionPane(Object *message*, int *messageType*, int *optionType*) |
| | public JOptionPane(Object *message*, int *messageType*, int *optionType*, Icon *icon*) |

| Constructor | Syntax |
|---|---|
| | `public JOptionPane(Object message, int messageType,`<br>`                    int optionType, Icon icon,`<br>`                    Object[] options)` |
| | `public JOptionPane(Object message, int messageType,`<br>`                    int optionType, Icon icon,`<br>`                    Object[] options, Object initialValue)` |

`JOptionPane()` creates a `JOptionPane` object. The `message` is generally a `String` such as `"Are you sure?"` and appears inside the `JOptionPane` object. The `icon` appears inside the `JOptionPane` object. To have no icon appear, pass `JOptionPane.PLAIN_MESSAGE` as the message type. In this case, the `null` value can be used as the `icon` argument. The `options` array allows an arbitrary number of buttons to be specified. Generally an array of `Strings` or `Icons` is passed for this argument.

## JOptionPane Class Constants

The `JOptionPane` class has a series of constants to defined the class property values. The message type, option type, and intial value are of type `int`. The bound property constants are `Strings`.

- **Message type**. This parameter indicates the type of dialog to create. It can have values of:
  - `JOptionPane.ERROR_MESSAGE`
  - `JOptionPane.INFORMATION_MESSAGE`
  - `JOptionPane.PLAIN_MESSAGE`
  - `JOptionPane.QUESTION_MESSAGE`
  - `JOptionPane.WARNING_MESSAGE`

- **Option type**. Specifies the number and type of buttons places inside the `JOptionPane` object. It can have values of:
  - `JOptionPane.DEFAULT_OPTION`
  - `JOptionPane.OK_CANCEL_OPTION`
  - `JOptionPane.YES_NO_CANCEL_OPTION`
  - `JOptionPane.YES_NO_OPTION`

The default option provides on an OK button. The other three indicate by their names which buttons are provided.

- **Initial value**. Specifies which selection is initially selected or which button initially has focus. It terms of buttons, the available values are:
  - `JOptionPane.CANCEL_OPTION`
  - `JOptionPane.CLOSED_OPTION`
  - `JOptionPane.NO_OPTION`

- ❏     `JOptionPane.OK_OPTION`

- ❏     `JOptionPane.YES_OPTION`

- ❏     `JOptionPane.UNINITIALIZED_VALUE` (This constant has type `Object`.)

- ❏   **Bound properties**. These are of type `String`. Two of the more useful ones are:

  - ❏     `JOptionPane.INPUT_VALUE_PROPERTY`

  - ❏     `JOptionPane.VALUE_PROPERTY`

## Methods to Create an Associated JDialog or JinternalFrame

| Method | Syntax |
| --- | --- |
| `createDialog()` | `public JDialog createDialog(Component parent, String title)` |
| `createInternalFrame()` | `public JInternalFrame createInternalFrame (Component parent, String title)` |

`createDialog()` creates a `JDialog` object containing the invoking `JOptionPane` object. The `JDialog` object is centered on the parent `Component`. This method is called by a `JOptionPane` object that was created using a constructor. It is called automatically by the static dialog display methods.

`createInternalFrame()` creates a `JInternalFrame` object containing the invoking `JOptionPane` object. The `JInternalFrame` object is centered on the parent `Component`. This method is called by a `JOptionPane` object that was created using a constructor. It is called automatically by the static dialog display methods.

# Static JOptionPane Display Methods

These methods create temporary instances of `JDialog` and `JInternalFrame` objects that contain `JOptionPane` objects. The input parameters are:

- ❏   `parent` – The parent container of the `JOptionPane` object. The dialog or internal frame will be centered on the parent.

- ❏   `message` – A `String` or `Icon` that is placed inside the dialog.

- ❏   `title` – A `String` that appears in the title bar.

- ❏   `messageType` – Indicates the type of dialog to create.

- ❏   `optionType` – Determines that types of buttons that will be displayed. This parameter is only relevant for Confirm and Option dialogs.

- ❏   `icon` – The `Icon` object that is displayed inside the dialog. Passing `null` means the `Icon` will be determined based on the value of `messageType`. A `messageType` of `PLAIN_MESSAGE` means no icon is displayed.

❑ selectionValues – This parameter is used only for Input dialogs. It allows a set of values to be provided to the user to choose from. The way the values are displayed is determined by the system. If selectionValues is set to null, a TextField is displayed.

❑ initialSelectionValue – which of the selectionValues is initially selected.

❑ options – This parameter is used for Option dialogs only. It allows for an arbitrary number of buttons to be displayed. An array of Strings or Icons is usually passed.

❑ initialValue – specifies a default option from the options list.

## showInputDialog() Method

| Method | Syntax |
|---|---|
| showInputDialog() | public static String showInputDialog(Object *message*) |
| | public static String showInputDialog<br>(Component *parent*, object *message*) |
| | public static String showInputDialog<br>(Component *parent*, object *message*,<br>String *title*, int *messageType*) |
| | public static Object showInputDialog<br>(Component *parent*, Object *message*,<br>String *title*, int *messageType*, Icon *icon*,<br>Object[] *selectionValues*,<br>Object *initialSelectionValue*) |

showInputDialog() creates a JDialog object containing an input-style JOptionPane object and returns the user input as a String. If an array of selection values is provided, it returns the selected item as an Object.

## showInternalInputDialog() Method

| Method | Syntax |
|---|---|
| showInternalInputDialog() | public static String showInternalInputDialog<br>(Component *parent*, Object *message*) |
| | public static String showInternalInputDialog<br>(Component *parent*, Object *message*,<br>String *title*, int *messageType*) |
| | public static Object showInternalInputDialog<br>(Component *parent*, Object *message*,<br>String *title*, int *messageType*,<br>con *icon*, Object[] *selectionValues*,<br>Object *initialSelectionValue*) |

showInternalInputDialog() creates a JInternalFrame object containing an input-type JOptionPane object and returns the user input as a String. If an array of selection values is provided, it returns the selected item as an Object.

## showMessageDialog() Method

| Method | Syntax |
|--------|--------|
| showMessageDialog() | public static void **showMessageDialog**<br>(Component *parent*, Object *message*) |
| | public static void **showMessageDialog**<br>(Component *parent*, Object *message*,<br>String *title*, int *messageType*) |
| | public static void **showMessageDialog**,<br>(Component *parent*, Object *message*,<br>String *title*, int *messageType*,<br>Icon *icon*) |

showMessageDialog() creates a JDialog object containing a message-style JOptionPane object. It returns no information.

## showInternalMessageDialog() Method

| Method | Syntax |
|--------|--------|
| showInternalMessage Dialog() | public static void **showInternalMessageDialog**<br>(Component *parent*, Object *message*) |
| | public static void **showInternalMessageDialog**<br>(Component *parent*, Object *message*,<br>String *title*, int *messageType*) |
| | public static void **showInternalMessageDialog**<br>(Component *parent*, Object *message*,<br>String *title*, int *messageType*,<br>Icon *icon*) |

showInternalMessageDialog() creates a JInternalFrame object containing a message-style JOptionPane object. It returns no information.

## showConfirmDialog() Method

| Method | Syntax |
|--------|--------|
| showConfirmDialog() | public static int **showConfirmDialog**<br>(Component *parent*, Object *message*) |
| | public static int **showConfirmDialog**<br>(Component *parent*, Object *message*,<br>String *title*, int *optionType*) |
| | public static int **showConfirmDialog**<br>(Component *parent*, Object *message*,<br>String *title*, int *optionType*,<br>int *messageType*) |
| | public static int **showConfirmDialog**<br>(Component *parent*, Object *message*,<br>String *title*, int *optionType*,<br>int *messageType*, Icon *icon*) |

showConfirmDialog() creates a JDialog object containing a confirm-style JOptionDialog object and returns either YES_OPTION, NO_OPTION, CANCEL_OPTION, OK_OPTION, or CLOSED_OPTION.

# showInternalConfirmDialog() Method

| Method | Syntax |
|---|---|
| showInternalConfirmDialog() | public static int showInternalConfirmDialog (Component *parent*, Object *message*) |
| | public static int showInternalConfirmDialog (Component *parent*, Object *message*, String *title*, int *optionType*) |
| | public static int showInternalConfirmDialog (Component *parent*, Object *message*, String *title*, int *optionType*, int *messageType*) |
| | public static int showInternalConfirmDialog (Component *parent*, Object *message*, String *title*, int *optionType*, int *messageType*, Icon *icon*) |

showInternalConfirmDialog() creates a JInternalFrame object containing a confirm-style JOptionPane object and returns either YES_OPTION, NO_OPTION, CANCEL_OPTION, OK_OPTION, or CLOSED_OPTION.

# showOptionDialog() Method

| Method | Syntax |
|---|---|
| showOptionDialog() | public static int showOptionDialog (Component *parent*, Object *message*, String *title*, int *optionType*, int *messageType*, Icon *icon*, Object[] *options*, Object *initialValue*) |

showOptionDialog() creates a JDialog object containing an option-style JOptionPane object and returns either YES_OPTION, NO_OPTION, CANCEL_OPTION, OK_OPTION, or CLOSED_OPTION, or if a list of options is provided it returns the index in the array of the option corresponding to the button pushed.

# showInternalOptionDialog() Method

| Method | Syntax |
|---|---|
| showInternalOptionDialog() | public static int showInternalOptionDialog (Component *parent*, Object *message*, String *title*, int *optionType*, int *messageType*, Icon *icon*, Object[] *options*, Object *initialValue*) |

showInternalOptionDialog() creates a JInternalFrame object containing an option-style JOptionPane object and returns either YES_OPTION, NO_OPTION, CANCEL_OPTION, OK_OPTION, or CLOSED_OPTION, or if a list of options is provided it returns the index in the array of the option corresponding to the button pushed.

9

javax.swing

## JOptionPane Property Methods

| Method | Syntax |
|---|---|
| getIcon() | public Icon getIcon() |
| getInitialSelectionValue() | public Object getInitialSelectionValue() |
| getInitialValue() | public Object getInitialValue() |
| getInputValue() | public Object getInputValue() |
| getMessage() | public Object getMessage() |
| getMessageType() | public int getMessageType() |
| getOptions() | public Object[] getOptions() |
| getOptionType() | public int getOptionType() |
| getSelectionValues() | public Object[] getSelectionValues() |
| getValue() | public Object getValue() |
| getWantsInput() | public boolean getWantsInput() |
| setIcon() | public void setIcon(Icon *icon*) |
| setInitialSelectionValue() | public void setInitialSelectionValue (Object *initialValue*) |
| setInitialValue() | public void setInitialValue (Object *initialValue*) |
| setInputValue() | public void setInputValue (Object *inputValue*) |
| setMessage() | public void setMessage(Object *msg*) |
| setMessageType() | public void setMessageType(int *messageType*) |
| setOptions() | public void setOptions(Object[] *options*) |
| setOptionType() | public void setOptionType(int *optionType*) |
| setSelectionValues() | public void setSelectionValues (Object[] *selectionValues*) |
| setValue() | public void setValue(Object *value*) |
| setWantsInput() | public void setWantsInput(boolean *b*) |

These methods return or set parameters associated with the invoking JOptionPane object. Setting the wantsInput parameter to true causes a textfield to appear in the JOptionPane object.

## selectInitialValue() Method

| Method | Syntax |
|---|---|
| selectInitialValue() | public void selectInitialValue() |

selectInitialValue() causes the default button to receive focus.

### Example: Using a JOptionPane to Confirm a Quit Command

In this example, a JButton is placed on a JFrame. When the JButton is pressed, the program terminates, however, before the program is allowed to terminate, a JOptionPane is created to confirm this intention. A static display method is used to create the JOptionPane.

The *WinClosing* class is used to terminate the program if the window is closed.
*See Section 7.3.8 on page 657 for more details.*

```java
import javax.swing.*;
import java.awt.*;
import java.awt.event.*;

public class TestJOP extends JFrame implements ActionListener {
  JButton quitButton;

  public TestJOP() {
    quitButton = new JButton("Quit");
    quitButton.setFont(new Font("Serif", Font.PLAIN, 12));
    quitButton.addActionListener(this);

    JPanel p = new JPanel();
    p.add(quitButton);

    getContentPane().add(p);

    // The WindowListener is used to terminate the program when the window
    // is closed.  Under Java 2 version 1.3, the addWindowListener() syntax
    // can be replaced by
    //
    // setDefaultCloseOperation(JFrame.EXIT_ON_CLOSE);

    addWindowListener(new WinClosing());
    setBounds(100, 100, 200, 200);
    setVisible(true);
  }

  public void actionPerformed(ActionEvent ae) {
    Container c = quitButton.getParent();

    // The showConfirmDialog() method creates a JOptionPane object and
    // displays it inside a dialog. The method blocks other activity
    // until the user presses either the "Yes" or "No" buttons inside
    // the dialog.

    int i =
      JOptionPane.showConfirmDialog(c, "Do you really want to quit?",
                                    "Quit?",
                                    JOptionPane.YES_NO_OPTION);

    if (i == JOptionPane.YES_OPTION) {
      System.exit(0);
    }
  }
```

9

javax.swing

```
    public static void main(String args[]) {
      TestJOP tjop = new TestJOP();
    }
  }

  // The WinClosing class terminates the program when the window is closed

  class WinClosing extends WindowAdapter {
    public void windowClosing(WindowEvent we) {
      System.exit(0);
    }
  }
```

**Output**

Here is the result with the JOptionPane:

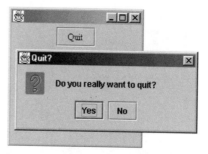

## Example: Using a JOptionPane to Save a File

In this example, a JButton is placed on a JFrame. When the JButton is pressed, the contents of a JTextArea are written to a file. Before this happens, a JOptionPane is created to obtain the name for the file. In this example, the JOptionPane object is created using a constructor.

*The WinClosing class is used to terminate the program if the window is closed. See Section 7.3.8 on page 657 for more details.*

```
import javax.swing.*;
import java.awt.*;
import java.awt.event.*;
import java.io.*;

public class TestJOP2 extends JFrame implements ActionListener {
  JButton saveButton;
  JOptionPane jop;
  JTextArea ta;
```

```
public TestJOP2() {

  // A JOptionPane object is created using the constructor

  jop = new JOptionPane("Save file as",
                        JOptionPane.QUESTION_MESSAGE,
                        JOptionPane.OK_CANCEL_OPTION, null);
  jop.setSelectionValues(null);
  jop.setWantsInput(true);

  ta = new JTextArea(5, 30);
  ta.setText("The weather outside was frightful");
  JPanel pn = new JPanel();
  pn.add(ta);

  saveButton = new JButton("Save");
  saveButton.setFont(new Font("Serif", Font.BOLD, 14));
  saveButton.addActionListener(this);
  JPanel ps = new JPanel();
  ps.add(saveButton);

  JPanel cp = (JPanel) getContentPane();
  cp.setLayout(new BorderLayout());
  cp.add(pn, BorderLayout.NORTH);
  cp.add(ps, BorderLayout.SOUTH);

  // The WindowListener is used to terminate the program when the window
  // is closed.  Under Java 2 version 1.3, the addWindowListener() syntax
  // can be replaced by
  //
  // setDefaultCloseOperation(JFrame.EXIT_ON_CLOSE);

  addWindowListener(new WinClosing());
  setBounds(100, 100, 400, 200);
  setVisible(true);
}

// When the "Save" button is pressed, the JOptionPane creates
// a JDialog.  The JOptionPane displays

public void actionPerformed(ActionEvent ae) {
  Container parent = saveButton.getParent();
  JDialog jd = jop.createDialog(parent, "Save");
  jd.show();
  String filename = (String) jop.getInputValue();
  try {
    FileWriter fw = new FileWriter(filename);
    fw.write(ta.getText());
```

9

javax.swing

```
          fw.flush();
      } catch (IOException ioe) {}
   }

   public static void main(String args[]) {
      TestJOP2 tjop = new TestJOP2();
   }
}

// The WinClosing class terminates the program when the window is closed

class WinClosing extends WindowAdapter {
   public void windowClosing(WindowEvent we) {
      System.exit(0);
   }
}
```

**Output**

Here is the result with the JOptionPane allowing the suer to save the contents of the
JTextArea:

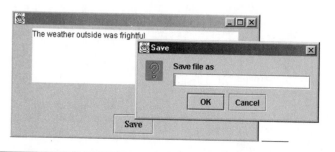

# 9.2.10 JPanel Class

```
public class JPanel extends JComponent implements Accessible
```

```
Object
   Component
      Container
         JComponent
            JPanel
```

**Interfaces**

```
ImageObserver, MenuContainer, Serializable, Accessible
```

A JPanel object is a simple Swing container. It does not have a JRootPane object
associated with it. Components can be added directly to the JPanel object. A JPanel is
often used for grouping components together before placing them in another
container.

Other than its constructor, the JPanel class defines no new methods.

**860**

# JPanel() Constructors

| Method | Syntax |
|--------|--------|
| JPanel() | public JPanel()<br>public JPanel(boolean *isDoubleBuffered*)<br>public JPanel(LayoutManager *lm*)<br>public JPanel(LayoutManager *lm*, boolean *isDoubleBuffered*) |

JPanel() creates a JPanel object. The default constructor generates a JPanel with a FlowLayout layout manager and double buffering enabled.

## Example: Using JPanel

In this example, we want to place three JButton objects in the center region of a JFrame's content pane. The JFrame object, however, uses a BorderLayout layout manager by default – which only permits one component to be placed in each region. To circumvent this, the JButtons are first placed in a JPanel and the JPanel is placed on the content pane of the JFrame.

*The WinClosing class is used to terminate the program if the window is closed. See Section 7.3.8 on page 657 for more details.*

```
import javax.swing.*;
import java.awt.event.*;
import java.awt.*;

public class TestJPanel extends JFrame {
   JButton b1, b2, b3;

   public TestJPanel() {
      b1 = new JButton("button 1");
      b2 = new JButton("button 2");
      b3 = new JButton("button 3");

      // The JButtons are first placed in a JPanel

      JPanel p = new JPanel();
      p.add(b1);
      p.add(b2);
      p.add(b3);

      // then the JPanel is placed in the content pane

      getContentPane().add(p, BorderLayout.CENTER);

      // The WindowListener is used to terminate the program when the window
      // is closed.  Under Java 2 version 1.3, the addWindowListener() syntax
      // can be replaced by
      //
```

9

javax.swing

```
//  setDefaultCloseOperation(JFrame.EXIT_ON_CLOSE);

    addWindowListener(new WinClosing());
    setBounds(100, 100, 400, 120);
    setVisible(true);
  }

  public static void main(String args[]) {
    TestJPanel tjp = new TestJPanel();
  }
}

// The WinClosing class terminates the program when the window is closed

class WinClosing extends WindowAdapter {
  public void windowClosing(WindowEvent we) {
    System.exit(0);
  }
}
```

**Output**

Here is the result:

# 9.2.11 JRootPane Class

```
public class JRootPane extends JComponent implements Accessible
```

```
Object
  Component
    Container
      JComponent
        JRootPane
```

**Interfaces**

```
ImageObserver, MenuContainer, Serializable, Accessible
```

Most of the higher level Swing Containers (JFrame, JWindow, JDialog, and JInternalFrame) contain a JRootPane object as their only component. A JRootPane object is itself a Container that contains a fixed number of other components including a content pane, a layered pane, a menu bar, and a glass pane.

GUI components are not placed on the higher-level Container itself, but instead are placed on one of the sub-panes of the JRootPane object associated with the higher-level Container. Most components are placed on the content pane.

The heirarchy of the sub-panes contained within the JRootPane object are as follows: At the bottom level are the content pane and menu bar. Above these is the layered pane. At the top level is the glass pane.

The glass pane is painted last. Anything placed on the glass pane will be displayed on top of anything placed on the layered or content panes. The glass pane is often used to block mouse events from components on the layered or content panes. This can be done by associated the glass pane with a MouseListener object. Since the glass pane is on top of the pane stack-up, the glass pane's MouseListener will receive any MouseEvent objects that are generated. To un-block the MouseEvent objects from reaching the underlying components, simply remove the MouseListener from the glass pane.

The default content pane is a JPanel with a BorderLayout layout manager. The default glass pane is a non-opaque, invisible JPanel with a FlowLayout layout manager. The default menu bar pane has no menu bar.

## JRootPane() Constructor

| Method | Syntax |
|--------|--------|
| JRootPane() | public JRootPane() |

JRootPane object constructor.

## Methods to Return the JRootPane Sub-Elements

| Method | Syntax |
|--------|--------|
| getContentPane() | public Container getContentPane() |
| getGlassPane() | public Component getGlassPane() |
| getJMenuBar() | public JMenuBar getJMenuBar() |
| getLayeredPane() | public JLayeredPane getLayeredPane() |

These methods return a reference to the content pane, glass pane, layered pane, or menu bar associated with the invoking JRootPane object.

## Methods to Set the JRootPane Sub-Elements

| Method | Syntax |
|--------|--------|
| setContentPane() | public void setContentPane(Container contentPane) |
| setGlassPane() | public void setGlassPane(Component glassPane) |
| setJMenuBar() | public void setJMenuBar(JMenuBar menuBar) |
| setLayeredPane() | public void setLayeredPane(JLayeredPane layeredPane) |

These methods are used to change the content pane, glass pane, layered pane, or menu bar associated with the invoking JRootPane object

9

javax.swing

## Default Button Methods

| Method | Syntax |
|--------|--------|
| getDefaultButton() | public JButton getDefaultButton() |
| setDefaultButton() | public void setDefaultButton(JButton *jb*) |

The default button is the JButton that will be pressed when the user hits the *Enter* key or any other specified key. This allows the user to use the *Enter* key rather than the mouse to press certain buttons.

getDefaultButton() returns a reference to the current default button.

setDefaultButton() is used to change the default button.

## UI Delegate Methods

| Method | Syntax |
|--------|--------|
| getUI() | public RootPaneUI getUI() |
| getUIClassID() | public String getUIClassID() |
| setUI() | public void setUI(RootPaneUI *ui*) |
| updateUI() | public void updateUI() |

getUI() returns the RootPaneUI object associated with the invoking RootPane object.

getUIClassID() returns the String "RootPaneUI" which is the suffix of the object used to render a RootPane object.

setUI() is used to change the RootPaneUI object associated the invoking RootPane object.

updateUI() is called when the look-and-feel of the invoking RootPane object has changed.

# 9.2.12 JScrollPane Class

```
public class JScrollPane extends JComponent
  implements ScrollPaneConstants, Accessible
```

```
Object
  Component
    Container
      JComponent
        JScrollPane
```

### Interfaces

ImageObserver, MenuContainer, Serializable, ScrollPaneConstants, Accessible

A JScrollPane object is a container that can have horizontal and/or vertical scrollbars. It can also have horizontal and vertical headers as well as active components in corners of the pane. JScrollPanes are often used to provide scrollbars for components that would not normally implement them.

## JScrollPane() Constructors

| Method | Syntax |
|---|---|
| JScrollPane() | public JScrollPane() |
| | public JScrollPane(Component child) |
| | public JScrollPane(Component child, int verticalScrollPolicy, int horizontalScrollPolicy) |

The child is the component placed inside the JScrollPane. The vertical and horizontal scroll policy inputs must be one of the following:

- ❑ ScrollPaneConstants.HORIZONTAL_SCROLLBAR_ALWAYS
- ❑ ScrollPaneConstants.HORIZONTAL_SCROLLBAR_AS_NEEDED
- ❑ ScrollPaneConstants.HORIZONTAL_SCROLLBAR_NEVER
- ❑ ScrollPaneConstants.VERTICAL_SCROLLBAR_ALWAYS
- ❑ ScrollPaneConstants.VERTICAL_SCROLLBAR_AS_NEEDED
- ❑ ScrollPaneConstants.VERTICAL_SCROLLBAR_NEVER

## Corner Component Methods

| Method | Syntax |
|---|---|
| getCorner() | public Component getCorner (String cornerLocation) |
| setCorner() | public void setCorner(String cornerLocation, Component c) |

Components can be placed in the corners of a JScrollPane object.

getCorner() returns a reference to the component, if any, that resides in the given corner location.

setCorner() method places a component in the specified corner of the invoking JScrollPane object. Valid arguments for the corner location are:

- ❑ ScrollPaneConstants.LOWER_LEFT_CORNER
- ❑ ScrollPaneConstants.LOWER_RIGHT_CORNER
- ❑ ScrollPaneConstants.UPPER_LEFT_CORNER
- ❑ ScrollPaneConstants.UPPER_RIGHT_CORNER

9

javax.swing

## Methods to Create a ScrollBar

| Method | Syntax |
|---|---|
| createHorizontalScrollBar() | public JScrollBar createHorizontalScrollBar() |
| createVerticalScrollBar() | public JScrollBar createVerticalScrollBar() |

createHorizontalScrollBar() and createVerticalScrollBar() are used by the UI delegate to create the scrollbars from the JScrollPane object. These can be overwritten if a non-default scrollbar is desired.

## Header Methods

| Method | Syntax |
|---|---|
| getColumnHeader() | public JViewport getColumnHeader() |
| getRowHeader() | public JViewport getRowHeader() |
| setColumnHeader() | public void setColumnHeader (JViewport columnHeader) |
| setColumnHeaderView() | public void setColumnHeaderView (Component c) |
| setRowHeader() | public void setRowHeader (JViewport rowHeader) |
| setRowHeaderView() | public void setRowHeaderView(Component c) |

A JScrollPane object can have row and column headers placed inside the view area. These methods are used to return a reference to or specify the column or row header. The header is set using a JViewport object that usually contains a label or icon.

## Methods to Return or Set ScrollBar Properties

| Method | Syntax |
|---|---|
| getHorizontalScrollBar() | public JScrollBar getHorizontalScrollBar() |
| getHorizontalScrollBarPolicy() | public int getHorizontalScrollBarPolicy() |
| getVerticalScrollBar() | public JScrollBar getVerticalScrollBar() |
| getVerticalScrollBarPolicy() | public int getVerticalScrollBarPolicy() |
| setHorizontalScrollBar() | public void setHorizontalScrollBar (JScrollBar jsb) |
| setHorizontalScrollBarPolicy() | public void setHorizontalScrollBarPolicy (int scrollBarPolicy) |
| setVerticalScrollBar() | public void setVerticalScrollBar (JScrollBar jsb) |
| setVerticalScrollBarPolicy() | public void setVerticalScrollBarPolicy (int scrollBarPolicy) |

getHorizontalScrollBar() and getVerticalScrollBar() return a reference to the horizontal and vertical scrollbars of the invoking JScrollPane object. The scrollbar policy determines if and how scrollbars will be displayed and will be one of the ScrollPane interface constants described in the JScrollPane() constructor section.

getHorizontalScrollBarPolicy() and getVerticalScrollBarPolicy() methods return the current horizontal and vertical scrollbar policy.

setHorizontalScrollBar() and setVerticalScrollBar() are used to change the horizontal and vertical scrollbars of the invoking JScrollPane object.

setHorizontalScrollBarPolicy() and setVerticalScrollBarPolicy() specify the horizontal and vertical scrollbar policy.

## Viewport Methods

| Method | Syntax |
|---|---|
| getViewport() | public JViewport getViewport() |
| getViewportBorder() | public Border getViewportBorder() |
| getViewportBorderBounds() | public Rectangle getViewportBorderBounds() |
| setViewport() | public void setViewport(JViewport jv) |
| setViewportBorder() | public void setViewportBorder (Border viewportBorder) |
| setViewportView() | public void setViewportView(Component c) |

A JScrollPane object uses a JViewPort object to determine which part of its contents are visible on the screen. These methods are used to return or set various view port properties.

## UI Delegate Methods

| Method | Syntax |
|---|---|
| getUI() | public ScrollPaneUI getUI() |
| setUI() | public void setUI(ScrollPaneUI ui) |

getUI() returns the ScrollPaneUI object associated with the invoking JScrollPane object.

setUI() method is used to change the ScrollPaneUI object associated the invoking JScrollPane object.

### Example: Using JScrollPane

A JScrollPane object is used to add scrollbars to a JList object. The JList object is passed to the JScrollPane constructor and the JScrollPane is added to the content pane of the JFrame.

*The WinClosing class is used to terminate the program if the window is closed. See Section 7.3.8 on page 657 for more details.*

9

javax.swing

```java
import javax.swing.*;
import java.awt.*;
import java.awt.event.*;

public class TestJSP extends JFrame {
  JList list;
  JScrollPane jsp;

  public TestJSP() {
    String[] names = {
      "Jackson", "Austin", "Allison", "Nathan", "Kelsen",
      "Marguerite", "Ellen", "Alex", "Lucas", "Mariah", "Tootsie"
    };
    list = new JList(names);

    // A JScrollPane object is wrapped around a JList object before
    // the JList is placed in a JFrame.  The JList object would not
    // otherwise be able to display scrollbars.

    JPanel p = new JPanel();
    p
      .add(new JScrollPane(list,
                               JScrollPane.VERTICAL_SCROLLBAR_ALWAYS,
                               JScrollPane
                                 .HORIZONTAL_SCROLLBAR_AS_NEEDED));

    getContentPane().add(p, BorderLayout.CENTER);

    // The WindowListener is used to terminate the program when the window
    // is closed.  Under Java 2 version 1.3, the addWindowListener() syntax
    // can be replaced by
    //
    // setDefaultCloseOperation(JFrame.EXIT_ON_CLOSE);

    addWindowListener(new WinClosing());
    setBounds(100, 100, 300, 300);
    setVisible(true);
  }

  public static void main(String args[]) {
    TestJSP tjsp = new TestJSP();
  }
}

// The WinClosing class terminates the program when the window is closed

class WinClosing extends WindowAdapter {
  public void windowClosing(WindowEvent we) {
    System.exit(0);
  }
}
```

### Output

Here is the resulting JList with the JScrollPane:

## 9.2.13 JToolBar Class

```
public class JToolBar extends JComponent
  implements SwingConstants, Accessible
```

```
Object
  Component
    Container
      JComponent
        JToolBar
```

### Interfaces

ImageObserver, MenuContainer, Serializable, SwingConstants, Accessible

A JToolBar object is a container that is used to hold other components. It is not connected to a menu, but the components a JToolBar object contains are often used to implement features also found in menus, such as changing text style to bold in a word processor.

Any Swing component can be added to a JToolBar object. The JToolBar class has an additional add() method to add Action objects to the JToolBar object.

## JToolBar() Constructors

| Method | Syntax |
|---|---|
| JToolBar() | public JToolBar() |
| | public JToolBar(int *orientation*) |
| | public JToolBar(String *name*) |
| | public JToolBar(String *name*, int *orientation*) |

JToolBar() creates a JToolBar object. The orientation of the JToolBar can be horizontal or vertical and is horizontal by default. Acceptable values for the orientation are SwingConstants.HORIZONTAL and SwingConstants.VERTICAL. A name can be given that is used as the title of the JToolBar.

## Methods to Add Components to a JToolBar

| Method | Syntax |
|---|---|
| add() | public JButton add(Action *action*) |
| addSeparator() | public void addSeparator() |
| | public void addSeparator<br>(Dimension *separatorSize*) |

add() adds an Action to the invoking JToolBar object. The method returns a JButton object that can be manipulated with JButton methods.

addSeparator() methods adds an invisible component to the JToolBar to provide some space between components. The size of the separator can be specified.

Other types of components can be added to the JToolBar using the add() methods defined in the Container class.

## Methods to Return JToolBar Properties

| Method | Syntax |
|---|---|
| getComponentAtIndex() | public Component getComponentAtIndex(int *index*) |
| getComponentIndex() | public int getComponentIndex(Component *c*) |
| getMargin | public Insets getMargin() |
| getOrientation() | public int getOrientation() |
| isBorderPainted() | public boolean isBorderPainted() |
| isFloatable() | public boolean isFloatable() |

getComponentAtIndex() returns a reference to the component at position index in the invoking JToolBar object.

getComponentIndex() returns the index of Component c.

getMargin() returns an Insets object containing the space between the JToolBar object's borders and the components it contains.

getOrientation() returns the orientation of the JToolBar, either SwingConstants.HORIZONTAL or SwingConstants.VERTICAL.

isBorderPainted() returns true if the border surrounding the JToolBar object is to be displayed.

isFloatable() returns true if the JToolBar object can be moved outside its parent container.

## Methods to Set JToolBar Properties

| Method | Syntax |
|---|---|
| setBorderPainted() | public void setBorderPainted(boolean *isPainted*) |
| setFloatable() | public void setFloatable(boolean *floatable*) |
| setMargin() | public void setMargin(Insets *insets*) |
| setOrientation() | public void setOrientation(int *orientationConstant*) |

setBorderPainted() is used to specify whether the border surrounding the JToolBar object is to be displayed.

setFloatable() specifies if the JToolBar object can be moved outside its parent container.

setMargin() changes the margin between the JToolBar object's borders and the components it contains.

setOrientation() changes the orientation of the JToolBar. Valid arguments to this method are SwingConstants.HORIZONTAL or SwingConstants.VERTICAL.

## UI Delegate Methods

| Method | Syntax |
|---|---|
| getUI() | public ToolBarUI getUI() |
| setUI() | public void setUI(ToolBarUI *ui*) |

getUI() returns the ToolBarUI object associated with the invoking JToolBar object.

setUI() is used to change the ToolBarUI object associated the invoking JToolBar object.

### Example: Using JToolBar

In this example, a JToolBar is created that contains two JComboBoxes and a JToggleButton. The JToolBar components control the font of a JLabel displayed at the bottom of the JFrame.

*The WinClosing class is used to terminate the program if the window is closed. See Section 7.3.8 on page 657 for more details.*

```
import javax.swing.*;
import java.awt.*;
import java.awt.event.*;

public class TestJToolBar extends JFrame implements ActionListener {
    JToolBar jtb;
```

9

javax.swing

```
JLabel lbl;
  JComboBox jcbF, jcbS;
  JToggleButton button;
  String name;
  int size;

  TestJToolBar() {

    // Three components are created that will be added to a JToolBar
    // and used to change the font of a JLabel

    String[] fonts = {
      "Courier", "Dialog", "Monospaced"
    };
    jcbF = new JComboBox(fonts);
    jcbF.setActionCommand("fonts");
    jcbF.addActionListener(this);

    Integer[] sizes = {
      new Integer(12), new Integer(14), new Integer(18)
    };
    jcbS = new JComboBox(sizes);
    jcbS.setActionCommand("sizes");
    jcbS.addActionListener(this);

    button = new JToggleButton("B");
    button.setFont(new Font("Serif", Font.BOLD, 14));
    button.setBorder(BorderFactory.createRaisedBevelBorder());
    button.setPreferredSize(new Dimension(30, 30));
    button.addActionListener(this);

    // A JToolBar is created and the components added to it.

    jtb = new JToolBar();
    jtb.setLayout(new FlowLayout());
    jtb.setBorder(BorderFactory.createEtchedBorder());
    jtb.add(jcbF);
    jtb.add(jcbS);
    jtb.add(button);

    // A JLabel is created.  The font of the JLabel will be controlled
    // by the JToolBar components

    lbl = new JLabel("Just some text");
    lbl.setForeground(Color.black);
    name = (String) jcbF.getSelectedItem();
    size = ((Integer) jcbS.getSelectedItem()).intValue();
    if (button.isSelected()) {
      lbl.setFont(new Font(name, Font.BOLD, size));
    } else {
      lbl.setFont(new Font(name, Font.PLAIN, size));
    }
```

```
    getContentPane().add(jtb, BorderLayout.NORTH);
    getContentPane().add(lbl, BorderLayout.SOUTH);

    // The WindowListener is used to terminate the program when the window
    // is closed.  Under Java 2 version 1.3, the addWindowListener() syntax
    // can be replaced by
    //
    // setDefaultCloseOperation(JFrame.EXIT_ON_CLOSE);

    addWindowListener(new WinClosing());
    setBounds(100, 100, 300, 150);
    setVisible(true);
  }

  // When the selection of any of the JToolBar components is changed,
  // the font of the JLabel is updated.

  public void actionPerformed(ActionEvent ae) {
    name = (String) jcbF.getSelectedItem();
    size = ((Integer) jcbS.getSelectedItem()).intValue();
    if (button.isSelected()) {
      lbl.setFont(new Font(name, Font.BOLD, size));
    } else {
      lbl.setFont(new Font(name, Font.PLAIN, size));
    }
    repaint();
  }

  public static void main(String args[]) {
    TestJToolBar tjtb = new TestJToolBar();
  }
}

// The WinClosing class terminates the program when the window is closed

class WinClosing extends WindowAdapter {
  public void windowClosing(WindowEvent we) {
    System.exit(0);
  }
}
```

**9**

javax.swing

## Output

Here is the result:

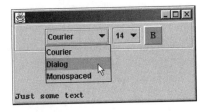

# 9.2.14 JWindow Class

```
public class JWindow extends Window
implements Accessible, RootPaneContainer
```

```
Object
  Component
    Container
      Window
        JWindow
```

### Interfaces

ImageObserver, MenuContainer, Serializable, RootPaneContainer, Accessible

A JWindow is a simple Container without any title, border, or other adornments. A common use for JWindow is to implement a splash, or start-up, screen.

Components are not added to the JWindow directly, but instead are added to one of the sub-panes of the JRootPane object associated with the JWindow object. Generally, objects are added to the content pane.

An error is thrown if an attempt is made to change the layout manager associated with the JWindow object. Changes to the layout manager should be made to the content, layered, or glass pane.

## JWindow() Constructors

| Method | Syntax |
| --- | --- |
| JWindow() | public JWindow() |
| | public JWindow(JFrame parent) |
| | public JWindow(Window parent) |

JWindow() creates a JWindow object. The JWindow object can be associated with a parent JFrame or JWindow object.

## Methods to Return the JRootPane and its Sub-Elements

| Method | Syntax |
| --- | --- |
| getContentPane() | public Container getContentPane() |
| getGlassPane() | public Component getGlassPane() |
| getLayeredPane() | public JLayeredPane getLayeredPane() |
| getRootPane() | public JRootPane getRootPane() |

These methods return a reference to the content pane, glass pane, layered pane, or JRootPane associated with the invoking JWindow object.

# Methods to Set the JRootPane Sub-Elements

| Method | Syntax |
|---|---|
| setContentPane() | public void setContentPane(Container *contentPane*) |
| setGlassPane() | public void setGlassPane(Component *glassPane*) |
| setLayeredPane() | public void setLayeredPane(JLayeredPane *layeredPane*) |

These methods are used to change the content pane, glass pane, or layered pane associated with the invoking JWindow object.

## Example: Using a JWindow as a Splash Screen

In this example, a JWindow object is used to display a splash screen at the beginning of a program. The JWindow is sized to fit the entire screen. In this example, the splash screen stays up for 10 seconds. More typically, the splash screen is displayed until a program finishes loading. The program load time could be obtained using a ProgressMonitor object and the splash screen would be put in its own thread.

*The WinClosing class is used to terminate the program if the window is closed. See Section 7.3.8 on page 657 for more details.*

```
import javax.swing.*;
import java.awt.*;
import java.awt.event.*;

public class TestJW extends JFrame {
  public TestJW() {
    addWindowListener(new WinClosing());
    setBounds(100, 100, 300, 300);
    splashScreen();
    setVisible(true);
  }

  // The splashScreen() method uses a JWindow to implement a splash screen

  public void splashScreen() {
    JWindow jw = new JWindow();

    Dimension screen = Toolkit.getDefaultToolkit().getScreenSize();
    jw.setSize(screen.width, screen.height);

    JLabel pict = new JLabel(new ImageIcon("gardening.jpg"),
                             JLabel.CENTER);

    JLabel lbl = new JLabel("Life on the Farm", JLabel.CENTER);
    lbl.setFont(new Font("Serif", Font.BOLD, 24));
    lbl.setForeground(Color.black);
```

9

javax.swing

```
        jw.getContentPane().add(pict, BorderLayout.CENTER);
        jw.getContentPane().add(lbl, BorderLayout.SOUTH);

        jw.setVisible(true);
        try {
          Thread.sleep(10000);
        } catch (InterruptedException e) {}

        jw.setVisible(false);
    }

    public static void main(String args[]) {
      TestJW tjw = new TestJW();
    }
}

// The WinClosing class terminates the program when the window is closed

class WinClosing extends WindowAdapter {
  public void windowClosing(WindowEvent we) {
    System.exit(0);
  }
}
```

The result is a picture that is displayed in the middle of a blank screen for ten seconds.

# 9.2.15 RootPaneContainer Interface

```
public interface RootPaneContainer
```

The top-level Swing containers (JFrame, JWindow, JDialog, and JInternalFrame) implement the RootPaneContainer interface which allows the top-level containers access to the content pane, glass pane, layered pane, and root pane directly.

Without the RootPaneContainer interface, access to the content pane, glass pane, and layered pane is only possible through a JRootPane object.

## Methods to Return the JRootPane Sub-Elements

| Method | Syntax |
|---|---|
| getContentPane() | public Container getContentPane() |
| getGlassPane() | public Component getGlassPane() |
| getLayeredPane() | public JLayeredPane getLayeredPane() |
| getRootPane() | public JRootPane getRootPane() |

These methods return a reference to the content pane, glass pane, layered pane, or root pane associated with the invoking top-level Swing container.

## Methods to Set the JRootPane Sub-Elements

| Method | Syntax |
|---|---|
| setContentPane() | public void setContentPane(Container contentPane) |
| setGlassPane() | public void setGlassPane(Component glassPane) |
| setLayeredPane() | public void setLayeredPane (JLayeredPane layeredPane) |

These methods are used to change the content pane, glass pane, or layered pane, associated with the invoking top-level Swing container.

# 9.2.16 WindowConstants Interface

```
public interface WindowConstants
```

The WindowConstants interface is implemented by the JFrame, JDialog, and JInternalFrame classes. It contains three constants of type int that describe what to do to the container object when its window is closed.

## Window Constants

| Syntax |
|---|
| public static final int DISPOSE_ON_CLOSE |
| public static final int DO_NOTHING_ON_CLOSE |
| public static final int HIDE_ON_CLOSE |

These constants define what happens to a container object when its window is closed.

# 9.3 Menu Classes

The javax.swing package provides Swing versions of the menu classes presented in the java.awt package. In addition, two new classes are introduced. The JSeparator class represents a horizontal or vertical line that can be used to separate menu elements. The JSeparator can also be used as a component to provide empty space between other components. A JRadioButtonMenuItem object is a radio button menu item that can be grouped together with other JRadioButtonMenuItem objects using a ButtonGroup object.

The other classes have similar functions to their AWT counterparts. JMenuItem objects are placed in JMenu objects. The JMenu objects are placed in a JMenuBar container which is placed in the display container. JMenuItem objects can be displayed as labels, icons, or both. The JMenu class is a sub-class of JMenuItem, so JMenu objects can contain other JMenu objects. The swing menu class hierarchy is shown in the following figure.

9

javax.swing

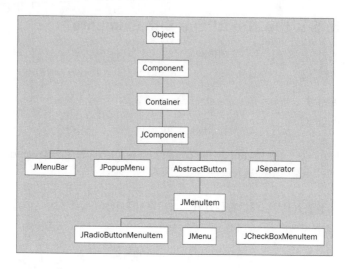

# 9.3.1 JCheckBoxMenuItem Class

```
public class JCheckBoxMenuItem extends JMenuItem
implements SwingConstants, Accessible
```

```
Object
  Component
    Container
      JComponent
        AbstractButton
          JMenuItem
            JCheckBoxMenuItem
```

### Interfaces

```
ImageObserver, MenuContainer, Serializable, SwingConstants, ItemSelectable,
MenuElement, Accessible
```

A JCheckBoxMenuItem is a menu item that can be toggled on and off. There is no
connectivity with other menu items meaning the checked state of a
JCheckBoxMenuItem has no affect on other menu items.

A JCheckBoxMenuItem fires an ItemEvent when it is toggled on or off.

## JCheckBoxMenuItem() Constructors

| Method | Syntax |
|--------|--------|
| JCheckBoxMenuItem() | public JCheckBoxMenuItem() |
| | public JCheckBoxMenuItem(Action *act*) |
| | public JCheckBoxMenuItem(Icon *icon*) |
| | public JCheckBoxMenuItem(String *text*) |

| Method | Syntax |
|--------|--------|
| | public **JCheckBoxMenuItem**(String *text*, Icon *icon*) |
| | public **JCheckBoxMenuItem**(String *text*, boolean *checked*) |
| | public **JCheckBoxMenuItem**(String *text*, Icon *icon*, boolean *checked*) |

JCheckBoxMenuItem constructor. The JCheckBoxMenuItem object may be displayed as a String, an Icon, or both. The initial state of the JCheckBoxMenuItem (checked or unchecked) can also be specified. The version that takes an Action obtains the necessary information from the Action object.

## Checked State Methods

| Method | Syntax |
|--------|--------|
| getState() | public boolean **getState**() |
| setState() | public void **setState**(boolean *isChecked*) |

getState() returns true if the invoking JCheckBoxMenuItem object is checked.

setState() is used to change the checked state of the invoking JCheckBoxMenuItem object.

### Example: Using JCheckBoxMenuItem

A JCheckBoxMenuItem object is created and placed in a menu named File. The menu is placed on the menubar of a JFrame. The JCheckBoxMenuItem object is registered with an ItemListener.

When the JCheckBoxMenuItem object is toggled on, the style of a JLabel placed in the center of the JFrame is changed to italic. When the JCheckBoxMenuItem object is toggled off, the style of a JLabel placed in the center of the JFrame is changed to plain.

*The WinClosing class is used to terminate the program if the window is closed. See Section 7.3.8 on page 657 for more details.*

```
import javax.swing.*;
import java.awt.*;
import java.awt.event.*;

public class TestJCBM extends JFrame {
    JMenuBar jmb;
    JMenu jm;
    JCheckBoxMenuItem italicMenuItem;
    JLabel label;
```

```
  public TestJCBM() {
    label = new JLabel("Italic is off");
    label.setFont(new Font("Serif", Font.PLAIN, 14));
    label.setForeground(Color.black);
    label.setHorizontalAlignment(SwingConstants.CENTER);

    // A JCheckBoxMenuItem is added to the menu bar under the "Font"
    // menu.  If the menu item is checked, the font of the Jlabel is
    // set to italic.

    italicMenuItem = new JCheckBoxMenuItem("Italic");
    italicMenuItem.addItemListener(new italicMenuHandler());

    jm = new JMenu("Font");
    jm.add(italicMenuItem);

    jmb = new JMenuBar();
    jmb.add(jm);

    getContentPane().add(jmb, BorderLayout.NORTH);
    getContentPane().add(label, BorderLayout.CENTER);

    addWindowListener(new WinClosing());
    setBounds(100, 100, 300, 150);
    setVisible(true);
  }

class italicMenuHandler implements ItemListener {
  public void itemStateChanged(ItemEvent ie) {
    if (italicMenuItem.getState()) {
      label.setFont(new Font("Serif", Font.PLAIN | Font.ITALIC,
                            14));
      label.setText("Italic is on");
    } else {
      label.setFont(new Font("Serif", Font.PLAIN, 14));
      label.setText("Italic is off");
    }
  }
}

  public static void main(String args[]) {
    TestJCBM tjcbm = new TestJCBM();
  }
}

// The WinClosing class terminates the program when the window is closed
```

```
class WinClosing extends WindowAdapter {
  public void windowClosing(WindowEvent we) {
    System.exit(0);
  }
}
```

### Output

The user interface of the program is shown below.

# 9.3.2 JMenu Class

```
public class JMenu extends JMenuItem implements MenuElement, Accessible
```

```
Object
  Component
    Container
      JComponent
        AbstractButton
          JMenuItem
            JMenu
```

### Interfaces

ImageObserver, MenuContainer, Serializable, SwingConstants, ItemSelectable, MenuElement, Accessible

A JMenu object represents a pull-down menu that can be placed in a container. The JMenu object can contain JMenuItem, String, or Action objects. A JMenu object is also a JMenuItem object which means a JMenu object can contain other JMenu objects.

A JMenu object generates MenuEvent objects when it is selected, deselected, or removed from the screen.

## JMenu() Constructors

| Method | Syntax |
|---|---|
| JMenu() | public JMenu() |
| | public JMenu(Action act) |
| | public JMenu(String name) |
| | public JMenu(String name, boolean tearoff) |

JMenu() creates a JMenu object. The name is what the JMenu object item will display when it is placed on a menu bar or inside another menu. The tearoff property indicates whether the JMenu object can be moved about the screen and is not currently implemented. The version that takes an Action obtains the necessary information from the Action object.

## add() Method

| Method | Syntax |
|--------|--------|
| add() | public JMenuItem add(JMenuItem menuItem) |
| | public JMenuItem add(String s) |
| | public JMenuItem add(Action a) |
| | public Component add(Component c) |
| | public Component add(Component c, int index) |

add() adds an element to the invoking JMenu object. If a String argument is passed, a JMenuItem with the String as its label is created. When an element is added to a JMenu object, a reference to a JMenuItem is returned, and can be used to modify the element.

## insert() Method

| Method | Syntax |
|--------|--------|
| insert() | public void insert(String s, int index) |
| | public JMenuItem insert(JMenuItem jmi, int index) |
| | public JMenuItem insert(Action a, int index) |

insert() inserts an element to the invoking JMenu object at position index. If a String argument is passed, a JMenuItem with the String as its label is created. When an element is added to a JMenu object, a reference to a JMenuItem is returned that can be used to modify the element.

## MenuListener Methods

| Method | Syntax |
|--------|--------|
| addMenuListener() | public void addMenuListener(MenuListener ml) |
| removeMenuListener() | public void removeMenuListener(MenuListener ml) |

MenuEvent objects are generated when a JMenu object is selected, deselected, or removed from the screen.

addMenuListener() method associates a MenuListener object to the invoking JMenu object to listen for MenuEvents.

removeMenuListener() disconnects the MenuListener object from the invoking JMenu object.

## Popup Menu Methods

| Method | Syntax |
|---|---|
| getPopupMenu() | public JPopupMenu getPopupMenu() |
| isPopupMenuVisible() | public boolean isPopupMenuVisible() |
| setPopupMenuVisible() | public void setPopupMenuVisible(boolean *visible*) |

A JPopupMenu object is used to display the JMenuItem objects contained by a JMenu. The JPopupMenu object becomes visible when the mouse is pressed while over the JMenu. It can also be made visible using the setPopupMenuVisible() method.

getPopupMenu() returns a reference to the JPopupMenu object that is used to display the JMenu element list.

isPopupMenuVisible() returns true if the JMenu element list is visible.

setPopupMenuVisible() is used to change the visible state of the JMenu element list.

## Methods to Remove Elements from a JMenu

| Method | Syntax |
|---|---|
| remove() | public void remove(JMenuItem *jmi*) |
|  | public void remove(int *index*) |
| removeAll() | public void removeAll() |

remove() removes an element from the invoking JMenu object based on either a reference to a JMenuItem object or an index.

removeAll() removes all of the elements from the invoking JMenu object.

## Methods that Return JMenu Elements

| Method | Syntax |
|---|---|
| getItem() | public JMenuItem getItem(int *index*) |
| getMenuComponent() | public Component getMenuComponent(int *index*) |
| getMenuComponents() | public Component[] getMenuComponents() |

These methods return one or more elements from the invoking JMenu object. The elements can be returned as either a JMenuItem, a Component, or an array of Components.

9

javax.swing

## Methods to Return JMenu Properties

| Method | Syntax |
|---|---|
| getDelay | public int getDelay() |
| getItemCount() | public int getItemCount() |
| getMenuComponentCount() | public int getMenuComponentCount() |
| isMenuComponent() | public boolean isMenuComponent(Component c) |
| isTearOff() | public boolean isTearOff() |
| isTopLevelMenu() | public boolean isTopLevelMenu() |

getDelay() returns the time in milliseconds an underlying menu waits to appear.

getItemCount() returns the number of JMenuItem objects contained by the invoking JMenu object.

getMenuComponentCount() returns the number of items (JMenuItems, separators, and other components) contained by the invoking JMenu object.

isMenuComponent() returns true if the Component c exists anywhere within the invoking JMenu object.

isTearOff() method returns true if the invoking JMenu object has the tear-off property enabled.

isTopLevelMenu() returns false if the invoking JMenu object is a sub-menu.

## Methods to Set JMenu Properties

| Method | Syntax |
|---|---|
| setDelay() | public void setDelay(int *delay*)<br>    throws IllegalArgumentException |
| setMenuLocation() | public void setMenuLocation(int *x*, int *y*) |

setDelay() changes the time in milliseconds an underlying menu waits to appear.

setMenuLocation() is used to position the invoking JMenu object on the screen.

## Separator Methods

| Method | Syntax |
|---|---|
| addSeparator() | public void addSeparator() |
| insertSeparator() | public void insertSeparator(int *index*) |

addSeparator() and insertSeparator() add or insert a separator to the invoking JMenu object. The separator is typically a horizontal line.

## Example: Using JMenu

In this example, two JMenuItem objects are placed on a JMenu object. The JMenu object is then placed on a JFrame. A separator is added to the JMenu between the two JMenuItem objects. The JMenuItem objects are given an accelerator key and each is given its own ActionListener. When the open menu item is selected, a larger version of the icon appears. When the quit menu item is selected, the program terminates.

*The WinClosing class is used to terminate the program if the window is closed. See Section 7.3.8 on page 657 for more details.*

```java
import javax.swing.*;
import java.awt.*;
import java.awt.event.*;

public class TestJM extends JFrame {
    JMenuBar jmb;
    JMenu jm;
    JMenuItem openMenuItem, quitMenuItem;
    JLabel lbl;
    JPanel p;

    public TestJM() {
        lbl = new JLabel(new ImageIcon("Big_Zack.jpg"));
        p = new JPanel();
        p.add(lbl);
        p.setVisible(false);

        // Two JMenuItem objects are created. The first is displayed using
        // both an image and a label. Both JMenuItem objects are given
        // accelerators.

        openMenuItem = new JMenuItem("open",
                            new ImageIcon("Zachary.jpg"));
        openMenuItem.setHorizontalTextPosition(SwingConstants.LEFT);
        openMenuItem.setAccelerator(KeyStroke.getKeyStroke('O',
                java.awt.Event.CTRL_MASK, false));
        openMenuItem.addActionListener(new openMenuHandler());

        quitMenuItem = new JMenuItem("quit");
        quitMenuItem.setAccelerator(KeyStroke.getKeyStroke('Q',
                java.awt.Event.CTRL_MASK, false));
        quitMenuItem.addActionListener(new quitMenuHandler());

        // The JMenuItem objects are added to a JMenu object. A separator
        // is placed between them
```

9

javax.swing

```
      jm = new JMenu("File");
      jm.add(openMenuItem);
      jm.addSeparator();
      jm.add(quitMenuItem);

      // The JMenu object is placed on a JMenuBar

      jmb = new JMenuBar();
      jmb.add(jm);

      getContentPane().add(jmb, BorderLayout.NORTH);
      getContentPane().add(p, BorderLayout.CENTER);

      addWindowListener(new WinClosing());
      setBounds(100, 100, 400, 200);
      setVisible(true);
    }

  class openMenuHandler implements ActionListener {
    public void actionPerformed(ActionEvent ae) {
      p.setVisible(true);
      p.revalidate();
    }
  }

  class quitMenuHandler implements ActionListener {
    public void actionPerformed(ActionEvent ae) {
      System.exit(0);
    }
  }

  public static void main(String args[]) {
    TestJM tjm = new TestJM();
  }
}

// The WinClosing class terminates the program when the window is closed

class WinClosing extends WindowAdapter {
  public void windowClosing(WindowEvent we) {
    System.exit(0);
  }
}
```

**Output**

Here is the result:

# 9.3.3 JMenuBar Class

```
public class JMenuBar extends JComponent implements MenuElement, Accessible
```

```
Object
    Component
        Container
            JComponent
                JMenuBar
```

### Interfaces

```
ImageObserver, MenuContainer, Serializable, MenuElement, Accessible
```

A JMenuBar object creates a horizontal menu bar. It may be placed anywhere on a JFrame, JDialog, or JApplet container. A JMenuBar object contains zero or more JMenu objects.

A JMenuBar object can be added to a container in one of two ways. The first is by the Container object invoking the setJMenuBar() method passing the JMenuBar object as the argument. The second is by simply adding it to the Frame like any other component. The first way always puts the JMenuBar at the top of the Container. The second way gives the flexibility to place the JMenuBar anywhere in the container.

## JMenuBar() Constructor

| Method | Syntax |
|---|---|
| JMenuBar() | public JMenuBar() |

creates a JMenuBar object.

9

javax.swing

## add() Method

| Method | Syntax |
|--------|--------|
| add() | public JMenu add(JMenu *menu*) |

add() adds a JMenu object to the invoking JMenuBar object. This method returns a JMenu reference allowing a menu item to be added to the menu the same time the menu is added to the invoking JMenuBar object:

```
menuBar.add(menu).add(menuItem);
```

## Methods to Return JMenuBar Components

| Method | Syntax |
|--------|--------|
| getComponent | public Component getComponent() |
| getComponentAtIndex() | public Component getComponentAtIndex (int *index*) |
| getHelpMenu() | public JMenu getHelpMenu() |
| getMenu(int index) | public JMenu getMenu(int *index*) |

getComponent() returns a reference to the invoking JMenuBar object.

getComponentAtIndex() returns a reference to the JMenu object at position index in the JMenuBar. This method is deprecated.

getHelpMenu() returns a reference to the JMenu object that has been designated as the help menu, or null if there has been no such designation. The help menu is placed as the right-most element on the JMenuBar.

getMenu() returns a reference to the JMenu object at position index in the JMenuBar.

## Methods to Return JMenuBar Properties

| Method | Syntax |
|--------|--------|
| getComponentIndex | public int getComponentIndex(Component *c*) |
| getMargin() | public Insets getMargin() |
| getMenuCount() | public int getMenuCount() |
| getSubElements() | public MenuElement[] getSubElements() |
| isBorderPainted() | public boolean isBorderPainted() |
| isSelected() | public boolean isSelected() |

getComponentIndex() returns the index of the JMenu object passed as an argument.

getMargin() returns an Insets object representing the space between the JMenuBar object's border and its contents.

getMenuCount() returns the number of JMenu objects contained by the invoking JMenuBar object.

getSubElements() returns a MenuElement array containing references to the JMenu objects contained by the invoking JMenuBar object.

isBorderPainted() returns true if the border around the invoking JMenuBar object is to be drawn.

isSelected() returns true if the invoking JMenuBar object is selected.

## Methods to Set JMenuBar Properties

| Method | Syntax |
|---|---|
| setBorderPainted() | public void setBorderPainted(boolean *painted*) |
| setHelpMenu() | public void setHelpMenu(Jmenu *helpMenu*) |
| setMargin() | public void setMargin(Insets *insets*) |
| setSelected() | public void setSelected(Component *selectedMenu*) |

setBorderPainted() specifies if the border around the invoking JMenuBar object is to be drawn.

setHelpMenu() specifies which menu should be the help menu.

setMargin() changes the spacing between the JMenuBar object's border and its contents.

setSelected() selects the JMenu object selectedMenu.

## UI Delegate Methods

| Method | Syntax |
|---|---|
| getUI() | public MenuBarUI getUI() |
| setUI() | public void setUI(MenuBarUI *ui*) |

getUI() returns the MenuBarUI object associated with the invoking JMenuBar object.

setUI() is used to change the MenuBarUI object associated the invoking JMenuBar object.

### Example: Using JMenuBar

See the *Using JMenu* example in the JMenu class Section 9.3.2 on page 885.

# 9.3.4 JMenuItem Class

```
public class JMenuItem extends AbstractButton implements MenuElement, Accessible
```

```
Object
  Component
    Container
      JComponent
        AbstractButton
          JMenuItem
```

### Interfaces

ImageObserver, MenuContainer, Serializable, SwingConstants, ItemSelectable, MenuElement, Accessible

A JMenuItem object is a wrapper class for the Strings and images that serve as menu elements. A JMenuItem is a type of button that is considered selected if the cursor is released while over the JMenuItem object. The JMenuItem class is also the parent class for the JCheckBoxMenuItem, JMenu, and JRadioButtonMenuItem, and provides methods common to those classes.

A JMenuItem object fires an ActionEvent when it is selected.

## JMenuItem() Constructors

| Method | Syntax |
|---|---|
| JMenuItem() | public JMenuItem() |
| | public JMenuItem(Icon *icon*) |
| | public JMenuItem(String *s*) |
| | public JMenuItem(String *s*, Icon *icon*) |
| | public JMenuItem(String *s*, int *mnemonic*) |
| | public JMenuItem(Action *action*) |

JMenuItem() creates a JMenuItem object. The JMenuItem can be initialized with a String or an icon that will be displayed inside the menu. The mnemonic is a keyboard sequence that will select the JMenuItem object. If an Action object is provided, the JMenuItem will take its properties from the Action object.

## Accelerator Methods

| Method | Syntax |
|---|---|
| getAccelerator() | public KeyStroke getAccelerator() |
| setAccelerator() | public void setAccelerator(KeyStroke *k*) |

An accelerator is a keyboard sequence that will select the invoking JMenuItem object. The KeyStroke class does not have a constructor but a KeyStroke object can be instantiated using the KeyStroke class method.

```
public static getKeyStroke(int keyCode, int modifiers,
         boolean fireEventOnKeyRelease)
```

getAccelerator() returns the accelerator KeyStroke associated with the invoking JMenuItem object.

setAccelerator() is used to set or change the accelerator KeyStroke associated with the invoking JMenuItem object.

## Armed Methods

| Method | Syntax |
|---|---|
| isArmed() | public boolean isArmed() |
| setArmed() | public void setArmed(boolean *armed*) |

A JMenuItem is considered "armed" if it will fire an event if the mouse is released while over the JMenuItem.

isArmed () returns true if the invoking JMenuItem is armed. An armed JMenuItem can be selected programmatically.

setArmed() is used to change the armed state of the invoking JMenuItem.

## Methods to Return JMenuItem Components

| Method | Syntax |
|---|---|
| getComponent() | public Component getComponent() |
| getSubElements() | public MenuElement[] getSubElements() |

getComponent() returns a reference to the Component used to paint the invoking JMenuItem object.

getSubElements() returns a MenuElement array containing any sub-menus contained by the invoking JMenuItem object.

## UI Delegate Methods

| Method | Syntax |
|---|---|
| getUI() | public ButtonUI getUI() |
| setUI() | public void setUI(MenuItemUI *ui*) |

getUI() returns the MenuItemUI object associated with the invoking JMenuItem object.

setUI() is used to change the MenuItemUI object associated the invoking JMenuItem object.

9

javax.swing

**891**

> ## Example: Using JMenuItem
>
> See the *Using JMenu* example in the JMenu class, Section 9.3.2 on page 885.

# 9.3.5 JPopupMenu Class

```
public class JPopupMenu extends JComponent implements MenuElement, Accessible
```

```
Object
  Component
    Container
      JComponent
        JPopupMenu
```

### Interfaces

```
ImageObserver, MenuContainer, Serializable, MenuElement, Accessible
```

A JPopupMenu object is a menu that is associated with another GUI component. JPopupMenus are displayed using the show() method in conjunction with a platform-dependent popup trigger, usually a mouse event. To determine which of the mouse events is the trigger, the mouse event can invoke the isPopupTrigger() method.

## JPopupMenu() Constructors

| Method | Syntax |
|--------|--------|
| JPopupMenu() | public JPopupMenu() |
| | public JPopupMenu(String *title*) |

JPopupMenu() creates a JPopupMenu object. A title can be provided.

## Methods that Add or Insert Menu Elements

| Method | Syntax |
|--------|--------|
| add() | public JMenuItem add(JMenuItem *menuItem*) |
| | public JMenuItem add(String *str*) |
| | public JMenuItem add(Action *a*) |
| insert() | public void insert(Component *c*, int *index*) |
| | public void insert(Action *a*, int *index*) |
| addSeparator() | public void addSeparator() |

add() is used to add an element to the bottom of the invoking JPopupMenu object, and returns a reference to the JMenuItem that was added; this can then be used to manipulate the JMenuItem.

insert() adds an element to the invoking JPopupMenu object at position index.

addSeparator() adds a separator to the invoking JPopupMenu object. The separator is typically a horizontal line.

## pack() Method

| Method | Syntax |
|--------|--------|
| pack() | public void pack() |

pack() reduces the size of the invoking JPopupMenu object to just fit its components.

## Methods to Return JPopupMenu Components

| Method | Syntax |
|--------|--------|
| getComponent() | public Component getComponent() |
| getComponentAtIndex() | public Component getComponentAtIndex(int *index*) |
| getInvoker() | public Component getInvoker() |

getComponent() returns a reference to the invoking JPopupMenu object.

getComponentAtIndex() returns a reference to the JMenuItem at position index in the invoking JPopupMenu object. This method is deprecated.

getInvoker() returns a reference to the parent Component of the invoking JPopupMenu object.

## Methods to Return JPopupMenu Properties

| Method | Syntax |
|--------|--------|
| getComponentIndex() | public int getComponentIndex(Component *c*) |
| getLabel() | public String getLabel() |
| getMargin() | public Insets getMargin() |
| getSubElements() | public MenuElement[] getSubElements() |
| isBorderPainted() | public boolean isBorderPainted() |
| isLightWeightPopupEnabled() | public boolean isLightWeightPopupEnabled() |

getComponentIndex() returns the index of the Component c.

getLabel() returns the label associated with the invoking JPopupMenu object.

getMargin() returns an Insets object representing the space between the JPopupMenu object's border and its contents.

getSubElements() returns a MenuElement array containing references to the JMenu objects contained by the invoking JPopupMenu object.

9

javax.swing

isBorderPainted() returns true if the border around the invoking JPopupMenu object is to be drawn.

isLightWeightPopupEnabled() returns true if lightweight components can be used to represent the popup menu.

## Methods to Set JPopupMenu Properties

| Method | Syntax |
|---|---|
| setBorderPainted() | public void setBorderPainted (boolean *painted*) |
| setInvoker() | public void setInvoker(Component *c*) |
| setLabel() | public void setLabel(String *label*) |
| setLightWeightPopupEnabled() | public void setLightWeightPopupEnabled (boolean *enabled*) |
| setPopupSize() | public void setPopupSize(int *width*, int *height*) |
| setPopupSize() | public void setPopupSize(Dimension *size*) |
| setSelected() | public void setSelected (Component *selectedComponent*) |

setBorderPainted() specifies if the border around the invoking JPopupMenu object is to be drawn.

setInvoker() is used to change or set the parent component of the invoking JPopupMenu object.

setLabel() method changes the label associated with the invoking JPopupMenu object.

setLightWeightPopupEnabled() specifies if lightweight components can be used to represent the popup menu. This method would be overridden to return false if an application wanted to mix heavyweight and lightweight components (this is not recommended).

setPopupSize() is used to change the size of the invoking JPopupMenu object.

setSelected() method selects the specified menu item.

## show() Method

| Method | Syntax |
|---|---|
| show() | public void show(Component *invoker*, int *x*, int *y*) |

show() displays the invoking JPopupMenu object. The integers x and y determine the location relative to the parent component where the JPopupMenu object will appear.

## UI Delegate Methods

| Method | Syntax |
|--------|--------|
| getUI() | `public PopupMenuUI getUI()` |
| setUI() | `public void setUI(PopupMenuUI ui)` |

`getUI()` returns the `PopupMenuUI` object associated with the invoking `JPopupMenu` object.

`setUI()` is used to change the `PopupMenuUI` object associated the invoking `JPopupMenu` object.

### Example: Using JPopupMenu

In this example, a `JPopupMenu` object is associated with a `JButton`. When the mouse pointer is over the `JButton` and the appropriate mouse event is generated, the `JPopupMenu` object appears and offers two `JMenuItem` objects to choose from.

The first, when selected, causes a panel containing a larger image to appear in the center region of the `JFrame`. This `JMenuItem` object has an accelerator key sequence attached to it. The second `JMenuItem` causes the program to terminate when it is selected. The popup trigger is somewhat system dependent but is generally either a `mouseClicked`, `mousePressed`, or `mouseReleased` mouse event. The `testEvent()` method tests these three events to obtain the popup trigger.

*The `WinClosing` class is used to terminate the program if the window is closed. See Section 7.3.8 on page 657 for more details.*

```
import javax.swing.*;
import java.awt.*;
import java.awt.event.*;

public class TestJPM extends JFrame {
    JButton clickButton;
    JPopupMenu jpm;
    JMenuItem openMenuItem, quitMenuItem;
    JPanel p;
    JLabel lbl;

    public TestJPM() {
        lbl = new JLabel(new ImageIcon("Big_Zack.jpg"));

        p = new JPanel();
        p.add(lbl);
        p.setVisible(false);
```

```
      // Two JMenuItem objects are created.  The first is displayed using
      // both an image and a label.  Both JMenuItem objects are given
      // accelerators.

      openMenuItem = new JMenuItem(new ImageIcon("Zachary.jpg"));
      openMenuItem.setHorizontalTextPosition(SwingConstants.LEFT);
      openMenuItem.setAccelerator(KeyStroke.getKeyStroke('O',
            java.awt.Event.CTRL_MASK, false));
      openMenuItem.addActionListener(new openMenuHandler());

      quitMenuItem = new JMenuItem("quit");
      quitMenuItem.addActionListener(new quitMenuHandler());

      // The JMenuItem objects are added to a JPopupMenu

      jpm = new JPopupMenu("File");
      jpm.add(openMenuItem);
      jpm.addSeparator();
      jpm.add(quitMenuItem);

      clickButton = new JButton("click");
      clickButton.addMouseListener(new MouseHandler());
      JPanel northPanel = new JPanel();
      northPanel.add(clickButton);

      getContentPane().add(p, BorderLayout.CENTER);
      getContentPane().add(northPanel, BorderLayout.NORTH);

      addWindowListener(new WinClosing());
      setBounds(100, 100, 300, 300);
      setVisible(true);
   }

   class openMenuHandler implements ActionListener {
     public void actionPerformed(ActionEvent ae) {
       p.setVisible(true);
       p.revalidate();
     }
   }

   class quitMenuHandler implements ActionListener {
     public void actionPerformed(ActionEvent ae) {
       System.exit(0);
     }
   }

   // When the mouse is over the "click" button and the appropriate
   // mouse event is generated, the JPopupMenu is shown.
```

```
class MouseHandler extends MouseAdapter {
    public void mouseClicked(MouseEvent me) {
        testEvent(me);
    }
    public void mousePressed(MouseEvent me) {
        testEvent(me);
    }
    public void mouseReleased(MouseEvent me) {
        testEvent(me);
    }

    private void testEvent(MouseEvent me) {
        if (me.isPopupTrigger()) {
            jpm.show(clickButton, me.getX(), me.getY());
        }
    }
}

    public static void main(String args[]) {
        TestJPM tjpm = new TestJPM();
    }
}

// The WinClosing class terminates the program when the window is closed

class WinClosing extends WindowAdapter {
    public void windowClosing(WindowEvent we) {
        System.exit(0);
    }
}
```

### Output

The user interface of the program is shown below.

# 9.3.6 JRadioButtonMenuItem Class

```
public class JRadioButtonMenuItem extends JMenuItem implements Accessible
```

```
Object
  Component
    Container
      JComponent
        AbstractButton
          JMenuItem
            JRadioButtonMenuItem
```

### Interfaces

ImageObserver, MenuContainer, Serializable, SwingConstants, ItemSelectable, MenuElement, Accessible

A JRadioButtonMenuItem object is a menu item with a radio button to the left of the text or icon. The radio button can be toggled on or off. A number of JRadioButtonMenuItem objects can be grouped together using a ButtonGroup object to ensure that only one of the group can be selected.

A JRadioButtonMenuItem object fires an ItemEvent when selected or de-selected.

## JRadioButtonMenuItem() Constructors

| Method | Syntax |
|---|---|
| JRadioButtonMenuItem() | public JRadioButtonMenuItem() |
| | public JRadioButtonMenuItem(Action *icon*) |
| | public JRadioButtonMenuItem(Icon *icon*) |
| | public JRadioButtonMenuItem(String *text*) |
| | public JRadioButtonMenuItem(String *text*, Icon *icon*) |
| | public JRadioButtonMenuItem(Icon *icon*, boolean *checked*) |
| | public JRadioButtonMenuItem(String *text*, boolean *checked*) |
| | public JRadioButtonMenuItem(String *text*, Icon *icon*, boolean *checked*) |

JRadioButtonMenuItem() object constructor. The JRadioButtonMenuItem object may be displayed as a String, an Icon, or both. The checked state of the JRadioButtonMenuItem can also be specified. The version that takes an Action obtains the necessary information from the Action object.

### Example: Using JRadioButtonMenuItem

In this example, two JRadioButtonMenuItem objects are created and placed on a JMenu. The JRadioButtonMenuItem objects are used to change the style of a JLabel object, and are made mutually exclusive by adding them to a ButtonGroup object. Because the JRadioButtonMenuItem objects use the same event handler, the call to the addItemListener() method must be performed after the JRadioButtonMenuItem objects are instantiated. If the plainMenuItem calls the addItemListener() method before the boldMenuItem object is created, a NullPointerException is thrown when the code is run.

*The WinClosing class is used to terminate the program if the window is closed. See Section 7.3.8 on page 657 for more details.*

```
import javax.swing.*;
import java.awt.*;
import java.awt.event.*;

public class TestJRBM extends JFrame {
    JMenuBar jmb;
    JMenu styleMenu;
    JRadioButtonMenuItem plainMenuItem, boldMenuItem;
    ButtonGroup styleGroup;
    JLabel label;

    public TestJRBM() {
        label = new JLabel("Style is plain");
        label.setFont(new Font("Serif", Font.PLAIN, 14));
        label.setForeground(Color.black);
        label.setHorizontalAlignment(SwingConstants.CENTER);

        // Two JRadioButtonMenuItem objects are created. They are made mutually
        // exclusive using a ButtonGroup and are registered with an
        // ItemListener

        plainMenuItem = new JRadioButtonMenuItem("Plain");
        plainMenuItem.setSelected(true);

        boldMenuItem = new JRadioButtonMenuItem("Bold");

        plainMenuItem.addItemListener(new RBMenuHandler());
        boldMenuItem.addItemListener(new RBMenuHandler());

        styleGroup = new ButtonGroup();
        styleGroup.add(plainMenuItem);
        styleGroup.add(boldMenuItem);
```

```
        styleMenu = new JMenu("Style");
        styleMenu.add(plainMenuItem);
        styleMenu.add(boldMenuItem);

        jmb = new JMenuBar();
        jmb.add(styleMenu);

        JPanel p = new JPanel();
        p.add(label);

        JPanel contentPane = (JPanel) getContentPane();
        contentPane.add(jmb, BorderLayout.NORTH);
        contentPane.add(label, BorderLayout.CENTER);

        addWindowListener(new WinClosing());
        setBounds(100, 100, 300, 200);
        setVisible(true);
    }

    // When one of the JRadioButtonMenuItem objects is selected, the font
    // style of the JLabel is changed to reflect the selection.

    class RBMenuHandler implements ItemListener {
        public void itemStateChanged(ItemEvent ie) {
            if (plainMenuItem.isSelected()) {
                label.setFont(new Font("Serif", Font.PLAIN, 14));
                label.setText("Label is plain");
            }
            if (boldMenuItem.isSelected()) {
                label.setFont(new Font("Serif", Font.BOLD, 14));
                label.setText("Label is bold");
            }
        }
    }

    public static void main(String args[]) {
        TestJRBM tjrbm = new TestJRBM();
    }
}

// The WinClosing class terminates the program when the window is closed

class WinClosing extends WindowAdapter {
    public void windowClosing(WindowEvent we) {
        System.exit(0);
    }
}
```

*Output*

Here is the result:

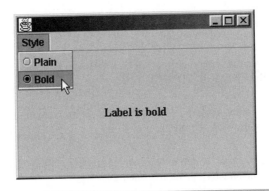

# 9.3.7 JSeparator Class

```
public class JSeparator extends JComponent implements SwingConstants, Accessible
```

```
Object
  Component
    Container
      JComponent
        JSeparator
```

### Interfaces

ImageObserver, MenuContainer, Serializable, SwingConstants, Accessible

A JSeparator object is a horizontal or vertical line. JSeparator objects are used in menus, but they also exist as standalone components and can be used to separate other GUI components.

## JSeparator() Constructors

| Method | Syntax |
|--------|--------|
| JSeparator() | public JSeparator()<br>public JSeparator(int *orientation*) |

JSeparator() object constructor. The orientation argument must be either SwingConstants.VERTICAL or SwingConstants.HORIZONTAL. The default is horizontal.

## Orientation Methods

| Method | Syntax |
|--------|--------|
| getOrientation() | public int getOrientation() |
| setOrientation() | public void setOrientation(int *orientation*) |

**901**

getOrientation() returns the orientation of the invoking JSeparator object. The return value will be either SwingConstants.VERTICAL or SwingConstants.HORIZONTAL.

setOrientation() is used to change the orientation of the invoking JSeparator object.

## Example: Using JSeparator

This example shows what a JSeparator object looks like when it is placed in a JMenu between two JMenuItem objects.

*The WinClosing class is used to terminate the program if the window is closed. See Section 7.3.8 on page 657 for more details.*

```java
import javax.swing.*;
import java.awt.*;
import java.awt.event.*;

public class TestJSeparator extends JFrame {
  JMenuBar jmb;
  JMenu jm;

  public TestJSeparator() {
    jm = new JMenu("File");
    jm.add(new JMenuItem("open"));
    jm.add(new JMenuItem("save"));
    jm.add(new JSeparator());
    jm.add(new JMenuItem("quit"));

    jmb = new JMenuBar();
    jmb.add(jm);

    getContentPane().add(jmb, BorderLayout.NORTH);

    addWindowListener(new WinClosing());
    setBounds(100, 100, 200, 200);
    setVisible(true);
  }

  public static void main(String args[]) {
    TestJSeparator tjs = new TestJSeparator();
  }
}

// The WinClosing class terminates the program when the window is closed
```

```
class WinClosing extends WindowAdapter {
  public void windowClosing(WindowEvent we) {
    System.exit(0);
  }
}
```

**Output**

Here is the result:

# 9.4 Component Managers and Models

The javax.swing package provides interfaces that define the data models, editors, and renderers used with the Swing components. Classes that provide default implementations of these interfaces are also provided. Some of these classes and interfaces are discussed in this section.

## 9.4.1 Cell Editor Interface

```
public interface CellEditor
```

The CellEditor interface defines the method that any class intended to serve as an editor should implement.

### CellEditorListener Methods

| Method | Syntax |
|---|---|
| addCellEditorListener() | public void addCellEditorListener (CellEditorListener cel) |
| removeCellEditorListener() | public void removeCellEditorListener (CellEditorListener cel) |

addCellEditorListener() registers the invoking CellEditor object with a CellEditorListener object. The CellEditorListener is notified if the invoking CellEditor object generates a ChangeEvent object due to the editor starting, stopping, or cancelling an editing session.

removeCellEditorListener() disconnects the CellEditorListener object from the invoking CellEditor object.

## Other CellEditor Methods

| Method | Syntax |
|---|---|
| cancelCellEditing() | public void cancelCellEditing() |
| getCellEditorValue() | public Object getCellEditorValue() |
| isCellEditable() | public boolean isCellEditable(EventObject *evt*) |
| stopCellEditing() | public boolean stopCellEditing() |

cancelCellEditing() ends the editing session without saving any changes.

getCellEditorValue() returns the value contained by the editor.

isCellEditable() returns true if editing can be started if the specified event occurs.

stopCellEditing() ends the editing session saving any changes and returns true if the editing session was successfully stopped.

# 9.4.2 DefaultButtonModel Class

```
public class DefaultButtonModel implements ButtonModel, Serializable
```

```
Object
  DefaultButtonModel
```

### Interfaces

```
ButtonModel, Serializable
```

The DefaultButtonModel is the default implementation of a button component's data model. It provides event handling methods and methods to access properties of the button.

## DefaultButtonModel() Constructor

| Method | Syntax |
|---|---|
| DefaultButtonModel() | public DefaultButtonModel() |

DefaultButtonModel() creates a DefaultButtonModel object.

## ActionCommand Methods

| Method | Syntax |
|---|---|
| getActionCommand() | public String getActionCommand() |
| setActionCommand() | public void setActionCommand<br>(String *actionCommand*) |

getActionCommand() returns the action command for the button associated with the invoking DefaultButtonModel object.

setActionCommand() is used to change the action for the button associated with the invoking DefaultButtonModel object.

## ActionListener Methods

| Method | Syntax |
| --- | --- |
| addActionListener() | public void addActionListener(ActionListener al) |
| removeActionListener() | public void removeActionListener<br>(ActionListener al) |

addActionListener() adds an ActionListener to the button associated with the invoking DefaultButtonModel object.

removeActionListener() disconnects the ActionListener object from the button associated with the invoking DefaultButtonModel object.

## ChangeListener Methods

| Method | Syntax |
| --- | --- |
| addChangeListener() | public void addChangeListener(ChangeListener cl) |
| removeChangeListener() | public void removeChangeListener<br>(ChangeListener cl) |

addChangeListener() adds a ChangeListener to the button associated with the invoking DefaultButtonModel object.

removeChangeListener() disconnects the ChangeListener object from the button associated with the invoking DefaultButtonModel object.

## Group Methods

| Method | Syntax |
| --- | --- |
| getGroup() | public ButtonGroup getGroup() |
| setGroup() | public void setGroup(ButtonGroup grp) |

getGroup() returns the ButtonGroup the button belongs to, or null if there is no ButtonGroup.

setGroup() changes the ButtonGroup to which the button belongs.

9

javax.swing

## ItemListener Methods

| Method | Syntax |
| --- | --- |
| addItemListener() | public void addItemListener(ItemListener *il*) |
| removeItemListener() | public void removeItemListener<br>  (ItemListener *il*) |

addItemListener() adds an ItemListener to the button associated with the invoking DefaultButtonModel object.

removeItemListener() disconnects the ItemListener object from the button associated with the invoking DefaultButtonModel object.

## Mnemonic Methods

| Method | Syntax |
| --- | --- |
| getMnemonic() | public int getMnemonic() |
| setMnemonic() | public void setMnemonic(int *keyCode*) |

getMnemonic() returns the keyboard mnemonic for the button associated with the invoking DefaultButtonModel object.

setMnemonic() is used to change the keyboard mnemonic for the button associated with the invoking DefaultButtonModel object.

## Methods to Access the State of a Button

| Method | Syntax |
| --- | --- |
| isArmed() | public boolean isArmed() |
| isEnabled() | public boolean isEnabled() |
| isPressed() | public boolean isPressed() |
| isRollover() | public boolean isRollover() |
| isSelected() | public boolean isSelected() |
| setArmed() | public void setArmed(boolean *armed*) |
| setEnabled() | public void setEnabled(boolean *enabled*) |
| setPressed() | public void setPressed(boolean *pressed*) |
| setRollover() | public void setRollover(boolean *rollover*) |
| setSelected() | public void setSelected(boolean *selected*) |

isArmed() returns true if releasing the button will cause an action to be performed.

isEnabled() returns true if the button can be interacted with.

isPressed() returns true if the button is currently being pressed.

isRollover() returns true if the mouse is currently over the button.

isSelected() returns true if the button is currently selected.

The set() methods are used to specfiy the armed, enabled, pressed, rollover, or selected state properties.

# 9.4.3 DefaultDesktopManager Class

```
public class DefaultDesktopManager extends Object
   implements DesktopManager, Serializable
```

```
Object
   DefaultDesktopManager
```

### Interfaces
```
DesktopManager
```

A `DefaultDesktopManager` object is the default implementation of the
`DesktopManager` interface. A user-defined `DeskTopManager` class is often a sub-class of
`DefaultDesktopManager` and overrides the appropriate `DefaultDesktopManager`
methods.

## DefaultDesktopManager() Constructor

| Method | Syntax |
|---|---|
| DefaultDesktopManager() | public DefaultDesktopManager() |

`DefaultDesktopManager()` creates a `DefaultDesktopManager` object.

## Frame Methods

| Method | Syntax |
|---|---|
| activateFrame() | public void activateFrame(JInternalFrame *frame*) |
| beginDraggingFrame() | public void beginDraggingFrame<br>(JComponent *frame*) |
| beginResizingFrame() | public void beginResizingFrame<br>(JComponent *frame*, int *direction*) |
| closeFrame() | public void closeFrame(JInternalFrame *frame*) |
| deactivateFrame() | public void deactivateFrame<br>(JInternalFrame *frame*) |
| deiconifyFrame() | public void deiconifyFrame<br>(JInternalFrame *frame*) |
| dragFrame() | public void dragFrame<br>(JComponent *frame*, int *newX*, int *newY*) |
| endDraggingFrame() | public void endDraggingFrame(JComponent *frame*) |
| endResizingFrame() | public void endResizingFrame(JComponent *frame*) |
| iconifyFrame() | public void iconifyFrame(JInternalFrame *frame*) |
| maximizeFrame() | public void maximizeFrame(JInternalFrame *frame*) |
| minimizeFrame() | public void minimizeFrame(JInternalFrame *frame*) |
| openFrame() | public void openFrame(JInternalFrame *frame*) |
| resizeFrame() | public void resizeFrame<br>(JComponent *frame*, int *x*, int *y*,<br>int *width*, int *height*) |
| setBoundsForFrame() | public void setBoundsForFrame(JComponent *frame*,<br>int *x*, int *y*, int *width*, int *height*) |

9

javax.swing

`activateFrame()` brings the specified `JInternalFrame` to the front of the desktop.

`deactivateFrame()` brings the specified `JInternalFrame` to the bottom of the desktop.

`beginDraggingFrame()` informs the `DefaultDesktopManager` to prepare any resources needed to drag a `JInternalFrame`. This is called prior to calling `dragFrame()`.

`beginResizingFrame()` informs the `DefaultDesktopManager` to prepare any resources needed to re-size a `JInternalFrame`. This is called prior to calling `resizeFrame()`.

`dragFrame()` moves the specified `frame` to a new location.

`resizeFrame()` resizes the specified `frame`.

`endDraggingFrame()` informs the `DefaultDesktopManager` that the dragging of the specified frame has ended.

`endResizingFrame()` informs the `DefaultDesktopManager` that the resizing of the specified frame has ended.

The other methods are used for manipulating a `JInternalFrame` that resides within a parent container. Their functions are self-explanatory.

# 9.4.4 DefaultListModel Class

```
public class DefaultListModel extends AbstractListModel
```

```
Object
  AbstractListModel
    DefaultListModel
```

### Interfaces

```
ListModel, Serializable
```

A `ListModel` provides the methods used to access elements of a List. A `JList` or `JComboBox` classes have an associated `ListModel` object. A `DefaultListModel` object is the default implementation of the `ListModel` interface. It defines a `Vector` object that stores the elements contained in an associated `JList` object.

## DefaultListModel() Constructor

| Method | Syntax |
|---|---|
| DefaultListModel() | public DefaultListModel() |

`DefaultListModel()` creates a `DefaultListModel` object.

## Size Methods

| Method | Syntax |
|--------|--------|
| size() | public int size() |
| getSize() | public int getSize() |
| setSize() | public void setSize(int *newSize*) |

size() and getSize() return the size of the invoking DefaultListModel object.

setSize() changes the size of the invoking DefaultListModel object.

## contains() Method

| Method | Syntax |
|--------|--------|
| contains() | public boolean contains(Object *obj*) |

contains() returns true if the invoking DefaultListModel object contains obj.

## Methods that Add or Remove List Elements

| Method | Syntax |
|--------|--------|
| add() | public void add(int *index*, Object *obj*) throws ArrayIndexOutOfBoundsException |
| addElement() | public void addElement(Object *obj*) |
| insertElementAt() | public void insertElementAt(Object *obj*, int *index*) throws ArrayIndexOutOfBoundsException |
| remove() | public Object remove(int *index*) throws ArrayIndexOutOfBoundsException |
| removeAllElements() | public void removeAllElements() |
| removeElement() | public boolean removeElement(Object *obj*) |
| removeElementAt() | public void removeElementAt(int *index*) |
| removeRange() | public void removeRange(int *startIndex*, int *endIndex*) throws ArrayIndexOutOfBoundsException, IllegalargumentException |

add() adds Object *obj* at position index in the list.

addElement() adds Object obj to the end of the vector.

insertElementAt() adds Object obj at position *index*.

remove() removes the element at position index and returns the removed object.

removeAllElements() removes all of the elements.

removeElementAt() removes the element at position index from the invoking DefaultListModel object.

removeElement() attempts to remove Object obj from the invoking DefaultListModel object and returns true if successful.

removeRange() removes the elements from startIndex to endIndex.

9

javax.swing

## Methods that Determine the Positions of List Elements

| Method | Syntax |
|--------|--------|
| indexOf() | public int indexOf(Object *obj*) |
| | public int indexOf(Object *obj*, int *startIndex*) |
| lastIndexOf() | public int lastIndexOf(Object *obj*) |
| | public int lastIndexOf<br>(Object *obj*, int *startIndex*) |

These methods determine the location of an object in the vector of the invoking DefaultListModel object.

indexOf() returns the index of the first occurrence of Object obj in the vector either from the beginning of the vector or from position startIndex.

lastIndexOf() returns the last occurrence of Object obj in the vector.

## Methods that Retrieve List Elements

| Method | Syntax |
|--------|--------|
| elementAt() | public Object elementAt(int *index*) |
| firstElement() | public Object firstElement() |
| lastElement() | public Object lastElement() |
| toArray() | public Object[] toArray() |

These methods return an element or elements from the invoking DefaultListModel object.

elementAt() returns the element at position index.

firstElement() and lastElement() return the first and last elements contained in the vector.

toArray() places all of the elements into an Object array.

# 9.5 Utility Classes and Interfaces

The javax.swing package offers several utility classes and interfaces that are used to support the application of the GUI component, container, and menu classes. The utility class hierarchy is shown in the following figure.

The AbstractAction class is used to create Action objects. Action objects are another way to implement the ActionListener interface and can be used to integrate the actions of toolbars, menu items, and other components that generate action events.

The BorderFactory class provides various types of border class objects that can be used to place borders around components.

The ImageIcon class is used to implement images in labels, buttons, and other objects that can display icons.

The KeyStroke class is used to create accelerator and shortcut keyboard sequences.

The SwingConstants interface provides alignment and positioning constants.

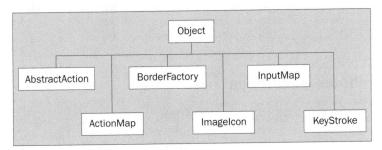

## 9.5.1 AbstractAction Class

```
public abstract class AbstractAction extends Object
   implements Action, Cloneable, Serializable
```

```
Object
   AbstractAction
```

### Interfaces
```
Action, ActionListener, EventListener, Cloneable, Serializable
```

An Action object implements the Action interface and can be used to bundle a procedure and some bound properties. Action objects implement the ActionListener interface and therefore can serve as an ActionListener for other components. The code to execute the procedure associated with an Action object is placed inside the actionPerformed() method that must be implemented by the Action object. See the Action interface section 9.5.2 on page 915 for more details on Action objects.

The AbstractAction class provides implementation of the methods declared in the Action interface. The AbstractAction class is often used as the parent class for user-defined Action classes, although the user-defined Action class needs only to implement the actionPerformed() method.

## AbstractAction() Constructors

| Method | Syntax |
|---|---|
| AbstractAction() | AbstractAction() |
| | AbstractAction(String *name*) |
| | AbstractAction(String *name*, Icon *icon*) |

An AbstractAction object is never instantiated, but the AbstractAction class constructor can be used to initialize Action objects using the super keyword.

9

javax.swing

## actionPerformed() Method

| Method | Syntax |
|---|---|
| actionPerformed() | public abstract void actionPerformed (ActionEvent *ae*) |

actionPerformed() is called when an Action object, which has been added to a menu or toolbar, is selected. It must be overridden in the AbstractAction sub-class. The code for whatever activity the Action object is intended to execute is placed inside this method.

## Enabled Property Methods

| Method | Syntax |
|---|---|
| isEnabled() | public boolean isEnabled() |
| setEnabled() | public void setEnabled (boolean *enabled*) |

isEnabled() returns true if the invoking Action object is enabled. A disabled Action object will do nothing if it is selected.

setEnabled() method is used to change the enabled state of the invoking Action object.

## PropertyChangeListener Methods

| Method | Syntax |
|---|---|
| addPropertyChangeListener() | public void addPropertyChangeListener (PropertyChangeListener *pcl*) |
| removePropertyChangeListener() | public void removePropertyChangeListener (PropertyChangeListener *pcl*) |

PropertyChangeEvent objects are generated when any of the Action object properties change.

addPropertyChangeListener() registers the invoking Action object with a PropertyChangeListener object. The PropertyChangeListener is notified if any of the Action object 's bound properties change.

removePropertyChangeListener() disconnects the PropertyChangeListener object from the invoking Action object.

## Value Methods

| Method | Syntax |
|---|---|
| getValue() | public Object getValue(String *key*) |
| putValue() | public void putValue(String *key*, Object *value*) |

The `Action` interface defines five constants (listed in Section 9.5.2 on page 916) which serve as the keys for key-value pairs, which are used to provide information about the `Action` object.

`getValue()` returns the value associated with the specified `key`.

`putValue()` is used to assign a value `Object` to a given `key`.

## Example: Using AbstractAction

In this example, an `AbstractAction` object is added to a `JMenu` and `JToolBar` object. When the GUI components associated with the `Action` are selected, the program terminates. The `Action` object is also used as the event handler for a `JButton`, and a `JRadioButton` object is provided to enable or disable the `Action`. If the `Action` is disabled, the corresponding element on both the `JMenu` and `JToolbar` objects is disabled. The `JButton`, which uses the `Action` as its event handler, is not disabled.

*The `WinClosing` class is used to terminate the program if the window is closed. See Section 7.3.8 on page 657 for more details.*

```
import javax.swing.*;
import java.awt.*;
import java.awt.event.*;

public class TestAction extends JFrame implements ItemListener {
  JMenuBar jmb;
  JMenu jm;
  JToolBar jtb;
  quitAction qa;
  JButton quitButton;
  JRadioButton jrb;

  public TestAction() {
    qa = new quitAction("quit");

    // The Action object is added to a JMenu.  The add() method returns
    // the JMenuItem that will be displayed on the toolbar.

    jm = new JMenu("File");
    JMenuItem quitMenuItem = jm.add(qa);

    jmb = new JMenuBar();
    jmb.add(jm);

    // The Action object is added to a JToolBar.  The add() method returns
    // the JButton that will be displayed on the toolbar.
```

```
      jtb = new JToolBar();
      jtb.setBorder(BorderFactory.createRaisedBevelBorder());
      JButton toolbarButton = jtb.add(qa);
      toolbarButton.setBorder(BorderFactory.createRaisedBevelBorder());

      // A JButton is created. It uses the Action object as its
      // ActionListener

      quitButton = new JButton("quit");
      quitButton.setBorder(BorderFactory.createRaisedBevelBorder());
      quitButton.addActionListener(qa);

      // A JRadioButton is created that will enable or disable the other
      // other components by using the Action object.

      jrb = new JRadioButton("enabled");
      jrb.setBorder(BorderFactory.createRaisedBevelBorder());
      jrb.setBorderPainted(true);
      jrb.setSelected(true);
      jrb.setPreferredSize(new Dimension(100, 40));
      jrb.setHorizontalAlignment(SwingConstants.CENTER);
      jrb.setVerticalAlignment(SwingConstants.CENTER);
      jrb.addItemListener(this);

      JPanel p = new JPanel();
      p.add(quitButton);
      p.add(jrb);

      getContentPane().add(jmb, BorderLayout.NORTH);
      getContentPane().add(jtb, BorderLayout.SOUTH);
      getContentPane().add(p, BorderLayout.CENTER);

      addWindowListener(new WinClosing());
      setBounds(100, 100, 300, 200);
      setVisible(true);
    }

  // When the JRadioButton is toggled on or off, an ItemEvent is
  // generated.  The Action object is enabled or disabled

  public void itemStateChanged(ItemEvent ie) {
    if (jrb.isSelected()) {
      qa.setEnabled(true);
    } else {
      qa.setEnabled(false);
    }
  }

  class quitAction extends AbstractAction {
    public quitAction(String name) {
      super(name);
    }
```

```
    public void actionPerformed(ActionEvent ae) {
      System.exit(0);
    }
  }

  public static void main(String args[]) {
    TestAction ta = new TestAction();
  }
}

// The WinClosing class terminates the program when the window is closed

class WinClosing extends WindowAdapter {
  public void windowClosing(WindowEvent we) {
    System.exit(0);
  }
}
```

**Output**

The user interface of the program is shown below.

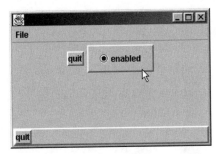

## 9.5.2 Action Interface

```
public interface Action extends ActionListener
```

An Action object can be used to bundle a procedure and some bound properties.
Examples of procedures that might be built in to an Action object are saving a file,
changing the look-and-feel, or terminating the program. Action objects implement the
ActionListener interface and therefore can serve as an ActionListener for other
components. The code to execute the procedure associated with an Action object is
placed inside the actionPerformed() method that must be implemented by the
Action object.

When an Action object is added to certain Swing containers (such as JMenu,
JPopupMenu, and JToolBar) using the add() method, a GUI component is returned:

❑   A JMenu or JPopupMenu object returns a JMenuItem.

❑   A JToolBar object returns a JButton.

The GUI component is what is visible in the container display area. The GUI component uses the `Action` object as its `ActionListener`. The `Action` object can register itself with a `PropertyChangeListener` which it will notify if any of the `Action` object's bound properties change.

An `Action` object must implement the `Action` interface. The `Action` interface defines the property change event, value, and enabled property methods used by `Action` objects.

## Enabled Property Methods

| Method | Syntax |
|---|---|
| `isEnabled()` | `public boolean isEnabled()` |
| `setEnabled()` | `public void setEnabled(boolean enabled)` |

`isEnabled()` returns `true` if the invoking `Action` object is enabled. A disabled `Action` object will do nothing if it is selected.

`setEnabled()` is used to change the enabled state of the invoking `Action` object.

## Key Constants

| Syntax |
|---|
| `public static final String DEFAULT` |
| `public static final String NAME` |
| `public static final String SHORT_DESCRIPTION` |
| `public static final String LONG_DESCRIPTION` |
| `public static final String SMALL_ICON` |

These constants serve as the keys in the `getValue()` and `putValue()` methods.

`DEFAULT` represents the default setting of the `Action`.

`NAME` corresponds to the name of the `Action`.

`SHORT_DESCRIPTION` and `LONG_DESCRIPTION` correspond to short and long descriptions of the `Action`.

`SMALL_ICON` represents an image that can be placed in a toolbar.

## PropertyChangeListener Methods

| Method | Syntax |
|---|---|
| `addPropertyChangeListener()` | `public void addPropertyChangeListener` `(PropertyChangeListener pcl)` |
| `removePropertyChangeListener()` | `public void removePropertyChangeListener` `(PropertyChangeListener pcl)` |

PropertyChangeEvent objects are generated when any of the Action object properties change.

addPropertyChangeListener() registers the invoking Action object with a PropertyChangeListener object  The PropertyChangeListener is notified if any of the Action object 's bound properties change.

removePropertyChangeListener() disconnects the PropertyChangeListener object from the invoking Action object.

## Value Methods

| Method | Syntax |
|---|---|
| getValue() | public Object getValue(String *key*) |
| putValue() | public void putValue(String *key*, Object *value*) |

The Action interface defines five constants (listed above) which serve as the keys for key-value pairs, which are used to provide information about the Action object.

getValue() returns the value associated with the specified key.

putValue() is used to assign a value Object to a given key.

# 9.5.3 ActionMap Class

public class **ActionMap** extends Object implements Serializable

    Object
      ActionMap

### Interfaces
    Serializable

An ActionMap object is used to map an Object key to a particular Action. They are used in conjunction with InputMap objects to associate an Action with a keyboard sequence. An ActionMap object can have a parent that can contain additional key–Action mappings.

## ActionMap() Constructor

| Method | Syntax |
|---|---|
| ActionMap() | public ActionMap() |

ActionMap() creates an ActionMap object with no parent and no key-Action mappings. An ActionMap object can also be obtained using the getActionMap() method defined in the JComponent class.

9

javax.swing

## Key Methods

| Method | Syntax |
|--------|--------|
| allKeys() | public Object[] allKeys() |
| keys() | public Object[] keys() |

allKeys() returns an Object array containing the keys defined by the invoking ActionMap object and its parent.

keys() returns an Object array containing the keys defined by the invoking ActionMap object . Any parent keys are not included.

## Key-Action Mapping Methods

| Method | Syntax |
|--------|--------|
| clear() | public void clear() |
| get() | public Action get(Object *key*) |
| put() | public void put(Object *key*, Action *action* ) |
| remove() | public void remove(Object *key*) |
| size() | public int size() |

clear() removes all of the key-Action mappings from the invoking ActionMap object.

get() returns the Action associated with the specified key.

put() adds a key-action mapping to the invoking ActionMap object.

remove() removes the key-Action mapping associated with the specified key.

size() returns the number of key-Action mappings defined by the invoking ActionMap object.

## Parent Methods

| Method | Syntax |
|--------|--------|
| getParent() | public ActionMap getParent() |
| setParent() | public void setParent(ActionMap *parent*) |

getParent() returns the parent of the invoking ActionMap object or null if it has no parent.

setEnabled() sets the parent of the invoking ActionMap object.

### Example: Using ActionMap

See the *Using Keyboard and Keystroke Methods* example on page 734 where an ActionMap object is used to map a keyboard sequence with an Action.

# 9.5.4 BorderFactory Class

```
public class BorderFactory extends Object
```

```
Object
   BorderFactory
```

The BorderFactory class provides static methods for creating border objects as an alternative to creating border objects using the constructors provided in by the javax.swing.border package. The use of static methods requires less memory because the static methods return references to previously created and stored border objects.

For a picture of what the various borders look like, see the screen output from the example at the end of this section.

## Bevel Border Methods

| Method | Syntax |
|---|---|
| createBevelBorder() | public static Border createBevelBorder (int *bevelType*) |
| | public static Border createBevelBorder (int *bevelType*, Color *highlight*, Color *shadow*) |
| | public static Border createBevelBorder (int *bevelType*, Color *highlightOuter*, Color *highlightInner*, Color *shadowOuter*, Color *shadowInner*) |
| createLoweredBevelBorder() | public static Border createLoweredBevelBorder() |
| createRaisedBevelBorder() | public static Border createRaisedBevelBorder() |

A BevelBorder object represents a raised or lowered beveled border.

createBevelBorder() returns a reference to a BevelBorder object. The bevelType is either BevelBorder.RAISED or BevelBorder.LOWERED. The highlight color is used on the upper and left-hand edges. The shadow color is used on the lower and right-hand edges.

createLoweredBevelBorder() and createRaisedBevelBorder() methods return a reference to a default lowered or raised BevelBorder object.

## createCompoundBorder() Method

| Method | Syntax |
|---|---|
| createCompoundBorder() | public static CompoundBorder createCompoundBorder(Border *insideBorder*, Border *outsideBorder*) |

A CompoundBorder object is a combination of two previously defined borders.

createCompoundBorder() returns a reference to a CompoundBorder object. The insideBorder or outsideBorder arguments can themselves be compound borders.

**9**

javax.swing

**919**

# createEmptyBorder() Method

| Method | Syntax |
|---|---|
| createEmptyBorder() | public static Border createEmptyBorder() |
| | public static Border createEmptyBorder(int topSpace, int leftSpace, int bottomSpace, int rightSpace) |

An EmptyBorder object is used to place an empty outline around a component.

createEmptyBorder() returns a reference to an EmptyBorder object. It is possible to specify different line widths to the top, bottom , left, and right sides.

# createEtchedBorder() Method

| Method | Syntax |
|---|---|
| createEtchedBorder() | public static Border createEtchedBorder() |
| | public static Border createEtchedBorder (Color highlight, Color shadow) |

An EtchedBorder object represents an etched line that is drawn around a component.

createEtchedBorder() returns a reference to an EtchedBorder object. The highlight color is used on the upper and left-hand edges. The shadow color is used on the lower and right-hand edges.

# createLineBorder() Method

| Method | Syntax |
|---|---|
| createLineBorder() | public static Border createLineBorder(Color c) |
| | public static Border createLineBorder(Color c, int thickness) |

A LineBorder object is a solid line drawn around a component.

createLineBorder() returns a reference to a LineBorder object. The thickness and/or color of the line can be specified.

# createMatteBorder() Method

| Method | Syntax |
|---|---|
| createMatteBorder() | public static MatteBorder createMatteBorder (int topSpace, int leftSpace, int bottomSpace, int rightSpace, Color c) |
| | public static MatteBorder createMatteBorder (int topSpace, int leftSpace, int bottomSpace, int rightSpace, Icon i) |

A `MatteBorder` object is a rectangular area placed around a component that is used to separate the component from its frame. The rectangular area is filled with a solid color or with an icon that is repeated around the rectangular area.

`createMatteBorder()` returns a reference to a `MatteBorder` object. The size of the rectangular area is also specified.

## createTitledBorder() Method

| Method | Syntax |
|--------|--------|
| createTitledBorder() | public static TitledBorder createTitledBorder<br>    (String *title*) |
|  | public static TitledBorder createTitledBorder<br>    (Border *border*) |
|  | public static TitledBorder createTitledBorder<br>    (Border *border*, String *title*) |
|  | public static TitledBorder createTitledBorder<br>    (Border *border*, String *title*,<br>    int *titleJustification*, int *titlePosition*) |
|  | public static TitledBorder createTitledBorder<br>    (Border *border*, String *title*,<br>    int *titleJustification*, int *titlePosition*,<br>    Font *titleFont*) |
|  | public static TitledBorder createTitledBorder<br>    (Border *border*, String *title*,<br>    int *titleJustification*, int *titlePosition*,<br>    Font *titleFont*, Color *titleColor*) |

A `TitledBorder` object superimposes a title on another type of border.

`createTitledBorder()` returns a reference to a `TitledBorder` object. The `titleJustification` parameter must be one of the following:

- ❑   `TitledBorder.DEFAULT_JUSTIFICATION`

- ❑   `TitledBorder.LEFT`

- ❑   `TitledBorder.CENTER`

- ❑   `TitledBorder.RIGHT`

- ❑   `TitledBorder.LEADING` (This is the default.)

- ❑   `TitledBorder.TRAILING`

9

javax.swing

The `titlePosition` parameter must be one of the following:

- ❏ `TitledBorder.DEFAULT_POSITION`
- ❏ `TitledBorder.ABOVE_TOP`
- ❏ `TitledBorder.TOP` (This is the default.)
- ❏ `TitledBorder.BELOW_TOP`
- ❏ `TitledBorder.ABOVE_BOTTOM`
- ❏ `TitledBorder.BOTTOM`
- ❏ `TitledBorder.BELOW_BOTTOM`

## Example: Using BorderFactory

In this example, six different borders are displayed on `JButton` objects. The `TitledBorder` constants are contained in the `javax.swing.border` package, which must be imported.

*The `WinClosing` class is used to terminate the program if the window is closed. See Section 7.3.8 on page 657 for more details.*

```
import javax.swing.*;
import java.awt.*;
import java.awt.event.*;
import javax.swing.border.*;

public class TestBorFac extends JFrame {
    JButton b1, b2, b3, b4, b5, b6;

    public TestBorFac() {
        b1 = new JButton("Bevel Border");
        b1.setBorder(BorderFactory.createRaisedBevelBorder());

        b2 = new JButton("Empty Border");
        b2.setBorder(BorderFactory.createEmptyBorder());

        b3 = new JButton("Etched Border");
        b3.setBorder(BorderFactory.createEtchedBorder(Color.cyan,
                Color.blue));

        b4 = new JButton("Line Border");
        b4.setBorder(BorderFactory.createLineBorder(Color.green, 25));

        b5 = new JButton("Matte Border");
        b5.setBorder(BorderFactory.createMatteBorder(20, 20, 20, 20,
                new ImageIcon("Zachary.jpg")));
```

```
      b6 = new JButton("Titled Border");
      b6
        .setBorder(BorderFactory
          .createTitledBorder(BorderFactory.createRaisedBevelBorder(),
                              "Title Here", TitledBorder.LEFT,
                              TitledBorder.TOP));

      JPanel p1 = new JPanel();
      p1.add(b1);
      JPanel p2 = new JPanel();
      p2.add(b2);
      JPanel p3 = new JPanel();
      p3.add(b3);
      JPanel p4 = new JPanel();
      p4.add(b4);
      JPanel p5 = new JPanel();
      p5.add(b5);
      JPanel p6 = new JPanel();
      p6.add(b6);

      JPanel p = new JPanel();
      p.setLayout(new GridLayout(3, 2));
      p.add(p1);
      p.add(p2);
      p.add(p3);
      p.add(p4);
      p.add(p5);
      p.add(p6);

      getContentPane().add(p, BorderLayout.CENTER);

      addWindowListener(new WinClosing());
      setBounds(100, 100, 300, 300);
      pack();
      setVisible(true);
    }

  public static void main(String args[]) {
    TestBorFac tbf = new TestBorFac();
  }
}

// The WinClosing class terminates the program when the window is closed

class WinClosing extends WindowAdapter {
  public void windowClosing(WindowEvent we) {
    System.exit(0);
  }
}
```

**Output**

Here we can see the different types of border we have created:

# 9.5.5 ImageIcon Class

```
public class ImageIcon extends Object implements Icon, Serializable, Accessible
```

```
Object
    ImageIcon
```

### Interfaces

```
Icon, Serializable, Accessible
```

A `ImageIcon` object is a concrete implementation of the `Icon` interface. It uses an `Image` object to store and display any graphic. An `ImageIcon` object can be loaded into `JLabel`, `JButton`, and `JMenuItem` objects to name just a few.

## ImageIcon() Constructors

| Method | Syntax |
|---|---|
| ImageIcon() | `public ImageIcon()` |
| | `public ImageIcon(Image image)` |
| | `public ImageIcon(Image image, String description)` |
| | `public ImageIcon(String filename)` |
| | `public ImageIcon(String filename, String description)` |
| | `public ImageIcon(URL location)` |
| | `public ImageIcon(URL location, String description)` |
| | `public ImageIcon(byte[] imageData)` |
| | `public ImageIcon(byte[] imageData, String description)` |

ImageIcon() creates an ImageIcon object. The constructor must be provided with an image file in an acceptable format. The .jpg or .gif formats, for example, are supported by the ImageIcon class. The image format may be passed to the constructor as an Image object, a String containing the file name, a URL object containing the location of the image file, or as a byte array of image data.

## paintIcon() Method

| Method | Syntax |
|--------|--------|
| paintIcon() | public synchronized void paintIcon(Component c, Graphics g, int x, int y) |

paintIcon() paints the invoking ImageIcon object at the specified location by calling the drawImage() method defined in the Graphics class.

## Methods to Return ImageIcon Properties

| Method | Syntax |
|--------|--------|
| getDescription() | public String getDescription() |
| getIconHeight() | public int getIconHeight() |
| getIconWidth() | public int getIconWidth() |
| getImage() | public Image getImage() |
| getImageLoadStatus() | public int getImageLoadStatus() |
| getImageObserver() | public ImageObserver getImageObserver() |

getDescription() returns a String that is intended to contain a description of the invoking ImageIcon object.

getIconHeight() and getIconWidth() return the height and width in pixels of the invoking ImageIcon object.

getImage() returns a reference to the Image object rendered by the icon.

getImageLoadStatus() returns the status of the image load process. It will return one of the following three constants:

❑ MediaTracker.ABORTED

❑ MediaTracker.ERRORED

❑ MediaTracker.COMPLETE

getImageObserver() returns a reference to the object that is serving as the image observer for the invoking ImageIcon object. If none has been specified, the component containing the ImageIcon is treated as the image observer.

9

javax.swing

# Methods to Set ImageIcon Properties

| Method | Syntax |
|---|---|
| setDescription() | public void setDescription(String *description*) |
| setImage() | public void setImage(Image *image*) |
| setImageObserver() | public void setImageObserver(ImageObserver *io*) |

setDescription() returns a String that is intended to contain a description of the invoking ImageIcon object.

setImage() changes the Image object associated with the invoking ImageIcon object.

setImageObserver() changes the object that is serving as the image observer for the invoking ImageIcon object.

## Example: Using ImageIcon

In this example, an image is placed on a JLabel using an ImageIcon object. In this case, the image file must reside in the same directory as the .class file.

*The WinClosing class is used to terminate the program if the window is closed. See Section 7.3.8 on page 657 for more details.*

```
import javax.swing.*;
import java.awt.event.*;
import java.awt.*;

public class TestImage extends JFrame {
    JLabel lbl;

    public TestImage() {
        lbl = new JLabel(new ImageIcon("Halloween.jpg"));

        JPanel p = new JPanel();
        p.add(lbl);

        getContentPane().add(p, BorderLayout.CENTER);

        addWindowListener(new WinClosing());
        setBounds(100, 100, 300, 300);
        setVisible(true);
    }

    public static void main(String args[]) {
        TestImage ji = new TestImage();
    }
}
```

```
// The WinClosing class terminates the program when the window is closed

class WinClosing extends WindowAdapter {
  public void windowClosing(WindowEvent we) {
    System.exit(0);
  }
}
```

### Output

Here is the image displayed on the JLabel:

# 9.5.6 InputMap Class

```
public class InputMap extends Object implements Serializable
```

```
Object
  InputMap
```

### Interfaces

```
Serializable
```

An InputMap object is used to map an Object key to an input event. Currently, only KeyStroke objects are used as the input event. An InputMap object can be used in conjunction with an ActionMap object to associate an Action with a keyboard sequence. An InputMap object can have a parent that can contain additional key-input event mappings.

## InputMap() Constructor

| Method | Syntax |
|---|---|
| InputMap() | public InputMap() |

Creates an InputMap object with no parent and no key-input event mappings. An InputMap object can also be obtained using the getInputMap() method defined in the JComponent class.

## Key Methods

| Method | Syntax |
|--------|--------|
| allKeys() | public KeyStroke[] allKeys() |
| keys() | public KeyStroke[] keys() |

allKeys() returns a KeyStroke array from the mappings defined by the invoking InputMap object and its parent.

keys() returns a KeyStroke array from the mappings defined by the invoking InputMap object . Any parent mappings are not included.

## Key-Input Event Mapping Methods

| Method | Syntax |
|--------|--------|
| clear() | public void clear() |
| get() | public Object get(KeyStroke keystroke) |
| put() | public void put(KeyStroke keystroke, Object key) |
| remove() | public void remove(KeyStroke keystroke) |
| size() | public int size() |

clear() removes all of the key-Action mappings from the invoking InputMap object.

get() returns the key associated with the specified input event, which is a KeyStroke object.

put() adds a key-input event mapping to the invoking InputMap object.

remove() removes the key-input event mappng associated with the specified KeyStroke object.

size() returns the number of key-input event mappngs defined by the invoking InputMap object.

## Parent Methods

| Method | Syntax |
|--------|--------|
| getParent() | public InputMap getParent() |
| setParent() | public void setParent(InputMap parent) |

getParent() returns the parent of the invoking InputMap object, or null if it has no parent.

setParent() sets the parent of the invoking InputMap object.

## Example: Using ActionMap

See the *Using Keyboard and Keystroke Methods* example on page 734 where an
InputMap object is used to map a keyboard sequence with an Action.

# 9.5.7 KeyStroke Class

```
public class KeyStroke extends Object implements Serializable
```

```
Object
   KeyStroke
```

### Interfaces

```
Serializable
```

A KeyStroke object provides a keyboard sequence that can be used to create an
accelerator or menu shortcut. They can also be used to associate a keyboard sequence
with a particular action through the use of a KeyMap object. The KeyStroke class does
not provide a constructor: a reference to a KeyStroke object is obtained by using the
static methods defined in the KeyStroke class.

## KeyStroke Object Creation Methods

| Method | Syntax |
|---|---|
| getKeyStroke() | public static KeyStroke **getKeyStroke**(char *keyChar*) |
| | public static KeyStroke **getKeyStroke**(char *keyChar*, boolean *activateOnRelease*) |
| | public static KeyStroke **getKeyStroke**(int *keyCode*, int *modifiers*) |
| | public static KeyStroke **getKeyStroke**(int *keyCode*, int *modifiers*, boolean *activateOnRelease*) |
| | public static KeyStroke **getKeyStroke**(String *keystroke*) |
| getKeyStrokeFor Event() | public static KeyStroke **getKeyStrokeForEvent** (KeyEvent *ke*) |

getKeyStroke() returns a reference to a KeyStroke object. If a char is specified, it
should be one of the keyboard elements, 'A' for instance. If a keyCode is specified, it is
one of the constants defined in the KeyEvent class. If activateOnRelease is set to
true, the action corresponding to the KeyStroke object is triggered when the key is
released. If it is false, the action is triggered when the key is pressed. The modifiers
are one of the control key masks:

- ❑ InputEvent.ALT_MASK

- ❑ InputEvent.CTRL_MASK

- ❑ InputEvent.META_MASK

- ❑ InputEvent.SHIFT_MASK

9

javax.swing

The second version is deprecated, and the first version should be used instead.

getKeyStrokeForEvent() returns a reference to a KeyStroke object based on a specified KeyEvent.

## Methods That Return KeyStroke Properties

| Method | Syntax |
|---|---|
| getKeyChar() | public char getKeyChar() |
| getKeyCode() | public int getKeyCode() |
| getModifiers() | public int getModifiers() |
| isOnKeyRelease() | public boolean isOnKeyRelease() |

getKeyChar() returns the char associated with the invoking KeyStroke object.

getKeyCode() returns the KeyEvent constant associated with the invoking KeyStroke object.

getModifiers() returns the modifier keys, if any, associated with the invoking KeyStroke object.

isOnKeyRelease() returns true if the action associated with the invoking KeyStroke object is triggered when the key is released and false if the action is triggered when the key is pressed.

## Example: Using KeyStroke

A KeyStroke object is used to create an accelerator for a JMenuItem object. When *Ctrl-Q* is pressed, the JMenuItem is selected and the program terminates. The WindowListener is used to terminate the program if the window is closed

```
import javax.swing.*;
import java.awt.*;
import java.awt.event.*;

public class TestKS extends JFrame {
  JMenuBar jmb;
  JMenu jm;
  JMenuItem quitMenuItem;

  public TestKS() {
    quitMenuItem = new JMenuItem("quit");
    quitMenuItem.setAccelerator(KeyStroke.getKeyStroke('Q',
        Event.CTRL_MASK, false));
    quitMenuItem.addActionListener(new quitMenuHandler());

    jm = new JMenu("File");
    jm.add(quitMenuItem);
```

```
     jmb = new JMenuBar();
     jmb.add(jm);

     getContentPane().add(jmb, BorderLayout.NORTH);

     addWindowListener(new WinClosing());
     setBounds(100, 100, 200, 200);
     setVisible(true);
   }

   class quitMenuHandler implements ActionListener {
     public void actionPerformed(ActionEvent ae) {
       System.exit(0);
     }
   }

   public static void main(String args[]) {
     TestKS tks = new TestKS();
   }
 }

// The WinClosing class terminates the program when the window is closed

class WinClosing extends WindowAdapter {
  public void windowClosing(WindowEvent we) {
    System.exit(0);
  }
}
```

### Output

The user interface of the program is shown below.

## 9.5.8 SwingConstants Interface

```
public interface SwingConstants
```

The SwingConstants interface provides alignment and position constants that are used by many Swing classes.

## Alignment Constants

| Syntax |
| --- |
| public static final int CENTER |
| public static final int TOP |
| public static final int LEFT |
| public static final int BOTTOM |
| public static final int RIGHT |

These constants are used to align Swing components, text, and icons.

## Orientation Constants

| Syntax |
| --- |
| public static final int HORIZONTAL |
| public static final int VERTICAL |

These constants are used to set or change the orientation of Swing components.

## Position Constants

| Syntax |
| --- |
| public static final int NORTH |
| public static final int NORTH_EAST |
| public static final int EAST |
| public static final int SOUTH_EAST |
| public static final int SOUTH |
| public static final int SOUTH_WEST |
| public static final int WEST |
| public static final int NORTH_WEST |
| public static final int LEADING |
| public static final int TRAILING |

These constants are used to position components.

# 9.6 Swing Layout Managers

Swing components have access to the layout managers contained in the java.awt package, but the javax.swing package introduces some additional layout managers; the BoxLayout, OverlayLayout, and ScrollPaneLayout classes. These layout managers can be used with both Swing and AWT containers. One of them, the BoxLayout class is discussed here. A BoxLayout object adds elements to a container either left-to-right or top-to-bottom. As seen in the figure below, the BoxLayout class is a sub-class of Object.

# 9.6.1 BoxLayout Class

```
public class BoxLayout extends Object implements LayoutManager2, Serializable
```

```
Object
    BoxLayout
```

### Interfaces

```
LayoutManager2, Serializable
```

A BoxLayout object adds elements to a container either left-to-right or top-to-bottom. It behaves similarly to the GridLayout class except the cells can be different sizes

## BoxLayout() Constructor

| Method | Syntax |
|---|---|
| BoxLayout() | public BoxLayout(Container *target*, int *orientation*) |

Creates a BoxLayout. The orientation determines how components are laid out, either along the x-axis or y-axis. Valid values for the orientation are:

- ❑   BoxLayout.X_AXIS
- ❑   BoxLayout.Y_AXIS

## Alignment Methods

| Method | Syntax |
|---|---|
| getLayoutAlignmentX() | public float getLayoutAlignmentX(Container *c*) |
| getLayoutAlignmentY() | public float getLayoutAlignmentY(Container *c*) |

getLayoutAlignmentX() returns how components are aligned along the x-axis. This method is only relevant for a horizontal BoxLayout.

getLayoutAlignmentY() returns how components are aligned along the y-axis. This method is only relevant for a vertical BoxLayout.

## invalidateLayout() Method

| Method | Syntax |
|---|---|
| invalidateLayout() | public void invalidateLayout(Container target) throws AWTError |

invalidateLayout() is invoked when any of the child components has changed its layout properties. The Container reference passed to this method must be the same as was passed to the BoxLayout constructor or an AWTError is thrown.

## Sizing Methods

| Method | Syntax |
|---|---|
| maximumLayoutSize() | public Dimension maximumLayoutSize<br>(Container *target*) throws AWTError |
| minimumLayoutSize() | public Dimension minimumLayoutSize<br>(Container *target*) throws AWTError |
| preferredLayoutSize() | public Dimension preferredLayoutSize<br>(Container *target*) throws AWTError |

maximumLayoutSize(), minimumLayoutSize(), and preferredLayoutSize() return the maximum, minimum, and preferred sizes of the Container target based on the maximum, minimum, or preferred sizes of the container's child components. The Container reference passed to these methods must be the same as was passed to the BoxLayout constructor or an AWTError is thrown

### Example: Using BoxLayout

Two JButton objects and a JTextField object are placed on a JFrame using a BoxLayout layout manager. The components are placed on JPanel objects before being placed in the BoxLayout panel to preserve their preferred size and centers the components in the JFrame. The WindowListener is used to terminate the program if the window is closed.

```
import javax.swing.*;
import java.awt.*;
import java.awt.event.*;

public class TestBL extends JFrame {
   JButton b1, b2;
   JTextField jtf;

   public TestBL() {
      b1 = new JButton("button 1");
      b1.setBorder(BorderFactory.createRaisedBevelBorder());

      b2 = new JButton("button 2");
      b2.setBorder(BorderFactory.createRaisedBevelBorder());

      jtf = new JTextField(15);
      jtf.setBorder(BorderFactory.createLineBorder(Color.black, 3));

      JPanel p1 = new JPanel();
      p1.add(b1);

      JPanel p2 = new JPanel();
      p2.add(jtf);
```

```
    JPanel p3 = new JPanel();
    p3.add(b2);

    JPanel p = new JPanel();
    p.setLayout(new BoxLayout(p, BoxLayout.Y_AXIS));
    p.add(p1);
    p.add(p2);
    p.add(p3);

    getContentPane().add(p);

    addWindowListener(new WinClosing());
    setBounds(100, 100, 300, 300);
    setVisible(true);
  }

  public static void main(String args[]) {
    TestBL tbl = new TestBL();
  }
}

// The WinClosing class terminates the program when the window is closed

class WinClosing extends WindowAdapter {
  public void windowClosing(WindowEvent we) {
    System.exit(0);
  }
}
```

### Output

The user interface of the program is shown below.

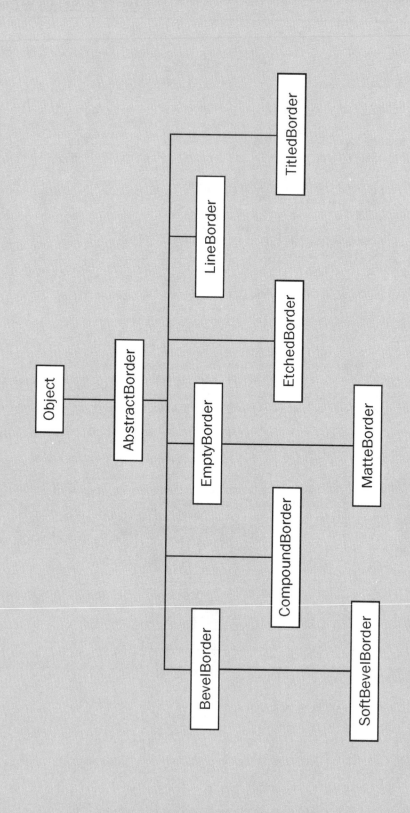

# 10

# javax.swing.border

Borders are used to frame Swing components. They are also used to create the appearance of depth. Any component that extends the JComponent class may have a border placed around it. The borders are added to a Swing component using the JComponent class method setBorder(). All borders can be instantiated directly, and some of them can also be created using the static methods defined in the BorderFactory class from the javax.swing package. (See Section 9.5.4 on page 919 for details.)

The border classes are contained in the javax.swing.border package. The border class hierarchy is shown in the figure opposite.

All of the concrete border classes are sub-classes of the AbstractBorder class, which provides methods that are used by its sub-classes.

❑ The BevelBorder and SoftBevelBorder classes represent a raised or lowered panel.

❑ The EmptyBorder class places an empty space around its associated component.

❑ The LineBorder class represents a solid line drawn around the component.

❑ An EtchedBorder object is an etched line that is drawn around its component.

❑    A MatteBorder object can use a repeated icon as a border.

❑    The TitledBorder class provides a means to place a label on another border type.

❑    Two borders can be combined to form a CompoundBorder object.

This chapter covers:

# 10.1 AbstractBorder Class

```
public abstract class AbstractBorder implements Border, Serializable
```

```
Object
    AbstractBorder
```

### Interfaces

```
Border, Serializable
```

AbstractBorder is the super-class for all Swing border classes. It also serves as the base class for user-defined border classes.

## AbstractBorder() Constructor

| Constructor | Syntax |
|---|---|
| AbstractBorder() | public AbstractBorder() |

Because AbstractBorder is an abstract class, an AbstractBorder object is never instantiated. Sub-classes of AbstractBorder can invoke this constructor by using the super keyword.

## getBorderInsets() Method

| Method | Syntax |
|---|---|
| getBorderInsets() | public Insets getBorderInsets (Component c) |
| | public Insets getBorderInsets(Component c, Insets insets) |

getBorderInsets() is implemented in the AbstractBorder sub-classes to return an Insets object containing the required distance between the border boundary and the component boundary. This information is useful to ensure that the border is not painted over the component. If an Insets object is provided, it is re-initialized with the border's current insets.

## getInteriorRectangle() Method

| Method | Syntax |
|---|---|
| getInteriorRectangle() | public static Rectangle getInteriorRectangle (Component c, Border b, int x, int y, int width, int height) |
| | public Rectangle getInteriorRectangle (Component c, int x, int y, int width, int height) |

getInteriorRectangle() returns a Rectangle object containing the area of the component the border is drawn around. The non-static version calls the static version using a reference to the border associated with Component c.

## isBorderOpaque() Method

| Method | Syntax |
|---|---|
| isBorderOpaque() | public boolean isBorderOpaque() |

isBorderOpaque() returns true if the invoking Border object is opaque. This method returns false by default. To obtain an opaque border, a sub-class should override this method to return true.

10

javax.swing.border

## paintBorder() Method

| Method | Syntax |
|---|---|
| paintBorder() | public void **paintBorder**(Component *c*, Graphics *g*, int *x*, int *y*, int *width*, int *height*) |

paintBorder() is overridden in each AbstractBorder sub-class to render the border.

# 10.2 BevelBorder Class

public class **BevelBorder** extends AbstractBorder

```
Object
    AbstractBorder
        BevelBorder
```

### Interfaces

Border, Serializable

A BevelBorder object is used to give a component the appearance of being raised or lowered. The BevelBorder object simulates a light source above and to the left of the component. The default bevel edge is two pixels wide on either edge. To give the illusion of being raised or lowered, the two edges that are exposed to the light source are colored with a highlight color. The two edges shielded from the light source are colored using a shadow color.

## BevelBorder() Constructors

| Constructor | Syntax |
|---|---|
| BevelBorder() | public **BevelBorder**(int *bevelType*) |
| | public **BevelBorder**(int *bevelType*, Color *highlight*, Color *shadow*) |
| | public **BevelBorder**(int *bevelType*, Color *highlightOuter*, Color *highlightInner*, Color *shadowOuter*, Color *shadowInner*) |

BevelBorder() creates a BevelBorder object. The bevel type and color of the highlight and shadow can be specified. Valid bevelType inputs are:

❑ BevelBorder.RAISED

❑ BevelBorder.LOWERED

## Color Methods

| Method | Syntax |
|---|---|
| getHighlightInnerColor() | `public Color getHighlightInnerColor()` |
| | `public Color getHighlightInnerColor` `(Component c)` |
| getHighlightOuterColor() | `public Color getHighlightOuterColor()` |
| | `public Color getHighlightOuterColor` `(Component c)` |
| getShadowInnerColor() | `public Color getShadowInnerColor()` |
| | `public Color getShadowInnerColor` `(Component c)` |
| getShadowOuterColor() | `public Color getShadowOuterColor()` |
| | `public Color getShadowOuterColor` `(Component c)` |

`getHighlightInnerColor()` returns the inner highlight color for the invoking `BevelBorder` object. If a `Component` is specified, the method returns the inner highlight color when the border is rendered on the `Component`.

`getHighlightOuterColor()` returns the outer highlight color for the invoking `BevelBorder` object. If a `Component` is specified, the method returns the outer highlight color when the border is rendered on the `Component`.

`getShadowInnerColor()` returns the inner shadow color for the invoking `BevelBorder` object. If a `Component` is specified, the method returns the inner shadow color when the border is rendered on the `Component`.

`getShadowOuterColor()` returns the outer shadow color for the invoking `BevelBorder` object. If a `Component` is specified, the method returns the outer shadow color when the border is rendered on the `Component`.

## getBevelType() Method

| Method | Syntax |
|---|---|
| getBevelType() | `public int getBevelType()` |

`getBevelType()` returns the bevel type of the invoking `BevelBorder` object. The return value will be either `BevelBorder.RAISED` or `BevelBorder.LOWERED`.

## getBorderInsets() Method

| Method | Syntax |
|---|---|
| getBorderInsets() | `public Insets getBorderInsets(Component c)` |
| | `public Insets getBorderInsets(Component c,` `Insets insets)` |

10

javax.swing.border

getBorderInsets() returns an Insets object containing the required distance between the border boundary and the component boundary. This information is useful to ensure that the border is not painted over the component. If an Insets object is provided, it is re-initialized with the border's current insets.

## isBorderOpaque() Method

| Method | Syntax |
|---|---|
| isBorderOpaque() | public boolean isBorderOpaque() |

isBorderOpaque() returns true if the invoking BevelBorder object is opaque. This method returns false by default. To obtain an opaque border, this method should be overridden to return true.

## paintBorder() Method

| Method | Syntax |
|---|---|
| paintBorder() | public void paintBorder(Component c, Graphics g, int x, int y, int width, int height) |

paintBorder() renders the border. This method does not normally need to be called by the user. A sub-class of BevelBorder would override this method.

### Example: Using BevelBorder

A raised BevelBorder object is placed around a JButton object. The highlight and shadow colors are set to cyan and blue in the constructor. The getInsets() method provides an outer margin to the JFrame. The WindowListener object terminates the program if the window is closed; see Section 7.3.8 on page 657 for more details.

```java
import javax.swing.*;
import javax.swing.border.*;
import java.awt.*;
import java.awt.event.*;

public class TestBevel extends JFrame {
    JButton button;

    public TestBevel() {
        BevelBorder bb = new BevelBorder(BevelBorder.RAISED,
                                         Color.cyan, Color.blue);

        button = new JButton("BevelBorder");
        button.setFont(new Font("Serif", Font.PLAIN, 12));
```

```
// The setBorder() method is used to set the border of the JButton

    button.setBorder(bb);

    JPanel p = new JPanel();
    p.add(button);
    getContentPane().add(p);

    addWindowListener(new WinClosing());
    setBounds(100, 100, 200, 120);
    setVisible(true);
  }

// The getInsets() method is overridden to place the button more
// in the center of the frame

  public Insets getInsets() {
    return new Insets(30, 50, 30, 50);
  }

  public static void main(String args[]) {
    TestBevel tb = new TestBevel();
  }
}

// The WinClosing class terminates the program if the window is closed

class WinClosing extends WindowAdapter {
  public void windowClosing(WindowEvent we) {
    System.exit(0);
  }
}
```

### Output

Here is the button that has been created:

# 10.3 CompoundBorder Class

```
public class CompoundBorder extends AbstractBorder
```

```
Object
    AbstractBorder
        CompoundBorder
```

### Interfaces

```
Border, Serializable
```

A CompoundBorder object allows the combination of two other Border types into an inner border and an outer border. The inner and outer borders can themselves be CompoundBorder objects. This border can be used to place blank space around a border by making the outer border of type EmptyBorder.

## CompoundBorder() Constructor

| Constructor | Syntax |
|---|---|
| CompoundBorder() | public CompoundBorder(Border *outsideBorder*, Border *insideBorder*) |

CompoundBorder() creates a CompoundBorder object. The insideBorder and outsideBorder objects can be any border type including CompoundBorder.

## getBorderInsets() Method

| Method | Syntax |
|---|---|
| getBorderInsets() | public Insets getBorderInsets(Component *c*) |
| | public Insets getBorderInsets(Component *c*, Insets *insets*) |

getBorderInsets() returns an Insets object containing the required distance between the border boundary and the component boundary. This information is useful to ensure that the border is not painted over the component. If an Insets object is provided, it is re-initialized with the border's current insets.

## isBorderOpaque() Method

| Method | Syntax |
|---|---|
| isBorderOpaque() | public boolean isBorderOpaque() |

isBorderOpaque() returns true if the invoking CompoundBorder object is opaque. This method returns false by default. To obtain an opaque border, this method should be overridden to return true.

# paintBorder() Method

| Method | Syntax |
|---|---|
| paintBorder() | public void paintBorder(Component *c*, Graphics *g*, int *x*, int *y*, int *width*, int *height*) |

paintBorder() renders the border. This method does not normally need to be called by the user. A sub-class of CompoundBorder would override this method.

# Methods to Return the Constituent Borders

| Method | Syntax |
|---|---|
| getInsideBorder() | public Border getInsideBorder() |
| getOutsideBorder() | public Border getOutsideBorder() |

getInsideBorder() and getOutsideBorder() return the inner and outer borders of the invoking CompoundBorder object.

## Example: Using CompoundBorder

In this example, three JButton objects are created and placed on a JFrame. Two of the JButton objects are provided with BevelBorder objects as their border. The third JButton object uses a CompoundBorder object to place some empty space around the JButton by wrapping an EmptyBorder 20 pixels wide on the outside of a BevelBorder object. The WindowListener object terminates the program if the window is closed; see Section 7.3.8 on page 657 for more details. The getInsets() method provides an outer margin to the JFrame.

```
import javax.swing.*;
import javax.swing.border.*;
import java.awt.*;
import java.awt.event.*;

public class TestComp extends JFrame {
    JButton button, b2;

    public TestComp()
    {
        BevelBorder bb = new BevelBorder(BevelBorder.RAISED);
        LineBorder lb = new LineBorder(Color.blue, 10);
        CompoundBorder cb = new CompoundBorder(lb, bb);

        button = new JButton("CompoundBorder");
        button.setFont(new Font("Serif", Font.PLAIN, 12));
// The setBorder() method is used to set the border of the JButton
```

```
            button.setBorder(cb);

            b2 = new JButton("BevelBorder");
            b2.setFont(new Font("Serif", Font.PLAIN, 12));
            b2.setBorder(bb);

            JPanel p = new JPanel();
            p.add(b2);
            p.add(button);
            getContentPane().add(p);

            addWindowListener(new WinClosing());
            setBounds(100, 100, 300, 120);
            setVisible(true);
        }

    // The getInsets() method is overridden to place the button more
    // in the center of the frame

        public Insets getInsets() {
            return new Insets(30, 20, 30, 20);
        }

        public static void main(String args[]) {
            TestComp tb = new TestComp();
        }
    }

    // The WinClosing class terminates the program if the window is closed

    class WinClosing extends WindowAdapter {
        public void windowClosing(WindowEvent we) {
            System.exit(0);
        }
    }
}
```

### Output

Here is the result:

# 10.4 EmptyBorder Class

```
public class EmptyBorder extends AbstractBorder implements Serializable
```

```
Object
    AbstractBorder
        EmptyBorder
```

### Interfaces
```
Border, Serializable
```

An EmptyBorder object is used to place empty space around a component. The border insets are set using the parameters given to the constructor.

## EmptyBorder() Constructors

| Constructor | Syntax |
|---|---|
| EmptyBorder() | public EmptyBorder(int *topSpace*, int *leftSpace*, int *bottomSpace*, int *rightSpace*) |
| | public EmptyBorder(Insets *insets*) |

EmptyBorder() creates an EmptyBorder object. The size of the border is provided either by specifying the width of each side or by an Insets object containing these dimensions.

## getBorderInsets() Method

| Method | Syntax |
|---|---|
| getBorderInsets() | public Insets getBorderInsets(Component *c*) |
| | public Insets getBorderInsets(Component *c*, Insets *insets*) |

getBorderInsets() returns an Insets object containing the required distance between the border boundary and the component boundary. This information is useful to ensure that the border is not painted over the component. If an Insets object is provided, it is re-initialized with the border's current insets.

## isBorderOpaque() Method

| Method | Syntax |
|---|---|
| isBorderOpaque() | public boolean isBorderOpaque() |

isBorderOpaque() returns true if the invoking EmptyBorder object is opaque. This method returns false by default. To obtain an opaque border, this method should be overridden to return true.

## paintBorder() Method

| Method | Syntax |
|---|---|
| paintBorder() | public void **paintBorder**(Component *c*, Graphics *g*, int *x*, int *y*, int *width*, int *height*) |

paintBorder() renders the border. This method, in its default implementation, does nothing. A sub-class of EmptyBorder would override this method.

### Example: Using EmptyBorder

An EmptyBorder object 20 pixels wide is placed around a JButton object. EmptyBorder objects can be used to place some empty space between components. The WindowListener object terminates the program if the window is closed; see Section 7.3.8 on page 657 for more details.

```
import javax.swing.*;
import javax.swing.border.*;
import java.awt.*;
import java.awt.event.*;

public class TestEmpty extends JFrame {
    JButton button;

    public TestEmpty() {
        EmptyBorder eb = new EmptyBorder(new Insets(20, 20, 20, 20));

        button = new JButton("EmptyBorder");
        button.setFont(new Font("Serif", Font.PLAIN, 12));
        button.setBackground(Color.cyan);

//  The setBorder() method is used to set the border of the JButton

        button.setBorder(eb);

        JPanel p = new JPanel();
        p.add(button);
        getContentPane().add(p);

        addWindowListener(new WinClosing());
        setBounds(100, 100, 200, 120);
        setVisible(true);
    }
```

```
        public static void main(String args[]) {
           TestEmpty te = new TestEmpty();
        }
    }

    //  The WinClosing class terminates the program if the window is closed

    class WinClosing extends WindowAdapter {
       public void windowClosing(WindowEvent we) {
          System.exit(0);
       }
    }
```

**Output**

Here is the button that is created:

# 10.5 EtchedBorder Class

```
public class EtchedBorder extends AbstractBorder
```

```
Object
    AbstractBorder
       EtchedBorder
```

### Interfaces
```
Border, Serializable
```

An EtchedBorder object creates an etched line around a component. Similar to the BevelBorder class, an EtchedBorder object renders itself by simulating a light source above and to the left. An EtchedBorder object can be either raised or lowered.

10

javax.swing.border

## EtchedBorder() Constructors

| Constructor | Syntax |
|---|---|
| EtchedBorder() | public EtchedBorder() |
| | public EtchedBorder(int *etchType*) |
| | public EtchedBorder(int *etchType*, Color *highlight*, Color *shadow*) |
| | public EtchedBorder(Color *highlight*, Color *shadow*) |

EtchedBorder() creates an EtchedBorder object. The etch type and color of the highlight and shadow can be specified. The etchType parameter must be one of the following constants:

❑ EtchedBorder.RAISED

❑ EtchedBorder.LOWERED

The default etch type is EtchedBorder.LOWERED.

## Color Methods

| Method | Syntax |
|---|---|
| getHighlightColor() | public Color getHighlightColor() |
| | public Color getHighlightColor(Component *c*) |
| getShadowColor() | public Color getShadowColor() |
| | public Color getShadowColor(Component *c*) |

getHighlightColor() returns the highlight color for the invoking EtchedBorder object. If a Component is specified, the method returns the highlight color when the border is rendered on the Component.

getShadowColor() returns the shadow color for the invoking EtchedBorder object. If a Component is specified, the method returns the shadow color when the border is rendered on the Component.

## getBorderInsets() Method

| Method | Syntax |
|---|---|
| getBorderInsets() | public Insets getBorderInsets(Component *c*) |
| | public Insets getBorderInsets(Component *c*, Insets *insets*) |

getBorderInsets() returns an Insets object containing the required distance between the border boundary and the component boundary. This information is useful to ensure that the border is not painted over the component. If an Insets object is provided, it is re-initialized with the border's current insets.

## getEtchType() Method

| Method | Syntax |
|---|---|
| getEtchType() | public int getEtchType() |

getEtchType() returns the etch type of the invoking EtchBorder object. The return value will be one of the following constants:

- ❏ EtchedBorder.RAISED
- ❏ EtchedBorder.LOWERED

## isBorderOpaque() Method

| Method | Syntax |
|---|---|
| isBorderOpaque() | public boolean isBorderOpaque() |

isBorderOpaque() returns true if the invoking EtchedBorder object is opaque. This method returns false by default. To obtain an opaque border, this method should be overridden to return true.

## paintBorder() Method

| Method | Syntax |
|---|---|
| paintBorder() | public void paintBorder(Component c, Graphics g, int x, int y, int width, int height) |

paintBorder() renders the border. This method does not normally need to be called by the user. A sub-class of EtchedBorder would override this method.

### Example: Using EtchedBorder

In this example, a lowered EtchedBorder object is placed around a JButton object. The WindowListener object terminates the program if the window is closed; see Section 7.3.8 on page 657 for more details. The getInsets() method provides an outer margin to the JFrame.

```
import javax.swing.*;
import javax.swing.border.*;
import java.awt.*;
import java.awt.event.*;
```

10

javax.swing.border

```
public class TestEtched extends JFrame {
    JButton button;

    public TestEtched() {
        EtchedBorder eb = new EtchedBorder();

        button = new JButton("EtchedBorder");
        button.setFont(new Font("Serif", Font.PLAIN, 12));

// The setBorder() method is used to set the border of the JButton

        button.setBorder(eb);

        JPanel p = new JPanel();
        p.add(button);
        getContentPane().add(p);

        addWindowListener(new WinClosing());
        setBounds(100, 100, 200, 120);
        setVisible(true);
    }

// The getInsets() method is overridden to place the button more
// in the center of the frame

    public Insets getInsets() {
        return new Insets(30, 50, 30, 50);
    }

    public static void main(String args[])
    {
        TestEtched te = new TestEtched();
    }
}


// The WinClosing class terminates the program if the window is closed

class WinClosing extends WindowAdapter {
    public void windowClosing(WindowEvent we) {
        System.exit(0);
    }
}
```

**Output**

Here is the JButton with the etched border, that has been created:

# 10.6 LineBorder Class

```
public class LineBorder extends AbstractBorder
```

```
Object
    AbstractBorder
        LineBorder
```

### Interfaces

```
Border, Serializable
```

A LineBorder object draws a solid line around a component. The thickness of the line is specified in the constructor. The line is a single color and is not shaded. A LineBorder object can be created using the constructor or by one of two static object creation methods.

## LineBorder() Constructors

| Constructor | Syntax |
|---|---|
| LineBorder() | public LineBorder(Color c) |
| | public LineBorder(Color c, int *thickness*) |
| | public LineBorder(Color c, int *thickness*, boolean *roundedCorners*) |

LineBorder() creates a LineBorder object. The thickness, or thickness and color, of the line can be specified. If roundedCorners is true, the corners of the border are rounded.

10

javax.swing.border

## Static LineBorder Object Creation Methods

| Method | Syntax |
|---|---|
| createBlackLineBorder() | public static Border createBlackLineBorder() |
| createGrayLineBorder() | public static Border createGrayLineBorder() |

These static methods create a black or gray LineBorder object 1 pixel thick.

## getBorderInsets() Method

| Method | Syntax |
|---|---|
| getBorderInsets() | public Insets getBorderInsets(Component c) |
| | public Insets getBorderInsets(Component c, Insets insets) |

getBorderInsets() returns an Insets object containing the required distance between the border boundary and the component boundary. This information is useful to ensure that the border is not painted over the component. If an Insets object is provided, it is re-initialized with the border's current insets.

## isBorderOpaque() Method

| Method | Syntax |
|---|---|
| isBorderOpaque() | public boolean isBorderOpaque() |

isBorderOpaque() returns true if the invoking LineBorder object is opaque. This method returns false by default. To obtain an opaque border, this method should be overridden to return true.

## paintBorder() Method

| Method | Syntax |
|---|---|
| paintBorder() | public void paintBorder(Component c, Graphics g, int x, int y, int width, int height) |

paintBorder() renders the border. This method does not normally need to be called by the user. A sub-class of LineBorder would override this method.

## LineBorder Property Methods

| Method | Syntax |
|---|---|
| getLineColor() | public Color getLineColor() |
| getRoundedCorners() | public boolean getRoundedCorners() |
| getThickness() | public int getThickness() |

getLineColor() returns the color of the invoking LineBorder object.

getRoundedCorners() returns true if the invoking LineBorder object will be drawn with rounded corners.

getThickness() returns the thickness of the invoking LineBorder object.

## Example: Using LineBorder

A blue line three pixels wide is placed around a JButton object using a LineBorder object. The WindowListener object terminates the program if the window is closed; see Section 7.3.8 on page 657 for more details. The getInsets() method provides an outer margin to the JFrame.

```
import javax.swing.*;
import javax.swing.border.*;
import java.awt.*;
import java.awt.event.*;

public class TestLine extends JFrame {
    JButton button;

    public TestLine() {
        LineBorder lb = new LineBorder(Color.blue, 3);

        button = new JButton("LineBorder");
        button.setFont(new Font("Serif", Font.PLAIN, 12));

//  The setBorder() method is used to set the border of the JButton

        button.setBorder(lb);

        JPanel p = new JPanel();
        p.add(button);
        getContentPane().add(p);

        addWindowListener(new WinClosing());
        setBounds(100, 100, 200, 120);
        setVisible(true);
    }

//  The getInsets() method is overridden to place the button more
//  in the center of the frame
```

10

javax.swing.border

```
        public Insets getInsets() {
            return new Insets(30, 50, 30, 50);
        }

        public static void main(String args[]) {
            TestLine tl = new TestLine();
        }
    }


    //   The WinClosing class terminates the program if the window is closed

    class WinClosing extends WindowAdapter {
        public void windowClosing(WindowEvent we) {
            System.exit(0);
        }
    }
```

**Output**

Here is the result of this program:

# 10.7 MatteBorder Class

```
public class MatteBorder extends EmptyBorder
```

```
Object
    AbstractBorder
        EmptyBorder
            MatteBorder
```

**Interfaces**

```
Border, Serializable
```

A `MatteBorder` object fills the border area with either a solid color or an `Icon` that is repeated to form a wallpaper effect.

## MatteBorder() Constructors

| Constructor | Syntax |
|---|---|
| MatteBorder() | public MatteBorder(Icon *i*) |
| | public MatteBorder(int *topWidth*, int *leftWidth*, int *bottomWidth*, int *rightWidth*, Color *c*) |
| | public MatteBorder(Insets *insets*, Color *c*) |
| | public MatteBorder(int *topWidth*, int *leftWidth*, int *bottomWidth*, int *rightWidth*, Icon *i*) |
| | public MatteBorder(Insets *insets*, Icon *i*) |

`MatteBorder()` creates a `MatteBorder` object. If the widths or an `Insets` object are not provided, the top, left, bottom, and right widths are based on the size of the `Icon` object.

## getBorderInsets() Method

| Method | Syntax |
|---|---|
| getBorderInsets() | public Insets getBorderInsets() |
| | public Insets getBorderInsets(Component *c*) |
| | public Insets getBorderInsets(Component *c*, Insets *insets*) |

`getBorderInsets()` returns an `Insets` object containing the required distance between the border boundary and the component boundary. This information is useful to ensure that the border is not painted over the component. If an `Insets` object is provided, it is re-initialized with the border's current insets. The no argument version returns the insets of the border by itself.

## isBorderOpaque() Method

| Method | Syntax |
|---|---|
| isBorderOpaque() | public boolean isBorderOpaque() |

`isBorderOpaque()` returns `true` if the invoking `MatteBorder` object is opaque. This method returns `false` by default. To obtain an opaque border, this method should be overridden to return `true`.

10

javax.swing.border

## paintBorder() Method

| Method | Syntax |
|---|---|
| paintBorder() | public void **paintBorder**(Component *c*, Graphics *g*, int *x*, int *y*, int *width*, int *height*) |

paintBorder() renders the border. This method does not normally need to be called by the user. A sub-class of MatteBorder would override this method.

## MatteBorder Property Methods

| Method | Syntax |
|---|---|
| getMatteColor() | public color **getMatteColor**() |
| getTileIcon() | public Icon **getTileIcon**() |

getMatteColor() returns the color of the invoking MatteBorder object or null if an icon is being used.

getTileIcon() returns the icon used by the invoking MatteBorder object or null if a solid color is being used.

### Example: Using MatteBorder

A MatteBorder object is created using a repeated icon. In this example, the icon is based on a JPEG format image file named zachary.jpg, although any small JPEG or GIF format image file could be used.Because the border widths are not specified, they are computed based on the size of the icon. The WindowListener object terminates the program if the window is closed; see Section 7.3.8 on page 657 for more details. The getInsets() method provides an outer margin to the JFrame.

```
import javax.swing.*;
import javax.swing.border.*;
import java.awt.*;
import java.awt.event.*;

public class TestMatte extends JFrame {
    JButton button;

    public TestMatte() {
        MatteBorder mb = new MatteBorder(new ImageIcon("Zachary.jpg"));

        button = new JButton("MatteBorder");
        button.setFont(new Font("Serif", Font.PLAIN, 12));

// The setBorder() method is used to set the border of the JButton
```

```
        button.setBorder(mb);

        JPanel p = new JPanel();
        p.add(button);
        getContentPane().add(p);

        addWindowListener(new WinClosing());
        setBounds(100, 100, 200, 120);
        setVisible(true);
    }

// The getInsets() method is overridden to place the button more
// in the center of the frame

    public Insets getInsets() {
        return new Insets(15, 30, 15, 30);
    }

    public static void main(String args[]) {
        TestMatte tm = new TestMatte();
    }
}

// The WinClosing class terminates the program if the window is closed

class WinClosing extends WindowAdapter {
    public void windowClosing(WindowEvent we) {
        System.exit(0);
    }
}
```

### *Output*

The user interface of the program is shown below:

# 10.8 SoftBevelBorder Class

`public class SoftBevelBorder extends BevelBorder`

```
Object
    AbstractBorder
        BevelBorder
            SoftBevelBorder
```

### Interfaces

Border, Serializable

A SoftBevelBorder object is similar to a BevelBorder object except that the SoftBevelBorder has small rounded corners and two of the four edges are slightly thinner.

## SoftBevelBorder() Constructors

| Constructor | Syntax |
|---|---|
| SoftBevelBorder() | public SoftBevelBorder(int *bevelType*) |
| | public SoftBevelBorder(int *bevelType*, Color *highlight*, Color *shadow*) |
| | public SoftBevelBorder(int *bevelType*, Color *highlightOuter*, Color *highlightInner*, Color *shadowOuter*, Color *shadowInner*) |

SoftBevelBorder() creates a SoftBevelBorder object. The bevel type and color of the highlight and shadow can be specified. Valid bevelType inputs are:

- ❏  BevelBorder.RAISED
- ❏  BevelBorder.LOWERED

## getBorderInsets() Method

| Method | Syntax |
|---|---|
| getBorderInsets() | public Insets getBorderInsets(Component *c*) |

getBorderInsets() returns an Insets object containing the required distance between the border boundary and the component boundary. This information is useful to ensure that the border is not painted over the component. A SoftBevelBorder object also has access to the version of getBorderInsets() from the BevelBorder class that takes an Insets argument.

## isBorderOpaque() Method

| Method | Syntax |
|---|---|
| isBorderOpaque() | public boolean isBorderOpaque() |

isBorderOpaque() returns true if the invoking SoftBevelBorder object is opaque. This method returns false by default. To obtain an opaque border, this method should be overridden to return true.

## paintBorder() Method

| Method | Syntax |
|---|---|
| paintBorder() | public void paintBorder(Component c, Graphics g, int x, int y, int width, int height) |

paintBorder() renders the border. This method does not normally need to be called by the user. A sub-class of SoftBevelBorder would override this method.

### Example: Using SoftBevelBorder

A raised SoftBevelBorder object is placed around a JButton object using the default colors. The WindowListener object terminates the program if the window is closed; see Section 7.3.8 on page 657 for more details. The getInsets() method provides an outer margin to the JFrame.

```
import javax.swing.*;
import javax.swing.border.*;
import java.awt.*;
import java.awt.event.*;

public class TestSoftBevel extends JFrame {
    JButton button;

    public TestSoftBevel() {
        SoftBevelBorder bb = new SoftBevelBorder(BevelBorder.RAISED);

        button = new JButton("SoftBevelBorder");
        button.setFont(new Font("Serif", Font.PLAIN, 12));

//  The setBorder() method is used to set the border of the JButton

        button.setBorder(bb);

        JPanel p = new JPanel();
```

```
      p.add(button);
        getContentPane().add(p);

        addWindowListener(new WinClosing());
        setBounds(100, 100, 200, 120);
        setVisible(true);
    }

//  The getInsets() method is overridden to place the button more
//  in the center of the frame

    public Insets getInsets() {
        return new Insets(30, 25, 30, 25);
    }

    public static void main(String args[]) {
        TestSoftBevel tsb = new TestSoftBevel();
    }
}

//  The WinClosing class terminates the program if the window is closed

class WinClosing extends WindowAdapter {
    public void windowClosing(WindowEvent we) {
        System.exit(0);
    }
}
```

*Output*

Here is the result that demonstrates the SoftBevelBorder:

# 10.9 TitledBorder Class

```
public class TitledBorder extends AbstractBorder
```

```
Object
    AbstractBorder
        TitledBorder
```

### Interfaces
```
Border, Serializable
```

A `TitledBorder` object takes another border object and adds a label to it. The label can be placed in one of six positions and can have one of three vertical alignments.

## TitledBorder() Constructors

| Constructor | Syntax |
|---|---|
| TitledBorder() | public **TitledBorder**(String *title*) |
| | public **TitledBorder**(Border *border*) |
| | public **TitledBorder**(Border *border*, String *title*) |
| | public **TitledBorder**(Border *border*, String *title*, int *titleJustification*, int *titlePosition*) |
| | public **TitledBorder**(Border *border*, String *title*, int *titleJustification*, int *titlePosition*, Font *titleFont*) |
| | public **TitledBorder**(Border *border*, String *title*, int *titleJustification*, int *titlePosition*, Font *titleFont*, Color *titleColor*) |

`TitledBorder()` creates a `TitledBorder` object. In addition to the `Border` object and title, the title justification and position can be specified. The `titleJustification` parameter is the horizontal alignment of the title and must have one of these values:

❑ `TitledBorder.LEFT`

❑ `TitledBorder.CENTER`

❑ `TitledBorder.RIGHT`

❑ `TitledBorder.DEFAULT_JUSTIFICATION`

10

javax.swing.border

**963**

The default justification is `TitledBorder.LEFT`. The position must be one of these values:

- ❏ `TitledBorder.ABOVE_TOP`
- ❏ `TitledBorder.TOP`
- ❏ `TitledBorder.BELOW_TOP`
- ❏ `TitledBorder.ABOVE_BOTTOM`
- ❏ `TitledBorder.BOTTOM`
- ❏ `TitledBorder.BELOW_BOTTOM`
- ❏ `TitledBorder.DEFAULT_POSITION`

The default position is `TitledBorder.TOP`.

## getBorderInsets() Method

| Method | Syntax |
|---|---|
| getBorderInsets() | `public Insets getBorderInsets(Component c)` |
| | `public Insets getBorderInsets(Component c, Insets insets)` |

`getBorderInsets()` returns an `Insets` object containing the required distance between the border boundary and the component boundary. This information is useful to ensure that the border is not painted over the component. If an `Insets` object is provided, it is re-initialized with the border's current insets.

## isBorderOpaque() Method

| Method | Syntax |
|---|---|
| isBorderOpaque() | `public boolean isBorderOpaque()` |

`isBorderOpaque()` returns `true` if the invoking `TitledBorder` object is opaque. This method returns `false` by default. To obtain an opaque border, this method should be overridden to return `true`.

## paintBorder() Method

| Method | Syntax |
|---|---|
| paintBorder() | `public void paintBorder(Component c, Graphics g, int x, int y, int width, int height)` |

`paintBorder()` renders the border. This method does not normally need to be called by the user. A sub-class of `TitledBorder` would override this method.

# Methods to Change TitledBorder Properties

| Method | Syntax |
|--------|--------|
| setBorder() | public void setBorder(Border *border*) |
| setTitle() | public void setTitle(String *title*) |
| setTitleColor() | public void setTitleColor(Color *titleColor*) |
| setTitleFont() | public void setTitleFont(Font *titleFont*) |
| setTitleJustification() | public void setTitleJustification (int *justificationConstant*) |
| setTitlePosition() | public void setTitlePosition (int *positionConstant*) |

setBorder() changes the border associated with the invoking TitledBorder object.

setTitle() changes the title associated with the invoking TitledBorder object.

setTitleColor() and setTitleFont() are used to alter the title color and font.

setTitleJustification() and setTitlePosition() specifiy the justification and position of the title. The arguments to these methods must be one of the constants described under *TitledBorder() Constructors* on page 963.

# Methods to Return TitledBorder Properties

| Method | Syntax |
|--------|--------|
| getBorder() | public Border getBorder() |
| getTitle() | public String getTitle() |
| getTitleColor() | public Color getTitleColor() |
| getTitleFont() | public Font getTitleFont() |
| getTitleJustification() | public int getTitleJustification() |
| getTitlePosition() | public int getTitlePosition() |

getBorder() returns the Border object associated with the invoking TitledBorder object.

getTitle() returns the title associated with the invoking TitledBorder object.

getTitleColor() and getTitleFont() return the title color and font.

getTitleJustification() and getTitlePosition() return the justification and position of the title. The return values will be one of the constants described under *TitledBorder() Constructors* above on page 963.

10

javax.swing.border

**965**

## Example: Using TitledBorder

A title is placed on a `BevelBorder` object using a `TitledBorder` object. The title is placed in the upper left-hand corner of the border. The `WindowListener` object terminates the program if the window is closed; see Section 7.3.8 on page 657 for more details. The `getInsets()` method provides an outer margin to the `JFrame`.

```java
import javax.swing.*;
import javax.swing.border.*;
import java.awt.*;
import java.awt.event.*;

public class TestTitled extends JFrame {
    JButton button;

    public TestTitled() {
        TitledBorder tb = new TitledBorder(
                            new BevelBorder(BevelBorder.RAISED),
                            "Title here",
                            TitledBorder.LEFT, TitledBorder.BELOW_TOP);
        tb.setTitleColor(Color.black);
        tb.setTitleFont(new Font("Serif", Font.PLAIN, 10));

        button = new JButton("TitledBorder");
        button.setFont(new Font("Serif", Font.PLAIN, 12));

// The setBorder() method is used to set the border of the JButton

        button.setBorder(tb);

        JPanel p = new JPanel();
        p.add(button);
        getContentPane().add(p);

        addWindowListener(new WinClosing());
        setBounds(100, 100, 200, 120);
        setVisible(true);
    }

// The getInsets() method is overridden to place the button more
// in the center of the frame

    public Insets getInsets() {
        return new Insets(30, 50, 30, 50);
    }
```

```
    public static void main(String args[]) {
        TestTitled tt = new TestTitled();
    }
}

//  The WinClosing class terminates the program if the window is closed

class WinClosing extends WindowAdapter {
    public void windowClosing(WindowEvent we) {
        System.exit(0);
    }
}
```

**Output**

Here is the resulting button using the titled border:

# 10.10 User-Defined Borders

It is relatively simple to create a user-defined border class. The class should extend the AbstractBorder class or one of the AbstractBorder sub-classes. The getBorderInsets(), isBorderOpaque(), and paintBorder() methods must be overridden within the class.

### Example: User-Defined Borders

In this example, a user-defined border class, FourColorBorder, is created that places a line border around a component with each side of the border having a different color. The user supplies four Color objects and a line width to the constructor.

```
import javax.swing.*;
import javax.swing.border.*;
import java.awt.*;
import java.awt.event.*;
```

```
public class TestFour extends JFrame {
   JButton button;

   public TestFour() {

// A FourColorBorder object is created.  FourColorBorder is a
// user-defined border class

      FourColorBorder fb = new FourColorBorder(Color.black, Color.green,
                                          Color.yellow, Color.gray, 5);

      button = new JButton("Gotcha");
      button.setFont(new Font("Serif", Font.PLAIN, 12));
      button.setBorder(fb);

      JPanel p = new JPanel();
      p.add(button);
      getContentPane().add(p);

      addWindowListener(new WinClosing());
      setBounds(100, 100, 200, 120);
      setVisible(true);
   }

// The getInsets() method is overridden to place the button more
// in the center of the frame

   public Insets getInsets() {
      return new Insets(30, 50, 30, 50);
   }

   public static void main(String args[]) {
      TestFour tr = new TestFour();
   }
}


// FourColorBorder is a user-defined border class.  It is a
// variation of the LineBorder class with a different colored line
// on each side of the border.

class FourColorBorder extends AbstractBorder
{
   Color topColor, bottomColor, leftColor, rightColor;
   int lineWidth;
```

```
// The FourColorBorder constructor takes four Color objects and the
// line width as arguments

   public FourColorBorder(Color tc, Color bc, Color lc, Color rc, int width)
   {
      topColor = tc;
      bottomColor = bc;
      leftColor = lc;
      rightColor = rc;
      lineWidth = width;
   }

// The getBorderInsets() method is overridden.  The Insets object
// that is returned contains the lineWidth property as its elements

   public Insets getBorderInsets(Component c)
   {
      return new Insets(lineWidth, lineWidth, lineWidth, lineWidth);
   }

   public Insets getBorderInsets(Component c, Insets insets)
   {
      insets.top = lineWidth;
      insets.bottom = lineWidth;
      insets.left = lineWidth;
      insets.right = lineWidth;
      return insets;
   }

// The isBorderOpaque() method is overridden to make the border opaque

   public boolean isBorderOpaque()
   {
      return true;
   }

// User-defined border classes must override the paintBorder() method
// to render the border as desired.

   public void paintBorder(Component c, Graphics g, int x, int y,
                                          int width, int height)

   {
      Insets i = getBorderInsets(c);

// The border is drawn by drawing four rectangles around the component.
```

```
//  The fillRect() method is defined in the java.awt.Graphics class

    g.setColor(topColor);
    g.fillRect(x, y, width, i.top);

    g.setColor(bottomColor);
    g.fillRect(x, y+height-i.bottom, width, i.bottom);

    g.setColor(leftColor);
    g.fillRect(x, y, i.left, height);

    g.setColor(rightColor);
    g.fillRect(x+width-i.right, y, i.right, height);
  }
}


//  The WinClosing class terminates the program if the window is closed

class WinClosing extends WindowAdapter {
  public void windowClosing(WindowEvent we) {
    System.exit(0);
  }
}
```

The getBorderInsets(), isBorderOpaque(), and paintBorder() methods are overridden within the FourColorBorder class. Note that the width and height passed to the paintBorder() are the width and height bounded by the component including the border. The location and extent of the component are obtained by adding or subtracting the inset values from this width and height. The WindowListener object terminates the program if the window is closed; see Section 7.3.8 on page 657 for more details.

### Output

Here is the resulting button with a four color border:

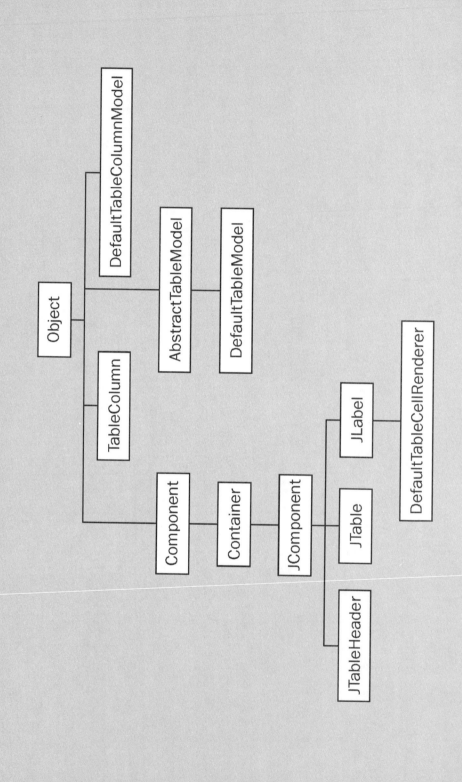

# 11

# javax.swing.table

The Java Foundation Classes provide the ability to create tables for the purpose of viewing data as a 2-D array of cells. The classes and interfaces provided in the javax.swing.table package are used to define the properties associated with a JTable object, including how the table is constructed, how the individual columns of the table are generated, and how the cells are rendered and edited.

The JTable class is a user-interface component that presents data in a two-dimensional table format. A JTable object is created, and can be customized, using the classes and interfaces contained in the javax.swing.table package. The JTable class is defined in the javax.swing package, but for purposes of continuity it will be described in this chapter.

The JTable classes are shown in the figure opposite.

This chapter covers:

# 11.1 JTable and JTableHeader Classes

The JTable class is a GUI component that represents a 2-D table of data. The JTable class is contained in the java.swing package, but for reasons of continuity it is described in this chapter. A JTable object is what is displayed on the screen, but the data contained in the table is managed by the underlying TableModel. The manner in which the table cells are rendered and edited is specified by the associated TableCellRenderer and TableCellEditor objects. The JTable class does provide some methods to control the appearance and behavior of the table; column spacing, color, resizability, etc.

The JTableHeader class represents the header component for a table. In addition to specifying the color and font used for the header, a JTableHeader object can also be used to control whether the columns that make up the table can be resized and/or moved.

The JTable and JTableHeader class hierarchy is shown in the following diagram.

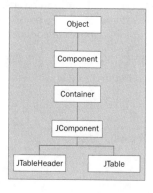

# 11.1.1 JTable Class

```
public class JTable extends JComponent implements TableModelListener, Scrollable,
   TableColumnModelListener, ListSelectionListener, CellEditorListener, Accessible
```

```
    Object
      Component
        Container
          JComponent
            JTable
```

### Interfaces

```
Accessible, CellEditorListener, EventListener, ImageObserver,
ListSelectionListener, MenuContainer, Scrollable, Serializable,
TableColumnModelListener, TableModelListener
```

A JTable object is a GUI component that represents a 2-D array of cells that contain data. The basic unit of a JTable object is a column. The appearance and behavior of the JTable object is controlled by a TableModel object and a TableColumnModel object.

The JTable class is contained in the javax.swing package but, for continuity, it is discussed in this chapter rather than Chapter 9.

Because the JTable class implements the relevant event listener interfaces, a JTable object will act as a CellEditorListener, EventListener, ListSelectionListener, TableColumnModelListener, and TableModelListener and will provide implementations of the methods declared by those interfaces.

## JTable() Constructor

| Constructor | Syntax |
|---|---|
| JTable() | public JTable() |
| | public JTable(TableModel *tm*) |
| | public JTable(TableModel *tm*, TableColumnModel *tcm*) |
| | public JTable(TableModel *tm*, TableColumnModel *tcm*, ListSelectionModel *lsm*) |
| | public JTable(int *numRows*, int *numColumns*) |
| | public JTable(Vector *data*, Vector *columnNames*) |
| | public JTable(Object[][] *data*, Object[] *columnNames*) |

Creates a JTable object. If the table, table column, and list selection models are not provided, the JTable object is created using DefaultTableModel, DefaultTableColumnModel, and DefaultListSelectionModel objects for its models. Initial data can be provided to the table using the last two versions.

11

javax.swing.table

## Methods to Access the Table, TableColumn, and ListSelection Models

| Method | Syntax |
|---|---|
| createDefaultColumnModel() | protected TableColumnModel createDefaultColumnModel() |
| createDefaultColumnsFromModel() | public void createDefaultColumnsFromModel() |
| createDefaultDataModel() | protected TableModel createDefaultDataModel() |
| createDefaultSelectionModel() | protected ListSelectionModel createDefaultSelectionModel() |
| getAutoCreateColumnsFromModel() | public boolean getAutoCreateColumnsFromModel() |
| getColumnModel() | public TableColumnModel getColumnModel() |
| getModel() | public TableModel getModel() |
| getSelectionModel() | public ListSelectionModel getSelectionModel() |
| setAutoCreateColumnsFromModel() | public void setAutoCreateColumnsFromModel (boolean *create*) |
| setColumnModel() | public void setColumnModel (TableColumnModel *tcm*) |
| setModel() | public void setModel(TableModel *tm*) |
| setSelectionModel() | public void setSelectionModel (ListSelectionModel *lsm*) |

createDefaultColumnModel() returns a reference to the default TableColumnModel. This method is sometimes overridden to specify a different default model.

createDefaultDataModel() returns a reference to the default TableModel. This method is sometimes overridden to specify a different default model.

createDefaultSelectionModel()returns a reference to the default ListSelectionModel. This method is sometimes overridden to specify a different default model.

createDefaultColumnsFromModel() creates default columns for the table using the data and methods contained in the TableModel.

getAutoCreateColumnsFromModel() returns true if the table can create default columns from its TableModel.

getColumnModel() returns the current TableColumnModel associated with the invoking JTable object. The TableColumnModel contains information about the table columns.

getModel() returns the current TableModel associated with the invoking JTable object. The TableModel contains the data displayed by the JTable.

getSelectionModel() returns the current ListSelectionModel associated with the invoking JTable object.

setAutoCreateColumnsFromModel() specifies if the table will create default columns from its TableModel.

setColumnModel() changes the TableColumnModel object associated with the invoking JTable object.

setModel() changes the TableModel associated with the invoking JTable object.

setSelectionModel() changes the ListSelectionModel associated with the invoking JTable object.

## Methods to Add or Remove Columns

| Method | Syntax |
| --- | --- |
| addColumn() | public void addColumn(TableColumn *tc*) |
| removeColumn() | public void removeColumn(TableColumn *tc*) |

addColumn() appends the specified TableColumn object to the end of the invoking JTable object.

removeColumn() removes the specified TableColumn object from the invoking JTable object.

## Cell Editing Methods

| Method | Syntax |
| --- | --- |
| editCellAt() | public boolean editCellAt<br>    (int *rowIndex*, int *columnIndex*) |
| | public boolean editCellAt<br>    (int *rowIndex*,<br>      int *columnIndex*, EventObject *e*) |
| getCellEditor() | public TableCellEditor getCellEditor() |
| | public TableCellEditor getCellEditor<br>    (int *rowIndex*, int *columnIndex*) |
| getDefaultEditor() | public TableCellEditor<br>    getDefaultEditor(Class *columnClass*) |
| getEditingColumn() | public int getEditingColumn() |

11

javax.swing.table

| Method | Syntax |
|---|---|
| getEditingRow() | public int getEditingRow() |
| getEditorComponent() | public Component getEditorComponent() |
| isCellEditable() | public boolean isCellEditable<br>    (int *rowIndex*, int *columnIndex*) |
| isEditing() | public boolean isEditing() |
| prepareEditor() | public Component<br>    prepareEditor(TableCellEditor *tce*,<br>                  int *rowIndex*,<br>                  int *columnIndex*) |
| removeEditor() | public void removeEditor() |
| setCellEditor() | public void setCellEditor<br>    (TableCellEditor *tce*) |
| setDefaultEditor() | public void setDefaultEditor<br>    (Class *columnClass*,<br>    TableCellEditor *tce*) |
| setEditingColumn() | public void setEditingColumn<br>    (int *columnIndex*) |
| setEditingRow() | public void setEditingRow(int *rowIndex*) |

editCellAt() starts editing the cell at rowIndex and columnIndex. An EventObject can be provided that will be passed to the shouldSelectCell() method. This method returns false if the cell cannot be edited.

getCellEditor() returns the TableCellEditor object associated with the invoking JTable object. If a row and column index are specified, the TableCellEditor will be for that specific cell.

getDefaultEditor() returns a default TableCellEditor object if no editor has been set.

getEditingColumn() method returns the index of the column being edited, or -1 if no column is being edited.

getEditingRow() method returns the index of the row being edited, or -1 if no row is being edited.

getEditorComponent() method returns that Component that is used for the editing session. This Component is set by the cell editor.

isCellEditable() returns true if the cell at rowIndex and columnIndex is editable.

isEditing() returns true if the table is editing a cell.

prepareEditor() initializes the editor with the current value of the cell and gets the editor ready to edit the cell.

`removeEditor()` cancels the editing session and removes the editing component from the table.

`setCellEditor()` specifies the `TableCellEditor` object that will be used for editing.

`setDefaultEditor()` species a default `TableCellEditor` object for a particular class.

`setEditingColumn()` and `setEditingRow()` methods specify the row and column to be edited.

## Cell Renderer Methods

| Method | Syntax |
|--------|--------|
| getCellRenderer() | public TableCellRenderer<br>    getCellRenderer(int *rowIndex*,<br>                  int *columnIndex*) |
| getDefaultRenderer() | public TableCellRenderer<br>    getDefaultRenderer(Class *columnClass*) |
| prepareRenderer() | public Component<br>    prepareRenderer(TableCellRenderer *tcr*,<br>                int *rowIndex*,<br>                int *columnIndex*) |
| setDefaultRenderer() | public void setDefaultRenderer<br>    (Class *columnClass*,<br>    TableCellRenderer *cr*) |

`getCellRenderer()` returns the `TableCellRenderer` object associated with the specified cell.

`getDefaultRenderer()` returns a default `TableCellRenderer` object if no renderer has been set. This method can be overridden to return a specific renderer for a specific class.

`prepareRenderer()` initializes the renderer with such information as whether the cell is selected and has focus. The method gets the renderer ready to render the cell.

`setDefaultRenderer()` species a default `TableCellRenderer` object for a particular class.

## Cell Value Methods

| Method | Syntax |
|--------|--------|
| getValueAt() | public Object getValueAt(int *rowIndex*,<br>                      int *columnIndex*) |
| setValueAt() | public void setValueAt(Object *value*,<br>                int *rowIndex*,<br>                int *columnIndex*) |

getValueAt() returns the value of the cell located at rowIndex, columnIndex (according to the view) as an Object.

setValueAt() is used to change the value of the cell located at rowIndex, columnIndex.

## Color Methods

| Method | Syntax |
|---|---|
| getGridColor() | public Color getGridColor() |
| getSelectionBackground() | public Color getSelectionBackground() |
| getSelectionForeground() | public Color getSelectionForeground() |
| setGridColor() | public void setGridColor(Color c) |
| setSelectionBackground() | public void setSelectionBackground (Color c) |
| setSelectionForeground() | public void setSelectionForeground (Color c) |

getGridColor() returns the grid line color of the invoking JTable object. The default color is Color.gray.

getSelectionBackground() returns the background color for selected cells.

getSelectionForeground() returns the foreground color for selected cells.

setGridColor() changes the grid line color of the invoking JTable object.

setSelectionBackground() specifies the background color for selected cells.

setSelectionForeground() specifies the foreground color for selected cells.

## Column Selection Methods

| Method | Syntax |
|---|---|
| addColumnSelectionInterval() | public void addColumnSelectionInterval (int startIndex, int endIndex) |
| getColumnSelectionAllowed() | public boolean getColumnSelectionAllowed() |
| getSelectedColumn() | public int getSelectedColumn() |
| getSelectedColumns() | public int[] getSelectedColumns() |
| getSelectedColumnCount() | public int getSelectedColumnCount() |
| isColumnSelected() | public boolean isColumnSelected (int columnIndex) |

| Method | Syntax |
|--------|--------|
| removeColumnSelectionInterval() | public void<br>    removeColumnSelectionInterval<br>    (int *startIndex*, int *endIndex*) |
| setColumnSelectionAllowed() | public void setColumnSelectionAllowed<br>    (boolean *allowed*) |
| setColumnSelectionInterval() | public void<br>    setColumnSelectionInterval<br>    (int *startIndex*, int *endIndex*) |

addColumnSelectionInterval() adds the columns from startIndex to endIndex to the currently selected group of columns.

getColumnSelectionAllowed() returns true if the columns of the invoking JTable object can be selected. The default is false.

getSelectedColumn() returns the index of the first selected column, or -1 if no column is selected.

getSelectedColumns() returns an int array containing the indices of the selected columns.

getSelectedColumnCount() returns the number of selected columns.

isColumnSelected() returns true if the column at position columnIndex is selected.

removeColumnSelectionInterval() de-selects the columns from startIndex to endIndex.

setColumnSelectionAllowed() is used to specify whether the columns can be selected.

setColumnSelectionInterval() selects the columns from startIndex to endIndex.

## Event Listener Support Methods

| Method | Syntax |
|--------|--------|
| columnAdded() | public void<br>columnAdded(TableColumnModelEvent *tcme*) |
| columnMarginChanged() | public void<br>columnMarginChanged(ChangeEvent *ce*) |
| columnMoved() | public void<br>columnMoved(TableColumnModelEvent *tcme*) |

11

javax.swing.table

| Method | Syntax |
|---|---|
| columnRemoved() | public void columnRemoved(TableColumnModelEvent *tcme*) |
| columnSelectionChanged() | public void columnSelectionChanged (ListSelectionEvent *lse*) |
| editingCanceled() | public void editingCanceled (ChangeEvent *ce*) |
| editingStopped() | public void editingStopped(ChangeEvent *ce*) |
| tableChanged() | public void tableChanged (TableModelEvent *tme*) |
| valueChanged() | public void valueChanged(ListSelectionEvent *lse*) |

These methods are defined in the TableModelListener, TableColumnModelListener, ListSelectionListener, and CellEditorListener interfaces. They are generally not called by application code but are used internally by the JTable class. They are called when their corresponding event is generated by the JTable object.

## General Selection Methods

| Method | Syntax |
|---|---|
| changeSelection() | public void changeSelection(int *rowIndex*, int *columnIndex*, boolean *toggle*, boolean *append*) |
| clearSelection() | public void clearSelection() |
| getCellSelectionEnabled() | public boolean getCellSelectionEnabled() |
| isCellSelected() | public boolean isCellSelected( int *rowIndex*, int *columnIndex*) |
| selectAll() | public void selectAll() |
| setCellSelectionEnabled() | public void setCellSelectionEnabled(boolean *enabled*) |
| setSelectionMode() | public void setSelectionMode(int *mode*) |

changeSelection() changes the selected state of the cell at rowIndex, columnIndex. The change made depends on the values of toggle and append. See the table opposite:

| toggle | append | action |
|--------|--------|--------|
| false | false | Current selections are cleared. Cell at `rowIndex`, `columnIndex` is selected. |
| false | true | Cell at `rowIndex`, `columnIndex` is added to the current selection. |
| true | false | The selected state of the cell at `rowIndex`, `columnIndex` is toggled on or off. |
| true | true | Selection is unchanged. Anchor index is moved to the cell at `rowIndex`, `columnIndex`. |

`clearSelection()` de-selects all selected columns and rows.

`getCellSelectionEnabled()` returns `true` if both rows and columns can be selected.

`isCellSelected()` returns `true` if the cell located at `rowIndex`, `columnIndex` is selected.

`selectAll()` selects all of the rows and columns.

`setCellSelectionEnabled()` specifies whether a rectangular region of cells can be selected.

`setSelectionMode()` method specifies the selection mode of the invoking `Jtable` object. Valid argument values are:

- ❑ `ListSelectionModel.MULTIPLE_INTERVAL_SELECTION`
- ❑ `ListSelectionModel.SINGLE_INTERVAL_SELECTION`
- ❑ `ListSelectionModel.SINGLE_SELECTION`

## Grid Line Methods

| Method | Syntax |
|--------|--------|
| getShowHorizontalLines() | `public boolean getShowHorizontalLines()` |
| getShowVerticalLines() | `public boolean getShowVerticalLines()` |
| setShowGrid() | `public void setShowGrid(boolean showGrid)` |
| setShowHorizontalLines() | `public void setShowHorizontalLines (boolean showHLines)` |
| setShowVerticalLines() | `public void setShowVerticalLines (boolean showVLines)` |

`getShowHorizontalLines()` returns `true` if horizontal lines will be drawn between cells.

getShowVerticalLines() returns true if vertical lines will be drawn between cells.

setShowGrid() specifies whether the grid lines will be drawn.

setShowHorizontalLines() and setShowVerticalLines() specify whether horizontal or vertical lines will be drawn between cells.

## Row Selection Methods

| Method | Syntax |
|---|---|
| addRowSelectionInterval() | public void addRowSelectionInterval (int startIndex, int endIndex) |
| getRowSelectionAllowed() | public boolean getRowSelectionAllowed() |
| getSelectedRow() | public int getSelectedRow() |
| getSelectedRows() | public int[] getSelectedRows() |
| getSelectedRowCount() | public int getSelectedRowCount() |
| isRowSelected() | public boolean isRowSelected (int rowIndex) |
| removeRowSelectionInterval() | public void removeRowSelectionInterval (int startIndex, int endIndex) |
| setRowSelectionAllowed() | public void setRowSelectionAllowed(boolean allowed) |
| setRowSelectionInterval() | public void setRowSelectionInterval (int startIndex, int endIndex) |

addRowSelectionInterval() adds the rows from startIndex to endIndex to the group of currently selected rows.

getRowSelectionAllowed() returns true if the rows of the invoking JTable object can be selected.

getSelectedRow() returns the index of the first selected row, or -1 if no row is selected.

getSelectedRows() returns an int array containing the indices of the selected rows.

getSelectedRowCount() returns the number of selected rows.

isRowSelected() returns true if the row at position rowIndex is selected.

removeRowSelectionInterval() de-selects the rows from startIndex to endIndex.

setRowSelectionAllowed() is used to specify whether the rows can be selected.

setRowSelectionInterval() selects the rows from startIndex to endIndex.

# Methods to Return or Change Column Properties

| Method | Syntax |
|---|---|
| columnAtPoint() | public int columnAtPoint(Point *p*) |
| getColumn() | public TableColumn getColumn<br>    (Object *columnIdentifier*) |
| getColumnClass() | public Class getColumnClass<br>    (int *columnIndex*) |
| getColumnCount() | public int getColumnCount() |
| getColumnName() | public String getColumnName<br>    (int *columnIndex*) |
| moveColumn() | public void moveColumn(int *oldIndex*,<br>                          int *newIndex*) |

columnAtPoint() returns the index of the column that lies over Point p, or -1 if there is no column over Point p.

getColumn() returns a TableColumn object representing the column corresponding to the specified column identifier.

getColumnClass() returns a Class object representing the data type of the members of column columnIndex.

getColumnCount() returns the number of columns in the table.

getColumnName() returns the name of the column at view index columnIndex. The first viewable column is at index 0.

moveColumn() moves the column at position oldIndex to position newIndex.

# Methods to Return or Change Row Properties

| Method | Syntax |
|---|---|
| getRowCount() | public int getRowCount() |
| getRowHeight() | public int getRowHeight() |
| getRowMargin() | public int getRowMargin() |
| rowAtPoint() | public int rowAtPoint(Point *p*) |
| setRowHeight() | public void setRowHeight(int *height*) |
| | public void setRowHeight(int *rowIndex*,<br>                            int *height*) |
| setRowMargin() | public void setRowMargin(int *margin*) |

getRowCount() returns the number of rows in the table.

getRowHeight() returns the height of a table row in pixels.

getRowMargin() returns the amount of empty space between rows.

11

javax.swing.table

rowAtPoint() returns the index of the row that is positioned over Point p, or -1 if there is no row over Point p.

setRowHeight() changes the row height. This can be done globally or for a specified row.

setRowMargin() changes the space between rows.

## Sizing and Spacing Methods

| Method | Syntax |
|---|---|
| getAutoResizeMode() | public int getAutoResizeMode() |
| getIntercellSpacing() | public Dimension getIntercellSpacing() |
| resizeAndRepaint() | protected void resizeAndRepaint() |
| setAutoResizeMode() | public void setAutoResizeMode (int *resizeMode*) |
| setIntercellSpacing() | public void setIntercellSpacing (Dimension *newSpacing*) |
| sizeColumnsToFit() | public void sizeColumnsToFit (int *resizingColumnIndex*) |

getAutoResizeMode() returns the auto re-size mode of the invoking JTable object.

getIntercellSpacing() returns a Dimension object containing the horizontal and vertical spacing between cells.

resizeAndRepaint() revalidates and repaints the table.

setAutoResizeMode() is used to specify the re-size mode. The re-size mode will be one of the following constants:

- ❏ JTable.AUTO_RESIZE_ALL_COLUMNS
- ❏ JTable.AUTO_RESIZE_LAST_COLUMN
- ❏ JTable.AUTO_RESIZE_NEXT_COLUMN
- ❏ JTable.AUTO_RESIZE_OFF
- ❏ JTable.AUTO_RESIZE_SUBSEQUENT_COLUMNS

sizeColumnsToFit() resizes one or more columns to fit a resized window or JTable object. See the Sun Java documentation for the JTable class for details on the resizing algorithm used.

setIntercellSpacing() is used to set the horizontal and vertical spacing between cells.

## Table Header Methods

| Method | Syntax |
|---|---|
| getTableHeader() | public JTableHeader getTableHeader() |
| createDefaultTableHeader() | protected JTableHeader createDefaultTableHeader() |
| setTableHeader() | public void setTableHeader (JTableHeader *jth*) |

getTableHeader() returns the JTableHeader object associated with the invoking JTable object.

createDefaultTableHeader() returns a reference to the default TableHeader object. This may can be overridden to implement a different default table header.

setTableHeader() is used to associate a JTableHeader object with the invoking JTable object.

## UI Delegate Methods

| Method | Syntax |
|---|---|
| getUI() | public TableUI getUI() |
| getUIClassID() | public String getUIClassID() |
| setUI() | public void setUI(TableUI *ui*) |
| updateUI() | public void updateUI() |

getUI() returns the TableUI object associated with the invoking JTable object.

getUIClassID() returns a String "TableUI", which is the suffix used to construct the name of the look-and-feel class used to render a JTable object.

setUI() is used to change the TableUI object associated the invoking JTable object.

updateUI() is used to refresh the appearance of the table if the look-and-feel has been changed.

## Example: Using JTable

In this example, a JTable object is created that contains three columns, for a name, an age, and a birthday, and allows you to add rows to the table. The columns can be re-ordered by dragging the mouse on the header tiles and can be re-sized by dragging the mouse between the header tiles.

```
import javax.swing.*;
import javax.swing.table.*;
import java.awt.*;
import java.awt.event.*;
```

```
public class TestJTable extends JFrame implements ActionListener {
  JTable jt;
  DefaultTableModel dtm;
  JLabel nameLabel, ageLabel, birthdayLabel;
  JTextField nameTF, ageTF, birthdayTF;
  JButton addButton;

  public TestJTable() {
    Object[][] data = {
      {
        "Jackson", new Integer(4), "March 21"
      }, {
        "Zachary", new Integer(2), "May 12"
      }
    };
    String[] headers = {
      "Name", "Age", "Birthday"
    };

    // A DefaultTableModel object is created and initialized with some
    // data and headers.

    dtm = new DefaultTableModel(2, 3);
    dtm.setDataVector(data, headers);

    // A JTable object is created using the DefaultTableModel object
    // as its data model.

    jt = new JTable(dtm);
    jt.setGridColor(Color.red);
    jt.setRowSelectionAllowed(true);
    jt.setRowSelectionInterval(1, 1);

    // Some GUI components are added that are used to add rows to
    // the JTable.

    nameLabel = new JLabel("Name: ");
    nameLabel.setForeground(Color.black);
    ageLabel = new JLabel("  Age: ");
    ageLabel.setForeground(Color.black);
    birthdayLabel = new JLabel("  Birthday: ");
    birthdayLabel.setForeground(Color.black);

    nameTF = new JTextField(10);
    ageTF = new JTextField(3);
    birthdayTF = new JTextField(12);

    addButton = new JButton("add");
    addButton.addActionListener(this);

    JPanel p = new JPanel();
```

```
      p.add(nameLabel);
      p.add(nameTF);
      p.add(ageLabel);
      p.add(ageTF);
      p.add(birthdayLabel);
      p.add(birthdayTF);
      p.add(addButton);

      // The JTable is placed inside a JScrollPane before it is placed
      // within the JFrame

      JPanel pc = new JPanel();
      pc.add(new JScrollPane(jt, JScrollPane.VERTICAL_SCROLLBAR_ALWAYS,
                             JScrollPane.HORIZONTAL_SCROLLBAR_AS_NEEDED));

      getContentPane().add(pc, BorderLayout.CENTER);
      getContentPane().add(p, BorderLayout.SOUTH);

      addWindowListener(new WinClosing());
      setBounds(100, 100, 700, 500);
      setVisible(true);
  }

  // whenever the "add" JButton is pressed, the actionPerformed()
  // method is called and a new row is added to the JTable

  public void actionPerformed(ActionEvent ae) {
    String name = nameTF.getText();
    Integer age = new Integer(ageTF.getText());
    String birthday = birthdayTF.getText();

    Object[] newData = {
      name, age, birthday
    };
    dtm.addRow(newData);
  }

  public static void main(String[] args) {
    TestJTable tjt = new TestJTable();
  }
}

// The WinClosing class terminates the program when the window is closed

class WinClosing extends WindowAdapter {
  public void windowClosing(WindowEvent we) {
    System.exit(0);
  }
}
```

For this simple example, a `DefaultTableModel` object was used for the `TableModel`. The grid lines of the table are set to be red, and the first row is initially selected. New data is added to the table by typing input into the three `JTextField` objects at the bottom of the window. When the add button is pressed, a new row is added to the table containing the `JTextField` data.

### Output

Here's the result:

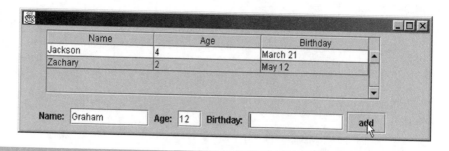

## 11.1.2 JTableHeader Class

```
public class JTableHeader extends JComponent
    implements TableColumnModelListener, Accessible
```

```
Object
  Component
    Container
      JComponent
        JTableHeader
```

### Interfaces

Accessible, EventListener, ImageObserver, MenuContainer, Serializable, TableColumnModelListener

A `JTableHeader` object represents the header for a table, and controls the font and color used to display the header. It can also be used to change column width and ordering. The `JTableHeader` class implements the `TableColumnModelListener` interface and therefore provides implementations of the methods declared in that interface.

## JTableHeader() Constructor

| Constructor | Syntax |
|---|---|
| JTableHeader() | public JTableHeader() |
| | public JTableHeader(TableColumnModel *tcm*) |

Creates a JTableHeader object. If a TableColumnModel object is not provided, a DefaultTableColumnModel object is used.

## columnAtPoint() Method

| Method | Syntax |
|---|---|
| columnAtPoint() | public int columnAtPoint(Point *p*) |

columnAtPoint() returns the index of the column that contains Point p, or -1 if there is no such column.

## Column Model and Renderer Methods

| Method | Syntax |
|---|---|
| createDefaultColumnModel() | protected TableColumnModel createDefaultColumnModel() |
| getColumnModel() | public TableColumnModel getColumnModel() |
| getDefaultRenderer() | public TableCellRenderer getDefaultRenderer() |
| setColumnModel() | public void setColumnModel(TableColumnModel *tcm*) |
| setDefaultRenderer() | public void setDefaultRenderer(TableCellRenderer *tcr*) |

createDefaultColumnModel() returns a reference to a DefaultTableColumnModel object. This method can be overridden to return a different column model.

getColumnModel() returns a TableColumnModel object that contains information about the invoking JTableHeader object.

getDefaultRenderer() returns a reference to the default cell renderer .

setColumnModel() changes the column model for the table associated with the invoking JTableHeader object.

setDefaultRenderer() changes the default cell renderer associated with the invoking JTableHeader object.

11

javax.swing.table

## Methods to Change Header Properties

| Method | Syntax |
|---|---|
| setDraggedColumn() | public void setDraggedColumn (TableColumn *tc*) |
| setDraggedDistance() | public void setDraggedDistance (int *distance*) |
| setReorderingAllowed() | public void setReorderingAllowed (boolean *reorderingAllowed*) |
| setResizingAllowed() | public void setResizingAllowed (boolean *resizingAllowed*) |
| setResizingColumn() | public void setResizingColumn (TableColumn *tc*) |
| setTable() | public void setTable(JTable *table*) |

setDraggedColumn() specifies which column will be the dragged column. The dragged column is a column that has been moved from its previous position.

setDraggedDistance() specifies the distance the dragged column has been moved, in terms of its index, from its original position.

setReorderingAllowed() specifies if the user can re-arrange columns by dragging the header.

setResizingAllowed() determines if the user can re-size headers by dragging between headers.

setResizingColumn() sets the column that can be re-sized.

setTable() associates a JTable object with the invoking JTableHeader object.

## Methods to Get Header Properties

| Method | Syntax |
|---|---|
| getDraggedColumn() | public TableColumn getDraggedColumn() |
| getDraggedDistance() | public int getDraggedDistance() |
| getHeaderRect() | public Rectangle getHeaderRect (int *columnIndex*) |
| getReorderingAllowed() | public boolean getReorderingAllowed() |
| getResizingAllowed() | public boolean getResizingAllowed() |
| getResizingColumn() | public TableColumn getResizingColumn() |
| getTable() | public JTable getTable() |
| getToolTipText() | public String getToolTipText (MouseEvent *me*) |

`getDraggedColumn()` and `getDraggedDistance()` are used when a column is being dragged and return a reference to the `TableColumn` object or the distance the column has been dragged.

`getHeaderRect()` returns a `Rectangle` object representing the header tile for the column at position `columnIndex`.

`getReorderingAllowed()` returns `true` if the user can re-arrange columns by dragging the header.

`getResizingAllowed()` return `true` if the user can re-size headers by dragging between headers.

`getResizingColumn()` returns a reference to a column that is being re-sized.

`getTable()` returns a reference to the `JTable` object that is associated with the invoking `JTableHeader` object.

`getToolTipText()` returns the text displayed by the tooltip associated with the invoking `JTableHeader` object. The `MouseEvent` is the event that triggered the tooltip display.

## resizeAndRepaint() Method

| Method | Syntax |
|---|---|
| `resizeAndRepaint()` | `public void resizeAndRepaint()` |

`resizeAndRepaint()` causes the table and header to be re-displayed by invoking the `revalidate()` and `repaint()` methods.

## TableColumnModelListener Interface Methods

| Method | Syntax |
|---|---|
| `columnAdded()` | `public void columnAdded` `(TableColumnModelEvent tcme)` |
| `columnMarginChanged()` | `public void columnMarginChanged` `(ChangeEvent ce)` |
| `columnMoved()` | `public void columnMoved` `(TableColumnModelEvent tcme)` |
| `columnRemoved()` | `public voidcolumnRemoved` `(TableColumnModelEvent tcme)` |
| `columnSelectionChanged()` | `public void columnSelectionChanged` `(ListSelectionEvent lse)` |

The `JTableHeader` class implements the `TableColumnModelListener` interface and therefore provides implementations of the methods declared in that interface. These methods are called when various types of `TableColumnEvent` objects are fired. Application code will not normally call these methods. They are generally used internally by the `JTableHeader` object.

11

javax.swing.table

## UI Delegate Methods

| Method | Syntax |
|---|---|
| getUI() | public TableHeaderUI getUI() |
| getUIClassID() | public String getUIClassID() |
| setUI() | public void setUI(TableHeaderUI *ui*) |
| updateUI() | public void updateUI() |

getUI() returns the TableHeaderUI object used to render the invoking JTableHeader object.

getUIClassID() returns a String "TableHeaderUI", which is the suffix used to construct the name of the look-and-feel class used to render a JTable object.

setUI() is used to change the TableHeaderUI object used to render the invoking JTableHeader object.

updateUI() is used to refresh the appearance of the header if the look-and-feel has been changed.

# 11.2 Column and ColumnModel Classes

In Java, a **column** is the basic building block of a table. The cell values down the column will generally be of the same type, for example the column may represent a list of names, which would be of type String. However, every column in a table may be of a different type. The Column and ColumnModel classes are used to describe the structure and behavior of table columns, while the data displayed in a given table is contained in a TableModel object The Column and ColumnModel class hierarchy is shown in the diagram below.

A TableColumn object is used to store all of the attributes of a given table. A TableColumnModel object, one that implements the TableColumnModel interface, is used to manage column attributes such margins, selection properties, event listeners, and column addition and removal. The DefaultTableColumnModel class is the default implementation of the TableColumnModel interface.

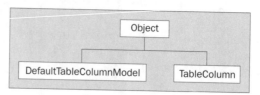

# 11.2.1 DefaultTableColumnModel Class

public class DefaultTableColumnModel extends Object implements TableColumnModel, PropertyChangeListener, ListSelectionListener, Serializable

```
Object
   DefaultTableColumnModel
```

### Interfaces

```
EventListener, ListSelectionListener, PropertyChangeListener, Serializable,
TableColumnModel
```

The DefaultTableColumnModel class is the default implementation of the TableColumnModel interface. User-defined table column model classes are often implemented as sub-classes of the DefaultTableColumnModel class.

The DefaultTableColumnModel class implements the ListSelectionChangeListener and PropertyChangeListener interfaces and therefore provides implementations of the methods declared in those interfaces.

## DefaultTableColumnModel() Constructor

| Constructor | Syntax |
|---|---|
| DefaultTableColumnModel() | public DefaultTableColumnModel() |

Creates a DefaultTableColumnModel object.

## Methods to Add, Move, or Remove Columns

| Method | Syntax |
|---|---|
| addColumn() | public void addColumn(TableColumn *column*) |
| moveColumn() | public void moveColumn(int *oldIndex*, int *newIndex*) |
| removeColumn() | public void removeColumn (TableColumn *column*) |

addColumn() appends TableColumn column to the end of the associated JTable object's table column array.

moveColumn() moves the column at position oldIndex to position newIndex. Any TableColumn object that was at position newIndex is shifted to the right.

removeColumn() deletes the TableColumn column from the associated JTable object's table column array.

## Column Count and Index Methods

| Method | Syntax |
|---|---|
| getColumnCount() | public int getColumnCount() |
| getColumnIndex() | public int getColumnIndex (Object *identifier*) |
| getColumnIndexAtX() | public int getColumnIndexAtX (int *xLocation*) |

getColumnCount() returns the number of columns associated with the TableColumnModel.

getColumnIndex() returns the index of the first column with the designated identifier.

getColumnIndexAtX() returns the index of the column at the specified x location, or -1 if there is no column at that location.

## ColumnModelListener Methods

| Method | Syntax |
|---|---|
| addColumnModelListener() | public void addColumnModelListener TableColumnModelListener *tcml*) |
| removeColumnModelListener() | public void removeColumnModelListener (TableColumnModelListener *tcml*) |

addColumnModelListener() registers the invoking DefaultTableColumnModel object with a ColumnModelListener object. The ColumnModelListener is notified if the DefaultTableColumnModel object generates a TableColumnModelEvent. A TableColumnModelEvent is generated if a column is added, moved, removed, or has its margin changed.

removeColumnModelListener() removes an ColumnModelListener object from the DefaultTableColumnModel object. TableColumnModelEvent objects generated by the DefaultTableColumnModel object will no longer be received by the ColumnModelListener.

## getListeners() Method

| Method | Syntax |
|---|---|
| getListeners() | public EventListener[] getListeners (Class *listenerClass*) |

getListeners() returns any listeners of the specified type registered to the invoking DefaultTableColumnModel object as an EventListener array.

## Methods Used to Fire Events

| Method | Syntax |
|---|---|
| fireColumnAdded() | protected void fireColumnAdded (TableColumnModelEvent *tcme*) |
| fireColumnMarginChanged() | protected void fireColumnMarginChanged() |
| fireColumnMoved() | protected void fireColumnMoved (TableColumnModelEvent *tcme*) |

| Method | Syntax |
|--------|--------|
| fireColumnRemoved() | protected void fireColumnRemoved (TableColumnModelEvent *tcme*) |
| fireColumnSelectionChanged() | protected void fireColumnSelectionChanged (ListSelectionEvent *lse*) |

These methods are used to fire events when columns are added, moved, removed or have their margins or selections changed. They are most often used in TableColumnModel classes that are sub-classes of the DefaultTableColumnModel class.

## Margin and Width Methods

| Method | Syntax |
|--------|--------|
| getColumnMargin() | public int getColumnMargin() |
| getTotalColumnWidth() | public int getTotalColumnWidth() |
| setColumnMargin() | public void setColumnMargin(int margin) |

getColumnMargin() returns the space in pixels that is placed between columns.

getTotalColumnWidth() returns the combined width of all of the columns.

setColumnMargin() is used to change the margin size. This method will cause a TableColumnModelEvent object to be generated.

## propertyChange() Method

| Method | Syntax |
|--------|--------|
| propertyChange() | public propertyChange(PropertyChangeListener *pcl*) |

propertyChange() is defined in the PropertyChangeListener interface, and is called whenever the value of a bound property changes.

## Methods to Return One or All Columns

| Method | Syntax |
|--------|--------|
| getColumn() | public TableColumn getColumn(int *index*) |
| getColumns() | public Enumeration getColumns() |

getColumn() returns a reference to the TableColumn object at position index.

getColumns() returns an Enumeration object containing all of the columns contained by the invoking DefaultTableColumnModel object.

11

javax.swing.table

## Column Selection Methods

| Method | Syntax |
|---|---|
| getColumnSelectionAllowed() | public boolean getColumnSelectionAllowed() |
| getSelectedColumnCount() | public int getSelectedColumnCount() |
| getSelectedColumns() | public int[] getSelectedColumns() |
| setColumnSelectionAllowed() | public void setColumnSelectionAllowed (boolean *allowed*) |

getColumnSelectionAllowed() returns true if the columns can be selected.

getSelectedColumnCount() returns the number of selected columns.

getSelectedColumns() returns an int array containing the indices of the selected columns.

setColumnSelectionAllowed() is used to specify whether columns can be selected.

## Selection Model Methods

| Method | Syntax |
|---|---|
| createSelectionModel() | protected ListSelectionModel createSelectionModel() |
| getSelectionModel() | public ListSelectionModel getSelectionModel() |
| setSelectionModel() | public void setSelectionModel(ListSelectionModel *model*) |

createSelectionModel() returns a default ListSelectionModel object to manage the selection methodolgy of the DefaultTableColumnModel object. See Section 9 for a discussion of the ListSelectionModel interface.

getSelectionModel() returns a reference to the current selection model.

setSelectionModel() method is used to change the selection model of the invoking DefaultTableColumnModel object.

## valueChanged() Method

| Method | Syntax |
|---|---|
| valueChanged() | public void valueChanged(ListSelectionEvent *lse*) |

valueChanged() is defined in the ListSelectionListener interface, and is called when the column selection changes.

## Example: Using DefaultTableColumnModel

This example creates a simple table using a DefaultTableColumnModel object.

```java
import javax.swing.*;
import javax.swing.table.*;
import java.awt.*;
import java.awt.event.*;
import java.util.*;

public class TestColumnModel extends JFrame {
    JTable jt;
    DefaultTableColumnModel dtcm;
    TableColumn column1, column2, column3;
    DefaultTableModel dtm;
    Vector v1, v2;

    public TestColumnModel() {

        // Three TableColumn objects are created.  The preferred
        // width of the first and second TableColumns are changed

        column1 = new TableColumn(0);
        column1.setHeaderValue("First Name");
        column1.setPreferredWidth(50);

        column2 = new TableColumn(1);
        column2.setHeaderValue("Last Name");
        column2.setPreferredWidth(100);

        column3 = new TableColumn(2);
        column3.setHeaderValue("Member Since");

        // A DefaultTableColumnModel object is created and the three
        // TableColumn Objects are added to it.

        dtcm = new DefaultTableColumnModel();
        dtcm.addColumn(column1);
        dtcm.addColumn(column2);
        dtcm.addColumn(column3);

        // Create two Vector objects and load them with the data
        // to be placed on each row of the table

        v1 = new Vector();
        v1.addElement("Lisa");
        v1.addElement("Reid");
        v1.addElement(new Integer(1990));
```

11

javax.swing.table

```
      v2 = new Vector();
      v2.addElement("Cheryl");
      v2.addElement("Spada");
      v2.addElement(new Integer(1979));

      // A DefaultTableModel object is created initally with 0 rows and
      // 3 columns.  Two rows are added containing the data in the
      // Vector objects.

      dtm = new DefaultTableModel(0, 3);
      dtm.addRow(v1);
      dtm.addRow(v2);

      // A JTable object is created using the DefaultTableModel and
      // DefaultTableColumnModel objects.

      jt = new JTable(dtm, dtcm);

      // The JTable is placed inside a JScrollPane and the JScrollPane
      // is placed on the JFrame.  The JScrollPane is valuable if the
      // size of the JTable is increased beyond the size of its display
      // window.

      JScrollPane jsp = new JScrollPane(jt);
      getContentPane().add(jsp, BorderLayout.CENTER);

      addWindowListener(new WinClosing());
      setBounds(100, 100, 400, 200);
      setVisible(true);
   }

   public static void main(String[] args) {
      TestColumnModel tcm = new TestColumnModel();
   }
}

// The WinClosing class terminates the program when the window is closed

class WinClosing extends WindowAdapter {
   public void windowClosing(WindowEvent we) {
      System.exit(0);
   }
}
```

Three TableColumn objects are created with different attributes and added to the DefaultTableColumnModel object. The preferred width of the first TableColumn is set to be half that of the second.

A JTable object is generated using the DefaultTableColumnModel object and a DefaultTableModel object that contains a first name, last name, and date on each row. The JTable is placed inside a JScrollPane object before it is placed on the JFrame. This is a good idea for tables, such as a database of names, that might grow beyond the size of the window.

### Output

Here's the result:

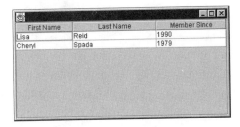

# 11.2.2 TableColumn Class

```
public class TableColumn extends Object implements Serializable
```

```
Object
    TableColumn
```

### Interfaces

```
Serializable
```

A TableColumn object is used to contain all attributes of a column in a table including the column width, the cell editor and renderer, whether the column is resizable, and header information.

A TableColumn object is used to store information about the structure of a table column, but it doesn't contain the actual data: the data is stored in a TableModel object.

## TableColumn() Constructor

| Constructor | Syntax |
|---|---|
| TableColumn() | public TableColumn() |
| | public TableColumn(int modelIndex) |
| | public TableColumn(int modelIndex, int columnWidth) |
| | public TableColumn(int modelIndex, int columnWidth, TableCellRenderer tcr, TableCellEditor tce) |

Creates a TableColumn object. If they are not provided, the default cell renderer and cell editor is used. The modelIndex is the index of the column in the model which will supply the data for this column in the table. The default model index is 0; if the column is moved to a different location in the table, the model index stays the same. The default column width is 75 pixels.

11

javax.swing.table

## Editing and Rendering Methods

| Method | Syntax |
|---|---|
| getCellEditor() | public TableCellEditor getCellEditor() |
| getCellRenderer() | public TableCellRenderer getCellRenderer() |
| getHeaderRenderer() | public TableCellRenderer getHeaderRenderer() |
| setCellRenderer() | public void setCellRenderer (TableCellRenderer *tcr*) |
| setCellEditor() | public void setCellEditor (TableCellEditor *tce*) |
| setHeaderRenderer() | public void setHeaderRenderer (TableCellRenderer *tcr*) |

getCellEditor() and setCellEditor() are used to return or change the TableCellEditor object associated with the invoking TableColumn object. The TableCellEditor is a sub-class of a GUI component that implements the TableCellEditor interface and is used to edit the cell values.

getCellRenderer() and setCellRenderer() are used to return or change the TableCellRenderer object associated with the invoking TableColumn object. The TableCellRenderer is a sub-class of a GUI component that implements the TableCellRenderer interface and is used to render the cells.

getHeaderCellRenderer() and setHeaderCellRenderer() are used to return or change the TableCellRenderer object for the headers associated with the invoking TableColumn object.

## Header Value Methods

| Method | Syntax |
|---|---|
| getHeaderValue() | public Object getHeaderValue() |
| setHeaderValue() | public void setHeaderValue(Object *value*) |

The header value is accessed by the header renderer for drawing the appropriate header. The default renderer displays a String representation of the Object specified as the header value.

getHeaderValue() returns the Object that serves as the header value for the invoking TableColumn object.

setHeaderValue() is used to change the header value.

## IdentifierMethods

| Method | Syntax |
|---|---|
| getIdentifier() | public Object getIdentifier() |
| setIdentifier() | public void setIdentifier(Object *value*) |

The identifier is used to uniquely identify the column.

getIdentifier() returns the Object that serves as the identifier for the invoking TableColumn object.

setIdentifier() is used to change the identifier.

## Model Index Methods

| Method | Syntax |
|---|---|
| getModelIndex() | public int getModelIndex() |
| setModelIndex() | public void setModelIndex(int *modelIndex*) |

The model index is used internally by the editor and renderer to associate the proper data values with a given column if the column is moved about in the table.

getModelIndex() returns the model index of the invoking TableColumn object.

setModelIndex() is used to change the model index.

## PropertyChangeListener Methods

| Method | Syntax |
|---|---|
| addPropertyChangeListener() | public void addPropertyChangeListener (PropertyChangeListener *pcl*) |
| removePropertyChangeListener() | public void removePropertyChangeListener (PropertyChangeListener *pcl*) |

addPropertyChangeListener() registers the invoking TableColumn object with a PropertyChangeListener object. The PropertyChangeListener is notified if the TableColumn object generates a PropertyChangeEvent. A PropertyChangeEvent is generated if the value of a TableColumn object property changes.

removePropertyChangeListener() removes a PropertyChangeListener object from the invoking TableColumn object. PropertyChangeEvent objects generated by the component will no longer be received by the PropertyChangeListener.

11

javax.swing.table

**1003**

## Resizing Methods

| Method | Syntax |
|--------|--------|
| getResizable() | public boolean getResizable() |
| setResizable() | public void setResizable<br>(boolean *resizable*) |
| sizeWidthToFit() | public void sizeWidthToFit() |

getResizable() returns true if the invoking TableColumn object can be resized. (This is the default.)

setResizable() is used to specify whether the TableColumn can be resized. Note that if the window is resized, the column wil be resized regardless of the value of the resizable property.

sizeWidthToFit() resizes the invoking TableColumn object to fit the width of its header cell. This method works under Java 2 version 1.2 but has problems under the beta release of Java 2 version 1.3.

## Column Width Methods

| Method | Syntax |
|--------|--------|
| getMaxWidth() | public int getMaxWidth() |
| getMinWidth() | public int getMinWidth() |
| getPreferredWidth() | public int getPreferredWidth() |
| getWidth() | public int getWidth() |
| setMinWidth() | public void setMinWidth(int *minWidth*) |
| setMaxWidth() | public void setMaxWidth(int *maxWidth*) |
| setPreferredWidth() | public void setPreferredWidth<br>(int *preferredWidth*) |
| setWidth() | public void setWidth(int *width*) |

getMaxWidth()returns the maximum width of the invoking TableColumn object. The width of a column cannot be made larger than this value.

getMinWidth() returns the minimum width of the invoking TableColumn object. The width of a column cannot be made smaller than this value.

getPreferredWidth() returns the preferred width.

getWidth() returns the current width of the invoking TableColumn object.

setMaxWidth() sets the maximum allowable width of the invoking TableColumn object.

setMinWidth() sets the minimum allowable width of the invoking TableColumn object.

setWidth() is used to change the column width. This method is not recommended since the layout manager may override the value set by this method if the table changes size of if the preferred size of the column changes. The use of setPreferredWidth() to suggest a column width is recommended.

setPreferredWidth() is used to change the preferred width. setPreferredWidth() is a better method to use than setWidth() to set the column width.

---

**Example: Using TableColumn**

See the *Using DefaultTableColumnModel* example on page 999, where three TableColumn objects with different attributes are added to a DefaultTableColumnModel object.

---

# 11.2.3 TableColumnModel Interface

```
public interface TableColumnModel
```

TableColumnModel interface defines methods for controlling the column margins, total column width, and for managing the selection properties of a column. It also contains event listener methods and methods to add, move, or remove columns.

A class that is intended to be used as a TableColumnModel must either implement this interface or extend a class that implements this interface, such as DefaultTableColumnModel.

## Methods to Add, Move, or Remove Columns

| Method | Syntax |
|---|---|
| addColumn() | public void addColumn(TableColumn *column*) |
| moveColumn() | public void moveColumn(int *oldIndex*, int *newIndex*) |
| removeColumn() | public void removeColumn (TableColumn *column*) |

addColumn() appends TableColumn column to the end the associated JTable object's table column array.

moveColumn() moves the column at position oldIndex to position newIndex. Any TableColumn object that was at position newIndex is shifted to the right.

removeColumn() deletes a TableColumn from the associated JTable object's table column array.

11

javax.swing.table

## Column Count and Index Methods

| Method | Syntax |
|--------|--------|
| getColumnCount() | public int getColumnCount() |
| getColumnIndex() | public int getColumnIndex<br>(Object *identifier*) |
| getColumnIndexAtX() | public int getColumnIndexAtX<br>(int *xLocation*) |

getColumnCount() returns the number of columns associated with the TableColumnModel.

getColumnIndex() returns the index of the first column whose header matches the Object identifier.

getColumnIndexAtX() returns the index of the column at the specified x location on the screen.

## ColumnModelListener Methods

| Method | Syntax |
|--------|--------|
| addColumnModelListener() | public void addColumnModelListener<br>(TableColumnModelListener *tcml*) |
| removeColumnModelListener() | public void removeColumnModelListener<br>(TableColumnModelListener *tcml*) |

addColumnModelListener() registers the invoking TableColumnModel object with a ColumnModelListener object. The ColumnModelListener is notified if the TableColumnModel object generates a TableColumnModelEvent. A TableColumnModelEvent is generated if a column is added, moved, removed, or has its margin changed.

removeColumnModelListener() removes an ColumnModelListener object from the TableColumnModel object. TableColumnModelEvent objects generated by the TableColumnModel object will no longer be received by the ColumnModelListener.

## Margin and Width Methods

| Method | Syntax |
|--------|--------|
| getColumnMargin() | public int getColumnMargin() |
| getTotalColumnWidth() | public int getTotalColumnWidth() |
| setColumnMargin() | public void setColumnMargin(int *margin*) |

getColumnMargin() returns the space in pixels that should be placed between columns.

setColumnMargin() is used to change the margin.

getTotalColumnWidth() returns the width of all of the columns.

## Methods to Return One or All Columns

| Method | Syntax |
|---|---|
| getColumn() | public TableColumn getColumn(int *index*) |
| getColumns() | public Enumeration getColumns() |

getColumn() returns a reference to the TableColumn object at position index.

getColumns() returns an Enumeration object containing all of the columns contained by the TableColumnModel.

## Column Selection Methods

| Method | Syntax |
|---|---|
| getColumnSelectionAllowed() | public boolean getColumnSelectionAllowed() |
| getSelectedColumnCount() | public int getSelectedColumnCount() |
| getSelectedColumns() | public int[] getSelectedColumns() |
| setColumnSelectionAllowed() | public void setColumnSelectionAllowed (boolean *allowed*) |

getColumnSelectionAllowed() returns true if the columns can be selected.

setColumnSelectionAllowed() is used to specify whether columns can be selected.

getSelectedColumnCount() returns the number of selected columns.

getSelectedColumns() returns an int array containing the indices of the selected columns.

## Selection Model Methods

| Method | Syntax |
|---|---|
| getSelectionModel() | public ListSelectionModel getSelectionModel() |
| setSelectionModel() | public void setSelectionModel (ListSelectionModel *model*) |

getSelectionModel() returns a reference to the ListSelectionModel object that is associated with the invoking TableColumnModel object. The ListSelectionModel is used manage the selection methodolgy of the column. See the Section 9.4.4 on page 908 for a discussion of the ListSelectionModel interface.

setSelectionModel() method is used to change the selection model of the invoking TableColumnModel object.

**11**

javax.swing.table

# 11.3 TableModel Classes and Interfaces

The `TableModel` classes and interfaces provide support for the management of data stored in a table;.the data stored in a table is loaded and accessed using a `TableModel` object. For an object to serve as a `TableModel`, it must implement the methods defined in the `TableModel` interface.

❏ The `AbstractTableModel` class is the super-class of all `TableModel` objects and provides implementations for most of the methods defined in the `TableModel` interface.

❏ The `DefaultTableModel` class is a `TableModel` that is provided as part of the `javax.swing.table` package. User-defined `TableModel` classes often are written as sub-classes of the `AbstractTableModel` class.

The `TableModel` class hierarchy is shown in the following diagram.

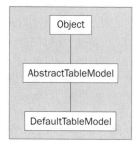

# 11.3.1 AbstractTableModel Class

```
public abstract class AbstractTableModel extends Object implements TableModel,
Serializable
```

```
Object
  AbstractTableModel
```

### Interfaces
```
Serializable, TableModel
```

The `AbstractTableModel` class provides default implementations for most of the methods defined in the `TableModel` interface. Methods are also provided for firing vaious types of `TableModelEvent` objects. Implementations are not provided for the `getColumnCount()`, `getRowCount()`, and `getValueAt()` methods; a user-defined `TableModel` class that extends the `AbstractTableModel` must, as a minimum, provide implementations for these three methods.

For an example of a user-defined `TableModel` class, see the *User-Defined TableCellRenderer* example on page 1020.

# AbstractTableModel() Constructor

| Constructor | Syntax |
|---|---|
| AbstractTableModel() | public AbstractTableModel() |

Because AbstractTableModel is an abstract class, an AbstractTableModel object is never instantiated. Sub-classes of the AbstractTableModel can access this constructor using the super keyword.

# Column and Row Methods

| Method | Syntax |
|---|---|
| getColumnClass() | public Class getColumnClass (int columnIndex) |
| getColumnName() | public String getColumnName (int columnIndex) |

getColumnClass() returns a Class object corresponding to the class of the elements in the specified column. The Class object is used to set the cell renderer and editor for the column.

getColumnName() method returns a String object containing the name of the column at the specified index. The String object is used to initialize the header name. Different columns can use the same name. Remember that the getColumnCount() and getRowCount() methods must be implemented by the AbstractTableModel sub-class.

# getListeners() Method

| Method | Syntax |
|---|---|
| getListeners() | public EventListener[] getListeners (Class listenerClass) |

getListeners() returns any listeners of the specified type registered to the invoking TableModel object as an EventListener array.

# isCellEditable() Method

| Method | Syntax |
|---|---|
| isCellEditable() | public boolean isCellEditable (int rowIndex, int columnIndex) |

isCellEditable() returns true if the cell at rowIndex, columnIndex can be edited. The default implementation of this method returns false. It can be overridden to return true if the cells are intended to be edited.

## Methods to Return or Change a Cell Value

| Method | Syntax |
|--------|--------|
| setValueAt() | public void setValueAt(Object *value*,<br>    int *rowIndex*, int *columnIndex*) |

setValueAt() is used to change the value of the cell at rowIndex, columnIndex. Note that if the isCellEditable() method returns false for the cell, the setValueAt() method will not be able to change its value. Remember that the getValueAt() method from the TableModel interface must be implemented by the AbstractTableModel subclass.

## TableModelEvent Methods

| Method | Syntax |
|--------|--------|
| fireTableCellUpdated() | public void fireTableCellUpdated<br>    (int *rowIndex*, int *columnIndex*) |
| fireTableDataChanged() | public void fireTableDataChanged() |
| fireTableRowsDeleted() | public void fireTableRowsDeleted<br>    (int *firstRow*, int *lastRow*) |
| fireTableRowsInserted() | public void fireTableRowsInserted<br>    (int *firstRow*, int *lastRow*) |
| fireTableRowsUpdated() | public void fireTableRowsUpdated<br>    (int *firstRow*, int *lastRow*) |
| fireTableStructureChanged() | public void fireTableStructureChanged() |
| fireTableChanged() | public void fireTableChanged<br>    (TabelModelEvent *tme*) |

The first six methods generate various types of TableModelEvent objects and fire the object to the fireTableChanged() method. The fireTableChanged() method sends the TableModelEvent object to any registered TableModelListener objects.

## TableModelListener Methods

| Method | Syntax |
|--------|--------|
| addTableModelListener() | public void addTableModelListener<br>    (TableModelListener *tml*) |
| removeTableModelListener() | public void removeTableModelListener<br>    (TableModelListener *tml*) |

addTableModelListener() registers the invoking TableModel object with a TableModelListener object. The TableModelListener is notified if the TableModel object generates a TableModelEvent. A TableModelEvent is generated whenever the table changes.

`removeTableModelListener()` removes a `TableModelListener` object from the invoking `TableModel` object. `TableModelEvent` objects generated by the component will no longer be received by the `TableModelListener`.

# 11.3.2 DefaultTableModel Class

`public class DefaultTableModel extends AbstractTableModel implements Serializable`

```
Object
  AbstractTableModel
    DefaultTableModel
```

### Interfaces

`Serializable, TableModel`

The `Swing` documentation recommends the use of a user-defined `TableModel` that is a sub-class of `AbstractTableModel`. However, the `DefaultTableModel` class is provided as a built-in implementation of the `TableModel` interface that uses a `Vector` of `Vectors` to store the cell value objects.

## DefaultTableModel() Constructor

| Constructor | Syntax |
|---|---|
| DefaultTableModel() | public DefaultTableModel() |
| | public DefaultTableModel<br>(int *numRows*, int *numCols*) |
| | public DefaultTableModel<br>(Vector *columnNames*, int *numRows*) |
| | public DefaultTableModel<br>(Object[] *columnNames*, int *numRows*) |
| | public DefaultTableModel<br>(Vector *data*, Vector *columnNames*) |
| | public DefaultTableModel<br>(Object[][] *data*, Object[] *columnNames* |

Creates a `DefaultTableModel` object. The number of rows and columns can be specified as well as the column names and the cell values. The column names and cell values can be provided either as a `Vector` object or an `Object` array.

## addColumn() Method

| Method | Syntax |
|---|---|
| addColumn() | public void addColumn<br>    (Object *columnIdentifier*) |
| | public void addColumn<br>    (Object *columnIdentifier*,<br>    Object[] *data*) |
| | public void addColumn<br>    (Object *columnIdentifier*, Vector *data*) |

addColumn() methods are used to add a column to the invoking DefaultTableModel object. The column can be created with or without data.

## Methods to Add or Insert a Row

| Method | Syntax |
|---|---|
| addRow() | public void addRow(Object[] *data*) |
| | public void addRow(Vector *data*) |
| insertRow() | public void insertRow(int *rowIndex*,<br>                    Object[] *data*) |
| | public void insertRow(int *rowIndex*,<br>                    Vector *data*) |

addRow() adds a row containing the data inside the Vector object or Object array to the end of the invoking DefaultTableModel object. The size of the row data is extended or truncated to match the number of columns in the table.

insertRow() is used to insert a row at position rowIndex. The size of the row data is extended or truncated to match the number of columns in the table.

## isCellEditable() Method

| Method | Syntax |
|---|---|
| isCellEditable() | public boolean isCellEditable<br>    (int *rowIndex*, int *columnIndex*) |

isCellEditable() returns true if the cell at rowIndex, columnIndex can be edited. The default implementation of this method returns false. It can be overwridden to return true if the cells are intended to be edited.

## Methods to Move or Remove Rows

| Method | Syntax |
|---|---|
| moveRow() | public void moveRow(int *startIndex*, int *endIndex*, int *toIndex*) |
| removeRow() | public void removeRow(int *index*) |

moveRow() moves the rows from startIndex to endIndex to position toIndex.

removeRow() is used to remove the row at the specified index from the model.

## Methods to Return or Change Row and Column Properties

| Method | Syntax |
|---|---|
| getColumnCount() | public int getColumnCount() |
| getColumnName() | public String getColumnName(int *index*) |
| getRowCount() | public int getRowCount() |
| setColumnCount() | public void setColumnCount(int *numColumns*) |
| setNumRows() | public void setNumRows(int *numRows*) |
| setRowCount() | public void setRowCount(int *numRows*) |

getColumnCount() returns the number or columns in the invoking DefaultTableModel object data table.

getColumnName() returns a String representation of the column identifier for the column at the specified index.

getRowCount() returns the number or rows in the invoking DefaultTableModel object data table.

setColumnCount() sets the number or columns in the invoking DefaultTableModel object data table. Columns will be added or truncated from the end of the model to match the value of numColumns.

setNumRows() is used to change the number of rows in the invoking DefaultTableModel object. If numRow is less than the current table size, rows are truncated from the table. This method is obsolete as of Java 2 version 1.3; the setRowCount() method should be used instead.

setRowCount() sets the number or rows in the invoking DefaultTableModel object data table. Rows will be added or truncated from the end of the model to match the value of numRows.

11

javax.swing.table

## Methods Used to Change Table Data

| Method | Syntax |
| --- | --- |
| setColumnIdentifiers() | public void setColumnIdentifiers<br>    (Object[] *columnIDs*) |
| | public void setColumnIdentifiers<br>    (Vector *columnIDs*) |
| setDataVector() | public void setDataVector<br>    (Object[][] *newData*,<br>    Object[] *columnNames*) |
| | public void setDataVector(Vector *newData*,<br>    Vector *columnNames*) |
| setValueAt() | public void setValueAt(Object *value*,<br>    int *rowIndex*,<br>    int *columnIndex*) |

setColumnIdentifiers() is used to change the column identifiers associated with the invoking DefaultTableModel object. The column identifiers are a way to uniquely identify a column and are different from the column headers that appear on the display.

setDataVector() replaces the data values contained in the table model with the specified Vector object or Object array. The Vector newData is a Vector of Vectors containing the data for each row.

setValueAt() method is used to change the value for the cell at rowIndex, columnIndex.

## Methods that Return Table Data

| Method | Syntax |
| --- | --- |
| getDataVector() | public Vector getDataVector() |
| getValueAt() | public Object getValueAt(int *rowIndex*,<br>    int *columnIndex*) |

getDataVector() returns a Vector object that contains the Vectors containing the data contained by the invoking DefaultTableModel object.

getValueAt() returns the value at rowIndex, columnIndex as an Object.

### Example: Using DefaultTableModel

See the *Using DefaultTableColumnModel* example on page 999, where a DefaultTableModel object. is used to provide the data model for a JTable object.

# 11.3.3 TableModel Interface

```
public interface TableModel
```

The TableModel interface defines row, column, event listener, value, and property methods that are common to all TableModel objects. If a class is to serve as a TableModel object, it must implement the TableModel interface.

## Column and Row Methods

| Method | Syntax |
|---|---|
| getColumnClass() | public Class getColumnClass (int columnIndex) |
| getColumnCount() | public int getColumnCount() |
| getColumnName() | public String getColumnName (int columnIndex) |
| getRowCount() | public int getRowCount() |

getColumnClass() returns a Class object corresponding to the class of the elements in the specified column. The Class object is used to set the cell renderer and editor for the column.

getColumnCount() returns the number of columns in the table model.

getColumnName() returns a String object containing the name of the column at the specified index. The String object is used to initialize the header name. Different columns can use the same name.

getRowCount() returns the number of rows managed by the table model. The number of rows can also be thought of as the number of data records.

## isCellEditable() Method

| Method | Syntax |
|---|---|
| isCellEditable() | public boolean isCellEditable (int rowIndex, int columnIndex) |

isCellEditable() returns true if the cell at rowIndex, columnIndex can be edited.

## Methods to Return or Change a Cell Value

| Method | Syntax |
|---|---|
| getValueAt() | public Object getValueAt(int rowIndex, int columnIndex) |
| setValueAt() | public void setValueAt(Object value, int rowIndex, int columnIndex) |

getValueAt() returns the value of the cell at rowIndex, columnIndex as an Object.

setValueAt() is used to change the value of the cell at rowIndex, columnIndex. Note that if the isCellEditable() method returns false for the cell, the setValueAt() method will not be able to change its value.

## TableModelListener Methods

| Method | Syntax |
|---|---|
| addTableModelListener() | public void addTableModelListener (TableModelListener *tml*) |
| removeTableModelListener() | public void removeTableModelListener (TableModelListener *tml*) |

addTableModelListener() registers the invoking TableModel object with a TableModelListener object. The TableModelListener is notified if the TableModel object generates a TableModelEvent. A TableModelEvent is generated whenever the table changes.

removeTableModelListener() removes a TableModelListener object from the invoking TableModel object. TableModelEvent objects generated by the component will no longer be received by the TableModelListener.

# 11.4 Cell Editors and Renderers

**Cell renderers** are used to specify how table cells are displayed. For a class to be used as a cell renderer, it must implement the methods defined in the TableCellRenderer interface. The usual convention is for a cell renderer to extend a GUI component class and implement the TableCellRenderer interface.

**Cell editors** are similar in nature to cell renderers and are used to edit table cells. For a class to be used as a cell editor, it must implement the methods defined in the TableCellEditor interface. The usual convention is for a cell editor to extend a GUI component class and implement the TableCellEditor interface.

The javax.swing.table package provides a default cell renderer, the DefaultTableCellRenderer class. The class hierarchy for this class is shown in the following diagram:

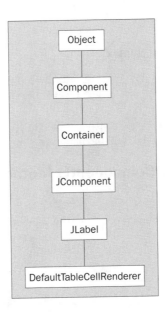

## 11.4.1 DefaultTableCellRenderer Class

```
public class DefaultTableCellRenderer extends JLabel implements
TableCellRenderer, Serializable
```

```
Object
  Component
    Container
      JComponent
        JLabel
          DefaultTableCellRenderer
```

### Interfaces

```
Accessible, ImageObserver, MenuContainer, Serializable, SwingConstants,
TableCellRenderer
```

The DefaultTableCellRenderer Class provides the default mechanism for displaying
the cells of a JTable object. A DefaultTableCellRenderer object uses JLabel objects
to display String representations of Number, Icon, and Object objects.

### DefaultTableCellRenderer() Constructor

| Constructor | Syntax |
|---|---|
| DefaultTableCellRenderer() | public DefaultTableCellRenderer() |

DefaultTableCellRenderer object constructor.

## Color Methods

| Method | Syntax |
|---|---|
| setBackground() | public void setBackground(Color c) |
| setForeground() | public void setForeground(Color c) |

setBackground() and setForeground() are used to specify the un-selected foreground and background that will be displayed.

## getTableCellRendererComponent() Method

| Method | Syntax |
|---|---|
| getTableCellRendererComponent() | public Component getTableCellRendererComponent (JTable *table*, Object *value*, boolean *isSelected*, boolean *hasFocus*, int *row*, int *column*) |

getTableCellRendererComponent() configures and returns the Component that will be used to render the cell at the specified row and column. The JTable object passed as an argument is the table requesting the renderer to draw. The Object value is the value to be displayed. The boolean arguments isSelected and hasFocus are used to determine the foreground and background colors and the type of border. This method returns a reference to the Component being drawn.

## setValue() Method

| Method | Syntax |
|---|---|
| setValue() | protected void setValue(Object *value*) |

setValue() is called by the getTableCellRendererComponent() method to return the text to display in the cell. A custom cell renderer might override this method.

# 11.4.2 TableCellEditor Interface

public interface TableCellEditor extends CellEditor

CellEditor
    TableCellEditor

The TableCellEditor interface defines one method that is to return a component that is used to edit cell values. Often the class that implements the TableCellEditor will be a sub-class of a GUI component class such as JButton or JScrollBar. This class would also have to implement the methods defined in the CellEditor interface. See the Section 9.4.1 on page 903 NN for more discussion on the CellEditor interface.

## getTableCellEditorComponent() Method

| Method | Syntax |
|---|---|
| getTableCellEditorComponent() | public Component<br>getTableCellEditorComponent<br>(JTable *table*, Object *value*,<br>boolean *isSelected*, int *row*,<br>int *column*) |

getTableCellEditorComponent() is used to return a Component capable of editing a cell value. The JTable object passed as an argument is the table requesting the editor. The Object value is the value of the cell to be edited. The boolean argument isSelected is true if the cell is to be rendered with selection highlighting. The row and column indicate the row and column of the cell to be edited.

# 11.4.3 TableCellRenderer Interface

```
public interface TableCellRenderer
```

This interface defines the getTableCellRendererComponent() method that must be implemented by a TableCellRenderer class.

## getTableCellRendererComponent() Method

| Method | Syntax |
|---|---|
| getTableCellRendererComponent() | public Component<br>getTableCellRendererComponent<br>(JTable *table*, Object *value*,<br>boolean *isSelected*,<br>boolean *hasFocus*, int *row*,<br>int *column*) |

getTableCellRendererComponent() configures and returns the Component that will be used to render the cell at the specified row and column. The JTable object passed as an argument is the table requesting the renderer to draw. The Object value is the value to be displayed. The boolean arguments isSelected and hasFocus are used to determine the foreground and background colors and the type of border. This method returns a reference to the Component being drawn.

11

javax.swing.table

## Example: User-Defined TableCellRenderer

In this example, a simple JTable object is created with two rows and two columns. The first column contains the names of the author's children, and the second column indicates whether they are taking their nap.

```java
import javax.swing.*;
import javax.swing.table.*;
import java.awt.*;
import java.awt.event.*;

public class TestRender extends JFrame {
  JTable jt;
  MyTableModel mtm;

  public TestRender() {

    // A JTable object is created using a data model provided by
    // an instance of the MyTableModel class

    jt = new JTable(new MyTableModel());

    // The setDefaultRenderer() method, which is called by the
    // JTable object, sets the cell renderer for the Nap class to
    // be a NapRenderer object. Other classes will still use the
    // default renderer.

    jt.setDefaultRenderer(Nap.class, new NapRenderer());

    JPanel p = new JPanel();
    p.add(jt);
    getContentPane().add(p, BorderLayout.CENTER);

    addWindowListener(new WinClosing());
    setBounds(100, 100, 200, 160);
    setVisible(true);
  }

  public static void main(String[] args) {
    TestRender tr = new TestRender();
  }
}


// The Nap class is a user-defined class that encapsulates
// whether my children are taking their naps.

class Nap {
  private boolean takingNap;
```

```
    public Nap(boolean b) {
      takingNap = b;
    }

    public boolean isTakingNap() {
      return takingNap;
    }

    public void setTakingNap(boolean b) {
      takingNap = b;
    }

    public String toString() {
      return "" + takingNap;
    }
}

class NapRenderer extends JCheckBox implements TableCellRenderer {

  // The NapRenderer constructor simply calls the JCheckBox constructor

  public NapRenderer() {
    super("Nap");
  }

  // The getTableCellRendererComponent() method configures and returns
  // the component that will be used to render the Nap objects.  In
  // this case, a NapRenderer is returned.  NapRenderer is a sub-class
  // of JCheckBox
  //
  // The Object value is the Object to be rendered.  It is a Nap object.
  // To determine if the checkbox should be checked or not, the Nap
  // object calls the isTakingNap() method from the Nap class.

  public Component getTableCellRendererComponent(JTable table,
         Object value, boolean isSelected, boolean hasFocus,
         int row, int column) {
    boolean b = ((Nap) value).isTakingNap();
    setSelected(b);

    return this;
  }
}


// This is a user-defined TableModel that extends the
// AbstractTableModel class. The data model contains
// two rows, each row containing a String and a Nap object.
```

```
class MyTableModel extends AbstractTableModel {

  Object[][] data = {
    {
      "Jackson", new Nap(true)
    }, {
      "Zachary", new Nap(false)
    }
  };

  String[] headers = {
    "Name", "Nap"
  };
  Class[] columnClasses = {
    String.class, Nap.class
  };

  MyTableModel() {}

  public Class getColumnClass(int column) {
    return columnClasses[column];
  }

  public String getColumnName(int column) {
    return headers[column];
  }

  public int getColumnCount() {
    return data[0].length;
  }
  public int getRowCount() {
    return data.length;
  }

  public Object getValueAt(int row, int column) {
    return data[row][column];
  }
}


// The WinClosing class terminates the program when the window is closed

class WinClosing extends WindowAdapter {
  public void windowClosing(WindowEvent we) {
    System.exit(0);
  }
}
```

A `Nap` class is defined that contains a `boolean` property, `takingNap`, that is set to `true` if the children are napping. A custom cell renderer is created to display a `JCheckBox` object that is checked if `takingNap` is `true`. The `JTable` method `setDefaultRenderer()` method is used to set the cell renderer for the `Nap` class to be a `NapRenderer` object.

The `NapRenderer` class is an extension of `JCheckBox`. Because `NapRenderer` implements the `TableCellRenderer` interface, it implements the `getTableCellRendererComponent()` method. This method obtains the value of `takingNap` and sets the checked state of the `JComboBox` using the `setSelected()` method from the `JComboBox` class. The `JTable` object is initialized with a `MyTableModel` table model. This class is used to specify the cell values and to provide column header and column class information.

If the `NapCellRenderer` was not used, the `DefaultCellRenderer` class would use a `JLabel` to display the second column, and the `Nap` objects would be displayed as a `String` containing either `true` or `false` depending on the value of the boolean `takingNap`.

### Output

Here is the result:

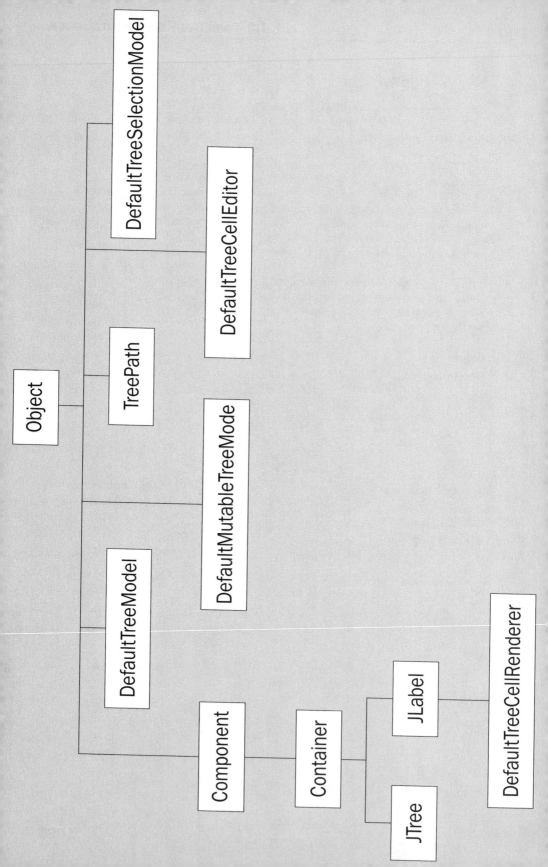

# 12

# javax.swing.tree

The `javax.swing.tree` package provides the classes and interfaces for creating, managing, and manipulating a hierarchical data structure called a tree. The `JTree` class provides a GUI representation of the tree. Although the `JTree` class is contained in the `javax.swing` package, for reasons of continuity, the discussion of the `JTree` class is presented in this chapter.

This chapter covers:

The basic building block of a tree is a **node**. A node is used to store a piece of data at a particular position in the tree. It has information about its parent node and any child nodes for which it may be the parent. The `javax.swing.tree` package provides the `DefaultMutableTreeNode` class as a default tree node, and user-defined `TreeNode` classes can be created by implementing the appropriate interface or extending the appropriate `TreeNode` class.

A `TreeModel` object is used to create and manage the data model associated with the tree. It defines methods for adding and removing nodes, for listening for `TreeModelEvent` objects, and for accessing general information about the data model.

The tree nodes (also called cells) are displayed using a `TreeCellRenderer` object. A `TreeCellRenderer` class is an extension of a Swing GUI component that implements the `TreeCellRenderer` interface. The `javax.swing.tree` package provides a `DefaultTreeCellRenderer` class that displays a `String` representation of the tree node. Similarly, a `TreeCellEditor` object is a GUI component that is used to edit a tree node.

In order to see the relationship between nodes, here we have a sample tree:

A tree is made up of nodes.

- ❏ A **sibling** node is one that is on the same hierarchical level as the invoking node.

- ❏ A **related** node is one that is in the same tree as the invoking node.

- ❏ An **ancestor** node is one that is along the path to the root node from the invoking node.

- ❏ A **descendant** node is a child node, grandchild node, and so on, further down the tree from the current node, away from the root.

For example in the previous diagram:

- ❏ My Company is the **root** node.

- ❏ Finance is a **child** node of My Company.

- ❏ My Company is a **child** node of Finance.

- ❏ Bob Wood is a **grandchild** or **ancestor** of My Company.

- ❏ Bob Wood is a **sibling** node of Sue Mi and Joe King.

- ❏ Finance is a sibling node of Accounting and Research.

- ❏ All nodes in this diagram are **related**

Selections of tree elements are based on **rows** and **paths**.

The path is the list of nodes from the root node to the current node (rather like the path of a file within folders on a file system). `TreeSelectionModel` objects must implement the `TreeSelectionModel` interface. The `DefaultTreeSelectionModel` class is provided in the `javax.swing.tree` package to serve as a default `TreeSelectionModel`. For example, the path to Sue Mi could be written as:

My Company/Finance/Sue Mi

A row represents one line in the window display of the tree. Each visible node of the tree is placed on a different row. If a parent node is collapsed causing its child nodes to disappear, the row indexes for the nodes below the parent node change. So, Finance, Joe King, and Accounting are all separate rows.

# 12.1 The JTree Class

The JTree class is a GUI component that displays a set of hierarchal data. A JTree object is just the graphical display of a tree component. The data displayed by a JTree object is stored in and managed by an associated TreeModel object. The JTree class hierarcy is shown in this figure:

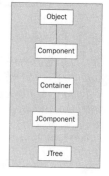

Although the JTree class is contained in the java.swing package, for continuity reasons it is discussed in this chapter.

# 12.1.1 JTree Class

```
public class JTree extends JComponent implements Scrollable, Accessible
```

```
Object
    Component
        Container
            JComponent
                JTree
```

### Interfaces

```
Accessible, ImageObserver, MenuContainer, Scrollable, Serializable
```

A JTree object is a graphical representation of a hierarchical data structure. The tree is made up of nodes that are implementations of the MutableTreeNode and/or TreeNode interfaces. A node can have a user object associated with it and can have child nodes. The nodes of a JTree object are displayed in rows. The data model of a JTree object is controlled by a TreeModel object.

## JTree() Constructors

| Constructor | Syntax |
|---|---|
| JTree() | public **JTree**() |
| | public **JTree**(Object[] *value*) |
| | public **JTree**(Hashtable *hash*) |
| | public **JTree**(Vector *value*) |
| | public **JTree**(TreeNode *root*) |
| | public **JTree**(TreeModel *model*) |
| | public **JTree**(TreeNode *root*, boolean *asksAllowsChildren*) |

JTree() creates a JTree object. The no-argument constructor creates a tree using a DefaultTreeModel object for the model. As shown in the next three constructors, the JTree object can also be initialized with data contained in an Object array, Vector object, or Hashtable – in which case, the data is displayed as the children of a root node, which is not shown. The JTree can also be created containing only a root node or it can be initialized with a data model contained in a TreeModel object.

If asksAllowChildren is set to true, nodes will be asked if they allow children before a child node is added to them.

## convertValueToText() Method

| Method | Syntax |
|---|---|
| convertValueToText() | public String convertValueToText(Object *value*, boolean *selected*, boolean *expanded*, boolean *leaf*, int *rowIndex*, boolean *hasFocus*) |

convertValueToText() is used by renderers to convert the value contained by a node to a String object. The default implementation of this method calls the toString() method. The method can be overwritten to provide an alternative String representation.

## Editing and Rendering Methods

| Method | Syntax |
|---|---|
| cancelEditing() | public void cancelEditing() |
| getCellEditor() | public TreeCellEditor getCellEditor() |
| getCellRenderer() | public TreeCellRenderer getCellRenderer() |
| getInvokesStopCellEditig() | public boolean getInvokesStopCellEditing() |
| isEditable() | public boolean isEditable() |
| isEditing() | public boolean isEditing() |
| setCellEditor() | public void setCellEditor(TreeCellEditor *editor*) |
| setCellRenderer() | public void setCellRenderer(TreeCellRenderer *renderer*) |
| setEditable() | public void setEditable(boolean *editable*) |
| setInvokesStopCellEditing() | public void setInvokesStopCellEditing(boolean *flag*) |
| startEditingAtPath() | public void startEditingAtPath(TreePath *path*) |
| stopEditing() | public boolean stopEditing() |

`cancelEditing()` cancels the current editing session without saving any changes that have been made.

`getCellEditor()` returns a reference to the cell editor associated with the invoking `JTree` object.

`getCellRenderer()` returns a reference to the `TreeCellRenderer` object used to render the cells.

`getInvokesStopCellEditing()` returns the boolean flag that indicates what occurs when editing is stopped. The method returns `true` if changes are saved when the editing session is interrupted and false if changes are lost.

`isEditable()` returns `true` if the invoking `JTree` object is editable.

`isEditing()` returns `true` if the tree is being edited.

`setCellEditor()` and `setCellRenderer()` are used to change the editor and renderer associated with the invoking `JTree` object.

`setEditable()` determines if the tree can be edited.

`setInvokesStopCellEditing()` determines what happens to changes that were made if the editing seesion is interrupted. If the method is set to `true`, `stopCellEditing()` is invoked when editing is interrupted and changes are lost. Setting it to `false` causes the `cancelEditing()` method to be invoked and changes are saved.

`startEditingAtPath()` initiates editing on the node corresponding to the specified path.

`stopEditing()` stops the current editing session and saves any edits currently in progress. It returns `true` if there was editing in progress and it was stopped successfully.

## Event Listener Methods

| Method | Syntax |
|--------|--------|
| `addTreeExpansionListener()` | `public void addTreeExpansionListener` `(TreeExpansionListener tel)` |
| `addTreeSelectionListener()` | `public void addTreeSelectionListener` `(TreeSelectionListener tsl)` |
| `addTreeWillExpandListener()` | `public void addTreeWillExpandListener` `(TreeWillExpandListener twel)` |
| `removeTreeExpansionListener()` | `public void removeTreeExpansionListener` `(TreeExpansionListener tel)` |
| `removeTreeSelectionListener()` | `public void removeTreeSelectionListener` `(TreeSelectionListener tsl)` |

| Method | Syntax |
|---|---|
| removeTreeWillExpandListener() | public void removeTreeWillExpandListener<br>(TreeWillExpandListener *twel*) |
| createTreeModelListener() | protected TreeModelListener<br>createTreeModelListener() |

addTreeExpansionListener(), addTreeSelectionListener(), and addTreeWillExpandListener() are used to add listeners for TreeExpansion, TreeSelection, and TreeWillExpand events.

removeTreeExpansionListener(), removeTreeSelectionListener(), and removeTreeWillExpandListener() are used to remove listeners for TreeExpansion, TreeSelection, and TreeWillExpand events.

createTreeModelListener() creates and returns an instance of TreeModelHandler.

## Methods to Fire Tree Events

| Method | Syntax |
|---|---|
| fireTreeCollapsed() | public void fireTreeCollapsed(TreePath *path*) |
| fireTreeExpanded() | public void fireTreeExpanded(TreePath *path*) |
| fireTreeWillCollapse() | public void fireTreeWillCollapse(TreePath *path*)<br>throws ExpandVetoException |
| fireTreeWillExpand() | public void fireTreeWillExpand(TreePath *path*)<br>throws ExpandVetoException |
| fireValueChanged() | protected void<br>fireValueChanged(TreeSelectionEvent *tse*) |

These methods are used to fire various types of events to registered listeners. The fireTreeWillCollapse() and fireTreeWillExpand() methods indicate that a tree node is about to expand or collapse.

## General Selection Methods

| Method | Syntax |
|---|---|
| clearSelection() | public void clearSelection() |
| getSelectionCount() | public int getSelectionCount() |
| isSelectionEmpty() | public boolean isSelectionEmpty() |

clearSelection() clears all selected paths and rows.

getSelectionCount() returns the number of nodes that are currently selected.

isSelectionEmpty() returns true if nothing is currently selected.

12

javax.swing.tree

## Path Methods

| Method | Syntax |
|---|---|
| collapsePath() | public void collapsePath(TreePath *path*) |
| expandPath() | public void expandPath(TreePath *path*) |
| getClosestPathForLocation() | public TreePath getClosestPathForLocation (int *x*, int *y*) |
| getEditingPath() | public TreePath getEditingPath() |
| getPathBounds() | public Rectangle getPathBounds (TreePath *path*) |
| getPathForLocation() | public TreePath getPathForLocation (int *x*, int *y*) |
| getPathForRow() | public TreePath getPathForRow (int *rowIndex*) |
| hasBeenExpanded() | public boolean hasBeenExpanded (TreePath path) |
| isCollapsed() | public boolean isCollapsed(TreePath *path*) |
| isExpanded() | public boolean isExpanded(TreePath *path*) |
| isPathEditable() | public boolean isPathEditable (TreePath *path*) |
| isVisible() | public boolean isVisible(TreePath *path*) |
| makeVisible() | public void makeVisible(TreePath *path*) |
| scrollPathToVisible() | public void scrollPathToVisible (TreePath *path*) |

A collapsed node is one whose child nodes are not visible. An expanded node is one that displays its children.

collapsePath() collapses the node corresponding to the specified path and makes the node viewable.

expandPath() expands the node corresponding to the specified path and makes the node viewable.

getClosestPathForLocation() returns the path for the node closest to the specified x and y location. The x and y distances are from the upper left hand corner of the display area.

getEditingPath() returns the path to the element currently being edited.

getPathBounds() returns a Rectangle object representing the area that the node identified by the specified path will be drawn into.

getPathForLocation() returns the path for the node at the specified x and y location or null if there is no path at that location. The x and y distances are from the upper left hand corner of the display area.

getPathForRow() returns the path for the node at the specified row index.

hasBeenExpanded() returns true if the node identified by the specified path has ever been expanded.

isCollapsed() returns true if the node identified by the specified path is currently collapsed.

isExpanded() returns true if the node identified by the specified path is currently expanded.

isPathEditable() returns true if every node identified by the specified path can be edited.

isVisible() returns true if the node identified by the specified path is currently viewable.

makeVisible() ensures that the node identified by the specified path is currently viewable.

scrollPathToVisible() is used f the tree is contained in a scroll pane, to scroll until the the node identified by the specified path is made visible. If necessary, the path is also expanded.

## Path Selection Methods

| Method | Syntax |
| --- | --- |
| addSelectionInterval() | public void addSelectionInterval<br>(int startRowIndex,<br>int endRowIndex) |
| addSelectionPath() | public void addSelectionPath(TreePath path) |
| addSelectionPaths() | Public void addSelectionPaths(<br>TreePath[] paths) |
| getAnchorSelectionPath() | public TreePath getAnchorSelectionPath() |
| getExpandsSelectedPaths() | public boolean getExpandsSelectionPath() |
| getLastSelectedPathComponent() | public Object<br>getLastSelectedPathComponent() |
| getLeadSelectionPath() | public TreePath getLeadSelectionPath() |
| getSelectionPath() | public TreePath getSelectionPath() |
| getSelectionPaths() | public TreePath[] getSelectionPaths() |

| Method | Syntax |
|---|---|
| isPathSelected() | public boolean isPathSelected(TreePath *path*) |
| removeSelectionInterval() | public void removeSelectionInterval<br>(int *startRowIndex*,<br>int *endRowIndex*) |
| removeSelectionPath() | public void removeSelectionPath(<br>TreePath *path*) |
| removeSelectionPaths() | public void removeSelectionPaths(<br>TreePath[] *paths*) |
| setAnchorSelectionPath() | public void setAnchorSelectionPath(<br>TreePath *path*) |
| setExpandsSelectedPaths() | public void setExpandsSelectionPath(<br>boolean *expand*) |
| setLeadSelectionPath() | public void setLeadSelectionPath<br>(TreePath *path*) |
| setSelectionInterval() | public void setSelectionInterval(<br>int *startRowIndex*, int *endRowIndex*) |
| setSelectionPath() | public void setSelectionPath(TreePath *path*) |
| setSelectionPaths() | public void setSelectionPaths(<br>TreePath[] *paths*) |

addSelectionInterval() adds the paths for the rows between startRowIndex and startRowIndex to the currently selected paths.

addSelectionPath() and addSelectionPaths() add one or more paths to the current selection.

getAnchorSelectionPath() returns the path identified as the anchor for the invoking JTree object.

getExpandsSelectedPaths() returns true if the parent path of a selected node is automatically expanded to make the parent nodes visible.

getLastSelectedPathComponent() returns a reference to the node that is the last path entry in the current selection.

getLeadSelectionPath() returns the path of the most recently selected node.

getSelectionPath() returns the TreePath for the first selected node or null if nothing is currently selected.

getSelectionPaths() returns a TreePath array containing the paths of all selected nodes or null if nothing is currently selected.

isPathSelected() returns true if the node identified by the specified path is currently selected.

removeSelectionInterval() removes the paths for the rows between startRowIndex and startRowIndex from the currently selected paths.

removeSelectionPath() and removeSelectionPaths() remove one or more paths from the current selection.

setAnchorSelectionPath() specifies the path that will serve as the anchor for the invoking JTree object.

setExpandsSelectedPaths() specifies whether the parent path of a selected node is automatically expanded to make the parent nodes visible.

setLeadSelectionPath() changes the lead selection path.

setSelectionInterval() sets the current selection to the node whose paths are between rows startRowIndex and startRowIndex.

setSelectionPath() and setSelectionPaths() sets the selection to the nodes identified by the path or paths passed as an argument.

## JTree Property Methods

| Method | Syntax |
|---|---|
| getShowsRootHandles() | public boolean getShowsRootHandles() |
| getScrollsOnExpand() | public boolean getScrollsOnExpand() |
| getToolTipText() | public String getToolTipText(MouseEvent me) |
| getToggleClickCount() | public int getToggleClickCount() |
| isLargeModel() | public boolean isLargeModel() |
| setExpandedState() | protected void setExpandedState(TreePath path, boolean expanded) |
| setLargeModel() | public void setLargeModel(boolean useLargeModel) |
| setScrollsOnExpand() | public voids setScrollsOnExpand(boolean scroll) |
| setShowsRootHandles() | public void setShowsRootHandles(boolean showHandles) |
| setToggleClickCount() | public void getToggleClickCount(int numClicks) |

A handle is a small icon displayed adjacent to the node that allows the user to expand or collapse the node.

getShowsRootHandles() returns true if the node handles will be displayed.

`getScrollsOnExpand()` returns `true` if when a node is expanded as many of its descendants as possible are scrolled to be visible.

`getToolTipText()` returns the tooltip text from the cell renderer. For this to work properly, the `JTree` object must be a registered component with the `ToolTipManager`.

`getToggleClickCount()` returns the number of mouse clicks required to expand or collapse a node.

`isLargeModel()` returns `true` if the tree is configured for a large model. A large model is an optimization mechanism that can be used if the cell height is the same for all nodes.

`setExpandedState()` marks all parents of the specified path as expanded if the argument is `true`.

`setLargeModel()` is used to specify whether a large-model methodology should be used. This would be appropriate if, for instance, all of the nodes displayed the same object type. Not all platforms support the large model optimization.

`setScrollsOnExpand()` determines if, when a node is expanded, as many of its descendants as possible are scrolled to be visible.

`setShowsRootHandles()` specifies whether the node handles will be displayed. Node handles are useful display if a node is expanded or collapsed.

`setToggleClickCount()` sets the number of mouse clicks required to expand or collapse a node.

## Root Node Methods

| Method | Syntax |
| --- | --- |
| `isRootVisible()` | `public boolean isRootVisible()` |
| `setRootVisible()` | `public void setRootVisible(boolean rootVisible)` |

`isRootVisible()` returns `true` if the root node of the tree is displayed.

`setRootVisible()` is used to change the visible state of the node.

## Row Methods

| Method | Syntax |
| --- | --- |
| `collapseRow()` | `public void collapseRow(int rowIndex)` |
| `expandRow()` | `public void expandRow(int rowIndex)` |
| `getClosestRowForLocation()` | `public int getClosestRowForLocation(int x, int y)` |
| `getRowBounds()` | `public Rectangle getRowBounds(int rowIndex)` |

| Method | Syntax |
|---|---|
| getRowCount() | public int getRowCount() |
| getRowForLocation() | public int getRowForLocation(int x, int y) |
| getRowForPath() | public int getRowForPath(TreePath path) |
| getRowHeight() | public int getRowHeight() |
| getVisibleRowCount() | public int getVisibleRowCount() |
| isCollapsed() | public boolean isCollapsed(int rowIndex) |
| isExpanded() | public boolean isExpanded(int rowIndex) |
| isFixedRowHeight() | public boolean isFixedRowHeight() |
| scrollRowToVisible() | public void scrollRowToVisible(int rowIndex) |
| setRowHeight() | public void setRowHeight(int height) |
| setVisibleRowCount() | public void setVisibleRowCount(int count) |

A collapsed node is one whose child nodes are not visible. An expanded node is one that displays its children.

collapseRow() collapses the node corresponding to the specified row index.

expandRow() expands the node corresponding to the specified row index and makes it viewable.

getClosestRowForLocation() returns the row index for the node closest to the specified x and y location. The x and y distance is from the upper left hand corner of the display area.

getRowBounds() returns a Rectangle object representing the area that the node identified by the specified row index will be drawn into.

getRowCount() returns the number of rows currently displayed.

getRowForLocation() returns the row index for the node at the specified x and y location or -1 if there is no row at that location.

getRowForPath() returns the row index for the node at the specified path.

getRowHeight() returns the height of each row in pixels. If the return value is less than or equal to zero, the height of each row is determined by the renderer.

getVisibleRowCount() returns the number of rows that can be seen in the display.

isCollapsed() returns true if the node identified by the specified row index is currently collapsed.

isExpanded() returns true if the node identified by the specified row index is currently expanded.

isFixedRowHeight() returns true if the height of each display row is a fixed size.

scrollRowToVisible() is used it the tree is contained in a scroll pane, to scroll until the the node identified by the specified row index is made visible.

setRowHeight() method is used to set the row height. If the argument passed to this method is less than or equal to zero, the height of each row is determined by the renderer.

setVisibleRowCount() method is used to specify the number of rows to be displayed.

## Row Selection Methods

| Method | Syntax |
| --- | --- |
| addSelectionRow() | public void addSelectionRow(int *rowIndex*) |
| addSelectionRows() | public void addSelectionRows(int[] *rowIndices*) |
| getLeadSelectionRow() | public int getLeadSelectionRow() |
| getMaxSelectionRow() | public int getMaxSelectionRow() |
| getMinSelectionRow() | public int getMinSelectionRow() |
| getSelectionRows() | public int[] getSelectionRows() |
| isRowSelected() | public boolean isRowSelected(int *rowIndex*) |
| removeSelectionRow() | public void removeSelectionRow(int *rowIndex*) |
| removeSelectionRows() | public void removeSelectionRows (int[] *rowIndices*) |
| setSelectionRow() | public void setSelectionRow(int *rowIndex*) |
| setSelectionRows() | public void setSelectionRows(int[] *rowIndices*) |

addSelectionRow() adds the path at the specified row index to the current selection.

addSelectionRows() adds the paths at each of the specified rows to the current selection.

getLeadSelectionRow() returns the row index of the most recently selected node.

getMaxSelectionRow() returns the index of the last selected row.

getMinSelectionRow() returns the index of the first selected row.

getSelectionRows() returns an int array containing the row indices of all selected nodes or null if nothing is currently selected.

isRowSelected() returns true if the node identified by the specified row index is currently selected.

removeSelectionRow() removes the path at the specified row index from the current selection.

`removeSelectionRows()` removes the paths at each of the specified rows from the current selection.

`setSelectionRow()` and `setSelectionRows()` sets the selection to the nodes identified by the row or rows passed as an argument.

# Methods to Access the Tree and Selection Models

| Method | Syntax |
|--------|--------|
| createTreeModel() | protected static TreeModel createTreeModel( Object *value*) |
| getDefaultTreeModel() | protected static TreeModel getDefaultTreeModel() |
| getModel() | public TreeModel getModel() |
| getSelectionModel() | public TreeSelectionModel getSelectionModel() |
| setModel() | public void setModel(TreeModel *model*) |
| setSelectionModel() | public void setSelectionModel(TreeSelectionModel *model*) |

`createTreeModel()` creates a `DefaultTreeModel` object and initializes it with the value `Object`. The value `Object` can be an `Object` array, `Vector` object, or `Hashtable`. This method is called by the constructors which take an initial value argument.

`getDefaultTreeModel()` returns a sample `TreeModel`.

`getModel()` returns the `TreeModel` object that provides the data model for the invoking `JTree` object.

`getSelectionModel()` returns the `TreeSelectionModel` object that provides the selection model for the invoking `JTree` object.

`setModel()` is used to change the `TreeModel` associated with the invoking `JTree` object.

`setSelectionModel()` is used to specify the `TreeSelectionModel` associated with the invoking `JTree` object.

# UI Delegate Methods

| Method | Syntax |
|--------|--------|
| getUI() | public TreeUI getUI() |
| getUIClassID() | public String getUIClassID() |
| setUI() | public void setUI(TreeUI *ui*) |
| updateUI() | public void updateUI() |

getUI() returns the TreeUI object that renders the invoking JTree object.

getUIClassID() returns the String TreeUI which is the suffix of the class that renders the invoking JTree object.

setUI() is used to change the TreeUI object associated the invoking JTree object.

updateUI() is used to refresh the appearance of the tree if the look-and-feel has been changed.

## Example: Using JTree

In this example, a three-level JTree object is constructed. The root node has three child nodes representing company departments. The Research node is a leaf node with no child nodes of its own. The Finance and Accounting nodes have child nodes representing employees of the company. The first row, corresponding to the Finance node, is initially expanded.

The JTree object is registered with a TreeSelectionListener to listen for TreeSelectionEvent objects. When the selected node changes, the valueChanged() method is called. The text inside a JTextField object placed at the bottom of the JFrame is set to the label of the selected node.

```java
import javax.swing.*;
import javax.swing.tree.*;
import javax.swing.event.*;
import java.awt.*;
import java.awt.event.*;

public class TestJTree extends JFrame
  implements TreeSelectionListener {
  private JTree tree;
  private JTextField jtf;

  public TestJTree() {
    jtf = new JTextField(15);
    jtf.setEditable(false);

    // Eight DefaultMutableTreeNode objects are created

    DefaultMutableTreeNode root =
      new DefaultMutableTreeNode("My Company");
    DefaultMutableTreeNode fin =
      new DefaultMutableTreeNode("Finance");
    DefaultMutableTreeNode acc =
      new DefaultMutableTreeNode("Accounting");
    DefaultMutableTreeNode res =
      new DefaultMutableTreeNode("Research");
    DefaultMutableTreeNode Bob =
      new DefaultMutableTreeNode("Bob Wood");
    DefaultMutableTreeNode Sue = new DefaultMutableTreeNode("Sue Mi");
    DefaultMutableTreeNode Joe =
```

```
      new DefaultMutableTreeNode("Joe King");
DefaultMutableTreeNode Moe =
  new DefaultMutableTreeNode("Moe Knee");

// The node hierarchy is loaded into a DefaultTreeModel object using
// the insertNodeInto() method.

DefaultTreeModel dtm = new DefaultTreeModel(root);
dtm.insertNodeInto(fin, root, 0);
dtm.insertNodeInto(acc, root, 1);
dtm.insertNodeInto(res, root, 2);
dtm.insertNodeInto(Bob, fin, 0);
dtm.insertNodeInto(Sue, fin, 1);
dtm.insertNodeInto(Joe, fin, 2);
dtm.insertNodeInto(Moe, acc, 0);

// A JTree object is created using the previously created
// DefaultTreeModel object.  Root handles are shown and the
// row at index 1 is expanded.

tree = new JTree(dtm);
tree.setShowsRootHandles(true);
tree.expandRow(1);

// The JTree object is registered with a TreeSelectionListener
// that will be notified if the selected node changes

tree.addTreeSelectionListener(this);

getContentPane().add(new JScrollPane(tree), BorderLayout.CENTER);
getContentPane().add(jtf, BorderLayout.SOUTH);

// The WindowListener is used to terminate the program when the window
// is closed.  Under Java 2 version 1.3, the addWindowListener() syntax
// can be replaced by
//
// setDefaultCloseOperation(JFrame.EXIT_ON_CLOSE);

addWindowListener(new WinClosing());
setBounds(100, 100, 300, 300);
setVisible(true);
}

// The valueChanged() method is called if the selected node changes.
// The method sets the text of the JTextField to the value of the
// selected node.

public void valueChanged(TreeSelectionEvent tse) {
  DefaultMutableTreeNode dmtn =
    (DefaultMutableTreeNode) tree.getLastSelectedPathComponent();
  String name = (String) dmtn.getUserObject();
```

```
jtf.setText("name is: " + name);
jtf.setForeground(Color.black);
  }

  public static void main(String args[]) {
    TestJTree tjt = new TestJTree();
  }
}

// The WinClosing class terminates the program when the window is closed

class WinClosing extends WindowAdapter {
  public void windowClosing(WindowEvent we) {
    System.exit(0);
  }
}
```

### Output

The user interface of the program is shown below. The `JTextField` at the bottom of the window displays the `String` associated with the node **Bob Wood**.

## 12.2 Tree Models, Nodes, and Paths

The tree model, node, and path classes and interfaces define the objects and methods used to create and manage the tree hierarchical data structure that is displayed by a `JTree` object. The model, node, and path class hierarchy is shown in the figure below:

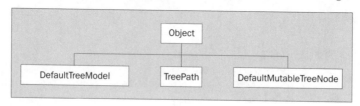

A node is used to store a piece of data at a particular position in the tree. It has information about its parent node and any child nodes for which it may be the parent. Node objects are implementations of the TreeNode interface.

A **Mutable** tree node is one that can change its parent node and the data that it stores. Mutable tree nodes must also implement the methods defined in the MutableTreeNode interface The javax.swing.tree package provides the DefaultMutableTreeNode class as a default tree node, and user-defined TreeNode classes can be created by implementing the appropriate interface or extending the appropriate TreeNode class.

A node with no parent is the **root** node of the hierarchy. A node with no children is known as a **leaf**.

A TreeModel object is used to create the data model associated with the tree. TreeModel objects must implement the TreeModel interface. The DefaultTreeModel class is an implementation of this interface and provides a good starting point for user-defined TreeModel classes.

The JTreePath class represents a path to a node.

# 12.2.1 DefaultMutableTreeNode Class

```
public class DefaultMutableTreeNode extends Object
  implements Cloneable, MutableTreeNode, Serializable, Treenode

    Object
      DefaultMutableTreeNode
```

### Interfaces

```
    Cloneable, MutableTreeNode, Serializable, TreeNode
```

A DefaultMutableTreeNode object represents a mutable tree node, one that can change by adding or removing child nodes, or by changing the contents of a user object stored in the node.

## DefaultMutableTreeNode() Constructors

| Constructor | Syntax |
|---|---|
| DefaultMutableTreeNode() | public DefaultMutableTreeNode() |
| | public DefaultMutableTreeNode(Object *obj*) |
| | public DefaultMutableTreeNode(Object *obj*, boolean allowsChildren) |

DefaultMutableTreeNode() creates a DefaultMutableTreeNode object. The DefaultMutableTreeNode object can be initialized with an object; any class object can be stored by the node. If allowsChildren is set to false, the DefaultMutableTreeNode object will not allow child nodes to be added to it.

## Methods to Access Child Nodes

| Method | Syntax |
|---|---|
| children() | public Enumeration children() |
| getAllowsChildren() | public boolean getAllowsChildren() |
| getChildAfter() | public TreeNode getChildAfter(TreeNode *childNode*) |
| getChildAt() | public TreeNode getChildAt(int *index*) |
| getChildBefore() | public TreeNode getChildBefore(TreeNode *childNode*) |
| getChildCount() | public int getChildCount() |
| getFirstChild() | public TreeNode getFirstChild() |
| getIndex() | public int getIndex(TreeNode *childNode*) |
| getLastChild() | public TreeNode getLastChild() |
| isNodeChild() | public boolean isNodeChild(TreeNode *node*) |
| setAllowsChildren() | public void setAllowsChildren(boolean *allows*) |

children() returns an Enumeration object containing references to the child nodes.

getAllowsChildren() returns true if the node can have child nodes.

getChildAfter() returns the child in the node's child array immediately after the specified child node.

getChildBefore() returns the child in the node's child array immediately preceding the specified child node.

getChildAt() returns the a reference to the child node at the specified index.

getChildCount() returns the number of child nodes.

getFirstChild() and getLastChild() return the first or last child nodes in the child node array.

getIndex() returns the index of the specified child node.

isNodeChild() returns true if the specified node is a child node of the invoking DefaultMutableTreeNode object.

setAllowsChildren() specifies if the invoking DefaultMutableTreeNode object can have child nodes.

## Methods to Add or Insert Child Nodes

| Method | Syntax |
|---|---|
| add() | public void add(MutableTreeNode *child*) |
| insert() | public void insert(MutableTreeNode node, int *index*) |

add() removes the specified child node from its parent and makes it a child of the invoking `DefaultMutableTreeNode` object by adding the child node to the end of the child node array.

insert() adds the child node to the invoking `DefaultMutableTreeNode` objects child node array at the specified index.

## Enumeration Methods

| Method | Syntax |
|---|---|
| breadthFirstEnumeration() | public Enumeration breadthFirstEnumeration() |
| depthFirstEnumeration() | public Enumeration depthFirstEnumeration() |
| pathFromAncestorEnumeraton() | public Enumeration pathFromAncestorEnumeration (TreeNode *ancestorNode*) throws IllegalArgumentException |
| postOrderEnumeration() | public Enumeration postOrderEnumeration() |
| preOrderEnumeration() | public Enumeration preOrderEnumeration() |

breadthFirstEnumeration() returns an Enumeration object that traverses the subtree rooted at the invoking node in breadth-first order. The first element in the Enumeration will be the invoking node. The next elements will be the child nodes of the invoking nodes, and so on.

depthFirstEnumeration() returns an Enumeration object that traverses the subtree rooted at the invoking node in depth-first order. The resulting Enumeration works from the leaf nodes inwards.

pathFromAncestorEnumeration() returns an Enumeration object that follows the path from the specified ancestor node to the invoking node.

postOrderEnumeration() returns the same Enumeration object as depthFirstEnumeration().

preOrderEnumeration() returns an Enumeration object that traverses the subtree rooted at the invoking node in preorder – the Enumeration starts at the root node and goes along the path of the first child node all the way to the leaf node at the end of the path, it then goes along the path of the root node's second child node and so on.

## Leaf Node Methods

| Method | Syntax |
|--------|--------|
| getFirstLeaf() | public DefaultMutableTreeNode getFirstLeaf() |
| getLastLeaf() | public DefaultMutableTreeNode getLastLeaf() |
| getLeafCount() | public int getLeafCount() |
| getNextLeaf() | public DefaultMutableTreeNode getNextLeaf() |
| isLeaf() | public boolean isLeaf() |
| getPreviousLeaf() | public DefaultMutableTreeNode getPreviousLeaf() |

A leaf node is one that has no child nodes.

getFirstLeaf() returns the first leaf node that is a descendant of the invoking DefaultMutableTreeNode object.

getLastLeaf() returns the last leaf node that is a descendant of the invoking DefaultMutableTreeNode object.

getLeafCount() returns the number of leaf nodes that are descendants of the invoking node.

getNextLeaf() returns the next leaf node after the invoking node or null if the invoking node is the last leaf in the tree.

isLeaf() returns true if the invoking node is a leaf node.

getPreviousLeaf() returns the first leaf node preceding the invoking node or null if the invoking node is the first leaf in the tree.

## Lineage Methods

| Method | Syntax |
|--------|--------|
| getNextNode() | public DefaultMutableTreeNode getNextNode() |
| getNextSibling() | public DefaultMutableTreeNode getNextSibling() |
| getPreviousNode() | public DefaultMutableTreeNode getPreviousNode() |
| getPreviousSibling() | public DefaultMutableTreeNode getPreviousSibling() |
| getSharedAncestor() | public TreeNode getSharedAncestor<br>(DefaultMutableTreeNode node) |
| getSiblingCount() | public int getSiblingCount() |
| isNodeAncestor() | public boolean isNodeAncestor(TreeNode node) |

| Method | Syntax |
|--------|--------|
| isNodeDescendant() | public boolean isNodeDescendant<br>(DefaultMutableTreeNode *node*) |
| isNodeRelated() | public boolean isNodeRelated<br>(DefaultMutableTreeNode *node*) |
| isNodeSibling() | public boolean isNodeSibling(TreeNode *node*) |

These methods provide information about a node's relatives. They are used to return sibling node objects or to return information about the invoking nodes lineage.

❑ A **sibling** node is one that is on the same hierarchical level as the invoking node.

❑ A **related** node is one that is in the same tree as the invoking node.

❑ An **ancestor** node is one that is along the path to the root node from the invoking node.

❑ A **descendant** node is a child node, grandchild node, and so on, further down the tree from the current node, away from the root.

## Parent Node Methods

| Method | Syntax |
|--------|--------|
| getParent() | public TreeNode getParent() |
| setParent() | public void setParent(MutableTreeNode *newParent*) |

getParent() returns the nodes parent node.

setParent() assigns the node to a new parent node but does not change the parents child array.

## Node Property Methods

| Method | Syntax |
|--------|--------|
| getDepth() | public int getDepth() |
| getLevel() | public int getLevel() |
| getPath() | public TreeNode[] getPath() |

getDepth() returns the number of levels between the invoking node and the furthest leaf node.

getLevel() returns the number of levels between the invoking node and the root node.

getPath() returns a TreeNode array containing the path from the root node to the invoking node.

## Methods to Remove Nodes

| Method | Syntax |
|---|---|
| remove() | public void remove(int *index*) <br>    throws ArrayIndexOutOfBoundsException |
| | public void remove(MutableTreeNode *childNode*) |
| removeAllChildren() | public void removeAllChildren() |
| removeFromParent() | public void removeFromParent() |

remove() removes a child node and all of the child node's descendants from the invoking DefaultMutableTreeNode object based on either a specified index or a reference to the child node.

removeAllChildren() removes all of this child nodes.

removeFromParent() removes the invoking node from its parent node.

## Root Node Methods

| Method | Syntax |
|---|---|
| getRoot() | public TreeNode getRoot() |
| isRoot() | public boolean isRoot() |

getRoot() returns the root node of the tree that contains the invoking DefaultMutableTreeNode object.

isRoot() returns true if the invoking node is the root node.

## User Object Methods

| Method | Syntax |
|---|---|
| getUserObject() | public Object getUserObject() |
| getUserObjectPath() | public Object[] getUserObjectPath() |
| setUserObject() | public void setUserObject(Object *obj*) |

getUserObject() returns the Object stored by the invoking DefaultMutableTreeNode object.

setUserObject() is used to specify the Object stored by the invoking DefaultMutableTreeNode object.

getUserObjectPath() returns an Object array containing the objects stored by the nodes along the path from the root node to the invoking node.

# toString() Method

| Method | Syntax |
|---|---|
| toString() | public String toString() |

toString() returns the result of sending the toString() method to the Object stored by the invoking DefaultMutableTreeNode object.

## Example: Using DefaultMutableNode

This example creates the same JTree object as the *Using JTree* example on page 1040, except that the DefaultMutableTreeNode objects create the node hierarchy themselves by using the add() method to add child nodes starting from the root node. The DefaultTreeModel object is created by passing the root node to the DefaultTreeModel constructor. The entire node hierarchy is imported into DefaultTreeModel object along with the root node.

This demonstrates that there is more than one way to build a tree.

```
import javax.swing.*;
import javax.swing.tree.*;
import java.awt.*;
import java.awt.event.*;

public class TestDMN extends JFrame {
  private JTree tree;

  public TestDMN() {
    DefaultMutableTreeNode root =
      new DefaultMutableTreeNode("My Company");
    DefaultMutableTreeNode fin =
      new DefaultMutableTreeNode("Finance");
    DefaultMutableTreeNode acc =
      new DefaultMutableTreeNode("Accounting");
    DefaultMutableTreeNode res =
      new DefaultMutableTreeNode("Research");
    DefaultMutableTreeNode Bob =
      new DefaultMutableTreeNode("Bob Wood");
    DefaultMutableTreeNode Sue = new DefaultMutableTreeNode("Sue Mi");
    DefaultMutableTreeNode Joe =
      new DefaultMutableTreeNode("Joe King");
    DefaultMutableTreeNode Moe =
      new DefaultMutableTreeNode("Moe Knee");

    // The DefaultMutableTreeNode objects create the node hierarchy by
    // using the add() method to add child nodes starting from the root
    // node
```

```
          root.add(fin);
          root.add(acc);
          root.add(res);
          fin.add(Bob);
          fin.add(Sue);
          fin.add(Joe);
          acc.add(Moe);

          // The node hierarchy is loaded into a DefaultTreeModel object by
          // passing the root node to the DefaultTreeModel constructor. The node
          // hierarchy is imported along with the root node.

          DefaultTreeModel dtm = new DefaultTreeModel(root);

          tree = new JTree(dtm);
          tree.setShowsRootHandles(true);
          tree.expandRow(1);

          getContentPane().add(new JScrollPane(tree), BorderLayout.CENTER);

          // The WindowListener is used to terminate the program when the window
          // is closed.  Under Java 2 version 1.3, the addWindowListener() syntax
          // can be replaced by
          //
          // setDefaultCloseOperation(JFrame.EXIT_ON_CLOSE);

          addWindowListener(new WinClosing());
          setBounds(100, 100, 300, 200);
          setVisible(true);
        }

      public static void main(String args[]) {
        TestDMN tn = new TestDMN();
      }
    }

// The WinClosing class terminates the program when the window is closed

class WinClosing extends WindowAdapter {
  public void windowClosing(WindowEvent we) {
    System.exit(0);
  }
}
```

### Output

The user interface of the program is shown below. The tree looks the same as the *Using JTree* example, but the tree was created using a different methodology.

## 12.2.2 DefaultTreeModel Class

```
public class DefaultTreeModel extends Object implements Serializable, TreeModel
```

```
Object
    DefaultTreeModel
```

### Interfaces

```
Serializable, TreeModel
```

The DefaultTreeModel class implements the methods defined in the TreeModel interface and is used to create a data model for a JTree object. User-defined TreeModel classes are often written as sub-classes of the DefaultTreeModel class.

## DefaultTreeModel() Constructors

| Constructor | Syntax |
|---|---|
| DefaultTreeModel() | public DefaultTreeModel(TreeNode *root*) |
| | public DefaultTreeModel(TreeNode *root*, boolean *asksAllowsChildren*) |

DefaultTreeModel() creates a DefaultTreeModel object. The root is the parent node of the tree. If asksAllowsChildren is false, any node can have children. If it is true, each node will be asked if it allows children.

**12**

javax.swing.tree

## Child Node Methods

| Method | Syntax |
|---|---|
| asksAllowsChildren() | public boolean asksAllowsChildren() |
| getChild() | public Object getChild(Object *parent*, int *index*) |
| getChildCount() | public int getChildCount(Object *parent*) |
| getIndexOfChild() | public int getIndexOfChild(Object *parent*, Object *child*) |
| setAsksAllowsChildren() | public void setAsksAllowsChildren (boolean ask) |

asksAllowsChildren() provides information on how leaf nodes are defined. It returns true if leaf nodes are nodes which do not allow children and false if leaf nodes are nodes which don't currently have children (but they may allow children).

getChild() returns the child node at the specified index for the designated parent node.

getChildCount() returns the number of child nodes attributed to the specified parent node. If the parent node is a leaf node, this method would return 0.

getIndexOfChild() returns the index of a designated child node.

setAsksAllowsChildren() determines how leaf nodes are defined. If set to true, leaf nodes are nodes which do not allow children. If set to false, leaf nodes are nodes which don't currently have children (but they may allow children).

## Event Methods

| Method | Syntax |
|---|---|
| fireTreeNodeChanged() | protected void fireTreeNodeChanged (Object source, Object[] *path*, int[] *childIndices*, Object[] *children*) |
| fireTreeNodeInserted() | protected void fireTreeNodeInserted (Object source, Object[] *path*, int[] *childIndices*, Object[] *children*) |
| fireTreeNodeRemoved() | protected void fireTreeNodeRemoved (Object source, Object[] *path*, int[] *childIndices*, Object[] *children*) |

| Method | Syntax |
|---|---|
| fireTreeStructureChanged() | protected void fireTreeStructureChanged<br>(Object source, Object[] *path*,<br>int[] *childIndices*,<br>Object[] *children*) |

These methods are used to fire TreeModelEvent objects to the corresponding method defined in the TreeModelListener interface.

## getListeners() Method

| Method | Syntax |
|---|---|
| getListeners() | public EventListener[] getListeners(<br>Class *listenerClass*) |

getListeners() returns any listeners of the specified type registered to the invoking DefaultTreeModel object as an EventListener array.

## getPathToRoot() Method

| Method | Syntax |
|---|---|
| getPathToRoot() | public TreeNode[] getPathToRoot(TreeNode *node*) |

getPathToRoot() returns a TreeNode array containing the nodes along the path from the root node to the node passed as an argument.

## Methods to Inform the Model of a Node Change

| Method | Syntax |
|---|---|
| nodeChanged() | public void nodeChanged(TreeNode *node*) |
| nodesChanged() | public void nodesChanged(TreeNode *node*,<br>int[] *childIndices*) |
| nodeStructureChanged() | public void nodeStructureChanged(TreeNode *node*) |
| nodesWereInserted() | public void nodesWereInserted(TreeNode *node*,<br>int[] *childIndices*) |
| nodesWereRemoved() | public void nodesWereRemoved(TreeNode *node*,<br>int[] *childIndices*,<br>Object[] *removedChildren*) |

nodeChanged() is called to inform the model that the representation of the specified node has been changed, possibly because the value was edited.

nodesChanged() is called to tell the model that the child nodes of the specified node have been changed.

nodeStructureChanged() is called to indicate a change in the child node structure.

nodesWereInserted() is called to inform the model that child nodes have been inserted into the specified node.

nodesWereRemoved() is called to indicate that child nodes have been removed from the specified node.

## insertNodeInto() Method

| Method | Syntax |
|---|---|
| insertNodeInto() | public void insertNodeInto(MutableTreeNode child, MutableTreeNode *parent*, int *index*) |

insertNodeInto() is used to insert a child node at the specified index into the parent node's collection of child nodes.

## isLeaf() Method

| Method | Syntax |
|---|---|
| isLeaf() | public boolean isLeaf(Object *node*) |

isLeaf() returns true if the specified node is a leaf node. A leaf node is one that has no child nodes.

## reload() Method

| Method | Syntax |
|---|---|
| reload() | public void reload() |
| | public void reload(TreeNode *node*) |

reload() is used to refresh the tree either from the root node down or from the specified node down.

## removeNodeFromParent() Method

| Method | Syntax |
|---|---|
| removeNodeFromParent() | public void removeNodeFromParent (MutableTreeNode *node*) |

removeNodeFromParent() removes the specified child node from its parent node.

## Root Node Methods

| Method | Syntax |
|--------|--------|
| getRoot() | public Object getRoot() |
| setRoot() | public void setRoot(TreeNode *root*) throws IllegalArgumentException |

getRoot() returns the root node of the tree.

setRoot() is used to change the root node of the tree.

## TreeModelListener Methods

| Method | Syntax |
|--------|--------|
| addTreeModelListener() | public void addTreeModelListener (TreeModelListener *tml*) |
| removeTreeModelListener() | public void removeTreeModelListener (TreeModelListener *tml*) |

A TreeModelEvent is fired if nodes are changed, inserted, or removed.

addTreeModelListener()registers the invoking DefaultTreeModel object with a TreeModelListener object. The TreeModelListener is notified if the DefaultTreeModel generates an TreeModelEvent object.

removeTreeModelListener()removes a TreeModelListener object from the invoking Checkbox object. TreeModelEvent objects generated by the DefaultTreeModel will no longer be received by the TreeModelListener.

## valueForPathChange() Method

| Method | Syntax |
|--------|--------|
| valueForPathChanged() | public void valueForPathChanged(TreePath *path*, Object *newValue*) |

valueForPathChanged() changes the Object stored by the node at TreePath *path*.

### Example: Using DefaultTreeModel

In this example, a DefaultTableModel object is used to set up the data model for a JTree object, which is populated with a three-level hierarchy of DefaultMutableNode nodes created using the insertNodeInto() method. A JButton is also provided to remove selected child nodes from their parent nodes, removing the child nodes from the display.

12

javax.swing.tree

When the `JButton` is pressed, the path to the selected node is obtained using the `getSelectionPath()` method. A reference to the selected node is then obtained using the `TreePath` object and the `getLastPathComponent()` method. The node is then removed from its parent in the data model using the `removeNodeFromParent()` method.

Trying to remove the root node from the tree causes an exception to be thrown. To prevent this, the selected node is tested to see if it is the root node with the `isRoot()` method before it is removed.

```
import javax.swing.*;
import javax.swing.tree.*;
import java.awt.*;
import java.awt.event.*;

public class TestDTM extends JFrame implements ActionListener {
  private DefaultTreeModel dtm;
  private JTree tree;
  private JButton removeButton;

  public TestDTM() {
    DefaultMutableTreeNode root =
      new DefaultMutableTreeNode("My Company");
    DefaultMutableTreeNode fin =
      new DefaultMutableTreeNode("Finance");
    DefaultMutableTreeNode acc =
      new DefaultMutableTreeNode("Accounting");
    DefaultMutableTreeNode res =
      new DefaultMutableTreeNode("Research");
    DefaultMutableTreeNode Bob =
      new DefaultMutableTreeNode("Bob Wood");
    DefaultMutableTreeNode Sue = new DefaultMutableTreeNode("Sue Mi");
    DefaultMutableTreeNode Joe =
      new DefaultMutableTreeNode("Joe King");
    DefaultMutableTreeNode Moe =
      new DefaultMutableTreeNode("Moe Knee");

    // A DefaultTreeModel object is created and a node hierarchy is
    // loaded into it.

    dtm = new DefaultTreeModel(root);
    dtm.insertNodeInto(fin, root, 0);
    dtm.insertNodeInto(acc, root, 1);
    dtm.insertNodeInto(res, root, 2);
    dtm.insertNodeInto(Bob, fin, 0);
    dtm.insertNodeInto(Sue, fin, 1);
    dtm.insertNodeInto(Joe, fin, 2);
    dtm.insertNodeInto(Moe, acc, 0);

    tree = new JTree(dtm);
    tree.setShowsRootHandles(true);
    tree.setSelectionRow(1);
```

```
        removeButton = new JButton("Remove");
        removeButton.setBorder(BorderFactory.createRaisedBevelBorder());
        removeButton.addActionListener(this);
        JPanel p = new JPanel();
        p.add(removeButton);

        getContentPane().add(new JScrollPane(tree), BorderLayout.CENTER);
        getContentPane().add(p, BorderLayout.SOUTH);

        // The WindowListener is used to terminate the program when the window
        // is closed.  Under Java 2 version 1.3, the addWindowListener() syntax
        // can be replaced by
        //
        // setDefaultCloseOperation(JFrame.EXIT_ON_CLOSE);
        addWindowListener(new WinClosing());
        setBounds(100, 100, 300, 300);
        setVisible(true);
    }

    // The actionPerformed() method is called when the "Remove" button
    // is pressed.  It tests to see if the selected node is the root
    // node, and if not it removes the node.

    public void actionPerformed(ActionEvent ae) {
        TreePath path = tree.getSelectionPath();
        DefaultMutableTreeNode node =
            (DefaultMutableTreeNode) path.getLastPathComponent();
        if (!node.isRoot()) {
            dtm.removeNodeFromParent(node);
        }
    }

    public static void main(String args[]) {
        TestDTM tjt = new TestDTM();
    }
}

// The WinClosing class terminates the program when the window is closed

class WinClosing extends WindowAdapter {
    public void windowClosing(WindowEvent we) {
        System.exit(0);
    }
}
```

---

**Output**

The user interface of the program is shown below. The node Joe King is about to be removed.

# 12.2.3 MutableTreeNode Interface

```
public interface MutableTreeNode extends TreeNode
```

The MutableTreeNode interface defines methods used by a mutable tree node; one that can change by adding or removing child nodes, or by changing the contents of a user object stored in the node.

## insert() Method

| Method | Syntax |
|--------|--------|
| insert() | public void insert(MutableTreeNode *node*, int *index*) |

insert() adds a child node into the child array maintained by the node at the specified index.

## remove() Method

| Method | Syntax |
|--------|--------|
| remove() | public void remove(int *index*) |
| | public void remove(MutableTreeNode *childNode*) |

remove() removes a child node from the node based on either a specified index or a reference to the child node.

### removeFromParent() Method

| Method | Syntax |
|---|---|
| removeFromParent() | public void removeFromParent() |

removeFromParent() removes the node from its parent node.

### setParent() Method

| Method | Syntax |
|---|---|
| setParent() | public void setParent(MutableTreeNode *newParent*) |

setParent() assigns the node to a new parent node.

### setUserObject() Method

| Method | Syntax |
|---|---|
| setUserObject() | public void setUserObject(Object *obj*) |

setUserObject() is used to specify the Object stored by the invoking TreeNode object.

## 12.2.4 RowMapper Interface

```
public interface RowMapper
```

The RowMapper interface defines a method for converting tree paths to display rows.

### getRowsForPaths() Method

| Method | Syntax |
|---|---|
| getRowsForPaths() | public int[] getRowsForPaths(TreePath[] *path*) |

getRowsForPaths() returns an int array containing the display rows corresponding to the specified group of paths.

## 12.2.5 TreeModel Interface

```
public interface TreeModel
```

The TreeModel interface defines methods that are used to create a data model for a JTree object.

## Child Node Methods

| Method | Syntax |
|---|---|
| getChild() | public Object getChild(Object *parent*, int *index*) |
| getChildCount() | public int getChildCount(Object *parent*) |
| getIndexOfChild() | public int getIndexOfChild(Object *parent*, Object *child*) |

getChild() returns the child node at the specified index for the designated parent node.

getChildCount() returns the number of child nodes attributed to the specified parent node. If the parent node is a leaf node, this method would return 0.

getIndexOfChild() returns the index of a designated child node.

## getRoot() Method

| Method | Syntax |
|---|---|
| getRoot() | public Object getRoot() |

getRoot() returns the root node of the tree. The root node is the ultimate parent node of the tree.

## isLeaf() Method

| Method | Syntax |
|---|---|
| isLeaf() | public boolean isLeaf(Object *node*) |

isLeaf() returns true if the specified node is a leaf node. A leaf node is one that has no child nodes.

## TreeModelListener Methods

| Method | Syntax |
|---|---|
| addTreeModelListener() | public void addTreeModelListener (TreeModelListener *tml*) |
| removeTreeModelListener() | public void removeTreeModelListener (TreeModelListener *tml*) |

A TreeModelEvent is fired if nodes are changed, inserted, or removed.

addTreeModelListener() registers a TreeModelListener with the invoking TreeModel object to listen for TreeModelEvent objects.

removeTreeModelListener() dissociates a TreeModelListener from the invoking TreeModel object.

## valueForPathChange() Method

| Method | Syntax |
|---|---|
| valueForPathChanged() | public void valueForPathChanged(TreePath *path*, Object *newValue*) |

valueForPathChanged() notifies the tree when the value for the node designated by the TreePath path has been changed.

# 12.2.6 TreeNode Interface

```
public interface TreeNode
```

The TreeNode interface defines methods used to access information about a tree node.

## Child Node Methods

| Method | Syntax |
|---|---|
| children() | public Enumeration children() |
| getAllowsChildren() | public boolean getAllowsChildren() |
| getChildAt() | public TreeNode getChildAt(int *index*) |
| getChildCount() | public int getChildCount() |
| getIndex() | public int getIndex(TreeNode *childNode*) |

children() returns an Enumeration object containing references to the child nodes.

getAllowsChildren() returns true if the node can have child nodes.

getChildAt() returns the a reference to the child node at the specified index.

getChildCount() returns the number of child nodes.

getIndex() returns the index of the specified child node.

## getParent() Method

| Method | Syntax |
|---|---|
| getParent() | public TreeNode getParent() |

getParent() returns the parent node for the node.

## isLeaf() Method

| Method | Syntax |
|--------|--------|
| isLeaf() | public boolean isLeaf() |

isLeaf() returns true if the invoking node is a leaf. A leaf node is one that has no child nodes.

# 12.2.7 TreePath Class

public class **TreePath** extends Object implements Serializable

Object
  TreePath

### Implements
Serializable

A TreePath object represents a path to a node. The properties it manages are set in the constructor and cannot be changed once the TreePath object is instantiated.

## TreePath() Constructors

| Constructor | Syntax |
|-------------|--------|
| TreePath() | protected TreePath() |
| | public TreePath(Object *path*) |
| | public TreePath(Object[] *path*) |
| | protected TreePath(Object[] *path*, int *length*) |
| | protected TreePath(TreePath *parent*, Object *lastElement*) |

TreePath() creates a TreePath object. The no-argument constructor is primarily intended to be used by sub-classes. The public constructors build the TreePath object from one or more Objects in the path.

## equals () Method

| Method | Syntax |
|--------|--------|
| equals() | public boolean equals(Object *obj*) |

equals() returns true if Object is a TreePath object with the same path as the invoking TreePath object.

## getParentPath() Method

| Method | Syntax |
|---|---|
| getParentPath() | public TreePath getParentPath() |

getParentPath() returns a TreePath object containing all the path elements except the last path component.

## getPathCount() Method

| Method | Syntax |
|---|---|
| getPathCount() | public int getPathCount() |

getPathCount() returns the number of elements in the path of the invoking TreePath object.

## hashCode () Method

| Method | Syntax |
|---|---|
| hashCode() | public int hashCode() |

hashCode() returns the hash code for the invoking TreePath object.

## isDescendant() Method

| Method | Syntax |
|---|---|
| isDescendant() | public boolean isDescendant(TreePath path) |

isDescendant() returns true if the path represented by TreePath path is a sub-set of the path presented by the invoking TreePath object.

## pathByAddingChild() Method

| Method | Syntax |
|---|---|
| pathByAddingChild() | public TreePath pathByAddingChild(Object child) |

pathByAddingChild() returns a new path containing the elements of the invoking TreePath object plus the specified child object.

## Methods to Return Path Components

| Method | Syntax |
|---|---|
| getLastPathComponent() | public Object getLastPathComponent() |
| getPath() | public Object[] getPath() |
| getPathComponent() | public Object getPathComponent(int index) |

getLastPathComponent() returns the last component in the path represented by the invoking TreePath object.

getPath() returns an Object array containing all of the elements in the path.

getPathComponent() returns the component at the specified index in the path.

## toString() Method

| Method | Syntax |
|--------|--------|
| toString() | public String toString() |

toString() returns a String representation of the invoking TreePath object.

### Example: Using TreePath

See the DefaultTreeModel example in the DefaultTreeModel section on page 1055, where a TreePath object is used to determine which node has been selected.

# 12.3 Selection Models

A TreeSelectionModel governs how selections are made within the elements of a tree. Selections are based on rows and paths.

A row represents one line in the window display of the tree. Each visible node of the tree is placed on a different row. If a parent node is collapsed causing its child nodes to disappear, the row indices for the nodes below the parent node change.

The path is the list of nodes from the root node to the current node. TreeSelectionModel objects must implement the TreeSelectionModel interface. The DefaultTreeSelectionModel class is provided in the javax.swing.tree package to serve as a default TreeSelectionModel. The DefaultTreeSelectionModel class hierarchy is shown in the following figure.

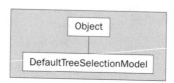

# 12.3.1 DefaultTreeSelectionModel Class

```
public class DefaultTreeSelectionModel extends Object
  implements Cloneable, Serializable, TreeSelectionModel
```

```
Object
  DefaultTreeSelectionModel
```

### Interfaces

```
Serializable, Cloneable, TreeSelectionModel
```

The `DefaultTreeSelectionModel` class is an implementation of the `TreeSelectionModel` interface. Listeners are notified whenever the paths in the selection change, not the rows.

## DefaultTreeSelectionModel() Constructor

| Constructor | Syntax |
|---|---|
| `DefaultTreeSelectionModel()` | `public DefaultTreeSelectionModel()` |

The initial selection is empty. The initial selection mode is `DISCONTIGUOUS_TREE_SELECTION`.

## General Selection Methods

| Method | Syntax |
|---|---|
| `clearSelection()` | `public void clearSelection()` |
| `getSelectionMode()` | `public int getSelectionMode()` |
| `isSelectionEmpty()` | `public boolean isSelectionEmpty()` |
| `setSelectionMode()` | `public void setSelectionMode(` `int selectionMode)` |

`clearSelection()` empties the current selection.

`isSelectionEmpty()` returns `true` if the selection is currently empty.

`getSelectionMode()` returns the selection mode.

`setSelectionMode()` is used to change the selection mode. The selection mode is one of the following constants:

- ❏ `TreeSelectionModel.SINGLE_TREE_SELECTION`
- ❏ `TreeSelectionModel.CONTIGUOUS_TREE_SELECTION`
- ❏ `TreeSelectionModel.DISCONTIGUOUS_TREE_SELECTION`

## getListeners() Method

| Method | Syntax |
|---|---|
| `getListeners()` | `public EventListener[] getListeners(` `Class listenerClass)` |

getListeners() returns any listeners of the specified type registered to the invoking DefaultTreeSelectionModel object as an EventListener array.

## PropertyChangeListener Methods

| Method | Syntax |
|---|---|
| addPropertyChangeListener() | public void addPropertyChangeListener (PropertyChangeListener *pcl*) |
| removePropertyChangeListener() | public void removePropertyChangeListener (PropertyChangeListener *pcl*) |

An PropertyChangeEvent is fired if an explicit setFont(), setBackground(), or SetForeground() command is performed on the current component.

addPropertyChangeListener() registers a PropertyChangeListener with the invoking TreeSelection object to listen for PropertyChangeEvent objects.

removePropertyChangeListener() dissociates a PropertyChangeListener from the invoking TreeSelection object.

## RowMapper Methods

| Method | Syntax |
|---|---|
| getRowMapper() | public RowMapper getRowMapper() |
| setRowMapper() | public void setRowMapper(RowMapper *newMapper*) |

getRowMapper() returns a RowMapper object that is used to map a path to a row. See Section 12.2.4, *RowMapper Interface* on page 1059, for more details.

setRowMapper() is used to change the RowMapper.

## Selection Path Methods

| Method | Syntax |
|---|---|
| addSelectionPath() | public void addSelectionPath(TreePath *path*) |
| addSelectionPaths() | public void addSelectionPaths(TreePath[] *paths*) |
| getLeadSelectionPath() | public TreePath getLeadSelectionPath() |
| getSelectionCount() | public int getSelectionCount() |
| getSelectionPath() | public TreePath getSelectionPath() |
| getSelectionPaths() | public TreePath[] getSelectionPaths() |

| Method | Syntax |
|---|---|
| isPathSelected() | public boolean isPathSelected(TreePath *path*) |
| removeSelectionPath() | public void removeSelectionPath(TreePath *path*) |
| removeSelectionPaths() | public void removeSelectionPaths(<br>TreePath[] *paths*) |
| setSelectionPath() | public void setSelectionPath(TreePath *path*) |
| setSelectionPaths() | public void setSelectionPaths(TreePath[] *paths*) |

addSelectionPath() and addSelectionPaths() add one or more paths to the current selection and notifies any TreePathListeners if the paths were newly selected.

getLeadSelectionPath() returns the last path that was added.

getSelectionCount() returns the number of paths that are selected.

getSelectionPath() returns the first path in the selection.

getSelectionPaths() returns all of the paths in the selection.

isPathSelected() returns true if the specified path is in the current selection.

removeSelectionPath() and removeSelectionPaths() remove one or more paths from the current selection and notify any TreePathListeners if paths are successfully removed.

setSelectionPath() and setSelectionPaths() set the selection to the specified path or paths.

## Selection Row Methods

| Method | Syntax |
|---|---|
| getLeadSelectionRow() | public int getLeadSelectionRow() |
| getMaxSelectionRow() | public int getMaxSelectionRow() |
| getMinSelectionRow() | public int getMinSelectionRow() |
| getSelectionRows() | public int[] getSelectionRows() |
| isRowSelected() | public boolean isRowSelected(int *rowIndex*) |
| resetRowSelection() | public void resetRowSelection() |

getLeadSelectionRow() returns the index of the row that was last added.

getMaxSelectionRow() returns the index of the last selected row.

getMinSelectionRow() returns the index of the first selected row.

getSelectionRows() returns an int array containing the indices of all selected rows.

isRowSelected() returns true if the specified row is selected.

resetRowSelection() updates what rows are selected.

## Selection Support Methods

| Method | Syntax |
|---|---|
| arePathsContiguous() | protected boolean arePathsContiguous (TreePath[] *paths*) |
| canPathsBeAdded() | protected boolean canPathsBeAdded (TreePath[] *paths*) |
| canPathsBeRemoved() | protected boolean canPathsBeRemoved (TreePath[] *paths*) |
| fireValueChanged() | protected void fireValueChanged (TreeSelectionEvent *tse*) |
| insureRowContinuity() | protected void insureRowContinuity() |
| insureUniqueness() | protected void insureUniqueness() |
| notifyPathChange() | protected void notifyPathChange (Vector *changedPaths*, TreePath *oldLeadSelection*) |
| updateLeadIndex() | protected void updateLeadIndex() |

arePathsContiguous(), canPathsBeAdded(), and canPathsBeRemoved() return information about the specified group of paths.

fireValueChanged() is used to notify registered TreeSelectionListener objects that the selection has changed.

insureRowContinuity() insures that the selection is made up of continuous rows.

insureUniqueness() removes duplicate entries in the selection.

notifyPathChange() notifies listeners of a change of path.

updateLeadIndex() is used to update the lead index.

## toString() Method

| Method | Syntax |
|---|---|
| toString() | public String toString() |

toString() returns a String representation of the invoking TreeSelectionListener object.

## TreeSelectionListener Methods

| Method | Syntax |
|---|---|
| addTreeSelectionListener() | public void addTreeSelectionListener<br>(TreeSelectionListener *tsl*) |
| removeTreeSelectionListener() | public void removeTreeSelectionListener<br>(TreeSelectionListener *tsl*) |

A TreeSelectionEvent is fired when the selection changes.

addTreeSelectionListener() registers a TreeSelectionListener with the invoking DefaultTreeSelectionModel object to listen for TreeSelectionEvent objects.

removeTreeSelectionListener() dissociates a TreeSelectionListener from the invoking DefaultTreeSelectionModel object.

# 12.3.2 TreeSelectionModel Interface

public interface TreeSelectionModel

The TreeSelectionModel interface defines methods for accessing the selection properties of a tree including the selection row, path, and mode. A class that is intended to serve as a TreeSelectionModel must implement this interface.

## General Selection Methods

| Method | Syntax |
|---|---|
| clearSelection() | public void clearSelection() |
| getSelectionMode() | public int getSelectionMode() |
| isSelectionEmpty() | public boolean isSelectionEmpty() |
| setSelectionMode() | public void setSelectionMode(int *selectionMode*) |

clearSelection() empties the current selection.

isSelectionEmpty() returns true if the selection is currently empty.

getSelectionMode() returns the selection mode.

setSelectionMode() method is used to change the selection mode. The selection mode is one of the following constants

❑   TreeSelectionModel.SINGLE_TREE_SELECTION

❑   TreeSelectionModel.CONTIGUOUS_TREE_SELECTION

## PropertyChangeListener Methods

| Method | Syntax |
|--------|--------|
| addPropertyChangeListener() | public void addPropertyChangeListener (PropertyChangeListener *pcl*) |
| removePropertyChangeListener() | public void removePropertyChangeListener (PropertyChangeListener *pcl*) |

A PropertyChangeEvent is fired if an explicit setFont(), setBackground(), or SetForeground() command is performed on the current component.

addPropertyChangeListener() registers a PropertyChangeListener with the invoking TreeSelection object to listen for PropertyChangeEvent objects.

removePropertyChangeListener() dissociates a PropertyChangeListener from the invoking TreeSelection object.

## RowMapper Methods

| Method | Syntax |
|--------|--------|
| getRowMapper() | public RowMapper getRowMapper() |
| setRowMapper() | public void setRowMapper(RowMapper *newMapper*) |

getRowMapper() returns a RowMapper object that is used to map a path to a row. See Section 12.2.4, *RowMapper Interface*, on page 1059 for more details.

setRowMapper() method is used to change the RowMapper.

## Selection Row Methods

| Method | Syntax |
|--------|--------|
| getLeadSelectionRow() | public int getLeadSelectionRow() |
| getMaxSelectionRow() | public int getMaxSelectionRow() |
| getMinSelectionRow() | public int getMinSelectionRow() |
| getSelectionRows() | public int[] getSelectionRows() |
| isRowSelected() | public boolean isRowSelected(int *rowIndex*) |
| resetRowSelection() | public void resetRowSelection() |

getLeadSelectionRow() returns the index of the row that was last added.

getMaxSelectionRow() returns the index of the last selected row.

getMinSelectionRow() returns the index of the first selected row.

getSelectionRows() returns an int array containing the indices of all selected rows.

isRowSelected() returns true if the specified row is selected.

resetRowSelection() updates what rows are selected.

## Selection Path Methods

| Method | Syntax |
| --- | --- |
| addSelectionPath() | public void addSelectionPath(TreePath *path*) |
| addSelectionPaths() | public void addSelectionPaths(TreePath[] *paths*) |
| getLeadSelectionPath() | public TreePath getLeadSelectionPath() |
| getSelectionCount() | public int getSelectionCount() |
| getSelectionPath() | public TreePath getSelectionPath() |
| getSelectionPaths() | public TreePath[] getSelectionPaths() |
| isPathSelected() | public boolean isPathSelected(TreePath *path*) |
| removeSelectionPath() | public void removeSelectionPath(TreePath *path*) |
| removeSelectionPaths() | public void removeSelectionPaths<br>(TreePath[] *paths*) |
| setSelectionPath() | public void setSelectionPath(TreePath *path*) |
| setSelectionPaths() | public void setSelectionPaths(TreePath[] *paths*) |

addSelectionPath() and addSelectionPaths() add one or more paths to the current selection and notifies any TreePathListeners if the paths were newly selected.

getLeadSelectionPath() returns the last path that was added.

getSelectionCount() returns the number of paths that are selected.

getSelectionPath() returns the first path in the selection.

getSelectionPaths() returns all of the paths in the selection.

isPathSelected() returns true if the specified path is in the current selection.

removeSelectionPath() and removeSelectionPaths() remove one or more paths from the current selection and notify any TreePathListeners if paths are successfully removed.

setSelectionPath() and setSelectionPaths() set the selection to the specified path or paths.

## TreeSelectionListener Methods

| Method | Syntax |
|---|---|
| addTreeSelectionListener() | public void **addTreeSelectionListener** (TreeSelectionListener *tsl*) |
| removeTreeSelectionListener() | public void **removeTreeSelectionListener** (TreeSelectionListener *tsl*) |

A TreeSelectionEvent is fired when the selection changes.

addTreeSelectionListener() registers a TreeSelectionListener with the invoking TreeSelection object to listen for TreeSelectionEvent objects.

removeTreeSelectionListener() dissociates a TreeSelectionListener from the invoking TreeSelection object.

# 12.4 Tree Editors

A TreeCellEditor object is used to edit tree nodes. For a class to serve as a TreeCellEditor object, it must implement the TreeCellEditor interface. User-defined TreeCellEditors can be written as an extension of one of the JComponent classes, so any Swing GUI component can be used to perform the node editing. For instance, a JSlider might be used to change the value of tree node Object that ranges between two integer values. The DefaultTreeCellEditor class is a default implementation of the TreeCellEditor interface. The DefaultTreeCellEditor class hierarchy is shown in the following figure.

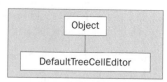

# 12.4.1 DefaultTreeCellEditor Class

```
public class DefaultTreeCellEditor extends Object
  implements ActionListener, TreeCellEditor, TreeSelectionListener
```

```
Object
  DefaultTreeCellEditor
```

### Interfaces

ActionListener, TreeCellEditor, TreeSelectionListener

The `DefaultTreeCellEditor` class is the default tree cell editor provided by the `javax.swing.tree` package. It uses a text field to edit cells. Editing is started on a triple mouse click, or after a click, pause, click and a delay of 1200 miliseconds.

## DefaultTreeCellEditor() Constructors

| Constructor | Syntax |
| --- | --- |
| DefaultTreeCellEditor() | public DefaultTreeCellEditor(JTree *tree*, DefaultTreeCellRenderer *renderer*) |
| | public DefaultTreeCellEditor(JTree *tree*, DefaultTreeCellRenderer *renderer*, TreeCellEditor *editor*) |

`DefaultTreeCellEditor()` creates a `DefaultTreeCellEditor` object. The `DefaultTreeCellEditor` object is associated with a `JTree` object. A reference to a `DefaultTreeCellRenderer` object must be provided. A `TreeCellEditor` can also be specified.

## actionPerformed() Method

| Method | Syntax |
| --- | --- |
| actionPerformed() | public void actionPerformed(ActionEvent *ae*) |

`actionPerformed()` is defined in the `ActionListener` interface and is called when an `ActionEvent` is generated from a registered source. For a `DefaultTreeCellEditor`, the `ActionEvent` will generated when the editing session begins.

## CellEditor and TreeCellEditor Interface Methods

| Method | Syntax |
| --- | --- |
| cancelCellEditing() | public void cancelCellEditing() |
| getCellEditorValue() | public Object getCellEditorValue() |
| getTreeCellEditorComponent() | public Component getTreeCellEditorComponent (JTree *tree*, Object *value*, boolean *isSelected*, boolean *expanded*, boolean *leaf*, int *row*) |
| isCellEditable() | public isCellEditable(EventObject *event*) |
| shouldSelectCell() | public shouldSelectCell(EventObject *event*) |
| stopCellEditing() | public boolean stopCellEditing() |

The `DefaultTreeCellEditor` class implements the `TreeCellEditor` interface and must therefore provide implementation to the methods defined in the `TreeCellEditor` and `CellEditor` interfaces.

cancelCellEditing() cancels the current editing session without saving any changes that have been made.

getCellEditorValue() returns the current value of the tree cell being edited.

getTreeCellEditorComponent() is used to configure the Component that will be used to edit the node and returns a reference to the component.

isCellEditable() is written to return true if the EventObject passed to the method is a valid trigger for starting the editor.

shouldSelectCell() is written to return true if the node to be edited should also be selected.

stopEditing() stops the current editing session and saves any edits currently in progress. It returns true if there was editing in progress and it was stopped successfully.

## CellEditorListener Methods

| Method | Syntax |
|---|---|
| addCellEditorListener() | public void addCellEditorListener<br>(CellEditorListener cl) |
| removeCellEditorListener() | public void removeCellEditorListener<br>(CellEditorListener c?) |

addCellEditorListener() registers a CellEditorListener with the invoking DefaultTreeCellEditor object to listen for ChangeEvent objects. A ChangeEvent is generated when the editor changes the value of a node.

removeCellEditorListener() dissociates a CellEditorListener from the invoking DefaultTreeCellEditor object.

## Color Methods

| Method | Syntax |
|---|---|
| getBorderSelectionColor() | public Color getBorderSelectionColor() |
| setBorderSelectionColor() | public void setBorderSelectionColor<br>(Color color) |

getBorderSelectionColor() returns the color that is used to draw the border.

setBorderSelectionColor() is used to change the border color.

## Font Methods

| Method | Syntax |
|--------|--------|
| getFont() | public Font getFont() |
| setFont() | public void setFont(Font *editingFont*) |

getFont() returns a Font object representing the font used for editing.

setFont() is used to set the editing font.

## valueChanged() Method

| Method | Syntax |
|--------|--------|
| valueChanged() | public void valueChanged(TreeSelectionEvent *tse*) |

valueChanged() is called when a TreeSelectionEvent is generated, it is defined in the TreeSelectionListener interface.

### Example: Using DefaultTreeCellEditor

In this example, a DefaultTreeCellEditor object is created to edit the String objects associated with the nodes of a tree. The setInvokesStopCellEditing() method is set to true to save any changes when the editor exits. To start the editor, select a node and then either click three times over the String or click-pause-click.

```java
import javax.swing.*;
import javax.swing.tree.*;
import java.awt.*;
import java.awt.event.*;
public class TestEdit extends JFrame {
  private JTree tree;
  private JLabel lbl;
  private DefaultTreeCellEditor editor;
  private DefaultTreeModel dtm;

  public TestEdit() {

// A JTree model is created using the same methodolgy as the
    // "Using JTree" example.  Eight DefaultMutableTreeNode objects are
    // created containing String objects.  The nodes hierarchy is loaded
    // into a DefaultTreeModel object which in turn is passed to the JTree
    // constructor
    DefaultMutableTreeNode root =
      new DefaultMutableTreeNode("My Company");
    DefaultMutableTreeNode fin =
      new DefaultMutableTreeNode("Finance");
    DefaultMutableTreeNode acc =
      new DefaultMutableTreeNode("Accounting");
  DefaultMutableTreeNode res =
```

```
    new DefaultMutableTreeNode("Research");
    DefaultMutableTreeNode Bob =
      new DefaultMutableTreeNode("Bob Wood");
    DefaultMutableTreeNode Sue = new DefaultMutableTreeNode("Sue Mi");
    DefaultMutableTreeNode Joe =
      new DefaultMutableTreeNode("Joe King");
    DefaultMutableTreeNode Moe =
      new DefaultMutableTreeNode("Moe Knee");

    dtm = new DefaultTreeModel(root);
    dtm.insertNodeInto(fin, root, 0);
    dtm.insertNodeInto(acc, root, 1);
    dtm.insertNodeInto(res, root, 2);
    dtm.insertNodeInto(Bob, fin, 0);
    dtm.insertNodeInto(Sue, fin, 1);
    dtm.insertNodeInto(Joe, fin, 2);
    dtm.insertNodeInto(Moe, acc, 0);

    tree = new JTree(dtm);
    tree.setShowsRootHandles(true);
    tree.expandRow(1);
    tree.setEditable(true);

    // A DefaultTreeCellEditor is set to be the editor of the JTree object.
    // The setInvokesStopCellEditing() is set to save changes if the
    // editing session is interrupted.
    editor = new DefaultTreeCellEditor(tree,
                                       new DefaultTreeCellRenderer());
    tree.setCellEditor(editor);
    tree.setInvokesStopCellEditing(true);

    getContentPane().add(new JScrollPane(tree), BorderLayout.CENTER);

    // The WindowListener is used to terminate the program when the window
    // is closed.  Under Java 2 version 1.3, the addWindowListener() syntax
    // can be replaced by
    //
    // setDefaultCloseOperation(JFrame.EXIT_ON_CLOSE);

    addWindowListener(new WinClosing());
    setBounds(100, 100, 300, 300);
    setVisible(true);
  }

  public static void main(String args[]) {
    TestEdit te = new TestEdit();
  }
}

// The WinClosing class terminates the program when the window is closed

class WinClosing extends WindowAdapter {
  public void windowClosing(WindowEvent we) {
    System.exit(0);
  }
}
```

**Output**

The user interface of the program is shown below. The node Bob Wood is being edited.

# 12.4.2 TreeCellEditor Interface

`public interface TreeCellEditor extends CellEditor`

The `TreeCellEditor` interface extends the `CellEditor` interface to provide the ability to configure an editor for a tree. It defines one method, `getTreeCellEditorComponent()`, that is used to return a `Component` that will be used to edit the tree node.

A custom tree editor would generally be a sub-class of a GUI component that would implement the `TreeCellEditor` interface and provide implementations of the methods defined in both the `TreeCellEditor` and `CellEditor` interfaces.

## getTreeCellEditorComponent() Method

| Method | Syntax |
|---|---|
| `getTreeCellEditorComponent()` | `public Component`<br>  `getTreeCellEditorComponent`<br>    `(JTree tree, Object value,`<br>      `boolean isSelected, boolean expanded,`<br>      `boolean leaf, int row)` |

`getTreeCellEditorComponent()` returns a component that can be used to edit a `JTree` node. The argument list provides the information needed to properly configure the editor. The `Object value` is the value of the cell to be edited. The `isSelected` and `expanded` flags inform the editor if the cell should be rendered with selection highlighting and if the node is expanded. The `leaf` flag is `true` if the node to be edited is a leaf node. The `row` is the row index of the node being edited.

To create a user-defined `TreeCellEditor`, write a class that extends a GUI component class and implements the `TreeCellEditor`. Override the `getTreeCellEditorComponent()` method to configure the component, and return a reference to it (that is, `return this;`).

# 12.5 Tree Renderers

A `TreeCellRender` object dictates how each tree node is rendered on the screen. User-defined `TreeCellRenderers` can be written as an extension of one of the `JComponent` classes, so that any GUI component can be used to perform the node rendering. The User-defined `TreeCellRenderer` would have to provide implementation of the methods defined in the `TreeCellRenderer` interface. The `DefaultTreeCellRenderer` class is an implementation of the `TreeCellRenderer` interface that uses `JLabel` objects to render the nodes. The `DefaultTreeCellRenderer` class hierarchy is shown in the following figure.

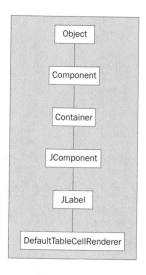

# 12.5.1 DefaultTreeCellRenderer Class

```
public class DefaultTreeCellRenderer extends JLabel implements TreeCellRenderer
```

```
Object
    Component
        Container
            JComponent
                JLabel
                    DefaultTreeCellRenderer
```

### Interfaces

```
ImageObserver, MenuContainer, Serializable, Accessible, SwingConstants,
TreeCellRenderer
```

The `DefaultTreeCellRenderer` class represents the default `TreeCellRenderer`. It uses `JLabel` objects to render the nodes.

## DefaultTreeCellRenderer() Constructor

| Constructor | Syntax |
|---|---|
| `DefaultTreeCellRenderer()` | `public DefaultTreeCellRenderer()` |

`DefaultTreeCellRenderer()` creates a `DefaultTreeCellRenderer` object. The alignment is set to left; the icons and text color are determined from the `UIManager`.

## Color Methods

| Method | Syntax |
|---|---|
| getBackgroundNonSelection Color() | public Color getBackgroundNonSelectionColor() |
| getBackgroundSelection Color() | public Color getBackgroundSelectionColor() |
| getBorderSelection Color() | public Color getBorderSelectionColor() |
| getTextNonSelection Color() | public Color getTextNonSelectionColor() |
| getTextSelectionColor() | public Color getTextSelectionColor() |
| setBackground() | public void setBackground<br>(Color *backgroundColor*) |
| setBackgroundNonSelection Color() | public void setBackgroundNonSelectionColor<br>(Color *backgroundColor*) |
| setBackgroundSelection Color() | public void setBackgroundSelectionColor<br>(Color *backgroundColor*) |
| setBorderSelectionColor() | public void setBorderSelectionColor<br>(Color *borderColor*) |
| setTextNonSelection Color() | public void setTextNonSelectionColor<br>(Color textColor) |
| setTextSelection Color() | public void setTextSelectionColor<br>(Color *textColor*) |

These methods are used to return or change the background, border, or text color. Different colors can be displayed for selected and non-selected nodes.

## getTreeCellRendererComponent() Method

| Method | Syntax |
|---|---|
| getTreeCellRenderer Component() | public Component getTreeCellRendererComponent<br>(JTree *tree*, Object *value*,<br>boolean *isSelected*, boolean *expanded*,<br>boolean *leaf*, int *row*,<br>boolean *hasFocus*) |

12

getTreeCellRendererComponent() returns a component that can be used to render a JTree node. The argument list provides the information needed to properly configure the renderer. The Object value is the value of the cell to be edited. The isSelected and expanded flags inform the editor if the cell should be rendered with selection highlighting and if the node is expanded. The leaf flag is true if the node to be edited is a leaf node. The row is the row index of the node being edited. The boolean hasFocus flag informs the renderer if the node has focus. The Component returned will be a JLabel object.

## Icon Methods

| Method | Syntax |
|---|---|
| getClosedIcon() | public Icon getClosedIcon() |
| getDefaultClosedIcon() | public Icon getDefaultClosedIcon() |
| getDefaultLeafIcon() | public Icon getDefaultLeafIcon() |
| getDefaultOpenIcon() | public Icon getDefaultOpenIcon() |
| getLeafIcon() | public Icon getLeafIcon() |
| getOpenIcon() | public Icon getOpenIcon() |
| setClosedIcon() | public void setClosedIcon(Icon closedIcon) |
| setLeafIcon() | public void setLeafIcon(Icon leafIcon) |
| setOpenIcon() | public void setOpenIcon(Icon openIcon) |

The DefaultTreeCellRenderer class uses different icons to represent different node states. These methods are used to return or set the various types of icon.

getclosedIcon() and setClosedIcon() return and set non-leaf icons that aren't expanded.

getleafIcon() and setleafIcon() is used to display leaf node icons.

getOpenIcon() and setOpenIcon() are used to show non-leaf nodes that are expanded.

There are also default icons for each of these icon types.

## paint() Method

| Method | Syntax |
|---|---|
| Paint() | public void paint(Graphics g) |

paint() paints the current value. The background is painted based on its selected status.

## setFont() Method

| Method | Syntax |
|---|---|
| setFont() | public void setFont(Font *font*) |

setFont() changes the display font. The Font object passed as an argument cannot be a FontUIResource.

# 12.5.2 TreeCellRenderer Interface

```
public interface TreeCellRenderer
```

The TreeCellRenderer interface defines one method that is used to configure a tree cell renderer. User-defined TreeCellRenderer objects will implement this interface

## getTreeCellRendererComponent() Method

| Method | Syntax |
|---|---|
| getTreeCellRendererComponent() | public Component<br>  getTreeCellRendererComponent<br>    (JTree *tree*, Object *value*,<br>    boolean *isSelected*,<br>    boolean ex*panded*,<br>    boolean *leaf*, int *row*,<br>    boolean *hasFocus*) |

getTreeCellRendererComponent() returns a component that can be used to render a JTree node. The argument list provides the information needed to properly configure the renderer. The Object value is the value of the cell to be edited. The isSelected and expanded flags inform the editor if the cell should be rendered with selection highlighting and if the node is expanded. The leaf flag is true if the node to be edited is a leaf node. The row is the row index of the node being edited. The boolean hasFocus flag informs the renderer if the node has focus.

To create a user-defined TreeCellRenderer, write a class that extends a GUI component class and implements the TreeCellRenderer. Override the getTreeCellRendererComponent() method to configure the component, and return a reference to it (that is, return this;).

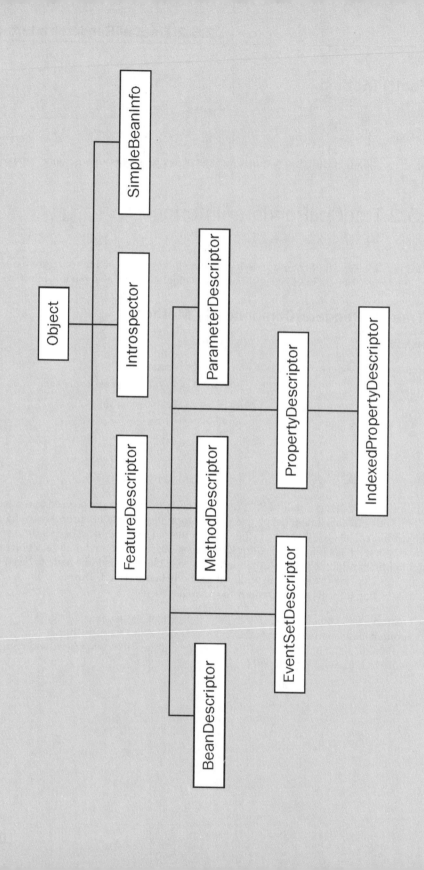

# 13

# java.beans

The java.beans package contains classes and interfaces for creating and analyzing reusable components called Java Beans. A Java Bean is a class object that adheres to a certain design architecture. The java.beans package provides event classes and interfaces for handling property change and vetoable property change events. A property change event occurs when the value of a property that is bound to a PropertyChangeListener object changes. Other associated components can be notified of the change and alter their own properties to reflect the change. A vetoable property change event is a property change that can be vetoed by registered components.

The java.beans package also provides classes and interfaces for analyzing the nature and behavior of a Bean. Information can be returned on the methods, properties, event listeners, and parameters of the Bean. The property editor classes and interfaces can be used to create an editor that can change a Bean's properties in the context of a visual programming environment.

The java.beans package hierarchy is illustrated in the figure opposite.

This chapter covers:

# 13.1 Bean Fundamentals

Before going into the detail of the classes and interfaces in the `java.beans` package, let's begin with some basics of Beans themselves.

# 13.1.1 What is a Bean

A **Java Bean** is a reusable **component** that adheres to a standard (i.e. JavaBeans) design architecture. A Bean is a class object that may or may not be visible at run time. They are intended to be compact and portable. They support the standard Java multi-threading, security, and event models as well as the concepts of persistence and customization.

**JavaBeans** provides a component architecture, a standard framework for developing components. There is a standard design pattern for naming methods and interfaces. Most properties, for instance, will have get`Property()` and set`Property()` methods associated with them to return or change the value of that property. A boolean property often has an is`Property()` method in place of the get`Property()` method.

A Java Bean utilizes the Java 1.1 event model. In addition to the event types defined in the `java.util`, `java.awt`, `java.awt.event`, and `javax.swing.event` packages, a Bean may fire a `PropertyChangeEvent` or `VetoableChangeEvent`. These events are defined in the `java.beans` package and are used to monitor or limit changes to a Bean property.

## Example: A Simple Bean

The following code represents a simple Bean. The `ZackButton` class defines a `JButton` object with the label **Zack** on it. It has one additional property, an `int` named `amount`. The specifics of the implementation, for instance the use of the `Serializable` interface, the syntax of the `get()` and `set()` methods, will be discussed in subsequent sections.

```java
import java.io.*;
import javax.swing.*;

public class ZackButton extends JButton implements Serializable {
  private int amount;

  public ZackButton() {
    super("Zack");
    amount = 2;
  }

  public int getAmount() {
    return amount;
  }

  public void setAmount(int amt) {
    amount = amt;
  }
}
```

*Output*

The picture below shows the `ZackButton` bean loaded into the BeanBox.

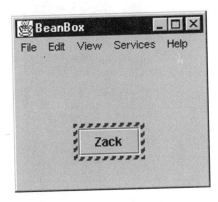

## The JavaBeans Development Kit (BDK)

The **JavaBeans Development Kit (BDK)** provides tools to support the development of JavaBeans components. The BDK provides a reference Bean container, the **BeanBox** which allows the user to create, modify, and connect Beans. The BDK also provides example Beans and a variety of other reusable example source code. The BDK can be downloaded from the JavaBeans website at

http://java.sun.com/beans/software/bdk_download.html

## The BeanBox

The BeanBox is a simple Bean container that is provided by the BDK. It permits Beans to be examined, modified, and connected to one another. The BeanBox is not intended to be an application development tool but rather it is a simple tool to test Beans. To run BeanBox, the BDK provides two scripts in the /beans/beanbox directory of the BDK hierarchy. The run.sh script is for running under the UNIX environment and the run.bat script is for running under Windows.

When the BeanBox is started, three windows appear:

The first is the toolbox which contains the available Beans. These Beans are read from the JAR files contained in the BDK1.1\jars directory (on Windows).

The second window is the main window and is the container that Beans can be placed into.

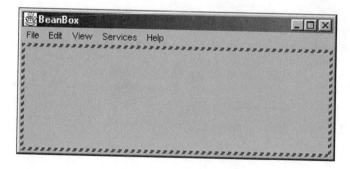

The third window is a property sheet which is used as a default property editor.

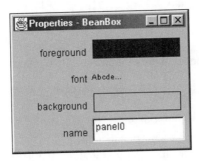

There is also a "method tracing" window.

To place a Bean from the toolbox into the main window, click on the desired Bean in the toolbox. The cursor will change to a cross-hair indicating that the Bean has been selected. Clicking the mouse at a spot in the main window places a copy of the Bean at that spot. The Beans properties can be edited by changing the values that appear in the property sheet.

## Loading a Bean into the BeanBox

Beans are loaded into the BeanBox by enclosing them in a JAR file and placing the JAR file in the jars directory of the BDK hierarchy. The JAR file must also contain a manifest file identifying the Bean as such: see Section 13.1.2 below for more information on JAR and manifest files. The syntax for creating a JAR file for the ZackButton Bean (see the example *A Simple Bean* on page 1084) is:

```
jar cfm zackbutton.jar ZackButton.mf ZackButton.class
```

The manifest file, ZackButton.mf, must contain these lines:

```
Manifest-Version: 1.1

Name: ZackButton.class
Java-Bean: True
```

When the zackbutton.jar file is placed in the jars directory of the BDK hierarchy (for example, C:\BDK1.1\jars on a typical Windows installation) and the BeanBox is started, the label **zackbutton** appears in the toolbox. A ZackButton object may now be placed in the main window just as the existing Beans can.

## 13.1.2 JAR Files

A Java Archive, or JAR, file is an archive that can contain any number of files using compression based on the ZIP format. One use of a JAR file is to package a series of Beans and their related BeanInfo and PropertyEditor files into a single file. To load a Bean into the BeanBox, the Bean .class file and its related files must first be placed into a JAR file. A JAR file will normally also contain a manifest file describing its contents; this can either be specified by the user or generated automatically by the jar tool.

**13**

java.beans

The jar program, provided as part of the JDK, is used to create, examine, and extract files from JAR files. The syntax is:

```
jar {command}{options} [jar file] [manifest file] file1, file2, file3, ...
```

The command must be one of these three letters. Only one command may be specified:

| Command | Description |
|---------|-------------|
| c | Create a new JAR file. |
| t | List the contents of a JAR file. |
| x | Extract the named file from the JAR file or all of the files if no names are provided. |

More than one option can be specified. The allowable options include:

| Option | Description |
|--------|-------------|
| f | Used to specify the name of the JAR file. If this option is not used, the standard input and output streams are used. |
| m | Used to specify that a manifest file will be included in the JAR file. |
| M | Indicates that a manifest file is not to be created. |
| v | Verbose output will be generated. |
| 0 | Compression will not be used with the JAR file. |

For an example of how to create a JAR file, see the *Using PropertyEditor* example on page 1152.

Unless the m option is specified, the jar program will automatically create a manifest file when the JAR file is created. The manifest file is stored in a directory called META-INF within the JAR file, and contains a series of attribute/value pairs that provide information about the contents of the JAR file. If a user-specified manifest file is provided when the JAR file is created, this information will be used to create the manifest file generated by the jar program; any additional information needed that is not contained in the user-specified manifest file will be generated by the jar program. Using a user-specified manifest file allows extra options to be specified that are not automatically generated, such as specifying that a particular class is a Java Bean.

# 13.1.3 Properties

A **property** is a named characteristic or attribute that helps to define the behavior or state of an object – for instance, a button has an action command property associated with it. A property does not have to correspond to a data member of the class, but often the data members do represent properties.

Properties are accessed by defining methods that return or change the value of the property. The standard naming convention is to define a get() method to return the value of the property, and a set() method is to change the value. For boolean properties, an is() method is often defined to return the value of the property.

## Example: Using Properties

The following code:

```
import java.io.*;
import java.awt.*;

public class ColorManager implements Serializable {
  protected Color fontColor;

  public ColorManager() {
    fontColor = Color.black;
  }

  public Color getFontColor() {
    return fontColor;
  }

  public void setFontColor(Color color) {
    fontColor = color;
  }
}
```

represents a simple Bean that defines one property, a Color object named
fontColor. Three methods are implemented, a no-argument constructor that sets
the initial color to black and get() and set() methods to access the fontColor
property. A program that uses this bean is listed below. In this case, the Bean is
non-visible and simply contains the color used when displaying a label:

```
import javax.swing.*;
import java.awt.*;
import java.awt.event.*;

public class DriverBean extends JFrame {
    private ColorManager lm;
    private JLabel nameLabel;

    public DriverBean() {
       lm = new ColorManager();

// A Label object is created and placed inside the JFrame.
// The ColorManager object is used to set the label color.

       nameLabel = new JLabel("Label");
       nameLabel.setFont(new Font("Serif", Font.PLAIN, 12));
```

```
            nameLabel.setForeground(lm.getFontColor());

        JPanel p = new JPanel();
        p.add(nameLabel);
        getContentPane().add(p, BorderLayout.CENTER);

    //  The WindowListener is used to terminate the program when the window
    //  is closed.  Under Java 2 version 1.3, the addWindowListener() syntax
    //  can be replaced by
    //
    //      setDefaultCloseOperation(JFrame.EXIT_ON_CLOSE);

        addWindowListener(new WinClosing());
        setBounds(100, 100, 200, 120);
        setVisible(true);
    }

    public static void main(String args[]) {
        DriverBean db = new DriverBean();
    }
}

//  The WinClosing class terminates the program when the window is closed

class WinClosing extends WindowAdapter {
    public void windowClosing(WindowEvent we) {
        System.exit(0);
    }
}
```

This code creates a JFrame object containing a JLabel object and a ColorManager object. The color of the text contained by the JLabel is obtained from the ColorManager object using the getFontColor() method. The WindowListener object is used to terminate the program if the window is closed.

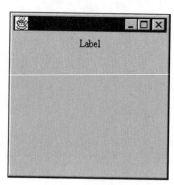

Properties do not have to be single entities. Arrays, vectors, or collections can be used to group similar properties together. A grouped property such as this is called an **indexed** property. Methods can be provided to access the entire group and/or individual elements of the indexed property, and may include a `throws` clause to include array-type exceptions such as an `ArrayIndexOutOfBoundsException`.

## Bound Properties

In the example shown in the previous section, changes to the `fontColor` property are made independent of the driver program. It is often desirable for a Bean to notify interested parties when one of its properties has been changed. For instance, since the purpose of the `ColorManager` class was to specify the color of the `JLabel` objects displayed by the driver program, if the `fontColor` property is changed, the color of any `JLabel` objects should be changed as well.

A property that supports change notifications is known as a **bound** property. The property change is reflected by the firing of a `PropertyChangeEvent` object. An object that is registered with a `PropertyChangeListener` can receive the `PropertyChangeEvent` object. The `PropertyChangeEvent` object contains the event source, the property name, and the old and new values of the property.

Unlike the AWT and Swing components where the event listening and firing methods were largely built in to the classes, when creating a Java Bean that supports bound properties, these methods must be implemented within the bean itself. Specifically, methods must be provided that add and remove a `PropertyChangeListener` and to fire events to any registered `PropertyChangeListener` object.

The syntax for the methods to add or remove a `PropertyChangeListener` object from the Bean is

| Method | Syntax |
|---|---|
| `addPropertyChangeListener()` | `public void addPropertyChangeListener` `(PropertyChangeListener pcl)` |
| `removePropertyChangeListener()` | `public void removePropertyChangeListener` `(Property ChangeListener pcl)` |

These methods can also be written as `synchronized` methods. The method to fire the `PropertyChangeEvent` first creates the `PropertyChangeEvent` object containing information about the property change and then sends the event to the `propertyChange()` method of any registered `PropertyChangeListener` objects.

### Example: Using Bound Properties

In this example, the `ColorManager` class (see the example *Using Properties* on page 1089) is revised such that the `fontColor` property is a bound property. Several changes have been made to the code in this example, and are highlighted below.

13

java.beans

```java
import java.io.*;
import java.util.*;
import java.awt.*;
import java.awt.event.*;
import javax.swing.*;
import java.beans.*;

public class ColorManager2 extends JPanel implements Serializable,
        ItemListener {
  protected Color fontColor, oldColor;
  protected JComboBox colorList;
  protected Vector listeners;

  public ColorManager2() {
    fontColor = Color.black;

    // A JComboBox is created with a selection of colors to choose from.
    // The JComboBox is registered with an ItemListener that receives
    // an ItemEvent when the selection changes.

    String[] colors = {
      "black", "red", "green", "blue"
    };
    colorList = new JComboBox(colors);
    colorList.addItemListener(this);
    add(colorList);

    listeners = new Vector();
  }

  public Color getFontColor() {
    return fontColor;
  }

  // When the color is changed witht the setFont() method,
  // a PropertyChangeEvent is sent to any PropertyChangeListener objects

  public void setFontColor(Color color) {
    oldColor = fontColor;
    fontColor = color;

    firePropertyChangeEvent(this, "Color", oldColor, fontColor);
  }

  public void itemStateChanged(ItemEvent ie) {
```

```
      String newColor = (String) colorList.getSelectedItem();

    if (newColor.equals("red")) {
      setFontColor(Color.red);
    }
    if (newColor.equals("black")) {
      setFontColor(Color.black);
    }
    if (newColor.equals("green")) {
      setFontColor(Color.green);
    }
    if (newColor.equals("blue")) {
      setFontColor(Color.blue);
    }
  }

  public synchronized void addPropertyChangeListener
            (PropertyChangeListener pcl) {
    if (!listeners.contains(pcl)) {
      listeners.addElement(pcl);
    }
  }

  public synchronized void removePropertyChangeListener
            (PropertyChangeListener pcl) {
    if (listeners.contains(pcl)) {
      listeners.removeElement(pcl);
    }
  }

  // This method sends a PropertyChangeEvent object containing
  // information about the color change to the propertyChange()
  // method of any registered PropertyChangeListener objects.

  public void firePropertyChangeEvent(Object source,
                                      String propertyName,
                                      Object oldValue,
                                      Object newValue) {
    PropertyChangeEvent pce = new PropertyChangeEvent(source,
            propertyName, oldValue, newValue);

    Vector listenerCopy;

    synchronized (this) {
      listenerCopy = (Vector) listeners.clone();
    }
```

```
    for (int i = 0; i < listeners.size(); ++i) {
      PropertyChangeListener pcl =
        (PropertyChangeListener) listenerCopy.elementAt(i);
      pcl.propertyChange(pce);
    }
  }
}
```

❑ In addition to the Color object, a JComboBox and Vector object are included as data members. The JComboBox allows the user to select the color.

❑ The ColorManager2 class extends the JPanel class to allow the JComboBox to be visible in the container that instantiates a ColorManager2 object.

❑ The Vector object is used to store the PropertyChangeListener references. This allows more than one PropertyChange Listener to be registered with the ColorManager object.

❑ The class now implements the addPropertyChangeListener() and removePropertyChangeListener() methods.

❑ The addPropertyChangeListener() method adds a reference to the PropertyChangeListener passed as an argument to the Vector if it is not already stored in the Vector.

❑ The removePropertyChangeListener() method deletes a reference to the PropertyChangeListener object passed as an argument from the Vector if it is currently stored in the Vector.

The JComboBox object is registered with an ItemListener. When a color selection is made, the setFontColor() method is called with the appropriate Color argument. In the setFontColor() method, the value of the fontColor property is changed and the firePropertyChangeEvent() method is called. In the firePropertyChangeEvent() method, a PropertyChangeEvent object is created and sent to the propertyChange() method of all the registered PropertyChangeListener objects.

Care must be taken that the Vector containing the PropertyChangeListener references is not accessed simultaneously by multiple threads. This is accomplished by declaring the add() and remove() methods as synchronized methods. A copy of the Vector is used when the events are fired to avoid the possibility of the Vector changing during the event firing process. To avoid multi-thread access to the clone() method, the call to the method is placed within a synchronized block.

A PropertyChangeSupport object can be used to simplify the registering and de-registering of PropertyChangeListener objects as well as the firing of PropertyChangeEvent objects. See Section 13.2.3 on page 1116 for more details.

The driver program that uses the `ColorManager2` class is listed below; major changes are again highlighted.

```java
import javax.swing.*;
import java.awt.*;
import java.awt.event.*;
import java.beans.*;

public class DriverBean2 extends JFrame
  implements PropertyChangeListener {

    private ColorManager2 lm;
    private JLabel nameLabel;
    private JPanel p;

    public DriverBean2() {

        // A ColorManager2 object is created and registered with a
        // PropertyChangeListener object.

        lm = new ColorManager2();
        lm.addPropertyChangeListener(this);

        // A JLabel object is created.  The ColorManager2 object sets
        // the color of the text.

        nameLabel = new JLabel("Label");
        nameLabel.setFont(new Font("Serif", Font.PLAIN, 12));
        nameLabel.setForeground(lm.getFontColor());

        p = new JPanel();
        p.add(nameLabel);
        getContentPane().add(p, BorderLayout.CENTER);
        getContentPane().add(lm, BorderLayout.WEST);

        // The WindowListener is used to terminate the program when the window
        // is closed. Under Java 2 version 1.3, the addWindowListener() syntax
        // can be replaced by
        //
        // setDefaultCloseOperation(JFrame.EXIT_ON_CLOSE);

        addWindowListener(new WinClosing());
        setBounds(100, 100, 200, 200);
        setVisible(true);
    }
```

```
    // Because the DriverBean2 class serves as a PropertyChangeListener,
    // it provides an implementation of the propertyChange() method.
    // In this case, the method changes the foreground color of the JLabel.

    public void propertyChange(PropertyChangeEvent pce) {
      nameLabel.setForeground((Color) pce.getNewValue());
      p.revalidate();
    }

    public static void main(String args[]) {
      DriverBean2 db = new DriverBean2();
    }
  }

  // The WinClosing class terminates the program when the window is closed

  class WinClosing extends WindowAdapter {
    public void windowClosing(WindowEvent we) {
      System.exit(0);
    }
  }
```

### Output

When the ColorManager2 object is added to the content pane, the JComboBox object containing the list of colors appears. When a color is selected, a PropertyChangeEvent containing the new Color object is sent to the propertyChange() method. The color of the JLabel text is changed to this new color.

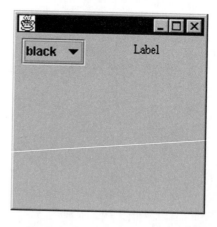

# Constrained Properties

Sometimes it is desirable to limit the changes that can be made to a property. Setting an array index to a negative number is an example of a change that should be prohibited. A property that is limited in the changes it can accept is known as a **constrained property**. The java.beans package provides the ability for client objects, or for the object containing the constrained property itself, to **veto** any proposed changes.

The mechanism for processing vetoable changes is similar to that for processing unconstrained property changes. The class containing the constrained property must provide addVetoableChangeListener() and removeVetoableChangeListener() methods to register or remove a VetoableChangeListener object. When a change is attempted on a constrained property, a PropertyChangeEvent containing the proposed change is sent to the vetoableChange() method of all registered VetoableChangeListener objects. The change is evaluated in the vetoableChange() method and if it is unacceptable, a PropertyVetoException object is thrown back to the class containing the constrained property.

A VetoableChangeListener object is one that implements the VetoableChangeListener interface. The object must provide an implementation of the vetoableChange() method. This method evaluates a proposed change to a constrained property and throws a PropertyVetoException if the change is unacceptable.

## Example: Using Constrained Properties

Making the fontColor property in the ColorManager class a constrained property results in further changes to the code shown in the example *Using Bound Properties* on page 1091; the changes are again highlighted below.

```
import java.io.*;
import java.util.*;
import java.awt.*;
import java.awt.event.*;
import javax.swing.*;
import java.beans.*;

public class ColorManager3 extends JPanel implements Serializable,
        ItemListener {
  protected Color fontColor, oldColor;
  protected JComboBox colorList;
  protected Vector propertyChangeListeners, vetoableChangeListeners;
  protected int oldIndex;

  public ColorManager3() {
    fontColor = Color.black;
```

13

java.beans

```
      // A JComboBox is created with a selection of colors to choose from.
      // The JComboBox is registered with an ItemListener that receives
      // an ItemEvent when the selection changes.

      String[] colors = {
        "black", "red", "green", "blue"
      };
      colorList = new JComboBox(colors);
      colorList.addItemListener(this);
      add(colorList);

      propertyChangeListeners = new Vector();
      vetoableChangeListeners = new Vector();

      oldIndex = colorList.getSelectedIndex();
    }

    public Color getFontColor() {
      return fontColor;
    }

    public void setFontColor(Color color) {

      oldColor = fontColor;

      // This method first determines if any VetoableChangeListener
      // object will veto the change.  If none do, the change is made.

      try {
        fireVetoableChangeEvent(this, "Color", oldColor, color);
        fontColor = color;
        oldIndex = colorList.getSelectedIndex();
      } catch (PropertyVetoException pve) {
        colorList.setSelectedIndex(oldIndex);
      }

      firePropertyChangeEvent(this, "Color", oldColor, fontColor);
    }

    public void itemStateChanged(ItemEvent ie) {
      String newColor = (String) colorList.getSelectedItem();

      if (newColor.equals("red")) {
        setFontColor(Color.red);
      }
```

```
      if (newColor.equals("black")) {
        setFontColor(Color.black);
      }
      if (newColor.equals("green")) {
        setFontColor(Color.green);
      }
      if (newColor.equals("blue")) {
        setFontColor(Color.blue);
      }
    }

    public synchronized void addPropertyChangeListener
              (PropertyChangeListener pcl) {
      if (!propertyChangeListeners.contains(pcl)) {
        propertyChangeListeners.addElement(pcl);
      }
    }

    public synchronized void removePropertyChangeListener
              (PropertyChangeListener pcl) {
      if (propertyChangeListeners.contains(pcl)) {
        propertyChangeListeners.removeElement(pcl);
      }
    }

    // This method sends a PropertyChangeEvent object containing
    // information about the color change to the propertyChange()
    // method of any registered PropertyChangeListener objects.

    public void firePropertyChangeEvent(Object source,
                                        String propertyName,
                                        Object oldValue,
                                        Object newValue) {
      PropertyChangeEvent pce = new PropertyChangeEvent(source,
              propertyName, oldValue, newValue);

      Vector listenerCopy;

      synchronized (this) {
        listenerCopy = (Vector) propertyChangeListeners.clone();
      }

      for (int i = 0; i < listenerCopy.size(); ++i) {
        PropertyChangeListener pcl =
          (PropertyChangeListener) listenerCopy.elementAt(i);
```

```
        pcl.propertyChange(pce);
    }
}

public synchronized void addVetoableChangeListener
          (VetoableChangeListener vcl) {
  if (!vetoableChangeListeners.contains(vcl)) {
    vetoableChangeListeners.addElement(vcl);
  }
}

public synchronized void removeVetoableChangeListener
          (VetoableChangeListener vcl) {
  if (vetoableChangeListeners.contains(vcl)) {
    vetoableChangeListeners.removeElement(vcl);
  }
}

// This method sends a PropertyChangeEvent object containing
// information about the color change to the vetoableChange()
// method of any registered VetoableChangeListener objects.

public void fireVetoableChangeEvent(Object source,
                                    String propertyName,
                                    Object oldValue,
                                    Object newValue)
        throws PropertyVetoException {
  PropertyChangeEvent pce = new PropertyChangeEvent(source,
        propertyName, oldValue, newValue);

  Vector listenerCopy;

  synchronized (this) {
    listenerCopy = (Vector) vetoableChangeListeners.clone();
  }

  try {
    for (int i = 0; i < listenerCopy.size(); ++i) {
      VetoableChangeListener vcl =
        (VetoableChangeListener) listenerCopy.elementAt(i);
      vcl.vetoableChange(pce);
    }
  } catch (PropertyVetoException pve) {
    throw pve;
  }
```

```
            }

        }
```

When a new color is selected in the JComboBox and the setFontColor() method is
called, the change is first evaluated for its acceptability before it is implemented.
The fireVetoableChangeEvent() method fires a PropertyChangeEvent containing
the proposed change to all registered VetoableChangeListener objects. As with
the bound property example, the VetoableChangeListener objects are contained in
a Vector and care is taken, by using the synchronized keyword, to prevent multi-
thread access to the Vector.

If any of the VetoableChangeListener objects reject the change, a
PropertyVetoException is sent back to the fireVetoableChangeEvent() method
which then re-throws the exception to the setFontColor() method and no change
to the fontColor value takes place. Otherwise, the fontColor value is changed. In
either case a PropertyChangeEvent is fired to update or re-set the color that is
displayed by the JLabel. If the change is rejected, the JComboBox object is re-set to
display the previous color.

A VetoableChangeSupport object can be used to simplify the registering and de-
registering of VetoableChangeListener objects as well as the firing of
PropertyChangeEvent objects associated with attempts to change the constrained
property. See Section 13.2.5 on page 1122 for more details.

The driver class for the constrained property example is shown below; again, the
major changes are highlighted. The class is used as the VetoableChangeListener
by implementing the VetoableChangeListener interface. The vetoableChange()
method is written to fire a PropertyVetoException if a change is attempted to the
color green.

```
import javax.swing.*;
import java.awt.*;
import java.awt.event.*;
import java.beans.*;

public class DriverBean3 extends JFrame
    implements PropertyChangeListener, VetoableChangeListener {
    private ColorManager3 lm;
    private JLabel nameLabel;
    private JPanel p;

    public DriverBean3() {

        // A ColorManager3 object is created and registered with both a
        // PropertyChangeListener and VetoableChangeListener object.

        lm = new ColorManager3();
```

```
       lm.addPropertyChangeListener(this);
       lm.addVetoableChangeListener(this);

       // A JLabel object is created.  The ColorManager3 object sets
       // the color of the text.

       nameLabel = new JLabel("Label");
       nameLabel.setFont(new Font("Serif", Font.PLAIN, 12));
       nameLabel.setForeground(lm.getFontColor());

       p = new JPanel();
       p.add(nameLabel);
       getContentPane().add(p, BorderLayout.CENTER);
       getContentPane().add(lm, BorderLayout.WEST);

       // The WindowListener is used to terminate the program when the window
       // is closed.  Under Java 2 version 1.3, the addWindowListener()
       // syntax can be replaced by
       //
       // setDefaultCloseOperation(JFrame.EXIT_ON_CLOSE);

       addWindowListener(new WinClosing());
       setBounds(100, 100, 200, 200);
       setVisible(true);
    }

// Because the DriverBean3 class serves as a PropertyChangeListener,
// it provides an implementation of the propertyChange() method.
// In this case, the method changes the foreground color of the JLabel.

public void propertyChange(PropertyChangeEvent pce) {
  nameLabel.setForeground((Color) pce.getNewValue());
  p.revalidate();
}

// Because the DriverBean3 class serves as a VetoableChangeListener,
// it provides an implementation of the vetoableChange() method.
// If the chosen color is green, a PropertyVetoException is thrown
// vetoing the change.

public void vetoableChange(PropertyChangeEvent pce)
        throws PropertyVetoException {
  Color c = (Color) pce.getNewValue();
  if (c.equals(Color.green)) {
    throw new PropertyVetoException("Bad Color", pce);
```

```
      }
    }

    public static void main(String args[]) {
      DriverBean3 db = new DriverBean3();
    }
  }
```

**Output**

The user interface of this program is the same as that of the *Using Bound Properties* example on page 1091.

# 13.1.4 Persistence

**Persistence** refers to a Bean's ability to be saved and restored. Generally this means that the Bean can be read from or written to a disk. Java Beans utilize the Java Serialization mechanisms to implement persistence. If an object is to be saved and/or restored it must implement either the `Serializable` or `Externalizable` interfaces.

# 13.1.5 The Serializable Interface

```
public interface Serializable
```

The `Serializable` interface, contained in the `java.io` package, defines no methods but is used as a marker to indicate that the implementing class is serializable and therefore can be saved and restored.

## Example: Using Serialization to Store a Bean

```
import java.io.*;
import javax.swing.*;
import java.awt.event.*;

public class TestSerial extends JFrame {
  ZackButton zb1, zb2;
  JLabel lbl;
  JPanel p;

  public TestSerial() {

    // A ZackButton object is created and added to a JPanel

    zb1 = new ZackButton();
    zb1.setValue(4);
```

```
lbl = new JLabel();

p = new JPanel();
p.add(zb1);

// The ZackButton object is written to a file named "boo.obj"

try {
  ObjectOutputStream oos =
    new ObjectOutputStream(new FileOutputStream("boo.obj"));
  oos.writeObject(zb1);
} catch (IOException ioe) {}

// A second ZackButton object is created by reading in the
// "boo.obj" file.

try {
  ObjectInputStream ois =
    new ObjectInputStream(new FileInputStream("boo.obj"));
  zb2 = (ZackButton) ois.readObject();
  lbl.setText("value is " + zb2.getValue());
} catch (FileNotFoundException fnfe) {
  System.out.println("Error: " + fnfe);
} catch (IOException ioe) {
  System.out.println("Error: " + ioe);
} catch (ClassNotFoundException cnfe) {
  System.out.println("Error: " + cnfe);
}

p.add(zb2);
p.add(lbl);
getContentPane().add(p);

// The WindowListener is used to terminate the program when the window
// is closed.  Under Java 2 version 1.3, the addWindowListener()
// syntax can be replaced by
//
// setDefaultCloseOperation(JFrame.EXIT_ON_CLOSE);

addWindowListener(new WinClosing());
setBounds(100, 100, 200, 150);
setVisible(true);
}
```

```
      public static void main(String args[]) {
        TestSerial ts = new TestSerial();
      }
    }

// The ZackButton class is a Bean that extends the JButton
// class.  It has one property, an int named value, and
// displays itself as a button with an icon.  Because the
// ZackButton class implements the Serializable interface,
// a ZackButton object can be saved and restored.

class ZackButton extends JButton implements Serializable {
  private int value;

  public ZackButton() {
    super(new ImageIcon("Zachary.jpg"));
    value = 2;
  }

  public int getValue() {
    return value;
  }

  public void setValue(int v) {
    value = v;
  }
}

// The WinClosing class terminates the program when the window is closed

class WinClosing extends WindowAdapter {
  public void windowClosing(WindowEvent we) {
    System.exit(0);
  }
}
```

A simple Java Bean called ZackButton is created. The ZackButton class is an
extension of the Jbutton class and also contains an int data member called value.
The value property is set to be 2 in the constructor, but is changed to be 4 using the
setValue() method. The ZackButton object is written to a file named boo.obj.

A second ZackButton object is created, not by using the constructor, but by reading
the previously saved ZackButton object. The value property of the new ZackButton
object is 4, the same as the initial object.

*Output*

Here is the result:

Implementing the Serializable interface does not guarantee that the class object can be saved and restored. It merely indicates that this is the intention. Whether a Bean is serializable depends on whether its data members are serializable. Primitive data types and most standard Java class objects are serializable, but some are not. For instance, a FileInputStream object is not serializable because the file associated with the FileInputStream object may not exist at some future date or on a different machine. Attempting to save or restore a Bean that contains a non-serializable object results in a NotSerializableException being thrown.

## Static and Transient Data Members

Static and transient data members are not automatically serialized. A static data member is associated with the class and only instance-specific data members are serialized. The transient keyword is used to designate a data member that is not part of the persistent state of the object, for example a temporary variable used in a for loop. The transient designation can also be applied to non-serializable objects to allow the rest of the object to be saved and restored.

## Extending the Default Serialization

It is possible to write information about an object that would normally not be serializable to a file by extending the default serialization mechanism. This is accomplished by having the class implement its own writeObject() method. The syntax for this method is:

| Method | Syntax |
|--------|--------|
| writeObject() | ```private void writeObject(ObjectOutputStream oos)```<br>```        throws IOException {```<br>```oos.defaultWriteObject();```<br><br>```// code to write additional information to the file```<br><br>```}``` |

The `defaultWriteObject()` method writes the non-static, non-transient data members of the class object using the default serialization mechanism. To restore the object, the class must also implement its own `readObject()` method. The syntax for this method is:

| Method | Syntax |
|--------|--------|
| readObject() | ```private void readObject(ObjectInputStream ois)```<br>```        throws IOException, ClassNotFoundException```<br>```{```<br>```  ois.defaultReadObject();```<br><br>```// code to read additional information from the file```<br><br>```}``` |

The `defaultReadObject()` method reads the non-static, non-transient data members of the class using the default serialization mechanism. This method can throw a `ClassNotFoundException` if the class of the object being restored is not found.

# 13.1.6 The Externalizable Interface

```
public interface Externalizable extends Serializable
```

```
Serializable
  Externalizable
```

Implementing the `Externalizable` interface is another way to serialize class objects. Unlike when using the `Serializable` interface, the `Externalizable` interface provides no default mechanism for saving and restoring objects. The code to save and restore the data members of the class objects must be provided inside implementations of the `readExternal()` and `writeExternal()` methods.

## readExternal() Method

| Method | Syntax |
|--------|--------|
| readExternal() | ```public void readExternal(ObjectInput inputStream)```<br>```        throws IOException, ClassNotFoundException``` |

`readExternal()` is called when the `Externalizable` object is being restored and contains the code for reading the data members of the class object.

## writeExternal() Method

| Method | Syntax |
|---|---|
| writeExternal() | public void **writeExternal**(ObjectOutput *outputStream*) throws IOException |

writeExternal() is called when the Externalizable object is being saved and contains the code for writing the data members of the class object.

### Example: Using Externalizable

This example is the same as the *Using Serialization to Store a Bean* example on page 1103 except the ZackButton class now implements the Externalizable interface. The value property is saved and restored using the writeExternal() and readExternal() methods.

```java
import java.io.*;
import javax.swing.*;
import java.awt.event.*;

public class TestExtern extends JFrame {
  ZackButton zb1, zb2;
  JLabel lbl;
  JPanel p;

  public TestExtern() {

    // A ZackButton object is created and added to a JPanel

    zb1 = new ZackButton();
    zb1.setValue(4);

    lbl = new JLabel();

    p = new JPanel();
    p.add(zb1);

    // The ZackButton object is written to a file named "boo.obj"

    try {
      ObjectOutputStream oos =
        new ObjectOutputStream(new FileOutputStream("boo.obj"));
      oos.writeObject(zb1);
    } catch (IOException ioe) {}

    // A second ZackButton object is created by reading in the
```

```
      // "boo.obj" file.

      try {
        ObjectInputStream ois =
          new ObjectInputStream(new FileInputStream("boo.obj"));
        zb2 = (ZackButton) ois.readObject();
        lbl.setText("value is " + zb2.getValue());
      } catch (FileNotFoundException fnfe) {
        System.out.println("Error: " + fnfe);
      } catch (IOException ioe) {
        System.out.println("Error: " + ioe);
      } catch (ClassNotFoundException cnfe) {
        System.out.println("Error: " + cnfe);
      }

      p.add(zb2);
      p.add(lbl);
      getContentPane().add(p);

      // The WindowListener is used to terminate the program when the window
      // is closed.  Under Java 2 version 1.3, the addWindowListener()
      // syntax can be replaced by
      //
      // setDefaultCloseOperation(JFrame.EXIT_ON_CLOSE);

      addWindowListener(new WinClosing());
      setBounds(100, 100, 200, 150);
      setVisible(true);
    }

  public static void main(String args[]) {
    TestExtern te = new TestExtern();
  }
}

// The ZackButton class is a Bean that extends the JButton
// class.  It has one property, an int named value, and
// displays itself as a button with an icon.  The readExternal()
// and writeExternal() methods are provided to restore and save
// the value property.

class ZackButton extends JButton implements Externalizable {
  private int value;

  public ZackButton() {
```

```
      super(new ImageIcon("Zachary.jpg"));
      value = 2;
   }

   public int getValue() {
     return value;
   }

   public void setValue(int v) {
     value = v;
   }

   public void readExternal(ObjectInput inputStream)
           throws IOException, ClassNotFoundException {
     value = inputStream.readInt();
   }

   public void writeExternal(ObjectOutput outputStream)
           throws IOException {
     outputStream.writeInt(value);
   }
}

// The WinClosing class terminates the program when the window is closed

class WinClosing extends WindowAdapter {
   public void windowClosing(WindowEvent we) {
     System.exit(0);
   }
 }
```

### Output

The user interface of this program is the same as that of the *Using Serialization to Store a Bean* example on page 1103.

# 13.1.7 Beans Class

```
public class Beans extends Object
```

```
Object
  Beans
```

The Beans class provides static methods to instantiate a Bean object, as well as methods to return or change certain Bean or system properties.

## Beans() Constructor

| Constructor | Syntax |
|---|---|
| Beans() | public Beans() |

Beans object constructor. Since all of the methods defined in the Beans class are static, they can be accessed without instantiating a Beans object.

## Design Time Methods

| Method | Syntax |
|---|---|
| isDesignTime() | public static boolean isDesignTime() |
| setDesignTime() | public static void setDesignTime (boolean *isDesignTime*) throws SecurityException |

isDesignTime() returns true if the system is running in design-time mode (as opposed to run-time mode).

setDesignTime() is used to specify whether to run in design time mode. An application builder environment would be an example of when design-time mode would be used.

## GUI Availability Methods

| Method | Syntax |
|---|---|
| isGuiAvailable() | public static boolean isGuiAvailable() |
| setGuiAvailable() | public static void setGuiAvailable (boolean *isGuiAvailable*) throws SecurityException |

isGuiAvailable() returns true if the Beans can assume a GUI is available to them.

setGuiAvailable() is used to specify whether the Beans should assume a GUI is available.

## instantiate() Method

| Method | Syntax |
|---|---|
| instantiate() | public static Object instantiate (ClassLoader *cl*, String *beanName*) throws IOException, ClassNotFoundException |
| | public static Object instantiate (ClassLoader *cl*, String *beanName*, BeanContext *bc*) throws IOException, ClassNotFoundException |
| | public static Object instantiate (ClassLoader *cl*, String *beanName*, BeanContext *bc*, AppletInitializer *ai*) throws IOException, ClassNotFoundException |

13

java.beans

instantiate() returns a `Bean` object based on a `ClassLoader` object and a `String` containing the Bean name. If the `ClassLoader` is `null`, the system class loader is used. A `BeanContext` and `AppletInitializer` object can also be provided.

## Example: Using the Beans Class

This example uses the `instantiate()` method from the `Beans` class to create a `ZackButton` object.

```java
import javax.swing.*;
import java.beans.*;
import java.io.*;
import java.awt.event.*;

public class TestBeans extends JFrame {
  private ZackButton zb;

  public TestBeans() {

    // A ZackButton object is created using the instantiate() method

    try {
      zb = (ZackButton) Beans.instantiate(null, "ZackButton");
    } catch (IOException ioe) {
      System.out.println("Error: " + ioe);
    } catch (ClassNotFoundException cnfe) {
      System.out.println("Error: " + cnfe);
    }

    JPanel p = new JPanel();
    p.add(zb);
    getContentPane().add(p);

    // The WindowListener is used to terminate the program when the window
    // is closed.  Under Java 2 version 1.3, the addWindowListener()
    // syntax can be replaced by
    //
    // setDefaultCloseOperation(JFrame.EXIT_ON_CLOSE);

    addWindowListener(new WinClosing());
    setBounds(100, 100, 200, 150);
    setVisible(true);
  }

  public static void main(String args[]) {
```

```
        TestBeans tb = new TestBeans();
    }
}

// The WinClosing class terminates the program when the window is closed

class WinClosing extends WindowAdapter {
  public void windowClosing(WindowEvent we) {
    System.exit(0);
  }
}
```

A ZackButton object is created using the instantiate() method. Because the ClassLoader argument is set to null, the system class loader is used. The instantiate() method returns an Object so the return value must be cast to a ZackButton object.

The code for the ZackButton class used in this example is given below. This file will have to be compiled (generating the ZackButton.class file) before the TestBeans code is run.

```
import java.io.*;
import javax.swing.*;

public class ZackButton extends JButton implements Serializable {
  private int amount;

  public ZackButton() {
    super("Zack");
    amount = 2;
  }

  public int getAmount() {
    return amount;
  }

  public void setAmount(int amt) {
    amount = amt;
  }
}
```

**Output**

The output of this example is:

# 13.2 Event Classes and Interfaces

The java.beans package provides classes and interfaces for dealing with events associated with bound and constrained property changes. The PropertyChangeListener and VetoableChangeListener interfaces provide methods for receiving and processing PropertyChangeEvent objects. The PropertyChangeSupport and VetoableChangeSupport classes make it easier to add or remove event listeners and fire PropertyChangeEvent objects.

## 13.2.1 PropertyChangeEvent Class

```
public class PropertyChangeEvent extends EventObject
```

```
Object
    EventObject
        PropertyChangeEvent
```

**Interfaces**

```
Serializable
```

A PropertyChangeEvent is fired whenever a bound or constrained property is changed. It contains a reference to the event source, the property name, and the old and new values of the property.

### PropertyChangeEvent() Constructor

| Constructor | Syntax |
|---|---|
| PropertyChangeEvent() | public PropertyChangeEvent(Object *source*, String *propertyName*, Object *oldValue*, Object *newValue*) |

Creates a PropertyChangeEvent object. The source refers to the object that fired the PropertyChangeEvent object.

### Property Methods

| Method | Syntax |
|---|---|
| getPropertyName() | public String getPropertyName() |
| getNewValue() | public Object getNewValue() |
| getOldValue() | public Object getOldValue() |

getPropertyName() returns the name of the property associated with the invoking PropertyChangeEvent object.

getNewValue() returns the new value of the property associated with the invoking PropertyChangeEvent object.

getOldValue() returns the old value of the property associated with the invoking PropertyChangeEvent object.

---

**Example: Using PropertyChangeEvent**

See the *Using Bound Properties* example on page 1091 and the *Using Constrained Properties* example on page 1097.

---

# 13.2.2 PropertyChangeListener Interface

```
public interface PropertyChangeListener extends EventListener
```

```
EventListener
    PropertyChangeListener
```

An object that implements the PropertyChangeListener interface can be used to monitor for and receive PropertyChangeEvents. It defines one method that is called when a PropertyChangeEvent object is generated by a registered source.

### propertyChange() Method

| Method | Syntax |
|---|---|
| propertyChange() | public void propertyChange (PropertyChangeEvent *pce*) |

13

java.beans

propertyChange() is called when a PropertyChangeEvent object is fired by a registered source. It is used to either implement the property change for a bound property or to evaluate the acceptability of the proposed change for a constrained property.

# 13.2.3 PropertyChangeSupport Class

public class PropertyChangeSupport extends Object implements Serializable

    Object
      PropertyChangeSupport

### Interfaces

    Serializable

The PropertyChangeSupport class provides methods to facilitate the addition and removal of PropertyChangeListeners from an associated Java Bean as well as the firing of PropertyChangeEvent objects. The Bean may either extend the PropertyChangeSupport class or use a PropertyChangeSupport object as one of its data members.

## PropertyChangeSupport() Constructor

| Constructor | Syntax |
| --- | --- |
| PropertyChangeSupport() | public PropertyChangeSupport(Object *sourceBean*) |

Creates a PropertyChangeSupport object. The Object sourceBean will generally be the this reference, meaning a reference to the class object containing the PropertyChangeSupport object as a data member.

## firePropertyChange() Method

| Method | Syntax |
| --- | --- |
| firePropertyChange() | public void firePropertyChange(String *propertyName*, Object *oldValue*, Object *newValue*) |
| | public void firePropertyChange(String *propertyName*, int *oldValue*, int *newValue*) |
| | public void firePropertyChange(String *propertyName*, boolean *oldValue*, boolean *newValue*) |
| | public void firePropertyChange(PropertyChangeEvent *pce*) |

firePropertyChange() sends a PropertyChangeEvent to all registered listeners. No event is sent if oldValue and newValue are the same. The final version is used to re-fire an existing PropertyChangeEvent object.

## hasListeners() Method

| Method | Syntax |
|---|---|
| hasListeners() | public boolean hasListeners(String *propertyName*) |

hasListeners() returns true if the specified property has any
PropertyChangeListener objects associated with it.

## PropertyChangeListener Methods

| Method | Syntax |
|---|---|
| addPropertyChangeListener() | public void addPropertyChangeListener<br>    (PropertyChangeListener *pcl*) |
| | public void addPropertyChangeListener<br>    (String *propertyName*,<br>      PropertyChangeListener *pcl*) |
| removePropertyChangeListener() | public void<br>    removePropertyChangeListener<br>    (PropertyChangeListener *pcl*) |
| | public void<br>    removePropertyChangeListener<br>    (String *propertyName*,<br>      PropertyChangeListener *pcl*) |

addPropertyChangeListener() registers a PropertyChangeListener object with the
Bean. The PropertyChangeListener is notified if the Bean generates a
PropertyChangeEvent object.

removePropertyChangeListener() disconnects the PropertyChangeListener object
from the Bean.

If a property name is provided, the PropertyChangeListener will receive
PropertyChangeEvent objects associated with that property.

### Example: Using PropertyChangeSupport

This is a modified version of the Bean from the *Using Bound Properties* example on
page 1091. The use of a PropertyChangeSupport object considerably simplifies the
code.

```
import java.io.*;
import java.util.*;
import java.awt.*;
import java.awt.event.*;
import javax.swing.*;
import java.beans.*;
```

```java
public class ColorManager4 extends JPanel implements Serializable,
        ItemListener {
  protected Color fontColor, oldColor;
  protected JComboBox colorList;
  protected PropertyChangeSupport pcs;

  public ColorManager4() {
    fontColor = Color.black;

    // A JComboBox is created with a selection of colors to choose from.
    // The JComboBox is registered with an ItemListener that receives
    // an ItemEvent when the selection changes.

    String[] colors = {
      "black", "red", "green", "blue"
    };
    colorList = new JComboBox(colors);
    colorList.addItemListener(this);
    add(colorList);

    pcs = new PropertyChangeSupport(this);
  }

  public Color getFontColor() {
    return fontColor;
  }

  // When the color is changed with the setFont() method,
  // a PropertyChangeEvent is sent to any PropertyChangeListener objects

  public void setFontColor(Color color) {
    oldColor = fontColor;
    fontColor = color;

    // The PropertyChangeSupport object creates and fires the
    // PropertyChangeEvent object.

    pcs.firePropertyChange("Color", oldColor, fontColor);
  }

  public void itemStateChanged(ItemEvent ie) {
    String newColor = (String) colorList.getSelectedItem();

    if (newColor.equals("red")) {
```

```
      setFontColor(Color.red);
    }
    if (newColor.equals("black")) {
      setFontColor(Color.black);
    }
    if (newColor.equals("green")) {
      setFontColor(Color.green);
    }
    if (newColor.equals("blue")) {
      setFontColor(Color.blue);
    }
  }

  // The PropertyChangeSupport object handles the addition and removal
  // of PropertyChangeListeners

  public synchronized void addPropertyChangeListener
          (PropertyChangeListener pcl) {
    pcs.addPropertyChangeListener(pcl);
  }

  public synchronized void removePropertyChangeListener
          (PropertyChangeListener pcl) {
    pcs.removePropertyChangeListener(pcl);
  }
}
```

The PropertyChangeListener objects no longer have to be stored in a Vector object. The addPropertyChangeListener() and removePropertyChangeListener() methods now call the same methods defined in the PropertyChangeSupport class, and the firePropertyChangeEvent() method has been eliminated. The firePropertyChange() method of the PropertyChangeSupport class is used to send the PropertyChangeEvent objects to the registered listeners.

The driver program is unchanged from that shown in the *Using Bound Properties* example on page 1091 except the references to ColorManager2 are now references to ColorManager4.import javax.swing.*;

```
import java.awt.*;
import java.awt.event.*;
import java.beans.*;

public class DriverBean4 extends JFrame
  implements PropertyChangeListener {
```

```
      private ColorManager4 lm;
      private JLabel nameLabel;
      private JPanel p;

      public DriverBean4() {

        // A ColorManager4 object is created and registered with a
        // PropertyChangeListener object.

        lm = new ColorManager4();
        lm.addPropertyChangeListener(this);

        // A JLabel object is created.  The ColorManager4 object sets
        // the color of the text.

        nameLabel = new JLabel("Label");
        nameLabel.setFont(new Font("Serif", Font.PLAIN, 12));
        nameLabel.setForeground(lm.getFontColor());

        p = new JPanel();
        p.add(nameLabel);
        getContentPane().add(p, BorderLayout.CENTER);
        getContentPane().add(lm, BorderLayout.WEST);

        // The WindowListener is used to terminate the program when the window
        // is closed. Under Java 2 version 1.3, the addWindowListener() syntax
        // can be replaced by
        //
        // setDefaultCloseOperation(JFrame.EXIT_ON_CLOSE);

        addWindowListener(new WinClosing());
        setBounds(100, 100, 200, 200);
        setVisible(true);
      }

    // Because the DriverBean4 class serves as a PropertyChangeListener,
    // it provides an implementation of the propertyChange() method.
    // In this case, the method changes the foreground color of the JLabel.

    public void propertyChange(PropertyChangeEvent pce) {
      nameLabel.setForeground((Color) pce.getNewValue());
      p.revalidate();
    }
```

```
    public static void main(String args[]) {
      DriverBean4 db = new DriverBean4();
    }
  }

  // The WinClosing class terminates the program when the window is closed

  class WinClosing extends WindowAdapter {
    public void windowClosing(WindowEvent we) {
      System.exit(0);
    }
  }
```

**Output**

The user interface of this program is the same as that of the *Using Bound Properties* example on page 1091.

# 13.2.4 VetoableChangeListener Interface

```
public interface VetoableChangeListener extends EventListener
```

```
EventListener
    VetoableChangeListener
```

An object that implements the VetoableChangeListener interface can be used to monitor for and receive PropertyChangeEvents that occur when a change is attempted to a constrained property. It defines one method that is called whenever a vetoable change event is generated by a registered source.

## vetoableChange() Method

| Method | Syntax |
| --- | --- |
| vetoableChange() | public void **vetoableChange**(PropertyChangeEvent *pce*) throws PropertyVetoException |

vetoableChange() is called when a change is attempted on a constrained property. The PropertyChangeEvent representing the proposed change can be evaluated, and if found to be unacceptable a PropertyVetoException can be thrown.

### Example: Using VetoableChangeListener

See the *Using Constrained Properties* example on page 1097.

# 13.2.5 VetoableChangeSupport Class

public class **VetoableChangeSupport** extends Object implements Serializable

```
Object
    VetoableChangeSupport
```

### Interfaces

```
Serializable
```

The VetoableChangeSupport class provides methods to facilitate the addition and removal of VetoableChangeListeners from an associated Java Bean as well as the firing of PropertyChangeEvent objects generated when an attempt is made to change a constrained property. The Bean may either extend the VetoableChangeSupport class or use a VetoableChangeSupport object as one of its data members.

## VetoableChangeSupport() Constructor

| Constructor | Syntax |
|---|---|
| VetoableChangeSupport() | public VetoableChangeSupport (Object *sourceBean*) |

Creates a VetoableChangeSupport object. The Object sourceBean will generally be the this reference, meaning a reference to the class object containing the VetoableChangeSupport object as a data member.

## fireVetoableChange() Method

| Method | Syntax |
|---|---|
| fireVetoableChange() | public void fireVetoableChange (String *propertyName*, Object *oldValue*, Object *newValue*) throws PropertyVetoException |
| | public void fireVetoableChange (String *propertyName*, int *oldValue*, int *newValue*) throws PropertyVetoException |
| | public void fireVetoableChange (String *propertyName*, boolean *oldValue*, boolean *newValue*) throws PropertyVetoException |
| | public void fireVetoableChange (PropertyChangeEvent pce) throws PropertyVetoException |

fireVetoableChange() sends a PropertyChangeEvent associated with an attempted change to a constrained property to all registered listeners. No event is sent if oldValue and newValue are the same. The final version is used to re-fire an existing PropertyChangeEvent object.

## hasListeners() Method

| Method | Syntax |
|---|---|
| hasListeners() | public boolean hasListeners (String *propertyName*) |

hasListeners() returns true if the specified propertyName has any
VetoableChangeListener objects associated with it.

## VetoableChangeListener Methods

| Method | Syntax |
|---|---|
| addVetoableChangeListener() | public void addVetoableChangeListener (VetoableChangeListener *pcl*) |
| | public void addVetoableChangeListener (String *propertyName*, VetoableChangeListener *pcl*) |
| removeVetoableChangeListener() | public void removeVetoableChangeListener VetoableChangeListener *pcl*) |
| | public void removeVetoableChangeListene (String *propertyName*, VetoableChangeListener *pcl*) |

addVetoableChangeListener() registers the invoking Bean object with a
VetoableChangeListener object. The VetoableChangeListener is notified if the Bean
generates a PropertyChangeEvent involving an attempted change to the value of a
constrained property.

removeVetoableChangeListener() disconnects the VetoableChangeListener object
from the invoking Bean object.

If a propertyName is provided, the VetoableChangeListener will only listen for
PropertyChangeEvents associated with that constrained property.

### Example: Using VetoableChangeSupport

This is a modified version of the *Using Constrained Properties* example on page 1097.
It uses both PropertyChangeSupport and VetoableChangeSupport objects to
simplify the code.

```
import java.io.*;
import java.util.*;
import java.awt.*;
import java.awt.event.*;
import javax.swing.*;
```

```java
import java.beans.*;

public class ColorManager5 extends JPanel implements Serializable,
        ItemListener {
  protected Color fontColor, oldColor;
  protected JComboBox colorList;
  protected PropertyChangeSupport pcs;
  protected VetoableChangeSupport vcs;
  protected int oldIndex;

  public ColorManager5() {
    fontColor = Color.black;

    // A JComboBox is created with a selection of colors to choose from.
    // The JComboBox is registered with an ItemListener that receives
    // an ItemEvent when the selection changes.

    String[] colors = {
      "black", "red", "green", "blue"
    };
    colorList = new JComboBox(colors);
    colorList.addItemListener(this);
    add(colorList);

    // A PropertyChangeSupport and VetoableChangeSupport objects are
    // created

    pcs = new PropertyChangeSupport(this);
    vcs = new VetoableChangeSupport(this);

    oldIndex = colorList.getSelectedIndex();
  }

  public Color getFontColor() {
    return fontColor;
  }

  public void setFontColor(Color color) {

    oldColor = fontColor;

    // This method first determines if any VetoableChangeListener
    // object will veto the change.  If none do, the change is made.
    // The PropertyChangeSupport and VetoableChangeSupport objects
    // generate and fire the PropertyChangeEvent objects.
```

```
    try {
      vcs.fireVetoableChange("Color", oldColor, color);
      fontColor = color;
      oldIndex = colorList.getSelectedIndex();
    } catch (PropertyVetoException pve) {
      colorList.setSelectedIndex(oldIndex);
    }

    pcs.firePropertyChange("Color", oldColor, fontColor);
  }

  public void itemStateChanged(ItemEvent ie) {
    String newColor = (String) colorList.getSelectedItem();

    if (newColor.equals("red")) {
      setFontColor(Color.red);
    }
    if (newColor.equals("black")) {
      setFontColor(Color.black);
    }
    if (newColor.equals("green")) {
      setFontColor(Color.green);
    }
    if (newColor.equals("blue")) {
      setFontColor(Color.blue);
    }
  }

  // The PropertyChangeSupport object handles the addition and removal
  // of PropertyChangeListeners

  public synchronized void addPropertyChangeListener
          (PropertyChangeListener pcl) {
    pcs.addPropertyChangeListener(pcl);
  }

  public synchronized void removePropertyChangeListener
          (PropertyChangeListener pcl) {
    pcs.removePropertyChangeListener(pcl);
  }

  // The VetoableChangeSupport object handles the addition and removal
  // of VetoableChangeListeners
```

```
        public synchronized void addVetoableChangeListener
            (VetoableChangeListener vcl) {
        vcs.addVetoableChangeListener(vcl);
    }

    public synchronized void removeVetoableChangeListener
            (VetoableChangeListener vcl) {
        vcs.removeVetoableChangeListener(vcl);
    }
}
```

The VetoableChangeListeners no longer have to be stored in a Vector object. The addVetoableChangeListener() and removeVetoableChangeListener() methods now call the same methods defined in the VetoableChangeSupport class. The fireVetoableChangeEvent() has been eliminated and the PropertyChangeEvent objects associated with trying to change the constrained property are sent using the fireVetoableChange() method of the VetoableChangeSupport object.

The driver program is unchanged from that shown in the *Using Constrained Properties* example on page 1097, except the references to ColorManager3 are now references to ColorManager5.

```
import javax.swing.*;
import java.awt.*;
import java.awt.event.*;
import java.beans.*;

public class DriverBean5 extends JFrame
    implements PropertyChangeListener, VetoableChangeListener {
    private ColorManager5 lm;
    private JLabel nameLabel;
    private JPanel p;

    public DriverBean5() {

        // A ColorManager5 object is created and registered with both a
        // PropertyChangeListener and VetoableChangeListener object.

        lm = new ColorManager5();
        lm.addPropertyChangeListener(this);
        lm.addVetoableChangeListener(this);

        // A JLabel object is created.  The ColorManager5 object sets
        // the color of the text.

        nameLabel = new JLabel("Label");
```

```
   nameLabel.setFont(new Font("Serif", Font.PLAIN, 12));
   nameLabel.setForeground(lm.getFontColor());


   p = new JPanel();
   p.add(nameLabel);
   getContentPane().add(p, BorderLayout.CENTER);
   getContentPane().add(lm, BorderLayout.WEST);


   // The WindowListener is used to terminate the program when the window
   // is closed.  Under Java 2 version 1.3, the addWindowListener()
   // syntax can be replaced by
   //
   // setDefaultCloseOperation(JFrame.EXIT_ON_CLOSE);


   addWindowListener(new WinClosing());
   setBounds(100, 100, 200, 200);
   setVisible(true);
}

// Because the DriverBean5 class serves as a PropertyChangeListener,
// it provides an implementation of the propertyChange() method.
// In this case, the method changes the foreground color of the JLabel.

public void propertyChange(PropertyChangeEvent pce) {
  nameLabel.setForeground((Color) pce.getNewValue());
  p.revalidate();
}

// Because the DriverBean5 class serves as a VetoableChangeListener,
// it provides an implementation of the vetoableChange() method.
// If the chosen color is green, a PropertyVetoException is thrown
// vetoing the change.

public void vetoableChange(PropertyChangeEvent pce)
        throws PropertyVetoException {
  Color c = (Color) pce.getNewValue();
  if (c.equals(Color.green)) {
    throw new PropertyVetoException("Bad Color", pce);
  }
}

public static void main(String args[]) {
  DriverBean5 db = new DriverBean5();
}
}
```

> **Output**
>
> The user interface of this program is the same as that of the *Using Bound Properties* example on page 1091.

# 13.3 Introspection Classes and Interfaces

The introspection classes and interfaces provide the ability to investigate the contents and behavior of a Bean without having to look at the source code listing. The description of the methods, events, parameters, and properties of a Bean are contained in an object that implements the BeanInfo interface. The SimpleBeanInfo class is provided as a built-in implementation of the BeanInfo interface. The Introspector class can be used to generate a BeanInfo object. The descriptor classes hold the information pertinent to specific features of the Bean.

## 13.3.1 BeanDescriptor Class

```
public class BeanDescriptor extends FeatureDescriptor
```

```
Object
    FeatureDescriptor
        BeanDescriptor
```

A BeanDescriptor object provides information about the Bean class and its customizer class. It is one of the descriptor classes available to a BeanInfo object.

### BeanDescriptor() Constructor

| Constructor | Syntax |
|---|---|
| BeanDescriptor() | public BeanDescriptor(Class *beanClass*) |
| | public BeanDescriptor(Class *beanClass*, Class *customizerClass*) |

Creates a BeanDescriptor object. If the Bean has a customizer, it can be provided to the constructor.

### getBeanClass() Method

| Method | Syntax |
|---|---|
| getBeanClass() | public Class getBeanClass() |

getBeanClass() returns a Class object representing the Bean class associated with the invoking BeanDescriptor object.

## getCustomizerClass() Method

| Method | Syntax |
|--------|--------|
| getCustomizerClass() | public Class getCustomizerClass() |

getCustomizerClass returns a Class object representing the customizer class associated with the invoking BeanDescriptor object. The method returns null if there is no customizer class.

### Example: Using BeanDescriptor

See the *Using SimpleBeanInfo* example on page 1144.

# 13.3.2 BeanInfo Interface

public interface BeanInfo

An object that implements the BeanInfo interface is used to obtain information about the methods, properties, events, etc. of a Bean. Not all of the methods in the BeanInfo interface need to be given a concrete implementation. If any of the methods returns null, a low-level reflection is used to obtain that piece of information. The SimpleBeanInfo class (see Section 13.3.10 on page 1142) is provided in the java.beans package as an implementation of the BeanInfo interface.

## BeanInfo Icon-Type Constants

| Constant |
|----------|
| public static final int ICON_COLOR_16x16 |
| public static final int ICON_COLOR_32x32 |
| public static final int ICON_MONO_16x16 |
| public static final int ICON_MONO_32x32 |

These constants are used to specify an icon type. The numbers refer to the size of the icon in pixels.

## getAdditionalBeanInfo() Method

| Method | Syntax |
|--------|--------|
| getAdditionalBeanInfo() | public BeanInfo[] getAdditionalBeanInfo() |

getAdditionalBeanInfo returns any additional BeanInfo objects associated with it. A BeanInfo object may have an arbitrary number of additional BeanInfo objects associated with it.

## Default Index Methods

| Method | Syntax |
| --- | --- |
| getDefaultEventIndex() | public int getDefaultEventIndex() |
| getDefaultPropertyIndex() | public int getDefaultPropertyIndex() |

A Bean may have a default event that is most commonly generated and a default property that is most commonly updated. These methods return the index of the default event or property in the EventDescriptor and PropertyDescriptor arrays returned by the getEventSetDescriptors() and getPropertyDescriptors() methods. If the defaults do not exist, these methods return -1.

## Descriptor Methods

| Method | Syntax |
| --- | --- |
| getBeanDescriptor() | public BeanDescriptor getBeanDescriptor() |
| getEventSetDescriptors() | public EventSetDescriptor[] getEventSetDescriptors() |
| getMethodDescriptors() | public MethodDescriptor[] getMethodDescriptors() |
| getPropertyDescriptors() | public PropertyDescriptor[] getPropertyDescriptors() |

getBeanDescriptor() returns a BeanDescriptor object providing Bean and customizer class information.

getEventSetDescriptors() returns an array of EventDescriptor objects containing information on the types of events fired by the Bean.

getMethodDescriptors() returns an array of MethodDescriptor objects providing information on the externally visible methods of the Bean.

getPropertyDescriptors() returns an array of PropertyDescriptor objects describing the editable properties of the Bean.

## getIcon() Method

| Method | Syntax |
| --- | --- |
| getIcon() | public Image getIcon(int iconType) |

getIcon() returns the image that will represent the Bean in a toolbox, toolbar, etc. The image is typically a .gif file. The iconType is one of the BeanInfo Icon-Type Constants described on page 1129.

# 13.3.3 EventSetDescriptor Class

```
public class EventSetDescriptor extends FeatureDescriptor
```

```
Object
   FeatureDescriptor
      EventSetDescriptor
```

An EventSetDescriptor object contains information about the event listeners and event types (the event set) fired by the Bean.

## EventSetDescriptor() Constructor

| Constructor | Syntax |
|---|---|
| EventSetDescriptor() | public EventSetDescriptor(Class *sourceClass*, String *eventSetName*, Class *listenerType*, String *listenerMethodName*) throws IntrospectionException |
| | public EventSetDescriptor(Class *sourceClass*, String *eventSetName*, Class *listenerType*, String[] *listenerMethodNames*, String *addListenerMethodName*, String *removeListenerMethodName*) throws IntrospectionException |
| | public EventSetDescriptor(String *eventSetName*, Class *listenerType*, Method[] *listenerMethods*, Method *addListenerMethod*, Method *removeListenerMethod*) throws IntrospectionException |
| | public EventSetDescriptor(String *eventSetName*, Class *listenerType*, MethodDescriptor[] *listenerMethodDescriptors*, Method *addListenerMethod*, Method *removeListenerMethod*) throws IntrospectionException |

Creates an EventSetDescriptor object. The sourceClass is the class firing the event. The eventSetName is the name of the event, for example Action or PropertyChange. The listenerType is the target interface to which the event will be delivered. The listenerMethodName is the name of the method that will be called when the event is fired. The addListener() and removeListener() methods can be provided as either a String or a Method object.

## Methods to Set Default Properties

| Method | Syntax |
|---|---|
| isInDefaultEventSet() | public boolean isInDefaultEventSet() |
| setInDefaultEventSet() | public void setInDefaultEventSet (boolean *isInDefaultEventSet*) |

isInDefaultEventSet() returns true if the event set is in the default set. This method defaults to true.

setInDefaultEventSet() specifies whether an event set is in the default set.

## Methods that Return Information about Listener Methods

| Method | Syntax |
|---|---|
| getAddListenerMethod() | public Method getAddListenerMethod() |
| getListenerMethodDescriptors() | public MethodDescriptor[] getListenerMethodDescriptors() |
| getListenerMethods() | public Method[] getListenerMethods() |
| getListenerType() | public Class getListenerType() |
| getRemoveListenerMethod() | public Method getRemoveListenerMethod() |

getAddListenerMethod() and getRemoveListenerMethod() return a Method object representing the addListener() or removeListener() method of the Bean.

getListenerMethodDescriptors() returns a MethodDescriptor object array for the methods defined by the listener interface that are called when events are fired.

getListenerMethods() method returns a Method object array representing the methods defined by the listener interface that are called when events are fired.

getListenerType() method returns the Class object of the target listener interface.

## Unicast Methods

| Method | Syntax |
|---|---|
| isUnicast() | public boolean isUnicast() |
| setUnicast() | public void setUnicast(boolean unicast) |

isUnicast() returns true if the event set is unicast. Normally event sources are multi-cast.

setUnicast() specifies whether an event set is unicast or not.

# 13.3.4 FeatureDescriptor Class

public class FeatureDescriptor extends Object

```
Object
   FeatureDescriptor
```

The FeatureDescriptor class is the parent class of the other descriptor classes found in the java.beans package. It provides methods common to the other descriptor classes. The FeatureDescriptor class also provides methods for assigning attribute/value pairs to a design feature.

# FeatureDescriptor() Method

| Method | Syntax |
|---|---|
| FeatureDescriptor() | public FeatureDescriptor() |

Creates a FeatureDescriptor object.

# Description Methods

| Method | Syntax |
|---|---|
| getShortDescription() | public String getShortDescription() |
| setShortDescription() | public void setShortDescription (String *description*) |

getShortDescription() returns a short description of the property, method, or event. If no short description has been specified, this method returns the display name.

setShortDescription() is used to provide a short description of the property, method, or event.

# Name Methods

| Method | Syntax |
|---|---|
| getDisplayName() | public String getDisplayName() |
| getName() | public String getName() |
| setDisplayName() | public void setDisplayName (String *displayName*) |
| setName() | public void setName(String *name*) |

getName() and setName() return or change the programmatic name associated with the property, method, or event.

getDisplayName()and setDisplayName() are used to return or change the localized display name associated with the property, method, or event. The displayName is often a simpler version of the programmatic name, JButton instead of javax.swing.JButton for instance. The default display name is to set it the same as the programmatic name.

# Methods to Return Feature Properties

| Method | Syntax |
|---|---|
| isExpert() | public boolean isExpert() |
| isHidden() | public boolean isHidden() |
| isPreferred() | public boolean isPreferred() |

isExpert() returns true if the feature is to be marked as being for expert users only.

isHidden() returns true if the feature is to be hidden from human interaction.

isPreferred() returns true if the feature is to be preferentially displayed to human users.

## Methods to Set Feature Properties

| Method | Syntax |
|---|---|
| setExpert() | public void setExpert(boolean *forExperts*) |
| setHidden() | public void setHidden(boolean *hidden*) |
| setPreferred() | public void setPreferred(boolean *preferred*) |

setExpert() is used to specify if the feature is to be marked as being for expert users only.

setHidden() designates if the feature is to be hidden from human interaction.

setPreferred() specifies if the feature is to be preferentially displayed to human users.

## Value/Attribute Methods

| Method | Syntax |
|---|---|
| attributeNames() | public Enumeration attributeNames() |
| getValue() | public Object getValue(String *attributeName*) |
| setValue() | public void setValue(String *attributeName*, Object *value*) |

attributeNames() returns an Enumeration object containing all of the attribute names.

getValue() returns the value associated with the specified attribute.

setValue() is used to designate an attribute/value pair.

# 13.3.5 IndexedPropertyDescriptor Class

```
public class IndexedPropertyDescriptor extends PropertyDescriptor
```

```
Object
    FeatureDescriptor
        PropertyDescriptor
            IndexedPropertyDescriptor
```

An IndexedPropertyDescriptor object is used to describe an indexed property such as an array or Vector object.

## IndexedPropertyDescriptor() Constructor

| Constructor | Syntax |
|---|---|
| IndexedPropertyDescriptor() | public IndexedPropertyDescriptor<br>    (String *propertyName*, Class *beanClass*)<br>    throws IntrospectionException |
| | public IndexedPropertyDescriptor<br>    (String *propertyName*, Class *beanClass*,<br>    String *getMethodName*,<br>    String *setMethodName*,<br>    String *indexedGetMethodName*,<br>    String *indexedSetMethodName*)<br>    throws IntrospectionException |
| | public IndexedPropertyDescriptor<br>    (String *propertyName*, Method *getMethod*,<br>    Method *setMethod*,<br>    Method *indexedGetMethod*,<br>    Method *indexedSetMethod*)<br>    throws IntrospectionException |

IndexedPropertyDescriptor constructor. The propertyName is the programmatic name of the property. The beanClass is a Class object representing the target Bean. The getMethod and setMethod parameters refer to the methods used to return or change the property as an array. The indexedGetMethod and indexedSetMethod parameters refer to the methods used to return or change individual elements of the property array.

## getIndexedPropertyType() Method

| Method | Syntax |
|---|---|
| getIndexedPropertyType() | public Class<br>getIndexedPropertyType() |

getIndexedPropertyType() returns a Class object representing the type of the indexed property

## Methods to Return Read and Write Methods

| Method | Syntax |
|---|---|
| getIndexedReadMethod() | public Method getIndexedReadMethod() |
| getIndexedWriteMethod() | public Method getIndexedWriteMethod() |

getIndexedReadMethod() and getIndexedWriteMethod() return a Method object representing the methods used to read or write an indexed property value.

13

java.beans

## Methods to Set Read and Write Methods

| Method | Syntax |
|---|---|
| setIndexedReadMethod() | public void setIndexedReadMethod<br>(Method *readMethod*)<br>throws IntrospectionException |
| setIndexedWriteMethod() | public void setIndexedWriteMethod<br>(Method *writeMethod*)<br>throws IntrospectionException |

setIndexedReadMethod() and setIndexedWriteMethod() are used to specify the methods used to read or write an indexed property value.

# 13.3.6 Introspector Class

```
public class Introspector extends Object
```

```
Object
    Introspector
```

The Introspector class is used to build a BeanInfo object containing information about the Bean. The Introspector object searches the Bean's class and super-classes for explicit or implicit information about the Bean. If a BeanInfo object exists for the Bean, the explicit information contained in the BeanInfo object is used. Low-level reflection is used to fill in any information not explicitly provided.

The methods provided by the Introspector class are all static which means they can be accessed without instantiating an Introspector object. No Introspector constructor is provided.

## Introspector Class Constants

| Constant |
|---|
| public static final int USE_ALL_BEANINFO |
| public static final int IGNORE_IMMEDIATE_BEANINFO |
| public static final int IGNORE_ALL_BEANINFO |

These constants are used to define the type of introspection used.

- ❏ USE_ALL_BEANINFO indicates that information contained in any BeanInfo class found will be used.

- ❏ IGNORE_IMMEDIATE_BEANINFO indicates that information contained in the local BeanInfo class associated with the Bean will be ignored.

- ❏ IGNORE_ALL_BEANINFO tells the introspector to ignore the information in any BeanInfo class found.

## decapitalize() Method

| Method | Syntax |
|---|---|
| decapitalize() | public static String decapitalize (String *name*) |

decapitalize() changes the first character of a String object from upper case to lower case to conform with the Standard Java convention of variable and method names. String objects with the first two letters being capitalized (for example, URL) are left alone.

## Methods to Flush an Introspector's Internal Cache

| Method | Syntax |
|---|---|
| flushCaches() | public static void flushCaches() |
| flushFromCaches() | public static void flushFromCaches(Class *cl*) |

flushCaches() and flushFromCaches() flush the internal caches of an Introspector. It is used if it is desired to have the Introspector re-analyze an existing class object.

## Methods that Return a BeanInfo Object

| Method | Syntax |
|---|---|
| getBeanInfo() | public static BeanInfo getBeanInfo (Class *beanClass*) throws IntrospectionException |
| | public static BeanInfo getBeanInfo(Class *beanClass*, int *flag*) throws IntrospectionException |
| | public static BeanInfo getBeanInfo (Class *beanClass*, Class *stopClass*) throws IntrospectionException |

getBeanInfo() returns a BeanInfo object containing information about a Bean. The beanClass is a Class object representing the target Bean. The flag is one of the Introspector class constants described at the top of this section. The stopClass defines how far down the class hierarchy to continue the introspection.

## Search Path Methods

| Method | Syntax |
|---|---|
| getBeanInfoSearchPath() | public static String[] getBeanInfoSearchPath() |
| setBeanInfoSearchPath() | public static void setBeanInfoSearchPath(String[] *path*) |

getBeanInfoSearchPath() returns the list of package names that will be used to search for BeanInfo classes.

setBeanInfoSearchPath() is used to change the list of package names that will be used to search for BeanInfo classes.

## Example: Using Introspector

```
import java.beans.*;

public class TestIntrosp {
  BeanInfo bi = null;

  public TestIntrosp() {

    // A BeanInfo object is obtained using the getBeanInfo() method
    // from the Introspector class

    try {
      bi = Introspector.getBeanInfo(SimpleBean.class);
    } catch (IntrospectionException ie) {
      System.out.println("Error: " + ie);
    }

    // The BeanInfo object is used to obtain information about the
    // methods and properties of the SimpleBean class

    MethodDescriptor[] md = bi.getMethodDescriptors();
    for (int i = 0; i < md.length; ++i) {
      System.out.println("Method programmatic name: "
                      + md[i].getName());
      System.out.println("Method display name: "
                      + md[i].getDisplayName());
      System.out.println("Description: "
                      + md[i].getShortDescription());
      System.out.println();
    }

    PropertyDescriptor[] pd = bi.getPropertyDescriptors();
    for (int i = 0; i < pd.length; ++i) {
      System.out.println("property programmatic name: "
                      + pd[i].getName());
      System.out.println("property display name: "
                      + pd[i].getDisplayName());
      System.out.println("Description: "
                      + pd[i].getShortDescription());
      System.out.println();
    }
```

```
    }

  public static void main(String args[]) {
    TestIntrosp ti = new TestIntrosp();
  }
}
```

The `Introspector` class is used to generate a `BeanInfo` object for a Bean named `SimpleBean`. The `Introspector` will first search for an existing `BeanInfo Class` object named `SimpleBeanBeanInfo.class`. If such an object exists, the Introspector will extract the information from it. The Introspector will fill in any missing information by performing a low-level introspection of the `SimpleBean` class.

See the *Using SimpleBeanInfo* example on page 1144 for a listing of the `SimpleBean` and `SimpleBeanBeanInfo` classes. These files will have to be compiled (generating the `SimpleBean.class` and `SimpleBeanBeanInfo.class` files) before this example can be run

# 13.3.7 MethodDescriptor Class

```
public class MethodDescriptor extends FeatureDescriptor
```

```
Object
  FeatureDescriptor
    MethodDescriptor
```

A `MethodDescriptor` object contains information about a single public method of a Bean.

## MethodDescriptor() Constructor

| Constructor | Syntax |
|---|---|
| MethodDescriptor() | public MethodDescriptor(Method *method*) |
| | public MethodDescriptor(Method *method*, ParameterDescriptor[] *parameterDesc*) |

Creates `MethodDescriptor` object. The `Method` object passed to the constructor provides low-level information, such as the programmatic and display names or description of the method. `ParameterDescriptor` objects containing descriptive information on the paramters used by the method can also be specified.

## getMethod() Method

| Method | Syntax |
|---|---|
| getMethod() | public Method getMethod() |

getMethod() returns a Method object representing the method associated with the MethodDescriptor object.

## getParameterDescriptors() Method

| Method | Syntax |
|---|---|
| getParameterDescriptors() | public ParameterDescriptor[] getParameterDescriptors() |

getParameterDescriptors() returns an array of ParameterDescriptor objects that contain information about the method's parameters, or returns a null array if the parameter names are not known.

### Example: Using MethodDescriptor

See the *Using Introspector* example on page 1138 or the *Using SimpleBeanInfo* example on page 1144.

# 13.3.8 ParameterDescriptor Class

```
public class ParameterDescriptor extends FeatureDescriptor
```

```
Object
    FeatureDescriptor
        ParameterDescriptor
```

A ParameterDescriptor object contains information about method parameters. Beyond the constructor, the ParameterDescriptor class defines no new methods.

## ParameterDescriptor() Constructor

| Constructor | Syntax |
|---|---|
| ParameterDescriptor() | public ParameterDescriptor() |

Creates a ParameterDescriptor object.

# 13.3.9 PropertyDescriptor Class

```
public class PropertyDescriptor extends FeatureDescriptor
```

```
Object
    FeatureDescriptor
        PropertyDescriptor
```

A PropertyDescriptor object contains information about one property associated with a Java Bean.

# PropertyDescriptor() Constructor

| Constructor | Syntax |
|---|---|
| PropertyDescriptor() | public PropertyDescriptor<br>(String *propertyName*, Class *beanClass*)<br>throws IntrospectionException |
| | public PropertyDescriptor<br>(String *propertyName*, Class *beanClass*,<br>String *getMethodName*, String *setMethodName*)<br>throws IntrospectionException |
| | public PropertyDescriptor<br>(String *propertyName*, Method *getMethod*,<br>Method *setMethod*)<br>throws IntrospectionException |

Creates a PropertyDescriptor object. The propertyName is the programmatic name of the property, the beanClass is the Class object representing the target Bean, and the getMethod and setMethod parameters refer to the methods used to return or change the property.

## PropertyEditor Methods

| Method | Syntax |
|---|---|
| getPropertyEditorClass() | public Class getPropertyEditorClass() |
| setPropertyEditorClass() | public void setPropertyEditorClass<br>(Class *propertyEditorClass*) |

getPropertyEditorClass() returns a Class object representing the PropertyEditor class, if any, that has been registered with the property.

setPropertyEditorClass() is used to associate a PropertyEditor class with the property.

## Property Type Methods

| Method | Syntax |
|---|---|
| getPropertyType() | public Class getPropertyType() |
| isBound() | public boolean isBound() |
| isConstrained() | public boolean isConstrained() |
| setBound() | public void setBound(boolean bound) |
| setConstrained() | public void setConstrained<br>(boolean *constrained*) |

getPropertyType() returns a Class object representing the property type.

isBound() returns true if the property is bound.

isConstrained() returns true if the property is constrained.

setBound() and setConstrained() are used to specify whether the property is bound and/or constrained.

## Methods to Return Read and Write Methods

| Method | Syntax |
|---|---|
| getReadMethod() | public Method getReadMethod() |
| getWriteMethod() | public Method getWriteMethod() |

getReadMethod() and getWriteMethod()return a Method object representing the methods used to read or write the property value.

## Methods to Set Read and Write Methods

| Method | Syntax |
|---|---|
| setReadMethod() | public void setReadMethod(Method *readMethod*) throws IntrospectionException |
| setWriteMethod() | public void setWriteMethod(Method *writeMethod*) throws IntrospectionException |

setReadMethod() and setWriteMethod() are used to specify the methods used to read or write the property value.

### Example: Using PropertyDescriptor

See the *Using Introspector* example on page 1138 or the *Using SimpleBeanInfo* example on page 1144.

# 13.3.10 SimpleBeanInfo Class

```
public class SimpleBeanInfo extends Object implements BeanInfo
```

```
Object
    SimpleBeanInfo
```

### Interfaces

```
BeanInfo
```

The SimpleBeanInfo class provides a framework for creating BeanInfo objects. The default implementation of the methods defined in the BeanInfo class provide no information. A sub-class of the SimpleBeanInfo class can overridden one or more of the SimpleBeanInfo methods to create a BeanInfo object. If the default methods are not overridden, low-level introspection is used to analyze the Bean.

## SimpleBeanInfo() Constructor

| Constructor | Syntax |
|---|---|
| SimpleBeanInfo() | public SimpleBeanInfo() |

Creates a SimpleBeanInfo object.

## getAdditionalBeanInfo() Method

| Method | Syntax |
|---|---|
| getAdditionalBeanInfo() | public BeanInfo[] getAdditionalBeanInfo() |

getAdditionalBeanInfo() returns any additional BeanInfo objects. A BeanInfo object may have an arbitrary number of additional BeanInfo objects associated with it.

## Default Index Methods

| Method | Syntax |
|---|---|
| getDefaultEventIndex() | public int getDefaultEventIndex() |
| getDefaultPropertyIndex() | public int getDefaultPropertyIndex() |

A Bean may have a default event that is most commonly generated and a default property that is most commonly updated. These methods return the index of the default event or property in the EventDescriptor and PropertyDescriptor arrays returned by the getEventSetDescriptors() and getPropertyDescriptors() methods.

## Descriptor Methods

| Method | Syntax |
|---|---|
| getBeanDescriptor() | public BeanDescriptor getBeanDescriptor() |
| getEventSetDescriptors() | public EventSetDescriptor[] getEventSetDescriptors() |
| getMethodDescriptors() | public MethodDescriptor[] getMethodDescriptors() |
| getPropertyDescriptors() | public PropertyDescriptor[] getPropertyDescriptors() |

getBeanDescriptor() returns a BeanDescriptor object providing Bean class and customizer class information.

getEventSetDescriptors() returns an array of EventDescriptor objects containing information on the types of events fired by the Bean.

getMethodDescriptors() returns an array of MethodDescriptor objects providing information on the externally visible methods of the Bean.

getPropertyDescriptors() returns an array of PropertyDescriptor objects describing the editable properties of the Bean.

## Image Methods

| Method | Syntax |
|---|---|
| getIcon() | public Image getIcon(int *iconType*) |
| loadImage() | public Image loadImage(String *imageName*) |

getIcon() returns the image that will represent the Bean in a toolbox, toolbar, etc. The image is typically a .gif file. The iconType is one of the BeanInfo Icon-Type Constants described on page 1129.

loadImage() method returns an Image object based on a String representation of the image file name.

### Example: Using SimpleBeanInfo

This example demonstrates how to provide a BeanInfo class by extending SimpleBeanInfo. The SimpleBean Bean and its accompanying SimpleBeanBeanInfo class are used in the *Using Introspector* example on page 1138.

```
import java.beans.*;
import java.awt.*;
import java.lang.reflect.*;

public class SimpleBeanBeanInfo extends SimpleBeanInfo {

   // The SimpleBeanInfo class overwrites the getBeanDescriptor(),
   // getMethodDescriptors(), and getPropertyDescriptors() methods
   // from the BeanInfo interface.

   public BeanDescriptor getBeanDescriptor() {
     BeanDescriptor bd = new BeanDescriptor(SimpleBean.class);
     bd.setDisplayName("simple");
     return bd;
   }

   public MethodDescriptor[] getMethodDescriptors() {
     Class simpleBeanClass = SimpleBean.class;

     try {
       Method getAmount = simpleBeanClass.getMethod("getAmount", null);
       MethodDescriptor getAmountDesc =
         new MethodDescriptor(getAmount);
```

```
       getAmountDesc.setShortDescription("returns the amount");

    Method getName = simpleBeanClass.getMethod("getName", null);
    MethodDescriptor getNameDesc = new MethodDescriptor(getName);
    getNameDesc.setShortDescription("returns the name");

    Class[] amtParams = {
      java.lang.Integer.TYPE
    };
    Method setAmount = simpleBeanClass.getMethod("setAmount",
           amtParams);
    MethodDescriptor setAmountDesc =
      new MethodDescriptor(setAmount);
    setAmountDesc.setShortDescription("changes the amount");

    Class[] nameParams = {
      String.class
    };
    Method setName = simpleBeanClass.getMethod("setName",
                                         nameParams);
    MethodDescriptor setNameDesc = new MethodDescriptor(setName);
    setNameDesc.setShortDescription("changes the name");

    MethodDescriptor[] mdArray = {
      getAmountDesc, setAmountDesc, getNameDesc, setNameDesc
    };
    return mdArray;
  } catch (SecurityException se) {
    return null;
  } catch (NoSuchMethodException nsme) {
    return null;
  }
}

public PropertyDescriptor[] getPropertyDescriptors() {
  try {
    PropertyDescriptor amount = new PropertyDescriptor("amount",
           SimpleBean.class, "getAmount", "setAmount");
    amount.setBound(false);
    amount.setConstrained(false);
    amount.setShortDescription("the amount");

    PropertyDescriptor name = new PropertyDescriptor("name",
           SimpleBean.class, "getName", "setName");
    name.setBound(false);
```

```
      name.setConstrained(false);
      name.setShortDescription("the name");

      PropertyDescriptor[] pdArray = {
        amount, name
      };

      return pdArray;
    } catch (IntrospectionException ie) {
      return null;
    }
  }

  public Image getIcon(int iconType) {
    return loadImage("Zachary.gif");
  }
}
```

This class provides a BeanInfo object for a Bean named SimpleBean. It overrides
the getBeanDescriptor(), getMethodDescriptors(),
getPropertyDescriptors(), and getIcon() methods. The MethodDescriptor
object constructor takes a Method object as an argument. The Method object is
obtained from the getMethod() method defined in the Class class.

The SimpleBean.java code listing is given below:

```
import java.io.*;

public class SimpleBean implements Serializable {
  private int amount;
  private String name;

  public SimpleBean() {
    amount = 2;
    name = "Jackson";
  }

  public String getName() {
    return name;
  }

  public void setName(String n) {
    name = n;
  }

  public int getAmount() {
```

```
        return amount;
    }

    public void setAmount(int amt) {
       amount = amt;
    }
}
```

# 13.4 Property Editor Classes and Interfaces

When a Bean is loaded into the BeanBox a default PropertyEditor is created. The
java.beans package also provides classes to create a user-defined PropertyEditor.

## 13.4.1 PropertyEditor Interface

```
public interface PropertyEditor
```

The PropertyEditor interface defines methods that are implemented by
PropertyEditor objects. The methods defined in the interface support several
different ways of displaying and updating property values. Depending on the type of
PropertyEditor desired some of the methods need not be implemented. For instance,
a simple PropertyEditor might only implement the getAsText() and setAsText()
methods.

### Methods that Access the Property Value as an Object

| Method | Syntax |
| --- | --- |
| getValue() | public Object getValue() |
| setValue() | public void setValue(Object value) |

getValue() returns the property value as an Object. Primitive data types are returned
as their corresponding wrapper class.

setValue() is used to set or change the property value.

### Methods that Access the Property Value as a String

| Method | Syntax |
| --- | --- |
| getAsText() | public String getAsText() |
| setAsText() | public void setAsText(String text) throws IllegalArgumentException |

getAsText() returns a String representation of the property value. If the
getAsText() method is set to return null, that indicates that the property value
cannot be represented as a text string.

`setAsText()` is used to change the property value by parsing the specified `String` object.

## Custom Editor Methods

| Method | Syntax |
|---|---|
| getCustomEditor() | public Component getCustomEditor() |
| supportsCustomEditor() | public boolean supportsCustomEditor() |

The default `PropertyEditor` implementation provides text fields and choice lists to change property values. A custom editor can be created that uses buttons or other GUI components to effect property changes. The default implementation of the `supportsCustomEditor()` method returns `false`. To use a custom editor, this method should be overridden within the `PropertyEditor` class to return `true`. The `getCustomEditor()` method should then be overwritten to return an instance of the desired custom editor object.

## getJavaInitializationString() Method

| Method | Syntax |
|---|---|
| getJavaInitializationString() | public String getJavaInitializationString() |

`getJavaInitializationString()` returns a `String` object containing a Java code fragment that can be used to initialize a variable with the current property value.

## getTags() Method

| Method | Syntax |
|---|---|
| getTags() | public String[] getTags() |

Sometimes it is desirable to limit the options available to change a property value.

`getTags()` is used to return a `String` array containing the available options. In the default `PropertyEditor`, these tags will be placed into a `Choice` list.

## Paint Methods

| Method | Syntax |
|---|---|
| isPaintable() | public boolean isPaintable() |
| paintValue() | public void paintValue(Graphics g, Rectangle rect) |

There are times when the property value cannot be adequately represented by a text string. It is possible to paint a suitable representation of the value. To enable the ability to paint, the `isPaintable()` method is overwritten within the class to return `true`. The `paintValue()` method is used to paint the representation of the value.

## PropertyChangeListener Methods

| Method | Syntax |
| --- | --- |
| addPropertyChangeListener() | public void addPropertyChangeListener (PropertyChangeListener pcl) |
| removePropertyChangeListener() | public void removePropertyChangeListener (PropertyChangeListener pcl) |

addPropertyChangeListener() registers the invoking PropertyEditor object with a PropertyChangeListener object. The PropertyChangeListener is notified if the PropertyEditor generates a PropertyChangeEvent object.

removePropertyChangeListener() disconnects the PropertyChangeListener object from the invoking PropertyEditor object.

# 13.4.2 PropertyEditorManager Class

```
public class PropertyEditorManager extends Object
```

```
Object
    PropertyEditorManager
```

There are two ways to associate a PropertyEditor with a property. The first way is through a PropertyDescriptor object. The PropertyEditorManager class provides methods for locating and registering a PropertyEditor for a given class.

## PropertyEditorManager() Constructor

| Constructor | Syntax |
| --- | --- |
| PropertyEditorManager() | public PropertyEditorManager() |

Creates a PropertyEditorManager object. Since the methods in the PropertyEditorManager class are static, they can be accessed without instantiating a PropertyEditorManager object.

## findEditor() Method

| Method | Syntax |
| --- | --- |
| findEditor() | public static PropertyEditor findEditor(Class target) |

findEditor() searches for a suitable PropertyEditor for the target class, or returns null if none can be found.

## registerEditor() Method

| Method | Syntax |
|--------|--------|
| `registerEditor()` | `public static void registerEditor`<br>`(Class target, Class editor)` |

`registerEditor()` registers a `PropertyEditor` class with a target class.

## Search Path Methods

| Method | Syntax |
|--------|--------|
| `getEditorSearchPath()` | `public static String[]`<br>`getEditorSearchPath()` |
| `setEditorSearchPath()` | `public static void`<br>`setEditorSearchPath(String[] path)` |

`getEditorSearchPath()` returns a `String` array containing the package names that will be searched for editors.

`setEditorSearchPath()` method is used to change the search path names.

# 13.4.3 PropertyEditorSupport Class

`public class PropertyEditorSupport extends Object implements PropertyEditor`

```
Object
    PropertyEditorSupport
```

### Interfaces

```
PropertyEditor
```

The `PropertyEditorSupport` class provides a default implementation of the methods defined in the `PropertyEditor` interface. A sub-class of the `PropertyEditorSupport` class need only overwrite the methods it has to instead of having to implement the entire `PropertyEditor` method list. The `PropertyEditorSupport` class has no public constructors but does have a protected no-argument constructor for use by derived classes and a protected constructor that takes an `Object` parameter that serves as the source for any events that are fired.

## Methods that Access the Property Value as an Object

| Method | Syntax |
|--------|--------|
| `getValue()` | `public Object getValue()` |
| `setValue()` | `public void setValue(Object value)` |

`getValue()` returns the property value as an `Object`. Primitive data types are returned as their corresponding wrapper class.

`setValue()` is used to set or change the property value.

## Methods that Access the Property Value as a String

| Method | Syntax |
|---|---|
| getAsText() | public String getAsText() |
| setAsText() | public void setAsText(String *text*) throws IllegalArgumentException |

getAsText() returns a String representation of the property value. If the getAsText() method is set to return null, that indicates that the property value cannot be represented as a text string.

setAsText() is used to change the property value by parsing the specified String object.

## Custom Editor Methods

| Method | Syntax |
|---|---|
| getCustomEditor() | public Component getCustomEditor() |
| supportsCustomEditor() | public boolean supportsCustomEditor() |

The default PropertyEditor implementation provides text fields and choice lists to change property values. A custom editor can be created that uses buttons or other GUI components to effect property changes. The default implementation of the supportsCustomEditor() method returns false. To use a custom editor, this method should be overridden within the PropertyEditor class to return true. The getCustomEditor() method should then be overridden to return an instance of the desired custom editor object.

## firePropertyChange() Method

| Method | Syntax |
|---|---|
| firePropertyChange() | public void firePropertyChange() |

firePropertyChange() sends a PropertyChangeEvent object to registered listeners to indicate that the PropertyEditor has changed a property value.

## getJavaInitializationString() Method

| Method | Syntax |
|---|---|
| getJavaInitializationString() | public String getJavaInitializationString() |

getJavaInitializationString() returns a String object containing a Java code fragment that can be used to initialize a variable with the current property value.

## getTags() Method

| Method | Syntax |
|---|---|
| getTags() | public String[] getTags() |

Sometimes it is desirable to limit the options available to change a property value.

getTags() is used to return a String array containing the available options. In the default PropertyEditor, these tags will be placed into a choice list.

## Paint Methods

| Method | Syntax |
|---|---|
| isPaintable() | public boolean isPaintable() |
| paintValue() | public void paintValue(Graphics g, Rectangle rect) |

There are times when the property value cannot be adequately represented by a text string. It is possible to paint a suitable representation of the value. To enable the ability to paint, the isPaintable() method is overwritten within the class to return true. The paintValue() method is used to paint the representation of the value.

## PropertyChangeListener Methods

| Method | Syntax |
|---|---|
| addPropertyChangeListener() | public void addPropertyChangeListener (PropertyChangeListener pcl) |
| removePropertyChangeListener() | public void removePropertyChangeListener (PropertyChangeListener pcl) |

addPropertyChangeListener() registers the invoking PropertyEditor object with a PropertyChangeListener object. The PropertyChangeListener is notified if the PropertyEditor generates a PropertyChangeEvent object.

removePropertyChangeListener() disconnects the PropertyChangeListener object from the invoking PropertyEditor object.

## Example: Using PropertyEditor

To run this example, compile the MyButton, MyButtonBeanInfo, and BorderEditor classes. Assemble the resulting .class files and the MyButton.mf file into a JAR file using the command:

```
jar cfm mybutton.jar MyButton.mf MyButton.class MyButtonBeanInfo.class
BorderEditor.class
```

Place the `mybutton.jar` file in the `jars` directory of the BDK hierarchy (such as `C:\BDK1.1\jars` on a typical Windows installation) and run the BeanBox. The code listings of the four classes are as follows

### MyButton Class

```
import java.io.*;
import javax.swing.*;
import java.beans.*;

public class MyButton extends JButton
        implements Serializable, PropertyChangeListener {
  protected String borderType;

  public MyButton() {
    super("Hello");
    setBorder(BorderFactory.createRaisedBevelBorder());

    borderType = "Bevel";

    addPropertyChangeListener(this);
  }

  public String getBorderType() {
    return borderType;
  }

  public void setBorderType(String type) {
    borderType = type;

    firePropertyChange("borderType", null, borderType);
  }

  public void propertyChange(PropertyChangeEvent pce) {
    String property = pce.getPropertyName();

    if (property.equals("borderType")) {
      String border = (String) pce.getNewValue();

      if (border.equals("Bevel")) {
        setBorder(BorderFactory.createRaisedBevelBorder());

      }
      if (border.equals("Etched")) {
        setBorder(BorderFactory.createEtchedBorder());
```

```
          }
        }
      }
    }
```

## BorderEditor Class

```java
import java.beans.*;

public class BorderEditor extends PropertyEditorSupport {
  protected String borderType;

  public String getAsText() {
    return borderType;
  }

  public void setAsText(String text) {
    borderType = text;
    firePropertyChange();
  }

  public Object getValue() {
    return borderType;
  }

  public void setValue(Object value) {
    borderType = (String) value;
  }

  public String[] getTags() {
    String[] borders = {
      "Bevel", "Etched"
    };
    return borders;
  }
}
```

## MyButtonBeanInfo Class

```java
import java.beans.*;
import java.awt.*;

public class MyButtonBeanInfo extends SimpleBeanInfo {
  public PropertyDescriptor[] getPropertyDescriptors() {
    try {
      PropertyDescriptor borderType = new PropertyDescriptor("borderType",
              MyButton.class);
```

```
      borderType.setPropertyEditorClass(BorderEditor.class);

      PropertyDescriptor[] pdArray = {
        borderType
      };

      return pdArray;
    } catch (IntrospectionException ie) {
      return null;
    }
  }
}
```

### MyButton.mf

```
Manifest-Version: 1.0

Name: MyButton.class
Java-Bean: True
```

*(There must be an end-of-line sequence at the end of this file.)*

The MyButton class defines a button Bean. It contains one property, a String object named borderType, which is used to specify the type of border drawn around the button. The MyButton class also serves as its own PropertyChangeListener. The value of borderType is changed with the setBorderType() method. When the value is changed, a PropertyChangeEvent is fired and the border is updated according to the value of borderType.

The BorderEditor class serves as the PropertyEditor for the borderType property. When The MyButton Bean is placed on the BeanBox main window, a PropertyEditor window appears containing one entry named borderType. The choices for borderType are limited to "Bevel" and "Border" by the getTags() method. When a selection is made, a PropertyChangeEvent is fired and the border surrounding the MyButton Bean.

The MyButtonBeanInfo class is used to associate the BorderEditor class with the borderType property of the MyButton class using a PropertyDescriptor object.

### Output

The BeanBox is shown below with a MyButton object placed on the user interface. The Properties window shows the PropertyEditor defined for the borderType property.

# 14

# Other Packages in the Standard Java API

For reasons of time, book length, and the Author's sanity, it was not possible to cover every package in the Standard Java API in detail in this book. This chapter provides a short description for those packages. The descriptions are sometimes taken directly from the Sun Java documentation: consult these for complete information on the classes and interfaces contained in these packages.

## 14.1 java.awt.color

The `java.awt.color` package provides support for color spaces based on International Color Consortium (ICC) Profile Format Specification, Version 3.4, August 15, 1997. It also contains color profiles based on the ICC Profile Format Specification. The International Color Consortium was established in 1993 to develop an open, vendor-neutral, cross-platform color management system architecture and components.

## 14.2 java.awt.datatransfer

The `java.awt.datatransfer` package provides interfaces and classes for transferring data between and within applications. It defines the notion of a "transferable" object, which is an object capable of being transferred between or within applications. It also provides a clipboard mechanism, which is an object that temporarily holds a transferable object that can be transferred between or within an application. The clipboard is typically used for copy and paste operations.

## 14.3 java.awt.dnd

The `java.awt.dnd` package provides classes and interfaces that support "Drag and Drop" operations. It defines classes for the drag-source and the drop-target, as well as events for transferring the data being dragged. This package also provides a means for giving visual feedback to the user throughout the duration of the Drag and Drop operation.

## 14.4 java.awt.font

The `java.awt.font` package provides classes and interface relating to fonts including glyphs, line metrics, text attributes, and text layout. It contains support for representing Type 1, Type 1 Multiple Master fonts, OpenType fonts, and TrueType fonts.

## 14.5 java.awt.geom

The `java.awt.geom` package provides classes for defining and performing operations on two-dimensional geometric entities including cubic curves, ellipses, and rectangles. It also provides classes for manipulating these geometries.

## 14.6 java.awt.im

The `java.awt.im` package provides classes and an interface for the input method framework. This framework enables all text editing components to receive Japanese, Chinese, or Korean text input through input methods. It defines an input context to manage the communication between text editing components and input methods and Unicode subsets for use by input methods.

## 14.7 java.awt.im.spi

The `java.awt.im.spi` package provides three interfaces that enable the development of input methods that can be used with any Java runtime environment. Input methods are components that allow text input in ways other than simple keyboard entry.

## 14.8 java.awt.image

The `java.awt.image` package provides classes for creating and modifying images. Images are processed using a streaming framework that involves an image producer, optional image filters, and an image consumer. This framework makes it possible to progressively render an image while it is being fetched and generated. This package provides classes that represent image producers, consumers, filters, and observers.

## 14.9 java.awt.image.renderable

The `java.awt.image.renderable` package contains classes and interfaces for producing rendering-independent images. It includes the `RenderedImageFactory` interface, implemented by classes that wish to produce rendered images.

## 14.10 java.awt.print

The `java.awt.print` package contains classes and interfaces for a general printing API including the ability to specify document types, mechanisms for control of page setup and page formats, and the ability to manage job control dialogs.

## 14.11 java.beans.beancontext

The `java.beans.beancontext` package provides classes and interfaces relating to bean context. A bean context is a container for beans and defines the execution environment for the beans it contains. This package also contains events and listener interface for beans being added and removed from a bean context.

## 14.12 java.lang.ref

The `java.lang.ref` package provides classes to create reference objects. A reference object encapsulates a reference to some other object and supports a limited degree of interaction with the garbage collector. A program may use a reference object to maintain a reference to some other object in such a way that the referred object may still be reclaimed by the collector. A program may also arrange to be notified some time after the collector has determined that the reachability of a given object has changed.

## 14.13 java.lang.reflect

The `java.lang.reflect` package contains classes and interfaces that are used to examine classes and objects. It allows the examination of the methods, constructors, and access modifiers of a class. The package also contains the `Array` class that provides static methods to dynamically create and access Java arrays.

## 14.14 java.math

The `java.math` package provides classes to perform arbitrary precision integer and decimal arithmetic. In addition to standard math operations, the classes contained in the package enable such things as modular arithmetic, GCD calculation, primality testing, prime generation, bit manipulation, and arbitrary-precision signed decimal numbers suitable for currency calculations.

## 14.15 java.rmi

The `java.rmi` package contains the three classes and one interface that permit Remote Method Invocation (RMI). RMI allows an object on one Java virtual machine to invoke methods on an object in another Java virtual machine.

## 14.16 java.rmi.activation

The `java.rmi.activation` package provides classes and interfaces that support RMI Object Activation. A remote object's reference can be made "persistent" and later activated into a "live" object using the RMI activation mechanism.

## 14.17 java.rmi.dgc

The `java.rmi.dgc` package provides two classes and one interface that support RMI distributed garbage-collection (DGC). When the RMI server returns an object to its client (caller of the remote method), it tracks the remote object's usage in the client. When there are no more references to the remote object on the client, or if the reference's "lease" expires and is not renewed, the server garbage-collects the remote object.

Other packages

# 14.18 java.rmi.registry

The `java.rmi.registry` package contains a class and two interfaces that are used to create an RMI registry. A registry is a remote object that maps names to remote objects. A server registers its remote objects with the registry so that they can be looked up. When an object wants to invoke a method on a remote object, it must first lookup the remote object using its name. The registry returns to the calling object a reference to the remote object, using which a remote method can be invoked.

# 14.19 java.rmi.server

The `java.rmi.server` package provides classes and interfaces that support the server side of RMI including client/server socket generation, failure handling, and remote/server object handles. There are also classes that implement the RMI Transport protocol and HTTP tunneling.

# 14.20 java.security

The `java.security` package provides classes and interfaces for the Java security framework. The security functionality includes keys, guards, and privileged actions. This package also supports the generation and storage of cryptographic public key pairs, as well as a number of exportable cryptographic operations including those for message digest and signature generation. The `java.security` package also provides for secure random number generation.

# 14.21 java.security.acl

The classes and interfaces in the `java.security.acl` package have been superceded by those in the `java.security` package.

# 14.22 java.security.cert

The `java.security.cert` package contains classes and interfaces for parsing and managing identity certificates, specifically X.509 v3 certificates.

# 14.23 java.security.interfaces

The `java.security.interfaces` package contains interfaces for generating Digital Signature Algorithm (DSA) or Rivest, Shamir and Adleman AsymmetricCipher algorithm (RSA) encryption keys.

# 14.24 java.security.spec

The `java.security.spec` package provides classes and interfaces for DSA and RSA key and algorithm parameter specification.

# 14.25 java.sql

The java.sql package implements the JDBC 2.0 package. JDBC is a standard API for executing Search Query Language (SQL) statements. (SQL is the industry standard for accessing relational databases.) The package contains classes and interfaces for creating SQL statements, and retrieving the results of executing those statements against relational databases.

# 14.26 java.text

The java.text package contains classes and interfaces for handling text, dates, numbers, and messages in a language-independent manner. Included are classes for formatting dates, numbers, and messages. Classes are also provided for searching and sorting String objects, and for iterating over characters, words, sentences, and line breaks.

# 14.27 java.util.jar

The java.util.jar package provides classes for reading and writing Java Archive (JAR) files. JAR files are used to bundle a collection of .class and manifest files into a single file. JAR files are based on the standard ZIP file format.

# 14.28 java.util.zip

The java.util.zip package provides classes for reading and writing the standard ZIP and GZIP file formats. Also included are classes for compressing and decompressing data using the DEFLATE compression algorithm and utility classes for computing the CRC-32 and Adler-32 checksums of arbitrary input streams.

# 14.29 javax.accessiblity

The javax.accessibility package provides classes that connect user-interface components and an assistive technology such as screen readers and screen magnifiers that provides access to those components.

# 14.30 javax.naming

The javax.naming package provides classes and interfaces for accessing naming services including composite and compound names, binding names to objects, and name references.

# 14.31 javax.naming.directory

The javax.naming.directory package provides classes and interfaces for accessing directory services.

Other packages

## 14.32 javax.naming.event

The `javax.naming.event` package provides the event classes and listener interfaces for naming and directory services.

## 14.33 javax.naming.spi

The `javax.naming.spi` package provides support for dynamic plug-in support for accessing the naming and directory services.

## 14.34 javax.rmi

The `javax.rmi` package contains user APIs for Remote Method Invocation (RMI).

## 14.35 javax.rmi.CORBA

The `javax.rmi.CORBA` package contains user APIs for Remote Method Invocation (RMI).

## 14.36 javax.sound.midi

The `javax.sound.midi` package contains interfaces and classes for managing Musical Instrument Digital Interface (MIDI) data.

## 14.37 javax.sound.midi.spi

The `javax.sound.midi.spi` package supplies interfaces for MIDI file readers, writers, and sound bank readers.

## 14.38 javax.sound.sampled

The `javax.sound.sampled` package contains interfaces and classes for managing sampled audio data.

## 14.39 javax.sound.sampled.spi

The `javax.sound.sampled.spi` package classes for sound file readers and writers or audio file converters.

## 14.40 javax.swing.colorchooser

The `javax.swing.colorchooser` package contains three classes and one interface used by the `JColorChooser` component including support for color chooser panels and color selection models.

# 14.41 javax.swing.event

The `javax.swing.event` package contains listener interfaces and event classes for events fired by Swing components. Included are the `CaretEvent`, `ChangeEvent`, `HyperlinkEvent`, `ListSelectionEvent`, `TableColumnModelEvent`, `TableModelEvent`, and `TreeModelEvent` classes.

# 14.42 javax.swing.filechooser

The `javax.swing.filechooser` package contains three classes used by the `JFileChooser` component. The classes provide file filter and file view functionality.

# 14.43 javax.swing.plaf

The `javax.swing.plaf` package provides the `ComponentUI` delegate classes that the Swing GUI component classes use to implement pluggable look-and-feel capability. This package is only used by look-and-feel developers who cannot create a new look-and-feel by subclassing existing look-and-feel components (such as "Basic" or "metal").

# 14.44 javax.swing.plaf.basic

The `javax.swing.plaf.basic` package provides UI delegate classes according to the "Basic" look-and-feel. The "Basic" look-and-feel is the default for Swing components.

# 14.45 javax.swing.plaf.metal

The `javax.swing.plaf.metal` package provides UI delegate classes according to the "metal" look-and-feel.

# 14.46 javax.swing.plaf.multi

The `javax.swing.plaf.multi` package provides UI delegate classes according to a multiplexing look-and-feel. This allows the combination of auxillary and default look-and-feels.

# 14.47 javax.swing.text

The `javax.swing.text` package provides classes and interfaces that deal with editable and noneditable text components such as text areas and text fields. The classes in this package support such things as selection, highlighting, editing, style, and key mapping.

# 14.48 javax.swing.text.html

The `javax.swing.text.html` package provides class for creating and supporting HTML text editors.

Other packages

14

## 14.49 javax.swing.text.html.parser

The `javax.swing.text.html.parser` package provides a default HTML parser and support classes

## 14.50 javax.swing.text.html.rtf

The `javax.swing.text.html.rtf` package contains the `RTFEditorKit` class that is used to create Rich Text Format text editors.

## 14.51 javax.swing.undo

The `javax.swing.undo` package contains classes and interfaces that support the undo and redo capabilities in an application such as a text editor. This allows, for instance, the restoration of deleted text.

## 14.52 javax.swing.transaction

The `javax.swing.transaction` package contains three transaction event classes.

## 14.53 org.omg.CORBA

The `org.omg.CORBA` package provides classes that map the OMG CORBA APIs to the Java, including the class ORB, which is implemented so that a programmer can use it as a fully-functional Object Request Broker (ORB). An ORB handles (or brokers) method invocations between a client and the method's implementation on a server.

## 14.54 org.omg.CORBA.DynAnyPackage

The `org.omg.CORBA.DynAnyPackage` package contains the exception classes used with the `DynAny` interface.

## 14.55 org.omg.CORBA.ORBPackage

The `org.omg.CORBA.ORBPackage` package contains the exception classes `InconsistenTypeCode` and `InvalidName`.

## 14.56 org.omg.CORBA.portable

The `org.omg.CORBA.portable` package contains classes and interfaces that enable portability making it possible for code generated by one vendor to run on another vendor's ORB.

## 14.57 org.omg.CORBA.TypeCodePackage

The `org.omg.CORBA.TypeCodePackage` package contains the `BadKind` and `Bounds` exception classes.

# 14.58 org.omg.CosNaming

The org.omg.CosNaming package provides the naming service for the Java IDL. It contains classes and interfaces that provide the means to bind or unbind names and object references, to retrieve bound object references, and to iterate through a list of bindings.

# 14.59 org.omg.CosNaming.NamingContextPackage

The org.omg.CosNaming.NamingContextPackage package provides the exception classes used by the classes in the org.omg.CORBA.CosNaming package as well as helper and holder classes for those exceptions.

# 14.60 org.omg.SendingContext

The org.omg.SendingContext package provides two interfaces for accessing value types between client and server machines.

# 14.61 org.omg.stub.java.rmi

The org.omg.stub.java.rmi package provides a stub class for use with Remote Method Invocation (RMI).

# Index A - Classes

# Index B- General

# B